W9-AAL-830

CONTEMPORARY INVESTMENTS

Security and Portfolio Analysis

THIRD EDITION

CONTEMPORARY INVESTMENTS
Security and Portfolio Analysis

THIRD EDITION

Douglas Hearth
University of Arkansas

Janis K. Zaima
San Jose State University

HARCOURT COLLEGE PUBLISHERS

Fort Worth   Philadelphia   San Diego   New York   Orlando   Austin   San Antonio
Toronto   Montreal   London   Sydney   Tokyo

PUBLISHER	Mike Roche
ACQUISITIONS EDITOR	Mike Reynolds
MARKET STRATEGIST	Charlie Watson
DEVELOPMENTAL EDITOR	Terri House
PROJECT EDITOR	Katherine Dennis
ART DIRECTOR	Scott Baker
PRODUCTION MANAGER	James McDonald

ISBN: 0-03-031528-x
Library of Congress Catalog Card Number: 00-104577

Address for Domestic Orders
Harcourt, Inc., 6277 Sea Harbor Drive, Orlando, FL 32887-6777
800-782-4479

Address for International Orders
International Customer Service
Harcourt, Inc., 6277 Sea Harbor Drive, Orlando, FL 32887-6777
407-345-3800
(fax) 407-345-4060
(e-mail) hbintl@harcourt.com

Address for Editorial Correspondence
Harcourt College Publishers, 301 Commerce Street, Suite 3700, Fort Worth, TX 76102

Web Site Address
http://www.harcourtcollege.com

Printed in the United States of America

0 1 2 3 4 5 6 7 8 9   048   9 8 7 6 5 4 3 2

Harcourt College Publishers

To my parents
Donald and Joan Hearth

In memory of my father
Kenneth H. Zaima

THE HARCOURT SERIES IN FINANCE

Amling and Droms
Investment Fundamentals

Berry and Young
Managing Investments: A Case Approach

Besley and Brigham
Essentials of Managerial Finance
Twelfth Edition

Besley and Brigham
Principles of Finance

Boone, Kurtz, and Hearth
Planning Your Financial Future
Second Edition

Brigham
Financial Management: Cases & Models

Brigham, Gapenski, and Ehrhardt
Financial Management: Theory and Practice
Ninth Edition

Brigham, Gapenski, and Daves
Intermediate Financial Management
Sixth Edition

Brigham and Houston
Fundamentals of Financial Management
Ninth Edition

Brigham and Klein
2001 Cases in Financial Management: Dryden Request

Brigham and Houston
Fundamentals of Financial Management: Concise Second Edition

Chance
An Introduction to Derivatives and Risk Management
Fifth Edition

Clark, Gerlach, and Olson
Restructuring Corporate America

Conroy
Finance Interactive

Cooley
Advances in Business Financial Management: A Collection of Readings
Second Edition

Dickerson, Campsey, and Brigham
Introduction to Financial Management
Fourth Edition

Eaker, Fabozzi, and Grant
International Corporate Finance

Gardner, Mills, and Cooperman
Managing Financial Institutions: An Asset/Liability Approach
Fourth Edition

Gitman and Joehnk
Personal Financial Planning
Eighth Edition

Greenbaum and Thakor
Contemporary Financial Intermediation

Hall
Effective Use of a Financial Calculator

Hayes and Meerschwam
Financial Institutions: Contemporary Cases in the Financial Services Industry

Hearth and Zaima
Contemporary Investments: Security and Portfolio Analysis
Third Edition

Hirschey
Investment Analysis and Management

Johnson
Issues and Readings in Managerial Finance
Fourth Edition

Kidwell, Peterson, and Blackwell
Financial Institutions, Markets, and Money
Seventh Edition

Koch and MacDonald
Bank Management
Fourth Edition

Leahigh
Pocket Guide to Finance

Maness and Zietlow
Short-Term Financial Management

Mayes and Shank
Financial Analysis with Lotus 1-2-3 for Windows

Mayes and Shank
Financial Analysis with Microsoft Excel
Second Edition

Mayo
Financial Institutions, Investments, and Management: An Introduction
Seventh Edition

Mayo
Investments: An Introduction
Sixth Edition

Osteryoung, Newman, and Davies
Small Firm Finance: An Entrepreneurial Analysis

Reilly and Brown
Investment Analysis and Portfolio Management
Sixth Edition

Reilly and Norton
Investments
Fifth Edition

Sandburg
Discovering Your Finance Career

Seitz and Ellison
Capital Budgeting and Long-Term Financing Decisions
Third Edition

Siegel and Siegel
Futures Markets

Smith and Spudeck
Interest Rates: Principles and Applications

Stickney and Brown
Financial Reporting and Statement Analysis: A Strategic Perspective
Fourth Edition

PREFACE

When we started writing the first edition of *Contemporary Investments* our overall objective was to create a comprehensive investments textbook, which, while covering much the same material as other texts, would have a much different writing style and focus. Years of teaching experience tells us that investments is often a course many students look forward to taking, only to be disappointed. The textbook is the usual suspect. Why?

Well, we believe the fundamental problem with most investments texts is that they appear to students to be detached from the real world of investments. Much of the material in existing texts seems to be cloaked in mysterious economic theory coupled with lots of statistics and mathematics. Too little time is devoted to discussing how *real* investors actually make decisions, whether these decisions are right or wrong. That's really too bad; we believe students want to learn more about the practice of investments, not just the theory.

What do we do differently than most investment texts? That's a fair question. For one thing, we've written *Contemporary Investments* in a more informal, conversational style. Let's face it, many textbooks, while sincere and technically correct, are just plain boring. Further, we place more emphasis on investing in common stocks than do most texts. Stocks are arguably the most complicated but also the most interesting investment instrument. The text is also replete with real companies and real investment situations. Whenever possible, we use real world examples to illustrate key points. We don't summarily dismiss successful investors as mere flukes, but rather try to understand why they're successful. Perhaps its mainly luck, but perhaps it's also superior investment skill.

Investment theory is presented in a more lucid, less intimating manner. You wouldn't need a degree in higher mathematics to understand the material. We show how investment theory can help investors better understand the world of investments and help them make better investment decisions. It's not that we don't believe theory is important; we do. In fact, we believe you need to solid foundation in investment theory in order to know how to properly apply it to real investment situations.

Investing can be fun. You can get a great deal of satisfaction from watching what you felt was a great investment exceed your expectations. At the same time, we never lose sight of the fact that investing is serious and important work. Many students aspire to a career in the investments field, and we accommodate them. But even if you don't want a career in investments, more likely than not you're going to be investor. In fact, you may already be. Today most employer sponsored retirement plans are so-called defined contribution plans, plans that often require employees to make investment decisions. Consequently, we don't neglect issues that apply mainly to the individual investor.

Finally, throughout the text, we never forget the historical context of investments. While, by its nature, investing is forward looking, we believe you often have to understand the past while looking toward the future. Sure, the past is never a guarantee of the future, but you can learn a great deal by studying past investment successes and failures.

In short, we've tried to create an investments text written in a more user-friendly, proactive manner, while still being complete and current. We hope this text not only gives you an operational knowledge of the current field of investments, but provides the stimulation for a lifetime of further study. It is our hope that you will find our text to be both interesting and understandable, and perhaps consider your reading assignments to be more joy than drudgery. You, the reader, will be the ultimate judge as to how well *Contemporary Investments* accomplishes this goal.

Intended Market and Use

We believe this text can be used in the first investments class at either the undergraduate or MBA level. The entire text can be covered in one semester (or quarter). At the same time, given the depth of the in-text examples and end of chapter problems, the text can easily fit into a two semester (or two quarter) sequence.

With close to 40 years of combined teaching experience, we know just how difficult it can be to cover all the material you want and need to cover. It often seems like there's never enough time to cover everything. We've tried to help by structuring the text material in such a way that topics can be covered generally, or in more depth, depending on the needs and preferences of instructors and their students. So, instructors can easily emphasize some topics and de-emphasize others.

The text is designed to be read in what we would call, for lack of a better term, a linear fashion—the chapters work best in the order presented. On the other hand, when designed and writing the text, we've tried to allow for some flexibility depending on instructor preferences. Comparing notes with instructors tells us that some prefer to cover modern portfolio theory in class earlier than we do in the text. This presents no problem; *Contemporary Investments* isn't, after all, a novel! One can read the chapters on modern portfolio theory (Chapters 17 through 19), before the chapters on security analysis (Chapters 11 through 14), without much loss in continuity. We know of other instructors who prefer to cover common stocks before bonds. Again, one can read the chapters devoted to stocks (11 through 14) before the two bond chapters (9 and 10), without becoming hopelessly confused.

Changes to the Third Editon

While we made several major changes to the third edition, our overriding goal while the writing the new edition of *Contemporary Investments* was to maintain our emphasis upon applications as the main "theme" behind the book. In other words, we haven't changed our basic philosophy. Rather, in the third edition, we concentrated on rearranging the text in a more logical order, adding some additional material, updating the extensive real-world data and examples, adding more computational problems, integrating the Internet, highlighting the applications features, and providing more instructional and ideas materials to professors in the supplements. Many of these changes were suggested by users of the prior editions. A sampling of the major changes to the third edition include:

✦ Presenting the material on bonds before the material on common stock investing. Many users have told us that they prefer to cover bonds before covering common stocks because bonds are simpler securities and are easier for students to understand.

✦ Adding a new chapter devoted specifically to the fundamentals of risk and return. This new chapter (Chapter 2) covers the basics of measuring risk and return for individual investments. In prior editions, this material was presented in the first chapter. In the third edition, we've expanded our coverage.

✦ Adding two new chapters devoted to managing investment portfolios. At the end of the text we discuss how to build investment portfolios and how to evaluate their performance.

✦ Moving the material on mutual funds. Our users agreed with us on the importance of mutual funds but felt that the material should be presented earlier. We agree, and the chapter on mutual fund investing is now Chapter 4.

✦ Presenting the material on derivative securities right after the section on common stock investing. This was another suggestion from users.

✦ Splitting the material on financial markets into two chapters. Chapter 3 of the second edition was a very long chapter. In this edition, we've taken the material and split it into two chapters: the first (now Chapter 5) describes the various financial markets while the second (now Chapter 6) discusses how investors participate in the financial markets.

✦ Adding more CFA problems and Internet-related exercises.

Features and Pedagogy

Contemporary Investments offers a number of unique and important features, some of which are new to the third edition, designed to aid in student learning and perk up student interest. Some of the most noteworthy of these features are:

✦ More emphasis on common stock investing and traditional security analysis (sometimes referred to as the Graham and Dodd approach). Not only have common stocks proven to be superior investments, they are also, in our view, the most interesting, albeit complicated investment instrument. The Graham and Dodd approach for valuing common stocks was first published more than 60 years ago, at the height of the Great Depression. It has easily withstood the test of time.

✦ The qualitative, as well as the quantitative, factors that may determine common stock values and prices are examined in depth, something most texts overlook. While it may be difficult to define what is meant by the quality of management, it is too important an topic to ignore, or even downplay. A company can appear to have good looking financial statements, but still be poorly managed.

✦ Modern portfolio theory (MPT) is presented in a more intuitive and realistic manner, compared to most texts, with a minimum of mathematics. We continually show how MPT can contribute to a better understanding of how the investment markets function. At the same time, we discuss how, when combined with traditional security analysis, MPT can help all types of investors make better investment decisions. If you can see how MPT relates to the real world, we believe you will take it more seriously and it will be easier to learn.

✦ More balanced treatment of how professional investors make their investment decisions (technical and fundamental analysis). We recognize, and point out, that professionals are often wrong. However, they've made more than their share of correct calls as well. Some professionals have excellent track records. Why professionals are right is as important as why they are wrong.

✦ The globalization of the financial markets and investing has been one of the most significant trends in recent years. Virtually all texts recognize this but address the globalization of investing by adding a chapter at the end. The international chapter then becomes a logical candidate for omission when time runs short. We've addressed globalization by attempting to integrate it throughout the text so international issues become a natural part of the material.

✦ Investing raises a number of ethical situations (such as those involving the use of inside or privileged information). Throughout the text there are numerous opportunities for class discussion involving ethical issues and investing. These are in the form of everything from boxes to end of chapter questions.

✦ Each chapter begins with a set of learning objectives—phrased as questions—designed to guide the student's reading. The chapter summary then repeats each objective individually and summarizes the chapter material that applies to it.

✦ At the beginning of each chapter is a feature called linkages. This feature consists of three parts—where we've been, what we're doing now, and where we're going in the future.

✦ Throughout each chapter there is extensive use of real companies and real investment situations to illustrate key points. Students will run into such well known companies as Applied Materials, Cisco Systems, Disney, General Electric, Home Depot, Intel, Johnson and Johnson, Microsoft, Nike, Sara Lee, Southwest Airlines, and Wal-Mart.

✦ Many exhibits are annotated. The notes explain what the figure, or graph, is showing and the point (or points) it is illustrating. This will make the exhibits clearer and easier to understand.

✦ All chapters contain two new boxes: Investment Insights and Investment History. Investment Insights provides practical advice or analysis of contemporary investments topics. The Investment History boxes relate stories of where we've been and what the past may mean for the future.

✦ In selected chapters, a brief one paragraph summary (Recap) follows difficult or complicated material. Practice questions are also given—the answers appear in an appendix to the text. These recap sections gives the reader a chance to catch his or her breath and review what was covered before pushing ahead.

✦ The most complicated, demanding material, whether it be mathematical or conceptual, has been placed in separate sections (indicated with a °). Readers can skip these sections without any loss of continuity. Instructors have the flexibility of covering or not covering this material.

✦ At the end of each chapter, there are extensive questions and problems. Most chapters have one or more mini-cases. These problems are designed to test student comprehension over large portions of material. All chapters have 10 to 20 review questions and problems designed to test knowledge over more specific points. Each chapter has at least one critical thinking exercise (most have more). Critical thinking exercises require Internet searches, library research, computer work, or all three. Not only are these exercises designed to see how well students comprehend the chapter material, they are also designed to give students some hands-on practice with real data and investment situations. We give students lots of opportunities to practice and improve their computer skills. Finally, new to this edition, each chapter contains a set of Internet related exercises.

Supplements

A number of excellent supplements have been developed and accompany Contemporary Investments. Our basic philosophy with the ancillary package is to enhance the learning experience by providing a wealth of material that can be used as examples, projects, and presentations. The ancillary package consists of:

✦ *Instructor's Resource Manual (IRM).* The IRM provides an outline of each chapter, a list of points to emphasize, and identifies areas where students often get confused. In addition, the IRM provides a list of possible student projects, worked out computational examples, integration of the lecture slides, mini-case solutions (on separate pages so they can be easily reproduced for distribution to students), and classroom information on the Investment Insights boxes (such as a summary of the issues raised and questions for discussion or testing). The IRM also contains a section on individual information handouts. These include a list of AIMR's standards for ethical behavior, a discussion of security price indexes, and a review of convexity.

✦ *Testbank.* A through, comprehensive text bank is available, both in paper and computerized versions. The test bank contains around 1,700 objective questions, short answer essay questions, and problems, along with several sample tests.

✦ *Data Disk.* A data disk is included with each book. It contains a set of Microsoft Excel worksheets designed to accompany many of the critical thinking exercises. The data disk also includes an entire security analysis report—in Microsoft Word format—and a file listing investment-oriented web sites. This file can be used in conjunction with popular web browsers such as Netscape and Microsoft Internet Explorer.

✦ *Investment Wizard.* Investment Wizard is a Microsoft Excel workbook and consists of a set of pre-built worksheets. Students enter data or information where indicated on the worksheet. The worksheet performs predetermined calculations—such as finding the duration of a bond or the standard deviation of a portfolio of stocks.

✦ *Lecture Presentation Slides.* Jorge Borge has prepared an outstanding set of computerized lecture slides for each individual chapter. These slides are in Microsoft Power Point format and are designed to be used to supplement class lectures. They provide a dynamic, multimedia lecture experience.

Acknowledgments

As with all books, we have many, many people to thank. At the risk of sounding like an acceptance speech at the Academy Awards, we want to start by thanking the individuals who reviewed various drafts of the first edition of the manuscript and participated in focus groups. Their comments and suggestions were invaluable and made Contemporary Investments better. They have our heart felt thanks. These individuals are:

Jerry Boswell *Metropolitan State College of Denver*
Larry Byerly *University of Pittsburg at Johnstown*
James D'Mello *Western Michigan University*
David Dubofsky *Virginia Commonwealth University*
John Emery *California State University—Fresno*
Stevenson Hawkey *Golden Gate University*
Jeffry Manzi *Ohio University*
Saeed Mortazavi *Humboldt State University*
Henry Oppenheimer *University of Rhode Island*
Aaron Phillips *American University*
Robert Ryan *Ithaca College*
Patricia Smith *University of New Hampshire*
Andrew Whitaker *North Central College*

We'd also like to thank the many users of the first and second editions, especially:

Ben Branch *University of Massachusetts*
David M. Ellis *Texas A&M University*
James F. Gatti *University of Vermont*
John M. Geppert *University of Nebraska – Lincoln*
Stephen P. Huffman *University of Wisconsin – Oshkosh*
Saeed Mortazavi *Humboldt State University*
Henry R. Oppenheimer *University of Rhode Island*
James Philpot *Ouachita Baptist University*
Steve Rich *Baylor University*
Linda L. Richardson *Siena College*
James N. Rimbey *University of Arkansas*
Edward L. Winn, Jr. *Belmont University*

These individuals helped to improve and strengthen the third edition:

Joseph Vu *De Paul University*
Marcelo Eduardo *Mississippi College*
Ann Rock *Wayne State University*
Indudeep Chhachhi *Western Kentucky University*
James M'Mello *Western Michigan University*
Ernest Swift *Georgia State University*
Richard Johnson *Colorado State University*

In addition, a number of other friends and colleagues provided a great deal of input and assistance to the earlier editions. These include, Professors Robert Kennedy, David Kurtz, and James Rimbey of the University of Arkansas, Professors BJ Campsey, Joe Black and Bruce Cochran of San Jose State University, Professor Mier Statman of Santa Clara University, Professor Stu Rosenstein of University of Colorado–Denver, Professor Ken Leong of San Francisco State University, Professor Nikihil Varaiya of San Diego State University, Professor Ronald Melicher of the University of Colorado, Professors Mac Clouse and Tomi Johnsen of the University of Denver, Professor John Claude Bosch of the University of Colorado-Denver, Professor Larry Johnson of the University of Tulsa, Professor Douglas Kaul at the University of Akron, Professor Don Nast of Florida State University, Professors Carl Schwser and J. Sa-Aadu of the University of Iowa, and Professor Darryl Gurley of Florida A&M University.

We received research and clerical help from a number of people at both the University of Arkansas and San Jose State University. We wish to thank Jason Katz, Donna Ludlow, Julie Ryan, and Lori Wilkin.

We've worked with some great people at the Dryden Press over the years. These include Mike Reynolds, Charles Watson, Terri House, Katherine Dennis, James McDonald, and Scott Baker. We appreciate their expertise, encouragement, and, goodness knows, their patience.

Finally, to our families, Karen, Alan & Eric, and Ken, Jana & Kelly, we acknowledge their love, encouragement, and understanding. Without their support, this project would never have gotten off the ground, much less it all to the way to a third edition.

Douglas Hearth
Janis K. Zaima

BRIEF CONTENTS

CONTENTS

Part 2   Financial Markets and Investment Selection   103

CHAPTER 5   ORGANIZATION OF THE FINANCIAL MARKETS   105

CHAPTER 10   MANAGING BOND PORTFOLIOS   242

Part 6   Modern Portfolio Theory   467

CHAPTER 17   RISK AND DIVERSIFICATION   469

CONTEMPORARY INVESTMENTS
Security and Portfolio Analysis

THIRD EDITION

Part 1

The World of Investments

THIS OPENING SECTION PRESENTS AN OVERVIEW OF THE SUBJECT OF INVESTMENTS. IT INTRODUCES SEVERAL IMPORTANT CONCEPTS AND IDEAS THAT REAPPEAR THROUGHOUT THE REMAINDER OF THE TEXT. WE DISCUSS THE IMPORTANCE OF INVESTMENT DECISIONS, THE GENERAL INVESTMENT PROCESS, AND SOME APPARENT TRUISMS IN INVESTMENTS. FROM THERE WE COVER THE ESSENTIAL CHARACTERISTICS OF RISK AND RETURN—THE TWO CONCEPTS THAT DOMINATE INVESTMENT DECISIONS. FINALLY, WE DESCRIBE IN DETAIL THE WIDE RANGE OF CONTEMPORARY INVESTMENT ALTERNATIVES FROM TREASURY BILLS TO COMMON STOCK TO MUTUAL FUNDS.

PRELUDE: INVESTING AND INVESTMENTS

IN THIS CHAPTER. . .

Our study of investments begins by asking the fundamental question of why investment decisions are important. Answering this question leads to a discussion of the history of investing and the steps involved in the investment process. We also introduce many of the basic themes carried throughout the book.

TO COME. . .

We continue to lay the foundation of investments study by discussing the concepts of risk and return (Chapter 2). Both are essential factors in determining how much and in what we invest. Next, we describe the wide array of investment instruments available today (Chapters 3 and 4).

Chapter Objectives

After reading Chapter 1, you should be able to answer the following questions:

1. Why are investment decisions important?
2. What is the history of investing?
3. What steps are involved in the investment process?
4. What are some important truisms in investments?

Over the next seven hundred pages or so, we plan to lead you on a journey through the fascinating world of investments. We look carefully at investment alternatives such as common stocks, bonds, options, and mutual funds. We examine how the security markets function and how professionals make investment decisions. We review some past follies of investors and develop an understanding of how investors should make investment decisions. We believe that you will find the journey to be rewarding intellectually and, perhaps at some point in the future, economically as well.

Why is investments an important and interesting topic of study? To help answer this question, consider the following story.

By all accounts, Donald and Mildred Othmer of New York lived quiet, unpretentious lives. Donald, who died in 1995, was a professor of chemical engineering at Brooklyn Polytechnic University. Mildred, a former teacher, died in 1998. When they died, they were both were in their nineties. What came as a shock to friends was that the Othmers left a combined estate worth about $800 million, the bulk of which was left to a variety of nonprofit organizations. How did they accumulate such an impressive amount of wealth? Simply put, the Othmers, like many other Americans, got rich by investing their money sensibly, leaving it invested for a long period of time, and living modestly.

In the early 1960s, the Othmers turned over their life savings, then fifty thousand dollars, to famed investor Warren Buffet, an old family friend. In the early 1970s, the Othmers received shares of Buffet's new company, Berkshire Hathaway. Berkshire Hathaway invests in other companies, such as American Express, Coca-Cola, and Gillette. When the Othmers received their Berkshire shares, the price was $42 per share; at the time of Mildred's death the price had risen to $77,000 per share. Although the Othmers were smart, or perhaps just lucky, to pick Buffet to manage their money, a similar investment, made at the same time, in the overall stock market would have grown to more than $100 million by the middle of 1998.

Although the rewards of investing are obvious, investing is not without risk. Between the middle of July 1998 and the end of September of 1998, common stocks lost almost 20 percent of their value. On October 19, 1987, stocks lost almost 21 percent of their value. During a four-week period during the late summer of 1999, the price of America Online shares, the leading Internet service provider, fell by close to 40 percent.

Over the long run, however, the rewards of investing far outweigh the risks. This chapter introduces you to the subject of investing and investments. Now, let's embark on our journey.

Why Invest?

Why do people invest? This seems like a simple question, and it can be answered by defining the word *invest*. According to the dictionary, *invest* means to commit money to earn a financial return; to make use of for future benefits or advantages.[1] In a nutshell, this definition explains why people commit money to investments: to increase their future wealth. By investing money to earn financial returns, people forgo current consumption but have more money to spend in future years. If you invest $1,000 today and earn 10 percent over the next year, you will have $1,100 one year from today. Had you invested $1,000 at the beginning of 1995 in a portfolio of common stocks of large companies, your investment would have been worth almost $5,500 by the end of 1999.

More specifically, someone might invest to accumulate funds to buy a home, to send their children to college, to retire comfortably, or to weather an unexpected crisis in their lives (for example, temporary unemployment). Also, even though investing is serious business and should never be taken lightly, some people find it a fun challenge.

---

[1]*Webster's Tenth New Collegiate Dictionary*, (Springfield, MA: Merriam-Webster, 1993), 616.

Investing also benefits society and the economy as a whole. By increasing personal wealth, investing can contribute to higher overall economic growth and prosperity. For example, if an investor increases the value of his or her pension fund, at retirement that person will have more disposable income and a higher standard of living, both of which benefit the economy as a whole. In addition, the process of investing helps create financial markets where companies can raise capital. This, too, contributes to greater economic growth and prosperity.

Specific types of investments provide other benefits to society as well. Common stocks, for example, provide a mechanism for stockholders to monitor the performance of company management. Municipal bonds benefit those who pay proportionally high income tax because interest from municipal bonds is exempt from federal tax. At the same time, municipal bonds provide capital for valuable public projects such as schools and roads.

The Importance of Investment Decisions

Investment decisions may be more critical today than ever before. The following sections discuss some of the more important reasons for this.

LARGER MENU OF INVESTMENT CHOICES

Today's investors choose among a dizzying array of investment alternatives, many of which have been around only a few years. Consider mutual funds, for example, which divide large portfolios of investments into small shares to allow investors to commit limited funds. In 1970, 361 mutual funds operated in the United States. Today, that number has grown to close to 9,000. Even to buy something as simple as a money market mutual fund, an investor has to choose from more than 850 different funds.

As the number of funds has grown, so has the diversity of their investment goals. The Investment Company Institute classifies mutual funds by investment objective. In 1975, it defined seven categories of mutual funds. Today, there are twenty-one different categories.

The larger menu of investment choices today means that most investors can find an investment instrument that suits personal needs. At the same time, however, the larger menu increases the potential for confusion and poor choices. Today's investors must do their homework extremely carefully.

LONGER LIFE EXPECTANCIES

Life expectancies in the United States and in most developed countries are rising. Since 1950, the life expectancy of an American has increased by about one-third. A sixty-five-year-old in good health can expect to live at least another twenty years.

One effect of longer life expectancies is an increase in the duration of the average person's retirement. Accumulating funds for retirement is one major reason that people invest. A longer retirement period means that they must accumulate more funds, which requires more careful investing. Further, the rising cost of health care will likely require tomorrow's retirees to set aside greater reserves, compared with today's retirees, to provide the same standard of living.

If you begin work tomorrow, the experts will tell you to plan on saving at least $1 million for retirement. What's more, much of the saving will be up to you. Do not count on Social Security or a company's pension to provide more than a small percentage of what you are going to need after you retire. In fact, the trend today has been toward defined contribution plans such as 401(k) plans and away from traditional pension plans, or defined benefit plans. You and your employer contribute to your retirement plan each year. You have a great deal of flexibility when it comes to deciding where to invest your retirement savings. In other words, the investment decisions you make during your working years will, to a large extent, determine whether you enjoy a financially secure retirement.

FLAT GROWTH IN PERSONAL INCOME

Adjusted for inflation, median per-capita U.S. income has increased at an annual rate of about 2 percent between 1980 and today. Real median per-capita income actually fell slightly between 1989 and 1991. Experts believe that average personal income is unlikely to substantially outpace the rate of inflation in the coming decades.

These personal income data suggest that one should not rely merely on increasing personal income to improve one's future standard of living. The key to improving a future standard of living may well be careful investing.

CHANGING LABOR MARKET

The average person entering the workplace today will change jobs about five times over his or her lifetime. Further, one in three workers will be unemployed at some point during their working years. The old ideal of going to work for a company right out of college and staying there until retirement will likely be the exception, not the rule, in tomorrow's labor market. Even IBM, which once had a reputation of virtually guaranteeing lifetime employment, has reduced its workforce by more than 100,000 in the past few years.

These sobering trends imply that people will have to rely more on their own resources and less on corporate paternalism to meet major financial goals. If nothing else, the changing labor market means everyone should accumulate a larger cushion of resources to break an unexpected fall. You never know when your employer is going to downsize your job out of existence!

A Brief History of Investing

Investing, itself, as a legitimate organized human endeavor, has a rather short history. Investing is an outgrowth of economic development and the maturation of modern capitalism. Three centuries ago, the world economy featured no stock exchanges or bond markets to speak of and had only a handful of banks. The Bank of England, for example, was not founded until 1694. It is considered to be history's first modern bank because it was the first institution empowered to accept deposits, issue notes to serve as paper money, make loans, and discount bills.

The London Stock Exchange, the first recognizable stock exchange, or *bourse*, was also chartered in 1694.[2] Stock markets were established in most other

---

[2]Before the establishment of the London Stock Exchange, a number of bourses, or financial markets, had operated. The first was established in Antwerp in 1531. These bourses were not, strictly speaking, stock exchanges. Rather, they were continuous fairs where dealings in commodities, bills of exchange, and insurance took place.

economically advanced countries over the next one hundred years or so. (The ancestor of the New York Stock Exchange [NYSE], for example, was founded in 1792.) Both the Bank of England and the London Stock Exchange were initially distrusted, and even despised, by many in English society. As recently as the middle of the past century, the London Stock Exchange was a struggling weakling, often threatened with extinction by Parliament.

The notion of individuals pooling their capital in an organized fashion to jointly finance and own a business venture is also a fairly new concept. Although some evidence suggests that joint-stock associations operated in ancient Rome, the evolution of common stock as we know it did not start until the European commercial revolution that sprang from the Renaissance. Joint-stock companies were first organized in Europe to finance sea voyages, exploration, and trade by providing large amounts of capital and distribution of the risks these voyages entailed.

The historical evidence suggests that the Dutch East India Company, founded in 1602, was the first corporation established with permanent capital stock. The idea of transferring shares from individual to individual soon followed. However, general incorporation laws and the notion of limited liability that protected stockholders from responsibility for all of a corporation's debts were not firmly established in either Europe or the United States until the mid-nineteenth century.

Less than a century ago, stock manipulation and insider trading were neither illegal nor uncommon in the United States. During 1929, for example, more than one hundred issues traded on the NYSE were subject to active pool, or syndicate, operations that involved overt manipulation of stock prices by members of the exchange.[3] Wildly overpriced, even fraudulent, securities were bought and sold openly, with little fanfare or government interference. In 1901, U.S. Steel is reported to have raised $1.4 billion in capital, including more than $500 million in common stock, supported by at least $700 million of intangible, even fictitious, assets.

Before the 1920s, those who thought of themselves as investors generally owned bonds to ensure income and safety of principal. Only the stocks of a few companies qualified as investment-grade securities. These consisted mostly of bank and insurance stocks, which were unlisted, backed by real capital, and could expect to raise dividends regardless of the economic environment. The stocks traded on the NYSE were generally considered to be speculative in nature. Railroads, for example, simply carried too much debt to be considered investments. Not until the 1920s did common stocks mature as investment vehicles.

Few Americans owned any securities, much less any common stocks, in the early part of this century. Even in the speculative frenzy that preceded the 1929 stock market crash, probably no more than 3 million individuals out of a population of about 122 million actually owned any shares of common stock. This fact contradicts the popular view that millions of ordinary Americans were playing the stock market in the late 1920s. Some historians doubt that the crash, in fact, caused, or even contributed significantly to, the Great Depression.[4]

Stock ownership, and investing in general, were not common in American households until after World War II. In 1952, 6.5 million individuals owned stocks (about 4 percent of the population). By 1970, that number had risen to about 31 million

---

[3]This practice is illegal today.

[4]See, for example, John K. Galbraith, *The Great Crash of 1929* (Boston: Houghton-Mifflin, 1954).

(almost 15 percent of the population). Still, the vast majority of household financial assets, about 80 percent in 1970, consisted of savings accounts and certificates of deposit from financial institutions.

During the 1970s and 1980s, millions of Americans finally made the transformation from savers to investors. This trend was stimulated by the explosive growth of money market mutual funds during the late 1970s. Fed up with earning 5.5 percent interest on savings deposits in banks, savers moved billions of dollars into money market funds that yielded 10 percent or more.[5] As interest rates began to fall during the 1980s, many of these individuals started buying stocks, bonds, and mutual fund shares; in short, they became investors. The number of mutual fund accounts grew from about 9 million in 1976 to more than 100 million today. By some estimates more than half of all American adults today could be classified as "investors."

THE INVESTMENT PROCESS

Before anyone begins an investment program, they must complete certain preliminary tasks. The first preparatory task is for the investor to inventory all assets and liabilities (both financial and nonfinancial). To do this, you would add up all current financial assets (checking and savings accounts, CDs, and so forth), and determine how much is already set aside for retirement (for example, the current balance of any pension plan, individual retirement account). In addition, assign rough market values to all physical, or real, assets (automobiles, home furnishings, and a home if the investor owns one). Next, add up all liabilities, including current balances on any mortgage, auto, or credit card loans and such. Subtracting liabilities from assets gives the investor's current net worth and a pretty good picture of your current financial situation. The net worth influences appropriate investment goals and helps with investment planning and selection.

Having inventoried assets and liabilities, the analysis should proceed by asking some questions about investment goals. What should investing accomplish? Having goals will help guide investment selection and management. These goals can be fairly specific (for example, to accumulate sufficient funds to send two children to college starting ten years from now) or they can be more general (for example, to fund a comfortable retirement in twenty years). Whether general or specific, investment goals should be realistic, and they should bear some relationship to the investor's present and expected future situation.

The next task is to review current insurance coverage. Most people can break all their insurance policies into three general areas: life, health and disability, and property and liability insurance. An investor needs adequate insurance in all three areas, but it should be the right kind of insurance. Many financial experts argue that few American households meet this goal; most are overinsured in some areas and underinsured in others. Many single people, for example, have life insurance, which they may not need, but no disability insurance, which they probably do need. Several books on personal financial planning discuss insurance in detail.[6]

---

[5]The assets of money market mutual funds grew from less than $4 billion in 1976 to more than $186 billion only five years later in 1981.

[6]See, for example, Louis Boone, David Kurtz, and Douglas Hearth, *Planning Your Financial Future*, 2nd edition (Ft. Worth: Harcourt, 2000).

Finally, the investor should establish an emergency fund before investing. This fund should consist of low-risk, short-term investments such as money market funds. The emergency fund has two basic purposes: to provide a financial safety net in the event of an unexpected emergency, such as a long-term illness or temporary unemployment, and to store funds to take advantage of changing financial conditions. Experts generally suggest that an adequate emergency fund should hold approximately three to six months of one's normal salary.

RISK AND RETURN ASSESSMENT

After performing these preliminary tasks, the next step in the investment process is an assessment of risk and return priorities. This assessment involves answering three specific questions: What holding period is appropriate? What expected return is necessary? How much risk is tolerable?

What Holding Period Is Appropriate?

Historically, security returns have behaved differently over short periods of time and longer periods. Returns over long holding periods have been far less volatile than returns over short holding periods. Between 1926 and today, stock returns for one-year holding periods have ranged between 54 percent and –43 percent. By contrast, annualized stock returns for twenty-five-year holding periods have ranged between 15 percent and 6 percent. The decision to invest for the short or long term could have a major impact on investment selection decisions.

What Expected Return Is Necessary?

Investing offers few guarantees, so we refer to future returns as expected returns. Everyone wants the highest return possible, but as we will see, higher expected returns come at a price. Investment choices depend, in part, on the return needed to achieve investment goals. For example, a parent who wants to accumulate $25,000 in ten years to send a child to college and who is willing to invest $1,500 per year (starting today) will need to earn a return of about 8 percent per year. If money market funds are yielding only 5 percent, what other alternatives would allow him or her to achieve this goal? Two solutions are to invest more each year or to find investment instruments that have expected returns higher than those of money market funds.

How Much Risk Is Tolerable?

The question of willingness to accept risk is difficult to answer, but it is critical. Someone who nearly suffers a nervous breakdown every time a stock drops one-eighth of a point (12.5 cents per share) shows low risk tolerance. However, someone who merely shrugs when a stock drops five points ($5 per share) can tolerate more risk. The point is that each investor must be comfortable with his or her investment selections.

Objective measurement of an individual's risk tolerance may be next to impossible. However, certain factors appear to influence tolerance for risk. These include age, marital status, family responsibilities, and income. For example, a retiree living on a fixed income may be less tolerant of risk than a young person with a rising income.

As we'll discuss in the next chapter, of the many types of investment risk, some can be measured and others cannot. A specific investment may expose you to substantial risk of one type but little of another. When making investment decisions, investors must be careful not to fear the wrong risks.

OTHER QUESTIONS

In addition to current financial status and risk and return preferences, three other questions guide preparation to invest. The first concerns tax status. An investor should always know his or her marginal tax rate (based on combined federal and state taxes).

Tax status can strongly influence investment selection. For example, someone who is investing for retirement in a tax-deferred account has no reason to buy municipal bonds, the interest from which is exempt from federal income taxes. However, someone in a high marginal tax bracket who is not investing for retirement may find that municipal bonds provide valuable protection from taxes.

After considering tax status, the analysis turns to preference for capital gains or income. As we will see, investment returns can come from both capital gains (price appreciation) and income (dividend and interest payments). Someone who prefers income is probably better off investing in bonds than stocks. Because capital gains receive preferential tax treatment for some taxable investors, tax status may greatly influence the choice between capital gains and income.

Finally, ask yourself how much time you can afford to spend on your investments. If you cannot or choose not to spend much time selecting and managing investments, you may be better off investing in mutual funds rather than in individual securities.

INVESTMENT SELECTION

asset allocation
The process of determining the appropriate mix of investments.

With preparations completed and questions about risk/return preferences, tax effects, and other background issues resolved, the investment process turns to selection of the most appropriate investment instruments. Sometimes called **asset allocation,** this is probably the most complex and time-consuming stage in the investment process.

One reason why investment selection can eat up so much time is the wealth of information available to today's investor. Computer technology, especially the Internet, has made it easier and cheaper to find information about various investments. In fact, today the problem isn't finding information, but sifting through the massive amount available. The Investment Insights box on page 11 lists some investment stops along the World Wide Web.

stocks
Securities that represent ownership in a corporation.

Although the menu of investments is long and diverse, most people invest in stocks, bonds, and money market instruments. **Stocks** represent ownership interest in corporations—such as Amazon.com, Home Depot, or Pfizer. Suppose you own 100 shares of Wal-Mart Stores, you actually own a tiny piece of the giant retailer. As a stockholder, you share in the company's profits in the form of cash dividends as well as potential increases in the stock price as the company's profits increase. Although income

INVESTMENT INSIGHTS

`0:00`   `0:00`

INVESTMENT STOPS ALONG THE WORLD WIDE WEB

The Internet is a bonanza for investors who use their personal computers to obtain business news, information, price quotes, and research. Often the most difficult task is knowing where to start. Below are some suggestions

quote.yahoo.com	Yahoo's investment site. You can get price quotes and other investment information in real time, or slightly delayed. Search the entire Internet using Yahoo's search engine.
investor.msn.com	Microsoft Network's investment site. Nonsubscribers have access to most of the site.
www.cnbc.wsj.com	A joint venture of CNBC and the *Wall Street Journal.* Excellent source of business news.
www.quicken.com	Quicken's personal finance site has an extensive investments section.
www.morningstar.net	Morningstar's Web site containing news, articles, and information. Users can screen stocks and mutual funds.
cnnfn.com	Web site of CNN's financial network. Source of news, advice, and information.
www.fidelity.com	Home page of Fidelity Investments, the nation's largest mutual fund company and a major discount broker.
www.schwab.com	Home page of Charles Schwab, a leading discount broker.
www.ml.com	Home page of Merrill Lynch, the nation's largest brokerage firm.
www.nasd.com	Home page of the National Association of Securities Dealers.
www.sec.gov	Home page of the U.S. Securities & Exchange Commission, access to the Edgar database (financial reports).

is a consideration, price appreciation is the main reason people invest in common stocks. As a company grows and prospers, the value of its stock should rise.

By contrast, if you a own a **bond,** you are actually lending money to an organization. Bonds are issued by governments (federal, state, and local) and corporations. You are paid a predetermined amount of interest each year for lending the organization your money. At some future certain date, the bond "matures" and you are paid a predetermined amount of money, called the **face value.** The face value of a bond is similar to a loan's principal. Because bonds pay fixed amounts of interest each year, the price of a bond—though not its face value—changes as interest rates change. Bond prices rise when interest rates fall and vice versa. Most people buy bonds for income, though under certain conditions bonds do rise in price.

Owning a **money market instrument** also means you're lending money to an organization. These are like bonds in the sense that you receive a predetermined amount of interest and the face value at maturity. Unlike bonds, however, all money market instruments mature within one year. Some investors even refer to market instruments as *cash* because they mature in a short amount of time. Examples of money market instruments include Treasury bills (T-bills) and bank savings accounts. A T-bill is a short-term IOU issued by the U.S. Treasury, so if you buy a T-bill you're lending money to the U.S. government. In the case of a bank savings account, you're lending money to a bank. The reasons for investing in money market instruments are liquidity, income, and safety of principal.

Exhibit 1.1 shows how stocks, bonds, and money market instruments compare on the basis of several investment characteristics (total return, stability of principal,

bond
A debt instrument issued by governments and corporations.

face value
The amount the bond is worth at maturity.

money market instrument
A debt instrument with a maturity of less than one year.

Exhibit 1.1 ✦ RISK AND RETURN CHARACTERISTICS OF STOCKS, BONDS, AND MONEY
MARKET INSTRUMENTS

(A is best or highest)

Characteristic	Stocks	Bonds	Money Market Instruments
1. Total return	A	B	C
2. Stability of principal	C	B	A
3. Current income	B	A	C
4. Stability of income	B	A	C
5. Growth in income	A	C	B

current income, stability of income, and growth of income). We'll discuss stocks, bonds, and money market instruments in more detail in subsequent chapters, starting with Chapter 3.

Strategic Asset Allocation

strategic asset allocation
The process of determining the general mix of investments.

The two phases of asset allocation are strategic and tactical. In **strategic asset allocation** the investor must decide on the general mix of investment instruments to include in the portfolio. Should it focus on stocks, bonds, money market instruments, or some combination of the three? If a combination of instruments is most appropriate, what proportion of each should the portfolio contain? For example, an investor's situation may dictate a mix of investment instruments in a portfolio of about 60 percent stocks, 30 percent bonds, and 10 percent money market instruments.

Tactical Asset Allocation

tactical asset allocation
The process of selecting specific investments within each general category.

The other phase of asset allocation, **tactical asset allocation,** involves the selection of specific investments within each general category. Although today's investment environment offers a wide range of choices, in general, an investor can take one of two approaches to the selection of investment instruments: passive or active.

A passive investor may try to "buy the market," usually in the form of a mutual fund that tries to replicate the performance of a broad market without many changes in portfolio composition. Such funds are called index funds. Vanguard, a large U.S. mutual fund company, offers several index funds that attempt to replicate the performance of well-known worldwide capital markets indexes, both stock and bond. In fact, the Vanguard 500 Index Fund (which tracks the Standard and Poor's 500) is one of the largest mutual funds in the United States, with more than $80 billion in assets. If a portfolio should contain 50 percent stocks and 50 percent bonds, a passive investor might buy equal amounts of two such funds, one that replicates the broad stock market and one that replicates the broad bond market.

Active investors take a more vigorous approach to investment selection. They look for specific investment instruments that offer superior risk/return characteristics. This approach requires a decision whether to invest in individual securities, mutual funds, or both. An active investor might decide that because so-called growth stocks are coming back into favor with investors, she should shift more money into growth stocks. Or perhaps, believing that long-term interest rates will fall in the next couple of years, she might invest all available funds in long-term corporate bonds. Active investing is more time-consuming and difficult than passive investing, but many investors believe that the payoff is worth the extra effort.

INVESTMENT MANAGEMENT

The last stage in the investment process involves monitoring investment performance and making changes when necessary. Investment management techniques fall into two categories: active portfolio management and buy-and-hold management.

Investors who actively manage their portfolios buy and sell more frequently than more passive investors. Active investors may shift funds between various types of instruments in anticipation of changing markets. To plan these moves, they tend to monitor investment performance more closely, and they may be more concerned about short-term performance than passive investors. A passive investor tends to buy a portfolio of securities and keep it pretty much intact for a long period of time. This investor may be less inclined to make changes to the portfolio in response to changing market conditions.

Those who select securities passively (for example, invest in index funds) are more likely to approach investment management passively as well. However, an investor could actively select securities and still take a passive buy-and-hold approach to investment management. This investor would buy a portfolio of specific securities that meet certain criteria and then hold the portfolio for a fairly long period of time, making few if any changes.

Financial experts agree that both active and passive investors should make changes to the contents of their investment portfolios as they go through life. What is best for a thirty-year-old may be inappropriate for someone who is sixty-five. A thirty-year-old investing for retirement should probably have most of his or her money invested in common stocks. By contrast, a sixty-year-old should probably have about half invested in stocks and about half invested in bonds and money market instruments.

Some Apparent Truisms in Investments

Although investments may sometimes appear a rational, precise, almost scientific field of study, much of investing actually involves ambiguity, subjective analysis, and opinion. One investor's favored security selection technique or other method may be scorned by another. Nevertheless, six major truisms, (as we call them), appear to characterize investments without much dispute. We briefly introduce each of these truisms below and continue talking about them throughout the entire book.

LESSONS OF HISTORY

As you read the pages that follow, you will confront the assumption that history teaches several important lessons about investments. In fact, the other five truisms that we discuss are all based, at least in part, on historical observation. Further, investment theory and analysis often involves the application of historical relationships. For example, much of modern portfolio theory, which we discuss in Chapters 17–19, was developed and tested using historical data.

TULIP MANIA

One of the most amazing speculative bubbles in history occurred in the early part of the seventeenth century and dealt with, of all things, tulips. Here's a brief history of the tulip mania that swept through Holland between 1635 and 1637.

Holland in the early seventeenth century was one of the most prosperous and economically advanced countries in Europe. Supposedly, tulips were introduced to European horticulture in Vienna about 1559 when an Austrian count brought some plants back from Turkey, where they had been grown for centuries. (*Tulip* comes from a Turkish word meaning "turban.") The Dutch fascination with tulips started soon after. Wealthy individuals began to order tulip bulbs directly from Constantinople, often paying exorbitant prices, and tulips in one's garden became a social necessity. The rage for tulips eventually caught on in the Dutch middle class, as

merchants and shopkeepers began to vie with one another for the most sought-after varieties of the plants. The resulting demand began to drive the prices of tulip bulbs sharply upward until, at some point, people started to view tulips as more than decorative additions to gardens, as investments whose prices were bound to go higher and higher; the frenzy had begun.

By about 1635, tulip mania was in full bloom in Holland. The normal business of the nation was neglected, and the population embarked in the tulip trade. People rushed to convert their property into cash, and invested it in flowers. Houses and lands were offered for sale at absurdly low prices. Traders in the bourses in Amsterdam, Rotterdam, and other Dutch towns abandoned mundane commodities such as loans and wheat and began actively trading tulip bulbs. Even call options were available—the right to buy tulips at a fixed price for a fixed period of time.

The prices of tulips reached absurd levels. One person is reported to have offered twelve acres of land in exchange for one especially glorious bulb. A *Semper Augustus* bulb, the most prized of all, sold for 5,500 florins in 1636 although it weighed less than half an ounce. At that time, in Amsterdam, 4,600 florins would have bought a new carriage complete with two horses!

Eventually, the more prudent Dutch citizens began to see that this folly could not last forever, and they began to sell their tulip bulbs. As this conviction spread in the early part of 1637, prices started to fall faster and faster. Dealers went bankrupt and refused to honor their commitments to buy bulbs. As more and more people tried to sell their tulips, a general panic took hold and prices plunged even further. When the dust finally settled, tulips were selling for no more than common onions, and Holland's economy plunged into a severe recession.

Consider some of the lessons that *speculative bubbles* teach us. A speculative bubble is the rapid increase in the price of an investment with no apparent justification other than a belief, or hope, that the price will go still higher. One of history's most amusing bubbles, at least in retrospect, is chronicled in the Investment History box above.

The history of speculative bubbles teaches us two important lessons. First, the price of an investment, in the long run, will reflect its true, or intrinsic value. In the short run, however, a substantial difference between price and value can exist. Eventually, the market will correct its mistake. All bubbles burst. The second lesson is that investor emotions affect investment performance. The psychological and emotional influences on investment decision making and valuation can be significant.

However, remember an important caveat whenever you apply historical observations or relationships to evaluate current and future investment situations. The past is no guarantee of the future; the past may repeat itself, but variations are common. For example, no two speculative bubbles have been identical, either in duration or magnitude. Some eras have seen many bubbles, whereas others have seen few. It may be easy to state that bubbles are inevitable, but predicting when and where they will occur is far more difficult.

As another example, consider the general history of security returns. Between 1989 and 1998, stocks outperformed T-bills by a substantial margin (almost 19 percent per year for stocks versus about 5.25 percent for T-bills). Does that mean that stocks will outperform T-bills over the next ten years? No one can answer yes for certain, although most believe stocks probably will. However, the next ten years could be quite different from the past ten years.

Here's another fact to consider, since 1972 stocks have passed through six bull markets and six bear markets.[7] Each market, however, has differed in both duration and magnitude. The 1990 bear market lasted less than five months, and the 1973–74 bear market lasted almost two years. The 1980 bull market lasted about a year. By contrast, the bull market that began in 1990 has lasted nine years and counting. Whenever some "expert" tells you he or she has a system that has regularly beaten the market, remember this warning: past performance is all well and good, but the past is no guarantee of the future.

POSITIVE RELATIONSHIP BETWEEN RISK AND RETURN

In general, a positive relationship exists between risk and return. Higher risk investments must offer investors higher potential returns. Although there may be some important exceptions, historically at least, the positive relationship between risk and return seems pretty clear.

Exhibit 1.2 graphs *cumulative wealth indexes* of stocks, Treasury bonds and Treasury bills and provides a comparison of risk levels and returns. (We'll talk about how a cumulative wealth index is constructed in the next chapter.) All these indexes assume that an investor started with $1,000 in 1926 and held each investment through June 30, 1999. The indexes show how much wealth the investments in stocks or bills would have produced at the end of each year. Stocks have clearly outperformed T-bonds and T-bills by a wide margin. A $1,000 investment in stocks at the beginning of 1926 would have been worth more than $2.5 million by the end of 1996. Similar investments in T-bonds and T-bills would have been worth about $39,000 and $15,000, respectively, by the middle of 1999. Measuring the averages, stock returns had an average return of about 13 percent per year versus 5.5 percent for T-bonds and 3.8 percent for T-bills. At the same time, however, stocks have shown far more year-to-year variation in returns than either T-bonds or T-bills. One measure of risk is the amount by which returns vary from period to period.

What explains the positive relationship between risk and return? The answer is risk aversion; all investors are risk averse to one degree or another (for example, they prefer to avoid risk that carries no enticement). Let's say you can play a game of chance for $100. Chances are fifty-fifty that if you play the game, you will either lose your $100 bet or double your money. Would you play the game? If you're risk averse, you probably would not. If you play the game, you are taking a risk and the total expected payoff from the game is zero.[8] This means your expected wealth will be the same regardless of whether or not you take the risk.

---

[7]A bull market is one where prices are generally rising; a bear market is one where prices are generally falling.

[8]The expected payoff from the game is found as follows: 0.5($100) + 0.5(−$100) = $0.

Exhibit 1.2 ✦ Cumulative Wealth Indexes of Stocks, Bonds, and Bills: 1926–1999

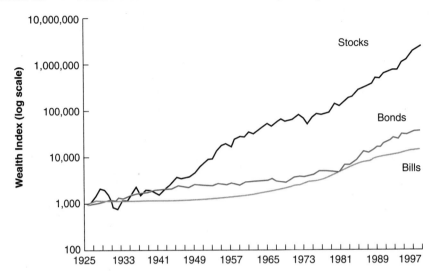

Now change the odds slightly. Suppose you have a one-in-three chance of losing $100 and a two-in-three chance of making $100. (The game still costs $100 to play.) If you are risk averse, you are more likely to play the game now because the expected payoff is now positive (it is about $34), meaning that your expected wealth will increase if you play. Risk aversion leads you to demand compensation, in the form of a positive expected payoff, to voluntarily take risk.

BENEFITS OF DIVERSIFICATION

The desire to avoid risk leads investors to resist putting all their investment nest eggs in one basket. Distributing available funds among several investments reduces the risk of harm from an adverse move in any one security. This diversification benefits investors, as both academics and practitioners widely agree. The well-known financial adviser and writer Andrew Tobias states that the goal of investing is to

> Buy low, sell high. Having said that, the fact remains that it's rarely possible to know with any real degree of confidence what is low or high. To know that you have to know what the future will bring and no one does. As a result, the only sensible strategy for all but the most avid risk takers is to diversify.[9]

In a nutshell, diversification is beneficial because it allows investors to beat the risk/return tradeoff, up to a point. Through diversification they can expose themselves to less risk, yet at the same time maintain about the same expected return. Alternatively, they can increase the expected return on their investments without significantly increasing risk.

---

[9]Andrew Tobias, *The Only Other Investment Guide You'll Ever Need* (New York: Bantam Books, 1989), p. 104.

Exhibit 1.3 ✦ The Benefits of Diversification

	Stock 1	Stock 2	Portfolio (half 1 and half 2)
Return	30.3%	33.7%	32.0%
Standard deviation (a measure of risk)	17.3%	16.0%	11.9%
Coefficient of variation (a measure of the risk/return tradeoff)	0.56	0.47	0.37

Notes: A higher standard deviation indicates more risk. A lower coefficient of variation indicates a better risk/return tradeoff.

Does diversification really work? The answer is clearly yes. In Exhibit 1.3 we show measures of risk and return for two stocks randomly drawn from the S&P 500. (We describe how these risk and return measures are calculated in the next chapter.) The same statistics are calculated for a portfolio consisting of an equal combination of the two stocks.

At first glance, the results might look like the result of magic. After all, the portfolio's return is about the same as returns from the two individual stocks. But the standard deviation is lower. The coefficient of variation is also lower, indicating a better risk/return tradeoff. This is the result, not of some sort of alchemy, but rather of diversification.

Not only do we know that diversification works, but perhaps more remarkably, we know why it works. Diversification works because returns on individual securities are not perfectly correlated over time. Just because one security's price rises by 10 percent this year, no one can say that all securities will perform exactly that way. Some securities prices will rise more, some will rise less, and some will fall. For example, between July 1984 and August 1987, the S&P 500 stock index more than doubled (up to 118 percent), yet stocks of drug companies were up more than 200 percent, and oil stocks rose less than 90 percent. Between October 1990 and December 1992, the S&P 500 rose about 42 percent, but computer stocks dropped about 40 percent. We have a lot more to say about diversification starting in Chapter 17.

INVESTING KNOWS NO NATIONAL BOUNDARIES

Throughout history intrepid investors have searched outside their own countries for good investment opportunities. During the 1800s, for example, English and Scottish investment trusts provided much of the capital to build the railroads in the western United States. In the 1960s, visionaries such as John Templeton started to open up foreign stock markets to U.S. investors. Nevertheless, even ten years ago few U.S. investors ever ventured beyond national boundaries.

This is no longer true. Today more and more U.S. investors are going international. For example, U.S. investors poured almost $5.5 billion into international stock mutual funds during the first six months of 1996. These investments are not limited to established foreign markets such as Canada, Germany, or Japan; intrepid investors have expanded to the emerging markets in countries such as Brazil, Malaysia, and Turkey.

Many forces are driving contemporary investing across national boundaries. Certainly the political and economic changes that swept over the world in the late 1980s and early 1990s contributed to the globalization of investments by opening up many parts of the world to foreign investment. Another factor has been the integration of security markets worldwide. Today, U.S. T-bonds are traded in Singapore, German stocks are traded in Tokyo, and Japanese stocks are traded in New York. An investor who wants to buy or sell several thousand shares of stock in a U.S. company may be as likely to trade the shares on the London Stock Exchange as on the New York Stock Exchange. Furthermore, most governments and large corporations raise capital by selling securities worldwide.

Although investing internationally can offer U.S. investors attractive returns, it is not without its share of risk. For one thing, international investing exposes you to foreign-exchange risk. Changes in the value of the U.S. dollar, relative to other currencies, can have either a positive or a negative impact on your returns. For example, during the first six months of 1996, Japanese stocks rose by 10 percent measured in yen. Measured in dollars, Japanese stocks rose by more than 25 percent.

Many international markets, especially the emerging markets, are notoriously volatile. As an example, in 1993 Fidelity's Emerging Markets Fund produced a total return of more than 65 percent. Investors who flocked to the fund during 1994 were, no doubt, disappointed; the fund's annual return since 1993 has averaged less than 5 percent.

FINANCIAL MARKETS FUNCTION PRETTY WELL

Despite the risk and novelty of international investing, our fifth truism states that the financial markets function quite well throughout most of the world, especially in the more developed countries. Although not perfect, financial markets are generally fair, orderly, and competitive, with many buyers and sellers. Furthermore, although investors should always be wary, unscrupulous traders are peddling far fewer outright fraudulent securities today compared with seventy-five years ago.

What makes a market function well? Three characteristics of today's financial markets illuminate this question. First, security prices adjust quickly, although not always correctly, to new information. For example, on June 9, 1993, Apple Computer's stock lost more than 10 percent of its value as investors reacted to negative news about the company's earnings. Had you owned Apple you could hardly have avoided the debacle, so rapidly did the stock drop after the announcement that day. In fact, a week before the June announcement, between June 2 and June 8, Apple had lost more than 14 percent of its value. The issue of how security prices react to new information is discussed extensively in Chapter 7.

A second characteristic of today's financial markets is the existence of several major equilibrium pricing relationships. If specific pricing relationships among different securities get out of line, in a well-functioning market, prices will quickly adjust to correct levels specified by the pricing relationships. Consider a simple example of an equilibrium pricing relationship. An investor might buy an option to buy 100 shares of some stock at, say, $50 per share. (This is referred to as a call option.) If the stock is currently trading for $60 per share, you know that the option must have a market price of at least $1,000 (60 minus 50, times 100). To see why, assume the option is selling for $700. Someone could buy the option, exercise it to buy the stock for $50 per share, paying $5,000 for 100 shares, and then immediately sell the stock for $60 per share. This risk free transaction would pay $300 (ignoring transaction costs). This is an example of arbitrage. Obviously, if one person could profit from this transaction, so could everyone else, and their purchases would drive the option's price upward quickly from $700 to at least $1,000. This kind of balance between supply and demand keeps price relationships among securities near equilibrium positions.

Finally, today's smoothly functioning financial markets leave no easy money on the table. Each investor competes with millions of other investors for great investments; many of these competitors devote substantial resources to the search. On-line trading and almost instant access to information make the financial markets even more competitive today. This does not mean, however, that small individual investors cannot compete with large institutional investors, nor that investors should not look for great investments. It means simply that great investments, those that are undervalued, meaning they offer better risk/reward characteristics than the market in general, are not easy to find. Undervalued securities typically don't stay undervalued for long.

MISTAKES HAPPEN

People make investment decisions, and people aren't perfect. Therefore, people make investment mistakes. One cynic noted that investments is really the study of mistakes in retrospect. Exhibit 1.4 lists some of the more common pitfalls investors should try to avoid. Here, we elaborate on some of them.

- ✦ *Fad Investing.* Investing in something just because everyone else is, is rarely a good idea. Fads become bubbles, and bubbles break. An old Wall Street expression reads something like this, "When you hear that everyone is buying, ask who's selling."
- ✦ *Chasing Returns.* Some investors continually move money in and out of investments on the basis of short-term returns. This strategy rarely works. Performance measured over a short period of time is often a poor predictor of future performance.
- ✦ *Ignoring the Effects of Taxes and Inflation.* Taxes and inflation can turn seemingly safe investments into money losers. For example, over the past twenty-five years the return from Treasury bills—what most people would

---

Exhibit 1.4 ✦ COMMON INVESTMENT PITFALLS

Investing has the potential to substantially increase your future wealth but is also fraught with danger. Here are some common investment pitfalls.

- ✦ Fad investing
- ✦ Chasing returns
- ✦ Ignoring the corrosive effect of inflation and taxes on investment returns.
- ✦ Buying after a major price increase
- ✦ Selling after a major price decline
- ✦ Keeping a loser in the hope of eventually breaking even
- ✦ Trusting self-appointed touts and investment gurus
- ✦ Not fully understanding investment risk
- ✦ Fearing the wrong risks
- ✦ Investing with no plan or goals
- ✦ Failing to diversify sufficiently
- ✦ Under investing in common stocks

consider to be a low-risk investment—is actually negative once taxes and inflation are taken into account.

✦ ***Selling after a Big Drop/Buying after a Big Increase.*** A great deal of evidence, both anecdotal and scientific, indicates that investors often overreact to new information, both positive and negative. Many savvy investors look to buy after major price declines and sell after major price advances.

✦ ***Hanging on to a Loser.*** Say you buy a stock for $50 a share. Almost immediately it drops to $40 a share, a decline of 20 percent. Would you sell? Many investors would hold onto the stock hoping for a rebound. Yet in order to get back to $50, the stock will have to rise in price by 25 percent. Maybe it will, but then again maybe it wouldn't. You must make that determination rationally. History is full of examples of investments that never bounced back. Polaroid, for example, reached its all-time high in 1972.

✦ ***Trusting the Self-Appointed Touts and Gurus.*** Lots of people out there would love to give you investment advice. Unfortunately, the quality of this advice can be quite variable and many advisors have a hidden agenda; they want to sell you something. As with all consumer purchases, let the buyer beware.

Outline of Future Chapters

This book is divided into seven parts. Part I, the World of Investments, reviews risk and return, direct investment alternatives, and indirect investment alternatives. Part II, Financial Markets and Investment Selection, discusses the organization of the financial markets, how securities are bought and sold, and how professional investors make investment decisions. Part III, Fixed Income Securities, explores the world of bonds. Part IV, Principles of Security Analysis, outlines in detail how common stocks are analyzed and valued. Part V is devoted to derivative securities and Part VI describes modern portfolio theory. Investment management is discussed in Part VII.

Chapter Summary

1. Why are investment decisions important?
   People invest to increase their future wealth. People also invest in order meet personal goals such as buying a home or sending children to college. Investment decisions are important today because people are living longer and thus will need more money when they retire; because personal income is rising slowly; because the job market has changed; and because we have a longer menu of investment choices.

2. What is the history of investing?
   As an organized legitimate endeavor, investing has a rather short history. The first recognizable banks and stock exchanges emerged only about 350 years ago. Until the 1920s, most stocks were considered wildly speculative investments. In fact, until recently, few Americans owned any stocks or other investments. During the late 1970s and 1980s many Americans made the transition from savers to investors. Today, more than half of all American adults would probably be classified as "investors."

3. What are the steps involved in the investment process?
   The first step in the investment process to complete some preliminary evaluating and assessment. These include preparing financial statements and a budget, making sure you have adequate and appropriate insurance coverage, and establishing an

emergency fund. The second step is to set some realistic investment goals. Third, you must assess your tolerance for risk and determine the return necessary to meet monetary goals. The fourth step is to choose the most appropriate investments; the fifth step is to manage your investments.

4. What are some of the important truisms in investments?

Six important investment truisms apply to investing. One, although history has much to teach us, the past is never a guarantee of the future. Two, risk and return are generally positively related in that higher risk investments must offer higher potential returns. Three, diversification is beneficial, it can reduce risk without significantly reducing returns. Fourth, investing takes place worldwide. Fifth, financial markets throughout much of the world function pretty well. And, sixth, mistakes happen. Investors should try to avoid common pitfalls.

Review Questions and Problems

1. What is the general reason people invest? Cite two or three more specific reasons why people invest.
2. How can investing benefit society as a whole? What are some of the societal benefits of municipal bonds?
3. List some of the reasons why investing is so important today. How have longer life expectancies affected investment decisions?
4. How long has investing been an organized, socially acceptable activity? When did millions of Americans finally make the transition from savers to investors?
5. Before you begin to invest, what preparations should you complete? What factors should influence your investment goals?
6. When you assess risk and return, what are some questions you need to ask yourself? What factors appear to explain differences in risk tolerance?
7. Explain the key investment differences between stocks, bonds, and money market instruments. Which of the three has produced the highest returns historically?
8. Explain the difference between strategic asset allocation and tactical asset allocation. How does a passive approach to investment management differ from an active approach?
9. Historically, have risk and return had a positive or negative relationship with one another? Why should we expect to see such a relationship?
10. List some of the more common investment mistakes. What is the relationship between fad investing and speculative bubbles?

CRITICAL THINKING EXERCISE

Most of the critical thinking exercises at the end of each chapter involve the analysis of actual investment data. Using Microsoft Excel, or a similar spreadsheet program, will make the exercises much less tedious. (You may wish to review how to use Excel and its key features.) For Chapter 1, complete the following tasks:

1. Open the Data Workbook (included on the disk that accompanies the text). Familiarize yourself with the various worksheets contained in the data workbook, including how the data are presented.
2. Open the Wizard Workbook (also included on the disk). The Wizard Worksheet consists of a series of prebuilt worksheets designed to solve common investment problems. Familiarize yourself with each worksheet.

THE INTERNET INVESTOR

1. The Internet contains a wealth of information and assistance on many investment topics. What's more, much of it is free. To help you get the most out of the "Internet Investor" exercises that appear at the end of every chapter, visit the following Web site. List three or four suggestions that will help you improve your "surfing" skills.

    www.msn.com/tutorial/default.html

    One excellent investment-oriented Web site is

    investor.msn.com

2. Visit the site and write a brief summary of some of the material and tools you found there.

3. One of the initial steps in the investment process is to assess your tolerance for risk. Visit the Web site, *www.investoreducation.org/quiz2a.htm*, and take the interactive quiz. According to the results, how much investment risk can you tolerate? Do you agree or disagree with the results?

FUNDAMENTALS OF RISK AND RETURN

PREVIOUSLY...

We provided an overview of investments, including a brief history of investing, the investment process, and some of the apparent truisms in investments.

IN THIS CHAPTER...

We introduce the concepts of risk and return in detail, the twin towers of investing. People invest in order to earn a rate of return. At the same time, however, all investing exposes you to risk. We'll review how to measure returns, how to summarize returns, the various types of risk, and how some types of risk can be measured.

TO COME...

The foundation of investments continues by discussing the characteristics of the major investment alternatives available today.

Chapter Objectives

After reading Chapter 2 you should be able to answer the following questions:

1. What are the sources of investment returns?
2. How are investment returns measured?
3. What is investment risk and how is it measured?
4. What is the relationship between risk and required return?
5. How can risk and return aid in investment selection?
6. What are the realized returns and risks from stocks and other investments?

One of the investment truisms we discussed in Chapter 1 was the positive relationship between risk and return. In a nutshell, higher risk investments must offer investors higher potential returns because investors, as a group, are risk averse. Risk aversion has two general implications. The first is that people will pay to avoid risk—something we all do when we buy insurance. We transfer risk from ourselves to the insurance company, in exchange for a fee (the insurance premium). Risk aversion also implies that people will accept risk only if they're offered some sort of inducement. Higher potential returns are one such inducement.

Historically the positive relationship between risk and return is easy to document. For example, between 1926 and today, stocks have had an average annual return of about 13 percent. By contrast, Treasury bill returns have averaged slightly less than 4 percent per year over the same period. At the same time, however, stock returns have shown far more year to year variation than have T-bills returns. (As we'll discuss in this chapter, a higher year to year variation is an indication of higher risk.) Since 1926, annual stock returns have ranged from a high of over 54 percent to a low of −43 percent. Annual T-bill returns, by comparison, have been relatively stable between a high of 14.5 percent and a low 0.1 percent since 1926.

Risk and return dominate the study of investments. Investors incur risk each time they exchange current income for future promised returns. Understanding risk and return is crucial when selecting and evaluating investment alternatives. In this chapter, we'll describe the sources of investment returns, how we measure investment returns, the many types of investment risk, and how investment risk is measured.

Sources of Investment Returns

Investments offer two potential sources of returns: income and price changes. Income is the periodic cash flow paid the investor. Some investments pay no income, and others pay a relatively high amount. Some investments pay a fixed amount each year, other investment incomes can vary quite a bit from year to year. If you own a stock, the income you receive is referred to as **dividends.** Companies that pay dividends typically pay them four times a year. The income received from bonds and money market instruments is referred to as **interest.** Most bonds pay interest twice a year.

dividends
Periodic income received from stock investments.

The other source of investment returns is price changes. The prices of most investments, though *not* all, usually rise or fall during a period of time. We refer to an increase in the price of an investment as a **capital gain;** a decrease in the price of an investment is referred to as a **capital loss.** When added to income, capital gains obviously increase investment returns, and capital losses decrease investment returns. Price declines can create negative investment returns even if the investment pays dividends or interest.

interest
Periodic income received from bonds and money market instruments.

capital gain
An increase in the price or value of an asset.

For example, during 1994 the return from Treasury bonds was −7.8 percent. The following year, T-bonds returned almost 29 percent. What happened? Bond prices fell throughout much of 1994, and these price declines more than offset interest payments. During 1995, by contrast, bond prices rose sharply. Interest payments combined with capital gains to produce an impressive return.

capital loss
A decrease in the price or value of an asset.

PAPER VERSUS REAL GAINS AND LOSSES

We stop for a moment here to distinguish between paper gains and losses, and real gains and losses. A simple example will illustrate the difference. Say you buy a stock for $50 a share. A year later, the stock is selling for $60 a share. In one sense you've earned $10 a share, but unless you sell the stock it's only a hypothetical, or paper profit, not a real one. Similarly, if the price of the stock had fallen from $50 to $40, your $10 loss would be only a paper loss unless you sold the stock.

The distinction between paper and real gains and losses has several important implications for investors, one of which is taxes. Only real, or using tax jargon, *realized* capital gains or losses have tax implications. Taxable investors must pay additional federal income taxes on realized capital gains. On the other hand, realized capital losses can be deducted.

Ex-Ante versus Ex-Post Returns

Between the beginning of 1990 and the end of 1999, stock returns have averaged close to 17 percent per year. What kind of return is this? It's a historical return, also known as an **ex-post return.** It's what someone *would* have earned had they invested in stocks during the 1990s. Let's say, an analyst forecasts that stocks will return an average of 15 percent over the next ten years. This return is an **ex-ante return.** It's the return we expect to earn over some future period of time.

    Obviously, the only investment returns we can accurately measure are ex-post returns. But we should base investment decisions today on ex-ante returns. It may sound like a cliché, but you can only go forward, not back in time when investing. All investors are constantly confronted with the question: how well do historical returns predict future returns? It's a hard question to answer. As we discussed briefly in Chapter 1, the past teaches us a great deal, but the past is never a guarantee of the future.

ex-post returns
Historical returns.

ex-ante returns
Expected future returns.

Measuring Investment Returns

Since investment returns can come from income and price changes, or both, any proper measure of investment needs to incorporate both. Exhibit 2.1. lists annual returns for the Fidelity Fund (a stock mutual fund) over a recent ten-year period. The returns listed are called **total returns** or **holding period returns.** Holding period returns incorporate both income as well as price changes.

total returns (holding period returns)
A measure of investment returns including both price changes and income.

Calculating Holding Period Returns

Holding period returns are calculated over a specific period of time, say a month, quarter, or year. The formula is as follows:

$$HPR_t = \frac{P_t - P_{t-1} + CF_t}{P_{t-1}},$$ (2.1)

where HPR_t is the holding period return over period t, P_t is the price at the end of the period, P_{t-1} is the price at the beginning of the period, and CF_t is the income, or cash flow, received from the investment during the period.

    The data necessary to calculate annual holding period returns for the Fidelity Fund are shown in Exhibit 2.2. Let's work an example. At the beginning of 1998, or the end of 1997, the Fidelity Fund had a net asset value (the net asset value is a mutual fund's price) of $30.87; at the end of 1998 the fund's net asset value had risen to $38.25. In addition, the fund had cash distributions of $2.11 during 1998. The holding period return for 1998 was:

$$\frac{\$38.25 - \$30.87 + \$2.11}{\$30.87} = 30.7\% \text{ (rounded)}.$$

Exhibit 2.1 ✦ ANNUAL RETURNS FOR FIDELITY FUND

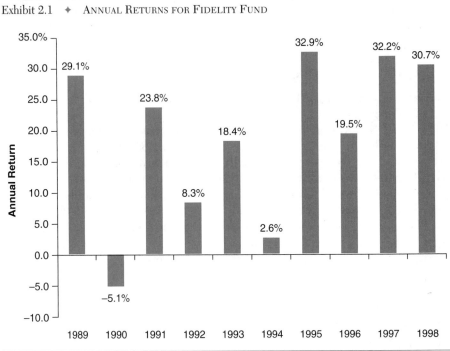

Exhibit 2.2 ✦ CALCULATING ANNUAL HOLDING PERIOD RETURNS FOR THE FIDELITY FUND

Year End	Net Asset Value	Cash Distributions	Holding Period Return
1988	15.40		
1989	17.93	1.95	29.1%
1990	16.28	0.74	−5.1
1991	18.51	1.65	23.8
1992	18.98	1.06	8.3
1993	19.48	2.99	18.4
1994	18.72	1.27	2.6
1995	23.06	1.82	32.9
1996	25.38	2.19	19.5
1997	30.87	2.67	32.2
1998	38.25	2.11	30.7

Equation 2.1 can be broken down into two components, one measuring the return from income and one measuring the return from price changes:

$$\text{HPR} = \text{Return from income} + \text{Return from price changes},$$

$$= \frac{CF_t}{P_{t-1}} + \frac{(P_t - P_{t-1})}{P_{t-1}}. \tag{2.2}$$

Breaking down the Fidelity Fund's 1998 return between income and price changes:

$$= \frac{\$2.11}{\$30.87} + \frac{\$38.25 - \$30.87}{\$30.87},$$

$30.7\% = 6.8\% + 23.9\%.$

The breakdown of the Fidelity Fund's holding period return between income and price changes for the entire ten-year period is shown in Exhibit 2.3.

Calculating Expected Returns

All of the holding period returns shown so far are ex-post returns—meaning actual historical returns. We can also use Equation 2.1 to calculate expected future returns, or ex-ante returns. For example, let's assume we expect the Fidelity Fund's net asset value to be $42.50 at the end of 1999. Further, we expect the fund to distribute $2.00 in cash to shareholders. Therefore, the expected holding period return for 1999 is:

$$\frac{\$42.50 - \$38.25 + \$2.00}{\$38.25} = 16.3\% \text{ (rounded)}.$$

Of course this is only an expected return; the actual 1999 return may be quite different! We'll discuss the importance of expected returns later in the chapter.

Annualizing Holding Period Returns

There is nothing magical about a one-year holding period. We can use Equation 2.1 to compute the return for a holding period shorter than one year. If you do that, however, it may be beneficial to annualize the holding period return, because investors typically think of returns on an annual basis. The general formula for annualizing a holding period return is:

$$(1 + HPR_t)^m - 1, \tag{2.3}$$

Exhibit 2.3 ✦ BREAKDOWN OF THE FIDELITY FUND'S HOLDING PERIOD RETURN BETWEEN INCOME AND PRICE CHANGES

Breakdown

Year	Holding Period Return	Income	Price Changes
1989	29.1%	12.6%	16.5%
1990	−5.1	4.1	−9.2
1991	23.8	10.1	13.7
1992	8.3	5.7	2.6
1993	18.4	15.7	2.7
1994	2.6	6.5	−3.9
1995	32.9	9.7	23.2
1996	19.5	9.5	10.0
1997	32.2	10.5	21.7
1998	30.7	6.8	23.9

where m is the number of periods per year. For example, in the case of monthly returns, m would equal 12.

At the beginning of the first quarter of 1999, the Fidelity Fund had a NAV of $36.69. At the end of the quarter, the fund's NAV has risen to $38.74. It made no cash distributions during the first quarter of 1999. Therefore, its quarterly holding period return was

$$(\$38.74 - \$36.69)/\$36.69 = 5.59\%$$

To annualize this quarterly return, we use Equation 2.3:

$$(1 + 0.059)^4 - 1 = 24.31\%.$$

Inflation Adjusted Returns

In your introductory finance class you may have discussed the difference between nominal returns and real returns. Nominal returns are dollar returns and tell us nothing about changes in the purchasing power of the dollars. Real returns that take out the effect of inflation are also referred to as inflation-adjusted returns.

You calculate a real holding period return, RHPR, as follows:

$$RHPR = \frac{(1 + HPR)}{(1 + IR)} - 1, \tag{2.4}$$

where HPR is the nominal holding period return and IR is the rate of inflation.[1] For example, in 1998 the nominal holding period return for large stocks was 23.14 percent and the rate of inflation was 3.1 percent. Therefore, the real holding period return (RHPR) for large stocks was

$$\frac{1.2314}{1.0310} - 1 = 19.44\%.$$

International Returns

Say you invest in a nondollar-denominated investment. Calculating the dollar return on this investment is more complicated and will be affected by changes in exchange rates. It is best illustrated with an example:

You bought a British government bond for £1,000 one year ago. Today the bond's price is £1,030. During the year, the bond also paid you £65 in interest. When you bought the bond the exchange rate was 1.65 ($ per £); today the exchange rate is 1.62. What was your holding period return, measured both in pounds and in dollars? Finding the HPR in pounds is simple if we use Equation 2.1:

$$(1,030 - 1,000 + 65)/1,000 = 9.5\%.$$

Now, let's find the HPR measured in U.S. dollars. First, calculate how many dollars it took to buy the bond a year ago: 1.65 × £1,000 = $1,650. Next, compute the dollar value of the bond's current price as well as the income you received: 1.62 × (£1,030

---

[1] A close approximation for the real holding period return can be found by simply subtracting the inflation rate from the nominal holding period return.

+ £65) = $1,773.90. Now we can find the holding period return in U.S. dollars using a slightly modified version of Equation 2.1. The dollar HPR equals: ($1,773.90 − $1,650)/$1,650 , or 7.51 percent.

In our example, the bond had a holding period return of 9.50 percent, measured in pounds, but only 7.51 percent measured in U.S. dollars. The difference is because the dollar strengthened relative to the pound (meaning it took more dollars to buy one pound at the beginning of the year than it did at the end of the year). At the beginning of the year, you had to pay $1.65 to buy one pound; at the end of the year, one pound bought only $1.62. Had the reverse occurred, and the pound strengthened relative to the dollar, the holding period return in dollars would have exceeded 9.5 percent, the holding period return in pounds. Had the exchange rate remained the same, the holding period return in dollars would have equaled 9.5 percent.

Total Return Indexes

A holding period return measures the change in wealth from the beginning of a period to the end of the period. Many times, when evaluating an investment, we want to measure the change in the level of wealth over a period of time. A total return index allows us to measure the cumulative effect of investment returns. The value of a total return index, I_t, at the end of period t, is defined as

$$I_t = I_{t-1} \times (1 + HPR_t). \tag{2.5}$$

The beginning index value, I_0, is arbitrary but is usually set at 1, 100, 1,000, or some other multiple of 10.

An example of a total return index is shown in Exhibit 2.4. The data show the cumulative change in the level of wealth for an investor in the Fidelity Fund between the beginning of 1989 and the end of 1998 (the initial index value is set at 1).

Total return indexes have various uses. For one thing, the total return index tells us the growth of a dollar investment. In the case of the Fidelity Fund the total return index tells us that each dollar invested in the fund at the beginning of 1989 was worth almost $5.50 by the end of 1998, so a $10,000 investment made at the beginning of 1989 would have grown to $54,778 by the end of 1998.[2]

Total return indexes also serve to calculate returns over holding periods of varying lengths. We can use the equation below to find a holding period return:

$$HPR_t = \left(\frac{I_t}{I_{t-1}}\right) - 1, \tag{2.6}$$

where I_t is the index value at the end of the period and I_{t-1} is the index value at the beginning of the period.

For example, at the beginning of 1989 the total return index for the Fidelity Fund was 1; at the end of 1998 the index was 5.4778. Therefore, the Fund's return over the entire ten-year period was: $(5.4778/1.0000) - 1 = 447.78\%$.

---

[2]Total return indexes assume that all cash distributions are reinvested.

Exhibit 2.4   ♦   Total Return Index for the Fidelity Fund: 1989–1998

Year	Holding Period Return	Total Return Index
1988		1.0000
1989	29.1%	1.2907
1990	−5.1	1.2251
1991	23.8	1.5172
1992	8.3	1.6430
1993	18.4	1.9448
1994	2.6	1.9956
1995	32.9	2.6525
1996	19.5	3.1708
1997	32.2	4.1905
1998	30.7	5.4778

Summarizing Returns

So far, we have discussed calculating holding period returns, real rates of return, returns from international investments, and total return indexes. Although all are useful measures of return and can aid in investment analysis and selection, we also need summary statistics of returns over a period of time. Two such statistics are the arithmetic mean and the geometric mean.

Arithmetic Mean

The arithmetic mean is simply the average of all observations in a data series. If we have a set of holding period returns for an investment, we can calculate the arithmetic mean by summing the returns and dividing by the number of observations. More formally, the arithmetic mean, or AM, is found using the following formula:

$$AM = \frac{\sum_{t-1}^{T} HPR_t}{T}, \qquad (2.7)$$

where T is the number of returns in the data series. Go back to the returns shown in Exhibit 2.2. We have ten years' worth of returns, so T is equal to 10. Summing the annual holding period returns (29.1% + −5.1% + 23.8%, and so on) equals 192.4 percent. Dividing the sum by 10 gives us the arithmetic mean, 19.2 percent.[3]

Let's say you have a series of monthly or quarterly returns. You can use Equation 2.7 to calculate the arithmetic mean. The arithmetic mean can then be annualized by using Equation 2.3. For example, the average monthly return on a stock is 1.7%. Annualized, the average return equals

$$(1.017)^{12} - 1 = 22.42\%.$$

---

[3]Any calculator with statistical functions—including all business or financial calculators—can find an arithmetic mean. Microsoft Excel also has built in statistical functions, including one that finds the arithmetic mean.

GEOMETRIC MEAN

Another measure of the "average" return over a period of time is called the geometric mean. The geometric mean is also called the compound average annual return. The geometric mean is found using the following formula:

$$GM = \left[\prod_{T=1}^{T} (1 + HPR_t) \right]^{1/T} - 1,$$ (2.8)

where Π is the product of the terms $(1 + HPR_1)$, $(1 + HPR_2)$, . . . , and $(1 + HPR_T)$. Between the beginning of 1989 and the end of 1998, the Fidelity Fund's geometric mean is

$$[5.4778]^{1/10} - 1 = 18.5\%.$$

Over this ten-year period the Fidelity Fund had a compound average annual return of 18.5 percent.

You may have already recognized that the number inside the bracket—the product of 1 plus holding period return—is the same as the total return index we found using Equation 2.4 (setting the initial index value equal to 1). It's no coincidence, the two are the same. The total return index measures the change in wealth over a period of time. The geometric mean measures the *average* annual change in wealth.

Equation 2.8 can also help find the compound average annual return over shorter time intervals. Let's go back to the Fidelity Fund. So far we've found that the compound average annual return over the ten years, ending in 1998, was 18.5 percent. What was the compound average annual return over the *five*-year period ending in 1998? To answer the question, we need the total return index at the beginning of the period (the end of 1993), 1.9448, and the total return index at the end of the period, 5.4778. The compound average annual return is

$$\left[\frac{5.4778}{1.9448} \right]^{1/5} - 1 = 23.01\%.$$

COMPARING THE GEOMETRIC AND ARITHMETIC MEANS

Let's review. Over the ten-year period ending in 1998, the Fidelity Fund had an arithmetic mean return of 19.2 percent and a geometric mean return of 18.6 percent. Why are the two different? The answer is because the two means measure different aspects. The geometric mean is backward looking, measuring the change in wealth over several periods of time, including compounding effects. By contrast, the arithmetic mean represents the typical return over time. In the case of the Fidelity Fund, the typical annual return is 19.2 percent. The arithmetic mean also provides an indication of the expected return for an investment for use in forecasting, discounting, or estimating the cost of capital.

In fact, the arithmetic and geometric means will be equal only if an investment provides a set of equal returns for each period. If the returns vary at all from period to period, the arithmetic mean will be higher than the geometric mean. Also, more variation in returns from period to period increases the difference between the arithmetic and geometric means. Because the arithmetic and geometric means measure different things and have somewhat different uses, it is a good idea to calculate both.

You will find that most historical data for investment returns include both the arithmetic and geometric means.

RECAP   So far we've discussed how to calculate holding period returns—a return measure that incorporates both price changes and income—how to adjust returns for inflation, how to compute returns for nondollar-denominated investments, how to construct a total return index, and how to summarize returns.

To see how well you understand the material you've read up to this point, answer the following questions:

1. At the beginning of 1999, a stock was selling for $50 a share; at the end of the year it was selling for $65 a share. If the stock paid $1.50 in dividends, what was its holding period return for 1999?
2. Is the return you calculated in Question 1 an ex-post or ex-ante return?
3. Assume the rate of inflation during 1999 was 3 percent. Find the inflation adjusted or real return for the stock in Question 1.
4. At the beginning of 1999, you bought shares of a Japanese stock, paying ¥1,500 per share. At the end of 1999, the price per share had risen to ¥1,750. Assuming the exchange rate between the dollar and yen (yen per dollar) was 125 at the beginning of the year and 130 at the end of the year, calculate your return measured in both yen and U.S. dollars.
5. A mutual fund produced the following annual holding period returns over the preceding five years: 15.5%, 20.0%, −10.5%, 35.0%, and 27.5%. Construct a total return index. If you had invested $10,000 in this stock at the beginning of the five-year period, how much would your investment have been worth at the end of the five-year period? Calculate the holding period return for the entire five-year period.
6. Using the information provided in the prior question, calculate both the arithmetic mean and the geometric mean. Why are the two different? What does each reflect?
7. Use the return data for the Fidelity Fund in Exhibit 2.4. Calculate the compound average annual return for the three-year period ending in 1998.

Investment risk

We have said that the concepts of risk and return dominate investments. We have also noted that all investing exposes investors to some degree of risk. But, what is risk and to what kinds of risk are investors exposed?

A Definition of Risk

risk
Uncertainty over an investment's return over some future period of time.

Risk simply means that some uncertainty exists regarding what an investment's actual return will be over some period in the future. The greater the uncertainty, the greater the risk. Risk, in and of itself, is neither good nor bad; it merely exists. Risk is also often a double-edged sword, having an upside as well as a downside.

To illustrate our general definition of risk, consider three hypothetical investments. We'll call them A, B, and C. We'll assume some uncertainty concerning their returns, but assume that all possible returns for the next year are known for all three, as are the probabilities of these returns occurring.

Exhibit 2.5 gives the probability distributions of next year's possible returns for all three securities. The probability distributions are shown graphically in Exhibit 2.6. Security A, has a 100 percent chance (probability = 1.00) that its return next year will be 10 percent. Security B has a 15 percent chance (probability = 0.15) that it will

---

Exhibit 2.5 ✦ PROBABILITY OF POSSIBLE RETURN

Possible Return	Security A	Security B	Security C
0%	0.00	0.00	0.10
5	0.00	0.15	0.20
10	1.00	0.70	0.40
15	0.00	0.15	0.20
20	0.00	0.00	0.10

Exhibit 2.6 ✦ BAR GRAPH OF THREE SECURITY RETURNS

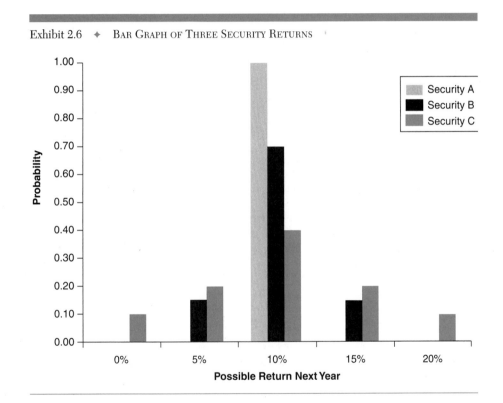

return 5 percent, a 70 percent chance that it will return 10 percent, and a 15 percent chance that it will return 15 percent. There is a 10 percent chance that Security C will return 0 percent, a 20 percent chance that it will return 5 percent, a 40 percent chance that it will return 10 percent, a 20 percent chance that it will return 15 percent, and a 10 percent chance that it will return 20 percent.

Recognize, initially, that all three securities have the same expected return next year, 10 percent. Next year's expected return for each security is simply the sum of the possible returns times the probability of each return occurring, as follows:

$$ER_A = (10\%)1.00 = 10\%,$$
$$ER_B = (5\%)0.15 + (10\%)0.70 + (15\%)0.15 = 10\%,$$
$$ER_C = (0\%)0.10 + (5\%)0.20 + (10\%)0.40 + (15\%)0.20$$
$$+ (20\%)0.10 = 10\%.$$

Given the general description of risk, which of the three securities is the riskiest? Looking at Exhibit 2.6, Security C certainly appears to be the riskiest of the three securities. It has the greatest range of possible returns, 0 percent to 20 percent, and it has the highest probability that its actual return will differ from its expected return. We see only a four in ten chance (probability 0.40) that Security C's actual return will equal its expected return. By contrast, there is a seven in ten chance that Security B's actual return will equal its expected return. Based on our general definition of risk, Security A appears to be risk free. We see no possibility that its actual return can differ from its expected return.

TYPES OF RISK

Although our general definition of risk is a starting point, you should realize that many types of risk exist. All of these types of risk create uncertainty about future investment returns. Further different investments are more sensitive to certain types of risk. The major types of investment risk are

- ✦ Default risk: the risk that an investment will become worthless.
- ✦ Credit risk: the risk that the financial health of the issuer of the security (a corporation or a government) will decline, causing the value of the investment to fall.
- ✦ Tax risk: the risk that some of your investment profits will be subject to taxes.
- ✦ Purchasing power risk: the risk that your investment returns will fail to keep pace with the rate of inflation.
- ✦ Interest rate risk: the risk that interest rates will rise, causing the value of the investment to fall.
- ✦ Market risk: the risk reflected in the periodic fluctuations of security prices.
- ✦ Event risk: the risk that something unexpected and beyond the control of the issuer of the security will occur causing the value of the investment to fall.
- ✦ Liquidity risk: the risk that you may be unable to convert an investment into cash at a price close to its fair value.
- ✦ Foreign exchange risk: the risk that the value of the dollar, relative to another currency, will change causing the dollar return on the investment to decline (applies mainly to nondollar-denominated investments).

As mentioned, different investments expose you to different types of risk, and to varying degrees. For example, common stocks have high amounts of market risk, moderate amounts of default, credit, tax, and event risk, and, for the most part, low amounts of liquidity risk. On the other hand, a Treasury bill exposes you to no default or credit risk, but high amounts of tax and purchasing power risk.

In addition, many types of risk have an upside as well as a downside. For example, interest rates can fall, unexpected events can be good news, and the financial health of the issuer can improve.

Total Risk, Systematic Risk, and Unsystematic Risk

The risks listed in the prior section make up the total risk of an investment. One of the cornerstones of modern portfolio theory, which we'll discuss starting in Chapter 17, is that the total risk of an investment can be broken into two parts. The first part, called unsystematic risk, can be eliminated through diversification that comes about when the security is added to a portfolio. The second part, called systematic risk, cannot be eliminated through diversification.

MEASURING RISK

The greater the uncertainty over future investment returns, the greater the risk of an investment. But how can you actually measure risk in order to compare various investments? In general, risk is associated with the variability of returns. The more variable the returns, the more risky the investment. Take a look at the chart in Exhibit 2.7. It shows the annual returns for large-company stocks and T-bills between 1984 and 1998. Annual stock returns showed much more year-to-year variation than T-bills, ranging from a high of 37.5 percent to a low of −3.2 percent. By contrast, T-bill returns ranged from a high of about 10 percent to a low of 3 percent. Based on these data, it would not be unreasonable to conclude that stocks are riskier than T-bills.

As another example, the chart in Exhibit 2.8 shows the monthly returns for two stocks over a recent five-year period. The two stocks are Staples (an office supply retailer) and Duke Energy (an electric and gas utility). Staples shows more month-to-month variation in returns and appears to be a riskier stock than Duke Energy. Even though we can often make visual judgments concerning the risk of an investment, we still need a statistical measure of risk. Standard deviation is one such measure.

Calculating the Standard Deviation

You may remember from your statistics class that standard deviation measures the dispersion of a set of observations around its arithmetic mean.[4] The greater the standard

Exhibit 2.7 ♦ GRAPH OF LARGE STOCKS AND T-BILLS

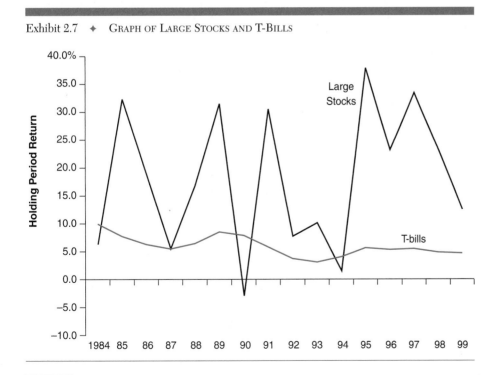

---

[4]The standard deviation is the square root of the variance. The variance also measures the dispersion of a distribution around its mean. Standard deviation is more widely used, however, because standard deviation is always in the same units as the mean. Thus, if we measure a mean rate of return, the standard deviation will also be a rate of return.

deviation, the more dispersed the distribution. Because risk is associated with the variability of returns, the higher the standard deviation of returns, the more risky the investment.

The standard deviation is found using the following formula:

$$SD = \left[\frac{1}{T-1} \sum_{t=1}^{T} (HPR_t - AM)^2 \right]^{1/2}. \tag{2.9}$$

Exhibit 2.9 shows the calculation of the standard deviation of returns for the Fidelity Fund.

Exhibit 2.8 ✦ GRAPH OF DUKE ENERGY AND STAPLES

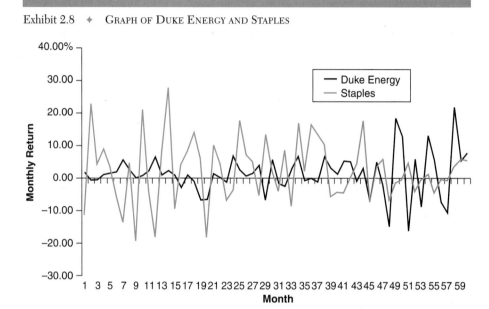

Exhibit 2.9 ✦ CALCULATING THE STANDARD DEVIATION OF RETURNS FOR THE FIDELITY FUND

Year	HPR	HPR − AM	$(HPR - AM)^2$
1989	29.1%	0.0983	0.0097
1990	−5.1	−0.2432	0.0592
1991	23.8	0.0460	0.0021
1992	8.3	−0.1095	0.0120
1993	18.4	−0.0087	0.0001
1994	2.6	−0.1663	0.0277
1995	32.9	0.1368	0.0187
1996	19.5	0.0030	0.0000
1997	32.2	0.1292	0.0167
1998	30.7	0.1148	0.0132
AM	19.2	Sum	0.1592
		Divided by $T - 1$	0.0177
		Square root	13.3%

Going back to the chart in Exhibit 2.7, T-bill returns exhibit less year-to-year variation than do stock returns over the period shown, suggesting that stocks have more risk than T-bills. The standard deviations confirm this. Stock returns have a standard deviation of 12.8 percent whereas the standard deviation of T-bill returns is only 1.9 percent.

Annualizing a Standard Deviation

Let's say you have a series of monthly or quarterly returns. In the prior section we saw how the arithmetic mean could be annualized. Annualizing the standard deviation is also fairly simple. You use Equation 2.9 to calculate the standard deviation (on a monthly or quarterly basis). You then annualize the standard deviation by multiplying the monthly or quarterly standard deviation by the square root of the periods per year,[5] or $SD \times \sqrt{m}$.

For example, based on the returns monthly shown in Exhibit 2.8, we concluded that Staples is a riskier stock than Duke Energy. Indeed, Staples has the higher standard deviation. The monthly standard deviation for Staples is 11.46 percent, whereas the monthly standard deviation for Duke Energy is only 3.65 percent. On an annual basis, the standard deviations of the two stocks are:

$$11.46\% \times \sqrt{12} = 39.68\% \text{ (Staples)}$$
$$3.65\% \times \sqrt{12} = 12.63\% \text{ (Duke Energy)}.$$

In the preceding section we've discussed a general definition of investment risk, the various types of investment risk, and how investment risk can be measured. Answer the following questions to see how well you understand the material on investment risk.

RECAP

8. Briefly explain credit risk, interest rate risk, and market risk.
9. A mutual fund produced the following annual returns over a recent ten year period: 3.94%, 54.92%, 15.89%, 21.43%, −1.12%, 36.28%, 21.94%, 23.00%, 31.57%, 20.71%. Calculate the standard deviation of the returns.
10. Assume two stocks had standard deviations—based on quarterly returns—of 7.89% and 8.45%. Annualize the standard deviations.

Risk and Required Return

As we have discussed, an investor buys a security in anticipation of earning a return over some future holding period. How does the investor determine whether or not the expected return is adequate? Essentially, the investor compares the security's expected return to the investor's required return. If the expected return is at least equal

---

[5]This is actually a close approximation. The more precise formula for annualizing a standard deviation is:

$$\sqrt{[SD^2 + (1 + AM)^2]^n - (1 + AM)^{2m}}.$$

to the required return, the investor will buy the security.[6] What then determines the required rate of return? Three influences on required rates of return are (1) the time value of money, (2) the expected rate of inflation, and (3) the risk of the security.

One underlying principle of finance is that money has a *time value*. This means that a dollar received today is worth more than a dollar received at some future point. Two reasons that money has time value are, of course, inflation and risk. Even with no inflation and absolutely no risk, however, required returns on securities would still be positive. We can call this required return, assuming no inflation or risk, the real rate of return.

Now, the assumption of no inflation may seem unreasonable. To adjust the real rate of return to account for inflation, while still assuming a security that is risk free, the required return would become

$$\text{Risk-free return} = (1 + \text{Real rate of return})(1 + \text{Expected rate of inflation}) - 1$$

This risk-free return is often referred to as the nominal rate of return. Thus, a higher expected rate of inflation increases the required return, even on a risk-free security. This should make sense, because investors want to be compensated for the expected erosion of the value of their returns due to inflation over a security's holding period. In other words, if they expect the rate of inflation to be 5 percent next year, they must earn at least 5 percent on their investments just to keep pace with inflation.

Exhibit 2.10 compares returns on T-bills between 1983 and 1998 to changes in the rate of inflation. (In many respects, a T-bill is the closest practical approximation to a risk-free security.) The figure shows both the nominal and real return on T-bills. The real return on T-bills is a reasonable approximation of the real rate of return.[7] Nominal T-bill returns and inflation generally moved in the same direction (that is, they rose and fell together).

However, notice that the real T-bill return fluctuated dramatically over the ten-year period, ranging from slightly more than 5 percent to about 0.2 percent.

The nominal rate of return still assumes a risk-free security. Few investors try to avoid risk entirely, however. The required return on a risky security can be written as

$$\text{Required return on a risky security} = (1 + \text{Risk free rate})(1 + \text{Risk premium}) - 1$$

The risk premium reflects compensation for the amount of risk for a particular security. More risk requires a higher risk premium, which boosts the required rate of return. Securities have many potential sources of risk, and the risk premium is a function of all of them. As an example of risk premiums, look at Exhibit 2.11. It shows the yields on T-bills, T-bonds, and Baa-rated corporate bonds between 1984 and 1999.

---

[6]In the terminology of security analysis, an investment whose expected return is greater than its required return is *undervalued*. An investment whose expected return is less than its required return is said to be *overvalued*. We'll cover security analysis in depth in Chapters 11–14.

[7]We used the actual rate of inflation to calculate the real return on T-bills, not the expected rate of inflation. While this may sound like semantics, it's an important distinction. Required returns are future returns, not historical ones. Whenever you invest you must form some expectation concerning future inflation and like all forecasts, your forecast of inflation may turn out to be incorrect. This is partly where purchasing power risk comes from.

Exhibit 2.10 ✦ NOMINAL AND REAL RETURNS ON T-BILLS

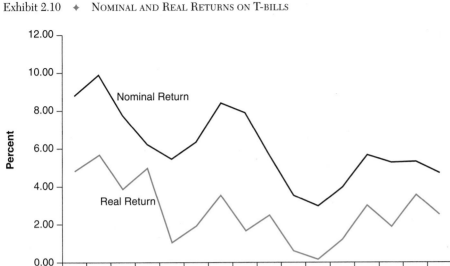

Exhibit 2.11 ✦ ANNUAL YIELDS ON Baa CORPORATE BONDS, T-BONDS, T-BILLS

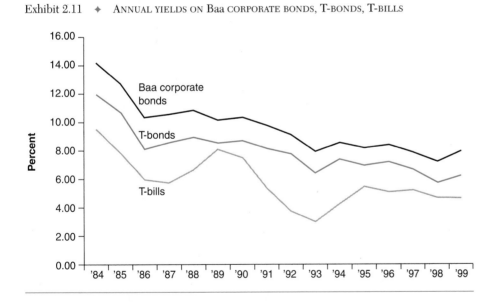

T-bill yields were consistently lower than T-bond yields, which, in turn, were lower than corporate bond yields. In 1992, for example, T-bills yielded 3.45 percent, T-bonds yielded 7.01 percent, and corporate bonds yielded 8.14 percent. Using the simple relationship shown in the above equation, investors assigned a risk premium of about 3.56 percent to T-bonds and about 4.69 percent to corporate bonds over the risk-free T-bill rate. This indicates investors' belief that T-bonds are less risky than corporate bonds. Notice also from Exhibit 2.11, however, that the risk premiums were not constant during the period.

Another way expressing the relationship between risk and required return is the *capital asset pricing model* (or CAPM). CAPM states that the required return on an investment equals

Risk free rate + beta (Market risk premium).

Beta is a measure of systematic risk (risk that cannot be diversified). By definition, the overall market has a risk of one; an investment with a beta greater than one is more risky than the market, and vice versa. The market risk premium equals the required return on the overall market minus the risk-free rate.

CAPM was developed from modern portfolio theory and is generally applied to common stocks. We'll discuss the derivation of CAPM, along with some of its uses, in more detail in later chapters.

Risk, Return, and Investment Selection

Investors can use the risk/return—expected, or mean return, and standard deviation—measures we've discussed so far in choosing between investments. To illustrate, consider these four hypothetical investments:

Investment	Expected Return	Standard Deviation
D	15%	10%
E	15	15
F	10	10
G	20	15

Clearly, a risk-averse individual should pick D over E. Why? D and E have the same expected return, but D has a lower standard deviation. In other words, because E offers you no incentive in the form of a higher expected return, D dominates E. What about D and F? Again, D should be the pick of a risk-averse individual. F has the same standard deviation as D but has a lower expected return. So, D also dominates F.

Now, would a risk-averse individual pick D or G? We really can't say, because, although G has a higher expected return than D, it also has a higher standard deviation. Neither D nor G dominates the other. One risk-averse individual might prefer D, whereas another risk-averse individual might just as legitimately prefer G.

coefficient of variation
A statistical measure of the risk/return trade-off offered by an investment.

Another statistic that may help clarify investment decisions similar to the choice between D and G is called the **coefficient of variation** (CV). The CV is the standard deviation divided by the mean. It measures an investment's risk/return trade-off: the lower the CV, the better the risk/return trade-off. The coefficient of variation for Investment D is 10%/15% = .67, whereas the coefficient of variation for Investment G is 15%/20% =.75. So, we could argue that D offers a slightly better risk/return trade-off than G, but we still can't say that D dominates G.

As another example of using risk and return statistics to make investment decisions, take a look at the historical return data shown below:

Stock	Bell Atlantic	Dow Chemical	Portfolio
Mean return	15.47%	17.95%	16.70%
Standard deviation	17.80	20.86	12.77
Coefficient of variation	1.15	1.16	0.76

Note: the portfolio consists of half Bell Atlantic and half Dow Chemical.

You can't say that Bell Atlantic dominates Dow Chemical, or vice-versa. For although Bell Atlantic has the lower standard deviation, it also has a lower mean return. In fact, you would have a hard time arguing that one stock offers a better risk/return trade-off than the other; the two stocks' coefficients of variation are virtually the same. But compare the individual stocks to the portfolio. Clearly the portfolio dominates Bell Atlantic; the portfolio has a higher mean return *and* a lower standard deviation. And, although the portfolio doesn't dominate Dow, it does offer a better risk/return trade-off (the portfolio's coefficient of variation is only 0.76 compared to 1.16 for Dow). The portfolio—which consists of half Bell Atlantic and half Dow—illustrates the magic of diversification, something we'll talk about in more detail in Chapter 17.

Although statistics such as mean, standard deviation, and coefficient of variation can help make investment decisions, real investment decisions are much more complicated than many of our examples. All investment decisions must relate to the goals of the individual or organization, as well as a host of other considerations. In addition, the impact of factors such as compounding, taxes, and inflation are taken into account. What appears to be the riskier investment, might, in reality, be the best investment once you consider all of the angles. And, remember many types of risk have upsides as well as downsides. The Investment Insights box on page 42, "Fearing the Wrong Risks," discusses what can happen if you focus on short-term volatility and lose sight of the bigger picture.

A Brief Review of Historical Returns

Having reviewed the fundamentals of risk and return, we conclude the chapter by comparing historical returns and risks for stocks, bonds, and money market instruments with a summary of the major highlights rather than a comprehensive review of the historical record. Remember one of the important truisms in investments: although very informative, the past is never a guarantee of the future.

CUMULATIVE WEALTH INDEXES

Let's begin our historical review by examining cumulative wealth indexes for large-company stocks, small-company stocks, Treasury bonds, and Treasury bills, beginning in the mid 1920s. As shown by the chart in Exhibit 2.12, stock returns have exceeded bond returns by a huge margin over the 70-plus year period shown.[8] Each dollar invested in large-company common stocks at the end of 1925 was worth over $2,700 dollars by the end of 1999. Put another way, a $1,000 investment in large stocks made at the end of 1925 would have grown to more than $2.7 million by the end of 1999. By contrast, each dollar invested in Treasury bonds at the end of 1925 was worth slightly more than $38 at the end of 1998 (a $1,000 investment made at the end of 1925 would have grown to only about $38,230 by the end of 1999).

Although large-company stocks have done well, small-company stocks have done even better. Each dollar invested in small stocks at the end of 1925 was worth over

---

[8]All total return indexes assume the reinvestment of dividends or interest. The y-axis in the chart is in a log scale. Equal distances along the y-axis represent the same percentage change. This makes it easier to compare the performance of different return series across time.

INVESTMENT INSIGHTS

FEARING THE WRONG RISKS

If you're saving for retirement or for a newborn's college education, which is a riskier place for your savings, stocks or Treasury bills? What a silly question, you may think. Everyone *knows* that stocks are much riskier than Treasury bills. After all, you can *lose* money in the stock market—prices dropped by more than 25 percent in *one* day, October 19, 1987. With a Treasury bill, or perhaps a certificate of deposit (CD), you're always guaranteed to get your money back. And, look at a chart of stock prices. They resemble a yo-yo: up and down, up and down, up and down. Yet, in some important ways, stocks are actually *less* risky than seemingly safe investments such as Treasury bills or CDs. Many people, in spite of investment horizons of 10, 20, 30 years, or even longer, avoid stocks because they consider stocks too risky. In truth, these people may be fearing the wrong risks. They worry about losing money in the short term, not whether they'll accumulate enough money to meet future needs.

For one thing, CDs and Treasury bills offer no growth potential. They provide income and a guarantee that you'll get your initial investment back, but nothing else. You have to pay taxes each year on the interest you receive and, of course, inflation erodes the purchasing power of your money. Over short periods of time—say, a month or a year—the impact of inflation and taxes is relatively minor. Over longer periods of time, taxes and inflation can devastate the real value of your savings.

During the 25-year period ending in 1998, Treasury bills had an average annual return of slightly more than 7 percent. This means an investment of $1,000 in T-bills at the beginning of 1973 would have been worth about $5,500 by the end of 1997. That may sound pretty good, but it ignores taxes and inflation. A taxable investor—and that's most of us—must pay federal income taxes on the interest received each year from Treasury bills. Assuming a 28 percent tax bracket—not an unrealistic assumption—a $1,000 investment in T-bills made at the beginning of 1973 was worth less than $3,500 by the end of 1997, after taxes.

Now let's factor in inflation. Between 1974 and 1998, inflation averaged about 5.5 percent per year. At that rate $1,000 would have had to have grown to over $3,800 by the end of 1998 just to *maintain* the same purchasing power. The bottom line is that, in real terms, taxable T-bill investors actually *lost* money between 1973 and 1997. The $1,000 invested at the beginning of 1974 would have been worth only about $650 by the end of 1998, after taxes and inflation.

People occasionally overlook another characteristic of T-bills and CDs: interest rates go down as well as up. So, although you'll never lose any money, at least in nominal terms, you could see big declines in your interest income from year to year. For example, the average interest rate paid by banks on one-year CDs fell from almost 7.5 percent in 1990, to less than 5 percent in 1991, to around 3.5 percent in 1992.

What about common stocks, taxes, and inflation? During the past 25 years, stocks, as measured by the Standard and Poor's 500, had an average annual return of slightly more than 13 percent. Although some of the return came from dividends, most came in the form of capital appreciation. And because you pay taxes only on dividends, not on unrealized capital gains, the after-tax return is only a little less than the before-tax return. After taking taxes and inflation into account, stocks still produced an average annual return of more than 8 percent. An investment of $1,000 made at the beginning of 1974 was worth more than $7,000 at the end of 1998 in real after-tax dollars. Put another way, after inflation and taxes, an investment in stocks was worth over 10 times as much as the same initial investment in Treasury bills.

Next, let's look more closely at the issue of stock market volatility. Over short periods of time, the stock market does indeed resemble a yo-yo. For example, during the past 25 years, stock investors made money in 189 out of 300 months (about 60 percent). Stretch the time horizon to one-year intervals, however, and stocks made money in all but five years. Over rolling five-year intervals, stocks made money in all but one five-year period. And in each and every rolling 10-year period or longer interval between 1974 and 1998, stock investors made money. The key point to remember is this: although stocks bounce up and down in the short run, stock prices rise much more than they fall. Focus on the long term, not the yo-yo of short-term ups and downs in stock prices.

The bottom line is that investors with longer time horizons should invest some of their money in stocks or stock mutual funds. Investors in their 20s or 30s saving for retirement, should invest at least 70 percent of their money in stocks. Investors in their 40s and 50s should keep at least half of their retirement funds in the stock market. Even investors in their 60s should still have some of their money in stocks.

Exhibit 2.12 ◆ GRAPH OF TOTAL RETURN INDEX

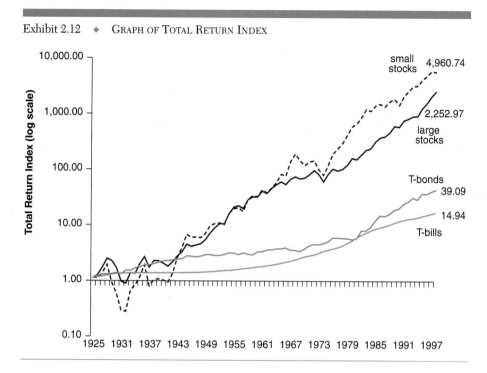

$6,000 by the end of 1999. So, a $1,000 investment in small stocks made at the end of 1925 was worth more than $6 million by the end of 1999.

Inflation-Adjusted Returns

The chart in Exhibit 2.13 shows total return indexes for large stocks, small stocks, T-bonds, and T-bills constructed using real (inflation-adjusted) returns. Not surprisingly, after adjusting for inflation, stocks still outperform bonds and bills by wide margins. For example, in real terms, $1,000 invested at the end of 1925 was worth in excess of $287,000 by the end of 1999. By contrast, in real terms $1,000 invested in T-bonds at the end of 1925 was worth only about $4,000 by the end of 1999. You may have noticed that the real total return index for T-bonds took a big dip between about 1968 and 1980. The 1970s were not the happiest of times for many bond investors, as the Investment History box, "The Agony of Bond Investors," recounts.

HISTORICAL MEANS AND STANDARD DEVIATIONS

Mean returns (both arithmetic and geometric), standard deviations, and range of returns, for large stocks, small stocks, T-bonds, and T-bills, are shown in Exhibit 2.14. The data confirm that stocks have outperformed other investments by a wide margin. Between the end of 1925 and the end of 1999, large stocks had a compound annual average return of over 11 percent. By contrast, bonds had a compound annual average return of less than 5.5 percent. The data also show that small stocks outperformed large stocks (a compound annual average return of 12.3 percent).

At the same time, the data show that stock returns varied far more from year to year than bond returns. For example, annual returns from large stocks ranged from a high of 54.0 percent to a low of –43.3 percent between 1926 and 1998. Annual bond

THE AGONY OF BOND INVESTORS:
1965-1981

Not *that* long ago, bonds were considered pretty dull investments. You simply bought bonds for income. Inflation was low and didn't vary much from year to year. Consequently, interest rates were fairly stable and bond prices rarely changed by much. In mid-1964 bonds were paying about 5.5 percent per year. In the face of 2.5 percent inflation, bond investors considered this an adequate real return. They never anticipated what was about to happen.

Between 1965 and 1981, inflation averaged over 7.5 percent per year, meaning bond investors earned negative real rates of return. To make matters worse, as inflation soared so did interest rates. Because as interest rates rise, bond prices fall; therefore the total return from bonds between 1965 and 1981 averaged only 2.4 percent per year. The total return from bonds adjusted for inflation, however, was −4.8 percent. Put another way, $1,000 invested in bonds at the beginning of 1965 was worth only about $500, in real terms, by the end of 1981. The chart below shows the agony of bond investors in graphic detail. And, to add insult to injury, most bond investors still had to pay income taxes on the interest they received, despite their negative real rates of return.

Even though inflation generally rose during the late 1960s and 1970s, it fluctuated a great deal from year to year. As inflation started to fluctuate substantially, so did interest rates. The increased volatility in interest rates led to a sharp increase in the volatility of bond prices. In fact, bond prices were often as volatile as stock prices during this period. For example, in 1965 the annualized standard deviation of bond returns was about 1.5 percent. By 1980 the annualized standard deviation of bond returns was over 21 percent. In comparison, the annualized standard deviation of stock returns was about 24 percent in 1980.

Although investors who bought bonds in the early 1960s suffered over the next fifteen years, those who bought bonds in the early 1980s have generally prospered. As inflation fell, so did interest rates. Between 1982 and 1998, the average annual nominal rate of return on bonds was over 13.5 percent. Even adjusting for inflation, bonds have returned an average of over 10 percent per year since 1982.

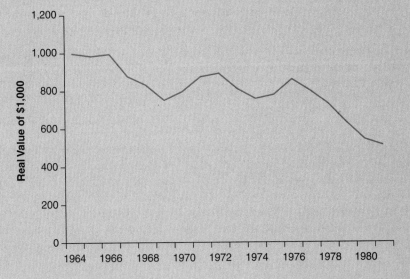

returns ranged between 40.4 percent and −9.2 percent over the same period. The standard deviations reflect this variability; large stocks have a standard deviation of 20.1 percent, whereas bonds have a standard deviation of 9.1 percent.

Real Rates of Return

A summary of real returns for stocks, bonds, and T-bills between 1926 and 1999 is shown in Exhibit 2.15.

The data confirm that even adjusted for inflation, stocks outperformed bonds by a large margin and that small-company stocks outperformed large-company stocks.

Exhibit 2.13 ✦ GRAPH OF REAL RETURN INDEX

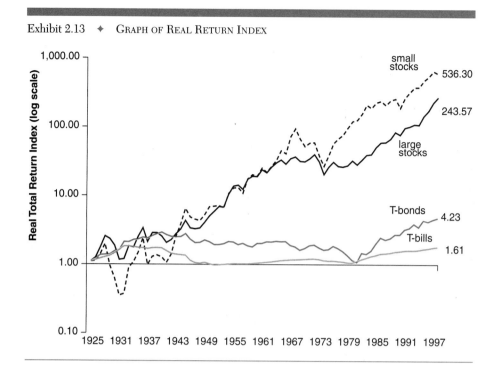

Exhibit 2.14 ✦ SUMMARY OF RETURNS FOR STOCKS, BONDS, AND TREASURY BILLS:
1926–1999

	Large stocks	Small stocks	T-bonds	T-bills
Arithmetic mean	13.2%	17.4%	5.4%	3.8%
Geometric mean	11.3	12.5	5.1	3.8
Standard deviation	20.1	33.4	9.1	3.2
Range:				
High	54.0	142.5	40.4	14.7
(year)	(1933)	(1933)	(1982)	(1981)
Low	−43.3	−58.0	−9.2	0.0
(year)	(1931)	(1937)	(1967)	(1938)

Exhibit 2.15 ✦ SUMMARY OF REAL RETURNS FROM STOCKS, BONDS, AND T-BILLS

	Arithmetic Means	Geometric Mean	Standard Deviation
Large stocks	9.9%	7.8%	20.4%
Small stocks	13.8	9.0	33.0
Treasury bonds	2.4	2.0	10.4
Treasury bills	0.8	0.7	4.1

Exhibit 2.16 ✦ SUMMARY OF RETURNS OVER VARYING HOLDING PERIODS

	Holding Period	Arithmetic Means (annualized)	Standard Deviation (annualized)	Coefficient of Variation
Large stocks	1 year	13.2%	20.1%	1.52
	2 years	12.2	14.5	1.19
	5 years	11.0	8.4	0.77
	10 years	11.1	5.5	0.50
	25 years	11.1	2.4	0.21
Small stocks	1 year	17.4	33.4	1.92
	2 years	15.3	24.8	1.62
	5 years	13.7	15.0	1.09
	10 years	14.1	7.3	0.52
	25 years	14.6	3.0	0.20
Treasury bonds	1 year	5.4	9.1	1.67
	2 years	5.3	6.3	1.19
	5 years	5.2	4.7	0.90
	10 years	5.1	3.9	0.78
	25 years	4.2	2.6	0.63
Treasury bills	1 year	3.8	3.2	0.83
	2 years	3.8	3.2	0.82
	5 years	3.8	3.1	0.80
	10 years	3.8	3.0	0.78
	25 years	3.8	2.5	0.66

The data also reveal that in real terms, the average annual return from T-bills was close to zero.

RISK, RETURN, AND HOLDING PERIOD

In the Investment Insights box on page 42, we noted that historically much of the short-term volatility in stock returns has disappeared over longer holding periods. To further illustrate this point, take a look at the data shown in Exhibit 2.16. Annualized mean returns, standard deviations, and coefficients of variations are shown for stocks, bonds, and T-bills over a variety of holding periods.

Notice that as the length of the holding period increases, both the standard deviation and the coefficient of variation decrease. This is especially true for stocks. The standard deviation of large-stock returns decreases from over 20 percent to less than 2.5 percent as the holding period increases from one year to 25 years. The coefficient of variation decreases from 1.53 to 0.21, indicating a better risk/return trade-off.

The decline in risk measures, as the holding period increases, is not nearly as dramatic for bonds or T-bills as it is for stocks. For example, the standard deviation of

T-bond returns declines from 9.1 percent to 2.6 percent as the holding period increases from one year to 25 years. The coefficient of variation for T-bond returns falls from 1.67 to 0.63.

The relationship between risk, return, and holding period led to the notion of diversification across time. That is, an investor can achieve the benefits of diversification merely by holding securities for longer periods of time. We'll discuss diversification across time, along with diversification across securities, in more detail in Chapter 17.

Risk and return dominate the subject of investments. This chapter has provided a basic overview of risk and return. We'll build on this material in subsequent chapters.

Chapter Summary

1. What are the sources of investment returns?

   Investment returns come from two sources: income (interest or dividends) and price changes. Some investments, such as common stocks, most of the return comes from price changes. For others, such as Treasury bills, virtually all returns come from interest income.

2. How are investment returns measured?

   The most appropriate measure of investment returns is the holding period return. It measures the total return from an investment over a specified period of time—most commonly a year. Holding period returns can be calculated on either an ex-post (meaning historical) basis or on an ex-ante basis. The latter is also referred to as the expected future return. Total return indexes help measure change in wealth over a period of time, and returns can be adjusted for inflation and exchange rates. The arithmetic mean and geometric mean are summaries of returns. The arithmetic mean measures the average, or typical return. The geometric mean measures the average compound return, or by how much an investor's wealth changed on average.

3. What is investment risk and how is it measured?

   Risk refers to uncertainty regarding an investment's future return. The more uncertainty, the more risk. Risk is neither good nor bad; it merely exists. Risk often has an upside as well as a downside. There are many different types of risk—including credit, market, purchasing power, and interest rate—and some investments are more sensitive to certain types of risk than others. A statistical measure of risk is standard deviation: the greater the standard deviation of security returns, the greater the risk.

4. What is the relationship between risk and required return?

   An investor buys a security in order to earn a rate of return over some future holding period. Three factors affect required rates of returns on securities: the time value of money, the expected rate of inflation, and the risk of the security. The nominal risk-free rate is a function of the real risk-free rate (representing the time value of money) and the expected rate of inflation. The required return on a risky security is a function of the nominal risk-free rate and the risk premium. The higher the risk of an investment, the higher the risk premium. The so-called capital asset pricing model is one way of expressing the relationship between risk and required return.

5. How can risk and return aid in investment selection?

   An investor can consider the risk and return measures when choosing between investments. If one investment offers a higher expected return, yet has the same risk as another investment, an investor would prefer the first investment. Similarly, if one investment has less risk but the same return as another investment, the first investment would be preferred. In the event that one investment offers a higher expected return and has more risk than another investment, the coefficient of variation may help us choose. The coefficient of variation shows the trade-off between risk and return; the lower the coefficient of variation the better the risk/return trade-off.

6. What are the realized returns and risks from stocks and other investments?
   A review of historical returns from stocks, bonds, and Treasury bills shows that stocks have outperformed bonds and T-bills by huge margins over the past 70-plus years. In fact, Treasury bill returns have, on average, barely exceeded the rate of inflation. Further, small-company stocks have outperformed large-company stocks. At the same time, stock returns have shown far more year-to-year variability than either bond or T-bill returns. However, much of the variability in stock returns disappears over longer holding periods.

Mini Cases

1. The table below lists month-end prices and cash dividends for Disney for a recent year. Using these data, complete the following:
   a. Find the holding period return for each month.
   b. Calculate the arithmetic mean return and the standard deviation. Annualize the arithmetic mean and standard deviation.
   c. Calculate the geometric mean. Explain why the geometric mean is less than the arithmetic mean.
   d. Calculate a total return index. Had you begun the year with $10,000 invested in Disney, how much would your investment have been worth at the end of the year?

Month	Price	Dividend
0	58.875	
1	62.000	0.090
2	66.000	
3	63.875	
4	59.000	0.110
5	60.750	
6	62.875	
7	58.000	0.110
8	57.000	
9	64.125	
10	65.500	0.110
11	73.875	
12	69.250	

2. Suppose you have the following probability distribution for three investments:

		Returns	
Probability	Investment A	Investment B	Investment C
0.1	−22.0%	−13.0%	−10.0%
0.2	−2.0	1.0	2.0
0.4	20.0	15.0	12.0
0.2	35.0	29.0	20.0
0.1	50.0	43.0	38.0

   a. Find the expected return for each investment.
   b. Find the standard deviation for each investment.

c. Find the coefficient of variation for each investment.
d. Does one investment represent a better risk/return tradeoff? Explain.

Review Questions and Problems

1. What are the two sources of investment returns? Which kind(s) of investment returns have potential tax implications?
2. Explain the difference between an ex-post return and an ex-ante return. Which is the only type of return that can be measured with certainty?
3. Find the holding period return of a mutual fund with a net asset value (NAV) of $12.00 at acquisition six months ago, a NAV of $12.75 today, and cash distributions during the six months of $0.50. Annualize the six-month holding period.
4. You bought a stock today for $100 a share. One year from now you expect the stock to be selling for $120 a share. In addition, you expect to receive a dividend of $5 per share. What is the expected rate of return on this stock? What is the breakdown between income and capital appreciation?
5. A mutual fund has the following net asset values and cash distributions:

Year	Net Asset Value (year end)	Cash Distributions
1988	$13.38	—
1989	14.06	$1.15
1990	12.27	0.84
1991	14.62	0.71
1992	15.63	1.02
1993	16.65	1.26
1994	15.98	1.40
1995	20.01	1.19
1996	23.08	0.61
1997	26.93	2.80
1998	28.93	0.49

Calculate the annual holding period return for 1989 through 1998. Starting with an initial index value of 100, compute a total return index from the end of 1988 through the end of 1998. Find the arithmetic mean and geometric mean. Why are the two different? What does each measure?

6. Using the total return index you calculated in the above question, what was the average annual compound return from this mutual fund between the beginning of 1994 and the end of 1998? What was the average annual compound return between the end of 1995 and the end of 1998?
7. Assume during 1999 an investment had a total return of 18.5 percent. If the rate of inflation was 2.5 percent, what was this investment's real rate of return?
8. Assume an investor purchased a Canadian government bond for CD1,000 a year ago. The bond pays CD60 in interest each year. Today she sold the bond for CD1,025. Calculate the holding period return in both Canadian dollars and U.S. dollars assuming the exchange rate (USD per one CD) was .65 when she bought the bond and .67 when she sold the bond.
9. Define risk. List three types of risk.
10. What is the difference between systematic and unsystematic risk?
11. Using the annual returns you calculated in question 5, find the standard deviation and coefficient of variation.

12. A set of monthly returns produces a standard deviation of 12.5 percent. Annualize the standard deviation.

13. Explain the difference between a required return and an expected return. What determines an investment's required return?

14. Below are annual return data for three stocks. Calculate the standard deviation and coefficient of variation for each stock. Does one stock represent a better risk/return trade-off than the other two? Explain.

Year	American Express	IBM	Sears
1	25.0%	13.0%	34.3%
2	34.3	−19.4	−2.3
3	−38.6	25.7	−29.1
4	3.4	−17.6	57.5
5	25.0	−38.0	25.4
6	28.1	15.3	53.0
7	11.1	31.9	−10.0
8	42.5	25.7	54.5
9	39.2	67.6	17.7
10	59.9	39.0	0.1

15. Reviewing historical return data for stocks, bonds, and T-bills, list three general conclusions. What is the relationship between risk and holding period?

CRITICAL THINKING EXERCISES

1. This exercise requires computer work. Open the Stock Returns 1 worksheet in the Data Workbook. The worksheet contains monthly price and income data for large U.S. stocks between December 1994 and December 1999. Using the data in the worksheet, perform the following calculations and answer the following questions.

   a. Calculate the monthly holding period return.

   b. Starting with an index value of 100, compute a total return index. If you had invested $10,000 in large stocks at the end of 1994, how much would you have had at the end of 1999?

   c. Calculate the arithmetic and geometric means. Annualize the arithmetic mean.

   d. Why are the two means different? In what situation would you prefer the arithmetic mean rather than the geometric mean, and vice-versa.

   e. Find the standard deviation. Annualize the standard deviation.

2. This exercise requires computer work. Open the Stock Returns 2 worksheet in the Data Workbook. The worksheet lists annual returns from large-company stocks, T-bonds, and T-bills, as well as annual inflation data between 1952 and 1999. Use the data to answer the following questions.

   a. Which were the five best years to have owned large-company stocks?

   b. Which were the five worst years to have owned large-company stocks?

   c. Answer questions a and b for T-bonds and T-bills.

   d. Which five years had the highest inflation rates? Which five years had the lowest inflation rates?

   e. What do your findings in questions a through d tell you about the historical performance of stocks and bonds, relative to one another and relative to inflation?

   f. Compute annualized returns over five- and ten-year holding periods.

   g. Calculate the mean, standard deviation, and coefficient of variation for annualized returns over one-, five-, and ten-year holding periods. Discuss your findings.

THE INTERNET INVESTOR

1. A great deal of investment information is available on the Internet. Visit the Microsoft Investor web site (*investor.msn.com*). On this site, find the information necessary to compute annual holding period returns for the most recent five years for the following stocks: AT&T, Cisco Systems, Ford, Pfizer, and Wal-Mart.

2. It is often difficult to explain to novice investors exactly what investment risk means. Many investment-oriented web sites contain investment education sections. Visit the following sites and read their explanations of risk. Write a brief report critiquing their explanations.

3. Assume you own some German government bonds denominated in Euros and some British government bonds denominated in pounds. Using your surfing skills, obtain recent exchange rate quotations. Compare the current exchange rates with the rates one year ago. Would your return, measured in dollars, have been higher than your return measured in either Euros or pounds?

DIRECT INVESTMENT ALTERNATIVES

PREVIOUSLY . . .

Following our overview of investments, and investing, we introduced the concepts of risk and return in detail, the two pillars of investing. People invest in order to earn a rate of return. At the same time, however, all investing exposes you to risk.

IN THIS CHAPTER . . .

We explore the wide array of direct investments today. To make intelligent decisions, an investor needs some basic understanding of investments from Treasury bills to futures contracts.

TO COME . . .

The foundation of investments continues as we discuss the characteristics of indirect investments, such as mutual funds.

Chapter Objectives

After reading Chapter 3 you should be able to answer the following questions:

1. What are money market instruments?
2. What are bonds and other long-term fixed income securities?
3. Why invest in common stocks?
4. What are derivative securities?
5. How is investing in real assets different from investments in paper assets?

Selecting between investment alternatives used to be pretty simple. For a typical individual, investing meant putting money into a savings account at a local bank, buying a home, monitoring a company-provided pension, holding a life insurance policy, and perhaps, for the adventuresome, owning a handful of stocks and bonds. Most Americans faced limited choices. Today, times have changed; investors choose among literally thousands of investment alternatives, many of which did not even exist twenty years ago. Money market mutual funds, emerging markets mutual funds, Ginnie Maes, stock options, financial futures, American Depository Receipts, and Eurobonds are a few relatively new possibilities. It is impossible to make intelligent investment decisions without some understanding of the various alternatives.

This chapter provides an overview of today's major direct investment alternatives. We will explore everything from Treasury bills to junk bonds, from blue chip stocks to call options, from pork bellies to gold.

Categorizing Investment Alternatives

How many alternative investments does the worldwide market offer today? Counting all the individual security issues and investment companies, both domestic and world-wide, the number is probably 50,000, or more.[1] To make the staggering number of choices more manageable, let us define some general categories in which to group investment alternatives, as illustrated in Exhibit 3.1.

First, we divide investment instruments into **financial assets** and **real assets.** We then divide financial assets between **direct investments** and **indirect investments.** A direct investment gives the buyer actual ownership of securities; indirect investment gives ownership of an entity that owns actual securities, for example investments companies such as mutual funds, closed-end funds, and unit investment trusts. (We'll defer our discussion of investment companies to the next chapter.) We divide direct investments in financial assets into nonmarketable assets (for example, bank deposits and U.S. savings bonds) and **marketable securities.** By marketable, we mean that an asset or security can be sold to another investor in a secondary market. We'll discuss the distinction between primary and secondary markets in detail in Chapter 5. Marketable securities include money market instruments (for example, Treasury bills and commercial paper), capital market instruments (for example, Treasury bonds and common stocks), and derivative securities (for example, options and futures contracts).

We can also divide real assets between direct and indirect investments. Direct investments in real assets give buyers actual ownership of such things as real estate (both owner-occupied housing and investment properties), gold, diamonds, and art works. Indirect investments in real assets provide ownership of entities such as real estate investment trusts and limited partnerships that own real assets.

Given the rather long menu of investment alternatives, it is interesting to take a brief look at what Americans actually own. Data from the Federal Reserve give us some insight into the distribution of financial assets of American households. The data are summarized in Exhibit 3.2.

Exhibit 3.2 illustrates an important transformation in what American households own. In 1980, Americans had more money in bank deposits, such as checking accounts, savings accounts, and certificates of deposit than they did in stocks, bonds, and mutual funds combined. By contrast today, although Americans still have a lot of money in bank deposits (more than $3.5 trillion), they now have far more money invested in stocks, bonds, and mutual funds. In the past fifteen years, many Americans have progressed from simple savers to investors.

financial asset
Nonmarketable assets such as bank deposits and marketable assets such as money market instruments, bonds, and common stocks.

real asset
Real property such as real estate.

direct investment
A direct investment gives the investor actual ownership of the securities.

indirect investment
Investment in an entity that owns actual securities, such as a mutual fund.

marketable security
A security that can be bought and sold in a secondary financial market.

---

[1]Just to give you an idea of this range of choices, there are over 8,000 mutual funds currently operating in the United States alone.

Exhibit 3.1 ✦ Contemporary Investment Alternatives

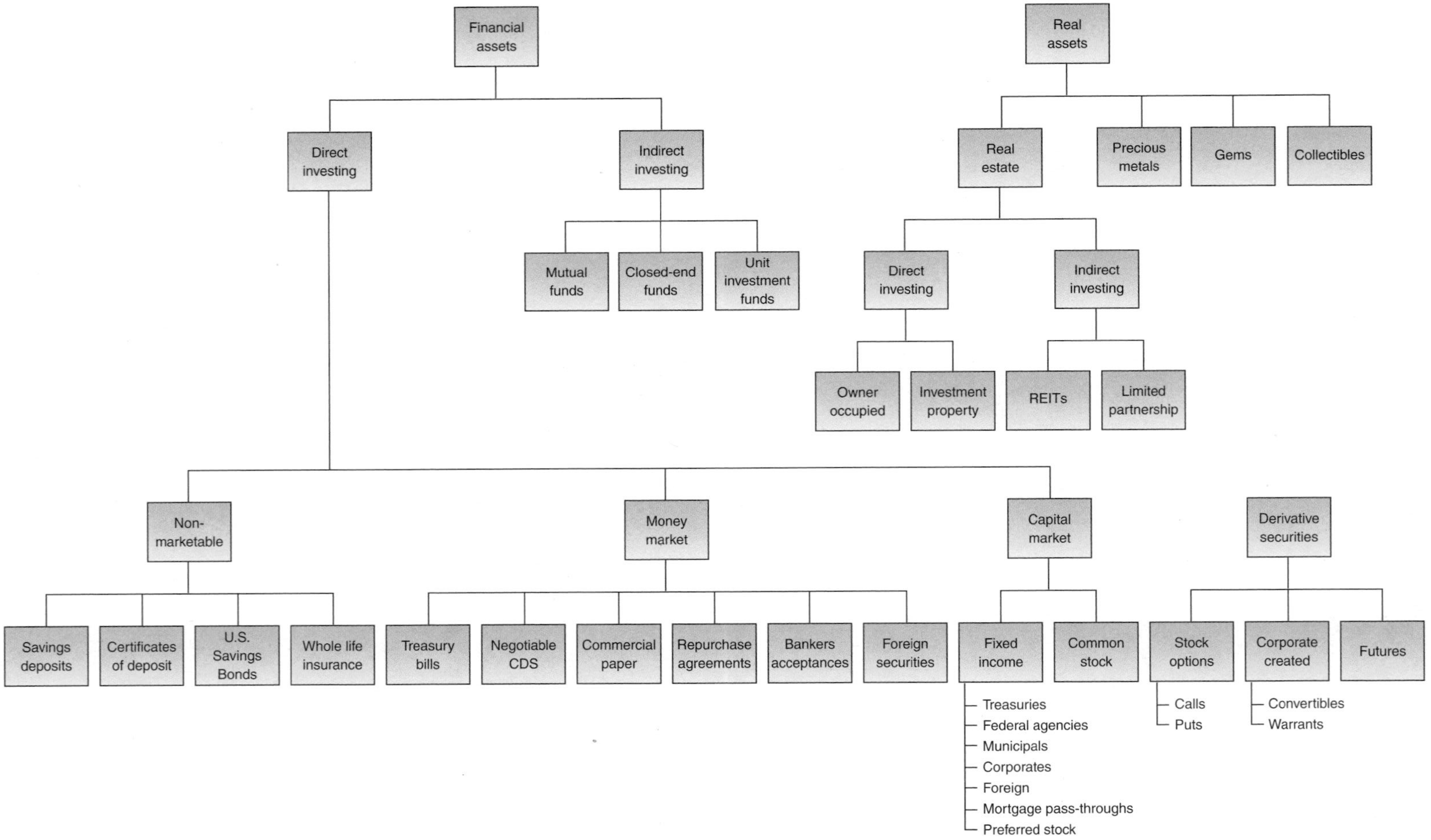

- **Financial assets**
  - **Direct investing**
    - **Non-marketable**
      - Savings deposits
      - Certificates of deposit
      - U.S. Savings Bonds
      - Whole life insurance
    - **Money market**
      - Treasury bills
      - Negotiable CDS
      - Commercial paper
      - Repurchase agreements
      - Bankers acceptances
      - Foreign securities
    - **Capital market**
      - Fixed income
        - Treasuries
        - Federal agencies
        - Municipals
        - Corporates
        - Foreign
        - Mortgage pass-throughs
        - Preferred stock
      - Common stock
    - **Derivative securities**
      - Stock options
        - Calls
        - Puts
      - Corporate created
        - Convertibles
        - Warrants
      - Futures
  - **Indirect investing**
    - Mutual funds
    - Closed-end funds
    - Unit investment funds
- **Real assets**
  - **Real estate**
    - Direct investing
      - Owner occupied
      - Investment property
    - Indirect investing
      - REITs
      - Limited partnership
  - Precious metals
  - Gems
  - Collectibles

Exhibit 3.2 ✦ Financial Assets of U.S. Households

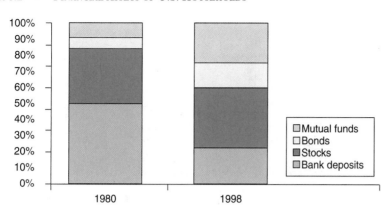

Money Market Instruments

Money market instruments are short-term debt securities. The category includes such securities as Treasury bills, large (or marketable) certificates of deposit, commercial paper, and banker's acceptances. Some recent yields on money market instruments are shown in Exhibit 3.3.

Of all the major categories of investments, money market instruments are arguably the most homogeneous. All share some important features, including

✦ **Maturity.** All money market instruments mature (that is, pay back their face values) within one year from the date of issue. Many money market instruments have maturities of only a few days.

✦ **Quality.** Most, although not all, money market instruments are high-quality securities. Their risk of default, or failure to repay principal, is low and in some cases effectively nonexistent.

✦ **Large denominations.** Another characteristic of money market instruments is their tendency to trade in large denominations. It is not unusual to see money market instruments sell in denominations of $1 million or more. This characteristic makes it difficult for small investors to own most money market instruments directly.[2]

✦ **Discount securities.** With the exception of bank deposits such as CDs, virtually all money market instruments are discount securities, meaning they sell for less than their face (or par) values and pay no periodic interest. When such an instrument matures, the investor receives the face value. The difference between the selling price and face value is the investor's return.

SHORT-TERM U.S. GOVERNMENT SECURITIES

The best-known short-term U.S. government security, and perhaps the best-known money market instrument in the world, is the U.S. **Treasury bill (T-bill).** T-bills are,

Treasury bill (T-bill)
A short-term security issued by the U.S. Treasury.

---

[2]In fact, until the late 1970s, small investors had virtually no access to the money market. Money market mutual funds changed that dramatically.

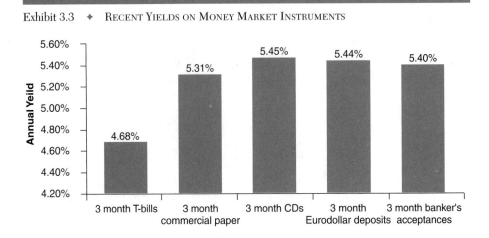

Exhibit 3.3 ✦ RECENT YIELDS ON MONEY MARKET INSTRUMENTS

in essence, IOUs issued by the U.S. Treasury and are backed by the full faith and credit of the U.S. government. As such, investors believe that T-bills have effectively no default risk. Given the large number of investors willing to buy them, T-bills are also highly liquid. Interest received from Treasury securities is taxable at the federal level, although it is exempt from state income taxes. Investors currently hold about $650 billion in outstanding T-bills.

T-bills are originally issued with three standard maturities: three months, six months, and one year. The Treasury sells bills to investors via an auction process. Three-month and six-month bills are auctioned weekly, whereas one-year bills are auctioned monthly. (We describe the Treasury's auction process in detail in Chapter 5.) T-bills are discount securities and have a minimum par value of $10,000.

T-Bill Yields and Prices

bank discount yield (BDY)
A method of computing the yield on T-bills.

Because T-bills are discount securities and make no periodic interest payments, their yields and prices are quoted differently than many securities. T-bill prices often are quoted on a bank discount basis. The **bank discount yield (BDY)** is computed as follows:

$$BDY = (D/F) \times (360/t)$$

where D is the discount (face value $\times$ price), F is the face value, and t is the number of days until the bill matures.

As an example, assume that a T-bill matures in 180 days and has a discount of $2,475 and a face value of $100,000. Its BDY equals

$$(2,475/100,000) \times (360/2) = 4.95\%$$

The above formula can be rewritten to find the price of a T-bill, given its BDY:

$$\text{Price} = F[1 - BDY \times (t/360)]$$

For example, if a 180-day T-bill has a BDY of 4.2 percent and a face value of $100,000, its price equals

$$\$100,000[1 - .0495(2/360)] = \$97,525$$

The bill's discount would be $100,000 minus $97,525 = $2,475.

The BDY is not a very meaningful measure of the real return an investor earns from owning a T-bill. For one thing, the BDY is based on a 360-day year, not 365 or 366. Also, the BDY bases the return on the face value of the T-bill, not the amount actually invested. An alternative way of stating the yield on a T-bill is the **bond equivalent yield (BEY)**:

$$BEY = (365 \times BDY)/[360 - (BDY \times t)]$$

A 180-day T-bill with a BDY of 4.95 percent would have a BEY of

$$(365 \times .0495)/[360 - (.0495 \times t)] = 5.15\%$$

The BEY is considered a truer estimate than the BDY of the return an investor would actually earn from owning a T-bill. Because it is based on a 365-day year and the actual amount paid for the T-bill, the BEY is always higher than the BDY.

bond equivalent yield (BEY)
An alternative method for computing the yield on a T-bill; closer to the actual return to the investor.

Short-Term Federal Agency Securities

In addition to the U.S. Treasury, several federal and quasi-federal agencies are empowered to issue debt securities called federal agency securities. About $800 billion in federal agency securities are outstanding; short-term obligations (that is, those with maturities of less than one year) make up approximately 20 percent of outstanding federal agency securities.

Short-term federal agency securities are similar to T-bills. They are discount securities and typically have a minimum face value of $10,000. Unlike T-bills, however, federal agency securities are not backed by the full faith and credit of the U.S. government. Although default is theoretically possible with federal agency securities, investment professionals see little likelihood that Congress would allow a federal agency to default on its debt.

COMMERCIAL PAPER

In essence, **commercial paper** is the corporate equivalent of a T-bill. It is a short-term IOU issued by a corporation to provide working capital. Corporations often issue commercial paper to supplement, or even as an alternative to, loans from commercial banks. Commercial paper has a maturity of less than 270 days; the most common maturity range is between 30 and 59 days.[3] Commercial paper is usually sold in large denominations ($100,000 or more) and is virtually always issued as a **discount security.** Today, more than $1,000 billion in commercial paper is outstanding, up

commercial paper
A short-term IOU issued by a corporation.

discount security
A security that is sold for less than its face value.

---

[3]Corporate securities with maturities of less than 270 days are exempt from SEC registration requirements. We'll describe SEC registration requirements in Chapter 5.

from less than $300 billion ten years ago. Approximately 80 percent of outstanding commercial paper was issued by financial companies. General Motors Acceptance Corporation (GMAC), General Motors' captive finance subsidiary, is the largest single issuer of commercial paper in the world.

Corporations issue commercial paper in one of two ways: as dealer-placed paper or directly placed paper. The difference is straightforward. Dealer-placed paper involves a third party, the commercial paper dealer, who purchases the paper from the issuing corporation and immediately resells it, at a slightly higher price, to investors. Directly placed paper bypasses dealers; the issuing corporation sells the paper directly to investors. Approximately 60 percent of outstanding commercial paper is dealer placed. Institutional investors (for example, mutual funds, pension funds, and banks) purchase virtually all newly issued commercial paper. Because most of these investors plan to hold the paper until maturity, trading is relatively light in previously issued commercial paper.

Traditionally, only companies with the strongest credit ratings have issued commercial paper.[4] Therefore, although defaults are not unknown, they are rare. In recent years, some companies with lower credit ratings have been able to issue commercial paper, pledging high-quality assets as collateral or backing the paper by bank letters of credit.

Banker's Acceptances

banker's acceptances
Instruments that facilitate commercial trade; bank accepts ultimate responsibility for paying off all the parties.

Banker's acceptances are instruments created to facilitate commercial trade transactions, many of which are international. The name comes from the fact that banks accept ultimate responsibility for paying off all the parties. Therefore, the default risk of a banker's acceptance depends more on the credit-worthiness of the bank than on the financial strength of the companies that conduct the commercial transactions. Banker's acceptances sell at discount, and their maturities range from a few days up to one year. Like commercial paper, virtually all banker's acceptances sell to institutional investors. Today, investors hold about $25 billion in banker's acceptances.

The easiest way to understand how banker's acceptances work is by looking at a hypothetical example. Suppose a California retail chain wants to import five thousand "genuine" Persian rugs from the manufacturer in China for sale in the United States. The manufacturer would like immediate payment, whereas the U.S. retailer would rather pay for the rugs after it sells them, say, in ninety days. The retailer and the manufacturer come up with the following arrangement: the retailer agrees to pay $5 million for the five thousand rugs in ninety days, and the manufacturer agrees to accept the present value of $5 million when the rugs are shipped. The retailer then obtains a letter of credit from its bank, Wells Fargo, which guarantees that the manufacturer will be paid ninety days after the rugs are shipped. Wells Fargo sends the letter of credit, called a time draft, to the manufacturer's Hong Kong bank, Heng Sen Bank. Heng Sen Bank notifies the manufacturer, who ships the rugs to the retailer. With proof of shipment, Heng Sen Bank pays the rug manufacturer the present value

---

[4]Commercial paper has been around since colonial times. Perhaps ironically, commercial paper was first issued by companies that could not qualify for bank loans. Over the years, however, commercial paper evolved into the high-quality instrument we see today.

of $5 million, and the manufacturer leaves the picture. Heng Sen Bank presents the time draft and shipping documents to Wells Fargo, which stamps *accepted* on the time draft, creating a banker's acceptance by which it agrees to pay $5 million to the holder of the banker's acceptance at maturity. Heng Sen Bank, the holder of the banker's acceptance, can either keep it, turn it over to Wells Fargo for its present value, or sell it to another money market investor. The retailer owes Wells Fargo $5 million in 90 days plus interest.

LARGE CERTIFICATES OF DEPOSIT

Certificates of deposit (CDs) are familiar to many individual and small investors. CDs are time deposits issued by financial institutions such as banks and credit unions. These instruments mature anywhere from a few weeks to a few years from the date of issue. Unlike other money market instruments, CDs are interest-bearing securities; they pay interest on their principal amounts at specified annual rates.

certificates of deposit (CDs)
A term savings deposit at a bank or other financial institution.

Although CDs can be issued in almost any denomination, an important distinction developed during the 1960s and 1970s between so-called small CDs and large CDs. Traditionally, all CDs were federally insured and could not be sold before maturity without substantial interest penalties. For a variety of historical reasons, interest rates on CDs were kept low and were subject to ceilings set by the Federal Reserve. During the 1960s and 1970s, CD rates started to fall well below rising money market rates. In an attempt to increase their direct access to the money market in the face of rising short-term rates, banks offered a new type of CD. These new CDs were not federally insured, their interest rates were not subject to Federal Reserve ceilings, and they could be sold before maturity in a secondary market. These became known as large CDs because they usually had face values of at least $1 million. Today, any CD with a face value in excess of $100,000 is considered a large CD. Investors currently hold more than $600 billion in large CDs outstanding, compared with almost $1 trillion in outstanding small CDs.

The credit risk associated with large CDs depends directly on the creditworthiness of the financial institutions that issue them. Because large CDs are not federally insured, a CD holder could lose principal if the financial institution fails. Although the overall credit risk of large CDs is low, some recent bank failures have cost large CD holders some, although rarely all, of their principal.

REPURCHASE AGREEMENTS

Repurchase agreements, or repos, are basically short-term loans with securities as collateral. In a repo, one party sells a package of securities (often U.S. government securities) to another party and agrees to buy back, or repurchase, the securities at a later date (ranging from overnight to months later) at a higher price. For example, suppose that a securities dealer has just purchased $10 million in U.S. government bonds to sell to customers and needs to finance the purchase for a couple of days. A city government is flush with cash from tax receipts that it must soon pay out for services, but it needs a short-term investment until that time. The securities dealer sells the bonds to the city for $9,975,000, agreeing to repurchase them in eighteen days for $10 million. The discount is found as follows:

repurchase agreements
Short-term loans with government securities pledged as collateral.

$$\text{Face value} - [\text{repurchase rate} \times (\text{term}/360) \times \text{face value}]$$

The repurchase rate in this example is 5 percent per annum, and the term is eighteen days:

$$\$10,000,000 - [.05 \times (18/360) \times \$10,000,000]$$

Today, more than $250 billion in repurchase agreements are outstanding. Because repos are collateralized—backed by another asset—they are considered safe investments.

SHORT-TERM MUNICIPAL SECURITIES

In addition to the federal Treasury and other federal agencies, thousands of state and local government units in the United States (states, cities, school districts, and such) issue securities, many of which are money market instruments. (In the terminology of investments, *government* refers to securities issued by the Treasury or federal agencies, whereas *municipal* refers to securities issued by all state and local government units.) Virtually all short-term municipals are called anticipation notes. They are issued in anticipation of revenue from another source (for example, property tax receipts) and are almost always discount securities. They sell in minimum denominations of at least $25,000.

The quality of short-term municipals varies, although the overall credit risk is low. Municipal securities may have some credit risk whereas government securities, specifically Treasury securities, have none. Although many issuers of municipal securities can levy taxes, unlike the federal government, they cannot legally print money. The Treasury could always print money to pay its bills (including the face value of maturing securities) if need be. State and local governments can rely only on receipt of tax payments and other revenue.

Like all municipal securities, short-term municipals have an important feature: the interest they pay is exempt from federal income taxes. As a result, short-term municipals typically have lower yields than even T-bills.

taxable equivalent yield (TEY)
Compares the yield on a tax-exempt security to the yield on a taxable security.

Because of this tax feature, taxable investors should compute the **taxable equivalent yield (TEY)** when comparing municipals with other securities. Compute the TEY as follows:

$$TEY = \text{Yield on the tax-exempt security}/(1 - T)$$

where T is the investor's marginal tax rate.[5] For example, if a short-term municipal security yields 3.5 percent and the investor has a marginal tax rate of 28 percent, the TEY equals 0.035/0.72, or 4.86 percent. Obviously as the investor's tax rate increases, the TEY increases, making municipal securities most attractive to investors in high tax brackets.

Foreign Money Market Instruments

Various money market instruments are sold in other countries. These instruments sell in either foreign currencies or U.S. dollars. Many foreign governments issue short-

---

[5]If the interest received is also exempt from state income taxes, T should reflect the investor's combined federal and state marginal tax rate.

term securities similar to U.S. T-bills. Canada, for example, sells Treasury bills weekly with maturities of 90, 180, and 360 days. These discount securities have denominations as small as C$1,000. Foreign and U.S. corporations also issue commercial paper throughout the world. For example, most U.S. finance companies, such as GMAC, have Canadian operations and issue commercial paper in Canada to finance those operations.

Two of the most significant foreign money market instruments are Eurodollar deposits and Eurodollar CDs. These are bank deposits and CDs denominated in U.S. dollars but issued and held outside the United States or in U.S. branches of foreign banks.[6] For example, a 180-day U.S. dollar CD issued by the London branch of Citibank would be a Eurodollar CD. Today, more than $125 billion in Eurodollars and Eurodollar CDs are outstanding.

One of the most widely followed money market interest rates, London Interbank Offered Rate (LIBOR), is the rate at which five large London banks are willing to lend dollar-denominated funds to one another in the interbank market. The rates on most Eurodollar deposits and CDs are tied to the LIBOR. Many other money market and loan rates worldwide also are tied to the LIBOR.

Many U.S. investors have been attracted to foreign money market instruments in recent years as U.S. money market rates have fallen well below rates in other countries. For example, in the middle of 1999 the yield on three-month T-bills was less than 5 percent. By contrast, short-term British government securities were yielding more than 6 percent. As we saw in the last chapter, however, investing in any foreign security, even a government security, exposes investors to foreign exchange risk.

Long-Term Fixed Income Securities (Bonds)

Money market instruments, by definition, have maturities of one year or less from the date of issue. Long-term fixed-income securities (often called *bonds*) include all debt instruments that have maturities longer than one year from the date they are originally sold.[7] Aside from this obvious difference, several other important characteristics separate money market instruments from long-term fixed-income securities. With the exception of CDs, money market instruments are typically discount securities. Bonds, by contrast, are usually interest-bearing securities. Most bonds pay regular interest payments at fixed rates, called **coupon rates.** Interest is computed and paid at regular intervals—usually twice a year—as a percentage of the security's par, or face value.

In addition, bond quality varies widely. Some bonds, such as Treasury bonds, have essentially no credit risk, and other bonds have a great deal of credit risk. Further, all bonds, regardless of the amount of credit risk, expose investors to more interest rate and purchasing power risk than money market instruments, and these risks generally increase as time to maturity increases. Finally, many bonds are **callable,** meaning the issuers can buy back the securities from investors, at prespecified prices,

coupon rates
Percentage of face value paid to bondholders each year as interest.

callable (call provision)
Gives the issuer the right to buy the bond back from investors, at a fixed price, prior to maturity.

---

[6]In addition to Eurodollars, Euroyen deposits and CDs are prominent in several major financial centers, especially in London. Euroyen deposits and CDs are deposits and CDs denominated in Japanese yen but issued and held outside Japan.

[7]Technically speaking, not all long-term fixed-income securities are bonds. The term *bond,* however, is often used generically to refer to any debt security with a maturity in excess of one year.

prior to maturity. Not surprisingly, issuers are far more likely to call bonds when interest rates are falling, which allows them to issue new bonds with lower coupon rates.

GOVERNMENT BONDS

government bond
A bond issued by the U.S. Treasury or a federal agency.

municipal bond
A bond issued by a state or local government.

In the language of investments, a **government bond** is a bond issued by the U.S. treasury or a federal agency. A **municipal bond** is one issued by a state or local government. The U.S. Treasury issues a variety of fixed-income securities with maturities ranging between two and thirty years. Treasuries issued with maturities between two and ten years are referred to as *notes;* those with original maturities of thirty years are referred to as *bonds.* Aside from maturity, bonds and notes differ only in that bonds are often callable starting five years before maturity; notes generally are not callable. Both notes and bonds bear interest, trade in vigorous secondary markets, and sell in denominations as small as $1,000. Like T-bills, T-notes and T-bonds are backed by the full faith and credit of the U.S. government and have no default risk. Currently, more than $2 trillion in notes and about $600 billion in bonds are outstanding.

Inflation-Indexed Securities

In 1996 the Treasury sold the first so-called inflation-indexed security. These securities pay investors a fixed real rate of interest plus additional interest as compensation for inflation. Therefore, unlike most fixed-income securities, inflation-indexed securities don't expose investors to purchasing power risk. They have proven quite popular with a variety of investors; currently more than $50 billion in inflation-indexed securities are outstanding.

Federal Agency Securities

Besides short-term securities, the federal agencies also issue a variety of longer-term fixed-income securities to finance their operations. Federal agency securities resemble T-notes and T-bonds. Remember, though, federal agency securities, not backed by the full faith and credit of the U.S. government, carry some, albeit minuscule, amount of credit risk.

MUNICIPAL BONDS

general obligation bond
Municipal bond backed by the full faith and credit of the governmental unit issuing the bond.

revenue bond
Municipal bond used to pay for revenue-producing projects; only revenues from the project are used to pay principal and interest.

Across the United States, thousands of state and local governments issue longer-term fixed-income securities in addition to the short-term securities discussed previously. The interest earned on these securities is also exempt from federal income tax. Municipal bonds are generally interest bearing, have par values of about $25,000, and are often callable.

Municipal bonds fall into two categories: general obligation bonds and revenue bonds. **General obligation bonds** are backed by the full faith and credit of the government that issues them. Because the issuer can spend any of its tax revenues to pay interest and principal on these bonds, general obligation bonds can be issued only by governments that have taxing authority. By contrast, **revenue bonds** help finance revenue-producing projects (from toll roads to sports facilities), and only revenues generated by the project may be used to pay bondholders. Revenue bonds can be issued by governmental units that lack authority to levy taxes. Thus, as a very general rule, revenue bonds have more credit risk than general obligation bonds. During a typical year, about two-thirds of all municipal bonds sold are revenue bonds.

Municipal bonds are often serial issues, as opposed to term issues. In a **serial bond** issue, a predetermined number of bonds mature each year until the final maturity date. All **term bonds** mature on the same date.

As we pointed out earlier, investors must realize that municipal bonds carry some credit risk, even when issued by a government with taxing authority. While rare, municipal bond defaults happen. One of the largest municipal bond defaults in history occurred in December 1994 when Orange County, California, defaulted on more than $1 billion of securities. To help investors assess credit risk, many municipal bonds carry **bond ratings** assigned by organizations such as Moody's and Standard and Poor. The highest rating—indicating the least amount of credit risk—is AAA (Aaa for Moody's). Bonds considered a higher credit risk receive lower ratings. We'll discuss bond ratings in more detail in Chapter 9.

CORPORATE DEBT ISSUES

Corporations issue a wide variety of longer-term debt securities to raise capital for company projects. Most corporate bonds are term issues that mature after anywhere between five and thirty years; most have par values of $1,000.[8] In addition, virtually all corporate bonds are callable. A large corporate may have several different debt issues outstanding at any one time. Shell Oil Company, for example, currently has more than fifteen different long-term debt issues outstanding.

All corporate bonds expose investors to some degree of credit risk, but the amount varies widely from issue to issue. Many corporate issues are considered almost as safe as government bonds, whereas others appear far more speculative. Like municipal bonds, most corporate bonds are rated. Corporate bonds with ratings above BB (or Ba) are considered investment grade; those with ratings below BBB are often called **junk bonds.**

In general, we can divide corporate bonds into categories based on their collateral provisions. Some bonds give their owners legal claims to specific assets in the event the issuers go bankrupt; these are secured bonds. A **mortgage bond** is secured by a lien on real assets, such as property or machinery. Unsecured bonds are known as **debentures.** Holders of debentures are general creditors of the issuers; if the company's assets are liquidated in bankruptcy, their claims are junior to mortgage bond holders. Owners of **subordinated debentures** have even lower claims to assets in the event of bankruptcy. Finally, **income bonds** are the corporate equivalent of municipal revenue bonds; they finance the purchase of income-producing assets. Unlike other corporate bonds, an income bond carries a commitment to pay interest and principal only if income from the asset is sufficient.

MORTGAGE PASS-THROUGH SECURITIES

One of the most dramatic changes to occur in the financial system over the past twenty years has been the so-called securitization of mortgages, especially home

---

[8]Occasionally a company will issue a bond with a maturity in excess of thirty years. In 1995 the Walt Disney Company issued a bond with a one-hundred-year maturity!

serial bond
A bond issue in which bonds mature over a period of time; commonly found in municipal bond issues.

term bond
A bond issue in which all bonds mature on the same date.

bond rating
An assessment made by an independent bond-rating agency of the bond's credit risk.

junk bond
A bond with a rating below BBB (or Baa); also called speculative-grade bond.

mortgage bond
A corporate bond in which specific assets are pledged as collateral.

debenture
A corporate bond in which no specific assets are pledged as collateral.

subordinated debenture
A bond in which investors have a junior claim to other bondholders in the event of bankruptcy.

income bond
Corporate equivalent of a revenue bond.

mortgages. Three federally sponsored organizations, the Federal National Mortgage Association (known as Fannie Mae), the Government National Mortgage Association (Ginnie Mae), and the Federal Home Loan Mortgage Corporation (Freddie Mac), played a major role. All three were created to purchase loans from primary mortgage lenders such as savings and loan associations to increase the supply of mortgage credit.

Traditionally all three organizations issued bonds to finance their mortgage purchases. However, in 1975, Ginnie Mae offered the first **mortgage pass-through security,** which pledged interest payments backed by a self-liquidating pool of mortgages, all with the same term and interest rate. As homeowners make their monthly house payments (consisting of both interest and principal), the pooled payment is "passed through" to the security holders. Owning a mortgage pass-through security is equivalent to owning a piece of a large pool of home mortgages. Today, Fannie Mae, Freddie Mac, and several other private financial institutions also issue mortgage pass-through securities. They have proved quite successful. Today, more than $2.3 trillion in mortgage pass-through securities are outstanding.

Mortgage pass-throughs are considered high-quality securities with minimal, if any, credit risk. All mortgages in the pool are insured, which means that the outstanding principal is paid by the insurer in the event of default. The organization that issues a mortgage pass-through security almost always guarantees timely payment of interest and principal to investors. Mortgage pass-throughs also offer attractive yields relative to Treasury securities. Also, many investors like the monthly income from pass-throughs. The main drawback with mortgage pass-throughs is their uncertain maturities. All loans in the pool have the same original term (usually thirty years); however, most homeowners pay off their mortgages early when they refinance or sell their homes. Because the pool is liquidated as mortgages are paid off, the pass-through could mature any time between one day and thirty years from the date of issue.

mortgage pass-through security
A fixed-income security backed by a self-liquidating pool of mortgages.

FOREIGN BONDS

Governments and corporations throughout the world issue debt securities outside their own countries. These bonds often have colorful names. For example, foreign bonds issued in the United States are called **Yankee** bonds, whereas foreign bonds issued in the United Kingdom are referred to as Bulldog bonds. Many U.S. corporations issue **Eurobonds** (bonds denominated in U.S. dollars but issued outside the United States). Companies also issue Euroyen bonds, bonds denominated in Japanese yen issued outside Japan. As for foreign money market instruments, foreign bond yields can seem attractive to U.S. investors, but they do expose investors to unique risks such as the risk of adverse changes in foreign exchange rates.

yankee bond
Foreign bond issued in the United States.

eurobond
Dollar-denominated bond issued outside the United States.

PREFERRED STOCK

Preferred stock is another security issued by corporations. Preferred stock is a hybrid security; it shares characteristics of both common stock and bonds. Legally, it is not a debt instrument but a class of stock, representing an ownership or equity claim on firm assets. We include it with other fixed-income securities, such as bonds, because from an investor's standpoint, preferred stock performs much more like a bond than a stock. Preferred stock pays a set annual dividend. This fixed amount almost never changes, regardless of the issuing firm's profitability. In addition, preferred shareholders have no voting rights, and their claim to firm assets in the event of bankruptcy is senior to common shareholders. However, failure to pay preferred stock dividends cannot force the issuer into bankruptcy, as failure to make principal and interest payments on bonds can. Although, in theory, preferred stock has no maturity, most issues are callable, and experience suggests that most preferred issues are eventually called.

Preferred stocks run the gamut from high to low quality. Like corporate and municipal bonds, preferred stocks are often rated by Standard & Poor's and Moody's. A rating reflects expert assessment of the issuer's ability to maintain the preferred stock dividend in the future. Preferred stock yields usually, although not always, exceed corporate bond yields.

For many reasons, preferred stock has long been viewed as an orphan security, not particularly popular with either issuers or investors. In fact, the total amount of preferred stock outstanding in the United States actually declined between 1970 and 1985. In recent years, however, preferred stock has made a modest comeback. In 1985, approximately $6.5 billion in new preferred stock was issued, representing less than three percent of all long-term corporate securities issued that year. Today, preferred stock represents slightly more than five percent of all long-term securities issued during a typical year.

COMMON STOCK

Common stock represents an ownership claim in a corporation; bondholders are creditors, but stockholders are owners. This leaves stockholders as residual claimants. If the company liquidates its assets, common stockholders get whatever remains after all creditors have been paid. Shares of publicly held companies (that is, shares that can be purchased by the investing public) are traded in markets known as stock exchanges. Unlike owners of sole proprietorships or partnerships, however, common stockholders have the advantage of limited liability. In the event the company goes bankrupt, stockholders can lose no more than what they paid for their stock. Stockholders are not fully liable for corporate debts.

Although the primary benefit to investors of fixed-income securities is clearly current income from interest payments, investors purchase common stocks primarily for potential capital appreciation.

Many common stocks do distribute some part of corporate net income as cash dividends; however, this income should be considered a secondary reason for investing in most stocks. In theory, as the company becomes more valuable (for example, as its earnings rise), shares of its common stock should also become more valuable, creating capital appreciation.

As an example, take a look at the two charts shown in Exhibit 3.4. It shows stock prices, earnings, and dividends for two well-known stocks: Home Depot and Johnson & Johnson. Both charts illustrate that, in the long run, stock prices follow earnings. As earnings for companies have risen, in general so has their stock prices. Between 1988 and 1998 Home Depot earnings rose by about 250 percent; over the same period of time Home Depot's stock price rose by 275 percent.

Although a clear *long-term* relationship exists between stock prices and earnings, the short term can show wide divergence between stocks and earnings. Speculative bubbles, which we discussed briefly in Chapter 1, can be extreme examples of

Exhibit 3.4a ✦ EARNINGS, DIVIDENDS, PER SHARE: HOME DEPOT

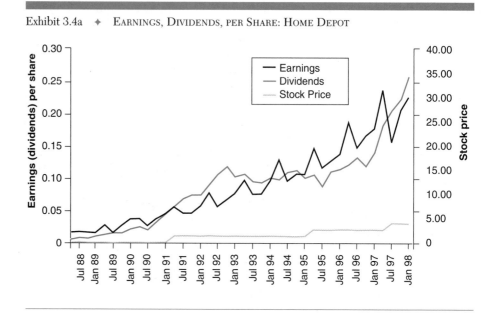

Exhibit 3.4b ✦ EARNINGS, DIVIDENDS, PER SHARE: J & J

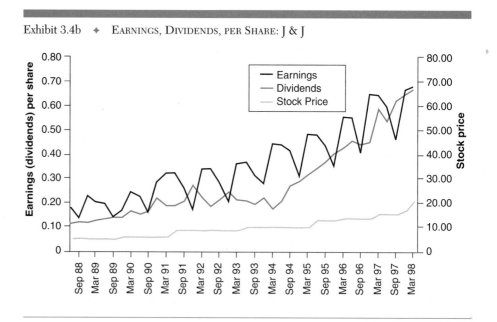

situations where stock prices get way ahead of earnings. The Investment History box, "The Nifty Fifty," on page 67, describes a famous speculative bubble. As with all bubbles, this one eventually broke.

Unlike fixed-income securities, it is difficult to categorize common stocks based on factors such as quality. Wall Street professionals use loose terms such as *cyclical, defensive, growth, value,* and *blue chip* to categorize individual common stocks. The

INVESTMENT HISTORY

The Nifty Fifty

Many stock investors would have preferred to forget the 1970s. Between the beginning of 1970 and the end of 1979, the S&P 500 had an average annual total return of 5.9 percent, less than the average rate of inflation for the period, 7.4 percent. The only major stock market fad, called the nifty fifty, came early in the decade.

Bounced by past bubbles, many investors, especially professional money managers and mutual fund managers, decided in the early 1970s to focus exclusively on sound rational investments, avoiding any fads. This notion led them to buy shares of companies with established growth records and familiar names, such as Disney, Hewlett-Packard, and Xerox. These stocks numbered about four dozen, thus the term nifty fifty. They were considered one-decision stocks, you bought them and held them forever. Unlike many past fads, the nifty fifty were quality stocks. Unfortunately, a bubble caused by excessive demand carried the prices of nifty fifty stocks well above values justified by their prospective growth rates.

Examples from the nifty fifty are shown in the table below. Between its low in 1970 and its high in 1972 to 1973, the S&P 500 gained about 57 percent. Nifty fifty stocks did much better, as the examples in the table illustrate. Disney and Hewlett-Packard, for example, each more than quadrupled between 1970 and 1972 to 1973. At its peak in late 1972, McDonald's was selling for eighty-two times earnings. Yet again, sophisticated investors fell into the trap of believing that whatever price they paid for a nifty fifty stock, it would continue to go up. Of course, that did not happen.

The market peaked in early 1973 and then declined sharply for most of the next two years. Between early 1973 and the end of 1974, the S&P 500 lost more than 43 percent of its value. The prices of the nifty fifty held up for a while and then collapsed. Avon Products and Disney, for example, each dropped more than 86 percent from their 1972 to 1973 highs. Polaroid lost more than 90 percent of its value between 1972 and 1974 as its price/earnings ratio fell from 115 to 16. In fact, Polaroid's stock has never recovered; it reached its all time high in the early 1970s.

Examples of the Nifty Fifty

	Low 1970		High 72/73		Low 1974		Percentage Change	
Stock	Price	P/E	Price	P/E	Price	P/E	70 to 72/73	72/73 to 74
Avon	59⅛	34	140	65	18⅝	10	136.8%	−86.7%
Disney	19⅜	24	111	82	15⅜	10	471.0	−86.1
Kodak	57⅝	23	152	44	57⅝	15	163.3	−62.0
Hewlett-Packard	19⅜	21	100	53	52	17	419.4	−48.3
McDonald's	9⅛	19	77 _	82	21 _	13	747.9	−72.5
Polaroid	51	25	150	115	14⅛	16	193.1	−90.6
Xerox	65 _	27	172	54	49	12	163.4	−71.5
S&P 500	75.6	14	118.4	19	67.1	7	56.6	−43.3

term blue chip, for example, was first introduced by the *Wall Street Journal* in 1904 to describe the stocks of the largest, most consistently profitable companies. In poker, the blue chips are always the most valuable. These terms are general, however, and not mutually exclusive. Any two investors are likely to put a single stock in different categories.

One goal of security analysis is to categorize individual common stocks, as well as estimate future earnings and dividends. We describe security analysis at more length in Chapters 11 through 14.

RIGHTS OF STOCKHOLDERS

Because common stockholders are legal owners of a corporation, their investments give them certain rights. Among these are voting rights. Each share normally gives its owner one vote in elections of the company's board of directors and on other significant issues facing the company.[9] Management retains responsibility for the day-to-day operation of the company within guidelines set by stockholders and the board of directors. The role of stockholders in corporate governance relative to the roles of the board of directors and management has become quite controversial in recent years as shareholders have asserted their will far more aggressively on issues such as management compensation and performance.

preemptive rights
Right of shareholders to purchase newly issued shares of stock before the general public buys.

Rights to retain a proportionate ownership in a company are known as **preemptive rights.** This concern stems from dilution of the percentage of shares controlled by existing shareholders, should a company decide to sell additional shares of common stock. For example, if a company with one million shares outstanding were to sell another five hundred thousand shares to new investors, the proportion of the company owned by existing shareholders would fall to 67 percent. Preemptive rights prevent dilution by giving existing shareholders the right to purchase any new share offerings before other investors. Preemptive rights eventually expire after set time periods, after which any remaining shares of a new issue can be sold to outside investors.

FOREIGN STOCKS

Americans interested in investing in a non-U.S. company have several options. Aside from international mutual funds, investors can buy the shares directly on the foreign exchange where shares are traded. For example, you could buy British Petroleum shares on the London Stock Exchange. The shares would be priced in British pounds (or rather, pence).

American depository receipt (ADR)
Surrogate for shares of a short company's stock held by a U.S. bank; denominated in U.S. dollars.

However, buying shares on foreign markets can be both cumbersome and expensive. Consequently, **American depository receipts (ADRs)** are often a better alternative. ADRs are denominated in U.S. dollars and trade on U.S. stock exchanges, so they eliminate some of the risk and complication of foreign investing. More than 125 ADR issues are traded on the New York Stock Exchange alone, including such well-known companies as Royal Dutch Shell, Unilever, and Honda Motor.

An ADR is a surrogate for the underlying shares. It represents a receipt for the shares of a foreign company held in the vault of a U.S. bank. ADR shareholders are entitled to all stock and cash dividends paid by the foreign shares. ADRs can be set up either by the bank at the request of the foreign company (known as a sponsored ADR) or can be set up at the request of U.S. market makers (known as an unsponsored ADR).

Derivative Securities

derivative security
A security whose value is tied to the value of an underlying asset; options and futures.

In recent years derivative securities have become more and more prominent. A **derivative security** is one whose value depends on the value of an underlying asset,

---

[9]The exception to this rule is a company with so-called dual classes of common stock. For example, Coors Brewing Company has two classes of common stock—Class A shares and Class B shares. Only the Class A shares carry with them voting rights, and they are all owned by members of the Coors family. Class B shares are available to the investing public.

such as an agricultural commodity, an individual common stock, a stock index, or a Treasury bond. Most derivative securities are considered riskier than more traditional investments, such as stocks and bonds. As a result, derivative securities are sometimes referred to as *speculative securities*. Derivative securities can be divided into three categories: stock options, corporate-created derivative instruments, and futures contracts.

STOCK OPTIONS

A stock option gives the holder the right, but not obligation, to buy or sell an individual stock, or stock index, at a fixed price for a fixed period of time. A **call option** is an option to buy, and a **put option** is an option to sell. Most options expire within one year after their issue dates.

Investors can buy or sell options to speculate that the underlying stocks will rise or fall in value over a short period of time. Options can also be used to hedge various stock positions, reducing their risk by gaining the right to buy or sell at set prices, despite market movements. Options are currently available on approximately 350 individual stocks as well as several well-known stock indexes. The most actively traded options are those on the Standard & Poor's 100 stock index (OEX options). Of course, you cannot buy or sell an index. These options are settled in cash and depend on the index value on the settlement date. This process is described in Chapter 15.

To illustrate how options work, consider a December call option on Microsoft at an exercise price of $100. This call option gives the holder the right to buy 100 shares of Microsoft at a price of $100 per share at any time before late December. If Microsoft's stock price were to rise above $100 per share before late December, the holder of the option could call the stock (that is, exercise the option). If Microsoft were to remain at or less than $90 per share before late December, the option would expire unexercised and worthless. By contrast, a December put option on Microsoft at an exercise price of $100 would give the holder the right to sell 100 shares of Microsoft at $100 per share until late December. If Microsoft's stock were to drop to $75 per share before late December, the holder of the put could buy 100 shares of Microsoft at $75 per share, then exercise the put option to sell the stock for $100 per share, earning $25 per share (ignoring transaction costs). However, if Microsoft's stock were to remain above $100 per share through late December, the put option would expire unexercised.

This simple example suggests generally how options work and how their value is tied to the value of the underlying stock (Microsoft, in the example). It leaves a number of important questions unanswered, however. For example, who sells the stock when someone exercises a call option or buys the stock when someone exercises a put? Other investors sell the same call or put option and accept the obligation to sell or buy in exchange for a fee. In Chapter 15 we answer many of the complex questions that options raise.

CORPORATE-CREATED DERIVATIVE SECURITIES

Corporations issue two kinds of securities that resemble options. These are convertible bonds or preferred stock issues and warrants. Like all derivative instruments, the value of these securities depends, in part, on the value of the underlying securities, which is the issuer's common stocks, for these derivatives.

call option
The right to buy stock at a fixed price, for a fixed period of time.

put option
The right to sell stock at a fixed price, for a fixed period of time.

Convertibles

convertible security
A bond or preferred stock that can be exchanged for a fixed number of shares of common stock.

A **convertible security** is just like a regular corporate bond or preferred stock issue with the added feature that the investor has the option of exchanging the convertible for a fixed number of shares of the issuing company's common stock. For example, Starbucks Corporation (the parent of Starbucks Coffee) has a convertible bond outstanding that can be converted into 43 shares of Starbucks common stock. Because it allows the investor to exchange a bond with a par value of $1,000 for 43 shares of common stock, this convertible has a conversion price of $23.25. The conversion price normally remains constant, regardless of the market price of the issuer's common stock, much like the exercise price on a call option. The value of the convertible depends, in part, on the value of the issuer's common stock. If Starbucks stock is trading at $25 per share, the convertible bond will sell for at least $1,075 (43 times $25).

Investors like convertibles because they combine characteristics of bonds (the Starbucks convertible pays interest at a coupon rate of 4.5 percent) with the potential to share in stock price appreciation. As a result, convertibles typically have lower coupon rates (or preferred stock dividends) than do similar straight bonds or preferred stock issues (that is, those that are not convertible).

Warrants

warrant
Long-term call option issued by corporations.

In essence, **warrants** are long-term call options issued by companies. The investor redeems the warrant with the issuing corporation and receives, for a preset price, a specified number of shares of common stock. Warrants typically have lives of five to ten years. They are often attached to other securities (especially bonds) to make them more marketable. Because an investor can sell the warrant and still keep the security to which it was attached, warrants trade on the major stock exchanges. Like all call options, the value of a warrant rises and falls as the price of the underlying common stock rises and falls.

FUTURES CONTRACTS

futures contract
A contract calling for the future delivery of an asset at a price agreed to today.

A **futures contract** is a real contract between parties for future delivery of a commodity at an agreed price, usually within one year. The party who agrees to deliver the commodity is said to have the *short position,* whereas the party who agrees to accept delivery has the *long position.* Let's say you go short and we go long in December corn. You agree to deliver, and we agree to accept, a specified amount of corn in December at a price on which we agree today.[10] In essence, the short position makes money if the price of the commodity falls between the contract date and the delivery date, whereas the long position makes money if the price of the commodity rises.

Futures contracts began in ancient Egypt and have historically involved only agricultural commodities such as corn, wheat, and livestock. Today, futures contracts are available on such diverse assets as foreign currencies, T-bonds, stock indexes, precious metals, and petroleum products, in addition to traditional agricultural products. The most actively traded futures contracts involve long-term T-bonds and currencies.

---

[10]The futures contract will also specify the grade of corn to be delivered and the delivery location as well as the amount to be delivered, the delivery date, and the price.

Futures contracts are traded throughout the world; the two largest futures exchanges are in Chicago (the Chicago Board of Trade and the Chicago Mercantile Exchange). The Singapore Futures Exchange is one of the world's largest markets for currency and other financial futures.

Basically, two groups of investors trade futures contracts: hedgers and speculators. A hedger owns or needs to buy the commodity that underlies the futures contract and uses the futures to reduce price uncertainty. A wheat farmer might use futures to guarantee the price at which a wheat crop would sell, prior to its harvest. Speculators have no need to trade commodities; they trade futures contracts hoping to profit from short-term movements in commodity prices. A speculator might go long in a wheat contract, believing that wheat is likely to rise in price over a short period of time. Another speculator might go short in T-bonds, believing that interest rates would soon climb higher, reducing the market prices of T-bonds.

We have a lot more to say about the investment uses of and trading in futures contracts in Chapter 16. Suffice to say at this point that although futures aren't for every investor, they can be quite useful in many investment situations.

Real Assets

The discussion so far has covered investing in financial assets, often called *paper assets*. To conclude our overview of investment alternatives, we turn our attention to real assets. *Real assets* are physical assets and include real estate, precious metals, gems, and collectibles (art, for example). Real assets have occasionally produced spectacular returns, but investing in them is problematic. The Investment Insights box on page 72 outlines some of the problems associated with investing in real assets.

REAL ESTATE

When we think of real assets, real estate may come to mind first. Land, commercial property, and housing units have long been considered viable investment options, and they have often provided attractive returns and even tax savings. Essentially, real investments fall into two categories: direct ownership of real estate and indirect ownership through a **real estate investment trust (REIT)** or limited partnership.

real estate investment trust (REIT)
An investment company that sells shares and uses the proceeds to purchase real estate investments.

Many Americans invest in real estate, even if they don't realize it. That's because more than 65 percent of all American households own their own homes. Owner-occupied housing has often been an excellent investment, but not always and not in every part of the country. In fact, many financial experts suggest you never buy a home *solely* on the basis of potential price appreciation. Owning a home has other advantages, including the pride of ownership and significant tax savings. Other direct real estate investments include farmland, rental property, and certain types of commercial property.

Just as with financial assets, you can also invest in real estate indirectly. REITs are corporations that invest in real estate. They pool funds from many investors and use the proceeds to purchase property, mortgage loans, or both. Shares of REITs trade on the major stock exchanges. A **limited partnership** consists of a general partner and several limited partners who invest funds in return for equity in property purchased by the partnership. The partners share in the income and/or capital appreciation produced by the property. The limited partners have limited liability; like corporate stockholders, they can lose only what they initially invested. The general partner has unlimited liability for all debts of the partnerships.

limited partnership
A form of indirect investment in real estate in which the partners have limited liability.

INVESTMENT INSIGHTS

THE TROUBLE WITH REAL ASSETS

Given the right set of circumstances, real assets can produce impressive returns. But, with exceptions, stocks and bonds have produced far better returns than real assets over long periods of time. The following are some other reasons why most investors should avoid real assets:

♦ No income. With the exception of some real estate investments, all returns from real assets come in the form of price appreciation.

♦ Value is subjective. It's much easier to put a fair value on a stock or bond than on a real asset.

♦ Lack of liquidity. Most real assets lack the liquidity of stocks and bonds. In addition, the cost of buying and selling real assets is high.

♦ Safekeeping. You're responsible when it comes to safekeeping real assets. Insurance can be quite expensive and difficult to obtain.

♦ Emotional bond. Many people who "invest" in collectibles, such as paintings, end up falling in love with them. Because they'll never sell their collectibles, they'll never make any money.

PRECIOUS METALS, GEMS, AND COLLECTIBLES

Investors have long been drawn to the glitter of gold, diamonds, and great works of art. Gold is one of the world's oldest investments and has long been considered a safe harbor in which money can weather any political or economic storm. Other precious metals—such as silver and platinum—have their advocates as well. Still others tout the investment potential of gems. What could be safer, they ask, than a bag full of diamonds? Some investors favor the investment potential of collectibles such as art, antiques, baseball cards, classic toys, and even Beanie Babies.

Although precious metals, gems, and collectibles have produced impressive returns at times, these investments, in our view, are even more risky than real estate. Liquidity, for example, is more of a problem with collectibles than it is with other real assets. Transaction costs can be high. And value is clearly in the eye of the beholder. Think about this, how much is an original Picasso painting really worth? The auction prices of many great art works fell sharply in the early 1990s when Japanese investors stopped buying art.

RETURNS FROM PAPER ASSETS AND REAL ASSETS

In the prior chapter we examined some of the historical returns produced by major categories of paper assets. Now let us compare the returns from paper assets to the returns from real assets. If you look at the chart shown in Exhibit 3.5 you'll see that over the past eighteen years returns from paper assets have exceeded returns from real assets by substantial margins. As the chart shows, even single-family homes, one of the best performing real assets, failed to keep pace with inflation over the 1981 through 1999 period. Gold and silver actually produced negative returns during these eighteen years. By contrast, paper assets such as stocks and bonds produced triple-digit returns, far exceeding the rate of inflation.

These relationships haven't always held true. If the 1980s and '90s can be described as the decades of paper assets, the 1970s was the decade of real assets, as shown in Exhibit 3.6. Between 1968 and 1979, the best performing asset was gold,

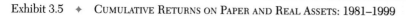

Exhibit 3.5 ✦ CUMULATIVE RETURNS ON PAPER AND REAL ASSETS: 1981–1999

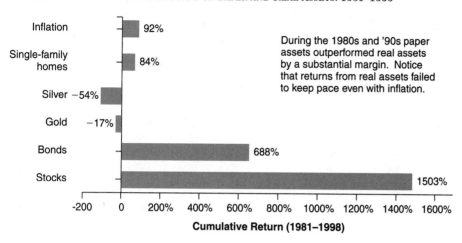

During the 1980s and '90s paper assets outperformed real assets by a substantial margin. Notice that returns from real assets failed to keep pace even with inflation.

Exhibit 3.6 ✦ AVERAGE ANNUAL RETURNS ON PAPER AND REAL ASSETS: 1968–1979

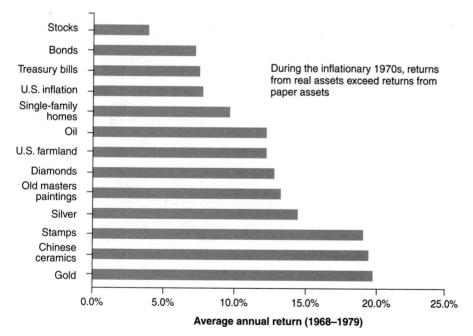

During the inflationary 1970s, returns from real assets exceed returns from paper assets

which achieved a compound return of almost 20 percent. Stocks and bonds ranked at the bottom, both failing to keep pace with inflation. Stocks, for example, produced an average annual compound return of only slightly more than 3 percent compared with an average inflation rate of 6.5 percent. What explains the difference between the 1970s and the 1980s and '90s? In a word, the answer is inflation. Historically, real assets often beat paper assets during periods of high inflation, especially if future rates of inflation seem difficult to predict. When inflation is low, and future inflation more predictable, paper assets tend to do much better than real assets.

In this chapter, you have been introduced to the wide array of direct investment alternatives available today. In the next chapter, we'll discuss how you can invest indirectly in paper assets by buying shares of investment companies.

Chapter Summary

1. What are money market instruments?
   Money market instruments are short-term debt securities issued by governments and corporations throughout the world. All money market instruments mature within one year, tend to be discount securities, and are generally high-quality instruments. Examples of money market instruments include Treasury bills, commercial paper, banker's acceptances, repurchase agreements, and Eurodollars.

2. What are bonds and other long-term fixed-income securities?
   Bonds and other fixed-income securities are debt instruments issued by governments and corporations throughout the world. All have maturities in excess of one year from the date of issue. Unlike money market instruments, most bonds are interest-bearing instruments. Bond quality can vary substantially, and most bonds are callable. Issuers of bonds include the U.S. treasury (government bonds), state and local governments (municipal bonds), and corporations.

3. Why invest in common stocks?
   Common stock represents ownership claims in corporations. The main reason for investing in common stock is expected price appreciation; over the long run stock prices tend to reflect a company's earnings. Owning common stock conveys certain rights, including voting rights and right to buy newly issued shares of common stock. U.S. investors can buy shares of foreign companies by investing in so-called ADRs.

4. What are derivative securities?
   Derivative securities are instruments that derive their value from another asset. Options give one the right to buy or sell stock at a fixed price, for a fixed period of time. Corporations issue securities with option-like features—convertibles and warrants. A futures contract is a real contract calling for the future delivery of some asset at a price agreed upon today. Futures are available in everything from agricultural commodities to currencies to financial instruments.

5. How is investing in real assets different from investments in paper assets?
   Many Americans already invest in real assets because they own their own homes. Other popular real asset investments include rental real estate, precious metals, gems, and collectibles. Real-asset investing often carries more risk than investing in paper assets. Historically, real assets have tended to outperform paper assets only in periods of high inflation.

Review Questions and Problems

1. What are the general characteristics of money market instruments? Give three examples of money market instruments.
2. Assume you purchased a ninety-day Treasury bill for $9,870 (face value of $10,000). Find the bank discount yield and the bond equivalent yield. Which yield comes closer to measuring your true rate of return?
3. A 180-day T-bill has a face value of $10,000 and a discount yield of 4.75 percent. Find the price, discount, and bond equivalent yield.
4. Assume a short-term municipal bond is yielding 3.75 percent. Find the security's taxable equivalent yield for an investor in a 33-percent tax bracket. When should the

marginal tax rate for this calculation reflect both the investor's state and federal income tax rates?

5. Define the terms *Eurodollar* and *LIBOR*. What is the relationship between Eurodollars and LIBOR?

6. What are the practical differences between federal agency securities and Treasury securities? Give an example of a federal agency security.

7. What are the differences between Treasury bills, notes, and bonds. Which of the three exposes an investor to the most risk?

8. Explain the difference between a general obligation bond and a revenue bond. Why are municipal bonds rated?

9. List several types of corporate bonds. Which type on your list is the safest?

10. What is a mortgage pass-through security? What are its investment advantages and drawbacks?

11. Why is preferred stock considered a hybrid security? Do investors consider preferred stock as more like a bond or more like common stock?

12. What is the main reason for investing in common stock? What major rights does common stock give its owner?

13. What is an American depository receipt (ADR)? Why would a U.S. investor purchase ADRs rather than buy the shares directly?

14. What rights do call and put options give their owners? Why are convertible securities and warrants considered options?

15. List the most popular real-asset investments. What are some general investment characteristics of real assets?

CRITICAL THINKING EXERCISE

This exercise requires library or Internet research. New stock issues—initial public offerings—can be quite risky and often disappointing. One of the most spectacular flops in recent years has been Planet Hollywood, the celebrity restaurant chain. The company went public in April 1996. The stock soared and then crashed. The company's fortunes sank along with its stock price. In 1999, the company filed for bankruptcy.

Research Planet Hollywood and try to identify why the stock was hot for a while and then cooled. What lessons does the Planet Hollywood debacle hold for investors?

THE INTERNET INVESTOR

1. Use your Web browser to research a company whose stock you may be interested in buying. Most companies provide financial results and other information on their Web sites. Other sites to visit include Quicken (www.quicken.com), Morningstar (www.morningstar.net), and Microsoft Investor (investor.msn.com). Prepare a brief report to your class about the company you selected.

2. As mentioned in the chapter, the U.S. Treasury recently began selling inflation-indexed securities. Visit the following Web site and read about these securities. Write a brief report explaining inflation-indexed securities in layman's terms. www.publicdebt.treas.gov/sec/seciis.htm

3. The largest options market in the world is the Chicago Board Options Exchange. Its Web site contains an extensive investor education section. Go to the CBOE's Web site and prepare a brief report on some of the uses and users of stock options. www.cboe.com/education

MUTUAL FUNDS

PREVIOUSLY . . .

We discussed the wide array of direct investment alternatives available today; everything from Treasury bills to junk bonds, from blue chip stocks to call options, from pork bellies to gold.

IN THIS CHAPTER . . .

We explore indirect investing through investment companies, especially mutual funds. Mutual funds are a significant part of today's investment landscape and many people invest a majority of their investment dollars in mutual funds. We'll also discuss two alternatives to mutual funds: unit investment trusts and closed-end funds.

TO COME . . .

We describe the world's financial markets, how investors participate in them, and how financial markets are regulated.

Chapter Objectives

After reading Chapter 4 you should be able to answer the following questions:

1. What is a mutual fund and how do mutual funds operate?
2. How much does mutual fund investing cost?
3. How should mutual fund performance be evaluated?
4. What are the other types of investment companies?

As we saw in Chapter 3, investors today must choose among a staggering number of investment alternatives. The stock market in the United States alone offers more than six thousand different stock issues. Throughout the international markets, the number of stock issues worldwide is closer to ten thousand. Add to that the thousands of money market, government, municipal, and corporate debt issues available, and investors face a bewildering task in choosing the right investments for their particular needs.

Many investors find that the best way to select securities intelligently in today's environment is to buy them indirectly by purchasing shares of mutual funds. Mutual funds pool the resources of many investors to purchase securities. Owning shares of a mutual fund means owning a small piece of a diversified portfolio; dividends (or interest income) and capital gains (or losses) flow through to the investor in proportion to the number of shares he or she owns.

Mutual funds are essentially creatures of the twentieth century, and they have become extremely popular in recent years. For example, net assets of mutual funds have increased at an annual rate of more than 25 percent between the end of 1988 and today, to more than $5.5 trillion. Mutual funds are larger today than life insurance companies, savings banks, and credit unions combined. The number of shareholder accounts has risen by over 250 percent during the past ten years. The fact that record numbers of Americans own stock today is due, in large part, to the existence and growth of mutual funds.

In this chapter we take a detailed look at mutual funds, how they operate, the kinds of funds available today, and how investors should choose the right fund. Although mutual funds are by far the largest type of investment company, two other types of investment companies exist: unit investment trusts and closed end funds.

Understanding Mutual Funds

The ancestors of today's mutual funds can be traced back to nineteenth-century Britain. Money invested in English and Scottish investment trusts (as these companies were known) contributed substantial financing to the U.S. economy following the Civil War. British investment trusts, for example, financed much of the railroad development that opened up America's western frontier.

HOW A MUTUAL FUND OPERATES

Today's mutual funds are fairly simple organizations. They raise money by selling shares of their own to the investing public. They use these funds to purchase various types of securities that help them achieve their stated investment objectives. For example, a money market mutual fund purchases only money market instruments such as commercial paper and Treasury bills. Mutual funds are also known as **open-end investment companies** because they continually sell new shares to investors. Shares of mutual funds do not trade on secondary financial markets such as the New York Stock Exchange (NYSE). If you wish to sell shares of a mutual fund, you sell them back to the fund. The term used is *redeeming shares.*

As the securities owned by the mutual fund pay interest or dividends, this income passes along to the mutual fund's shareholders. If the securities become more or less valuable, these capital gains or losses also pass along to the mutual fund's shareholders. Mutual funds work in a straightforward fashion, as the simple example in Exhibit 4.1 illustrates.

The mutual fund (let's call it The Fund) sells one million shares, at $10 per share, to the investing public, raising a total of $10 million. (Assume that The Fund charges no fees or expenses to investors.) The Fund uses the $10 million to purchase equal dollar amounts of five stocks with the initial purchase prices, annual dividends, and numbers of shares purchased shown in Exhibit 4.1.[1]

open-end investment companies
Another name for mutual funds; comes from the fact that mutual funds continually issue and redeem shares.

---

[1]To simplify the example, we'll make three assumptions: (1) investors pay no management fees or commissions, (2) the portfolio does not change during the year, and (3) the number of shares remains constant.

Exhibit 4.1 ✦ ILLUSTRATION OF A HYPOTHETICAL INVESTMENT COMPANY

The Fund initially sells 1 million shares priced at $10.00 per share. It buys equal dollar amounts of five stocks with the proceeds.

Stock	Purchase Price	Annual Dividend	Number of Shares Purchased	After Six Months		After One Year		Total Dividends
				Price	Total Value	Price	Total Value	
A	$ 20	$0.50	100,000	$ 30.00	$ 3,000,000	$ 34.00	$ 3,400,000	$ 50,000
B	25	0.50	80,000	24.75	1,980,000	22.50	1,800,000	40,000
C	50	1.00	40,000	67.50	2,700,000	80.00	3,200,000	40,000
D	50	1.25	40,000	48.00	1,920,000	45.00	1,800,000	50,000
E	100	2.00	20,000	100.00	2,000,000	120.00	2,400,000	40,000
Total portfolio value					$11,600,000		$12,600,000	$220,000
Per-share value					$11.60		$12.60	$0.22

Someone who buys 1,000 shares of The Fund, a total investment of $10,000, owns 0.1 percent of its equally weighted portfolio of five stocks. Assume that in six months, the total value of The Fund's portfolio rises to $11.6 million, even though only two of the five stocks in the portfolio actually rise in price. The value of 1,000 shares in The Fund also rises, to $11,600. If, at the end of one year, the total value of The Fund's portfolio rises to $12.6 million, the value of 1,000 shares becomes $12,600.

Now, assume that The Fund decides to liquidate at the end of one year. The investor receives $12,600 for 1,000 shares (the $10,000 initial investment plus $2,600 in capital gains) and $220 in dividends. The owner of 0.1 percent of The Fund receives 0.1 percent of its capital gains and 0.1 percent of the dividends produced by its portfolio. (Remember, this example assumes no transaction costs.) The investor's return for the year equals

$$(\$12,600 - \$10,000 + \$220)/\$10,000 = 28.2 \text{ percent}$$

Not a bad return for one year! Obviously, the operations of real mutual funds are more complicated than the example, but they all work in basically the same way.

net asset value (NAV)
Market value of the fund's assets, minus any liabilities, divided by the number of shares outstanding at any point in time.

The example emphasized the mutual fund's **net asset value (NAV).** NAV is simply the market value of the mutual fund's assets minus its liabilities (if any) divided by the number of outstanding shares. The Fund's NAV equals $10.00 when it begins operations, $11.60 in six months, and $12.60 in one year. (Remember, the number of outstanding shares stays constant at one million.)[2]

ADVANTAGES OF MUTUAL FUNDS

The popularity of mutual funds is no fluke. They offer some clear advantages to investors that more than justify their costs. We'll talk more about the costs associated

---

[2]Calculating the NAV for a real mutual fund can get quite complicated. It is a function of the number of new shares issued, the number of shares redeemed, and cash distributions, as well as the change in the value of the fund's assets.

with mutual funds later. For now, let's look at the three most obvious advantages of mutual funds.

Diversification

Perhaps the most important advantage of mutual funds is diversification. Time and time again, the markets confirm the value of diversification. We demonstrated in Chapter 2 how even simple diversification can substantially improve the risk/return trade-off associated with investing (for example, reducing an investor's risk without sacrificing too much expected return).

Because mutual funds own multiple securities, they offer investors diversification at a minimum. For example, Fidelity's Magellan Fund (the world's largest mutual fund) owns several hundred different stocks. To see the potential benefits of this kind of diversification, take another look at the hypothetical mutual fund shown in Exhibit 4.1. At the end of six months, two of the five stocks owned by The Fund have risen in price, two have fallen in price, and one is unchanged. Overall, the NAV of The Fund rises by $1.60 because the gain from stocks that rise in price more than offsets the loss from stocks that fall in price. At the end of one year, three stocks rise in price and two fall in price; the NAV rises another dollar. The Fund offers the advantage of diversification, as do most mutual funds.

Smaller Minimum Investments

Another advantage of mutual funds is their need for smaller minimum investments. Consider The Fund again; to create this portfolio independently, buying equal dollar amounts of all five stocks in round lots (multiples of 100 shares), an investor would have to spend $50,000. The mutual fund can give the investor some of the benefits of diversification while making a much smaller investment.

Of course, The Fund is hypothetical, but real mutual funds also offer the benefit of smaller minimum investments. For example, the Magellan mutual fund has a minimum investment of $2,500; for this relatively small investment, one can obtain a piece, albeit a small one, of a portfolio of several hundred different stocks. Another example is a money market mutual fund. As you may recall from Chapter 3, many money market instruments (for example, commercial paper and banker's acceptances) sell in large denominations ($1 million or more). Obviously, few individual investors can directly buy any of these instruments. Small investors who put up as little as $1,000 can buy these instruments indirectly, however, by purchasing shares of a money market fund. Simply put, mutual funds allow small investors access to large diversified portfolios and securities they could not purchase on their own.

Professional Management

All mutual funds provide some management services to their shareholders (for example, basic clerical services including the preparation of some relevant tax forms). Managing even a small investment portfolio can involve a substantial amount of time-consuming clerical work. Mutual funds relieve the individual investor of much of that work.

In addition to the clerical function, most mutual funds have professional portfolio managers who decide what securities to buy, when to buy them, and when to sell them. Does this relieve the investor of the sometimes arduous task of security analysis and selection? Yes, and no. The investor still must select a mutual fund that matches his or her objectives from among today's plethora of mutual funds and then monitor its performance.

Does professional management always imply superior performance? In general, no. In recent years, neither the average stock fund nor the average bond fund beat the appropriate market average. For example, during the ten-year period ending December 31, 1998, the average large-stock fund had an average annual return of about 16 percent. By contrast, the S&P 500 had an average annual return of almost 19.5 percent during the same period. Exceptions exist, however. Many funds have consistently beaten the overall market over long periods of time.

GROWTH AND DEVELOPMENT OF MUTUAL FUNDS

The Massachusetts Investment Trust, founded in 1924, is recognized as the first mutual fund organized in the United States. At the time, the financial community considered the idea of continuously offering and immediately redeeming shares a radical departure. Despite this, the idea took hold and other newly organized mutual funds soon followed. Most of the early mutual funds survived the 1929 stock market crash and the Great Depression.

The growth of the mutual fund industry accelerated after the end of World War II. At the end of 1940, mutual funds had net assets of $448 million; the net assets of mutual funds exceeded $2 billion by 1950, $17 billion by 1960, and $47 billion by 1970. At the end of 1970, 361 U.S. mutual funds served some 10.5 million shareholders.

Mutual funds continued to grow throughout the 1970s aided by two new types of mutual funds: money market funds and tax-exempt municipal bond funds. Money market funds became especially popular during the 1970s as small savers, who were used to earning 5 percent on their savings, were given the opportunity to earn market yields. In 1974, 16 money market funds had net assets of slightly more than $1.7 billion; by 1980, 96 money market funds had net assets in excess of $74.4 billion. By the end of the end of 1980, 564 U.S. mutual funds had net assets of $138.4 billion.

The 1980s saw extraordinary growth in the mutual fund industry, no doubt fueled in part by the historic bull market in paper assets. Between 1980 and 1988, the number of mutual funds and shareholder accounts more than tripled; the net assets of mutual funds increased by more than 250 percent. During the past decade, growth in the mutual fund industry has not abated. Between the end of 1988 and the end of 1998, mutual fund assets rose by almost 600 percent. Today, more than 7,000 mutual funds are in operation, with net assets exceeding $5.5 *trillion,* and almost 200 million shareholder accounts. Exhibit 4.2 illustrates the recent growth in U.S. mutual funds.

International Perspective

Mutual funds are also popular in other parts of the world, especially in France, Italy, Japan, Spain, and the United Kingdom. Today, net assets of non–U.S.-based mutual funds are closing in on $3 trillion. Like their U.S. counterparts, non-U.S. mutual funds have grown rapidly in recent years. The net assets of Italian mutual funds, for example, have risen from less than $65 billion in 1993 to almost $400 billion today.

TYPES OF MUTUAL FUNDS

In general, most mutual funds can be classified as one of four types: equity funds, hybrid funds (funds that invest in both stocks and bonds), bond and income funds, and money market funds. Exhibit 4.3 illustrates the distribution of mutual fund assets by

Exhibit 4.2 ✦ RECENT GROWTH IN U.S. MUTUAL FUNDS

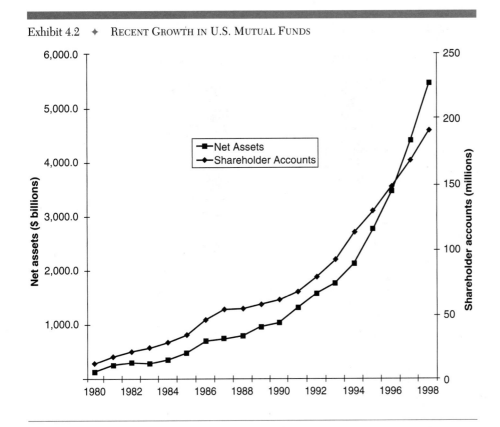

type of fund for 1988 and 1998. It also shows the rapid growth of equity funds relative to other types of mutual funds. In 1988, equity funds made up less than 25 percent of mutual fund assets; by 1998, equity funds made up close to 60 percent of mutual fund assets.

We can further classify mutual funds on the basis of their overall investment objectives and the types of securities they purchase to obtain that objective. Along with the rapid growth in mutual fund assets, the number of different categories of mutual funds has also expanded in recent years to meet changing investment needs. In 1975, all mutual funds fit neatly into seven categories established by the Investment Company Institute (a mutual-fund trade organization). The Investment Company Institute expanded the number of different categories of mutual funds to 16 in 1985 and to the current number of 22 by 1987. Examples of mutual fund categories include aggressive growth, equity income, general bond, growth, and tax-exempt bond.

Some argue that the traditional stock mutual fund categories can lump together funds that may be, in reality, significantly different. To further aid investors, Morningstar—one of the best-known mutual fund advisory services—classifies stock mutual funds on the basis of the kinds of stocks the fund typically buys (large-company stocks, mid-size-company stocks, or small-company stocks) and the fund manager's general approach to selecting stocks (growth, value, or a blend of growth and value).[3]

---

[3]Generally, a growth fund buys stocks the fund manager believes will grow faster than the overall market. A value-fund manager looks for stocks that he or she believes are in some way "undervalued" by the market.

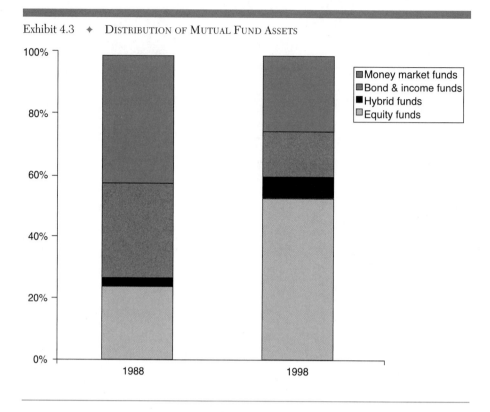

Exhibit 4.3   ✦   DISTRIBUTION OF MUTUAL FUND ASSETS

Index Funds

index funds
Mutual funds designed to closely track the performance of one of several indexes.

One of the fastest growing types of mutual fund today is **index funds.** The largest index fund—the Vanguard 500 Index Fund—has grown in size from about $1 billion in 1988 to more than $75 billion today. Index funds are designed to closely track the performance of a stock or bond market index. The most popular index funds are designed to track the S&P 500 stock index.

The case for index funds can be quite compelling. For one thing, index funds have much lower expenses than actively managed funds. For another, index funds often outperform actively managed mutual funds. As evidence, take a look at the chart shown in Exhibit 4.4, which shows the performance of the Vanguard 500 Index Fund compared with the performance of the average large-blend stock fund. The index fund outperformed its group average over each period shown, sometimes by quite a bit. Before you conclude that index funds are as close to a perfect investment as you can find, however, read the Investment Insights box on page 84, which lists the pros and cons of index fund investing.

SERVICES OFFERED

Mutual funds offer a variety of services to shareholders that vary from fund to fund. Five services are the most common:

✦   ***Automatic reinvestment of distributions.*** Instead of paying distributions (dividends and capital gains) to the shareholder in cash, the fund automatically reinvests the distributions, increasing the number of shares the shareholder owns.

Exhibit 4.4 ✦ PERFORMANCE OF THE VANGUARD 500 INDEX FUND COMPARED WITH THE PERFORMANCE OF THE AVERAGE LARGE-BLEND STOCK FUND

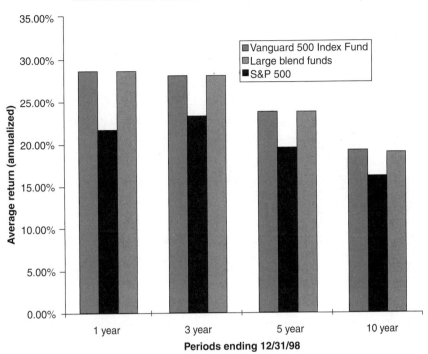

- *Automatic investment plans.* The shareholder can elect to have a specific dollar amount transferred periodically (usually either monthly or quarterly) from a bank account to the fund to purchase additional shares.
- *Check writing.* All money market funds, and many bond and income funds, allow shareholders to write checks (usually for at least $500). These checks can be used just like bank checks. Sufficient shares of the fund are redeemed to cover the check. Few equity funds offer check writing services.
- *Exchange privileges.* Many funds are part of mutual fund families. The same management company may offer several different mutual funds. Fidelity Investments, for example, offers more than 100 different mutual funds. Exchange privileges allow shareholders to transfer money from one fund to another. For example, let's say a money market fund shareholder believes that stocks are cheap. The exchange privilege would allow her to move all or part of her money from the money market fund to an equity fund managed by the same company. Many funds allow exchanges by telephone or PC.
- *Periodic statements.* All funds provide shareholders with periodic statements that show how much their shares have earned (dividends and capital gains), what their shares are currently worth, new shares purchased, shares redeemed, and so forth. Funds periodically distribute information on their expenses and portfolio compositions and also provide important year-end tax information to shareholders.

REGULATION AND TAXATION OF MUTUAL FUNDS

As with most investments, federal agencies impose the most significant regulation on mutual funds in the United States. Many of the federal securities laws that we'll

INVESTMENT INSIGHTS

0:00   0:00

THE DEBATE OVER INDEX FUNDS

Index funds are hugely popular, but are they a good investment for you? Some experts say yes while others say no. Here are some of the arguments in favor of, and against, investing in index funds to help you decide whether or not index funds are a good place to put your money.

Pro

1. Index funds charge low operating expenses compared to actively managed mutual funds (.4 percent versus 1.4 percent).
2. Index funds have outperformed actively managed funds over periods as long as the past ten years.
3. Index funds are more tax efficient than the typical actively managed fund.

4. Index funds are available that track small, mid-cap, and international stock indexes.

Con

1. Index funds will never make as much money as the indexes, due to transactions costs and taxes.
2. Index funds must adjust their portfolios in order to track their respective index. As a result, they tend to buy stocks when prices are high and sell when prices are low.
3. Index funds don't own a balanced portfolio of stocks. Their holdings tend to be concentrated in a few, large stocks. If these stocks soar in price, the index fund will end up buying more.
4. Index funds are more risky than many actively managed funds, meaning they're more volatile and can fall much more in price.

Sources: Beth Kobliner, Get a Financial Life, *(New York: Fireside Press, 1998), pp. 109–112; Ric Edelman,* The New Rules of Money, *(New York: Harper-Collins, 1998), pp. 95–103; Eric Tyson,* Personal Finance for Dummies, *2nd ed., (San Mateo: IDG Books), pp. 212–13.*

discuss in the next chapter apply to mutual funds. For example, federal law requires that every mutual fund provide potential investors with a current prospectus (the official offering document for the mutual fund) and limits the types of advertisements that mutual funds may use. Federal law and regulations also contain numerous provisions designed to protect the integrity of mutual fund assets and prevent funds from charging shareholders excessive fees. To buy shares, a mutual fund must be approved for sale in the investor's home state. Although most funds are approved for sale in every state, some exceptions exist.

Virtually all mutual funds choose to be taxed as regulated investment companies under Subchapter M of the Internal Revenue Service (IRS) code. To qualify, a mutual fund must meet several requirements on asset diversification, sources of income, short-term gains, and distribution of income. The last requirement has the most significant impact on investors; to qualify under Subchapter M, a mutual fund must distribute virtually all investment income to its shareholders each year.

Regulated mutual funds pay no taxes on investment income or capital gains; rather, income and capital gains pass through to individual shareholders, who assume the tax liability. Generally, for taxable individual investors, investment income (interest and dividends) is taxed as ordinary income and increases in the value of the fund's portfolio are taxed as either short-term or long-term capital gains. Distributions of these capital gains, which are called *dividends,* are taxable for individual investors. Mutual funds are allowed to pass through the federal tax exemption on interest from municipal securities to shareholders.

To illustrate this kind of pass through, let's look at an actual example. During 1998 the Fidelity Fund—a stock fund—distributed $2.11 per share to shareholders. Of this amount, $0.30 was dividend income and $1.81 was capital gains. Had you owned

100 shares of the fund, you would have had to report $30 in dividend income and capital gains of $181 on your 1998 federal and state tax returns. Also during 1998 the fund's net asset value rose. However, as with any investment, changes in the NAV are not taxed unless you sell your shares.

Mutual Fund Fees and Expenses

As you probably can guess, investing in a mutual fund is not free. All mutual funds charge shareholders fees and expenses, though some funds charge much more than others. Fees and expenses charged by mutual funds can be divided into two rough categories: load charges and annual operating expenses.

LOAD CHARGES

A **load charge** is a fee associated with buying or redeeming shares of a mutual fund. Some mutual funds charge a *front-end load,* in which the investor pays the load charge when purchasing shares initially. By law, a front-end load cannot exceed 8.5 percent of the fund's NAV. A front-end load effectively reduces the amount of the initial investment. For example, Fidelity's Contrafund has a 3 percent front-end load. If you initially invested $3,000 in the fund, you actually purchase only $2,910 worth of Contrafund shares, or 97 percent of $3,000.

    A *back-end load* refers to a fee assessed when an investor redeems shares of a mutual fund. Like a front-end load, a back-end load charge is stated as a percentage of NAV. If, for example, to redeem 1,000 shares of a fund with an NAV of $8.50 and a 3 percent back-end load, one would receive $8,245 for the shares [.97 × $8.50 × 1,000].

    One type of back-end load, a **contingent deferred sales charge (CDSC),** is assessed, usually on a declining scale, only if shares are redeemed during the first few years of ownership. For example, the Eaton Vance National Limited Maturity Tax Free Fund has a CDSC that starts at 3 percent for shares redeemed less than one year after purchase; the charge declines to zero for shares held at least four years. To determine whether a fund has a CDSC or other back-end load, look for an *r* after the name of the fund in a newspaper's listing of mutual funds. Of course, information on all fees and expenses is outlined in the fund's prospectus, which you should always read carefully before investing.

    Front-end loads often are designated, in part, as compensation for the brokers or dealers who sell mutual fund shares to investors. Back-end loads, especially CDSCs, are designed to discourage short-term trading by investors who might otherwise move money in and out of the fund frequently. Traditionally, all mutual funds have had load charges, especially front-end loads. However, no-load funds have become increasingly popular in recent years. Excluding money market funds, which are all no-load funds, about half of mutual fund assets today are held by no-load funds, up from about 20 percent 15 years ago.

OPERATING EXPENSES

All mutual funds assess shareholders annual management or advisory fees, along with fees to cover other operating expenses. These expenses are paid out of investment

load charge
Charge assessed when shares are purchased or sold.

contingent deferred sales charge (CDSC)
Back-end load that declines as the holding period increases.

income before it is distributed to shareholders. Instead of measuring operating expenses as a percentage of investment income, or in total dollars, a fund measures this charge as a percentage of NAV (or dollars per share). For example, the Safeco Equity Fund has annual operating expenses of 0.84 percent of NAV. The majority, 0.61 percent, goes to pay the fund's managers. The rest goes to pay for expenses such as postage, brokerage costs, and the cost of printing the annual report.

Operating expenses can, of course, vary from year to year. However, most mutual funds set their advisory fees at fixed percentages of net assets. Details on operating expenses are provided in a fund's prospectus.

12b-1 fee
Annual charge assessed by some funds; covers distribution costs and commissions to dealers and brokers.

Some mutual funds now assess **12b-1 fees** (named after the 1980 rule that allowed them). A 12b-1 fee can range up to 1.25 percent of NAV annually. It covers distribution costs, such as advertising, or commissions to brokers or dealers who sell the fund, in lieu of an initial load charge. Details on the 12b-1 fee, if a fund charges one, can be found in the prospectus.

Standardizing Fees and Expenses

The Fidelity Contrafund has a 3 percent front-end load and annual operating expenses of 0.83 percent. Another stock fund, the Heartland Value Fund, has no front-end load and annual operating expenses of 1.29 percent. Which fund would charge a shareholder more? This used to be a difficult question to answer until a few years ago when federal regulators began requiring mutual funds to publish in the prospectus a table listing fees and expenses over 1-, 3-, 5-, and 10-year periods using a standardized formula. This table allows a shareholder to compare the expenses charged by different funds.

Exhibit 4.5 shows the total expenses for both the Contrafund and Heartland Value fund over varying periods of time using the SEC's formula. Note that the Contrafund is more expensive over shorter holding periods due to its front-end load. However, the Heartland Value fund is more expensive over longer holding periods because it charges higher annual operating fees.

Evaluating Fees and Expenses

You have three things to remember when evaluating mutual fund fees and expenses. First, fees and expenses can have a dramatic impact on the value of your investment over time. This is especially true for funds with differences in annual operating expenses and similar investment returns. The hypothetical example in Exhibit 4.6 illustrates this point. We start with $10,000 in each fund and assume both funds earn 10 percent per year over a ten-year period. Fund A has annual operating expenses of .75 percent, and Fund B has annual operating expenses of 1.5 percent (we'll assume that neither fund charges any loads). At the end of 10 years you'll have $24,308 in Fund A but only $21,775 in Fund B.

Second, not all mutual funds with similar investment objectives charge the same. For example, the Heartland Value, Kaufmann, and Vanguard Explorer funds all are classified as small-stock growth funds. All three are no-load funds, but the Explorer fund charges annual operating expenses of 0.63 percent compared with 1.29 percent for the Heartland Value fund and 2.17 percent for the Kaufmann fund. Today annual operating expenses for stock funds average about 1.4 percent, yet they range from a low of .1 percent to a high of over 2.5 percent.

Exhibit 4.5 ✦ Total Expenses for Contrafund and Heartland Value

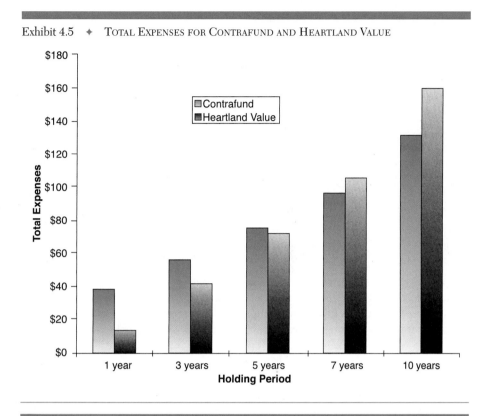

Exhibit 4.6 ✦ Differences in annual Wealth Due To Differences

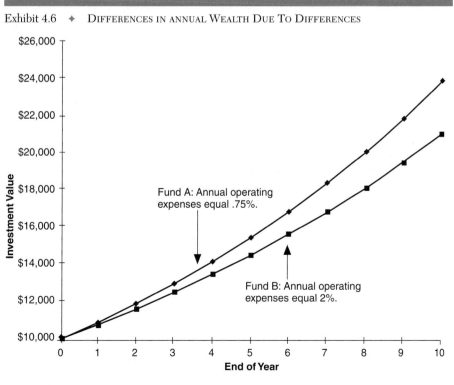

Third, no definitive evidence suggests that higher fees, or load charges, relate to superior performance, or vice-versa. For example, of the top 25 stock funds, based on their five-year performance ending December 31, 1998, about half were load funds and half were no-load funds. About half of the funds had lower than average annual operating expenses (1.4 percent per year) and half had higher than average annual operating expenses.

So, how do you evaluate mutual fund fees and expenses? For one thing, do not ignore them and do not assume you can nothing to limit fee increases; shareholders have the right to vote on proposed changes in fees and expenses. All things being equal, of course, you should buy funds with no loads and low annual operating expenses. If your holding period may be relatively short, it is especially important to avoid load charges. The trouble is, alas, that all things are rarely equal. The fund that best suits your investment objectives may charge more.

Performance

Performance is perhaps the single most important criterion for choosing among mutual funds. Investors must consider several factors when assessing performance. Absolute performance is obviously important, but so is relative performance (how well the fund's performance compares with an appropriate benchmark). Also the fund's performance consistency and its risk level are important considerations, as are the possible relationship between historical performance and future performance.

EVALUATING HISTORICAL PERFORMANCE

As an example of how to evaluate the historical performance of a mutual fund, we examine the track record of the Weitz Value fund. Now, although the Weitz Value fund's past performance has been for the most part exceptional, we're not recommending it to you or anyone else. We use it merely to illustrate how investors should go about evaluating historical performance.

Measuring Returns

Mutual fund returns can be measured the same way as the returns from any investment. Using the standard holding period return formula, introduced in Chapter 2, the one-period return from a mutual fund—for a single day, month, quarter, or year—is

$$(NAV_t - NAV_{t-1} + DIV_t)/NAV_{t-1}$$

where, NAV_{t-1} is the net asset value at the beginning of the period, NAV_t is the net asset value at the end of the period, and DIV_t is the amount of cash (capital gains and investment income) distributed during the period to shareholders.

At the beginning of 1998, the Weitz Value fund had a NAV of $25.15; it ended the year with a NAV of $29.07. During the year, the fund distributed $3.19 per share. Therefore, its 1998 holding period return was 28.3 percent [($29.07 − $25.15 + $3.19)/$25.15 = 28.3 percent].

Measuring performance over longer periods of time provides more valuable information to investors than performance over just one year. After all, one year's return may be an aberration. Even the best funds have occasional bad years and mediocre funds have rare days in the sun.

A way of measuring performance over longer periods is to construct a total return index. (We discussed how to do this in Chapter 2.) Exhibit 4.7 shows such an index for the Weitz Value fund from the end of 1988 through the end of 1998. This total return index can be interpreted as the current value of $1,000 in the Weitz Value fund from the end of 1988 through the end of 1998; such an investment would be worth more than $5,300 at the end of 1998. Annualized, the Weitz Value fund had a total return of about 18.3 percent during the ten-year period.

Performance Benchmark

The Weitz Value fund returned, on average, slightly more than 18 percent between the beginning of 1989 and the end of 1998. Although this sounds impressive, without a standard for comparison, it actually says little about how the Weitz fund performed relative to others. Therefore, the next step is to compare fund performance to appropriate benchmarks. Two commonly used benchmarks are a board market index and the average for the group to which the fund belongs. The S&P 500 is the most widely used "market" benchmark, but it is not the most appropriate for certain stock funds, nor is it an appropriate benchmark for bond and income funds. Exhibit 4.8 lists the appropriate market benchmark for major equity and bond fund categories. Now, let's see how the Weitz Value fund compared with its two benchmarks.

Exhibit 4.9 compares the average annual returns for the Weitz Value fund, the S&P Midcap 400, and the average midcap value fund (the Morningstar group to which the Weitz Value fund belongs) over varying periods ending December 31, 1998. In each of the periods shown, the Weitz Value fund beat the average midcap value fund, and in most periods, the fund also outperformed the S&P Midcap 400. For example, over the 10 years ending on December 31, 1998, the Weitz Value fund produced an average annual return of 18.3 percent compared to a group average of only 13.4 percent.

Performance and Risk

The other side of the investment question, of course, is risk. Perhaps the Weitz Value fund showed superior performance in the past decade because it is riskier than the market, a characteristic that would require the investor to evaluate fund risk as well as return. As we noted in Chapter 2, two common risk measures are standard deviation and beta. Using quarterly returns between 1989 and 1998, the Weitz Value fund had an annualized standard deviation of 16.4 percent and a beta of 0.61. By contrast, the S&P Midcap 400 index had an annualized standard deviation of 19.6 percent and a beta of one. Thus, both risk measures suggest that the Weitz Value fund was less risky than the overall market.[4]

ASSESSING FUTURE PERFORMANCE

Past performance is attractive, but it does not help today's investor. Future performance is much more interesting. Investors buy mutual funds not because of what they

---

[4]We can also assess the risk of a mutual fund, relative to its return, by using three performance measures based on modern portfolio theory. We'll discuss these three measures, Jensen's alpha, Treynor, and Sharpe, in Chapter 21.

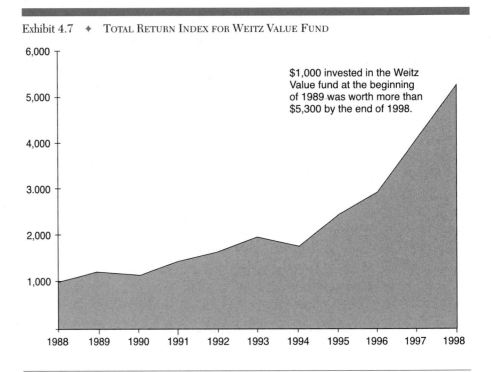

Exhibit 4.7 ✦ TOTAL RETURN INDEX FOR WEITZ VALUE FUND

$1,000 invested in the Weitz Value fund at the beginning of 1989 was worth more than $5,300 by the end of 1998.

Exhibit 4.8 ✦ APPROPRIATE PERFORMANCE BENCHMARKS

Type of Fund	Appropriate Benchmark for Comparison
Large domestic stock	S&P 500 index
Midcap domestic stock	S&P Midcap 400 index
Small domestic stock	Russell 2000 index
International stock	Morgan Stanley EAFE index
Taxable bond	Lehman Brothers aggregate bond index
Tax exempt bond	Lehman Brothers municipal bond index

did yesterday but how well they seem likely to do tomorrow. A key question, therefore, is how much investors should rely on the historical performance of mutual funds to assess future performance.

A school of thought especially popular in parts of the academic community argues that past performance is a poor predictor of future performance. Backed by some statistical evidence, the argument holds that individual mutual funds do not consistently, over long periods of time, post better risk-adjusted performances than the broad market averages. Some funds beat the averages some years, whereas others beat the averages in other years, but trying to predict which fund will beat the averages next year, or during the next five years, is a waste of time; random selection would do just as well. Too many investors have made the mistake of buying last year's hot fund, only to see it cool off this year. These critics claim that such investors are better off simply buying and holding shares of a well-diversified mutual fund that has

Exhibit 4.9 ✦ Compares the Average Annual Returns for Weitz Value and Benchmarks

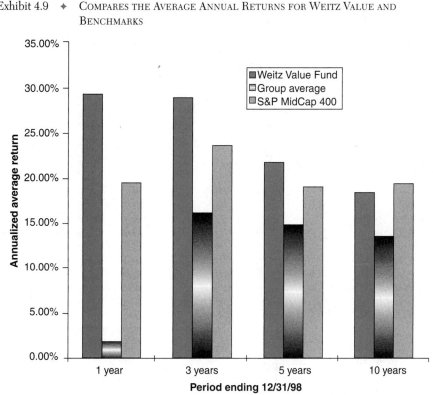

investment objectives consistent with individual objectives and tolerance for risk, or better yet an index fund. According to this school of thought, if a fund lags behind the averages for a couple of years, shareholders are still better off holding onto the fund instead of looking for a new fund. Past performance is simply no guarantee of future performance.

Others argue that this view is nonsense. They cite evidence that past performance is a reasonable, although not perfect, predictor of future performance. For example, one can point to the performance records of several mutual funds that have consistently beaten the averages in both up and down markets. These funds may not beat the averages *every* year, but over 5-year, 10-year, or 20-year periods, they have posted superior performance. This school of thought argues that past records must reflect more than just luck. A good track record, they argue, at the very least tilts the odds of success in the investor's favor.

By extension, this school of thought argues, if a fund lags behind the averages for three or four years, an investor may be wise to look elsewhere. The drop in performance may well indicate that the fund manager's investment philosophy or security selection process is not working. Further, if you believe that a fund's superior performance is due, in large part, to the superior skills of its manager, you should consider selling your shares if the fund manager leaves. The Investment History box on page 92, discusses one of the first mutual-fund superstars, Peter Lynch, and what happened to the fund he managed, Fidelity Magellan, after Lynch retired in 1990.

PETER LYNCH: THE FIRST CELEBRITY MUTUAL-FUND MANAGER

Ask investors to name a mutual-fund manager, many will name Peter Lynch of Fidelity Investments. Interestingly, Lynch hasn't actively managed a mutual fund in years. Yet even ten years after he "retired," Lynch's aura is incredibly strong. He was arguably the first celebrity mutual fund manager, and remains one today.

Lynch got his start in the investments business on the golf course, where he caddied while in high school and college for many of Boston's investment professionals, including Ned Johnson, his future employer. Lynch's experience with investment pros kindled his interest in the stock market but also ironically led to a deep skepticism of much professional investment advice. While attending Boston College Lynch bought his first stock, the air freight company Flying Tigers. Lynch claimed that he made enough money on the stock to finance his graduate studies at the University of Pennsylvania's Wharton School of Business. After a brief stint in the army, Lynch began his professional career with Boston-based Fidelity Investments in the late 1960s.

In 1980 Lynch became portfolio manager of Fidelity's Magellan Fund.

Even though Magellan, established in 1962, was one of Fidelity's older funds, it was fairly small and its performance record was generally pretty mediocre. Both the performance record and size of the fund, changed dramatically over the next 10 years. During the 1980s Magellan was the top-performing stock mutual fund, with an annualized return in excess of 30 percent. Magellan beat the S&P 500 by an astonishing 13 percent per year, on average. The size of the fund soared from less than $50 million to more than $11 billion. The number of shareholder accounts grew about five-fold.

How did Lynch achieve these results? In his best-selling book, *One Up on Wall Street*, Lynch explains his basic approach to investing. First, don't pay too much attention to the overall market; focus on individual stocks. Second, buy stocks that appear "cheap" and avoid fads. More specifically, Lynch looked for stocks of companies with superior products or services, companies with products or services you can easily understand, companies that show promise of above-average growth in future earnings, companies where insiders own a large portion of outstanding shares, and companies whose shares aren't heavily owned by institutional investors.

Lynch's approach to stock selection has been described by others as being "value-oriented, contrarian" in nature. But Lynch bought many different types of stocks while running Magellan, small-company stocks, cyclical stocks, growth stocks, high-dividend-yielding stocks, and even utilities. In other words, he bought any stock he thought was reasonably priced. Lynch also believed strongly in diversification. At one time Magellan owned close to 1,500 different stocks. That was probably a good thing since, by his own admission, about a third of the stocks Lynch bought while running Magellan turned out to be duds.

Tired of 14-hour days, Lynch stepped down from the day-to-day operations of running Magellan in 1990. Today he serves on Fidelity's board of directors and several other important investment committees. Fidelity still features Lynch prominently in advertising.

Since Lynch left Magellan's helm, the fund has had its ups and downs, not to mention three different managers. One manager invested heavily in technology stocks—an area Lynch tended to avoid—and bonds—another investment Lynch never thought much of. Performance suffered somewhat, but over the past five years Magellan has regained its position as one of the top-performing stock mutual funds. It now has about $100 billion in assets and is closed to new investors.

The evidence that past performance is related to future performance today goes beyond the claims of mutual-fund managers and other practitioners. One can also point to several recent scientific studies that suggest that the past performance of equity funds is a solid predictor of future performance.[5]

---

[5]See, for example, James Philpot, "Performance-Related Characteristics of Mutual Funds," Ph.D. dissertation, University of Arkansas, 1994.

Although we cannot resolve the controversy over how heavily investors should rely on past performance to gauge future performance, let's look at some anecdotal evidence. Exhibit 4.10 lists the top 10 performing mutual funds based on three-year returns ending December 31, 1993. It shows their performance over the three-year period, 1991 through 1993 and the three-year period 1994 through 1996. The exhibit also shows how each fund ranked within its mutual fund group. How well did 1995's stars perform during the more recent period? The record isn't pretty.

Only one of 1995's stars came close to matching the S&P 500 performance over the more recent three-year period. The percentile rankings also show erratic performance during 1996 through 1998. For example, Govett Smaller Companies, the top-ranked fund based on 1993–95 performance, ranked in the bottom quartile of its peer group in each of the subsequent three years.

Although many funds, including the Weitz Value fund, have impressive long-term performance records and investing in these funds may improve your odds, the past is never a guarantee of the future. Chasing returns from year to year rarely works.

PERFORMANCE AND TAXES

An issue the financial press is just starting to recognize is the relationship between taxes and mutual fund returns. As we noted earlier in the chapter, mutual funds are not taxed directly on investment income or on capital gains; shareholders pay taxes on income and capital gains distributions. A mutual fund's return can be broken down into the portion from distributions and the portion due to the change in the fund's NAV. The greater the portion of the return from distributions, the lower the after-tax return to the shareholder.

Exhibit 4.10　◆　SUBSEQUENT THREE YEAR PERFORMANCE OF 1995'S TOP PERFORMING FUNDS

Name of Fund	Annualized Three-Year Return (1993–95)	Annualized Three-Year Return (1996–98)	Peer Group Rank		
			1998	1997	1996
Govett Smaller Companies	51.1%	−11.7%	4	4	4
PBHG Growth	32.2	1.6	4	4	4
AIM Aggressive Growth	29.9	9.6	2	3	3
Robertson Stephens Value and Growth	28.8	18.4	3	4	4
Putnam OTC Emerging Growth	28.2	8.0	3	4	4
20th Century Gift Trust	27.3	−4.1	4	4	4
Franklin CA Growth	26.5	18.3	3	3	1
Smith Barney Special Equities	26.1	−1.4	3	4	4
Putnam New Opportunities	26.1	18.5	2	1	4
Excelsior Business & Industry	25.9	26.5	1	2	3
S&P 500	15.3	28.2			

Note: A peer group rank of 1 means the fund's performance ranked it in the top quarter of its peer group; a rank of 2 means the fund ranked in the second quarter; a rank of 3 means the fund ranked in the third quarter; and a rank of 4 means the fund ranked in the bottom quarter.

To illustrate the impact of taxes on mutual fund returns, consider the following hypothetical example:

	NAV (1998)	NAV (1999)	Distributions	Before-Tax Return	After-Tax Return°
Fund A	$10.00	$10.00	$2.00	20%	14.4%
Fund B	$10.00	$12.00	$0.00	20	20.0

°Assumes a 28 percent tax bracket.

Assume the value of particular securities owned by both funds rose by the equivalent of $2.00 per share during the year. The manager of fund A chose to sell the securities and distribute the profits to shareholders. Fund B's manager chose to keep the securities. As a result, the after-tax return to fund B's shareholders is higher. Of course, unrealized capital gains can turn into losses, so the fund manager has to weigh the risk of losing capital gains with the tax consequences to shareholders.

Experts suggest investors examine portfolio turnover, since higher turnover means greater capital gains distributions which are taxable to the investor. Information on portfolio turnover can be obtained from the fund's prospectus. Morningstar and other mutual fund advisory services also report tax information.

When Not to Buy Mutual Fund Shares

Most mutual funds make cash distributions at regularly scheduled intervals during the year; some make distributions monthly, others quarterly, and still others once a year. It is never a good idea to purchase shares of a mutual fund *right* before it makes a distribution (this information can be obtained from the fund). Why? Cash distributions reduce the fund's NAV by the amount of the distribution, which means, in effect, the total value of your investment remains the same. Unfortunately, you must pay taxes on the distribution.

Other Types of Investment Companies

Two other types of investment companies, although smaller than mutual funds, are worth some consideration. These are the unit investment trust and the closed-end investment company.

UNIT INVESTMENT TRUSTS

unit investment trust
Unmanaged portfolio of a specific type of security; investor purchases units or pieces of the portfolio.

A **unit investment trust** is typically an unmanaged portfolio of fixed-income securities put together by a sponsor and run by an independent trustee. The sponsor sells a fixed number of shares, called *units,* and uses the proceeds, less a sales charge, to purchase a portfolio of securities. All income from the securities held by the trust is distributed to the owners of the units, along with any principal repayments. The major advantages of unit investment trusts, compared with other investment companies, are generally lower annual fees and the routine return of principal.

The securities that make up a unit investment trust's portfolio almost always remain unchanged. Unit investment trusts are usually unmanaged passive investments. A unit investment trust with a portfolio of bonds ceases to exist when the last of the bonds in the portfolio mature. An investor can usually sell units prior to maturity. The sponsor typically makes a market in the units, buying and selling them at their current NAV, although sponsors are not obliged to do so. Shares of unit investment trusts are generally the least liquid of any investment company. In addition to the initial sales charge (typically 3 to 4 percent), some unit investment trusts charge small annual management fees. Some sponsors also charge commissions if units are sold early.

The first unit investment trust was created in 1961; since then, more than $250 billion in units have been sold. Only municipal bond unit investment trusts were available until 1972, when the first corporate bond trust was created; government bond trusts became available in 1978. Despite these developments, municipal bond trusts have remained the most popular. Municipal bond trusts have accounted for about 60 percent of the total amount of unit investment trusts sold since 1961.

A more recent development is the *stock trust*, a unit investment trust that purchases a fixed portfolio of stocks with the intention of liquidating the portfolio at some set point in time (usually after one to five years). The purpose is to offer small investors a way of purchasing a portfolio of common stocks. (Units are initially sold for as little as $1,000 each.) The units may represent diversified portfolios of stocks, specific sectors, or even stocks meeting certain investment criteria (for example, stocks with high dividend yields or low price/earnings ratios).

Another recent development is *index depository receipts*. These are unit investment trusts that purchase all the shares of stocks that make up several popular indexes—such as the Standard & Poor's 500 or Dow-Jones Industrials. Index depository receipts have an important difference from most other unit investment trusts. Although only a fixed number of units are sold, units trade on the major stock exchanges like individual shares of common stock. One of the most popular is *Spiders*, a unit investment trust that holds shares of all companies making up the S&P 500 index. *Spiders* trades on the American Stock Exchange.

CLOSED-END INVESTMENT COMPANIES

Like all investment companies, **closed-end investment companies** (or *closed-end funds*) raise money by selling shares to the investing public. They invest this money in a variety of securities consistent with their stated investment objectives. A closed-end fund usually does not sell additional shares after the initial public offering, however, and thus the number of outstanding shares is usually fixed. In addition, a closed-end fund will not redeem shares unless it liquidates. Shares of closed-end funds trade on various stock exchanges. (About 80 percent of closed-end fund shares are listed on the NYSE.) Investors can buy or sell shares of closed-end funds just like ordinary shares of common stock.

Some see advantages in limits on the number of shares that closed-end investment companies have outstanding. For one thing, this limits how large a closed-end investment company can get, unlike the potentially unlimited growth of a mutual fund. Another potential advantage of a closed-end investment company, with its limited number of shares, is potential to buy shares at a discount.

Unlike unit investment trusts, virtually all closed-end funds are actively managed. Each fund has a portfolio manager, or adviser, who buys and sells securities in an attempt to maximize return for what the adviser believes is an acceptable level of risk. For example, the manager of a closed-end fund that invests in government securities might increase the average duration of the portfolio if interest rates seem likely to decline. The manager of a closed-end fund that invests primarily in common stocks might increase the percentage of the portfolio held in money market instruments if

closed-end investment companies
Managed portfolios of securities with a fixed number of shares outstanding.

common stocks appear temporarily overvalued, making price declines likely in the near future.

More than 400 closed-end funds trade in the United States, with total net assets exceeding $150 billion. More than half of all closed-end funds invest in debt securities (either municipal or corporate bonds). However, one of the most rapidly growing type of closed-end funds is the single-country equity fund. Such a fund limits its investments to equity securities issued in a specific country.

Example of a Closed-End Fund

Exhibit 4.11 illustrates a closed-end fund, the France Fund. The France Fund is also an example of a single-country fund. It attempts to keep a minimum of 70 percent of its assets invested in common and preferred stocks of French companies, although currently it is more than 80 percent. Notice that the France Fund shares some characteristics with mutual funds. The fund does not pay U.S. taxes on investment income and realized capital gains so long as it distributes these to shareholders. The fund is actively managed, for which the fund's investment adviser receives an annual fee. The main difference between the two, however, is the fact that the France Fund has a fixed number of shares outstanding.

Net Asset Value Discount

Because the shares of closed-end funds trade on stock exchanges like ordinary common stocks, market prices are set by the sometimes mysterious interaction of supply and demand. In fact, the market prices of closed-end fund shares rarely equal their respective NAVs. Take another look at Exhibit 4.11 and compare the France Fund's year-end price with its NAV in recent years, the two were close together only at the end of 1993.

Historically, closed-end funds have generally sold at discounts from their respective NAVs. In recent years, the typical discount has narrowed, and some funds (for example, the France Fund) currently sell at premiums (that is, their share prices exceed their NAVs). In 1979, for example, equity closed-end funds sold at an average discount of 28 percent; today, the average discount is less than 5 percent. This raises several interesting questions. Why would a closed-end fund sell at a discount? Why does the discount vary from fund to fund? Why has the average discount narrowed in recent years?

There are no definitive answers to these questions, but several reasonable explanations have been offered. Some suggest that the discount relates, in part, to thin secondary markets. (Remember, shares of closed-end funds are traded on stock exchanges.) As the secondary markets for the shares of these funds have improved in recent years, the average discount has diminished. Others suggest that the discount relates to poor average historical performance; because the funds have exhibited better performance in recent years, the discount has shrunk. Other factors may help to explain the variation in the NAV discount, including distribution policies, taxes, management fees, and relative performance.

dual-purpose fund
A type of closed-end fund that sells two types of shares: income shares and capital shares.

Dual-Purpose Funds

A special type of closed-end fund is a **dual-purpose fund.** Unlike the typical investment company, a dual-purpose fund sells two types of shares and has a predetermined

Exhibit 4.11a ✦ EXAMPLE OF A CLOSED-END INVESTMENT COMPANY

STANDARD &POOR'S
STOCK REPORTS

Morgan Stanley Dean Witter Africa
NYSE Symbol **AFF**

15-APR-00 | **Industry:** Closed-end Fund | **Summary:** This closed-end fund seeks long-term capital appreciation by investing mainly in equity securities of African issuers.

Quantitative Evaluations

Outlook (1 Lowest—5 Highest)
• **NA**
Fair Value
• **NA**
Risk
• **Low**
Earn./Div. Rank
• **NR**

Technical Eval.
• **Bearish** since 2/00
Rel. Strength Rank (1 Lowest—99 Highest)
• **35**
Insider Activity
• **NA**

Net Asset Value • 13.03
Current Price • 8⅛
Prem./Disc. • -37.6%
Yield • 10.7%

Earnings vs. Previous Year
▲=Up ▼=Down ▶=No Change

10 Week Mov. Avg. — —
30 Week Mov. Avg. · · · ·
Relative Strength —

Principal Holdings - 13-MAR-00

At December 31, 1999, the fund's 10 largest holdings (42.0% of net assets), excluding short-term investments, were: Egyptian Company for Mobile Services (Egypt) 10.6%, State Bank of Mauritius Ltd. (Mauritius) 5.9%, Sechaba Breweries Ltd. (Botswana) 4.5%, Billiton plc (South Africa) 4.3%, Al-Ahram Beverages Co. (Egypt) 4.1%, Rembrant Group Ltd. (South Africa) 2.7%, Standard Chartered Bank (Ghana) 2.5%, B.O.E. Corp., Ltd. (South Africa) 2.5%, Bidvest Group Ltd. (South Africa) 2.5%, and Johnnies Industrial Corp., Ltd. (South Africa) 2.4%. The fund's current name was adopted in June 1999.

Operational Review - 13-MAR-00

Total investment income for 1999 amounted to $8.0 million. Expenses absorbed 39.8% of income, resulting in net investment income of $4.8 million ($0.34 a share). There was a net realized and unrealized gain on investments of $2.68 a share.

Stock Performance - 14-APR-00

In the past 30 trading days, AFF's shares have declined 19%, compared to a 4% fall in the S&P 500. Average trading volume for the past five days was 31,440 shares, compared with the 40-day moving average of 32,146 shares.

Key Stock Statistics

Dividend Rate/Share	0.87	Shareholders		NA
Shs. outstg. (M)	13.9	Market cap. (B)		$0.113
Avg. daily vol. (M)	0.026	Inst. holdings		59%
Beta	0.48			

Value of $10,000 invested 5 years ago: $ 12,949

Fiscal Year Ending Dec. 31

	1999	1998	1997	1996	1995	1994
Net Asset Value Per Share ($)						
1Q	9.43	17.42	--	16.95	--	12.12
2Q	12.96	15.67	21.19	16.04	16.04	--
3Q	12.46	12.78	20.42	—	--	--
4Q	14.51	11.69	14.45	16.86	17.05	14.43
Net Investment Income Per Share ($)						
1Q	--	--		0.12	0.12	0.06
2Q	0.18	0.23	0.16	0.11	0.11	0.21
3Q	—	—	—	—	0.13	0.14
4Q	—	—	—	—	0.22	0.13
Yr.	**0.34**	**0.40**	0.34	0.35	0.64	0.54

Dividend Data (Dividends have been paid since 1995.)

Amount ($)	Date Decl.	Ex-Div. Date	Stock of Record	Payment Date
0.050	Jun. 21	Jun. 28	Jun. 30	Jul. 09 '99
0.246	Dec. 10	Dec. 17	Dec. 21	Jan. 14 '00

  A Division of The **McGraw·Hill** *Companies*

Exhibit 4.11b ✦ EXAMPLE OF A CLOSED-END INVESTMENT COMPANY (*CONTINUED*)

STANDARD
&POOR'S

Morgan Stanley Dean Witter Africa Investment Fund

STOCK REPORTS

15-APR-00

Business Summary - 13-MAR-00

Morgan Stanley Dean Witter Africa Investment Fund (formerly Morgan Stanley Africa Investment Fund, Inc.) is a closed-end, non-diversified management investment company that seeks long-term capital appreciation by investing primarily in equity securities of African issuers and by investing, from time to time, in debt securities issued or guaranteed by African governments or governmental entities (Sovereign Debt).

Under normal market conditions, the fund will invest substantially all, but not less than 80%, of its total assets in African equity securities, which means common and preferred stock, bonds, notes and debentures convertible into common or preferred stock, stock purchase warrants and rights, equity interests in trusts and partnerships, and American, Global or other types of Depositary Receipts, and in Sovereign Debt.

The fund defines African equity securities as equity securities (i) of companies organized in, or for which the principal trading market is, Africa; (ii) denominated in an African currency issued by companies to finance operations in Africa; or (iii) of companies that derive 50% or more of their annual revenues from either goods produced, sales made or services performed in Africa.

Investments, which totaled $204.9 million (at market; 101.7% of net assets) at year-end 1999, were divided by country as follows: Botswana 4.5%, Egypt 21.3%,

Ghana 7.4%, Ivory Coast 1.4%, Kenya 1.7%, Malawi 0.5%, Maritius 9.7%, Mozambique 0.1%, Namibia 1.2%, Nigeria 0.2%, South Africa 40.9%, Tunisia 0.8%, U.K. 0.5%, U.S. 1.1%, Zambia 0.5%, Zimbabwe 8.1%, and other 1.8%.

Morgan Stanley Dean Witter Investment Management Inc., which acts as the fund's investment adviser, is paid a monthly fee at the annual rate of 1.20% of the average weekly net assets. In 1999, investment advisory fees amounted to $2.1 million.

Chase Manhattan Bank, through Chase Global Funds Services Co., provides administrative services. The administrator is paid a fee computed weekly and payable monthly at an annual rate of 0.06% of AFF's average weekly net assets, plus $100,000 per annum. In addition, the fund is charged certain out-of-pocket expenses by the administrator.

In September 1998, AFF began a share repurchase program intended to enhance shareholder value and reduce the discount to net asset value at which the fund's shares trade. In 1999, AFF purchased 455,300 shares (3.17% of its common stock) at an average price per share of $9.51, and an average discount of 23.59% from net asset value. In 1998, the fund bought back 1,102,056 shares (7.13%) at an average price of $10.83 a share, and an average discount of 25.62% from net asset value.

Per Share Data ($)

(Year Ended Dec. 31)	1999	1998	1997	1996	1995	1994	1993	1992	1991	1990
Net Asset Value	14.51	11.69	14.45	16.86	17.05	14.43	NA	NA	NA	NA
Yr. End Prices	10.38	8.38	11.50	13.63	12.88	11.38	NA	NA	NA	NA
% Difference	-28.50	-28.40	-20.50	-19.20	-24.50	-21.10	NA	NA	NA	NA
Dividends:										
Invest. Inc.	0.30	0.86	0.30	0.14	0.96	0.54	NA	NA	NA	NA
Capital Gains	NA	Nil	2.25	1.23	0.01	Nil	NA	NA	NA	NA
Portfolio Turned	135%	53%	40%	68%	66%	32%	NA	NA	NA	NA

Income Statement Analysis (Million $)

	1999	1998	1997	1996	1995	1994	1993	1992	1991	1990
Total Invest Inc.	8.5	10.3	11.0	10.3	14.2	11.8	NA	NA	NA	NA
Net Investment Income:										
Total	4.8	5.8	5.3	5.5	10.0	8.3	NA	NA	NA	NA
Per Share	0.34	0.40	0.34	0.35	0.64	0.54	NA	NA	NA	NA
Realized Cap. Gains:										
Total	0.4	3.0	25.0	22.7	6.9	-2.5	NA	NA	NA	NA
Per Share	0.03	0.21	2.15	1.47	0.45	-0.16	NA	NA	NA	NA
% Net Inv. Inc./Net Assets	2.70	2.56	1.70	2.10	4.20	4.50	NA	NA	NA	NA
% Expenses to:										
Net Assets	1.78	1.79	1.80	1.80	1.80	1.90	NA	NA	NA	NA
Invest. Inc.	44	43	49	46	30	30	NA	NA	NA	NA

Balance Sheet & Other Fin. Data (Million $)

	1999	1998	1997	1996	1995	1994	1993	1992	1991	1990
Net Assets	202	168	223	261	263	223	NA	NA	NA	NA
% Change NAV	27	-11.80	2.69	8.60	26	7.30	NA	NA	NA	NA
% Change S&P 500	21	29	33	23	38	1.30	NA	NA	NA	NA
% Change Bonds AAA	NA	NA	NA	NA	18	-13.70	NA	NA	NA	NA
Investments Cost	198	210	246	227	239	224	NA	NA	NA	NA
Investments Market	205	179	255	264	286	232	NA	NA	NA	NA
% Net Asset Distribution:										
Net Cash	-1.70	-6.90	-13.40	-1.30	-8.50	-4.20	NA	NA	NA	NA
ST Oblig.	2.4	8.5	14.2	2.1	8.3	5.8	NA	NA	NA	NA
Bonds & Pfd.	Nil	Nil	1.1	3.2	19.8	34.0	NA	NA	NA	NA
Common Stk.	99.3	98.4	98.1	96.0	80.4	64.4	NA	NA	NA	NA
Other Invest.	Nil	Nil	Nil	Nil	Nil	Nil	NA	NA	NA	NA

Data as orig reptd.; bef. results of disc opers/spec. items. Per share data adj. for stk. divs. Bold denotes diluted EPS (FASB 128)-prior periods restated. E-Estimated. NA-Not Available. NM-Not Meaningful. NR-Not Ranked.

Office—1221 Ave. of the Americas, New York, NY 10020. **Tel**—(800) 221-6726. **Website**—http://www.msdw.com **Chrmn**—B. M. Biggs. **Pres**—M. F. Klein. **Treas**—B. A. Brady. **Secy**—M. E. Mullin. **Dirs**—B. M. Biggs, P. J. Chase, J. W. Croghan, D. B. Gill, G. E. Jones, M. F. Klein, J. A. Levin, W. G. Morton Jr. **Transfer Agent & Registrar**—American Stock Transfer & Trust Co., NYC. **Incorporated**—in Maryland in 1993. **Empl**—0. **S&P Analyst:** M.I.

Exhibit 4.11c   ✦   EXAMPLE OF A CLOSED-END INVESTMENT COMPANY   *(CONTINUED)*

STANDARD &POOR'S
STOCK REPORTS

Morgan Stanley Dean Witter Africa Investment Fund

14-APR-00

NEWS HEADLINES

■ **07/06/99**   June 29, 1999, Morgan Stanley Africa Invstmt. Fund Inc. began trading under the new name, Morgan Stanley Dean Witter Africa Invstmt. Fund Inc. The company is listed on the New York Stock Exchange and trades under the ticker symbol AFF.

■ **12/19/95**   Morgan Stanley Africa Investment Fund Inc. (AFF) announced that its board declared an annual distribution of $0.9592 of net investment income and $0.0146 of long term capital gains, payable Jan. 9, 1996 shareholders of record on Dec. 29, 1995.

■ **06/28/95**   Morgan Stanley Africa Investment Fund Inc. (AFF) announced that its board declared a distribution of $0.0049 on common, payable July 17 to holders of record July 6.

■ **12/19/94**   Morgan Stanley Africa Investment Fund, Inc. (AFF) announced that its board declared the fund's first annual distribution of $0.5393 of net investment income, payable Jan. 10, 1995, to shareholders of record on Dec. 30, 1994.

■ **02/03/94**   Morgan Stanley Africa Investment Fund Inc. stated in a prospectus that 9,250,000 of its common shares were offered for initial public sale at $15 each to investors purchasing less than 100,000 shares. Minimum Purchase: 100 shares.   The New York Stock Exchange announced on February 4 that it admitted the shares to the list. Trading became available under the symbol AFF.   Concurrently, an additional 6,201,885 restricted shares were offered to investors purchasing more than 100,000 shares at an initial price of $14.45 each.   Morgan Stanley

Africa (AFF) was incorporated in Maryland on Dec. 14, 1993, as a non-diversified, closed-end management investment concern. AFF seeks to achieve its objective of long-term capital appreciation by investing primarily in equity securities of African issuers and by investing in debt securities issued or guaranteed by African governments or governmental entities. The offering of 9,250,000 shares was made through underwriters led by Morgan Stanley & Co. Inc.; Cowen & Co.; Crowell, Weedon & Co., Los Angeles; Janney Montgomery Scott Inc., Philadelphia; Kemper Securities, Inc., Chicago; Piper Jaffray Inc., Minneapolis; and Tucker Anthony Inc., Boston.   Address: 1221 Avenue of the Americas, New York, NY 10020 (212-296-7100).   INVESTMENT ADVISER: Standard New York, Inc.

---

lifespan (typically, 10 to 20 years). Investors who buy the fund's *income shares* receive all income (interest and dividends) from its assets plus a fixed redemption value when the fund liquidates. Investors who purchase the fund's *capital shares* receive everything else. Both sets of shares trade on the secondary markets. Only a handful of new dual-purpose funds have formed in the past few years; currently, the market offers about six dual-purpose funds.

Mutual funds, and other types of investment companies are significant and attractive investment options. Many investors will invest the bulk of their funds by buying shares of investment companies.

Chapter Summary

1.   What is a mutual fund and how do mutual funds operate?

Mutual funds, also known as open-end investment companies, pool investors' funds and invest in securities consistent with the fund's investment objective. Mutual fund shareholders share in the portfolio's value appreciation and income. Mutual funds continually issue new shares and redeem existing shares. The first mutual fund was created in the 1920s, but these companies have become a significant force in the investment field just during the past 20 years. Mutual funds also have become significant in many other countries. Mutual funds invest in money market instruments, bonds, small stocks, large-value stocks, foreign stocks, and so on. Domestic mutual funds are regulated by the Securities and Exchange Commission. Investment income and realized capital gains must be passed through to shareholders in the form of dividends who pay taxes on them.

2. How much does mutual fund investing cost?

    Mutual fund fees and expenses can be divided into two categories: sales charges (also called loads) and annual operating expenses. About half of all mutual funds charge an initial sales fee; a few charge a fee when shares are sold. All funds charge annual operating expenses. Fees and expenses must be reported using a standardized formula making it much easier to compare funds. Higher fees can significantly reduce the value of an investment. Further, fees and expenses vary widely from fund to fund, and no evidence indicates that higher fees are associated with better performance, or vice-versa.

3. How should mutual fund performance be evaluated?

    Performance is perhaps the most important criterion when selecting a mutual fund. Historical performance should be measured using holding period returns. Performance should be measured over long periods of time and compared with relevant benchmarks. Risk and the impact of taxes should also be factored in when assessing performance. Although good past performance may improve the odds of success, investors should always remember that past performance is never a guarantee of future performance.

4. What are the other types of investment companies?

    There are two other types of investment companies in addition to mutual funds. Unit investment trusts are unmanaged portfolios consisting of specific types of securities. The investor buys units, small pieces of the overall portfolio. The most popular type of unit investment trust consists of municipal bonds. A relatively recent development has been the creation of index depository shares—unit investment trusts holding shares of all the companies making up several popular indexes. Closed-end funds are similar to mutual funds in that most are actively managed. They are similar to unit investment trusts in that they have a fixed number of shares outstanding. Shares of closed-end funds trade on major stock exchanges. About half of closed-end funds invest in bonds. Single-country equity funds are also prominent today.

Review Questions and Problems

1. List the advantages of investing in mutual funds. Elaborate on one.
2. How are mutual funds regulated and taxed? How are individual cash distributions to shareholders taxed?
3. During the 1970s two new types of mutual funds appeared. What were they? Why were they so immediately popular with investors?
4. List some of the common services offered by mutual funds. What is a family of mutual funds?
5. Define *net asset value*. How is NAV affected by cash distributions?
6. List the criteria investors should use when selecting between mutual funds. What two should be examined in detail?
7. Define *sales load*. What is a contingent deferred sales charge (CDSC), or back-end load?
8. Why are mutual fund expenses standardized? Assume that you are trying to choose between a fund with a 3 percent initial load and annual operating expenses of 0.75 percent and a fund with no initial load and annual operating expenses of 1.5 percent. Which fund is likely going to be the more expensive over a one-year holding period? Over a 10-year holding period?
9. How should total returns for a mutual fund be measured? Assume that a fund began the year with a NAV of $20 and finished the year with a NAV of $25. During the year, it distributed $1 per share. Calculate the return to shareholders.

10. Assume that the total index on a stock fund rose from 1.6469 to 6.1403 between the end of 1989 and the end of 1999. Calculate the annual compound total rate of return. How much would an initial investment of $1,000 made at the end of 1989 been worth at the end of 1999?

11. Assume two funds began the year with NAVs of $30.00. Fund A distributed $2.00 to shareholders ($1.50 in realized in capital gains and $0.50 in investment income) and ended the year with a NAV of $32.00. Fund B distributed $0.50 to shareholders and ended the year with a NAV of $33.50. Calculate the before- and after-tax holding period returns (assume a marginal tax rate of 28 percent). If an investor owned 200 shares of Fund A, how much additional income would she report on her federal tax return?

12. Explain the purpose of performance benchmarks. What are the appropriate benchmarks for a growth and income stock fund and a small-stock fund?

13. Is past performance a good predictor of future performance for a mutual fund? Should you examine other factors to predict future performance?

14. Compare and contrast a unit investment trust and closed-end fund. What types of securities do most unit investment trusts purchase?

15. Define *net asset value discount*. Why do many closed-end funds trade at prices other than their respective NAVs?

CRITICAL THINKING EXERCISES

1. This exercise requires library or Internet research. Make a list of the 10 largest mutual funds—measured by net assets. How rapidly have these funds grown over the past five years? How well have they performed? Does your research lead you to any conclusions concerning the issue of size and performance? In other words, do you think a mutual fund can get too large?

2. This exercise requires library or Internet research. Using a well-known source of mutual fund information (for example, February issues of *Money* magazine), review data for the five-year period 1994 through 1998. Measured in terms of total one-year performance, find the five best-performing stock mutual funds each year (ignore sector funds and international funds). Record the fund and its one-year return. How well did each fund do the following year? For example, how did the top-performing funds of 1994 do in 1995? Do these one-year returns show any consistent patterns? Discuss your findings.

3. This exercise requires computer work. Open the Mutual Fund worksheet in the Data workbook. The worksheet contains quarterly returns for 10 mutual funds, along with quarterly returns from the S&P 500. Compute the arithmetic and geometric average returns for the funds and the S&P 500. Annualize the arithmetic mean. Calculate and annualize the standard deviation of returns for each fund and the S&P 500. Use these data to evaluate the performance of each of the funds.

THE INTERNET INVESTOR

1. Go to the Morningstar web site (www.morningstar.net). Click on the research tab and then the fund selector option. Screen the Morningstar database and find the 10 top-performing stock funds. Research each fund. Which would be the most appropriate for new mutual fund investors?

2. Virtually all mutual funds have web sites. Two of the most comprehensive are the Janus Funds (www.janus.com) and Vanguard (www.vanguard.com). Visit each site and write a brief report that answers the following questions: Do Janus and Vanguard appear to take different approaches to investing? What are some of the differences

between the types of funds offered by Janus and Vanguard? Which site did you think would be more helpful to a new investor?

3. The SEC's web site (www.sec.gov) has lots of information to help people make better investment decisions. Visit the SEC's web site and read the information on mutual fund investing. Did it improve your understanding of mutual funds? After reading the information, are you better prepared to make investment decisions?

Part 2

Financial Markets and Investment Selection

PART II IS DEVOTED TO A DISCUSSION OF THE FINANCIAL MARKETS AND HOW INVESTORS MAKE INVESTMENT DECISIONS. WE BELIEVE IT IS IMPORTANT TO UNDERSTAND NOT ONLY HOW INVESTORS ACTUALLY MAKE DECISIONS BUT HOW THEY *SHOULD* MAKE THEM AS WELL. WE BEGIN BY DESCRIBING THE MAJOR FINANCIAL MARKETS, BOTH PRIMARY AND SECONDARY. NEXT, WE DISCUSS HOW INVESTORS PARTICIPATE IN THE FINANCIAL MARKETS AND THE DEVICES IN PLACE TO PROTECT THEIR INTERESTS. THEN WE REVIEW THE CONCEPT OF MARKET EFFICIENCY. WE TRY BOTH TO DETERMINE WHETHER, AND TO WHAT DEGREE THE FINANCIAL MARKETS ARE EFFICIENT, AND WHAT MARKET EFFICIENCY IMPLIES FOR INVESTMENT SELECTION AND ANALYSIS. FINALLY, WE TAKE A LOOK AT TECHNICAL AND FUNDAMENTAL ANALYSIS—TWO TECHNIQUES PROFESSIONAL INVESTORS OFTEN RELY ON TO MAKE INVESTMENT DECISIONS. WE SHOW HOW TO APPLY THESE TECHNIQUES AND WHETHER THEY REALLY WORK.

ORGANIZATION OF THE FINANCIAL MARKETS

| PREVIOUSLY . . . | IN THIS CHAPTER . . . | TO COME . . . |

We described the wide array of investment alternatives available today, both direct investments and indirect investments, such as mutual funds.

We provide an overview of the world's financial markets, both primary and secondary. We describe how financial markets are classified, why financial markets are important, and how they function. We also speculate on the future evolution of financial markets.

We continue our discussion of the financial markets by describing how financial markets are regulated and investors participate in them.

Chapter Objectives

After reading Chapter 5, you should be able to answer the following questions:

1. What are the different types of financial markets?
2. How do primary financial markets function?
3. Why are secondary financial markets important?
4. How are secondary financial markets organized?
5. How are financial markets evolving?

Something remarkable happened in the early 1990s in a building that once housed offices of the central committee of the Polish communist party. After a recess of 50 years, the Warsaw Stock Exchange again commenced operations. The Exchange, originally founded in the early 1800s, was closed by Poland's new communist government in the late 1940s. The collapse of communism in the late 1980s changed both the political as well as economic landscape in Poland and throughout the Eastern Europe.

The Warsaw Stock Exchange reopened operations on a modest scale and has grown steadily. In 1996, the general public was allowed to purchase shares in newly privatized companies. The importance of the Warsaw Stock Exchange continues to grow as the privatization of state-owned companies continues. Poland views the Warsaw Stock Exchange as an important part of the country's transformation to a Western market-oriented democracy. Poland's leaders recognize that well developed financial markets, including a stock market, help foster increased economic growth and improved the opportunities for its citizens.

Compared to other world financial markets, however, the Warsaw Stock Exchange is still tiny. Currently, the Exchange lists shares of about 200 companies, and daily trading volume is less than one million shares. By contrast, the giant New York Stock Exchange lists close to 3,000 companies, and over 700 million shares, representing billions of dollars, are traded during a typical day.

In our view, no one can make informed, intelligent investment decisions without understanding the financial markets in which those decisions are implemented. And, as the reemergence of Poland's stock market illustrates, the economic prosperity of any society is enhanced by smoothly functioning financial markets. Consequently, some knowledge of the financial markets is important for everyone, not just active investors.

What Is a Financial Market

The dictionary defines a *market* as a meeting of people, or a place, for selling and buying goods or services. That rather broad definition suggests that a financial market exists almost any time and anywhere that anyone trades a security, but it does not imply that trading has to take place in a physical location. Buyers and sellers need only the ability and opportunity to communicate with one another. Nor does the definition imply that all buyers and sellers must receive the best price possible.

good market
A market where trading is conducted in a fair, orderly, and open manner.

Rather than ask what is a market, perhaps a more fundamental question would be what is a **good market?** We argue that a good financial market is one in which trading occurs in a fair, open, and orderly manner. To meet this standard, what characteristics should a good market have?

CHARACTERISTICS OF A GOOD MARKET

liquidity
The ability to quickly buy or sell an asset at a price justified by underlying supply and demand conditions.

Perhaps the single most important characteristic of a good market, for both buyers and sellers, is **liquidity.** Liquidity is the ability to quickly buy or sell an asset at a price justified by its underlying supply and demand conditions. In a liquid market, a seller should be able to quickly sell an asset for a cash price close to the market price. Let us say, for example, that you want to sell a house and you receive an offer of $100,000. Suppose, however, that local housing supply and demand suggests that the house should be worth about $150,000. This real estate market is not liquid. Although it allows you to sell your house for cash, it does not set a price that is justified by the underlying supply and demand conditions. Of course, liquidity does not prevent an asset from falling in price, nor does it mean that an investor never must sell an asset for a price well below the purchase price. One can lose lots of money even in the most liquid of markets.

A good financial market, to be considered fair, open, and orderly, should have the following characteristics:

✦ Sufficient information is available to determine the underlying supply and demand conditions, and this information is available to all market participants at about the same time. This implies that all trading should take place in full view of all market participants.

✦ Price continuity exists. This means that, assuming no new information has entered the market, one can buy or sell at a price close to that of the most recent similar trade.

✦ Transaction costs are low. All participants should have the opportunity to buy or sell at reasonable cost.

✦ All participants have equal access to the market. The market should not allow some participants to execute orders to buy or sell faster than others.

✦ Prices adjust quickly to new public information, and this information is disclosed at the same time to all participants.

These conditions are not absolute standards, and any assessment of how well any specific financial market meets these conditions is somewhat subjective. In the next chapter, we see that regulation of the financial markets, in both the United States and most other countries, is designed primarily to ensure that these conditions exist.

The conditions of a good market do not demand a **perfect market.** For one thing, a perfect market would have to eliminate frictions, with no transaction costs, taxes, or constraining regulations. In the real world, of course, market participants must pay transaction costs and taxes and contend with other conditions that impede their trading somewhat. Furthermore, a good market need not even always be an **efficient market.** Market efficiency is the extent to which security prices reflect all relevant information. Chapter 7 explores several versions of market efficiency theory, along with evidence supporting and contradicting the theory.

perfect market
One where trading is frictionless.

efficient market
A market where security prices reflect all relevant information.

CLASSIFICATION OF FINANCIAL MARKETS

Thousands of financial markets exist throughout the world. These markets, however, differ widely in terms of such characteristics as organization, trading practices, customers served, and types of securities traded. Let's discuss some of the ways financial markets can be classified.

Primary Markets versus Secondary Markets

One of the most obvious differences between financial markets is whether the market is a primary market or a secondary market. In a **primary financial market,** securities are sold to investors for the first time. The issuer of the security—a corporation or government—receives funds from the sale. For example, the United States Treasury auctions—sells—securities called Treasury bills—or T-bills—on almost every Monday of the year. This is a primary financial market because the Treasury receives funds from the security sale.

By contrast, a **secondary financial market** is one where securities are resold and bought after their initial sale. In other words, the issuer of the security receives no proceeds from the sale; all trades are between investors. The New York Stock Exchange (NYSE) is a secondary market. All of the shares of stock traded are being sold by one set of investors and bought by another set of investors. Most financial market transactions—about 80 percent by some estimates—occur on the secondary markets.

primary financial market
One where securities are sold to investors for the first time; the issuer receives the proceeds from the security sale.

secondary financial market
A market where securities are bought and sold after their initial sale; trades between investors.

Money versus Capital Markets

In Chapter 3 we described money market instruments, such as Treasury bills, and capital market instruments such as stocks and bonds. Thus, money markets are financial markets where money market instruments are traded, whereas capital markets are financial markets where stocks and bonds are traded.

Debt versus Equity

Financial markets where debt securities are traded are debt markets. Financial markets where equity securities are traded are equity markets. The NYSE, for example, is primarily an equity market.

Organized versus Over the Counter

The terms *organized* and *over the counter* are somewhat out of date. Traditionally, organized markets had established, fixed trading rules. Over-the-counter markets had looser trading rules. Today, most financial markets have established trading rules. However, **organized markets** today are those where trading takes place in a physical location. The NYSE is an example of an organized market. All trading takes place on a trading floor.

organized market
One where trading takes place in a specific location such as a trading floor.

    An **over-the-counter (OTC) financial market** is one where trading takes place in many locations with participants linked by a computerized communications system. The National Association of Securities Dealers Automated Quotation System (Nasdaq) stock market, the second largest stock market in the world, is an over-the-counter market. Traders throughout the world are linked by one of the most sophisticated computer Intranets. We'll discuss the Nasdaq is greater detail later in this chapter.

over-the-counter market
A market where trading takes place at many locations; traders are linked by a communications network.

Global versus Regional Markets

Many financial markets are global in scope. This means that the securities traded come from many countries throughout the world. Other markets are more national or regional in scope. For example, stocks from throughout the world, not just those located in the United Kingdom, trade on the London Stock Exchange. By contrast, stocks traded on the Frankfurt Stock Exchange tend to be those of German companies.

    In Chapter 3 we discussed derivative securities—securities that derive their value from another instrument. Examples of derivative securities include options and futures. Option and futures markets function somewhat differently from other financial markets, as we'll see in Chapters 15 and 16. For the rest of this chapter, we'll focus on stock and bond markets.

Primary Financial Markets

As noted, in a primary financial market investors buy newly issued securities and security issuers (for example, corporations) receive the proceeds from those sales. A popular misconception is that selling stock on the New York Stock Exchange (NYSE) takes money away from a corporation. This is not true; all NYSE trades involve one investor buying shares from another investor. The company received its money when it sold the stock initially in the primary market. Subsequent trades simply change the owners of the corporation and leave its financial condition unaffected.

Primary financial markets function as intermediaries between savers (investors) and borrowers (corporations and governments). Well-functioning primary markets allow borrowers to raise funds as cheaply as possible and at the same time give savers the opportunity to earn the highest possible expected rates of return. No modern economy can exist without well-functioning primary financial markets in which firms can raise capital to fund their operations.

Primary financial markets vary widely in size and organizational complexity. Generally, they process sales of new security issues in one of three ways: through open auctions, through underwriting by investment bankers, or through private placement with large institutional investors.

OPEN AUCTIONS

Several types of securities are sold primarily through **open auctions,** where investors bid on the basis of price or yield. The most significant new security auctions sell U.S. Treasury securities, federal agency securities, and mortgage-backed securities.

open auction
A market where investors bid on the basis of price or yield.

U.S. Treasury Security Auctions

As we discussed in Chapter 2, the U.S. Treasury issues a variety of debt instruments. Even though the federal budget deficit has shrunk dramatically during the past few years, the size of this market is still staggering. For example, during August 1999 the Treasury sold more than $144 billion in Treasury bills (T-bills) and almost $85 billion in T-notes and T-bonds.

Virtually all Treasury securities are initially sold to the investing public via an auction process. These auctions occur regularly, usually on a Monday. Auctions for three-month and six-month bills usually occur every Monday (excluding holidays), auctions for two-year and five-year notes occur monthly, and auctions for other securities (for example, thirty-year bonds) occur quarterly. The Treasury usually announces on the Wednesday before each auction how much of what types of securities it will sell the following Monday.

As the fiscal agent for the federal government, the Federal Reserve actually conducts the auctions, with the Federal Reserve Bank of New York taking the leading role. Buyers can submit two types of bids: competitive bids and noncompetitive bids. A competitive bid must specify a face amount and a bid price, whereas a noncompetitive bid specifies only the face amount the buyer wants to purchase, with maximums of $5 million for notes and bonds and $1 million for bills. The Treasury accepts all noncompetitive bids and reviews the competitive bids to determine the *stop-out bid,* the one with the lowest price (or highest investor yield) that it will accept. Those who submit noncompetitive bids agree to pay the average price on accepted competitive bids.

In theory, anyone can submit a competitive bid, but in reality only primary **government bond dealers** do so. (There are currently about 40 primary government bond dealers.) Despite the lack of formal restrictions, the Federal Reserve deals directly only with primary dealers, which the Federal Reserve itself designates. The Federal Reserve verifies that any firm requesting primary dealer status has adequate capital and handles a reasonable volume of trading in Treasuries (at least 1 percent of Treasury market activity).

government bond dealer
Institutions that make markets in U.S. government securities.

Primary dealers are expected to participate in every Treasury auction and are not allowed to bid for more than 35 percent of a total issue. Primary dealers may then resell the securities to other investors such as pension funds. To fulfill this function, primary dealers are expected to maintain inventories of Treasury securities at all times and to participate in secondary market trading.

Federal Agency Securities

As we discussed in Chapter 3, several federal and quasi-federal agencies are empowered to issue debt. These federal agency securities are sold in essentially the same manner as Treasury securities. Auctions generate competitive and noncompetitive bids, which are accepted based on a minimum price and funding needs. Again, the primary government bond dealers submit virtually all competitive bids and bid on almost every new issue. Dealers also are expected to maintain inventories of federal agency securities and to participate in secondary market trading. Because the amount of federal agency debt outstanding is much smaller than the amount of outstanding Treasury debt, sales of new federal agency issues are smaller than new Treasury issues, and the auctions are held less frequently.

Mortgage-Backed Securities

Virtually all mortgage-backed securities issued by the federally sponsored mortgage agencies GNMA, FNMA, and FHLMC (often referred to as Ginnie Mae, Fannie Mae, and Freddie Mac) are sold via auctions similar to those for Treasury and federal agency securities. The primary government bond dealers do most of the bidding and maintain inventories of mortgage-backed securities. Some mortgage-backed securities are issued by nongovernment entities such as large financial institutions; these securities are usually underwritten and sold through investment bankers.

UNDERWRITING AND INVESTMENT BANKING

Virtually all nongovernment security issues are sold to the investing public through investment bankers. This includes most municipal debt issues and public offerings of corporate debt and equity instruments. Bonds that are issued in other countries (for example, Eurobonds) also sell through investment bankers. Some foreign governments also tap the international credit markets by issuing bonds, which are typically underwritten, as well.

Role of the Investment Banker

investment banker
Institutions that help corporations and municipalities sell securities to investors.

underwriting
The purchase of a security issue by the investment banker who accepts responsibility for selling the issue to others.

The **investment banker** plays several important roles in the sale of new securities. These roles can be described as origination, risk bearing, and distribution. In the origination role, the investment banker helps the issuer design the terms and set the price of the new security issue. In the risk-bearing role, the investment banker purchases the issue (called **underwriting**) and accepts responsibility for reselling it to other investors. The risks associated with mispricing the issue are borne by the investment banker, not the issuer. Finally, in the distribution role, the investment banker distributes the issue to the public. The issuer could, of course, perform these functions itself. However, most issuers (for example, municipalities and corporations) find it much more efficient and less costly to sell new security issues through investment bankers.

Investment bankers do not provide their services for free. They charge **underwriting discounts,** purchasing securities from issuers below the prices at which they hope to resell them. Exhibit 5.1 shows the front page of a prospectus (the legally required document that accompanies a new issue) for a new issue of 2.6 million shares of common stock in Yahoo Corporation. Notice that the underwriting discount is stated as 91 cents per share (or about 7 percent of the value of the issue). The investment bankers stood to receive more than $2.3 million for their role in the deal.

underwriting discount
Difference between the price paid the security issuer and the price charged investors; fee paid to investment bankers.

Competitive versus Negotiated Arrangements

Issuers of securities employ investment bankers based on either competitive or negotiated arrangements. In a competitive arrangement, the issuer solicits bids from several investment bankers and chooses the firm that offers the smallest underwriting discount, and the least cost to the issuer. In a negotiated arrangement, the issuer selects the investment banking firm and negotiates all aspects of the issue, including the underwriting discount, with the firm. Some argue that, although competitive bidding might reduce the cost of a new security issue slightly, the extra services provided by the investment banking firm in a negotiated arrangement more than offset the extra expense to the issuer.

Most corporations issue securities by negotiated arrangements. In fact, most large corporations have ongoing business relationships with one or more investment banking firms. Public utility companies, however, are still required in many states to complete competitive bidding processes.

Many states require that municipal general obligation bonds be sold through competitive bidding as well, although this requirement seldom affects revenue bond issues. However, during the past 15 years or so a trend has increased the use of negotiated arrangements for sales of new municipal securities. The increasingly close relationship between some issuers of municipal bonds and their investment banking firms has been strongly criticized as not serving the best interests of either taxpayers or investors. Critics have accused some local officials of trading underwriting business for political contributions.

Syndication

For virtually any security issue, the investment banking firm selected by the issuer, whether by negotiation or competitive bidding, forms a **syndicate** to actually sell the issue to the public. The syndicate is a group of investment banking firms, each of which purchases a portion of the issue, accepting responsibility for reselling only that portion. For example, the syndicate for the Yahoo stock issue consisted of more than 70 firms, each of which purchased at least 20,000 shares for resale to the public. Syndicates allow investment bankers to spread the risk, limit their commitment of capital, and improve the marketing of the issue.

syndicate
A group of investment bankers who each buy, and try to resell, a portion of a new security issue.

A few corporate securities, mostly speculative equity issues, are sold by investment bankers on a best-efforts basis. In this arrangement, the investment banker does not underwrite the issue. The issuing corporation retains ownership of the stock, and the investment banking firm, or syndicate, merely acts as a broker to try to find buyers for the stock at the best possible price. The fees charged for a best-efforts issue are less than the underwriting discount, because the investment banker takes less risk.

Exhibit 5.1 ✦ FRONT PAGE OF A STOCK ISSUE PROSPECTUS

2,600,000 Shares

Yahoo! Inc.

Common Stock
(par value $0.001 per share)

All of the shares of Common Stock offered hereby are being offered by Yahoo! Inc. Prior to this offering, there has been no public market for the Common Stock of the Company. For factors considered in determining the initial public offering price, see "Underwriting".

In connection with this offering, the Underwriters have reserved approximately 200,000 shares of Common Stock for sale at the initial public offering price to persons associated with the Company.

See "Risk Factors" commencing on page 6 for certain considerations relevant to an investment in the Common Stock.

The Common Stock has been approved for quotation on the Nasdaq National Market under the symbol "YHOO".

THESE SECURITIES HAVE NOT BEEN APPROVED OR DISAPPROVED BY THE SECURITIES AND EXCHANGE COMMISSION OR ANY STATE SECURITIES COMMISSION NOR HAS THE SECURITIES AND EXCHANGE COMMISSION OR ANY STATE SECURITIES COMMISSION PASSED UPON THE ACCURACY OR ADEQUACY OF THIS PROSPECTUS. ANY REPRESENTATION TO THE CONTRARY IS A CRIMINAL OFFENSE.

	Initial Public Offering Price	Underwriting Discount(1)	Proceeds to Company(2)
Per Share	$13.00	$0.91	$12.09
Total(3)	$33,800,000	$2,366,000	$31,434,000

(1) The Company has agreed to indemnify the Underwriters against certain liabilities, including liabilities under the Securities Act of 1933. See "Underwriting".

(2) Before deducting estimated offering expenses of $700,000 payable by the Company.

(3) The Company has granted the Underwriters an option for 30 days to purchase up to an additional 390,000 shares at the initial public offering price per share, less the underwriting discount, solely to cover over-allotments. If such option is exercised in full, the total initial public offering price, underwriting discount and proceeds to the Company will be $38,870,000, $2,720,900 and $36,149,100, respectively. See "Underwriting".

The shares offered hereby are offered severally by the Underwriters, as specified herein, subject to receipt and acceptance by them and subject to their right to reject any order in whole or in part. It is expected that certificates for the shares will be ready for delivery in New York, New York, on or about April 17, 1996, against payment therefor in immediately available funds.

Goldman, Sachs & Co.

Donaldson, Lufkin & Jenrette
Securities Corporation

Montgomery Securities

The date of this Prospectus is April 12, 1996.

PRIVATE PLACEMENTS

Some new security issues may not be sold publicly but rather only to a small select group of large institutional investors (for example, pension funds and life insurance companies). These sales are referred to as **private placements.** Virtually all private placements involve corporate debt issues, although a small amount of municipal debt (less than 10 percent) is privately placed. In a typical year, about one-third of all new corporate debt issues are privately placed.

private placement
Private sale of securities directly to institutional investors.

A private placement typically provides some cost savings. The issuer avoids both the underwriting discount and the various costs associated with registering the issue with the Securities and Exchange Commission. (We'll describe SEC registration in the next chapter.) Institutions buy private placements because they usually carry slightly higher yields than publicly issued securities. In addition, the terms of the issue can be tailored to meet the specific needs of both the issuer and the institutional investor. Of course, the institutional investor gives up liquidity. Privately placed securities will not trade in any secondary market.

The Importance of Secondary Markets

Secondary financial markets handle trading of previously issued securities between investors. Like primary markets, secondary financial markets can be classified in several different ways: auction and negotiated markets, organized and over-the-counter markets, markets with face-to-face trading, and markets where trading takes place by computer.

The importance of secondary financial markets to investors is apparent. Many investors want, or need, to sell securities that they acquire in the primary markets. For example, an investor might purchase a five-year T-note with the full expectation of holding it until maturity. However, the investor's situation might change, and he or she might want to sell the note after, say, three years. The secondary market for U.S. Treasury securities provides liquidity for this investor by allowing him or her to sell the note for approximately its market value.

Although it is obvious why secondary markets are important to investors, their importance to issuers may not seem as obvious. Secondary markets benefit issuers of securities in the primary markets because if investors doubted that they could sell a newly issued security in a secondary market, they might refuse to purchase it or demand a substantially higher rate of return. By giving investors the option of selling their securities, a well-functioning secondary market lowers the cost of capital for issuers.

Aside from liquidity, secondary markets serve an important economic need for **price discovery.** Even if an investor plans to continue to hold a security, the secondary market still tells the investor what the security is currently worth. Furthermore, new issues of securities to be sold in the primary market are actually priced by the secondary market. For example, if five-year T-notes are yielding 5 percent in the secondary market, newly issued T-notes will have to yield about 5 percent to attract buyers.

price discovery
Secondary market information informing investors what securities are currently worth.

Any security issue that is not privately placed has some kind of secondary market. However, some secondary markets function better than others (that is, they provide more liquidity to investors). One way of seeing this is to look at the spread between the *bid* and *ask prices* of the market makers. Every secondary market has market

bid price
Price at which a market maker is willing to buy a security.

ask price
Price at which a market maker is willing to sell a security.

makers, dealers willing to buy and sell the securities traded on that market. The **bid price** is the price at which the market maker will buy the security, and the **ask price** is the price at which the market maker will sell the security. Market makers make their profits by selling securities at higher prices than they pay for them. A larger bid/ask spread, however, makes a secondary market less liquid.

Why, then, do some securities develop better secondary markets than others? Among several factors, the most important appears to be the size of the issue (for example, how many individual bonds or shares of stock were originally issued). Larger issues, in general, have more active and liquid secondary markets. Another important factor is the number of investors who originally purchased the issue. If, for example, ten large institutions buy up an entire new security issue, it is less likely that an active secondary market will develop than if the issue had been sold to thousands of investors, any of whom may decide to sell at any time.

Secondary Bond Markets

Domestic secondary bond markets trade U.S. government securities, municipal securities, corporate debt securities, and foreign debt securities. Most U.S. secondary bond markets are OTC markets. In such a market, trading takes place not in a physical location such as a trading floor but rather through computer-based communications systems that link dealers. These systems allow dealers, many of whom are widely dispersed geographically (sometimes in other countries), to exchange offers and make deals without meeting at a single location.

U.S. GOVERNMENT SECURITIES

U.S. government securities (Treasuries, federal agencies, and most mortgage-backed securities) are traded by government bond dealers, including the 40 or so primary dealers discussed earlier. Given the more than $3.5 trillion in outstanding Treasury, federal agency, and mortgage-backed securities, this secondary market is predictably large and active; it is considered the largest, most liquid financial market in the world.[1] Government bond dealers buy and sell billions of dollars' worth of government securities each day in a busy OTC financial market.

As you might expect, trading activity is heaviest in Treasuries and lightest in federal agencies, simply because of differences in amounts outstanding. This is reflected in the bid/ask spreads of each kind of security.[2] For example, the typical bid/ask spread for a Treasury security is about 4/32 (or 12.5 cents per $100 in par value), whereas the typical bid/ask spread for a federal agency security is about 6/32 (or 18.25 cents per $100 in par value).

---

[1] Some Treasury bonds are also listed and traded on the New York Stock Exchange. Trading volume, however, is minuscule. Less than one percent of secondary market trades in U.S. Treasury securities occurs on the NYSE.

[2] The bid/ask spread is the difference between the price at which a government bond dealer is willing to buy a particular government issue (bid) and the price at which the dealer is willing to sell the security (ask). As we noted. the bid/ask spread is often considered a barometer for the liquidity of a financial market—the narrower the spread, the more liquid the market.

MUNICIPAL BONDS

Like government securities, municipal securities are traded over the counter by municipal bond dealers. Commercial banks are large investors in municipal securities, and they often function as municipal bond dealers in some secondary market activity. As a rule, municipal bonds are not actively traded, and many issues lack good secondary markets. In fact, only a handful of municipal issues are traded in any particular day. Much of this trading occurs in large volumes between institutions (for example, mutual funds and commercial banks). This sparse trading activity is reflected in the bid/ask spread, which can be as high as 250 basis points (2.5 percent). The reason for this lack of trading activity is simply that most municipal issues are relatively small.

CORPORATE DEBT SECURITIES

Some corporate debt instruments trade over the counter. Others are listed and traded on some of the major stock exchanges. Today, the NYSE lists close to 2,000 corporate debt issues.

As the sizes of corporate debt issues vary, so does the trading activity in the secondary market. Like most municipal issues, small corporate issues do not trade frequently. The bonds listed on the NYSE tend to be the larger issues (the average par value of these issues is about $288 million). However, in a typical trading day only about $15 million in bonds change hands on the NYSE compared with more than $29 *billion* in common stock.

INTERNATIONAL BOND MARKETS

Bonds trade throughout the world. After those in the United States, the largest bond markets are located in Japan and Germany. Bond trading in Japan resembles bond trading in the United States. Trading takes place on both organized exchanges such as the Tokyo Stock Exchange (TSE) and over the counter. One difference between the U.S. and Japanese markets, however, is that a greater percentage of Japanese government bonds trade on organized exchanges in Japan than in the United States.

In Germany, banks make up the largest group of bond investors. In addition, unlike the United States and Japan, German law mandates no separation between banking and securities businesses. Banks dominate underwriting, trading, and investing in securities. As a result, secondary bond trading in Germany takes place in essentially an interbank market.

As you might expect, bonds issued in a particular country tend to trade in that country. The largest market for trading Canadian government bonds, for example, is in Toronto. However, globalization of the financial markets extends to the bond market as well. U.S. government bonds trade in London, as well as New York, and Eurobonds trade in Tokyo, as well as Zurich. The Tokyo Stock Exchange, for example, is an active secondary market for U.S. government bonds.

Domestic Stock Markets

The United States has several secondary stock markets, some with national, indeed international, operations and others that serve more regional needs. Trading on some U.S. stock markets is over the counter, whereas others trade on a trading floor.

Exhibit 5.2 ✦ DISTRIBUTION OF STOCK TRADING VOLUME AMONG MAJOR U.S. MARKETS

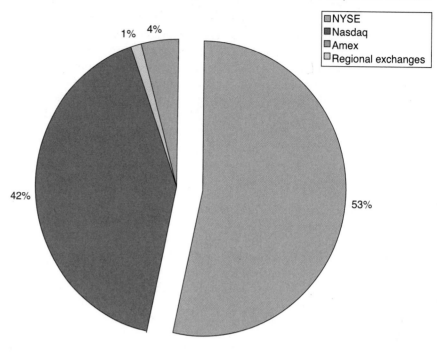

Exhibit 5.2 illustrates the distribution of stock trading volume among major U.S. markets for a recent year.

As illustrated in Exhibit 5.2, virtually all stock trading in the U.S. occurs on either the New York Stock Exchange or the Nasdaq Stock Market. Measured in dollar terms, the NYSE is the largest U.S. stock market, with about 50 percent to the total. Nasdaq likes to point out that, when trading is measured in terms of number of shares traded, the Nasdaq Stock Market is larger than the NYSE (see Exhibit 5.3). In addition, as Exhibit 5.3 illustrates, Nasdaq trading volume has grown faster over the past five years compared with NYSE trading volume.

Stock market indexes, the best known of which is the Dow-Jones Industrials (or Dow 30), are gauges of overall stock market activity and performance. In addition to the Dow 30, other well-known indexes include the Standard & Poor's 500 and the Nasdaq Composite. The various stock market indexes, however, are constructed differently and measure different segments of the stock market. Consequently, investors should use indexes with caution. The Investment Insights box on page 118 describes some of the key differences between the Dow 30 and the S&P 500.

NEW YORK STOCK EXCHANGE

The NYSE, founded in 1792, is arguably the most famous financial market in the world. It is also one of the largest. Today, shares of almost 3,000 companies trade on the NYSE, called the *big board* by some market participants. Most are U.S. companies; however, more than 300 stock issues of foreign companies also sell on the

Exhibit 5.3 ✦ Stock Trading Compared by Shares Traded on the NYSE and Nasdaq

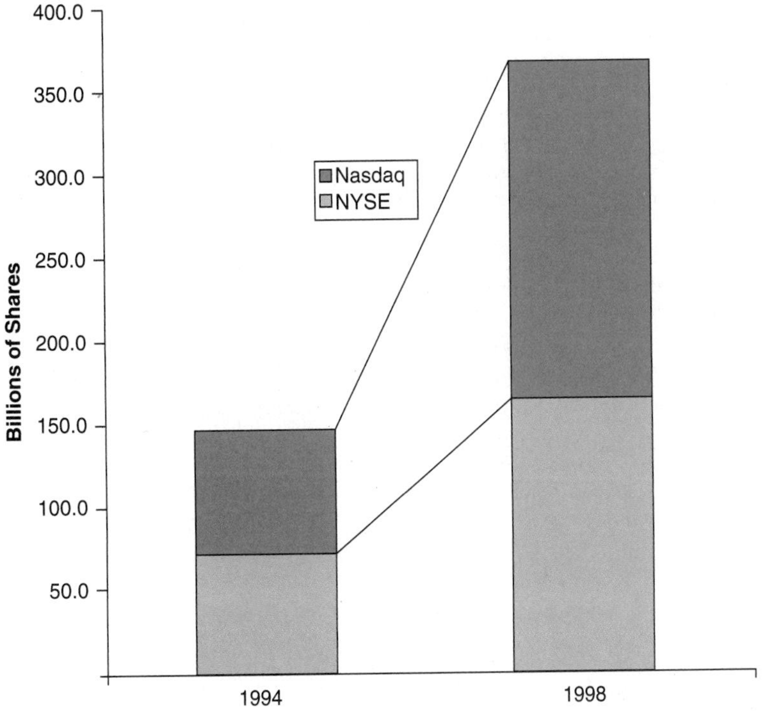

Billions of Shares

400.0 –

350.0 –

300.0 –

250.0 –

200.0 –

150.0 –

100.0 –

50.0 –

■ Nasdaq
□ NYSE

1994   1998

exchange. Companies listed on the NYSE have a combined market value in excess of $10.8 trillion. Companies that wish to have their securities traded on the NYSE must apply directly to the exchange and meet certain listing requirements. Companies must also meet annual certain requirements and pay annual listing fees. Why do companies choose to submit to the requirements and pay the cost to list their stocks on the NYSE? Four common reasons are liquidity for shareholders, access to capital, prestige, and exposure.

During an average day the NYSE accounts for more than 650 million shares traded, representing more than $29 billion worth of stock. The average trade is about 1,200 shares. On an annual basis, more than 170 billion shares of stock, representing more than $7.3 trillion dollars, trade. Trading volume has grown steadily over the past ten years. The number of shares traded annually, as well as the dollar value of these shares, has more than tripled since 1988.

The NYSE is an auction market. Unlike the secondary market for Treasury securities, all trading on the NYSE takes place on the exchange floor. Only members of the exchange (firms that own at least one of the 1,366 **seats**) are entitled to trade on the NYSE floor. Customer orders are delivered to the exchange by telephone, teletype, or computer. Buyers and sellers of an issue meet, face to face, at one of the 42 posts where that issue is traded, and bid against each other in an auction.

Each security listed on the NYSE is assigned to one of 42 **specialists.** A specialist acts as a market maker and assumes responsibility for maintaining an orderly and

seat
What gives a person or institution the right to trade stock on the floor of the New York Stock Exchange.

specialist
A NYSE market maker.

INVESTMENT INSIGHTS

0:00   0:00

STOCK MARKET INDEXES

Stock market indexes are widely reported in the financial and popular press and are a common tool for measuring the performance of the overall stock market. Probably the best-known stock market index is the so-called Dow-Jones Industrial Average (or Dow 30). It is made up of the stocks of 30 large, well-known companies, all of which trade on the New York Stock Exchange. (See the list of Dow 30 stocks in the table below.)

The Dow 30 a price-weighted index and is calculated as follows. The numerator is the sum of the prices of the 30 stocks making up the index. This sum is divided by a number, called the divisor. Each time the makeup of the Dow changes or any time a stock splits, the divisor changes and the index retains continuity.

The Dow's main drawback is that it doesn't represent a random sample of stocks. Certain sectors of the economy are over weighted and others are under weighted. Many times Dow stock performances have been higher, or lower, than the performance of the "typical" stock. Nevertheless, the Dow remains a popular gauge of the health of the stock market.

Another widely followed stock market index is the Standard & Poor's 500 (or S&P 500). The S&P's 500 stocks represent something like 95 percent of the total market value of all stocks traded in the United States. Stocks trading on both Nasdaq and the NYSE are included in the S&P 500.

The S&P 500 is calculated differently from the Dow. The numerator is the sum of the market values (price times number of outstanding shares) of each of the 500 stocks. The sum is divided by the so-called base period value. It is adjusted each time the composition of the index changes in order to ensure continuity.

Although most agree that the S&P 500 is a much broader measure of the overall stock market than the Dow, some still argue that the S&P 500 is an imperfect measure of the performance of stocks. Because the index is based on market values, stocks with higher market values have much more influence over the index than do stocks with low market values. The second table lists the 10 largest stocks in the S&P 500. Notice that these ten make up almost 25 percent of the index. A one percent price change for any of these 10 stocks will have a much greater impact on the index compared to a one percent price change for stocks with much smaller market values.

THE 30 STOCKS OF THE DOW JONES INDUSTRIAL AVERAGE

Allied Signal	Hewlett Packard
Alcoa	Home Depot
American Express	IBM
AT&T	International Paper
	Intel
Boeing	Johnson & Johnson
Caterpillar	McDonald's
	Merck
	Microsoft
Citigroup	3M
Coca-Cola	J.P. Morgan
Disney	Philip Morris
DuPont	Procter & Gamble
Eastman Kodak	SBC Communications
Exxon Mobil	
General Electric	United Technologies
General Motors	Wal-Mart Stores

THE 10 LARGEST STOCKS IN THE S&P 500

Stock	Market Value (millions)	Percent of Index
1. Microsoft	$462,205	4.39
2. General Electric	388,899	3.70
3. Intel Corporation	245,817	2.34
4. Cisco Systems	224,260	2.13
5. IBM	218,900	2.08
6. Wal-Mart Stores	211,648	2.01
7. Lucent Technologies	198,760	1.89
8. Exxon Mobil Corporation	184,512	1.75
9. Merck	152,013	1.44
10. Citigroup	148,601	1.41
Total	2,435,615	23.15

liquid market in each assigned security. Specifically, specialists have four roles: (1) they act as auctioneers, calling out quotes throughout the trading session; (2) they act as catalysts, bringing buyers and sellers together; (3) they act as agents for limit orders (discussed later in the chapter); and (4) they provide liquidity by buying or selling out of their own inventories when no other buyers or sellers are present. Specialists directly participate in only about 25 percent of all trades. A specialist must have sufficient capital to maintain an inventory of about 15,000 shares of each security assigned to it.

Like other market participants, specialists participate to make money. They earn money primarily in two ways: first, by acting as agents in limit orders, for which they receive part of the commissions (we'll talk about limit orders in the next chapter), and second, by buying and selling the stocks assigned to them. As mentioned earlier, a specialist offers to buy its assigned stock at a price (the bid price) slightly below the last trade price; at the same time, it offers to sell the stock at a price (the ask price) slightly above the last trade price. Over time, specialists should end up selling their stocks at higher prices than they pay for the shares. However, specialists must buy when no one else is willing to buy and sell when no one else is willing to sell to maintain liquidity in the market. In a period when prices are rising or falling sharply, specialists put their own capital at risk. For example, during the market break on October 19, 1987, NYSE specialists lost more than $100 million. Several specialist firms were forced to merge as a result.

NASDAQ STOCK MARKET

The Nasdaq Stock Market—owned by the National Association of Securities Dealers (NASD)—is a computer-based communications network that links the member firms to serve the vast OTC market for stocks. Trading volume on the Nasdaq Stock Market has increased sharply in recent years, growing at an annual rate of more than 20 percent.

Small-firm stocks, those that could not meet NYSE listing requirements, have traded over the counter for years. Various dealers make markets in these sometimes thinly traded stocks, earning the name market makers, by buying and selling from their own inventories. Before the Nasdaq Stock Market was established, a broker who wanted to buy or sell a stock traded over the counter would call around to the various market makers to receive current bid and ask prices. The broker would then buy from, or sell to, the market maker, offering the best apparent price. However, a customer could never tell whether a broker obtained the best price, because public trading information was incomplete.

As the OTC market grew in size and activity, this system became more and more cumbersome. In 1971, the NASD created the Nasdaq to gather all market maker quotes together for immediate reference by all member firms. The association also wanted to spruce up the somewhat unsavory reputation of the OTC market.

The current Nasdaq Stock Market offers three levels of information to members. Level 1 provides a median representative quote based on bid and ask prices that changes constantly as individual market makers adjust their prices. Level 1 is designed for firms that want current OTC quotes but do no heavy OTC trading for customers and are not OTC market makers. Level 2, designed for firms that do heavy OTC trading but are not market makers, provides a list of real-time quotes from all market makers in a particular stock. Level 3, designed for OTC market makers, resembles

Level 2 except that it allows dealers to change their bid and ask prices continually throughout the day.

Today, close to 5,000 stock issues trade on the Nasdaq Stock Market. The most actively traded issues, slightly fewer than 4,000, are listed on the Nasdaq National Market System (NMS). Stocks listed on the NMS must meet somewhat stricter listing requirements.

Nasdaq has been in the forefront among U.S. markets in participation in international activity. Today, more than 100 American depository receipt issues are listed on the Nasdaq system. Further, more than 250 issues are listed on both Nasdaq and foreign stock exchanges. In addition, Nasdaq has developed links with the Hong Kong Stock Exchange, the Singapore Stock Exchange, and the London Stock Exchange (LSE) that accommodate around-the-clock trading.

Unlike the NYSE, all Nasdaq-listed stocks have at least two market makers, and most have many more. Recently, an average of almost 11 market makers handled each Nasdaq stock. In addition, about 200 stocks have more than 25 market makers. Any Nasdaq member can become a market maker for any Nasdaq-listed stock, subject to minimum capital requirements. Today, Nasdaq has more than 500 qualified market makers, including all the well-known brokerage firms.

Traditionally, companies migrated from the Nasdaq to the NYSE once they met the NYSE's listing requirements. Today, however, many companies, including such well-knowns as Amgen, Cisco Systems, Dell Computer, Intel, Microsoft, Sun Microsystems, and WorldCom, have chosen to remain on the Nasdaq Stock Market even though they clearly would qualify for listing on the NYSE. Why? Each company probably has its own reasons, though some believe the prestige once associated with a NYSE listing is no longer significant.

Other Domestic Stock Markets

The American Stock Exchange (AMEX), sometimes referred to as the *curb*, was founded in New York City about 1910 to provide a market for unlisted securities. In fact, the AMEX did not have formal listing requirements until the 1930s, and it continued to trade unlisted securities until about 1946. Like the NYSE, the AMEX is considered a national market, and it conducts trading in much the same way as the NYSE. The AMEX began listing foreign securities and warrants before the NYSE, and since 1975 has become a major options market. Today, the AMEX does still trade stock issues, and it lists the shares of about 900 companies. Since 1985, trading volume on the AMEX has increased at an annual rate of about 10 percent.

Traditionally, the AMEX has traded the stocks of smaller, less well-known companies. That is still the case, as its listing requirements reflect. Although the NYSE requires that the total market value of a listed firm's publicly held shares exceed $18 million, the AMEX requires that it exceed only $3 million.

Even though AMEX trading volume rose throughout the 1990s, the AMEX's share of total stock trading volume declined. Trading on the AMEX represents less than 1 percent of total stock trading in the United States today. Faced with competition from the giant NYSE and Nasdaq Stock Markets, the AMEX gave up on its attempt to remain independent and sold out to the National Association of Securities Dealers in 1997. While the NASD merged some administrative functions, it continues to operate both the Nasdaq Stock Market and AMEX as independent markets.

Regional Exchanges

In addition to the two national exchanges, several smaller regional markets trade stocks in the United States. Virtually all trading on the regional exchanges (in excess of 95 percent) is in *dual-listed shares,* stocks listed on both a regional exchange and one of the national exchanges. For example, Disney's common stock is listed on the NYSE, along with the Boston, Cincinnati, Midwest (Chicago), Pacific (San Francisco), and Philadelphia stock exchanges. Buyers and sellers may get slightly better prices on a regional exchange, pay slightly lower transaction costs, or make trades when the NYSE is closed. The Chicago Stock Exchange, for example, remains open for 30 minutes after the NYSE closes. Some of the smaller regional brokerage firms, which are not NYSE members, often use the regional exchanges.

THIRD AND FOURTH MARKETS

During the 1970s, many large institutional investors became dissatisfied with the cost of trading stocks on the NYSE. Their objection gave birth to the **third market,** in which NYSE-listed stocks are traded off the exchange floor. It is considered an OTC market in which firms that are not NYSE members act as market makers for the institutional investors. More than 5 billion shares of stocks listed on the NYSE are traded in the third market each year. By most accounts, the third market is the third largest for NYSE listed stocks, after the Midwest Stock Exchange and, of course, the NYSE itself.

third market
Over the counter trading of listed shares off the floor of the NYSE.

The **fourth market** trades stocks listed on the NYSE or Nasdaq over the counter between institutions without the intervention of market makers. The fourth market is essentially a series of communications networks that directly match investors who want to trade large blocks of stock. Because the fourth market's trades are essentially private deals between buyers and sellers, it is difficult to obtain detailed data on its trading activity. However, by most estimates trading volume in the fourth market exceeds several billion shares per year.

fourth market
Private trades of NYSE listed stocks off the floor of the exchange.

Instinet

One of the largest and best-known fourth market networks is Instinet, a subsidiary of the Reuters Group. Instinet provides agency brokerage services to mostly large institutional investors and is always open for trading stocks listed on any of the exchanges to which Instinet belongs.[3] Investors pay as little as a penny a share to trade on Instinet.

Because it is an agent broker, Instinet remains neutral in its transactions. It neither buys nor sells for its own account, thus eliminating the market maker bid/ask spread. Because Instinet also offers anonymous trading, other market participants can't tell who is buying or selling.[4]

---

[3]Instinet is a member of the NASD, all U.S. regional exchanges, and the American, London, Paris, Toronto, Zurich, Hong Kong, Frankfurt, Stockholm, and Bermuda stock exchanges.

[4]Large investors have complained for years that traditional brokers often leaked who was transacting. Such leaks, investors contended, often affected prices.

Instinet trading volume often tops 100 million shares a day. Most Instinet trades are in Nasdaq-listed stocks. In fact, during a typical day Instinet trades accounts for about 25 percent of all Nasdaq trading volume.

In House Networks

in-house networks
Internal trading networks set up by institutional investors allowing the cross-trading between internal accounts.

An emerging trend today is the **in-house network**. In-house networks are internal trading networks that bypass brokers and stock markets and are set up by mutual funds, pension funds, and other large institutional investors. These networks allow an institution to cross-trade between its many funds or accounts. For example, an in-house network would allow the manager of a mutual fund to sell shares of stock to another fund owned by the same fund family.

International Stock Markets

As we've noted already, stock markets exist throughout the world. Virtually all developed countries, and many developing ones, have stock markets. Some markets are large with long histories and sophisticated trading practices. Others are much newer and smaller. The approximate international distribution of equity trading during a recent year is shown in Exhibit 5.4. Let's take a closer look at some of the major international stock markets.

THE LONDON STOCK EXCHANGE

The LSE is the world's third largest stock market and the largest in Europe. It is arguably the oldest stock exchange in the world, founded in the seventeenth century. The LSE lists approximately 2,900 issues, more than 500 of which are shares of companies based outside the United Kingdom and Ireland. In addition to stocks, the LSE trades bonds (especially Eurobonds), options, and futures contracts. The London market is very much an international market; more than 66 percent of the world's cross-border trading (for example, trading of U.S. stocks outside the United States) takes place in London. The figure rises to more than 95 percent for cross-border trading in European issues alone. Institutional investors in the United States have been known to deliberately bypass the NYSE or Nasdaq in favor of trading large blocks of stock on the LSE claiming they get better prices and faster order execution. Recently, the LSE has announced plans to combine some of its operations with the Frankfurt Stock Exchange in Germany.

For many years the LSE's trading practices virtually mirrored those of the New York Stock Exchange. That is no longer the case. On October 27, 1986 (known in London as the "Big Bang"), member firms gained the capability to trade off the exchange floor using an automated quotation system. Trading on the exchange floor dropped so sharply that it was closed on February 28, 1991. Today, all trading on the LSE is conducted "upstairs," using a Nasdaq-type computer system.

TOKYO STOCK EXCHANGE (TSE)

Based on the number of shares traded, can you guess which market was larger in 1994, the NYSE or the TSE? If you answered the NYSE, you are wrong! In fact, trading volume on the TSE exceeded Nasdaq and NYSE trading volume between 1985

Exhibit 5.4 ✦ TRADING VOLUME IN WORLD STOCK MARKETS

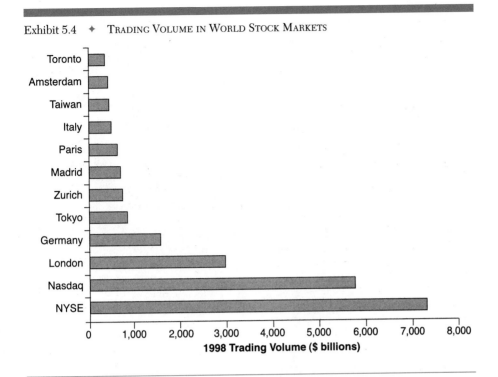

1998 Trading Volume ($ billions)

and 1996, sometimes by large margins. In 1988, for example, the number of shares traded on the TSE was more than twice the number of shares traded on the Nasdaq and NYSE combined.

Although the TSE is still one of the world's largest stock markets—and is by far the largest stock market in Asia—trading volume declined sharply during the early 1990s. For example, in 1992 trading volume was less than half what it was in 1989. The Tokyo Stock Exchange was the scene of a recent spectacular speculative bubble. The Investment History box on page 124 recounts the story of the Japanese bubble of the 1980s and early 1990s.

Currently, the TSE lists approximately 1,800 Japanese and 50 non-Japanese stock issues. It also trades bonds issued by the Japanese government and corporations, foreign bonds, options, and futures contracts. A few large American companies list their stock on the TSE, though the number has declined somewhat in recent years as TSE trading volume slowed.

Only the 150 most active issues, all Japanese companies, trade on the floor of the exchange in a NYSE auction-type market. The other issues trade by automatic computer matching of buy and sell orders. Besides this distinction, the TSE is also divided into a first section and a second section. Stocks in the first section are the approximately 1,200 more actively traded stocks of larger companies.

EMERGING MARKETS

One of the most interesting developments in recent years is the emergence of new equity markets in many developing nations. New markets have sprung up in places as diverse as the Chile, China, the Czech Republic, Malaysia, and Turkey. Returns from emerging markets can be quite impressive. During the first half of 1999, for example,

THE TOKYO STOCK MARKET BUBBLE

During the late 1980s, the Japanese stock market was infected by the madness of crowds. Like the economy as a whole, the Japanese stock market experienced an incredible bubble. Market historians have likened the Japanese stock market bubble of the late 1980s to the U.S. market in the years leading up to the Great Crash of 1929.

For many years, the Tokyo stock market was considered something of an investment backwater, even though Japanese stocks had risen fairly steadily throughout the 1970s and early 1980s. The Japanese economy was growing rapidly, corporate profits were high, and inflation and interest rates were low. Like the U.S. market in the 1920s, the Japanese bull market eventually became a speculative bubble, probably sometime in the mid-1980s.

Japanese stock prices soared between 1985 and 1989. From its low on January 4, 1985 to its high on December 18, 1989, the Tokyo Stock Price Index (TOPIX) more than tripled, increasing from a little more than 900 to almost 2,900. By contrast, the S&P 500 rose slightly more than 111 percent during the period. At the same time, the average price/earnings ratio of stocks listed on the Tokyo Stock Exchange rose from 35 to 71. Trading volume also exploded. In 1986, average daily trading volume was about 428 million shares; by 1988 it was more than 1 billion shares. The 1987 market break had only a temporary effect on the frenzy. Although the Tokyo market lost about 14 percent on October 20, 1987, it gained back almost 9.5 percent the next day. For all of 1987, the TOPIX increased by almost 11 percent. During the next two years, 1988 and 1989, the Japanese market rose another 50 percent.

Finally, Japanese stocks reached a point at which more and more investors began to realize that stock prices were far out of line with their intrinsic values and started selling. Fears of slower growth in the Japanese economy and falling real estate prices, coupled with higher interest rates, also helped to break the bubble in Japanese stocks in 1990. The TOPIX dropped by more than 60 percent, from 2,885 to 1,103, between late 1990 and October 1992. Trading volume also declined sharply, from 283 billion shares in 1988 to about 65 billion shares in 1992.

The Tokyo stock market has yet to recover from the bubble. Since 1992, the TOPIX has ranged between a high of about 1,700 to a low of 980. Annual trading volume has gradually increased, reaching 123 billion shares in 1998, still a far cry from the heady days of the late 1980s.

U.S. stocks rose about 10 percent. Venezuela and China's markets each rose more than 40 percent during the same period.

Investing in these markets exposes U.S. investors to additional risk, however. For one thing, a rapid change in the value of the local currency, relative to the U.S. dollar, can dramatically alter returns. For example, during the first half of 1999 the Brazilian stock market rose 40 percent, measured in Brazilian currency, but actually fell 20 percent when measured in U.S. dollars. For another, these markets can be quite volatile. The chart in Exhibit 5.5 shows the recent history of the Mexican stock market. Note the wide swings in the index from month to month.

At times liquidity is also a problem in emerging markets—this can partially explain the huge swings in prices. Further, neither trading practices nor regulation are as sophisticated in emerging markets as they are in more established stock markets.

The Future of The Financial Markets

As we enter the twenty-first century, it's difficult to know exactly what the financial markets will look like in the next 25 or 50 years; so many uncertainties cloud the crystal ball. However, given the rapid and dramatic changes the financial markets

Exhibit 5.5 ✦ PERFORMANCE OF THE MEXICAN STOCK MARKET: 1994–98

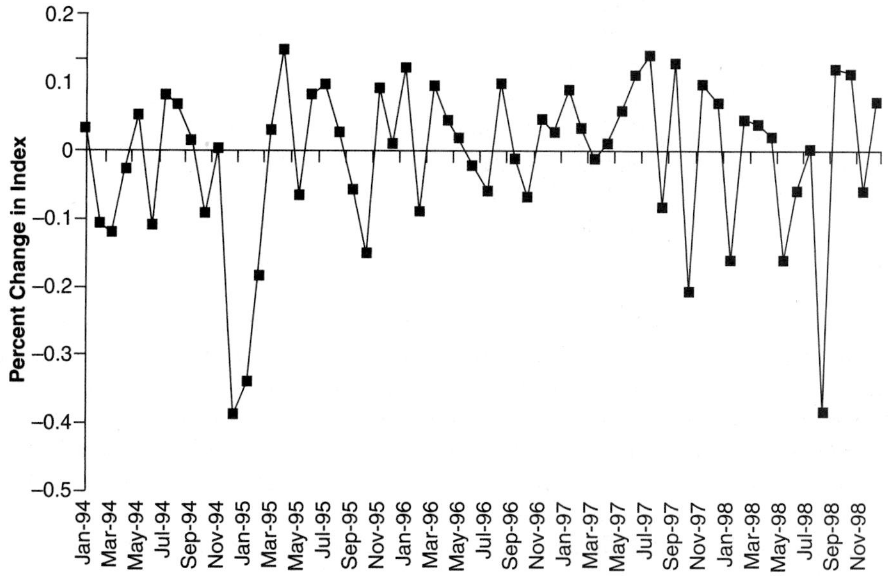

have experienced during the past 20 years, we can safely say that the financial markets will continue to evolve. Three factors appear to be driving the evolution of the financial markets: institutional investors, globalization, and technology.

Today the majority of stock in most companies is owned by institutional investors (life insurance companies, pension funds, mutual funds, and so forth). Compared with individual investors, institutions trade larger blocks of stocks and often trade more frequently. Each year institutions account for a larger and larger share of trading activity in the financial markets.[5] The speed at which orders can be executed, the trading price, and the cost of trading are critically important to institutional investors. Their dominance in the financial markets has already led to major changes in market structure and operations. One example is the increasing trading volume on Instinet and other fourth-market networks. These networks will likely continue to grow and expand in the coming years.

The second trend driving the evolution of the financial markets is globalization. The globalization of the financial markets is already virtually complete. Shares of more and more U.S. companies will likely be listed and traded in markets throughout the world, and shares of foreign companies will trade more widely in the United States. A future trading system will likely automatically route an order to buy an NYSE-listed stock to London or Hong Kong if one of those markets offers the best price. As trading moves worldwide, it moves toward around-the-clock activity. Already, as we have noted, Nasdaq has developed trading links with markets in

---

[5]For example, in 1998 a record 3.5 million blocks were traded on the floor of the NYSE—a block trade is defined as a trade that involves at least 10,000 shares—or more than double the number of blocks traded in 1994 on the NYSE.

London and Singapore. The London Stock Exchange has been in the forefront of development of a Pan-European stock market, one large European market linking all the continent's stock exchanges.

Driving many of these changes is technology. The pace of technological development in just the past few years has been astonishing. Continued technological change will make 24-hour global trading much easier and cheaper. Is continuous, 24-hour trading a good thing? Perhaps. Continuous trading may make the markets function even more smoothly than they do today. Say, for example, that a company makes a significant announcement after the NYSE closes. Without continuous trading, a supply/demand imbalance will likely make trading hectic when the NYSE opens the next day. Continuous trading would adjust prices to the new information as soon as announcements were made.

Some believe that these changes will destroy the exchange floor as we know it. Will all trading take place on computer networks rather than the stock exchange floor? It's hard to say. Trading in many world markets has moved away from exchange floors in recent years, most notably in London, Paris, and Toronto, and trades are matched by computer, not face-to-face agreements. After the Big Bang, the LSE tried to keep the floor open, but its trading volume vanished virtually overnight. In Tokyo, more issues are traded solely by computer each year. Could the floor trading system even cope with global 24-hour trading? Some doubt that it could. Like all floor markets, the NYSE depends on people, who have limited stamina and cannot function beyond the current number of trading hours. To extend the trading day too long, some argue, would be too burdensome and too expensive.

In response, the NYSE argues that no conclusive evidence demonstrates that computerized trading systems such as Nasdaq are any more efficient than its floor trading system, which is already quite automated. Bid/ask spreads, for example, are no larger on the NYSE than they are on Nasdaq, and are often smaller. Further, in defending its 200-year-old specialist system, the NYSE argues that the human element is still a critical part of trading. Computers cannot "feel" a stock, "work" a sensitive order, or take necessary risk. In short, computers cannot make all the critical decisions during the frenzy of trading. The exchange also likes to point out that during the 1987 market break, most specialists stayed at their posts and continued to fill orders, despite losing millions of dollars. (Specialists that failed to perform their market-making functions were disciplined by the NYSE.) Over on Nasdaq, critics allege that many market makers simply stopped answering their phones and ceased trading as stock prices plunged on October 19, 1987. Only time will tell who's right.

In this chapter we've described how the world's financial markets are organized and how they operate. How investors participate in the financial markets, and how they're protected, will be discussed in the next chapter.

Chapter Summary

1. What are the different types of financial markets?
   Financial markets exist throughout the world and can be classified in various ways. Financial markets can be classified as primary and secondary, money and capital, debt and equity, organized and over the counter, and global and regional. Many of the world's financial markets meet the criteria of "good" markets. A good, well-functioning market has the following characteristics: sufficient information is available to all participants, price continuity exists, transaction costs are low, all investors have equal access to the market, and prices adjust quickly to new information.

2. How do the primary financial markets function?

Securities are sold in the primary markets by open auction, through investment bankers, or through private placements. Treasury and other U.S. government securities are sold via open auction, whereas most corporate and municipal securities are sold (underwritten) through investment bankers Some corporate debt issues are privately placed.

3. Why are secondary financial markets important?

Secondary markets are important because they provide investors with liquidity—the ability to sell a security to another investor at a price close to the security's true value. Not all secondary markets, however, are equally liquid. Often the spread between the bid and ask price is an indication of a market's liquidity. Liquidity is beneficial for issuers as well, because liquidity lowers the cost of capital. Aside from liquidity, secondary markets provide a measure of a security's current worth. This is referred to as price discovery.

4. How are the secondary financial markets organized?

Secondary bond and stock markets exist throughout the world; some are organized exchanges where trading takes place face to face, and others are over-the-counter markets where trading takes place via a computerized communications network. One of the largest secondary markets is the over-the-counter market for U.S. Treasury securities. Major stock markets include the New York Stock Exchange, the Nasdaq Stock Market, the London Stock Exchange, and the Tokyo Stock Exchange.

5. How are financial markets evolving?

Financial markets have changed dramatically in recent years and will continue to evolve. This evolution is being driven by three factors: the emerging dominance of institutional investors, the globalization of the financial markets, and technology.

Review Questions and Problems

1. What are the major characteristics of a "good" market? Pick a major financial market; does it have most of these characteristics?

2. Explain how financial markets can be classified. Are most financial market transactions conducted in the primary or secondary markets?

3. Explain the auction process for U.S. Treasury securities. Can small investors participate in a Treasury auction?

4. How is a new security issue sold via an investment banker? Why do issuers use the services of an investment bank?

5. Define *liquidity*. Why are some markets more liquid than others?

6. Explain the differences between organized and over-the-counter financial markets. Where are the various types of bonds traded?

7. Compare and contrast the NYSE specialist with the Nasdaq market maker. How does a specialist make money?

8. Define the third and fourth markets. Explain how Instinet operates.

9. List several major foreign stock exchanges. Are these markets more like the NYSE or the Nasdaq Stock Market in their trading practices?

10. List and discuss the three factors that appear to be driving the evolution of the financial markets. What are some of the arguments for and against around-the-clock trading?

CRITICAL THINKING EXERCISE

This exercise requires Internet or library research. Three of the best-known stock market indexes are the Dow-Jones Industrials (Dow 30), the Standard & Poor's 500, and the Wilshire 5000. Research all three indexes and answer the following questions.

a. How have each of the indexes performed over the past five years? Can you explain any differences in performance?

b. How is each index constructed? How is the index adjusted whenever the contents of the index portfolio changes?

c. What is the Dow's current divisor? If one of the stocks in the index splits 2 for 1, will the divisor rise or fall?

d. When was the last time the Dow's portfolio changed? Which stocks were added, which were deleted? Why were the changes made?

e. In your opinion, which of the three indexes best represents the overall stock market? Explain your answer.

THE INTERNET INVESTOR

1. The two largest stock markets in the world are the New York Stock Exchange (www.nyse.com) and the Nasdaq Stock Market (www.nasdaqamex.com). Visit both web sites and prepare a report summarizing the similarities and differences between the two stock markets.

2. Most international stock markets have web sites. Pick an international market and visit its web site. Using only the information available on the Web, list some details about the market including the type of market, number of issues, traded, trading procedure, listing requirements, and so forth.

3. The U.S. Treasury allows "small" investors to buy newly issued Treasury securities directly from the Treasury. Visit www.publicdebt.treas.gov/sec/sectrdir.htm and write a brief report explaining the program, and its advantages (or disadvantages) to small investors.

INVESTOR PARTICIPATION IN THE FINANCIAL MARKETS

PREVIOUSLY . . .

We described how securities are issued and how they are bought and sold in the world's financial markets. We also speculated on the future of the financial markets.

IN THIS CHAPTER . . .

We examine how investors participate in the financial markets, including how to choose a broker, the various types of orders investors place, and cybertrading. We also discuss the regulation of the financial markets and other ways in which investors are protected.

TO COME . . .

We discuss the concept of market efficiency. Even if the markets aren't totally efficient, market efficiency has several important implications for investors.

Chapter Objectives

After reading Chapter 6 you should be able to answer the following questions:

1. How should investors choose a broker?
2. What are the various types of orders placed by investors?
3. What is cybertrading?
4. What are block trades and program trading?
5. Who regulates the financial markets and protects investors?

How Americans buy and sell securities has certainly changed over the past couple of decades. Gone are the days when the only way to buy or sell stocks, bonds, and most other investments was to use a traditional full-service brokerage firm such as Merrill Lynch or Dean Witter. Investors were forced to pay commissions equal to 2 percent or more of the value of their investments each time they bought or sold securities. These hefty commissions ate away at investment profits.

Since the mid-1970s, high, uniform commissions have been replaced by a three-tiered industry in the brokerage business. *Full-service firms* continue to offer their wide array of services, along with their high commissions. *Discount firms* such as Charles Schwab and Quick & Reilly offer fewer services but charge lower commissions. The so-called *deep discount firms* (Jack White and Brown & Company, for example) charge even lower commissions but provide almost no service.

In recent years a major new player, electronic brokerage firms, entered the brokerage business. Firms such as E*Trade (www.etrade.com) allow investors to buy and sell securities through the Internet using their personal computers. Once an investor sets up an account with an electronic broker, he or she can access real or delayed price quotations, information, and even place buy and sell orders. Not only is trading on line faster than using the phone, it's cheaper. For example, buying a 100 shares of stock using E*Trade costs about $15, which is one-half what a typical deep discount firm charges, one-fourth the cost per trade using a discount broker, and one-sixth the cost of a full-service broker. As E*Trade CEO Christos Cotsakos puts it, "For years, consumers have been paying exorbitantly high prices to get information that is selectively controlled by their brokers."

E*Trade and other electronic brokers have proven popular with investors. In just two years, more than 300,000 investors have opened accounts with E*Trade, and 500 more open new accounts each day. By one estimate, about 25 percent of all investment trades today use electronic brokers. Not to be left out, most discount, and even a few full-service brokerage firms have started on-line services.

In this chapter we describe how investors participate in the financial markets, including how investors should choose the right brokerage firm, the various types of orders investors can place, and investor protection. Each of these topics is important knowledge if investors are to make informed decisions.

Choosing a Broker

In order to buy or sell securities, investors must first open a brokerage account. This fairly simple and straightforward process does entail a few important decisions. The first decision, of course, is to choose a brokerage firm and, in many cases, a specific broker. Investors select firms and brokers on the basis of reputation, personal contact, referral, and similar criteria. All brokerage firms require each investor to fill out an application to provide minimal information regarding such characteristics as income and net worth. Many firms require that new customers have cash or cash-equivalent assets of at least $5,000.

TYPES OF BROKERAGE FIRMS

full-service brokerage firms
Brokerage firms that provide extensive advice to clients along with order execution and record keeping.

discount brokerage firms
Brokerage firms that provide much more limited advice to clients; charge less than full service firms.

Today there are several different types of brokerage firms. **Full-service brokerage firms,** such as Merrill Lynch and Smith Barney, offer investment advice to their customers in addition to order execution and record keeping. A full-service firm usually assigns a specific broker to each individual customer.[1] **Discount brokerage firms** such as Charles Schwab and Quick & Reilly provide mainly order execution and record-keeping services, although most provide information on investment opinions from independent sources. A customer of a discount firm must likely deal with many individual brokers. **Deep discount brokerage firms** provide order execution and

---

[1]Brokers at most full-service firms are called *account executives.*

record keeping, but almost no research or other services. Many deep discounters also require larger initial deposits to open accounts and a minimum number of trades per year. **Electronic brokerage firms** such as E°trade and Ameritrade allow investors to buy and sell securities over the Internet. We'll discuss electronic brokers a little later in the chapter along with the rest of cybertrading.

electronic brokerage firms
Brokerage firms that allow investors to buy and sell securities over the Internet.

Which type of brokerage should an investor choose? That depends on what type of investing the account will handle and the investor's need for services. Someone who is experienced in making personal investment decisions and trades frequently would probably be better off with a discount firm. However, someone who needs help making investment selections for infrequent trades may prefer a full-service firm. Because the customer of a full-service firm usually deals with one specific broker, it is just as important to select an appropriate broker as it is to select the right brokerage firm. The Investment Insights box on page 132 discusses some considerations when choosing a brokerage firm and a broker. The bottom line is that investors should look for a broker who understands and accepts their personal investment objectives and risk preferences.

It is true that full-service firms cost more, sometimes a great deal more, than discount and deep discount firms. Exhibit 6.1 lists some sample commissions.[2] Notice that full-service firms charge five to ten times what a deep discount firm charges. For an investor who trades infrequently and values investment advice, the difference in commissions may be a small price to pay. However, frequent traders who make their own decisions can save thousands of dollars by using discount, or deep discount firms. Most brokerage customers set up cash accounts that require them to pay the full cost, in cash, for all securities purchased, within three days. Some customers also set up margin accounts to finance portions of their securities purchases by borrowing from the brokerage firm. The customer repays the borrowed funds with interest. We talk more about buying securities on margin a little later in the chapter.

The typical brokerage firm allows investors to buy or sell stocks, bonds, and options. Many firms today also allow investors to buy and sell shares of mutual funds. Investors interested in trading futures contracts, however, may have to set up another account with a firm that specializes in futures trading; many traditional brokerage firms do not offer futures trading to their customers.

Most investors allow their brokers to hold securities in a **street name,** meaning the brokerage firm, not the investor, is technically listed as the owner of the security. The brokerage firm sends the investor a monthly statement detailing monthly transactions, how much cash is in the account, and the current market value of securities owned by the investor.

street name
System by which brokerage firms hold securities for investors in their names.

Virtually all brokerage firms belong to the **Securities Investor Protection Corporation (SIPC),** which insures brokerage accounts up to $500,000 to reimburse investors in the event the brokerage firm fails. Over the past 20 years, the SIPC has paid out more than $200 million to customers of failed brokerage firms. Of course, it does not repay customers for losses due to adverse market moves! In addition to SIPC insurance, most large brokerage firms carry private insurance to further protect

securities investor protection corporation (SIPC)
Organization that protects investors in the event their brokerage firm goes bankrupt.

---

[2]This may surprise you, but as recently as the mid-1970s, the New York Stock Exchange required all of its members to charge fixed commissions. This NYSE rule effectively meant that all investment firms charged the same. Congress, as part of the Securities Acts Amendments of 1975, eliminated fixed commissions.

INVESTMENT INSIGHTS

`0:00` `0:00`

PICKING A STOCKBROKER

Choosing a stockbroker is one of the most important decisions any investor makes. Here are some important considerations:

✦ Before selecting a broker, determine your investment goals, time horizon, and tolerance for risk. You should also prepare a financial profile (age, assets, liabilities, and so forth).

✦ Interview several brokers at several different firms. Ask about their experience, educational background, and a profile of their typical client.

✦ Ask if the broker has all necessary federal and state licenses. Call your state securities regulatory agency if you question what those are or

the answer you receive. The Securities and Exchange Commission (www.sec.gov) has a list of state securities regulatory agencies.

✦ Check to see if the broker has ever been subject to any disciplinary action by state or federal regulators. The National Association of Securities Dealers (800-289-9999; www.nasd.com) can provide this information.

✦ The broker should carefully explain the commissions and fees you will pay for various investment products. Ask if the broker receives higher commissions for certain products than for others. If you believe the broker is recommending a product just to earn a higher commission, change brokers.

✦ Don't submit to pressure to immediately open an account and begin investing. Take your time and do your homework.

✦ Be wary of unsolicited sales calls from brokers (known in the industry as "cold calling"). Some calls may be legitimate, but don't buy any investment based upon a telephone solicitation, no matter how much pressure the broker puts on you. Ask the broker to send you written information about the investment and his or her background. Check on the investment from another source (Value Line, Standard & Poor's, etc.). Check on the broker with state regulators or the National Association of Securities dealers.

customers from financial loss in the event the firm fails. We strongly recommend using only brokerage firms that are SIPC members *and* carry insurance.

BUYING SECURITIES WITHOUT A BROKER

You can buy some securities without using a broker and thus avoid paying the brokerage commission. In the prior chapter, we briefly described how individuals can buy U.S. government securities directly from the Treasury. Investors can also buy shares of many mutual funds directly from the fund, paying no sales charges in the process.[3]

However, you can also buy shares of common stock of many companies without paying brokerage commissions. Hundreds of companies offer **dividend reinvestment plans** (known as **DRIPs**). When an investor enrolls in a DRIP, the company uses the dividends paid on shares owned by the investor to buy more shares of the company's stock. The investor ends up buying more shares while paying no commissions.

dividend reinvestment plan (DRIP)
Program by which a company uses the dividends paid on shares owned by an investor to buy more shares of the company's stock.

---

[3]In Chapter 3 we discussed load funds and no-load funds. When you buy shares of a load fund you pay a sales charge; no sales charge applies to no-load fund purchases. Many discount and deep discount firms allow customers to purchase shares of hundreds of mutual funds, from dozens of fund families, without paying any brokerage fees or sales charges.

Exhibit 6.1 ✦ SAMPLE COMMISSIONS

Firm (type)	200 shares at $25 per share	300 shares at $20 per share	500 shares at $15 per share
E°Trade (cyberbroker)	$15.00	$15.00	$15.00
Fidelity Brokerage (discount)	88.50	95.10	101.00
Merrill Lynch (full service)	129.50	164.85	205.54
Solomon Smith Barney (full service)	139.61	166.39	212.15

Note: All of the above are based on published commission rates for market orders of listed and over-the-counter stocks. Actual commissions to specific investors may vary.

Another form of direct investment gaining popularity is no-load stock purchase programs. More than 100 companies allow first-time investors to buy shares directly from the company, often paying little if any transactions fees.

Types of Orders

Investors use various types of orders to buy or sell securities. They are *market orders, limit orders,* and *stop-loss* orders. Some investors also buy stocks on margin while others sell stocks short.

MARKET ORDERS

A **market order** instructs the broker to buy or sell a security at the best currently prevailing price—the lowest price for a purchase or the highest price for a sale. Market orders are executed somewhat differently on the organized exchanges from on the over-the-counter market, so let's look at an example of each.

market order
An order that instructs your broker to obtain the best possible price.

Organized Exchange Market Order

Let's assume that an investor would like to buy 100 shares of Home Depot, which trades on the NYSE.[4] In response to this request, the broker looks up the stock's symbol, HD, on a quote machine, which returns the following information: 68¼ bid, 68⁷⁄₁₆ ask, 68⅜ last trade.[5] Home Depot last traded at 68⅜ ($68.325 per share), and the

---

[4]Any order in a multiple of 100 shares (100; 200; 300; 500; 1,000; 10,000; and so on) is called a "round lot." Any order not in a multiple of 100 shares is called an "odd lot." Less than 1 percent of stock trading is in odd lots.

[5]All stocks have so-called ticker systems. NYSE-listed stocks have ticker symbols consisting of one, two, or three letters. Nasdaq listed stocks have four- or five-letter ticker symbols. Most ticker symbols are abbreviations of the company names (GE is General Electric, HD is Home Depot, and WMT is Wal-Mart Stores, for example). Some ticker symbols are a little more creative. For example, Anheuser-Busch trades under BUD and Harley-Davidson under HOG.

stock's specialist is currently offering to buy it at 68¼ ($68.25) or sell it at 68⁷⁄₁₆ ($68.4375). The investor enters a market order, which the broker transmits to the floor of the NYSE to be delivered (either physically or, more likely, electronically) to the post where HD is traded. If no sellers are present when the order arrives, the HD specialist sells 100 shares from inventory at the current ask price. If sellers are present, an auction takes place and the specialist may not be involved. Typically, specialists participated in less than 25 percent of all NYSE trades. The broker relays confirmation of the trade back to the investor, and the trade appears on the NYSE consolidated tape.[6] How long does all this take? More than 98 percent of all market orders are filled within two minutes!

This speed is possible because the NYSE has become highly automated in recent years. An electronic system helps to match buy and sell orders entered before the market opens and sets an opening price for each stock. The exchange has an electronic order-routing system called **SuperDot** that carries members' orders directly to the appropriate trading posts and returns trade confirmations.

SuperDot system
NYSE's automated order routing and matching system.

Over-the-Counter Markets

Now, assume that another investor wants to buy 100 shares of Cisco Systems, which trades on the Nasdaq NMS under the symbol CSCO. After the broker receives instructions to enter a market order, he or she consults the Nasdaq electronic quotation machine to find out the current bid and ask prices for CSCO. A broker who has access to Level 2 of the Nasdaq system sees the bid and ask prices for each CSCO market maker (which probably number more than 25). Assume that the broker finds the following quotes:

Market Maker	Bid Price	Ask Price
A	65	65⅛
B	64¹⁵⁄₁₆	65¹⁄₁₆
C	65	65⅛
D	65¹⁄₁₆	65³⁄₁₆

The broker contacts Market Maker B, either by telephone or electronically, because it is offering the best (that is, lowest) ask price for Cisco. To sell CSCO, the broker would contact Market Maker D, which currently has the highest bid price (that is, it is willing to pay the most for Cisco).

Today, entering small orders into the Nasdaq system is even simpler. In 1985, Nasdaq introduced its Small Order Execution System (SOES) to automatically execute small market orders (usually defined as orders for fewer than 1,000 shares) at the best possible price available in the Nasdaq system. SOES returns confirmation to the broker in a matter of seconds.

Spreads and Decimal Pricing

In the two prior examples you probably noticed that the NYSE specialist and Nasdaq market makers establish spreads between their respective bid and ask prices. This

---

[6]The NYSE consolidated tape lists all transactions in NYSE listed stocks that take place on the NYSE, the regional exchanges, or over the counter in the third market.

spread represents one way specialists and market makers make money, but what's a reasonable spread between a stock's bid and ask prices?

Critics have long complained that bid ask spreads are too wide, effectively costing investors millions of dollars a year. [7] Indeed a study published in 1994 suggested that Nasdaq market makers routinely avoided quoting prices in "odd-eights" quotes (such as ⅜ or ⅝). [8] Instead of, for example, offering to buy a stock at 25⅜ and sell it at 25⅝, a spread of 25 cents a share, the market maker might quote 25¼ bid and 25¾ ask, for a spread of 50 cents a share.

This study spurred action on the part of the brokerage industry, financial markets, and regulators. Nasdaq market makers were bluntly told by NASD officials to lower their spreads. Stock prices were traditionally quoted in eights (one eight is 12.5 cents) but under pressure from federal regulators and Congress, exchanges began quoting prices in sixteenths and, in some cases, thirty-seconds (one sixteenth is equal to 6.25 cents per share and one thirty-second is equal 3.125 cents per share). This change too effectively lowered bid-ask spreads.

Many international markets, such as the London, Paris, and Toronto stock exchanges, began quoting stock prices in decimals in the 1990s. Starting in the spring of 2000, U.S. stock markets began quoting prices of actively traded issues in decimals—meaning in dollars and cents. Soon all U.S. stock prices will quoted in decimals. Some suggest the move toward decimal pricing will further lower bid-ask spreads.

An often-asked question is why *were* stock prices traditionally quoted in eights? The exact origins of the system of eights is murky but one well-known story is as follows. When the New York Stock Exchange was established in 1792 the Spanish *peso duro* ("hard dollar") was the most widely used currency in the New World. The new United States dollar was in fact based on the *peso duro*. Although the United States Treasury adopted a decimal-based currency, the NYSE stuck with the Spanish system, which divided the *peso duro* into eights of a dollar—pieces of eight in pirate lore. More than 200 years passed before the U.S. markets moved from eights to decimals.

Clearing Procedures

Most market orders are settled three business days after the trade date. On the **settlement date,** the securities and funds are transferred between the buyer and the seller. The investor's brokerage firm is responsible for settling the transaction with the other party, either another brokerage firm or a market maker. To facilitate the clearing process, most brokerage firms use the services of a clearinghouse. The clearinghouse collects records of all transactions made by member firms, verifies each transaction, and nets outs securities and cash due, or owed, by the member firms.

LIMIT ORDERS

A **limit order** instructs a broker to buy a security for no more than a specific price or to sell for no less than a specific price. Let us return to the buyer of Home Depot

limit order
An order that puts a limit on the price at which an investor is willing to buy or sell.

---

[7]As we noted in Chapter 5, the size of bid-ask spreads is one explanation for growth in the fourth market.

[8]William Christie and Paul Schultz, "Why Do Nasdaq Market Makers Avoid Odd-Eight Quotes?" *Journal of Finance,* December 1994, pp. 1813–40.

stock but suppose that some analysis leads to the conclusion that the current ask price, 68⅝₆, is a little too high. The investor tells the broker to enter an order to buy Home Depot *limit* 68¼; the investor would willingly pay less than 68¼ for HD, but not more. The broker transmits the order to the post where HD is traded. If no one is willing to sell the stock for 68¼ (or less), the order remains with the specialist for entry into the *limit order book* (which today is an electronic data file). If HD eventually declines to 68¼, the specialist executes the order and informs the broker, who informs the customer. In return for this service, the specialist receives part of the commission.

In 1989, Nasdaq introduced a new limit-order service within its SOES. The service automatically accepts and stores limit orders for less than 1,000 shares, and it executes them when Nasdaq market-maker ask quotations reach or improve on the limit prices set by the customers.

Limit orders can be valid for periods of time varying from one trading day to several trading days, one week, or longer. A limit order can also be placed *on a good until canceled* (GTC) basis, which leaves the order open ended. Brokerage firm policies regarding limit orders vary, and many charge slightly higher commissions for limit orders than for market orders.

STOP (OR STOP-LOSS) ORDERS

stop (stop-loss) order
An order that automatically becomes a market order if the price of a stock drops below a specified price.

A **stop order** enters a market order that takes effect at a specified price. Stop orders are often referred to as *stop-loss orders* because they usually are used to sell stock if value drops below some threshold. For example, an investor may have bought Home Depot at $20 per share and watched it rise to more than $68 per share. The investor still likes the outlook for the stock but worries about a temporary setback due to other stockholders selling to realize their gains (sometimes called *profit taking*). Instead of selling the stock outright for about $68 per share, the investor instructs a broker to enter a sell order at "60 stop." Should HD decline below $60, this stop order would automatically become a market order, and the stock would be sold at the prevailing price, protecting most of the investor's profit. The stop order does not guarantee a sale at $60 per share, only that the stock will be sold quickly at the best price currently available should its price fall below $60. Stop orders can be valid for varying periods of time, or they can be open ended. As with limit orders, various brokerage firms have different policies on stop orders, and most charge higher commissions to execute them than to execute simple market orders.

MARGIN TRANSACTIONS

As we noted earlier, margin trading involves borrowing money to buy securities. Banks lend funds to brokerage firms, which in turn lend them to customers to buy securities on margin. Customers typically pay between 1 percent and 1½ percent over the rate the brokerage firm pays the bank. The brokerage firm specifies how and when the customer repays a margin loan. About $140 billion in margin debt is outstanding.

Technically, *margin* is the part of the total value of the securities that the investor pays with cash—the investor's *equity*. The Federal Reserve sets minimum initial margin requirements; in other words, it specifies how much the investor must put up initially to purchase a security on margin. The current requirement of 50 percent has not changed since 1974. To purchase 200 shares of Coca-Cola at $50 on margin, an investor would have to put up at least $5,000 in cash (plus the commission) and borrow the other $5,000. In addition, the NYSE requires that a margin customer maintain at least a 25 percent margin as a security's price changes; this is called the *maintenance margin requirement.* Most brokerage firms have higher maintenance requirements (30 to 40 percent).

Exhibit 6.2 illustrates how margin works. Assume you buy 200 shares of Coca-Cola at $50 on margin. Your initial margin is 50 percent, or $5,000. Your brokerage firm requires that you maintain a margin of 35 percent. Assume Coke rises to $60 per share. The value of your shares rises to $12,000. You now have $7,000 in your margin account ($12,000 − $5,000). Because you are only required to have $6,000 in your margin account (50 percent of $12,000), some brokerage firms might allow you to withdraw $1,000 in cash from your account.

Now, instead of rising, assume Coke falls to $40. The value of your shares is $8,000, and you have only $3,000 in your margin account ($8,000 − $5,000). This percentage is 37.5 ($3,000/$8,000), and although it is below the initial margin requirement, it is still above the maintenance requirement. You would not be required to deposit any additional cash but will probably not be able to make any further margin purchases. (This is called a *restricted account.*)

Assume that Coke continues to slide, falling to $35 per share. Now your margin is down to $2,000, which is only about 28.6 percent of the value of the stock. You now face the dreaded **margin call.** Your broker will require that you deposit another $450 in cash into your account to bring your margin back up to 35 percent. Failure to do so will result in the shares being sold and the proceeds being used to repay the margin loan.

margin call
Having to deposit additional cash into a margin account.

Why should anyone buy stock on margin and pay interest on a margin loan? The answer is simply because margin trading gives investors the potential benefit of leverage, as illustrated in Exhibit 6.3. Buying stock on margin might increase the return to the investor, but at the same time it increases the potential risk. Margin purchases do not suit every investor.

Exhibit 6.3 ignores the interest expense on the margin loan. Interest expense, of course, slightly reduces returns to the margin investor.

SHORT SALES

Someone who buys a security is said to be taking the *long position.* This investor purchases the stock with the expectation that it will provide a satisfactory return in the

Exhibit 6.2   ✦   ILLUSTRATION OF A MARGIN TRANSACTION

	Coke rises to $60	Coke falls to $40	Coke falls to $35
Value	$12,000	$8,000	$7,000
Margin	7,000	3,000	2,000
Required margin	6,000	2,800	2,450
The investor . . .	Can withdraw $1,000 in cash from the account	Is not required to deposit any additional cash but cannot make additional margin purchases	Must deposit another $450 in cash into the account or the shares will be sold

Exhibit 6.3 ✦ ILLUSTRATION OF CASH VERSUS MARGIN PURCHASE

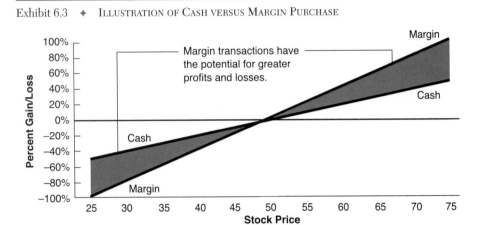

form of dividend payments plus price appreciation. What about taking the opposite position if a stock seems likely to fall in value? This is possible by executing a **short sale,** selling borrowed stock with the expectation of buying back shares at a lower price to return to the owner at some point in the future. This is a perfectly legal transaction, although certain conditions must be met. The NYSE reports that in recent years one share of stock is sold short for every ten shares purchased.

short sale
Selling shares with the intention of buying them back at a later date.

Exhibit 6.4 outlines the anatomy of a short sale. The shares sold short are borrowed from another account, and the short seller must keep at least 50 percent of the proceeds in a margin account as collateral. The short seller is free to use the balance for anything, although the brokerage firm sometimes pays the short seller interest (called a *rebate*) on the collateral. If the stock rises in price, the short seller must add to the collateral balance (much like maintaining a margin). The short seller is also responsible to the stock's owner for any cash dividends paid on the borrowed stock.

uptick
Most recent trade was either an increase or no change from the prior trade.

In addition to the requirements listed in Exhibit 6.4, the NYSE will allow a short sale only on an **uptick.** A short sale can take place at the last trade price only if that price exceeds the last different price before it. Although the example in Exhibit 6.4 worked out quite nicely and the short seller earned a profit of about $10,000, short selling can involve substantial risk and is recommended only for experienced, knowledgeable investors.

Cybertrading

With a click of a mouse and a few keystrokes, today's investors can trade securities using their personal computer and an on-line account as easily as they surf the Net. As even the most casual observor of the financial markets can tell you, cybertrading has exploded in recent years. Today more than 100 brokerage firms, including many of the most established names on Wall Street, offer on-line trading services. By some estimates about 20 percent of all trades are cybertrades today.

Establishing an on-line account requires you to complete an application and deposit a minimum amount of cash into the account. Once the account is established, you receive an account name and password. You go on the Internet, to the on-line broker's web site, enter your personal information, and you're ready to trade. We

Exhibit 6.4   ◆   ANATOMY OF A SHORT SALE

- ◆ Decide on the stock you want to sell short. It could be a poorly run company or simply one that you think is overpriced. You notice that AT&T has zoomed from 45 to 70 in just a few weeks. You believe that even though AT&T is a good company, its stock has risen too far, too fast. You decide to sell the 500 shares of AT&T short.
- ◆ Borrow the stock from another account. It must be selling for at least $5 per share and be marginable. Because AT&T is among the most widely held stocks, finding shares to borrow is no problem.
- ◆ Sell the stock. You receive $35,000, less commissions. You have to keep half of the proceeds in your account as margin. You deposit the other half in a money market account fund.
- ◆ Pay dividends to the owner of the stock—if dividends are paid while your short position is open. Assume AT&T pays a quarterly dividend of $0.33 while your short position is open. You pay the owner $165 ($0.33 × 500).
- ◆ Three months after you went short, AT&T announces that its earnings will be well below analysts' expectations. The stock price tumbles to 50. You decide to close out your short position buying 500 shares at 50 to replace the shares you borrowed. You make a profit of $20 per share—or $10,000. Your total profit is $10,000 minus commissions, plus the interest you earned over the three months, minus $165 in dividends.

should note that no money changes hands over the Internet, however. All monetary transactions take place the old fashion way.

HISTORY OF CYBERTRADING

Using your personal computer to trade stocks is not new. In the mid-1980s discount brokerages such as Schwab and Quick & Reilly began offering on-line trading using their own specialized software and networks. A few years later, brokerage firm Donalson, Lufkin & Jenrette began offering an on-line trading service called PC Financial Network. It made the service available to clients of commercial on-line services America Online, CompuServe, and Prodigy.

The Internet launched on-line trading. Trading on the Internet is both cheaper and faster than other on-line trading systems, because less specialized software is needed. And the Web has potentially much wider access to investors. E°Trade and Lombard Institutional Brokerage were among the first to use the Internet for on-line trading. Internet trading received a big boost in early 1996 when Schwab decided to permit stock trading over the World Wide Web. Other large discount brokerage firms followed suit later in the year.

ADVANTAGES AND DISADVANTAGES OF CYBERTRADING

Cybertrading offers several main advantages to investors. One is cost. Commissions on cybertrades average between $5 and $35, much less than the commissions charged by full-service and even discount brokerage firms. Another advantage of cybertrading is convenience. Investors can check account balances, research, or enter orders at any time, day or night, where ever they have access to a PC and the Internet. On-line trading has given individual investors ready access to market data and information that just a few years ago was available only to securities professionals. In addition, some claim that orders placed on line may be executed faster than orders placed through more traditional means, such as over the telephone or in person.

Although cybertrading offers advantages for investors, it has drawbacks as well. The mechanics of on-line trading are fairly fast and easy, but investing is still a time-consuming process. Investors still must do their homework. Many worry that investors will confuse the speed at which they can now trade with the speed at which they should make investment decisions.

Another potential problem with on-line trading services is access during volatile and busy markets. All on-line trading services warn investors that delays in order execution are possible. In fact, no government regulations require that orders be executed within a certain amount of time. On-line systems have limited capacity and can handle only so many orders at once. Consequently, the execution price can be quite different from the price when the investor placed his or her order. Experts suggest on-line traders use limit orders, rather than market orders during fast-paced trading. Before opening an on-line account, ask about delays and what options are available if you can't access your account on line.

On-line traders who buy on margin should be aware that margin calls are not required. In other words, your broker can sell your securities without giving you a margin call. Many on-line brokerage firms often don't provide margin calls. Read the margin agreement carefully and pay attention if your account is close to the maintenance margin requirement.

DAY TRADING

One of the by-products of on-line trading expansion and other technical innovations has been the emergence of day traders. Day traders sit in front of computer screens and, using computer software and fast Internet connections, look for short-term trends in security prices. What stocks a day trader buys or sells is of no consequence. If day traders think a stock is about to rise, they buy. If they think it's about to fall, they sell. Day traders rarely hold positions for more than a few minutes, and never over night. It is not uncommon for a day trader to buy or sell the same stocks several times during one trading day.

Day trading has been around for a long time. NYSE specialists have used day trading for years as a way of making some extra money.[9] But advances in computer software and hardware, along with on-line brokerage firms and their rock-bottom commissions, have allowed individuals to become day traders. Although it is impossible to come up with an exact figure on the number of full-time day traders, some estimates top 100,000.

So, should you quit school and become a day trader? Probably no. Day trading is extremely risky and, by most accounts, a majority of day traders lose money. Even more worrisome is the fact that many day traders rely heavily on borrowed money. As a full-time job, day trading is stressful. It requires a great deal of concentration to watch thousands of ticker symbols and prices trying to spot trends. Day traders have high fixed costs; many seriously underestimate how much money they need to make trading just to break even. We suggest you forget about day trading and stay in school.

---

[9]NYSE rules allow specialists to trade stocks not assigned to them for their own accounts.

Block Trades and Program Trading

As we've mentioned, institutional investors account for a larger and larger share of trading volume each year. The increased presence of institutional investors has led to increases in both *block trades* and *program trading*.

BLOCK TRADING

The increase in institutional investing in stocks has brought an increase in the number of giant **block trades,** which NYSE rules define as any trade of at least 10,000 shares with a minimum market value of $200,000. In 1970, block trades represented about 15 percent of NYSE trading volume; today, more than 50 percent of trades are block trades.[10] More than 40 percent of Nasdaq trading volume is made up of block trades.

block trade
Purchase or sale of 10,000 or more shares of stock.

Increases in block trading during the 1970s began to strain the specialist system. Many specialists lacked the capital necessary to buy large blocks and accommodate the huge trades. Even with sufficient capital, most specialists were reluctant to take the large risks involved. Consequently, institutions started trading blocks off the floor in other markets or even off the floor of the NYSE. The NYSE recognized this problem and started to allow member firms, with permission from the NYSE, to trade large blocks off the floor of the exchange.[11]

PROGRAM TRADING

Institutional investors also buy and sell large numbers of stocks through **program trading.** Program trading employs sophisticated computer programs that can make automatic decisions to buy or sell. To take advantage of an expected market-wide increase, a pension fund might execute a program trade to buy all 500 stocks that make up the Standard & Poor's 500. Program trades are usually executed directly, using the NYSE's electronic SuperDot system. Program trades make up about 15 percent of NYSE volume.

program trading
Trading via sophisticated computer programs that can make automatic buy or sell decisions.

Program trades serve several purposes. A pension fund manager might execute a program trade each time the fund's sponsor makes a monthly or quarterly contribution. The program trade would deploy new cash into the stock market without substantially altering the contents of the fund's portfolio. Another use of program trading, **index arbitrage,** attempts to gain risk-free returns by exploiting differences between the prices of stock index futures and prices of the underlying stocks. We take a closer look at index arbitrage in Chapter 16.

index arbitrage
Using stocks and stock index futures to make a guaranteed profit over a short period of time.

Program trading is controversial. Some small investors complain that program trades often get priority in execution, despite NYSE rules and policies that give priority to small orders. Critics also allege that program trading tends to exaggerate market

---

[10]This figure only includes block trades executed on the floor of the exchange or in the third market. Most trading activity in the fourth market consists of large blocks. Data on fourth-market activity is only fragmentary, but most likely block trades in the fourth market consists of a few billion shares each year.

[11]This rule change essentially created the third market. We described the third market in Chapter 5.

moves (both upward and downward), making stock prices more volatile. Some have even blamed program trading for contributing to the 1987 market break. However, no conclusive evidence links program trading to market volatility. Nevertheless, during periods of high market volatility the NYSE and other markets implement a series of so-called circuit breakers, many of which restrict program trades. Exhibit 6.5 lists some of the circuit breakers employed by the NYSE in an attempt to control highly volatile trading days.

Investor Protection

For the financial markets to function properly, investors must have confidence in them. To a large extent, investor confidence stems from a belief that the securities markets are sufficiently regulated. U.S. securities markets are regulated by both federal and state authorities, as well as industry self-regulation. Other countries, too, regulate financial markets, to a greater or lesser extent, through national government agencies. U.S. financial markets are considered among the best regulated and fairest financial markets in the world.

GOVERNMENT REGULATION IN THE UNITED STATES

Most government regulation of U.S. securities markets takes place at the federal level. Federal regulation grew out of various trading abuses during the 1920s. During the Great Depression, in an attempt to restore confidence and stability in the financial markets after the 1929 stock market crash, Congress passed a series of landmark legislative acts that formed the basis of federal securities regulation.

The U.S. Securities and Exchange Commission (SEC), created in 1934, is the principal federal regulatory overseer of the securities markets. The SEC's mission is to administer securities laws and protect investors in public securities transactions.

Exhibit 6.5 ✦ NYSE CIRCUIT BREAKERS

In the aftermath following the 1987 market break, the New York Stock Exchange instituted a series of so-called circuit breakers. These breakers are tripped during periods of extreme market volatility in an attempt to maintain an orderly market. The circuit breakers include

- *Rule 80A*. If the Dow Jones Industrial Average moves 50 points or more from the previous day's close, index arbitrage (a form of program trading) is subject to a tick test. In down markets sell orders cannot be executed on a downtick; in up markets buy orders cannot be executed on an uptick.
- *Sidecar*. If the S&P 500 futures contract declines by 12 points (equivalent to about 100 points on the Dow), all program trading market orders for S&P 500 stocks listed on the NYSE are diverted for five minutes. After the five-minute period, buy and sell orders are paired off and executed. If orderly trading cannot resume, trading in the stock is halted. New stop-loss orders in all stocks are banned for the rest of the trading day if they involve more than 2,100 shares.
- *Rule 80B*. If the Dow Jones Industrial Average declines by 10 percent, trading will halt for one hour (one-half hour if the decline occurs after 2 p.m.); if the Dow drops by 20 percent, trading will halt for two hours (if the decline occurs after 1 p.m., trading will be halted for one hour); and if the Dow drops by 30 percent, trading will be halted for the rest of the day.

The SEC is a quasijudicial agency with broad enforcement power, including the power to take civil action against individuals and corporations. Actions requiring criminal proceedings are referred to the U.S. Justice Department.

Some of the best-known cases of regulatory intervention have involved **insider trading,** broadly defined as the use of material nonpublic information to make investment profits. There have been many celebrated cases of insider trading over the past 15 years. Some of those convicted of insider trading in recent times actually spent time in prison. At times, however, difficulties arise in determining if an action constitutes insider trading. The Investment History box on page 144 describes a recent situation that may, or may not, have involved insider trading. Read the facts and decide for yourself whether the analyst's actions constituted insider trading.

insider trading
Using material nonpublic information to make investment profits.

In the primary security markets, the SEC requires that virtually all new public issues of corporate securities be *registered*.[12] Before offering securities for sale, an issuer must file a registration statement with the SEC. As part of the registration process for a new security issue, the issuer must prepare a **prospectus.** In Chapter 5 we reprinted the first page from the prospectus of Yahoo's IPO (Exhibit 5.1 on page 112). Exhibit 6.6 presents a couple more pages of the prospectus to give you an idea of the typical contents. (To read an entire prospectus, open the Yahoo.doc file on your data disk.) The typical prospectus gives a fairly detailed description of the company issuing the securities, including financial data, recent developments, products, research and development projects, pending litigation, and so forth. It also describes the security issue and underwriting agreement in detail.

prospectus
Official offering document for a new security sale.

The registration process seeks to guarantee **full and fair disclosure.** The SEC does not rule on the investment merits of a registered security issue. It is concerned only that an issuer gives investors enough information to make informed decisions.

full and fair disclosure
SEC requirement that investors be given enough information to make informed decisions.

In 1982, SEC Rule 415 introduced shelf registration to allow a large issuer to register a bundle of security issues once and then sell them piecemeal over a period as long as two years. The purpose is to reduce the time delays and expenses associated with registering individual security issues. Companies can now sell new securities on short notice to take advantage of favorable market conditions. Companies have used shelf registrations primarily to sell new corporate bond issues.

Besides primary market registration requirements, SEC regulation extends to the secondary markets as well, keeping tabs on trading activity to make sure it is fair to all participants. Every securities exchange, including Nasdaq, must, by law, follow a set of trading rules approved by the SEC. In response to the 1987 market break, Congress passed the Market Reform Act of 1990, giving the SEC emergency authority to halt trading and restrict practices such as program trading during periods of extreme volatility.

Securities laws also require every public corporation to file several reports each year with the SEC; the contents of these reports become public information. The best known, of course, is the annual report. Public corporations prepare annual reports for their shareholders, and they file another report containing essentially the same information, Form 10-K, with the SEC. The SEC requires additional reports each time certain officers and directors buy or sell a company's stock for their own accounts (Form 4) or any time an investor accumulates more than 5 percent of a company's outstanding stock (Form 13-d).

---

[12]The major exceptions are issues under $500,000 and those that mature in less than 270 days.

INVESTMENT HISTORY

A Case of Insider Trading?

On October 14, 1999, the *Wall Street Journal* story "Abercrombie & Fitch Ignites Controversy Over Possible Leak of Sluggish Sales Data" discussed the market's reaction to sluggish sales data announced the previous day by trendy retailer Abercrombie & Fitch. The company announced that same-store sales (sales in stores open for at least one year) rose only 12 percent for the current fiscal quarter, less than the 15 to 17 percent expected by investors. The stock, which had been among Wall Street's best performers, immediately lost almost 19 percent of its value.

But this wasn't the real story according to the *Wall Street Journal* article. Rather, it was the fact that an Abercrombie & Fitch official allegedly gave one analyst, Todd Slater of Lazard Freres, advance warning of the news on the Friday before the public announcement. Slater, the article suggests, told his firm's

sales force. Many of the firm's customers started to dump the stock; its price fell from about $39 a share to less than $33 a share during Friday afternoon.

Analysts at other firms were caught off guard by the sudden price drop and contacted the company. Senior management at Abercrombie & Fitch reassured these analysts that there were no major changes in sales trends. Some A & F senior managers called the Friday market reaction an anomaly and a few even issued buy recommendations. The announcement on Wednesday was followed by howls of protest, especially after it became evident that the information may have leaked.

The SEC is deeply concerned about the select disclosure of information on Wall Street. SEC Chairman, Arthur Levitt said in a speech in 1998 that he believes companies should not selectively disclose information to certain analysts in order to, in his words, "curry favor with them and reap a

tangible benefit." Levitt further stated that "no one who knows that information should be trading."

The Abercrombie & Fitch case illustrates problems with disseminating market-making news and raises a number of ethical and legal questions. Among these are

✦ Was the new sales data material nonpublic information?
✦ Did the official who may have leaked the information to Lazard Freres violate laws concerning insider trading?
✦ Did the analyst who passed along the news to his firm's sales force, have an obligation to disseminate the information more broadly or, at the least, keep it to himself?
✦ Did senior Abercrombie & Fitch management act properly reassuring investors only a couple of days before the Wednesday announcement?

State Regulation

blue sky laws
State securities laws.

All states have laws regulating securities markets. In 1911, Kansas became the first state to enact a set of comprehensive securities laws. State securities laws, often referred to as **blue sky laws,** vary widely. Some states have fairly lax laws, deferring virtually all regulatory power to the SEC, whereas other states impose much stricter regulations. Unlike federal regulation, which is concerned primarily with full and fair disclosure, these states empower regulators to pass judgment on the worthiness of new security issues as investments. Some states have prohibited sales of security issues approved by registration with the SEC. In one celebrated case in 1980, Massachusetts initially refused to allow sale of the first publicly issued shares of Apple Computer. [13]

---

[13]Massachusetts regulators relented a few days after Apple went public in December 1980 and allowed the stock to be sold to state residents.

SECURITIES REGULATION IN OTHER COUNTRIES

Most countries regulate securities. Generally, securities regulation throughout the world is modeled more or less closely after U.S. regulation. The main goal is to ensure fair, orderly, and open securities markets. Let's briefly look at securities regulation in three other countries.

In Canada, securities regulation is more a provincial than national responsibility. Because Toronto is Canada's largest business center and the home of the country's largest stock exchange, the Ontario Securities Commission is probably the most important regulatory body in the country. The Ontario Securities Commission is closely patterned after the U.S. SEC, often following the SEC's lead to adopt rule changes. For example, in 1993 the commission passed a series of rules concerning the disclosure of CEO pay similar to rules earlier passed by the SEC .

Japan's Ministry of Finance is that country's principal regulatory body for securities trading. All public security issues require the approval of the Ministry of Finance, and its reporting and public disclosure requirements are similar to the SEC's. Further, it licenses all securities firms and brokers. The ministry in the past imposed severe restrictions on foreign access to the Japanese capital markets, especially the bond markets. In recent years, however, the Ministry of Finance has liberalized some of these restrictions.

Germany differs from Japan and the United States in that no regulatory walls separate the banking and securities businesses. As we noted in Chapter 5, the secondary markets for both stocks and bonds in Germany are essentially interbank markets. Consequently, the German central bank, the Bundesbank, has the major responsibility for securities regulation in Germany. It must approve all public security issues, and it is responsible for maintaining orderly secondary markets. The German capital markets are among the most open in the world to foreign (that is, nonGerman) participants.

INDUSTRY SELF-REGULATION

In the United States and most other countries, the securities industry is heavily self-regulated by professional associations and the major financial markets. Industry participants recognize that rules and regulations designed to ensure fair and orderly markets will promote investor confidence to the benefit of all participants. Two examples of self-regulation are the rules of conduct established by the various professional organizations and the market surveillance techniques used by the major securities markets.

Professional Rules of Conduct

Prodded initially by federal legislation, the National Association of Securities Dealers (NASD) established, and periodically updates, rules of conduct for members (both individuals and firms). These rules try to ensure that brokers perform their basic functions honestly and fairly, under constant supervision. Failure to adhere to rules of conduct can result in a variety of disciplinary actions. The NASD also established a formal arbitration procedure through which investors can attempt to resolve disputes with brokers without litigation.[14]

---

[14]When an investor first opens an account, he or she may be required to sign a form agreeing to submit any future disputes to NASD-sponsored arbitration before filing a lawsuit.

Exhibit 6.6 ◆ CONTENTS OF *YAHOO!* PROSPECTUS

PROSPECTUS SUMMARY

The following summary should be read in conjunction with, and is qualified in its entirety by, the more detailed information and the Financial Statements and notes thereto appearing elsewhere in this Prospectus. Except as otherwise noted, all information in this Prospectus, including share and per share information, (i) assumes no exercise of the Underwriters' over-allotment option, (ii) reflects the conversion of all outstanding shares of the Company's convertible Preferred Stock into Common Stock upon closing of the offering, (iii) reflects a two-for-one stock split of the Company outstanding capital stock effected prior to the closing of the offering and (iv) reflects the exercise, prior to the closing of the offering, of warrants to purchase 12,000 shares of the Company's Convertible Preferred Stock at an exercise price of $0.20 per share (after giving effect to the two-for-one stock split).

The Company

Yahoo! offers a branded Internet navigational service that is among the most widely used guides to information and discovery on the World Wide Web (the "Web"). *Yahoo!,* one of the first comprehensive and popular navigational services for the Web, was developed and made available in 1994 by the company's founders, David Filo and Jerry Yang, while they were graduate students at Stanford University. The Company believes that by providing an intuitive, context-based guide to Web content, *Yahoo!* has played a significant role in the development and growth in usage of the Web. As a result, the Company believes that *Yahoo!* has achieved a strong, globally prominent brand presence among Web users and is one of the most visible and recognizable names generally associated with the Internet. According to an independent audit report, *Yahoo!* averaged in excess of 1 million user visits and 6 million page views per day in February 1996.

The large and rapidly growing number of Internet users and ease of creating Web sites have led to a dramatic increase in content available on the Web. This rapid growth of Web content presents significant challenges for users searching for information and for content providers attempting to reach their target audience. To address these challenges, *Yahoo!* developed a context-based directly structure, which permits users to search for information online within interest-area categories, as well as a Web-wide search engine that is seamlessly integrated with the *Yahoo!* directly service. *Yahoo!* offers these services free of charge to Web users. The Company believes that by providing a branded "navigational gateway" to Internet resources and a familiar context for user navigation of the Web. *Yahoo!* is well positioned to capitalize on the emergence of the Web as a new advertising mass medium.

The Company believes that the Web represents an important new medium for sponsors to reach consumers through targeted, interactive, and highly measurable advertising. Published industry sources estimate that the market for advertising on the Internet will reach $74 million in 1996 and will exceed $2 billion by the year 2000, or approximately 1% of projected advertising expenditures in traditional print, television, and radio broadcast media by the end of the decade. The Company's objective is to capitalize on this opportunity by providing the most popular and widely used guide to information on the Internet and to leverage the Company's strong brand position by developing a global family of branded media properties in targeted subject, demographic, and geographic areas. The Company also intends to enhance and extend the features and functionality of the *Yahoo!* main site, continue to promote its *Yahoo!* brand and build additional alliances with strategic third-party content, technology, and distribution partners. In March 1996, the Company introduced *Yahooligans!,* an Internet navigational guide for children ages 8 to 14, and, together with Ziff-Davis,

Many investment professionals—such as security analysts and mutual fund managers—are Chartered Financial Analysts (or CFAs). CFAs are required to adhere to the Association for Investment Management & Research (AIMR) Standards of Professional Conduct. CFAs who fail to adhere to the professional conduct standards can be disciplined and even lose their CFA certification.

Market Surveillance

Like all major financial markets, the NYSE uses a series of market surveillance techniques. Trading activity is monitored continuously throughout the trading day. A key technical tool is Stock Watch, an electronic monitoring system that flags unusual price and volume activity. NYSE personnel investigate possible explanations for unusual

Yahoo! Internet Life, a print and online magazine which provides in-depth editorial coverage, including Web site reviews, of particular subject areas of interest on the Internet. In April 1996, the company, in cooperation with SOFTBANK Corporation, introduced *Yahoo! Japan,* a localized version of *Yahoo!.* By mid-1996, the Company, with its strategic partners, expects to introduce *Yahoo! Canada,* another localized version of *Yahoo!,* and *Yahoo! Computing,* an online guide focused on computing topics. The Company also recently entered into an agreement with VISA International for the development of a Web navigational service, currently referred to as *Yahoo! MarketPlace,* to be focused on information and resources relating to the purchase of consumer products and services over the Internet.

The Company has established strategic alliances with prominent content, technology, distribution, and financial partners, including Ziff-Davis Publishing Company, Reuters New Media, Open Text Corporation, SOFTBANK Corporation, Rogers Communications, VISA International, Sequoia Capital, and The Capital Group. SOFTBANK Holdings Inc., a subsidiary of SOFTBANK Corporation (together "SOFTBANK"), one of the Company's principle shareholders, recently purchased 5,100,000 shares of the Company's capital stock from the Company for an aggregate purchase price of $63.73 million. In April 1996, SOFTBANK privately purchased 3,400,000 additional shares of the Company's capital stock from certain shareholders of the Company at a price of $12.50 per share. As a result of these purchases, SOFTBANK will own approximately 37% of the Company's outstanding common Stock upon completion of this offering (or 30.6% of the outstanding shares of Common Stock, assuming exercise of all currently outstanding options to purchase Common Stock). The Company also issued to VISA International a warrant to purchase 350,000 shares of Common Stock at an exercise price of $12.50 per share. As of March 1, 1996 the *Yahoo!* main site hosted over 80 advertisers, including American Express Company, Apple Computer, Colgate-Palmolive, Lexus, Netscape Communications Corporation and VISA. As of the date of this Prospectus, the Company's navigational guide was featured in a number of online and Internet access services and leading Web sites, including CompuServe/Spry, Global Network Navigator (a subsidiary of America Online, Inc.), Intuit's Quicken Financial Network, The Microsoft network, Netscape's directory and search pages and Pacific Bell Internet.

The company was incorporated in California in March 1995. The Company's executive offices are located at 635 Vaqueros Avenue, Sunnyvale, California 94086, and its telephone number at that location is (408) 328-3300. Unless the context otherwise requires, the terms "*Yahoo!*" and the "Company" refer to Yahoo! Inc. Unless the context otherwise requires, the term "*Yahoo!*" refer to the Company's Web site, located at "http://www.yahoo.com". Information contained in the Company's Web site shall not be deemed to be a part of this Prospectus.

Risk Factors

For a discussion of certain considerations relevant to an investment in the Common Stock, see "Risk Factors."

The Offering

Common Stock offered hereby	2,600,000 shares
Common Stock to be outstanding after the offering	25,702,798 shares (1)
Use of proceeds	General corporate purposes, including working capital and potential acquisitions, See "Use of Proceeds."
Nasdaq National Market symbol	YHOO

activity from the member firms and companies involved. In addition, all market participants must keep detailed records of every aspect of every trade (called an *audit trail*). The NYSE's enforcement division acts as its prosecutorial arm and may impose a variety of penalties on members. Further, the exchange turns evidence over to the SEC for further action if it believes that violations of federal securities laws may have occurred.

Unlike the NYSE, which probably has as effective a market surveillance system as any financial market in the world and carefully polices the activities of its members, the Nasdaq Stock Market has sometimes been criticized for lax enforcement of trading rules. After a two-year investigation, the SEC formally censured the Nasdaq in 1996. The SEC found that some market makers engaged in price fixing by not allowing some investors news of the best prices available for particular issues. The investigation also uncovered evidence of market makers refusing to honor public quotes to buy and sell stocks, even suspicious delays in reporting trades. In response, the NASD agreed to a sweeping set of reforms, including new oversight of market makers and greater penalties for violators. Many contend these changes have lowered, though not eliminated, chances of small investors being ripped off and have boosted investor confidence in the fairness of the Nasdaq Stock Market.

This chapter has outlined how investors participate in the financial markets, from choosing a broker to the types of orders investors can place. We also described the various ways investors are protected from abusive practices. In the next two chapters we take a look at how well the financial markets function and how investors make investment decisions.

Chapter Summary

1. How should investors choose a broker?

   In order to trade, investors usually establish an account with a brokerage firm. An investor should consider individual characteristics and needs when choosing a brokerage firm. Full-service firms offer detailed investment advice, along with order execution and record keeping. They also charge higher commissions. Discount brokerage firms offer less advice but charge lower commissions. Deep discount brokerage firms offer virtually no advice, but charge rock-bottom commissions. It is possible to buy some securities without a broker by investing directly with the company.

2. What are the various types of orders investors place?

   Most investors place market orders, which instructs their broker to obtain the best possible price. Market orders are executed slightly differently on the NYSE and the Nasdaq Stock Market. Other types of orders include limit orders and stop-loss orders. Investors may be able to buy securities on margin, meaning they are borrowing some of the funds used to purchase the securities. Margin buying increases the investor's potential return as well as the risk. A short sale is the process of selling a stock with the hope of buying it back later at a lower price. Short selling is a way of speculating on price declines and can be quite risky.

3. What is cybertrading?

   Today thousands of investors use their personal computers and the Internet to trade. Price and convenience are leading the rapid growth of on-line trading and brokerage firms. However, on-line trading has drawbacks and isn't for all investors. Day trading is the process of trading stocks over short periods of time to take advantage of expected short-term price movements. Day trading is extremely risky, and most day traders lose money.

4. What are block trades and program trading?

   Block trades are defined as trades that involve at least 1,000 shares or $100,000 worth of securities. About half of all trades in the stock market are block trades. Many block trades are handled off the exchange floors, in the third market. Program trading uses computer systems to execute trades at prespecified prices. One of the best-known forms of program trading involves the simultaneous trading of stocks and stock index futures. Some argue that program trading aggravates market volatility. The NYSE has rules to limit program trading during highly volatile trading days.

5. Who regulates the financial markets and protects investors?

   Financial markets are heavily regulated. In the United States, the federal Securities and Exchange Commission is the main regulatory body. Its regulations are designed to ensure fair and orderly markets where information is fully and fairly disclosed. Securities regulations in other countries follows the U.S. model. In addition, the financial markets are self-regulated. Most professional associations require members to adhere to a code of conduct.

Mini Case

The purpose of this mini-case is to illustrate the various types or orders and trades.

Today is Monday, January 6. You placed an order this morning to buy 500 shares of The Gap. Answer the following questions about the order, assuming that The Gap is currently trading for $65 a share and your broker charges a commission of .75 percent of the total trade value.

a. If you placed a market order, how much would you have owed your broker, and when would the payment have been due?
   Had you placed a limit order to buy (limit 64 1/2), and made it good until canceled, what would have happened to your order?

b. Had you bought the stock on margin, with an initial margin requirement of 50 percent and a maintenance requirement of 30 percent, how much cash would you have had to deposit initially?

c. Using the information from question 3, at what price would you have faced a margin call?

d. Compute your return on both a cash transaction and a margin transaction, assuming you had bought The Gap at 65 and sold it one year later for 75. Assume your margin loan carries an annual rate of interest of 6 percent.

Review Questions and Problems

1. Explain the various types of brokerage firms. In general, what type of investor is better off using a full-service firm? A discount, or deep discount firm?

2. Is it possible to buy stock without using a broker? Explain how dividend reinvestment plans work.

3. Explain how a market order would be executed on the NYSE and on the Nasdaq Stock Market. What role does the NYSE specialist and Nasdaq market maker play in market orders?

4. What is a limit order? How does a stop-loss order differ from a limit order?

5. Assume you buy 200 shares of stock at 100 on margin. Your broker requires a 50 percent initial margin and a 35 percent maintenance margin. If the stock rises to 110, how much money will you have in your margin account? Assuming the stock price falls to 90, how much money will you have in your margin account?

6. Using the same information in question 5, find the price where you will face a margin call. What will happen if you fail to meet the margin call?

7. Why has on-line trading grown so rapidly in recent years? What is day trading?

8. Explain block trades and program trading. Discuss why have both increased in recent years.

9. What federal agency has most of the regulatory responsibility over the financial markets? When and why was this agency created?

10. Define full and fair disclosure. Give an example of a trading practice that violates federal securities law.

CFA Questions

All of the following questions relate to standards of professional and ethical conduct adopted by the Association of Investment Management and Research. All members are required to adhere to these standards. You can review them at the AIMR web site: www.aimr.com/ethics/practice/standards.html

1. (Level I, 1992) Scott Hill, CFA, is a research analyst with a brokerage firm. He decided to change his recommendation on the common stock of Green, Inc., from buy

to sell. He mailed this change in investment advice to all his customers on Wednesday. The day after the mailing, one of his customers called with a buy order for 500 shares of Green, Inc. In this circumstance, Hill should

 a. accept the order because he has complied with the standard on fair dealing with customers.

 b. advise the customer of the change in recommendation before accepting the order.

 c. not accept the order until five days have elapsed after the communication of the change in recommendation.

 d. not accept the order because it is contrary to the firm's recommendation.

2. (Level I, 1992) Martha Halliburton, an analyst, is asked by her research director to increase the 1992 earnings estimate for Headley Electric, an important underwriting client. A violation of the AIMR Standards of Professional Conduct would result if the reason Halliburton increased her estimate was that

 a. her earnings estimate was inconsistent with the price/earnings ratio at which Headley management wishes its secondary offering to be made.

 b. her economic assumptions were more conservative than those used in her firm's investment strategy.

 c. her annual sales assumptions were more conservative than those indicated by the quarterly report just released by Headley.

 d. her estimate did not allow for a change in accounting rules, which her firm expects to be in effect by the time Headley reports earnings for the year.

3. (Level I, 1992) An analyst who receives material nonpublic information must make an effort to achieve public disclosure of the information if

 a. doing so would prevent a loss to those with whom the analyst has a fiduciary relationship.

 b. the analyst refrains from communicating or trading on the information until it becomes public.

 c. the information arises lawfully in the course of a special or confidential relationship with the issuer.

 d. the information is acquired through a breach of fiduciary duty.

4. (Level I, 1992) Ann Carter, CFA, recently became a portfolio manager at Riverside Bank. She has both ERISA-qualified retirement plans and personal trust accounts. She knows she will be acting in a fiduciary capacity for both kinds of accounts and that her duties and responsibilities for both kinds of accounts are similar.

Explain what a "fiduciary" is, and describe an investment manager's specific duties as a fiduciary under ERISA. In reviewing all of the accounts under her management, Carter notices that several of the personal trust portfolios have substantial holdings in Riverside Bank's own stock. When she accepted her new position at Riverside, she was told in confidence that a major national bank was seeking to take over Riverside. Carter is unsure what the effect of a takeover would be on the shareholders of Riverside or on her employment at Riverside. In view of her fiduciary responsibilities, Carter is concerned about how to apply the AIMR Standards of Professional Conduct in managing the portfolios that hold Riverside stock. She is particularly concerned about Standard II C—Compliance with Governing Laws and Regulations and the Code and Standards—Prohibition against Use of Material Nonpublic Information. Standard II C prohibits a financial analyst from using material nonpublic information in a breach of duty or if the information is misappropriated. She is also concerned about Standard V—Disclosure of Conflicts. Standard V requires a financial analyst to disclose to clients material conflicts of interest that could reasonably be expected to impair her ability to render unbiased and objective advice to clients.

 a. Describe *each* of these *two* standards. With reference to Carter's fiduciary responsibilities, explain how *each* standard applies to the management of her accounts in view of the information Carter possesses about the possible takeover.

The situation described above presents Carter with a dilemma in performing her fiduciary duties. Briefly discuss the dilemma that Carter faces. (Do not attempt to resolve the dilemma.)

5. (Level II, 1991) BanCo, a major public bank whose common shares tend to trade at a high yield, announced a substantial dividend cut on April 30, 1991. BanCo has had a record of steady dividend growth. The following descriptions outline how three individuals employed by investment banking firms derived information regarding BanCo.

   ✦ Karen Dawson, CFA, is an analyst in the Corporate Finance Department of DSP Ltd. On April 29, 1991, the chief financial officer (CFO) of BanCo, a long-standing client, told Dawson that the dividend was going to be cut, with an announcement planned for the next day.

   ✦ Joan Davidson, CFA, a security analyst with Equity Co., has covered the banking industry for 20 years. On April 29, 1991, she was having one of her usual quarterly management interviews with the CFO of BanCo and the CFO told her that the dividend was going to be cut.

   ✦ Sonia Black, CFA, a senior bank analyst with Security Co., has not talked to the company specifically about the dividend for the past two months. After extensive research on the economic environment and on the company, Black concluded BanCo's dividend would be cut. On April 26, 1991, she notified all her clients over the newswire of her conclusion.

   a. Define both the terms *material* and *nonpublic* as established by securities regulators and the courts. Your answer must include *two* criteria for the term *material* and *one* criterion for the term *nonpublic*. State whether BanCo's dividend cut was "material nonpublic" information.

   b. Based on AIMR's Standards of Professional Conduct, describe the duty of *each* of the three CFAs listed above regarding both their use of the information about the dividend cut and their required action after the receipt of this information. Identify the reason(s) for the differences in duty and required action among the three CFAs.

CRITICAL THINKING EXERCISES

1. This exercise requires library or Internet research. Major financial markets regularly publish information on "short interest." Markets list stocks with the largest short positions, along with issues that have seen the greatest change in short activity. Find a recent report on short interest and answer the following questions:
   List the three stocks with the largest short positions. Why do you believe these stocks show so much short activity?
   a. Identify the three stocks that have seen the greatest change in short activity (both increases as well as decreases in the number of short positions). List some reasons for so much change in these stocks' short activity.

2. This exercise requires library or Internet research. The Investment History box on page 144 discussed the question of whether an analyst improperly used inside information. Using information in the box, investigate whether, since the case came to light, the SEC or others have taken any action against the analyst, his firm, or the company involved. If any action was taken, what was the outcome? Do you agree or disagree with the action taken, or even the lack of action?

THE INTERNET INVESTOR

1. The National Association of Securities Dealers (NASD) is directly involved in industry self-regulation of the financial markets. Go to NASD's web site (www.nasd.com)

and read about NASD programs regarding dispute resolution between investors and brokerage firms. Prepare a short report on how the arbitration process works.

2. Visit the web site of a brokerage firm that offers on-line trading (such as E°Trade, www.etrade.com, or Charles Schwab, www.schwab.com) to learn more about on-line trading. Most electronic brokerage firms also offer a trading demonstration. Use the demonstration to see how you obtain price information, company news, place buy or sell orders, and check account balances.

3. Use your web browser to research a company whose stock you might be interested in buying. Most companies provide financial results and other information on their web sites. Other sites to visit include Quicken (www.quicken.com), Morningstar (www.morningstar.net), Microsoft Investor (investor.msn.com), and the SEC's Edgar database (www.sec.gov/edgar). Prepare a brief report to your class about the company you selected.

MARKET EFFICIENCY: CONCEPT AND REALITY

PREVIOUSLY . . .

We discussed how the financial markets are organized, regulated, and how investors participate in the financial markets.

IN THIS CHAPTER . . .

We examine the efficient markets hypothesis, the notion that security prices reflect all available information. This hypothesis has many important implications for investors. Although more and more evidence suggests that the markets are less efficient than often believed, one can still conclude that it is difficult to consistently beat the market on a risk-adjusted basis.

TO COME . . .

We discuss technical and fundamental analysis, the two techniques by which many professional investors make their decisions and recommendations. We will describe both techniques and examine their successes and failures.

Chapter Objectives

After reading chapter 7, you should be able to answer the following questions:

1. What is the efficient-markets hypothesis?
2. What are the three traditional forms of market efficiency?
3. How is the efficient-markets hypothesis tested?
4. Does any evidence support the efficient markets hypothesis?
5. Can investors profit from anomalies?

One of the most controversial and far-reaching concepts to have emerged from investments theory over the past 40 years is the **efficient-markets hypothesis (EMH),** sometimes referred to as the random walk theory. In a nutshell, EMH states that securities prices fluctuate randomly around their respective intrinsic values. Intrinsic values, in turn, rationally reflect all relevant publicly available information and perhaps even privately available information as well. Prices adjust quickly to new information, which also enters the market in a random fashion. A logical conclusion

efficient-markets hypothesis (EMH)
The notion that security prices reflect all available information.

153

from the efficient markets hypothesis is that no person or system can accurately and consistently predict short-term movements in securities prices.

The efficient markets hypothesis has many strong proponents; most financial economists, and many Wall Street practitioners, believe in the EMH, at least up to a point. The proponents cite large amounts of evidence, both scientific and anecdotal, to support the concept of market efficiency. A fair amount of evidence suggests, for example, that past price patterns provide virtually no information about future price patterns.

Not surprisingly, many others dismiss as nonsense ideas such as efficient markets and security prices following random walks. The detractors point to evidence, some anecdotal and some more scientific, and to many common situations that seem to contradict the concept of market efficiency. As Peter Lynch, the former star mutual fund manager, wrote:

> It's very hard to support the popular academic theory that the market is [unpredictable] when you know somebody who just made a twenty-fold profit in Kentucky Fried Chicken, and furthermore, who explained in advance why the stock was going to rise.[1]

In this chapter, we examine both the concept and reality of market efficiency. In doing so, we try to answer two big questions: just how efficient are the markets, and what does it all mean for investors?

Random Walks and Efficient Markets

In the early 1950s, a statistician named Maurice Kendall was analyzing several economic time series using a new tool, the computer, when he discovered, to his surprise, that changes in stock prices appeared almost random in nature. On any given day, a positive price change was as likely as a negative price change. Furthermore, Kendall concluded, past price patterns could not reliably predict future price patterns.

At first glance, Kendall's findings, which several other researchers replicated, seemed to suggest that stock markets behaved almost irrationally. Perhaps prices were determined, not by rational valuation, but by the erratic behavior of investors. Some financial economists soon realized, however, that Kendall's findings might mean something quite different. Perhaps random price changes were not the results of irrational markets but rather the results of well-functioning markets in which prices rationally reflect all available information and adjust quickly to new information. The concept of market efficiency was born.

WHAT IS A RANDOM WALK?

random walk
A stochastic time series in which each successive change in a variable is drawn independently from a distribution with a constant mean and variance.

Kendall's discovery about the time series behavior of stock prices is commonly referred to as a random walk. Mathematically, a **random walk** is a stochastic time series in which each successive change in a variable is drawn independently from a probability distribution with a constant mean and variance. What does it mean to say that stock prices follow a random walk?

To answer this question, assume the following time series best describes the behavior of stock prices:

---

[1]Peter Lynch, *One Up on Wall Street* (New York: Penguin Books), 1989, p. 35.

$$P_t = P_{t-1} + a_t, \text{ where } a \sim N(\mu, \sigma^2). \tag{7.1}$$

Equation 7.1 identifies a random walk—one of just many possibilities. It says that today's price is equal to yesterday's price, plus a random variable, a. Each random variable is drawn from a normally distributed population with a mean of μ and a variance of σ^2. The change in price, $P_t - P_{t-1}$ equals the random variable, a_t.

Take a look at the charts shown in Exhibit 7.1 and Exhibit 7.2. In the first chart, one of the two unlabeled series is the daily close for the S&P 500 between the beginning of 1998 and the end of October 1999. The other series consists of a random walk, much like the one defined by Equation 7.1. The random series begins at the same point, but each subsequent value equals the prior value plus a random variable. Each random variable is drawn from a normal distribution with a mean of 0.67 and a standard deviation of 14.36 (the same mean and standard deviation of the daily changes for the S&P 500). In the second chart, shown in Exhibit 7.2, one of the two series is the daily closing price for Applied Materials and the second is a random series constructed in a similar fashion to the random series shown in Exhibit 7.1.

Examining both charts, can you tell which series is which? If you guessed that the index and stock price are the blue series, you're correct. The black series are the random walks. This example demonstrates an important point: it's easy to see patterns in stock prices, even if none exist. The series produced by the random walks look a lot like the stock index and stock price series.

RANDOM WALKS AND FORECASTING

Suppose that a time series of stock prices is best described by the random walk model in Equation 7.1 and someone wants to forecast its behavior. What will the forecast look like? Assume that, based on a history of price observations, $P_0, P_1, P_2, \ldots, P_T$, an

---

Exhibit 7.1 ✦ COMPARISON OF S&P 500 DAILY CLOSE PRICE AND A RANDOM WALK SERIES

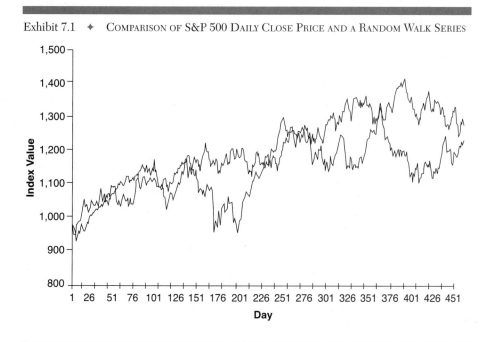

Exhibit 7.2 ✦ DAILY CLOSING PRICE FOR APPLIED MATERIALS COMPARED TO A RANDOM
WALK SERIES

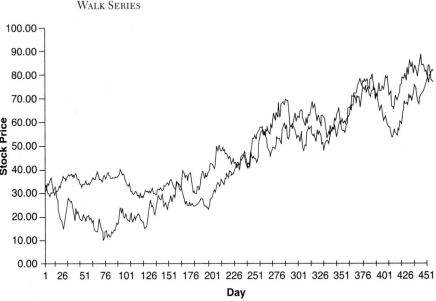

analyst wants to forecast tomorrow's price, P_{T+1}. Using all the information contained
in the historical price series, if the series follows a random walk, the best forecast of
tomorrow's price is actually today's price, P_T plus the mean of the random variable, a.
We'll talk about this a bit more later, but as you can probably already see, if stock
prices do follow a random walk, we can seriously question the value of investment
techniques that rely solely on historical price patterns.

SOURCE OF MARKET EFFICIENCY

Why should anyone expect financial markets to be efficient markets in which prices
reflect all available information? In a word, competition. Financial markets in most
parts of the world are heavily competitive. Literally millions of highly motivated participants (both individuals and institutions) hunt constantly for above-average profits
(the "best" investments).

After one participant discovers an investment with an above-average return, how
long will it be before other participants discover it, too? In a highly competitive market, probably not very long. As participants discover the investment, they quickly bid
up its price, eliminating the abnormal profit.

Further, many participants can devote substantial resources to search for the best
investments. Say that a stock mutual fund with $10 billion in assets believes that buy-
ing the right stocks will boost its annual performance by 0.5 percent. One-half of 1
percent of $10 billion is $50 million. How much will this fund be willing to spend on
research and analysis to uncover the best stocks? The fund probably would be willing
to spend up to $50 million. Beating so many deep-pocketed investors to the best in-
vestments is not easy. Perhaps this elusive search for abnormal profits by so many investors is the single most important source of market efficiency.

IMPLICATIONS OF MARKET EFFICIENCY

If the markets truly are efficient, and we'll look at the evidence shortly, what implications would the EMH have for popular investment techniques? For certain techniques, the EMH has quite a bit to say.

Technical Analysis

As we'll discuss in the next chapter, many professional investors and investment advisers rely on one of two techniques when making investment decisions: technical analysis and fundamental analysis. **Technical analysis** is based on the notion that security prices follow recurrent and fairly predictable patterns. Thus, by looking at historical prices an investor can reasonably predict future prices. As we've already seen, if stock prices follow a random walk, the best forecast of tomorrow's price is today's price plus the mean of some random variable. This is rarely the formula for a reliable forecast. Furthermore, the EMH argues that current security prices already reflect all available information. Therefore, even if historical prices contain usable information, the EMH concludes that current prices already reflect this information. Consequently, the EMH hypothesis argues that technical analysis will not produce above-average investment profits over the long run.

technical analysis
Investment technique based on the notion that security prices follow recurrent and predictable patterns.

Fundamental Analysis

The basis for **fundamental analysis** is the belief that every security eventually sells for its intrinsic value, and therefore fundamental analysts constantly hunt for under- or overvalued securities. The EMH argues that if analysts rely solely on historical data, and current publicly available information, their recommendations cannot consistently produce abnormal profits because security prices already reflect this information. Rather, an analyst must have superior forecasting ability to beat the market and gain insight into the fundamental factors that drive stock prices before other market participants recognize them. As we'll see in the next chapter, forecasting these fundamental factors is difficult.

fundamental analysis
Investment technique based on the notion that every security eventually sells for its intrinsic value.

Active versus Passive Portfolio Management

In Chapter 1 we briefly discussed the differences between passive and active portfolio management; a buy-and-hold philosophy versus more frequent trading in anticipation of price movements. The EMH casts doubts on the possibility that an actively managed portfolio can produce returns that are consistently superior to the returns of a passively managed one (assuming both have similar risk characteristics). Because the EMH argues that security prices already reflect all available information, regularly finding under- or overvalued securities is difficult, especially because active investors must pay higher transactions costs (brokerage commissions, for example) and perhaps taxes.[2]

---

[2]For taxable investors, capital gains are taxed only when realized, meaning a security is actually sold at a profit. Because active investors trade more frequently than passive investors, they'll realize more capital gains and, therefore, lose some of their profits to taxes.

Market efficiency, however, doesn't imply that a specific investor should never make changes to his or her portfolio. Changes should keep pace with changes in income, family situation, and other factors. Even in an efficient market, the appropriate portfolio for a twenty-five-year-old will differ greatly from that of a sixty-five-year-old.

Traditional Forms of Market Efficiency

Earlier, we noted that market efficiency implies that security prices rationally reflect all available information. Using different assumptions about the meaning of the phrase *all available information,* we've traditionally distinguished between three levels, or forms, of market efficiency: the weak form, the semistrong form, and the strong form. Let's briefly define each.

WEAK-FORM MARKET EFFICIENCY

weak-form market efficiency
Current prices fully reflect all historical information.

Weak-form market efficiency states that current security prices fully reflect all historical information. Further, weak-form efficiency states that investors cannot earn abnormal returns by using historical information. Historical information includes not just price information, but information on trading volume, short interest, odd lots, and other variables. Weak-form efficiency also implies that security prices do not follow either recurrent or predictable patterns, but rather a random walk.

A technical analyst may develop a trading model based on past prices over the prior 60 months, buying stock when his or her model gives one signal and selling when it gives another. Weak-form market efficiency does not imply that the trading model would not generate a profit, just that the profit would match that of someone who simply bought and held the same stock over the same period (adjusting for differences in risk and transactions costs).

SEMISTRONG-FORM MARKET EFFICIENCY

semistrong-form market efficiency
Prices fully reflect all public information.

Semistrong-form market efficiency states that security prices reflect all public information and react almost instantaneously to new public information. Public information includes all historical information and adds all public information on a company's product lines, its financial policies, the quality of its management, and so forth. Therefore, semistrong-form efficient markets are also weak-form efficient, although weak-form efficiency does not necessarily imply semistrong-form efficiency.

As an example of semistrong-form efficiency, consider a company that announces quarterly earnings 10 percent higher than analysts were forecasting. This is good news, and the price of the company's stock should increase after the announcement. Semistrong-form efficiency says, however, that buying the stock after the public earnings announcement would fail to consistently produce abnormal returns. Why? Simply because prices would quickly adjust to the new information, so the price at the time of the purchase would fully reflect the new information.

STRONG-FORM MARKET EFFICIENCY

strong-form market efficiency
Prices fully reflect all public and private information.

Strong-form market efficiency makes the extreme statement that security prices reflect not only all public information but all private information as well. Again, price reactions to new information, whether public or private, occur rapidly. Thus, even insiders who have access to confidential information (for example, corporate officers) cannot make abnormal returns consistently.

Few would dispute that corporate insiders may have access to valuable information before the general investing public. Indeed, as we discussed in the prior chapter, a principal focus of securities regulation is to prevent insiders from exploiting their potential information advantage through such practices as insider trading. Government regulators, as well as the NYSE and other major financial markets, closely monitor records of trading activity, looking for abuses of inside information.

Testing Market Efficiency

As you review the evidence on market efficiency in the next two sections, keep in mind several issues that make interpreting the evidence somewhat subjective, including the types of tests, the benchmarks used, and other topics covered in the following discussion. In our opinion, the debate on market efficiency is likely to continue indefinitely and may never be settled one way or the other.

Types of Tests

The EMH can be tested in several ways. Analysts have devised direct and indirect tests of market efficiency. *Direct tests* assess the success of specific investment strategies or trading rules. An example of a direct test would be to test the accuracy of predictions by some specific technical indicator, such as moving averages or filters. *Indirect tests* are statistical tests of prices or returns. For example, if prices follow a random walk, the serial correlation of returns should be close to zero.

One can also test the efficient-markets hypothesis by some scientific methodology or simply by looking for anecdotal evidence. A *scientific* experiment develops a research design based on a proven methodology. For example, we could scientifically examine market reactions to unexpected earnings announcements using a large sample over time. Results from the study would determine how rapidly the market responds to new public information. *Anecdotal evidence* involves looking for examples consistent, or inconsistent, with the EMH.

The conundrum, of course, is that any test can be criticized. Critics can argue that the test was applied improperly, was inadequate to measure its target, or both. For example, direct tests of technical trading rules can always be criticized because testing these trading rules requires applying them mechanically. These tests cannot hope to capture the subjective portion of technical analysis that, technicians argue, helps investors exploit historical price patterns. Even if a test provides evidence consistent with the EMH, critics can always argue that the results reflected the test used, not necessarily the truth of the EMH.

Establishing a Benchmark

Tests of the EMH must usually establish some sort of benchmark. For example, to assert that a particular trading rule works and provide evidence inconsistent with the EMH, a test must compare a portfolio that used the trading rule and outperformed a similar portfolio, the benchmark portfolio, which did not use the trading rule. Like the type of test used, critics can always question whether the benchmark chosen was appropriate.

The most common benchmark is the so-called buy-and-hold portfolio. As an example, a test may want to evaluate a trading rule that indicates when to switch between a stock index fund and a money market fund. How well does the trading rule perform? It would have to earn higher profits (or returns) than the profits from simply buying and holding the stock index fund over the same period of time. Of course, the test would have to account for differences in risk and transaction costs between the two investment strategies as well. Active trading strategies usually involve higher transaction costs, and they often expose a portfolio to more risk as well. Furthermore, most investors pay taxes on realized capital gains—active strategies are usually less tax efficient.

THE TIME FACTOR

On October 11, 1987, eight days before the market event popularly known as Meltdown Monday, Elaine Garzarelli, a well-known technical analyst, predicted the upcoming market break. Was this prediction the result of her special insight into the market, application of her trading rules, and market inefficiency, or was this prediction merely luck? Of course, we will never know. In retrospect, it is easy to find investment strategies that produced abnormal profits. Believers will call it skill, and skeptics will call it luck. The proper test evaluates how well the strategy works over different time periods.

The time period(s) selected can, of course, always be criticized. One analyst, when confronted with his less-than-stellar recent record, commented to a television audience, that the current market was "unusual" and his system would begin to work once the market returned to "normal." His assertion was, of course, unprovable without testing it over every single possible time period, a rather daunting task.

KISS AND TELL

Suppose that someone discovered an investment strategy that really worked and made a lot of money. Why would this person want to tell anyone? He or she could try to make money writing a book or an investment newsletter describing the strategy, but it would probably generate more money if kept secret. Suppose an analyst discovers that stocks beginning with the letter K rise on Wednesdays and fall on Fridays. Buying K stocks on Tuesdays and selling them on Thursdays will make the analyst lots of money. The dilemma, of course, is that once others know about the strategy, it will likely stop working. K stocks will probably start rising on Mondays and falling on Wednesdays as other investors try to anticipate the market. To avoid this, the analyst would probably keep the strategy a secret for as long as possible.

Seriously, some argue that the inclination to keep successful strategies secret introduces *sample selection bias* into tests of market efficiency and trading rules. Only those strategies that fail to work are widely reported and, consequently, tested. Strategies that work go unreported, which biases the results in favor of the EMH. In other words, the results, based on testing inferior trading rules, will quite understandably indicate that trading rules produce no abnormal profits. If the successful trading rules are kept secret, perhaps we can never fairly test the true ability of investors or the validity of the EMH.

QUALITATIVE VERSUS QUANTITATIVE EFFICIENCY

We know that some investors pay more to trade than others. We also know that some investors can obtain information more cheaply than others. Perhaps we should replace the quantitative question "are the markets efficient?" with the more qualitative question "how efficient are the markets?" In other words, market efficiency may hold different meanings for different investors.

We use an actual example to illustrate this point. One familiar NYSE specialist firm has a small trading operation in addition to its normal specialist duties. The trading operation attempts to make money for the firm by buying and selling NYSE-listed stocks other than those for which the firm is the specialist. The firm's traders use a variety of technical indicators and trading rules, and the trading operation appears to consistently make abnormal profits.

Does that mean that the NYSE is inefficient? Not necessarily. For one thing, the specialist, being a member of the NYSE, pays virtually no transaction costs when it trades. For another, the firm rarely holds a position for more than a few minutes and never overnight. Through electronic links with the NYSE's SuperDot System, the specialist firm's traders might buy 1,000 shares of Disney at 30 and sell the shares a minute later for 30¼, earning $250 (before transaction costs). The specialist tries to take advantage of what its traders believe are small temporary mispricings of NYSE-listed stocks. The vast majority of investors, even many so-called day traders, could never profitably duplicate this firm's trading strategy. Perhaps this suggests that the markets are efficient for the vast majority of investors, although not necessarily for a few investors with special advantages. In fact, one could argue that these investors help to contribute to market efficiency by correcting mispricing.

Traditional Tests of the Efficient-Markets Hypothesis

In this section, we review some traditional tests of the three forms of the EMH, most of which appear to support the concept of market efficiency, at least in its weak and semistrong forms. We examine tests based on historical prices, how rapidly the market reacts to new public information, and the value of private, or inside, information.

The vast majority of tests of the efficient-markets hypothesis have examined the efficiency of U.S. stock markets. A few studies have attempted to test the efficiency of non-U.S. markets for stocks and other securities. The studies suggest that foreign markets may be at least as efficient as U.S. markets.

USEFULNESS OF HISTORICAL PRICES

Tests of trading based on historical prices essentially evaluate the weak-form theory of market efficiency: that security prices fully reflect all historical information. These tests fall into two general categories: tests of the random nature of security prices and returns, and tests of specific trading rules.

Tests of the Random Nature of Security Prices and Returns

Tests of the randomness of securities prices over time have relied primarily on two statistical techniques: serial correlation and a so-called runs test. Both of these techniques have many other applications, as discussed in detail in most standard business statistics textbooks. Briefly, *serial correlation* measures the strength of the relationship between the current value of a time series (for example, stock returns) and past share values. If stock prices follow something like the random walk described in Equation 7.1, serial correlation coefficients should be close to zero.

A *runs test* counts the number of times that price changes, each one designated positive or negative, change sign over a specific time period. For example, say ten days of price changes produce this series: + +, +, −, −, −, +, −, +, +. This sequence has five runs (the first three positive changes, the next three negative changes, a positive change, a negative change, and the final two positive changes). Now consider the following sequence of ten price changes: +, +, +, +, +, +, −, −, −, −. This sequence has just two runs (the first six positive changes and the final four negative changes). Too many or too few runs suggests that a series is not random.

The results of these statistical tests from many studies have strongly suggested that stock prices and returns are essentially random, thus providing evidence in support of weak-form market efficiency. For example, a test of price changes for each of the Dow Jones Industrial Average's 30 stocks over several years found that the average serial correlation coefficient was virtually equal to zero. This study also conducted runs tests on price changes for each of the 30 Dow stocks (also over a period of several years) and found evidence supporting the contention that the price series were essentially random.

Let's conduct our own test of the randomness of security prices, using the two series shown in Exhibit 7.1, one the S&P 500 index, the other a random series. We compute several serial correlation coefficients and conduct a runs test on the daily changes for each series. We expect changes in the random walk should probably be random, but what about price changes for the index? The results are shown in Exhibit 7.3.

The serial correlation coefficients are essentially equal to zero. These results confirm that today's price change provides virtually no information about tomorrow's price change. The results of the runs tests reinforce the random nature of price changes for both series. The actual numbers of runs in both series are not significantly different from the number of runs expected for a random series.

Tests of Trading Rules

In addition to tests of the randomness of security prices and returns, several studies have examined trading rules based on historical prices to see if they produce abnormal profits. Weak-form efficiency, of course, states that such trading rules cannot produce abnormal profits. Again, the extensive evidence generally supports weak-form efficiency. Let's look at one example of a trading rule, filter rules.

Essentially, a *filter rule* states that if a stock rises X percent from its most recent low (what's called a support level), buy it, because it has defined an up trend. Similarly, if a stock declines by Y percent from its most recent high (called a resistance level), sell the stock and hold cash (or sell the stock short if you do not own it), because the stock has defined a down trend.

How well do filter rules perform? Not very well, suggests some of the scientific evidence. One study compared buy-sell filters between 0.5 percent and 5 percent on each of the Dow Jones Industrial Average's 30 stocks against a simple buy-and-hold portfolio of those stocks. Only the smallest filter, 0.5 percent, outperformed the buy-and-hold portfolio, on average. The difference in performance, however, disappeared once the authors considered the higher transaction costs associated with the actively

Exhibit 7.3 ♦ TEST OF RANDOMNESS: S&P 500 VERSUS A RANDOM SERIES

	Series	
Autocorrelation (lag)	S&P 500	Random Walk
−1	−0.020	0.000
−2	0.061	−0.002
−3	−0.074	−0.046
−4	−0.033	0.029
−5	−0.117	−0.015
Runs Test		
Actual	119	110
Expected[a]	114	114

[a]Assuming the series is random.

managed portfolio. Portfolios based on the larger filters all under performed the buy-and-hold portfolio, even before accounting for higher transaction costs.

We will repeat a caveat about tests of trading rules: to allow testing, mechanical buy-and-sell criteria must be established. As we discussed earlier in this chapter, forecasts based on trading rules often are by nature more subjective than objective, and they are difficult to replicate. No test can really evaluate the subjective portion.

MARKET REACTION TO NEW PUBLIC INFORMATION

A huge amount of widely varying new public information enters the financial markets each day. Semistrong-form market efficiency states that security prices reflect all this information and react quickly to it. The reaction is so fast, in fact, that no one can consistently earn abnormal profits simply by buying or selling in response to the new public information. Studies have examined market reactions to almost every conceivable type of new public information. Results of these studies generally support the semistrong form of market efficiency. Let's look at some anecdotal evidence first.

On October 20, 1999, IBM announced that its third-quarter earnings were substantially less than analysts had been expecting. Investors bolted for the doors, and the stock lost about 20 percent of its value, falling from over 112 to about 90. Could you have avoided this debacle by selling IBM shares on October 20? Probably not, unless you had access to the information early. You see, IBM made the announcement *after* the New York Stock Exchange closed for the day.[3] By the time the stock opened for trading the next day, October 21, the overnight flood of sell orders had already driven the opening price down to 90¼. IBM closed that day at 89.

This type of anecdotal evidence of semi-strong form market efficiency can be seen almost every day. Companies regularly make significant announcements with

---

[3]Significant information is often released after the close of trading. The fact that new, potentially market-moving information is released throughout the day is one reason cited by proponents of expanded after-hours trading. After the announcement, IBM's stock price dropped sharply on Instinet.

both negative and positive implications. In the majority of cases, much of the reaction takes place either before the announcement or so quickly that most investors can't profit from trading on the information. Scan today's business news on the Internet and you will probably find several examples similar to IBM's—rapid price changes in response to new public information.

Scientific Evidence

Of course, anecdotal evidence in and of itself fails to prove that investors cannot earn abnormal returns by acting on new public information. To find stronger evidence in support of semistrong-form market efficiency, we turn to the various scientific studies. These studies, often called *event studies,* typically examine market reactions to specific kinds of announcements. They analyze a large group of similar announcements using a statistical methodology that measures returns different from what would be expected, given no new information (called *abnormal returns* or *residuals*). Semistrong-form market efficiency implies that no abnormal returns should consistently occur after the announcement date.

To illustrate this approach, and the evidence presented by the vast majority of these studies, let's look at a classic study that examined market reactions to merger/takeover announcements.[4] As you know, shareholders of public companies that are taken over (often referred to as *target shareholders*) receive premium prices for their shares (prices higher than the existing market price). As a result, we would logically expect stock prices to jump in response to a takeover announcement. If the market is semistrong-form efficient, this jump should occur before, and/or on, the announcement date, not afterward.

Exhibit 7.4 summarizes the researchers' results. It plots the cumulative average abnormal residual (CAAR) against trading days relative to the announcement (day 0). The CAAR starts to rise, slowly at first, starting about 30 days before the announcement (day −30), and the trend continues right up to the announcement date (day 0).[5] The two largest increases occur on the day before the announcement date (day 21) and the announcement date itself. The CAAR exhibits random drift after the announcement date (day 11 through day 110). These findings suggest that any significant price reaction of a target company stock relevant to a takeover announcement occurs before the announcement date. No one can earn an abnormal profit by acting on this new public information after it enters the market. This study's results are, therefore, consistent with semistrong-form market efficiency.

Be careful not to over-interpret the results of this and other event studies. For example, let us assume that company A offers to buy company B for $50 cash per share. The price of company B's stock will jump on the announcement. If it does not jump to $50 per share, does that mean that the market is not semistrong-form efficient?

---

[4]Arthur Keown and John Pikerton, "Merger Announcements and Insider Trading," *Journal of Finance*, September 1981, pp. 855–70.

[5]The *CAAR* is the sum of the average abnormal residual up to day t, or $CAAR_t = AAR_t + CAAR_{t-1}$. In the absence of new information of the expected value of *AAR* is zero. Therefore, in the absence of new information, the *CAAR* should exhibit random drift around zero. If investors have reacted to the new information, the *CAR* should rise (positive information) or fall (negative information).

Exhibit 7.4 ✦ EXAMPLE OF THE MARKET REACTION TO NEW PUBLIC INFORMATION: TAKEOVERS

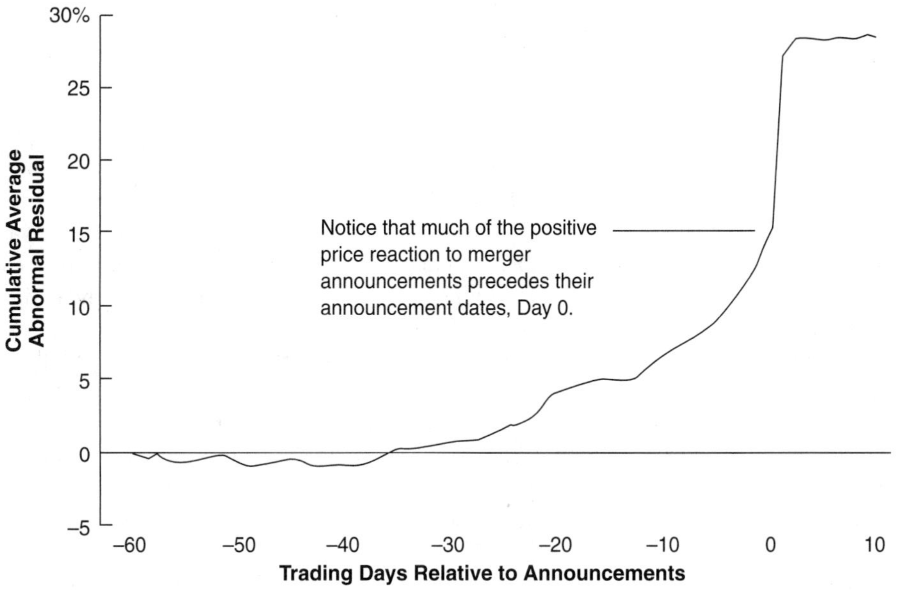

Source: Arthur Keown and John Pinkerton, "Merger Announcements and Insider Trading Activity," The Journal of Finance, September 1981, pp. 855–70.

Not necessarily; think of everything that can happen once a takeover offer becomes public. For one, company A's bid may fail. Even if A does buy B, when the announcement is first made, who can tell just how long the deal will take to complete. For another alternative, company A may be forced to raise its offer price. The point is that takeovers, and many other transactions, are complex and uncertain. As this uncertainty is resolved after the announcement, significant price reactions are likely to occur. We can think of the resolution of uncertainty as new public information.

VALUE OF PRIVATE INFORMATION

Tests of the value of inside, or private, information seek to evaluate strong-form market efficiency. These tests are perhaps the most difficult to conduct because we have no way to pinpoint exactly when new private information, or inside information, enters the market. Further, the definition of inside information is ambiguous. Not surprisingly, the results from these studies are quite mixed.

One group of studies began with the assumption that mutual fund managers and securities analysts may have access to information before the general investing public. Securities analysts, for example, constantly talk to the companies they follow and may be able to learn some new information before it is made public. These studies examined the performance of mutual funds or security analyst recommendations, compared with some benchmark.

Results from these studies generally show that neither mutual fund managers nor securities analysts appear, on average, to consistently outperform the overall market, after adjusting for risk. In fact, the average stock mutual fund has under performed the S&P 500 over the past 10 years.

Does this evidence support strong-form market efficiency, or does it cast doubt on the assumption that mutual fund managers have access to private information? Obviously, we can't answer this question.

Event Studies

Event studies have provided more evidence regarding strong-form efficiency. Notice that Exhibit 7.4 showed evidence of positive price movements in takeover stocks well before the public announcements. Does this suggest that insiders were using private information about upcoming takeovers to make abnormal profits? The authors of the study thought so. They wrote, "Impending merger announcements are poorly held secrets, and trading on this nonpublic information abounds."[6]

Many event studies show the same pattern as Exhibit 7.4. Prices rise, or fall, before the public announcement date. Further, the rise or fall in prices is often gradual, not immediate, suggesting that one can earn abnormal returns by possessing material nonpublic information. Perhaps the markets lack strong-form efficiency. However, because no one knows when private information becomes available, or even what really constitutes private information, perhaps these findings show only that some investors are good at anticipating significant new public information. We cannot say one way or the other.

Market Efficiency and Anomalies

anomaly
A situation that appears to violate the traditional view of market efficiency.

In recent years, many so-called **anomalies** have been identified in the marketplace. Anomalies are situations that appear to violate the traditional view of market efficiency, suggesting that it may be possible for careful investors to earn higher risk-adjusted returns.

Some of the better-known anomalies are listed in Exhibit 7.5. Most of the anomalies listed revolve around four themes:

1. Investors tend to overreact to new information, both positive and negative.
2. Value investing is contrarian in nature and is often profitable because investors tend to overreact.
3. The market consistently ignores certain stocks, especially small stocks.
4. All things being equal, sometimes it is more advantageous to buy stocks whereas other times it better to avoid stocks.

Let's examine some major anomalies, why they exist, and what they mean for investors and the concept of market efficiency.

DO INVESTORS OVERREACT?

One of the most intriguing issues to emerge in the past few years is the notion of market overreaction to new information, whether positive or negative. Many investment

---

[6]Keown and Pinkerton, "Merger Announcements," p. 855. Results of this and other studies prompted the SEC to crack down on insider trading starting in the mid 1980s.

Exhibit 7.5 ✦ SOME STOCK MARKET ANOMALIES

Low Price-Earnings Ratio	Stocks that are selling at price-earnings rations that are low relative to the market
Low Price-Sales Ratio	Stocks that have price-to-sales ratios that are lower compared with other stocks in the same industry or with the overall market
Low Price-to-Book Value Ratio	Stocks whose stock prices are less than their respective book values
High Dividend Yield	Stocks that pay high dividends relative to their respective share prices
Small Companies	Stocks of companies whose market capitalization is less than $100 million
Neglected Stocks	Stocks followed by only a few analysts and/or stocks with low percentages of institutional ownership
Stocks with High Relative Strength	Stocks whose prices have risen faster relative to the overall market
January Effect	Stocks do better during January than during any other month of the year
Day of the Week	Stocks do poorer during Monday than during other days of the week

Source: "Picking Stocks: Techniques That Stand the Test of Time," American Association of Individual Investors, *1994.*

professionals have insisted for years that markets do overreact. Some point to one momentous event, the 1987 market break, as an extreme example of investor overreaction. The Investment History box on page 168 recounts "Meltdown Monday."

Recent statistical evidence for both the market as a whole and individual securities has shown errors in security prices that are systematic and therefore fairly predictable. Overreactions are sometimes called reversals. Stocks that perform poorly in one period suddenly reverse direction and start performing well in a subsequent period, and vice versa.

For example, Merck was one of the poorest performing stocks among the Dow 30 during 1993, only to reverse direction and rank among the top performers during 1994. In 1997 DuPont ranked among the best performing stocks in the Dow 30 until it reversed direction in 1998 and finished close to the bottom of Dow 30 in terms of total performance.

Anecdotal Evidence of Market Overreaction

After the market closed on July 19, 1999, software giant Microsoft announced its quarterly earnings. On the surface the company's earnings were impressive. Earnings grew by over 60 percent, compared with the same quarter in 1998, beating analyst forecasts by 5 cents per share. Yet when stock opened for trading the following day, the price fell by more than 5 percent. Why? Apparently many investors were spooked by comments made by Microsoft's CFO forecasting a slowdown in future revenue growth. Most analysts immediately concluded that the market overreacted. They noted that even with a slowdown in revenue growth, Microsoft's earnings would continue to grow at an impressive rate due to lower costs and higher margins. Several

THE 1987 MARKET BREAK: MELTDOWN MONDAY

On October 19, 1987, stocks suffered their worst one-day decline in history. The Dow Jones Industrial Average lost more than 500 points that day. In percentage terms, the Dow's decline on October 19, 1987, was far greater than its decline on October 29, 1929 (23 percent versus 12 percent). The S&P 500 dropped more than 50 points (a decline of 20 percent). Even relatively stable utilities dropped sharply. The S&P utilities index, for example, fell by more than 19 points (18 percent) on October 19, 1987.

Much has already been written about the causes of the 1987 market break. Some have argued that it was the result of rampant speculation in stocks; others have blamed the break on program trading; still others have blamed it on simple investor panic. In our view, all three factors probably contributed to what became known as Meltdown Monday. Did it mark the end of a period of speculative frenzy similar to that of the 1920s or was it a simple, albeit extreme case of overreaction? Perhaps both.

The table below puts the 1987 market break into some perspective. Stocks had risen rapidly throughout 1987, before the break. The S&P 500 added more than 90 points (about 38 percent) between the end of 1986 and August 25, when the index peaked at 336.8. Many individual stocks did much better. Ford, for example, more than doubled between the end of 1986 and its high in the summer of 1987.

During the late summer and early fall of 1987, some investors began to worry that stocks were becoming overvalued. The average price/earnings ratio of the S&P 500 stocks had risen from 16.7 to 21.1. Interest rates were also rising. The yield on long-term Treasury bonds, for example, had risen 1.5 percent between January and August. Stocks started to drift lower throughout September and the first week of October. The S&P 500 lost about 30 points between August 25 and October 14.

Then matters got serious. Several reports of bad economic news were released, fueling fears of inflation and recession. Also, interest rates continued to climb; the yield on long-term Treasury bonds crossed a psychological barrier at 10 percent several days before the market break. Friday, October 16, was a bad day for stocks. The S&P 500 lost more than 16 points (about 5 percent), and trading volume was heavy.

Over the weekend, many investors apparently hit the panic button. By the time the U.S. markets opened Monday morning, thousands of sell orders were waiting. (Markets in Asia and Europe had already experienced sharp sell-offs.) Prices tumbled from the opening bell. Falling prices triggered sell commands in computer trading programs, driving prices even lower. By the time the dust settled, the S&P 500 had lost more than 58 points, or about 21 percent of its value. The stocks shown in the table below all took big hits. Ford, for example, dropped more than points, to about 34. NYSE trading volume on October 19, 1987, set a record, exceeding 600 million shares.

Following many anxious days after Meltdown Monday, the markets stabilized by the end of the year. The Federal Reserve quickly intervened to prevent any liquidity crisis. No major banks or brokerage firms failed. Interest rates started to fall (the yield on the long Treasury bond was down to about 9 percent by the end of 1987), and no recession materialized. Unlike the 1929 crash, which ushered in a prolonged bear market, the 1987 market break was only a temporary setback. The S&P 500 broke its earlier 1987 record on July 26, 1989, and crossed the 300-point mark again on April 14, 1989. The individual stocks listed in the table below had all recovered from Meltdown Monday by 1989. In retrospect, Meltdown Monday presented investors with a historic buying opportunity.

STOCK AND INDEX VALUES AROUND MELTDOWN MONDAY

Stock/Index	Opening (1987)	High (1987)	Closing Price (10/19/87)	High (1989)
Ford	28⅛	56⅜	34¼	56⅝
General Electric	43	66⅜	41⅞	64
Microsoft	24⅛	39⅝	22⅝	44⅝
Wal-Mart Stores	23	42⅞	26⅝	44⅞
S&P 500	242.2	336.8	224.8	359.8
Dow 30	1,895.95	2,722.42	1,738.74	2,791.41
Nasdaq Composite	348.83	455.26	291.88	485.73

investment firms reiterated buy recommendations on the stock. Within a few days, Microsoft's stock had recovered from the July 20th sell-off. This kind of anecdotal evidence of market overreaction arises almost daily.

Scientific Evidence of Market Overreaction

In addition to widespread anecdotal evidence of market overreaction, researchers have compiled considerable scientific evidence of reversals. Several studies have found that stock returns over longer time horizons (in excess of one year) display significant negative serial correlation. This means that high returns in one time period tend to be followed by low returns in the next period, and vice versa.

Others studies have tested for market overreaction by forming portfolios of winners and losers based on performance over a specific time period and measuring performance over subsequent periods of time. One study, for example, found that over the next year a portfolio of "losers" earned about 15 percent more than a portfolio of "winners."[7]

Reversals and Other Anomalies

Market overreaction may offer the best explanation for several of the anomalies listed in Exhibit 7.5. For example, low price-to-earnings ratio (P/E) stocks may be analogous to the losers described above, or they may simply be out of favor with investors. However, high-P/E stocks may be current investor favorites, or winners. As the market demonstrates almost daily, today's favorite stocks can fall from grace and quickly reverse direction.

Why Do Investors Overreact?

Behavioral finance is a fast-growing, relatively new field of study that considers the influence of psychology on investor behavior.[8] Behavioral finance explains investor overreaction in the context of **representativeness**—judgments based on stereotypes. In an investment context, some argue that representativeness leads investors to become overly optimistic about past winners while becoming overly pessimistic about past losers. Therefore, prices of past winners tend to get too high, relative to their fundamental value, while prices of past losers tend to get too low. Eventually, though the mispricing corrects itself and losers outperform winners over subsequent periods of time.

representativeness
Judgments based on stereotypes.

PROFITING FROM REVERSALS

Market overreaction and reversals suggest several possible investment strategies that may product abnormal profits for investors. Some possibilities include buying last

---

[7]See Werner DeBondt and Richard Thaler, "Does the Stock Market Overreact?" *Journal of Finance*, July 1985, p. 800.

[8]A good, readable guide to behavioral finance is Hersh Shefrin's *Beyond Freed and Greed: Understanding Behavioral Finance and the Psychology of Investing*, Boston, MA: Harvard Business School Press, 2000.

INVESTMENT INSIGHTS

THE DOW DIVIDEND STRATEGY

One popular investment strategy is clearly based on contrarian or value investing. It's called the Dow Dividend Strategy. It's a simple strategy consisting of three steps:

1. At the end of the year, rank the Dow 30 stocks from highest to lowest based on dividend yield. Dividend yield equals dividends divided by price per share, so a stock with a dividend of $1.50 per share and a price of $50 per share has a dividend yield of 5 percent ($1.50 divided by $50).
2. Buy equal dollar amounts of the ten Dow stocks with the highest dividend yields.
3. Hold the portfolio for one year; at the end of the following year repeat the first two steps (rank the Dow by dividend yield and buy—or

keep—the 10 stocks with the highest dividend yields).

Clearly the Dow Dividend Strategy is a contrarian/value-based investment strategy. High dividend yields have long been used as a measure of value, indicating stocks that are out of favor with the market. But does it work? According to Jeremy Siegel, the answer is a smashing yes. Take a look at the table below. It shows the average annual performance of the Dow 10, compared to the overall Dow 30 and S&P 500 (both buy and hold) over varying periods of time.

Before you invest next year's tuition money into the Dow's highest dividend-yielding stocks, consider the following: First, the Dow Dividend Strategy is extremely tax inefficient. Because you're buying and selling more frequently than you would if you bought and held, you'll end up losing more of your profits to taxes. Second, you'll pay more in transactions costs. And, as with all strategies, what worked in the past may not work in the future. Indeed, there is *some* evidence that the Dow Dividend Strategy isn't working as well now as it did in past years.

TIME PERIOD	DOW 10 STOCKS	DOW 30	S&P 500
1928–97	13.21%	11.40%	10.64%
1940–97	15.91	12.71	12.46
1970–97	18.04	13.75	12.83
1990–97	19.45	16.83	16.57

Source: Jeremy Siegel, Stocks for the Long Run, *2nd ed. (New York: McGraw-Hill, 1998), p. 66.*

contrarian (or value) investing
Buying what is out of favor with most investors.

year's worst-performing stocks, avoiding stocks with higher than average P/E ratios, or buying stocks on bad news. At the risk of oversimplifying, any investment strategy based on market overreaction represents a **contrarian,** or **value** approach to investing—buying what appears to be out of favor with the majority of investors. The Investment Insights box above describes one well-known contrarian approach to picking stocks.

Contrarian/value investing has several strong proponents in the investment community. Respected professionals such as Warren Buffet, Mario Gabelli, the late Benjamin Graham, Peter Lynch, and John Templeton all embrace aspects of contrarian/value investing. But can an investor consistently earn higher risk adjusted returns by following the popular value-oriented strategies, such as those listed in Exhibit 7.5?

Considerable evidence suggests that the answer to both questions may indeed be yes. The results of one study of value investing is shown in Exhibit 7.6. The study was conducted by respected investment professional James O'Shaughnessy. He compared the records of dozens of stock selection methods using data from 1952 through 1997. O'Shaughnessy's results generally support the notion that contrarian/value investing may indeed work. He found that buying stocks with low price-to-sales ratios, low

Exhibit 7.6 ✦ WHAT APPEARS TO WORK FOR INVESTORS

Strategy	Average Annual Return (1952–97)
High relative strength	14.28%
Low price-to-book value	14.30
Low price-to-cash flow	14.02
Low price to sales	13.67
Low price to earnings	13.61
Buy and hold (S&P 500)	11.51

Source: James O'Shaughnessy, What Works on Wall Street, *2nd ed. (New York: McGraw-Hill, 1998).*

price-to-book ratios, or low P/E ratios produced returns that were higher, on average, than those from the overall market, even after adjusting for higher transactions costs and differences in risk. For example, a strategy where an investor buys a set number of stocks with the lowest price-to-sales ratios produced an average annual compound return of 13.7 percent between 1952 and 1997. In comparison, a buy-and-hold strategy produced an average annual compound return of 11.5 percent over the sample period.[9]

SOME CAVEATS ABOUT CONTRARIAN/VALUE INVESTING

Although value investing appears quite attractive, it requires several caveats. First, it is important to remember that good fundamental reasons may be driving reversals. Reversing prices may be more a response to new information than the correction of an overreaction.

Second, stocks with low P/E ratios are not necessarily cheap, nor are stocks with high P/E ratios necessarily expensive. The inverse relationship between value and P/E ratios (or other measures such as price-to-book ratios) is far from perfect. Some stocks may have low (or high) P/E ratios for good reasons. Further, value is definitely in the eye of the beholder. Recently, one mutual fund manager described Cisco Systems as a value stock even though it had P/E ratio at the time in excess of 65!

Third, although we see evidence of overreactions and reversals, we *also* see evidence that stocks occasionally get stuck on one-way streets, meaning that poor or good performance persists for long periods of time. One study found evidence of significant positive serial correlation in security returns.[10] O'Shaughnessy's findings also bear this out. Although value measures based on investment strategies outperformed

---

[9]While 2.2 percent per year may not seem like much, compounded over 45 years it adds up to a huge difference in wealth. A thousand dollars invested in 1952 in a value portfolio—based on low price-to-sales—was worth almost $1.2 million by the end of 1997. A thousand dollars invested in a buy-and-hold portfolio in 1952 was worth *only* $398,000 by the end 1997.

[10]Andrew Lo and A. Craig MacKinlay, "Stock Prices do not Follow Random Walks," *Review of Financial Studies*, Spring 1988, pp. 41–66.

the overall market, he found that a strategy based on buying last year's winners beat all the value-oriented strategies.[11]

Finally, past success is never a guarantee of future success. Think about what would happen if every investor suddenly became a contrarian. If contrarian investing really does offer consistently higher investment returns, it would not be unreasonable to expect the wise investors to exploit these opportunities aggressively. Abnormal returns would eventually disappear and value investing would no longer work. On the other hand, according to behavioral finance, two behavioral phenomena make it difficult for most people to become contrarian investors: regret and hindsight bias.[12]

CALENDAR-BASED ANOMALIES

Are certain times better to own stocks than others? Should you avoid stocks on certain days? The evidence seems to suggest that several calendar-based anomalies exist. The two best known, and widely documented, are the weekend effect and the January effect.

Weekend Effect

Studies of daily returns began with the goal of testing whether the markets operate on calendar time or trading time. In other words, are returns for Mondays—which is actually the Friday-to-Monday period—different from returns for other days of the week? Some studies concluded that the answer was indeed yes.[13] One study found that returns on Mondays were substantially less than returns for any other day of the week.

The January Effect

Some evidence suggests that stock returns often exhibit seasonal return patterns meaning that returns are systematically higher in some months than in others. Initial studies found that returns were higher in January for all stocks (thus this anomaly was dubbed the **January effect**), whereas later studies found the January effect was more pronounced for small stocks than for large ones.[14]

For evidence of seasonal patterns in stock returns, look at the chart in Exhibit 7.7. The chart illustrates average monthly total returns between 1926 and 1999 for both

January effect
Stock returns are higher in January than during other months of the year.

---

[11]O'Shaughnessy used a common measure, relative strength, to identify winners and losers. (We'll talk more about relative strength and market momentum in the next chapter.) He found that buying the stocks with the highest relative strength produced an average annual compound return of 14.3 percent between 1952 and 1997. Interestingly, O'Shaughnessy also found that combining relative strength with various value measures greatly improved performance.

[12]See Shefrin, *Beyond Greed and Fear*, pp. 84–86.

[13]See Burton Malkiel, *A Random Walk Down Wall Street* (rev. ed.), New York: Norton, 1999, pp. 247–49; and Jeremy Siegel, *Stocks for the Long Run* (2nd ed.), New York: McGraw-Hill, 1998, pp. 264–66.

[14]See Malkiel, *A Random Walk Down Wall Street*, pp. 247–49; and Siegel, *Stocks for the Long Run*, pp. 254–63.

Exhibit 7.7 ✦ SEASONAL PATTERNS IN STOCK RETURNS

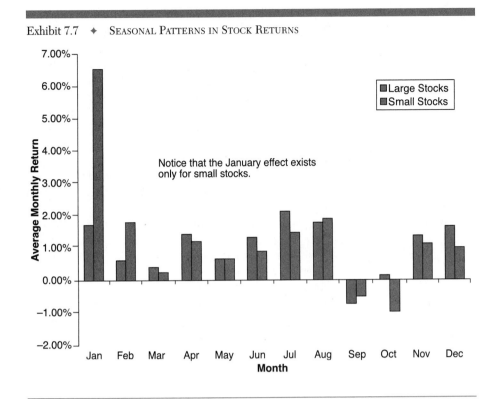

large and small stocks. Although average January returns from large stocks are impressive (about 21 percent on an annual basis), two other months (July and August) have provided higher average total returns. However, January returns from small stocks are four times higher than average total returns from any other month. (Average January returns are a stratospheric 119 percent on an annual basis.)

One widely accepted explanation for the January effect is tax-loss selling by investors at the end of December. Because this selling pressure depresses prices at the end of the year, it would be reasonable to expect a bounce-back in prices during January. Small stocks, the argument goes, are more susceptible to the January effect because their prices are more volatile, and institutional investors (many of whom are tax-exempt) are less likely to invest in shares of small companies.

CALENDAR-BASED TRADING STRATEGIES

Both seasonal and day-of-the-week effects are inconsistent with market efficiency because both suggest that historical information can generate abnormal profits. As with all anomalies, however, a more important issue is whether seasonal and day-of-the-week effects can create profit opportunities for investors. Should you, for example, always buy stocks at the close of trading on Mondays and sell them at the close of trading on Wednesdays?

Although differences in daily returns appear impressive, they are probably much too small to offset transaction costs. The daily mean return on Wednesdays, for example, is only 0.097 percent. A purchase at the end of trading on Tuesday followed by a sale at the end of trading on Wednesday, based on the mean Wednesday return, would earn only about $9.70 on a $10,000 investment, a profit that would be gobbled up by commissions. Even E*Trade charges about $15 per trade.

The January effect appears to have far more profit potential. For example, the average January return suggests that buying a portfolio of small stocks at the end of December and selling them at the end of January will produce an extra profit of about $679 per $10,000 invested, probably more than enough to offset the added transactions cost.

If this sounds too good to be true, that is because it probably is. The average January return of about 6.7 percent from small stocks is just that, a historical average. It hides substantial year-to-year variation in January returns. In January 1990, for example, small stocks produced a total return of −7.6 percent. Remember, the past is never a guarantee of the future.

Another reason we are skeptical that an investor can exploit the January effect to produce abnormal profits goes back to a point we have made over and over again in this chapter: Once profitable investment strategies are recognized, it is reasonable to expect other investors to aggressively exploit them, eventually eliminating the profit potential. This may be happening to the January effect. Entire books have been published about this widely recognized anomaly, and it may be disappearing.

For example, Exhibit 7.8 shows average monthly returns for small stocks between 1990 and 1999. Notice that the January effect appears far less pronounced during this more recent period. This suggests that investors have become aware of the January effect and have adjusted their buying and selling behavior accordingly.

THE SMALL-FIRM EFFECT

We saw in Chapter 2 that stocks of small companies have substantially outperformed stocks of large companies since 1926. An initial investment of $1,000 in large-firm stocks, made at the beginning of 1926, would be worth about $2.5 million today. By contrast, $1,000 invested in small-firm stocks at the same time would be worth in excess of $5 million today. Of course, history has also shown that small stocks have exhibited far more year-to-year variation than large stocks. However, even after correcting for differences in risk, some studies suggest that investors can earn abnormal profits by investing in shares of small companies, exploiting the small-firm effect.

Two explanations for the small-firm effect seem plausible to us. The first is that analysts have applied the wrong risk measures to evaluate returns from small stocks. Small stocks may well be riskier than these traditional risk measures indicate. If proper risk measures were used, the argument goes, the small-firm effect might disappear. Small-firm stocks may not generate larger risk-adjusted returns than large stocks. Although the risk of small stocks may not be adequately captured by standard risk measures, it is hard to believe that better measures of risk would eliminate the entire small-firm effect.

Another explanation for the small-firm effect is that large institutional investors (for example, pension funds) often overlook small-firm stocks. Consequently, less information is available on small companies. (They are also followed by fewer analysts.) One could argue that this information deficiency makes small-firm stocks riskier investments, but one could also argue that discovery of a neglected small-firm stock by the institutions could send its price rising as the institutions start buying it. The small-firm effect may arise from the continuous process of discovery of neglected small-firm stocks leading to purchases by institutional investors.

Exhibit 7.8　✦　AVERAGE MONTHLY RETURNS FROM SMALL STOCKS: 1990–97

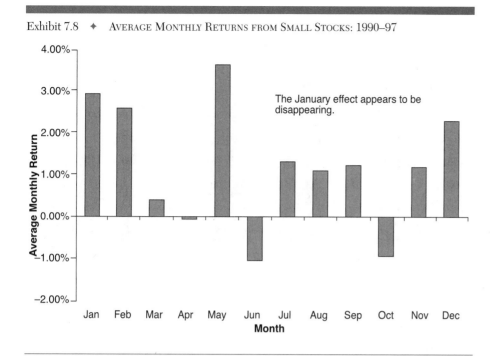

The January effect appears to be disappearing.

Whatever the explanation, small-firm stocks, although riskier than large-firm stocks, have historically provided substantial returns to investors, higher than those produced by large-firm stocks. Unfortunately, like other anomalies, the small-firm effect may have run its course. Take a look at the chart shown in Exhibit 7.9, which shows the annualized average returns for large and small stocks over varying periods, ending December 31, 1998. Although small stocks beat large stocks over the longer periods, the reverse has been true over more time periods. For example, during the five-year period, ending on December 31, 1998, large stocks outperformed small stocks by an average of more than 10 percent per year.

PERFORMANCE OF INVESTMENT PROFESSIONALS

As we have seen, both in the prior chapter and in this one, investments professionals such as pension fund managers or mutual fund managers seem to have a difficult time beating the overall market. We know that the performance of the average mutual fund has lagged the market over the past 10 years, for example.

Of course, this is an average figure. In any particular year, some professionals will beat the market and others will not. The key question is whether some professionals can consistently outperform the market. Some evidence suggests that the answer to this question may be yes.

The Value Line Enigma

The performance of investment advisory services has been examined as well. The well-known investment advisory firm Value Line gives each of the 1,700 or so stocks it follows a timeliness rating of between 1 and 5 (1 being the highest). Several studies

Exhibit 7.9 ✦ PERFORMANCE OF LARGE AND SMALL STOCKS

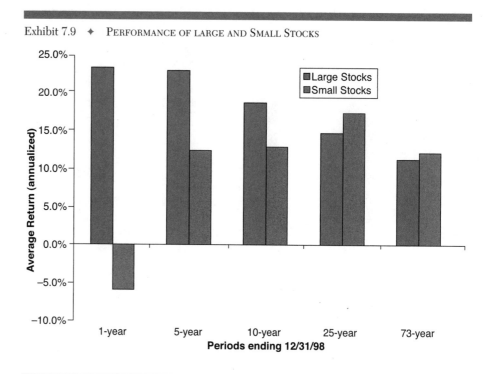

have examined the predictive value of the Value Line ranking system.[15] These studies have found that an investor who bought stocks with Value Line rankings of 1, and avoided or sold stocks with rankings of 5, would have earned abnormal returns. Financial columnist Mark Hulbert found that the Value Line system produced an average return about 4.5 percent higher than that of the overall stock market.

Playing Hot Hands

Several studies show that the past performance of mutual fund and pension fund managers is a good predictor of their future performance. For example, a comprehensive study of mutual fund performance found that the past performance of stock mutual funds was strongly, and positively, related to subsequent performance.[16] A study of pension fund managers found that more than 65 percent of the top-ranked managers, based on past performance, ranked above average in performance over subsequent periods.[17]

---

[15]See, for example, Thomas Copeland and David Myers, "The Value Line Enigma," *Journal of Financial Economics,* November 1982, pp. 289–321.

[16]James Philpot, *Performance Related Characteristics of Mutual Funds,* Ph.D. dissertation, University of Arkansas, Fayetteville, AR, 1994.

[17]Josef Lakonishok, et al., "The Structure and Performance of the Money Management Industry," *Brookings Papers on Economic Activity* (Washington, DC: Brookings Institute), pp. 339–79, 1992.

So, Are the Markets Efficient?

Today, it is fashionable, both in academia and on Wall Street, to discuss the pending demise of the old EMH. Well, we are not quite yet ready to bury it, but a considerable amount of evidence does contradict it, and more evidence seems to emerge daily. However, a considerable amount of evidence still supports the concept of market efficiency.[18] And even if the markets are not efficient in an academic sense, they may be efficient in a more practical sense. In most parts of the world, the financial markets are well-functioning, competitive institutions in which consistent abnormal profits based on public or historical information are rare.

There is an often-repeated joke about a Wall Street trader and a finance professor walking down the street. The trader notices a $100 bill lying on the street and stops to pick it up. "Why bother?" the finance professor says, "If it had really been a $100 bill, someone would already have grabbed it."

In one sense, this joke sums up the debate over market efficiency. An unquestioning acceptance of the EMH and subsequent rejection of all investment analysis and research as worthless can leave a lot of money lying on the street for someone else. Real-world situations and investor psychology defy a strict view of market efficiency often enough to justify the careful search for undervalued (and overvalued) securities. However, one should always be skeptical of someone who claims to have a clever system or special insight to consistently beat the market. Not too many $100 bills are lying on the sidewalk, waiting to be picked up. As Mark Hulbert, not exactly a true believer of the EMH, once observed, making money consistently in the stock market is darned hard, but it is possible.

Chapter Summary

1. What is the efficient-markets hypothesis?

    The efficient markets hypothesis (EMH) states that security prices fully reflect all available information and that thus it is impossible to earn above-average returns by using this information. Price changes may appear to follow a random walk. The source of market efficiency may be competition, thousands of investors constantly searching for the best investments. The efficient-markets hypothesis raises a number of questions concerning the value of the two techniques used by many professional investors: technical and fundamental analysis. Further, the efficient-markets hypothesis suggests that passive investing is superior to active investing.

2. What are the three traditional forms of market efficiency?

    There are three traditional forms of the efficient-markets hypothesis. The weak form states that security prices fully reflect all historical information and using historical information to make buy and sell decisions will not produce abnormal profits. The semistrong form states that prices reflect all historical information and react quickly to new public information. The strong form states that prices fully reflect all historical, public, and private information.

3. How is the efficient-markets hypothesis tested?

    The efficient-markets hypothesis can be tested either directly by assessing how well trading rules and investment strategies work. It can also be tested indirectly by examining the statistical properties of security returns. Numerous issues arise regarding

---

[18]See, for example, Eugene Fama, "Efficiency Survives the Attack of the Anomalies," *Alumni Bulletin*, Graduate School of Business, University of Chicago, Winter 1998, pp. 14–16.

testing the efficient-markets hypothesis. These include the type of test used, the establishment of a benchmark, and the time period used to test the EMH. In addition, investors have strong incentive to keep profitable trading strategies to themselves.

4. Does evidence support the efficient-markets hypothesis?

Considerable evidence supports at least the weak and semistrong forms of the EMH. Numerous tests suggest that past prices are of little value in predicting future prices. Evidence also shows that security prices adjust quickly to new public information. Some evidence, however, suggests that private information has value.

5. Can investors profit from anomalies?

An anomaly is a situation that appears to contradict the efficient markets hypothesis. Numerous anomalies have been identified. Many are based on the observation that investors overreact and thus a value or contrarian approach to investing can be profitable. Other anomalies include calendar-based effects and the small-firm effect. In addition, the fact that some professional investors—mutual fund and pension fund managers, for example—appear to consistently beat the market can also be considered to be an anomaly.

Review Questions and Problems

1. Define the term *random walk*. Does a random walk imply that stock prices will be independent of each other?

2. If a series follows a random walk, what is the best forecast of tomorrow's price? Why?

3. How does competition produce an efficient market? What does competition imply about the future success of trading rules?

4. What are the implications of market efficiency for technical and fundamental analysis? Why, in an efficient market, is a passive approach to investing superior to an active approach?

5. Distinguish between the weak, semistrong, and strong forms of market efficiency. What is meant by *all available information?*

6. Explain the difference between a direct test of market efficiency and an indirect test. What major issues affect the selection of methods to test the EMH?

7. What is meant by *sample selection bias?* How does sample selection bias apply to tests of market efficiency?

8. Define the term *serial correlation*. If security returns follow a random walk, what results should you obtain from a serial correlation test?

9. Compute the number of runs in the following series of 20 daily stock prices. Do the price changes appear to be random?

Day	Price	Day	Price
1	$30.25	11	$33.00
2	30.50	12	33.25
3	30.75	13	33.00
4	32.25	14	33.50
5	31.75	15	33.75
6	31.25	16	33.50
7	32.00	17	34.00
8	32.25	18	34.25
9	32.00	19	34.75
10	32.75	20	35.00

10. What is a filter rule? Describe how you would go about testing a filter rule.

11. Explain how you would go about testing how rapidly security prices respond to new public information. What would you look for?

12. What is meant by the term *reversal*? Explain how an investor might profit from a reversal.

13. Discuss an investment strategy that you would classify as contrarian. What are some issues regarding contrarian/value investing?

14. What is the January effect? How are the January and small-firm effects related?

15. Discuss the small-firm effect. What causes it?

CFA Questions

1. (Level I, 1993) A random walk occurs when
   a. stock price changes are random but predictable.
   b. stock prices respond slowly to both new and old information.
   c. future price changes are uncorrelated with past price changes.
   d. past information is useful in predicting future prices.

2. (Level I, 1993) The semistrong form of the efficient-markets hypothesis asserts that stock prices
   a. fully reflect all historical price information.
   b. fully reflect all publicly available information.
   c. fully reflect all relevant information, including insider information.
   d. may be predictable.

3. (Level I, 1993) Assume a company announces an unexpectedly large cash dividend to its shareholders. In an efficient market *without* information leakage, one might expect
   a. an abnormal price change at the announcement.
   b. an abnormal price increase before the announcement.
   c. an abnormal price decrease after the announcement.
   d. no abnormal price change before or after the announcement.

4. (Level III, 1994) Mrs. Goode is now very interested in learning about the background for investment decision making and has done extensive reading in textbooks as well as the popular investment-oriented press. However, she is confused about a number of terms and concepts, particularly as to how they interrelate. You have been asked to help her make sense out of some of these terms and concepts.
   ✦ Mrs. Goode has read that there are two traditional approaches to equity valuation: technical and fundamental. Define each of these approaches and discuss the key premise underlying each approach.
   ✦ Mrs. Goode favors the fundamental approach to valuation but has read that the efficient-markets hypothesis presents a challenge to that approach. Briefly describe the three forms of the EMH. Identify which of the three forms most directly challenges fundamental analysis and explain your choice.

CRITICAL THINKING EXERCISES

1. This exercise requires computer work. Open the Index worksheet in the Data Workbook. The worksheet lists daily values for the Nasdaq Composite Index over a recent two-year period. Use the data to perform the following exercises and answer the following questions.
   a. Compute the daily percentage change. Plot both the index and the percentage change against time.
   b. Compute the daily change in the index value. Plot the changes. Do they appear to be random? Explain your answer.
   c. Design a filter rule. Set your filter no lower than 0.5 percent and no higher than 2.5 percent.

    d.   Identify when the filter says to buy or sell.

    e.   Evaluate how well your filter worked. In other words, did your filter give you correct buy and sell signals?

    f.   If you had simply bought the Nasdaq Composite at the beginning of the period and held it until the end of the period, how well would you have done? Is the buy-and-hold approach performance better or worse than your filter's performance? (Ignore dividends.)

2. This exercise requires both computer work and library/Internet research. Open the Dow worksheet in the Data Workbook. The worksheet contains end-of-year dividend yields and annual total returns for the Dow 30 stocks between 1991 and 1999.

    a.   Rank the stocks by dividend yield.

    b.   Using library sources or a computer database, collect annual data on sales, earnings, dividends, and year-end prices for each of the Dow 30 stocks for the period 1990 through 1998.

    c.   Calculate the price earnings, sales-to-price, and market-to-book-value ratios for each stock for each year. Also, calculate the change in price from year to year. Rank the stocks by each measure.

    d.   Compare the rankings for one year with the total returns for the next. Do you see any patterns? For example, do stocks with low market-to-book-value ratios consistently outperform stocks with high market-to-book-value ratios?

    e.   Discuss your findings with respect to the market anomalies described in the chapter.

THE INTERNET INVESTOR

1. Visit one of the major on-line booksellers (www.amazon.com or www.bn.com). Search the available titles and identify those dealing with value or contrarian investing. Read the synopsis of each title and prepare a brief report, including whether or not you would recommend the title to a novice investor.

2. Review the recent financial news and identify an announcement that appears to offer significant new information. Look at a chart of the stock price for several days around the announcement. (A variety of investment-oriented web sites provide charts including quote.yahoo.com and investor.msn.com.) Using the information you collected, answer the following questions:

    a.   How did the company's stock react to the announcement?

    b.   How rapidly did the stock price react to the announcement?

    c.   Can you detect any leakage of new information before the announcement date? Why or why not?

    d.   Would you classify the stock price reaction as an overreaction? Explain your answer.

3. The efficient-markets hypothesis is not widely popular among many on Wall Street, yet almost every investment firm attempts to explain the EMH to investors. Visit the following two web sites. Go to the investor education section and read their descriptions of the EMH. Prepare a report comparing and contrasting each description.

      www.vanguard.com

      www.fidelity.com

TECHNICAL AND FUNDAMENTAL ANALYSIS: HOW THE PROS MAKE INVESTMENT DECISIONS

PREVIOUSLY . . .

We examined the efficient-markets hypothesis, the notion that security prices reflect all available information. We reviewed implications of the EMH, the evidence supporting it, and the evidence against it.

IN THIS CHAPTER . . .

Part 2 ends with a discussion of technical and fundamental analysis—the two techniques by which most professional investors make decisions. We will describe each technique, give some reasons why it might work, and review how well each technique works in actual practice.

TO COME . . .

We move on to a detailed examination of one of the major investment alternatives, fixed-income securities. We describe how fixed-income securities are priced and the major risks facing bond investors.

Chapter Objectives

After reading Chapter 8, you should be able to answer the following questions:

1. How do technical and fundamental analyses differ?
2. What are some technical indicators?
3. How well does technical analysis work?
4. What is the process of fundamental analysis?
5. How well does fundamental analysis work?

In Chapter 4 we made the point that, on average, mutual funds rarely outperform the overall market. These funds, actively managed by investment professionals, often fail to match the performance of an unmanaged stock portfolio. In 1998, for example, more than 70 percent of all domestic stock mutual funds failed to match the performance of the S&P 500 index. And 1998 was hardly unusual. Over the ten-year period ending December 31, 1998, the average domestic stock mutual fund had an average annual return of about 15.2 percent. By contrast, the S&P 500 Stock Index produced an average annual return of 19.2 percent over the same 10-year period.

This is not an isolated example. In late August 1996, a well-known market technician finally turned bullish on stocks.[1] He had recommended avoiding stocks since April 1994. Anyone who followed his advice missed out on a substantial increase in stock prices; between April 1994 and August 1996, the S&P 500 added more than 250 points, a 50 percent increase. Because professional investment advice is rarely free—managers of stock mutual funds collect an average fee of about 1 percent per year and an annual subscription to a technician's newsletter can costs several hundred dollars—you might legitimately ask if professional investment advice is worth the cost.

In prior chapters, we've argued that all investors should approach investment advice with a healthy degree of skepticism. Here we present a critical examination of the two techniques by which most professional investors make their investment recommendations and decisions. Most rely on either technical or fundamental analysis, or some combination of the two, to make decisions. Our discussion of fundamental analysis will be fairly general in this chapter. The process of fundamental analysis will be covered in depth in Part 4 (Chapters 11–14).

Technical Versus Fundamental Analysis

In Chapter 7 we broadly defined both technical and fundamental analysis. Now, let's be more specific. *Technical analysis* refers to a broad group of indicators, all based on the belief that past patterns in security prices can reliably predict future price patterns. Technical analysts believe that these patterns reflect the changing attitudes of investors to a variety of economic, political, and psychological factors. Technical analysis has been applied to stock indexes, individual stocks, bonds, foreign currencies, and many other investments. Those who believe in, or at least pay attention to, technical analysis are much more interested in a stock's past price record than how much the company is really worth.

Fundamental analysis, however, is based on the notion that every security has an intrinsic value. For common stocks, that value is based on the company's expected future earnings and dividend payments, the expected growth rate of those earnings and dividends, and the degree of uncertainty surrounding these forecasts. Fundamental analysts, or fundamentalists, believe that the intrinsic value of a security can be estimated and that it will eventually sell for this intrinsic value. Fundamentalists search for undervalued or overvalued securities, securities whose prices are out of line with their intrinsic values, hoping to profit from the price correction.

Both technical and fundamental analysts believe that security prices depend on the interaction of supply and demand, but they each look at different factors to evaluate supply and demand. Fundamentalists believe that supply and demand are determined, at least in the long run, by such factors as the growth rate in earnings and dividends. Although technicians agree that intrinsic value plays a role in determining supply and demand, they argue that a wide range of other rational and irrational factors (for example, investor emotions) governs these relationships. As a result, a technician would not hesitate to recommend a stock with indications of good technical strength, even if the stock appeared to be selling for more than its intrinsic value. In the technician's view, a favorable market supply-and-demand relationship is all that matters. Likewise, if the technician thought that a stock had poor supply-and-demand

---

[1] Mark Hulbert, "Long Term Bear Turns Bullish," *Forbes*, September 23, 1996, p. 238.

characteristics, he or she probably would not recommend the stock regardless of the relationship of its current price to its intrinsic value.

Understanding Technical Analysis

Double bottoms, head and shoulder formations, resistance levels, trend lines, and relative strength are all part of the sometimes strange language of technical analysis. No subject in investments has as many critics as technical analysis. At the same time, however, technical analysis has a core of almost fanatical believers.

Technicians have developed literally dozens of technical indicators. Sometimes it seems like there are more indicators than technicians. And often technicians disagree on how a particular indicator is calculated or interpreted. Given space constraints, we'll review just a few of the better-known indicators, divided into the following somewhat rough and arbitrary categories: charts, investor sentiment measures, and measures of market momentum.[2]

CHARTING

Perhaps the best-known form of technical analysis is *charting*. Technicians plot the past price history of a security or index and examine the chart for patterns that suggest shifts in the underlying supply and demand relationship and indicate shifts in investor attitudes. Anyone can draw a chart similar to the one shown in Exhibit 8.1. In fact, most investment-oriented web sites have excellent charting capabilities.

Although generating a chart may not be difficult, interpreting it is another matter. Because a technician believes that historical price patterns accurately predict the future, the key lies in recognizing the patterns and understanding what they mean. The history of charting can be traced back to a series of writings by Charles Dow in the late 1800s. These writings formed the basis for the so-called Dow Theory.[3]

Dow Theory

The Dow Theory is based on the assumption that a demonstrated trend in stock prices will continue until a reversal in investor attitudes—from bullish to bearish, or from bearish to bullish—occurs. The theory identifies three types of moves in stock prices: primary, secondary, and minor. The *primary movement* is the major, or overall trend in prices. The primary movement can be toward either rising prices (bull market) or falling prices (bear market). Within each primary move, prices can show secondary and minor movements. *Secondary movements* are defined as large changes (33 to 67 percent of the primary change) in the opposite direction from the primary move; secondary movements bring declines in bull markets or advances in bear markets. *Minor movements* are small advances or declines that last only a short period of

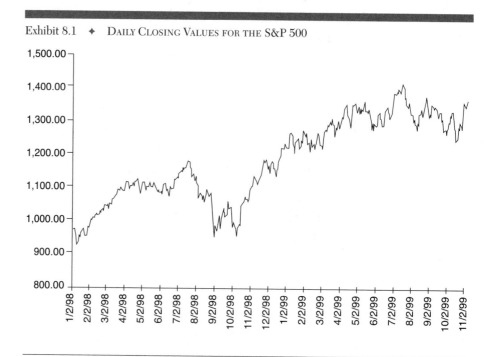

Exhibit 8.1 ✦ DAILY CLOSING VALUES FOR THE S&P 500

time. Dow Theory adherents believe minor moves can usually be ignored. The objective is to determine changes in the primary movement of stock prices. In other words, the theory attempts to ascertain when a secondary move is about to become a change in the primary direction of prices. One approach is to look at a price chart and establish **support levels,** below which prices tend not to fall, and **resistance levels,** above which prices tend not to rise.

support level
A level below which prices should not drop.

resistance level
A level above which prices should not rise.

Support and Resistance Levels

Exhibit 8.2 shows a price chart of the daily closing values of Applied Materials between the beginning of 1998 and the end of 1999. Notice that the primary move throughout the period was generally positive as Applied Materials rose from about $30 a share to over $95 a share. Initially the stock price rose to about $40 a share and then fell back, which established $40 as a resistance level. Prices bottomed at about $22 a share in October 1998 and then rose, establishing $22 as a support level. Prices rose sharply throughout the rest of 1998 and into early 1999, breaking through the resistance level (a buy signal) in January 1999. Another resistance level was established at about $70 a share and another support level was established about $50 a share. Prices rose and fell for a few weeks—never breaking either the support or resistance level. During the late summer and into the fall, Applied Materials rose sharply again, breaking through the resistance level in August. With only a few bumps, prices rose fairly steadily into the mid-90s by the end of the year—overall, a bullish chart.

Different technicians believe in support and resistance levels for different specific reasons, but they generally agree on the following explanation. As prices approach a support level, investors who failed to buy at the prior low start buying, which pushes prices upward. Similarly, when prices start to approach a resistance

Exhibit 8.2   ✦   DAILY PRICES FOR APPLIED MATERIALS

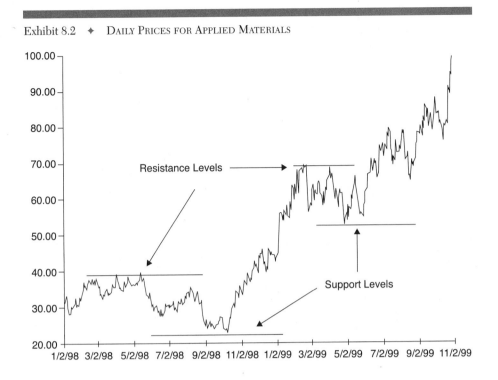

level, investors who failed to sell at the prior high start doing so, which pushes prices downward. If prices break through either a support or resistance level, this suggest a substantial change in investor attitude—from bullish to bearish (when a support level is breached) or from bearish to bullish (when a resistance level is breached).

More Complex Price Patterns

Beyond simple support and resistance levels, technicians may look for a variety of specific price patterns in their charts, many with colorful names. Some examples include fulcrum, compound fulcrum, head and shoulders, duplex horizontal, and inverse saucer. All of these more complex price patterns are merely variations, modifications, or extensions of the basic notion of support and resistance levels. All price patterns attempt to predict a coming change in the primary direction of prices (bullish to bearish or bearish to bullish).

Trendlines

A *trendline* is simply a line that connect secondary highs (upper trendline) or secondary lows (lower trendline). Both trendlines moving up tends to confirm a bull market; down tends to confirm a bear market. However, if the trendlines are moving together—called a narrowing formation—this might indicate that the bull market (if the trend is up) or the bear market (if the trend is down) will continue. One explanation for this conclusion is that plenty of buyers are waiting for any price decline to buy, and plenty of sellers are waiting for an increase to sell. However, trendlines moving

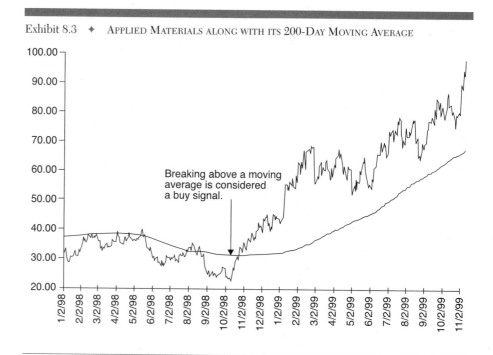

Exhibit 8.3 ✦ APPLIED MATERIALS ALONG WITH ITS 200-DAY MOVING AVERAGE

apart—called a broadening formation—might suggest that the market is about to reverse direction.

Moving Averages

moving average
An average price during a specified period of time that moves over time.

Another type of charting uses **moving averages**—averages of prices over a specified number of days (or weeks or months) that move over time. Each day (or week or month), the technician adds the most recent price and deletes the most distant price from the average. Exhibit 8.3 shows an example of a moving average based on the daily closing price of Applied Materials along with its 200-day moving average.

Because a moving average smoothes the variations in any time series, technicians argue that a moving average can better represent support and resistance levels. When prices break below or above the moving average, this may indicate that a support or resistance level has been breached and prices are going to head even lower or higher. For example, in October 1998, Applied Materials broke above its 200-day moving average—a bullish signal. The stock rose from the low 30s to over 95 during the next twelve months.

INVESTOR SENTIMENT INDICATORS

investor sentiment
Technical indicators that measure whether investors are optimistic or pessimistic.

Many technicians have moved beyond studying charts to looking at indicators that, they argue, measure **investor sentiment.** They seek to gauge whether investors are optimistic (bullish) or pessimistic (bearish). Some of these investor sentiment indicators are based on contrary opinion, whereas others are based on following the so-called smart money. Most technicians chart these indicators, often in conjunction with various price charts.

Contrary Opinion Theory

The notion behind contrary opinion theory is quite simple. As the market approaches a peak (that is, the primary upward move in prices is about over), the consensus among investors tends to be bullish. Likewise, as the market approaches a trough, the consensus among investors tends to be bearish. Two indicators that, according to technicians, measure contrary opinion are the odd-lot sales ratio and the cash positions of mutual funds. The *odd-lot sales ratio* is defined as odd-lot sales volume divided by odd-lot buying volume, in which volume is usually measured in numbers of shares. (An odd lot is a trade involving less than a round lot, or 100 shares.) The rationale behind this indicator is simply that small investors, who are much more likely to trade in odd lots, are generally less sophisticated and more conservative. As a result, technicians argue, small investors tend to sell toward the end of a bear market (that is, just before the primary downward move stops), and they tend to buy toward the end of a bull market (that is, just before the market peaks). Thus, a declining odd-lot sales ratio, indicating increasing margins of odd-lot purchases over sales, tells technicians that the bull market has about run its course, so they consider selling.

The *cash positions of mutual funds* are another contrary opinion indicator. Every mutual fund holds a percentage of its assets in cash or cash equivalent securities (such as Treasury bills). Mutual funds can affect stock prices significantly by moving cash in and out of stocks. Some technicians forecast an impending market top if the cash positions of mutual funds are shrinking or are near historic lows (say, less than 5 percent of total assets). In other words, they fear that demand for stocks is about to drop. However, if mutual funds have as much as 15 percent or so of their assets in cash, technicians may conclude that stocks are likely to enter, or continue, a primary bull market because the demand for stocks is likely to increase.

Smart Money Indicators

Other indicators of investor sentiment rely on the notion that investors should follow the *smart money,* investors who are more astute than average and are likely to lead bull and bear markets. Two examples of smart money indicators are short sales by specialists and the level of debit balances in brokerage accounts.

Specialists on the NYSE, as part of their market-making function, often engage in short selling. Specialists are also allowed, with certain restrictions, to sell stocks short for their own accounts. Technicians believe that specialists may have access to better, more timely information that gives them a better feel for the future direction of prices compared with average investors. Therefore, if technicians see specialists engaged in heavy short selling, they take this as a bearish signal. Likewise, if specialist short sales are relatively light, technicians take this as a sign of an impending bull market. To make this determination, technicians usually look at the ratio of specialist short sales to total short sales. This ratio is typically about 40 percent. If it rises above, say, 50 percent, technicians may conclude that specialists are selling short more heavily and the market is about to fall.

Finally, technicians often look at the debit balances in brokerage accounts (that is, total margin debt). This indicator is based on the notion that only more sophisticated investors use margin debt. Thus, if the amount of margin debt in brokerage accounts is rising, these investors are buying. In fact, these supposedly more astute investors are borrowing to buy stocks. Technicians take this as a definitely bullish indicator.

MARKET MOMENTUM INDICATORS

market momentum
Technical indicators that measure the level of energy behind the current trend.

The final group of technical indicators we review is based on a concept known as **market momentum**. Those who believe in market momentum equate the market for stocks, or any security, to a freight train: it takes a long time to get going (either upward or downward), and, once it gets going, it takes a long time to stop or change directions. Usually, measures of market momentum are plotted on charts along with prices.

Technicians use many other indicators to measure market momentum, the most obvious of which is trading volume. A technician sees a rising market on low, or perhaps, even falling, volume as a sign of an impending peak because it indicates weak upward momentum. However, a rising market on increasing volume is a sign that the market has strong momentum and that, therefore, prices are likely to go higher before peaking. As well-known technician Martin Zweig likes to say, "The trend is your friend."

Advance/Decline Ratio

Another simple indicator of market momentum is the relationship between advancing and declining stocks, called the *diffusion index*. The diffusion index is often calculated as the number of advancing stocks plus one-half the number of unchanged stocks divided by the total number of stocks trading. A rising diffusion index is usually interpreted as a bullish signal, a signal that a primary upward move in the market has substantial momentum behind it. By contrast, if the diffusion index is falling as the market rises, technicians see a sign that the bull market is losing its momentum and approaching a peak.

A variation of an advance/decline ratio is to determine the number of stocks that are selling above or below their respective moving averages. For example, assume that 90 percent of the stocks that make up the S&P 500 are selling at prices above their 13-week moving averages. Many technicians would argue that this strongly suggests that a trend has enough momentum to carry the overall market higher in the coming months.

Relative Strength Indicators

Another example of technical indicators that purport to measure market momentum are relative strength indicators. A simple measure of relative strength is price change. Another, somewhat more sophisticated measure of relative strength divides the price of stock (or group of stocks) by a broad market average and creates an index.[4]

Exhibit 8.4 shows the relative strength of Applied Materials and Ford between the beginning of 1998 and the end of 1999. Notice that Ford's relative strength generally declines, whereas Applied Materials' relative strength generally increases, during the period. Rising relative strength is bullish, whereas declining relative strength is bearish. Relative strength that starts to show signs of declining after rising for a period of time may indicate that the stock has topped out. However, if relative strength

---

[4]You could use the following formula to calculate relative strength: $RS_t = [(S_t/I_t)/(S_{t-1}/I_t - 1)] \times RS_{t-1}$, where S is the stock price, I is the index value, and RS is the relative strength measure. RS_0 is set at an arbitrary value, most commonly 100.

Exhibit 8.4   ✦   RELATIVE STRENGTH OF APPLIED MATERIALS AND FORD MOTOR COMPANY

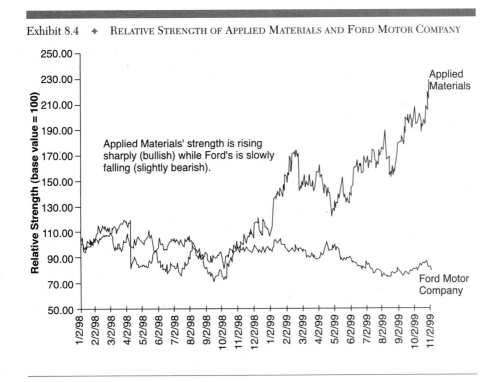

starts to show signs of rising after a sustained period of decline, this might indicate that it is time to buy the stock.

Assessment of Technical Analysis

We have described technical analysis and a few of the better-known technical indicators. Many technical indicators are simple to calculate, and their interpretations seem straightforward and full of common sense. For investors, however, the most important question is, how well does technical analysis work? This question evokes more than a little controversy. Many investors sincerely believe that technical analysis works, or least gives them an edge. And although technical analysis has attracted some individuals who can best be described as crackpots, even charlatans, the field also includes serious, almost scholarly professionals who carefully examine their technical indicators. Some of these individuals have built impressive track records.

On the other hand, some professionals regard technical analysis in much the same way astronomers view astrology. These critics argue that technical analysis is worthless. Burton Malkiel, one of the more articulate critics of technical analysis states flatly, "I, personally, have never known a successful technician, but I have seen the wrecks of several unsuccessful ones."[5] Malkiel adds, "With large numbers of technicians predicting the market, there will always be some who call the last turn, or the

---

[5]Burton Malkiel, *A Random Walk Down Wall Street,* (New York: Norton, 1999), p. 139.

last few turns, but none will consistently be accurate."[6] Indeed, as the Investment History box on page 191 points out, market guru fame on Wall Street can be fleeting.

Although we cannot hope to resolve the controversy over the value of technical analysis, we would like to provide some basic insight into the question of how well it works. We begin with a discussion of some of the reasons technical analysis might work, and some reasons why it might not work.

WHY TECHNICAL ANALYSIS MIGHT WORK

In describing technical indicators, we explained some of the basic rationales behind them, in other words, why they might work. For example, recall that the basic rationale for the Dow Theory is that investors who held back from buying a stock at its prior low (or support level) will be anxious to buy as the stock approaches that price level again. Other reasons why technical analysis might work, or at least appear to work, often relate to inadequacies of fundamental information.

It is quite possible that not all investors have equal access to fundamental information. Also, some investors might have access to relevant information before other investors. This suggests that a lag might separate the initial dissemination of information from the stock market reaction. Therefore, some investors may miss out on major moves if they wait for the fundamental information to reach them. Perhaps following the smart money (investors who presumably have better and more timely access to information) could produce higher returns than the general market over the long run.

Technical analysis might also work if fundamental information is incomplete or misleading. As we see in Chapter 12, accounting information can be manipulated to misrepresent a situation. In addition, fundamental information reveals little about nonquantitative factors such as employee morale. Past stock price patterns might provide better insight into these nonquantitative factors, technicians argue.

Beyond the inadequacies of fundamental information, technical analysis might work because investor emotions can have a major impact on stock prices. Remember, one of the important lessons of speculative bubbles is that people make investment decisions, and human psychology can affect prices. Behavioral finance argues that human psychology leads investors to make the same mistakes over and over again, creating the possibility of recurrent and predictable patterns in security prices.

Aside from these reasons, technical analysis might appear to work through the effects of a self-fulfilling prophecy. For example, assume that many investors believe in and follow moving averages. These investors abandon the market if a stock market index breaks below its moving average. Assume that the S&P 500's 200-day moving average is 1,500 and the index closes at 1,505. These investors are likely to sell. As a result, stock prices are likely to drop further, at least in the short run. Does this mean that the indicator works? One could argue that the answer is both yes and no.

Several strong arguments also give reasons why technical analysis might not work. Essentially, critics attack technical analysis on two points. First, critics label most recurrent patterns in short-term security prices as mere illusions. As an example, take a look at the chart in Exhibit 8.5. One series is the S&P 500; the other is a random walk, both of which we discussed in Chapter 7. Random walks can produce price series that

---

[6]Malkiel, *A Random Walk Down Wall Street*, p. 159.

WHERE HAVE ALL THE GURUS GONE?

Fame on Wall Street can be transitory for investment gurus. Make one big correct call and people will pay attention to you, at least for a while. After a few bad calls, however, people stop listening and your celebrity fades. Consider the fate of these two gurus.

Robert Prechter

Robert Prechter is best known for advocating something called the Elliot wave, which posits that stock prices exhibit basic wave characteristics common to all natural forces. Prechter, the story goes, rediscovered the Elliot wave—its murky origins supposedly go back to a thirteenth-century mathematician—while working as a technical analyst for Merrill Lynch in the 1970s. Excited by his "discovery," Prechter quit Merrill Lynch and began writing his one investment newsletter.

Prechter was one of the first market gurus to turn bullish during the early 1980s when the Dow was still under 1,000. His prediction of a 2,700-point Dow by the mid-1980s turned out to be pretty accurate (the Dow hit 2,722 in August 1987). Investors and the media flocked to Prechter and subscriptions to his newsletter soared.

Unfortunately some of Prechter's later forecasts were way off the mark. During the summer and early fall of 1987, when the market started to show signs of weakness, Prechter remained bullish. Even in early October 1987, he urged clients to aggressively buy stocks and boldly predicted a 3,600 Dow by the end of 1988. Those who took his advice probably wished they hadn't when the Dow dropped by more than 500 points on October 19, 1987.

After the 1987 market break, Prechter dramatically reversed direction, becoming staunchly bearish. "The message of October 1987," he said, "is that the great bull market is over." He predicted that the Dow would fall below 400, losing about 85 percent of its value, by the early 1990s. Obviously Prechter missed the major rebound in stock prices that occurred in 1988 and 1989. The Dow ended the 1980s at 2,753.20, an increase of more than 57 percent over its 1987 low.

Apparently, many investors wiped out trying to ride the Elliot wave to success during the late 1980s. When *Barron's* published an article in February 1991 that referred to Prechter as a top market guru, it received many letters attacking Prechter's track record as "crummy" and labeling the Elliot-wave theory as total nonsense. As stock prices climbed higher and higher during the 1990s, Prechter remained generally bearish and his star continued to fade.

Elaine Garzarelli

Unlike Robert Prechter's single-indicator forecast, Elaine Garzarelli bases her forecasts on at least a dozen indicators measuring such variables as monetary policy and investor psychology. In 1987, Elaine Garzarelli, then a vice president for Lehman Brothers, made the call of the century. On October 11, she became convinced that a major break was coming based on a steep drop in Japanese bond prices and hints from the Federal Reserve of higher interest rates to reduce inflationary pressures. In an interview on October 13, with the Dow at 2,508, Garzarelli told *USA Today* that she was convinced that a major market crash (possibly 500 points or more) would occur within a few days. Of course, on October 19, the Dow dropped more than 500 points; not a bad prediction as it turned out!

Garzarelli became an almost overnight sensation. She was deluged with interview requests, and her picture appeared on the cover of several magazines. Unfortunately, her forecasts right after the market break were not quite as accurate. Garzarelli told investors that she would not touch stocks for a while, expecting the Dow to drop another 200 to 400 points. In fact, the Dow hit its low for 1987 on October 19. The index ended 1987 at 1,938.83, actually up slightly for the year and up about 12 percent from the October low. Garzarelli remained bearish or neutral throughout 1988 and much of 1989 as the market continued to rise. Her more recent performance has also been mixed. She turned bearish on July 23, 1996, the date the market hit bottom. She remained bearish until the middle of 1997 while stocks rose by almost 20 percent. Today, Garzarelli's predictions rarely make news.

Exhibit 8.5 ♦ DAILY VALUES OF THE S&P VERSUS A RANDOM SERIES

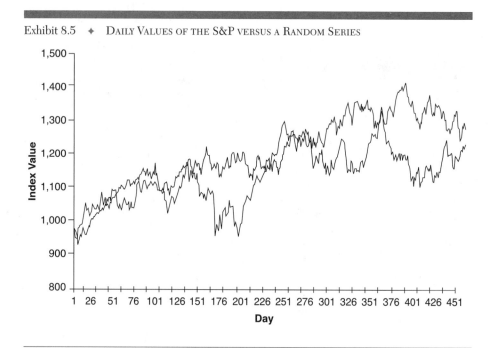

appear to show trends, recurring patterns, resistance levels, support levels, and so forth. It's easy to be fooled into seeing something where there is nothing.[7] Second, even if security prices followed recurrent and predictable patterns, many other investors would quickly recognize the patterns. Once that happened, any trading rule based on those patterns would rapidly self-destruct.

As an example of the second point, assume that a trading rule based on a historical price pattern indicates that a specific stock is about to rise from $50 to $55 per share. A technician who believes in the indicator would immediately buy the stock, as would other investors who recognize the price pattern. The price would jump almost instantaneously from $50 to $55 under the pressure of many buyers and no one willing to sell the stock at a price less than $55. (Remember, every buyer has to find a seller.) In fact, some investors might buy the stock in *anticipation* of the pattern. In any event, the trading rule would no longer produce an abnormal profit.

HOW WELL DO TECHNICAL INDICATORS WORK?

We have examined some reasons why technical analysis might work and some reasons why it might fail. To resolve some of the controversy, we evaluate the track record of

---

[7]Burton Malkiel likes to tell the following story: "One of the charts showed a beautiful upward breakout from an inverted head and shoulders (a strongly bullish formation). I showed it to a chartist friend of mine who practically jumped out of his skin. 'What is the company?' he exclaimed. 'We've got to buy immediately . . .' He did not respond kindly when I told him the chart had been produced by flipping a coin." Malkiel, *A Random Walk Down Wall Street,* pp. 143–44.

systems based on one popular technical indicator (moving averages). Again, our discussion makes no attempt to be comprehensive.

Before we get to the question of how well moving-average systems work, however, we need to define how to determine whether technical analysis does or doesn't work. It is not enough to say that technical analysis works if it correctly predicts an event—say, a bull market. One can say that technical analysis works only if it consistently produces above-average returns for investors who follow its signals. Above-average returns must exceed the returns that the investor would have earned by simply buying and holding a similar investment over the same period. Adjustments for differences in risk, transaction costs, and taxes should also be made.

We also have to note a problem with testing how well technical analysis works: the interpretation of many technical indicators is often ambiguous. In addition, most market technicians examine several indicators when making their forecasts. This can make it quite difficult to scientifically evaluate the forecasts. Most technicians admit that interpreting technical indicators is subjective, more of an art than a science. Consequently, it is not unheard of for one technician to argue that a particular indicator is giving a bullish signal while another, looking at the same data, concludes that the indicator is giving a bearish signal.

As we mentioned earlier, moving averages are another way of finding support and resistance levels. Breaking below the 200-day moving average is analogous to breaking below a support level (a bearish signal). Breaking above the 200-day moving average is the same as breaking through a resistance level (a bullish signal). But how well do moving averages work? According to critics, not too well. Substantial scientific evidence suggests that moving averages, as well as other technical indicators, fail to produce above-average returns consistently.[8]

However, recently evidence has begun to emerge suggesting that maybe it isn't time to put away your charts just quite yet. A recent scientific study found fairly strong support for moving-average systems.[9] The study found that breaking through resistance and support levels produced good buy and sell signals, respectively.

Jeremy Siegel, in his book *Stocks for the Long Run*, back-tested the moving-average strategy using a series of daily values of the Dow Industrials starting in 1885. He assumed that investors bought the Dow when the index crossed above its 200-day moving average, and left the market when the index fell below its 200-day moving average. Siegel assumed investors reinvested dividends when in the market and earned interest when not in the market. Exhibit 8.6 summarizes Siegel's findings.

At first glance, Siegel's results seem to suggest a mixed track record for moving-average systems. The active strategy produced higher average returns than a passive buy-and-hold strategy *only* if you ignore transaction costs and taxes. After adjusting for transaction costs and taxes, the performance of the passive strategy either matched or, in some cases, exceeded the performance of the active strategy.

The one exception was the 1926-45 time period. Even after adjusting for taxes and transaction costs, the active strategy beat the passive strategy by an average of more than 4 percent per year. According to Siegel, this is because the moving-average strategy would have gotten an investor out of the market prior to the 1929 crash, and kept

---

[8]Many of these studies are listed in Malkiel, *A Random Walk Down Wall Street*, pp. 432–35.

[9]William Brock, Blake LeBaron, and Josef Lakonishok, "Simple Technical Trading Rules and the Stochastic Properties of Stock Returns," *Journal of Finance*, December 1992, pp. 1731–64.

Exhibit 8.6 ✦ PERFORMANCE OF A MOVING AVERAGE STRATEGY: 1885–1997
(AVERAGE ANNUALIZED RETURNS)

		Active Strategy	
Period	Passive Strategy	Before Transaction Costs & Taxes	After Transaction Costs & Taxes
1886–1925	9.11%	10.01%	8.32%
1926–1945	6.24	11.98	10.42
1946–1997	12.16	12.50	11.26
1885–1997	9.98	11.51	10.05

Source: Jeremy Siegel, Stocks for the Long Run, 2nd ed. (New York: McGraw-Hill, 1998), p. 250.

the investor out of the market for most of the early 1930s—a dismal period for stock investors.[10] And this raises another important point about Siegel's findings. Although a moving-average-based system doesn't seem to improve performance, it does seem to reduce risk, especially helping investors avoid large losses (such as in 1929–32). In fact, the standard deviation of returns from the active strategy is 20 percent lower than the standard deviation of returns from the passive, buy-and-hold strategy.

What is Siegel's overall assessment of moving averages and technical analysis? He gives a cautious endorsement—so long as transactions costs aren't too high. However, he notes that throughout history actions of investors to advantage of the past, affect future returns. In other words, profitable trading strategies often disappear.

What is Fundamental Analysis?

In one sense, technicians focus exclusively on a stock's current and past price patterns. Intrinsic value, what the stock really should be worth, plays only a supporting role. Fundamental analysts, however, try to determine the true value of a stock under the belief that all stocks, in the long run, will sell for their fundamental values. Therefore, fundamentalists are less interested in passing effects such as investor sentiment than in, say, the company's five-year projected growth rate in earnings.

Benjamin Graham and David Dodd are considered the fathers of modern security analysis. The first edition of their seminal work, *Security Analysis*, argued that common stocks were not wildly speculative investments, but rather belonged in the portfolios of all prudent long-term investors.[11] Graham and Dodd presented a methodology—often referred to as the Graham and Dodd approach—to analyze and value common stocks. A remarkable fact about *Security Analysis* is that it was initially published during the depths of the Great Depression when interest in common stocks

---

[10]Unlike the 1987 market break—where stock prices bounced back fairly quickly—the 1929 Great Crash was only the beginning of a brutal bear market. Between the early September 1929 peak and the eventual bottoming out in 1932, the Dow Industrials lost about 90 percent of their value. More than 25 years passed before the Dow fully recovered from that crash.

[11]Benjamin Graham and David Dodd, *Security Analysis*, (New York: McGraw-Hill, 1934).

was weak. Graham and Dodd showed a great deal of faith in the long-run future of the capital markets and the American economy.

THE PROCESS OF FUNDAMENTAL ANALYSIS

Fundamental analysis is usually a three-stage process, beginning with economic and aggregate market analysis and proceeding to industry analysis and company analysis. The four major variables that generally drive stock prices are current earnings and dividends, future growth rates in earnings and dividends, uncertainty surrounding growth rates, and interest rates. One cannot forecast future earnings and dividends without some idea of the company's future sales, operating expenses, capital investment, and financing requirements.

We devote four chapters to a detailed description of the process of fundamental analysis (Chapters 11–14). Chapter 11 describes economic and industry analysis, and Chapters 12 and 13 deal with company analysis. Chapter 14 ties fundamental analysis together by presenting several stock valuation models.

AN EXAMPLE OF FUNDAMENTAL ANALYSIS IN ACTION

To give you an idea of how the process of fundamental analysis works, let's look at Peter Lynch's 1994 analysis of Johnson & Johnson.[12] Lynch is strongly devoted to fundamental analysis, and he has an excellent track record. Until 1989, Lynch ran Fidelity's Magellan Fund basing his investment decisions on fundamental analysis. Instead of looking at charts, he read company annual reports and listened for stories he liked. Lynch and his associates must have done something right; Magellan has one of the best performance records of any mutual fund since 1980. Since retiring from Magellan, Lynch has remained active in the investments game, publicly recommending stocks.

In late 1993, Lynch noticed that the price of Johnson & Johnson's stock had been falling since early 1992, losing almost one-third of its value. Lynch was puzzled, thinking something might be wrong with the company. Looking through its annual report, Lynch discovered that Johnson & Johnson's earnings had risen every year for the previous 10 years (more than doubling), that the company had raised dividends each year for the past 32 years, and that the company was becoming more efficient. He also noticed that the company had almost $1 billion in cash, $5.5 billion in equity, only $1.5 billion in long-term debt, and excellent products in the pipeline. In short, Johnson and Johnson had solid fundamentals. So, why was its stock not responding?

Lynch believed that the answer lay in the market's reaction to proposals for health-care reform. The market was worried that these proposals might have a negative impact on the earnings of health-care companies. Consequently, all health-care stocks were taking beatings. Yet, Lynch concluded, even if the proposals became law, Johnson & Johnson would be less affected than most health-care companies. One-half of its profits came from international sales and another 20 percent came from the sale of consumer products such as shampoo. Lynch decided that at about $10 a share (adjusted for subsequent stock splits), Johnson & Johnson was one of the great bargains of the decade. He recommended the stock publicly in spring 1994.

---

[12]Peter Lynch and John Rothchild, *Learn to Earn* (New York: Simon & Schuster, 1995), pp. 166–69.

Lynch was right. Johnson & Johnson's stock price has risen almost steadily since mid-1994, trading at more than $100 a share today. And Johnson & Johnson has raised its dividend each year since 1994.

Assessing Fundamental Analysis

Before we get to an assessment of fundamental analysis, we need to point out that the investment opinions of fundamental analysts can have dramatic impact on stock prices. For example, on Friday November 12, 1999, a Merrill Lynch analyst lowered his rating on Intel. The stock promptly lost about 5 percent of its value (see the chart in Exhibit 8.7). The Intel example is not an isolated case. A scientific study found that analyst recommendations significantly influence stock prices, not only around the announcement, but for several months following.[13]

TRACK RECORDS OF FUNDAMENTAL ANALYSTS: SOME EXAMPLES

A great deal of evidence, both anecdotal and scientific, lays out the records of fundamental analysts. This record appears somewhat mixed. As we've noted, the average stock mutual fund has under-performed the overall market over the past 10 years. Most of these funds are managed by individuals who rely primarily on fundamental analysts.

However, unlike critics of technical analysis, even the most severe detractors of fundamental analysis criticize not the process or technique but rather its execution. Critics often still find a great deal of value for investors in analyst commentaries on the overall market, or specific industries and companies. We have more to say about this in Part 4, but let's look at some examples of the successes and failures of fundamental analysis.

Forecasting Earnings

One of the more important tasks of an analyst is to forecast earnings. However, some evidence suggests that analysts have less-than-stellar records in forecasting earnings.[14] One study found that a naïve model that assumes next year's earnings will equal this year's earnings produced better forecasts than those of professional security analysts. Another study found that professional analysts' average forecast error of next year's earnings exceeded 30 percent.

Blown Calls

As a group, security analysts have a long, somewhat dubious history of blowing calls. There is the story of an analyst who kept recommending America West Airlines in the early 1990s even as the stock was losing more 70 percent of its value. The airline eventually filed for bankruptcy. Or the story of Sunbeam's first quarter 1998 earnings. Sunbeam had been touted by most analysts for its remarkable turnaround under "Chainsaw Al" Dunlap. The company had returned to profitability and growth prospects appeared strong. Most analysts had "strong buy" or "buy" recommendations

---

[13]Kent Womack, "Do Analyst Recommendations Have Investment Value?" *Journal of Finance*, March 1996, pp.137–67.

[14]For citations, see Malkiel, *A Random Walk Down Wall Street*, pp. 435–37.

Exhibit 8.7   ◆   INTEL STOCK PERFORMANCE, NOVEMBER 8–12, 1999

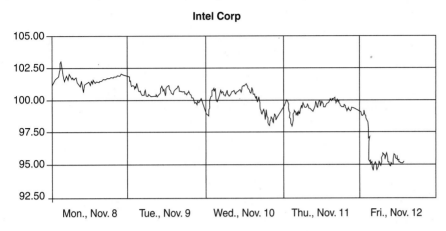

on the stock even though it had more than doubled since Dunlap took over in 1996. As it turned out, Sunbeam stunned many on Wall Street by announcing a loss for the first quarter of 1998. Moreover sales actually declined by 5 percent. Red-faced analysts immediately cut their ratings on Sunbeam, and investors stampeded for the exits. By the summer of 1998, the stock had dropped by more than 80 percent and Dunlap was out as CEO.

Success Stories

For every story of a failure of fundamental analysis, you'll hear at least one story where fundamental analysis has succeeded. Beyond Peter Lynch, many other pros with impressive track records rely on fundamental analysis. Consider Helen Young Hayes, who runs the Janus Overseas and Janus Worldwide funds. Hayes focuses less on specific countries (though this still a consideration) and more on individual companies and their earnings outlook. Like most of the Janus portfolio managers, she believes that stock prices follow earnings. Her funds own a wide range of different stocks located throughout the world. Both the Janus Overseas and Worldwide funds have impressive performance records; both have ranked in the top 10 percent of international stock funds in each of the past ten years.

Abby Joseph Cohen of Goldman Sachs is another star among analysts. Cohen is more of a market strategist than a security analyst, meaning she spends most of her time trying to forecast the overall market rather than the fortunes of individual companies. Her market forecasts have generally been right on the mark; she was one of the first to correctly call the great bull market of the 1990s. Cohen relies not on charts but on sophisticated economic analysis of the domestic economy. Her accurate prediction of noninflationary growth led to her successful forecast of the stock market.

WHY FUNDAMENTAL ANALYSIS MIGHT FAIL TO WORK

What makes fundamental analysis so difficult? Why do analysts "blow" calls? Essentially, we see two primary reasons: the nature of the task and data, and the behavior of the analysts themselves.

Analysts must attempt to forecast the future stream of earnings and dividends, often using incomplete and ambiguous data. Financial data reported by companies can be misleading, occasionally deliberately made so by the companies themselves. In several recent, well-publicized cases, companies, including Sunbeam, were forced to admit that some of their previously released financial reports were wrong. Analysts also try to anticipate changes to key macroeconomic variables and overall industry conditions. And random events can cloud even the best crystal ball.

Needless to say, accurately forecasting earnings in such an uncertain environment can be quite daunting. Let's look at a classic, albeit somewhat extreme example.

Delta Airlines' 1991 Earnings

In July 1990, the airline analyst for Standard & Poor's estimated that Delta Airlines would earn about $7.00 a share for the fiscal year ending on June 30, 1991, a healthy increase from its 1990 earnings of $5.79 per share. The analyst cited several reasons for the rosy forecast: moderate overall growth in airline passenger traffic due to continued economic expansion, an increase in average fare yields due to fewer price wars, and stable or perhaps even falling fuel prices. Then, on August 2, 1990, Iraq invaded Kuwait.

Perhaps the most significant of the initial effects of the Iraqi invasion, for the airline industry, was a sharp increase in oil, and thus jet fuel prices. The price index for crude petroleum was at 46.3 in July 1990 (1982 = 100); it shot up to 118.0 by October 1990, an increase of about 155 percent. The average July price of jet fuel of 56 cents per gallon (excluding taxes) increased to 114.4 cents per gallon by October. This increase significantly cut into airline operating margins, and thus earnings. By the end of September, S&P had cut its estimate of Delta's 1991 earnings from $7.00 per share to $2.75 per share.

The sharp increase in oil prices, and overall war fears, also helped push the U.S. economy into recession. Typically, passenger traffic slows during economic downturns, forcing airlines to reduce fares. This further depressed operating margins and earnings. Thus, by December 1990, even with slightly lower jet fuel prices (90.1 cents per gallon), S&P projected that Delta would lose $5.10 per share for the 1991 fiscal year.

After the Gulf War began in January 1991, oil prices again rose sharply but started to fall after it became apparent that the United States and its allies would defeat Iraq without disrupting oil supplies. The crude petroleum price index fell from 87.9 in January to 54.1 in March. Jet fuel prices fell, as well, from 82.2 cents per gallon in January to 62.2 cents per gallon in March. Unfortunately for the airlines, passenger traffic also fell as economic recession and fears of terrorism kept many travelers home. In fact, in the first three months of 1991, U.S. passenger traffic was down 7.7 percent compared with the same period in 1990. Even heavy price discounting and the end of the war offered little help. The U.S. economy started to grow again toward the summer of 1991, but slowly, and passenger traffic continued to be sluggish. By May 1991, S&P revised its forecast and said that Delta would lose about $6 per share for the 1991 fiscal year. As it turned out, even that forecast was somewhat optimistic; Delta ended up losing $7.73 per share in that period. Comparing the July 1990 forecast with the actual result, S&P overestimated Delta's 1991 earnings by almost $15 per share. As an airline analyst, how could you have predicted all that would happen when making your initial prediction?

Analyst Behavior

The other major reason we see for the periodic failure of fundamental analysis deals with the behavior of the analysts themselves. A fair amount of evidence indicates that analysts are overly optimistic and tend to exhibit a herd mentality in the face of uncertainty.

Analysts almost always have positive, or at least neutral opinions on the stocks they follow. Negative opinions are rare. One study, for example, found that over a 15-year period analyst "buy" recommendations exceeded "sell" recommendations by more than seven to one.[15]

Why do analysts tend to be so overly optimistic? For one thing, most analysts are employed by brokerage firms, which make most of their money through commissions on sales of stocks to investors. Brokers are always more interested in stocks with buy ratings than stocks with sell ratings. Further, it is much easier to sell stocks if brokers can tell clients that analysts are predicting a good year.

Another explanation for analyst optimism is the subtle, and not-so-subtle, pressure analysts receive from the companies they follow. Obviously, the companies want the analysts to say positive things about them. To do their jobs properly, analysts must be able to talk directly with company managers, not to obtain illegal inside information but rather to obtain more detailed explanations of public announcements and annual reports. An analyst may fear that if he or she fails to say positive things about a stock, management will refuse to talk in the future, putting the analyst at a competitive disadvantage against other analysts who follow the same company.

Analysts sometimes blow calls because of *herd instinct*. According to psychologists, a normal human reaction in the face of uncertainty is the tendency to stick together and follow the crowd. Analysts whose recommendations stick out from the pack expose themselves to risk—the cost to both themselves and their firms if they are wrong. Being wrong is a lot easier to take when all of your professional colleagues also were wrong. The following remark has been attributed to legendary economist John Maynard Keynes: "Worldly wisdom teaches that it is better for reputation to fail conventionally than to succeed unconventionally."[16]

Implications for Investors

We have seen mixed track records for both technical and fundamental analysis. Following technicians or fundamental analysts sometimes produces fantastic returns and sometimes poor returns. Some go so far as to argue that an investor who buys and holds a well-diversified portfolio of stocks will do as well as, and perhaps even better than someone who follows the advice of investment professionals over long periods of time. The Investment Insights box on page 200 raises another interesting point about the value of professional investment advice. Most professionals—whether technicians or fundamental analysts—are overwhelmed by their human nature and base their forecasts in large part on qualitative and intuitive methods. Yet ample evidence shows that actuarial, or quantitative, forecasts are usually better. Perhaps it's no fluke that unmanaged index funds often beat actively managed mutual funds.

---

[15]Womack, "Do Analyst Recommendations Have Investment Value?"

[16]Quoted in Malkiel, *A Random Walk Down Wall Street*, p. 176.

INVESTMENT INSIGHTS

0:00   0:00

The Limits of Human Judgment

Although some on Wall Street might think it heresy, professional money manager and investment analyst James O'Shaughnessy suggests that human judgment—or as he says "the unreliable experts"—may be the biggest obstacle to outstanding investment performance. In his book, *What Works on Wall Street*, O'Shaughnessy contends that models that require no subjective judgments consistently beat intuitive models.

Why are "experts" unreliable? According to O'Shaughnessy, "Successful investing runs contrary to human nature. We make the simple complex, follow the crowd, fall in love with the story, let our emotions dictate decisions, buy and sell on tips and hunches, and approach each investment decision on a case by case basis" (pp. 17–18). The following all contribute to the limits of human judgment:

◆ *People often ignore information contained in base rates*. Base rates are like averages—they tell you what to expect from a group but say nothing about each individual within the group. People tend to ignore base rate information in favor of their "feel" for an individual in the group. Here's an example. Say you flip a fair coin five times and come up with five heads in a row. If you flip the coin for the sixth time, what's your prediction? Because it's a fair coin, and each flip is independent of the others, the base rate

indicates a 50 percent chance the sixth flip will be heads and a 50 percent chance it will be tails. Even so, according to psychologists who have conducted similar experiments, most people will answer tails. Why? Because they "feel" a tails is due—given the run of five heads. In other words, they ignore the base rate and substitute their intuition, which has no real basis in fact.

Here's an investments example. After several years of above-average returns in the stock market, it is not uncommon to hear market strategists predict at least a couple of years of below-average returns. Why? Sometimes they base predictions on the outlook for interest rates and corporate profits and similar factors, but more often than not they believe that the market must regress to its mean. However, objectively reviewing past market history—the base rate—reveals no evidence that a series of above-average years is necessarily followed by several below-average years, or vice-versa.

◆ *Personal experience is preferred*. People place more weight on their personal experience than on the base rate and as a result are overconfident. For example, the data show that most initial public offerings under-perform the overall market and disappoint investors. However, an investor who had the

personal experience of making money on the last IPO he or she bought is likely to ignore the base rate information as well as any other objective financial data. The fact that the investor picked a winner last time is the main factor driving the decision to buy the next IPO.

◆ *Simple versus complex*. Psychologists argue that human nature makes people prefer the complex to the simple. This leads people to believe that successful investing requires the mastery of a wide of range of complicated variables. Yet that is rarely the case. Simple investing strategies—such as buying the Dow stocks with the highest dividend yields or lowest price-to-sales ratios—usually produce higher, more consistent returns than complicated investment strategies. One of the most important axioms of modern science is called Ockham's Razor: Most often the simplest theory is the best.

◆ *Herd instinct*. When confronted with uncertainty and incomplete information, people will imitate each other's behavior. Investing obviously involves a great deal of uncertainty. Many resolve this uncertainty by assuming that, for example, if others are buying an investment, they should, too. If you think everyone around you is getting rich from a particular investment, you may feel like a fool if you don't invest, too.

Critics often deride technicians as sellers of some modern-day snake oil. In this and the previous chapter, we have examined some of the evidence by which they argue that such methods are patently false and simply do not work. Although we agree that some technicians are flakes and perhaps even charlatans, we are not prepared to dismiss technical analysis entirely. Some technicians have impressive track records that indicate more than just luck. Listening investors may well hear something of value from serious technicians about both where they think the market is going and why.

Likewise, it's easy to pick on fundamental analysts; they have blown calls, too, sometimes quite badly. Nevertheless, analysts still have much to contribute to the investment analysis and selection process. You may not want to bet your financial future on their earnings forecasts, but they often have insightful and valuable comments concerning a company's current situation and its prospects for the future. Just remember for whom they work. Each investor must adapt his or her behavior to the inherent optimism of analysts.

In conclusion, we argue that some, although certainly not all, professional investment advice is worth your attention. Is professional investment advice worth the cost? Every investor must answer that question individually. All investors should heed the following: ask questions, think for yourself, be skeptical of anyone who claims to have a system that beats the market consistently, and remember that the past is never a guarantee of the future. Good luck!

Chapter Summary

1. How do technical and fundamental analyses differ?
   Technical analysis is based on the notion that past price patterns predict future price. Fundamental analysis is based on the belief that stocks have a fundamental or intrinsic value. The analyst seeks stocks selling for prices above or below their respective fundamental values.

2. What are some technical indicators?
   Technical indicators can be grouped into broad categories: charting, measures of investor sentiment, and measures of market momentum. Charting includes the notion of support and resistance levels, trendlines, and moving averages. Investor sentiment measures include contrary-opinion and smart-money indicators. Market momentum measures include trading-volume and relative-strength indicators.

3. How well does technical analysis work?
   Good reasons explain both why technical analysis might work and why it might not work. Interpreting technical indicators can be more of an art than a science, which adds to the difficulty of assessing how well technical analysis works. The evidence is mixed, though recent scientific evidence suggests that charting and moving averages are useful market timing devices.

4. What is the process of fundamental analysis?
   Fundamental analysis attempts to determine how much a stock should be worth. Fundamental analysis is usually a three-stage process of economic and aggregate market analysis, industry analysis, and company analysis. The most important determinant of the fundamental value of a stock is its future stream of earnings and dividends.

5. How well does fundamental analysis work?
   Fundamental analysis has a mixed track record, although stock prices do react to analyst comments. Analysts have a poor record of forecasting earnings and occasionally blow calls. However, many fundamental analysts have excellent records. Forecasting is made difficult by the nature of the task and the behavior of the analysts themselves.

Review Questions and Problems

1. What major assumptions underlie technical analysis? What roles do supply and demand play?

2. Define the terms *support level* and *resistance level*. What signals do price breaks through support and resistance levels send?

3. What is a trendline? If the upper and lower trendlines move closer together in a bull market, does this suggest that the bull market is likely to continue?

4. The table below lists 20 weekly stock prices. Find the four-week moving average. Plot both the moving average and the raw stock prices. Why is the moving average considered a better indicator of a trend than the raw data?

Week	Stock Price	Week	Stock Price
1	35.875	11	41.625
2	36.625	12	41.500
3	38.000	13	40.750
4	39.000	14	40.375
5	40.125	15	40.875
6	39.250	16	40.750
7	38.000	17	40.375
8	39.250	18	40.000
9	40.500	19	40.375
10	42.500	20	41.000

5. Define what technicians mean by investor sentiment. Give an example of an indicator that supposedly measures investor sentiment.

6. Why is trading volume considered an indicator of market momentum? Give an example of another market momentum indicator.

7. List several reasons why technical analysis might work. List and explain several reasons why it might not work.

8. Why is it so hard to determine whether technical analysis really works? By what standard should we test the effectiveness of technical analysis?

9. How does fundamental analysis differ from technical analysis? Why is intrinsic value so important to fundamental analysis?

10. Explain the three-step process of fundamental analysis. What four variables, in general, determine stock prices?

11. Why might fundamental analysis fail to work? Why are criticisms of fundamental analysis different from criticisms of technical analysis?

12. Why are analysts as a group optimistic? Explain the herd instinct.

CRITICAL THINKING EXERCISES

1. This exercise requires computer work. Open the Nasdaq worksheet in the Data Workbook. The worksheet contains daily values for the Nasdaq Composite index. Use the data to complete the following activities:

   a. Graph the original value with time as the *x* variable and the index value as the *y* variable.

   b. Compute the 10- and 200-day moving averages. Graph the moving averages and the original data against time.

   c. On the first graph, find the support and resistance levels. When did the Nasdaq Composite index break through a support or resistance level? Did stock prices behave as expected after breaking through support or resistance levels (for example, continue to drop after breaking through a support level)?

   d. On the second graph, determine when moving averages gave buy and sell signals. Did these signals coincide with the signals given by the first chart?

   e. Discuss what this exercise illustrates about the nature of technical analysis.

2. This exercise requires computer work. Open the Relative Strength worksheet in the Data Workbook. The worksheet contains daily price data for three stocks (Boeing, Disney, and Gap) along with daily data for the S&P 500. Use the data to answer the following questions:

    a. Compute relative-strength measures for each company. Use the formula given in the text.

    b. What do the relative-strength measures tell you about these companies? Do they indicate rising or falling momentum?

    c. Describe how you might use the relative-strength measures to develop buy and sell signals.

3. This exercise requires library/Internet research. Quarterly earnings announcements are available from a variety of sources. Most sources also identify earnings surprises—situations in which a firm's actual earnings were either higher or lower than analyst expectations.

    a. Go back over a recent month's announcements and identify the five largest earnings surprises on both the upside and downside. (Earnings announcements are concentrated in February, April, July, and October.)

    b. How much did the actual numbers differ from what analysts were expecting?

    c. Do you find any correlation between the number of analysts following a stock and the size of the error?

    d. Pick one company from each list. Why were the analysts wrong? What did they miss?

THE INTERNET INVESTOR

1. Visit the following web site: moneycentral.msn.com/articles/invest/derby. The site reports on an investment contest by several investment professionals. Read about each contestant's strategy to picking winners (technical, fundamental, or both). How well have they done?

2. Pick a stock you are interested in buying. Using your web browser to find out as much as you can about the stock, including what analyst opinions. Visit some of the investment-oriented web sites listed below:

    www.quicken.com
    www.morningstar.com
    investor.msn.com
    www.fidelity.com
    quote.yahoo.com

3. Visit the Morningstar web site (www.morningstar.com) section entitled "University." Read the section on technical analysis. Prepare a brief report on what you learned.

Part 3

Fixed

Income

Securities

UP TO THIS POINT, WE PROVIDED A GENERAL

DISCUSSION OF INVESTMENT ALTERNATIVES.

IT IS NOW TIME TO DISCUSS THESE INVEST-

MENT CHOICES IN GREATER DETAIL, BEGIN-

NING WITH FIXED INCOME SECURITIES OR

BONDS. THERE ARE GOOD REASONS TO INVEST IN BONDS, AND BONDS MAKE UP A

LARGE PERCENTAGE OF MANY INVESTORS' PORTFOLIOS. HOWEVER, BOND IN-

VESTING IS NOT WITHOUT ITS PITFALLS AND RISKS. THE NEXT TWO CHAPTERS

TAKE A MUCH CLOSER LOOK AT THE INVESTMENT CHARACTERISTICS AND

POTENTIAL OF BONDS.

FIXED-INCOME SECURITIES: VALUATION AND RISKS

PREVIOUSLY . . .

We concluded the section on financial markets and investment selection with a discussion of how the pros make investment decisions for various investment alternatives.

IN THIS CHAPTER . . .

Our discussion of fixed-income securities begins with an outline of the basic principles of bond valuation. We move on to a description of the two major risks bond investors face: interest rate and credit risk. We see that, regardless of the quality of the bond issuer, all investors are exposed to interest rate risk.

TO COME . . .

We continue our discussion of bond investing by describing both active and passive bond management strategies.

Chapter Objectives

After reading Chapter 9 you should be able to answer the following questions:

1. Why are bonds viable investment alternatives?
2. What risks do bond investors face?
3. How are bonds priced?
4. What are the basic bond pricing theorems?
5. How can interest rate risk be measured?
6. How can credit risk be evaluated?
7. How are bond risk and required return related?

Back in Chapter 3 we described many different types of fixed-income securities. The U.S. government issues bonds and notes through the Treasury Department and various federal agencies; state and local governments issue municipal bonds, and domestic corporations, foreign governments, and foreign corporations all issue their own bonds. Mortgage pass-through securities and preferred stock issues are also considered fixed-income securities.

The market offers literally thousands of different bonds.[1] The U.S. Treasury, for example, currently has more than 200 different bond and note issues outstanding. Billions of dollars' worth of new bonds are issued each year by a variety of corporations and governments.

At first glance, bonds may appear relatively simple securities, at least compared with common stocks. A bond represents a debtor/creditor relationship; the investor is the creditor and the issuer is the debtor. Most investors purchase bonds primarily for current income rather than capital appreciation. A bondholder collects interest payments, usually twice a year, and the issuer returns the principal—or par value—when the bond matures. In the process, the bondholder earns a fixed rate of return. Seems simple, right? Well, in the real world, bond investing can be quite complicated.

In this chapter, we concentrate on two basic issues: bond valuation and the major risks associated with investing in bonds (interest rate and credit risk). Before discussing how bonds are valued, we begin by answering what seems like a simple question: Why invest in bonds at all?

Why Bonds?

Even though bond trading makes up a substantial portion of total trading volume in the world's financial markets, bonds have a reputation as being rather dull, conservative investments. Images of people leisurely sitting by a pool clipping coupons might come to mind. Others argue that, compared with stocks, bonds offer poor risk/return trade-offs. Even legendary investment guru Peter Lynch has had less-than-kind words for investing in bonds: "In stocks you've got the company's growth on your side," he writes. "You're a partner in a prosperous and expanding business. When you lend money [buy bonds], the best you can hope for is to get it back, plus interest."[2] Lynch recites a list of all that can go wrong if one buys bonds and concludes that bond prices fluctuate as wildly these days as stock prices.

Although some of what Lynch and others have to say about bonds is probably true, we regret the attitude that bonds generally are dull or poor investments. For many investors, both individuals and institutions, bonds are a viable and important investment option. What do bonds offer investors?

INCOME

Investors who want predictable regular income must consider buying bonds. Although many common stocks do pay cash dividends, and these dividends often increase regularly, few common stocks have dividend yields that exceed the current yield on bonds. This is illustrated in Exhibit 9.1, which compares the Standard & Poor's (S&P) 500 dividend yield with the average yield on Treasury bonds (T-bonds) between 1967 and 1999. Notice that the dividend yield on the S&P 500 has generally been about half the current yield on long-term T-bonds.

---

[1]From now on, we will use the generic term *bond* to refer to all fixed-income securities.
[2]Peter Lynch, *One Up on Wall Street* (New York: Penguin Books, 1989, p. 57).

Exhibit 9.1 ✦ Yield on Long-Term Treasury Bonds versus the Dividend Yield from the Standard & Poor's 500

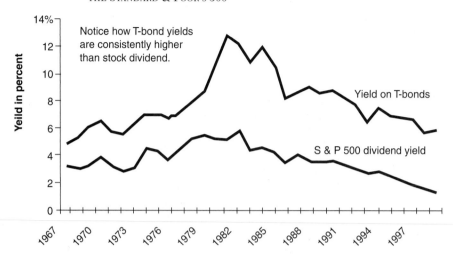

In addition, the financial trauma associated with reducing cash dividends on common stocks is much less than the trauma associated with suspending interest payments on bonds (which, of course, constitutes default). A source of reliable regular income can also improve the liquidity of any well-diversified portfolio.

POTENTIAL FOR CAPITAL GAINS

Looking over the data on historical returns presented in Chapter 3, it is difficult to argue that bonds have been dull investments in recent years. For example, during a three-year period from the beginning of 1991 through the end of 1993, bonds (both corporate and government) produced average annual compound returns that exceeded the average annual return on common stocks. In 1982, long-term T-bonds produced an annual return in excess of 40 percent. In periods of falling interest rates, bonds can produce spectacular returns.

PAPER VERSUS REAL LOSSES

Of course, rising interest rates can clobber bond prices—in 1994, for example, T-bonds produced a total return of −7.9 percent. Still, it is important to remember that rising interest rates produce only paper losses, not real losses, unless the investor sells the bond at the depressed price. Assume that you buy a bond for its face value of $1,000 and rising interest rates drop the bond's price to $900. This is only a paper loss, unless you sell the bond at the lower price. Furthermore, holding the bond to maturity guarantees return of your $1,000 (assuming that the issuer does not default). Like a bond, if you buy a stock at $50 per share and it declines to $40 per share, you suffer only a paper loss, not a real loss, of $10 per share. However, unlike a bond, you have no guarantee that the stock will *ever* get back to $50 per share, regardless of how long you hold it.

Exhibit 9.2 ✦ CORRELATIONS OF HISTORICAL RETURNS BETWEEN STOCKS AND BONDS: 1926–99

	Large Stocks	Small Stocks	Treasury Bonds	Treasury Bills
Large stocks	1.00			
Small stocks	0.79	1.00		
Treasury bonds	0.20	0.03	1.00	
Treasury bills	−0.03	−0.10	0.25	1.00

DIVERSIFICATION

Bonds may expand investors' risk/return opportunities by further diversifying a portfolio of common stocks. Exhibit 9.2 shows the correlation coefficients between stock and bond returns. Later, when you study common stocks, you will learn that any correlation coefficient less than 1.0 between two sets of returns indicates some diversification potential (or a potential to reduce risk). Correlation coefficients between stock and bond returns are generally quite small, ranging from −0.10 to 0.19.

TAX ADVANTAGES

The Tax Reform Act of 1986 eliminated many popular tax shelters. One that remained was the tax treatment of municipal bond interest: interest received from municipal bonds remains exempt from individual federal income taxes. Municipal bonds are one of the few tax shelters still available to a wide range of individual investors.

Risks Associated with Investing in Bonds

Although bonds have much to offer investors, buying bonds is not without risk. Further, some bonds expose investors to more risk than other bonds. U.S. government bonds, for example, have no default risk but still expose investors to other risks.

CREDIT RISK

credit risk
Possibility that the issuer of a bond will not make interest and principal payments when due.

default
Technical name for credit risk.

Whenever anyone lends money, their biggest concern is probably getting it back. Essentially, **credit risk** involves the possibility that the bond's issuer will not make interest and principal payments when due. (The technical term is **default.**) As we discussed in Chapter 3, bonds' credit risk levels vary widely. Some bonds, such as those issued by the U.S. Treasury, have no credit risk, whereas other bonds have much greater probabilities of default. Generally, we would expect to see a positive relationship between credit risk and expected returns. We have a lot more to say about credit risk later in this chapter.

INTEREST RATE RISK

As interest rates rise, bond prices fall, and vice versa. An investor forced to sell a bond when rates were high could suffer a capital loss. Even if the investor does not sell before maturity, rising interest rates also create an opportunity cost. For example, if someone buys a bond with a coupon rate of 8 percent and rates rise to, say, 10 percent, the bondholder loses the opportunity to get the higher rate; the bond is locked in at 8 percent. All bonds expose investors to interest rate risk, but, as we will see, some bonds have more interest rate risk than others. We also discover, in the next chapter, that investors can manage, and perhaps almost eliminate, interest rate risk.

REINVESTMENT RISK

If a bond promises a return (referred to as *yield to maturity*) of 8 percent, when it matures—assuming that the issuer does not default—will its actual rate of return equal 8 percent? Not necessarily, because, as we will see, part of the actual return from owning a bond comes from reinvesting the intermediate cash flows (that is, the coupon payments). Reinvesting the coupon payments at a rate higher than the bond's yield to maturity could raise the actual rate of return above the promised return when the bond was initially purchased. Note that interest rate risk and reinvestment risk tend to offset each other to some extent. The immunization techniques discussed in the next chapter are based on this offsetting effect.

PURCHASING POWER RISK

Purchasing power risk deals with the impact of future rates of inflation on cash flows. If a bond has a coupon rate of 6 percent when inflation is raging at 8 percent, the purchasing power of the invested money actually declines. Purchasing power risk hurts a bond investor if actual inflation exceeds the rate the investor expected when he or she first purchased the bond. Second, purchasing power risk and interest rate risk are closely related. As we know, rising expected inflation leads to higher interest rates.

purchasing power risk
Impact of inflation on a bond's cash flows.

CALL RISK

In Chapter 3, we pointed out that many bonds (especially corporate and municipal bonds) are *callable*. A call provision gives the issuer the option of buying the bond back from the investor at a specified price during a specified period of time, before maturity. Why should bond investors care about this **call risk?** An issuer is most likely to call a bond when interest rates are low or have fallen substantially from when the bond was initially issued. To replace the called bond in such an environment, the investor would probably accept a lower coupon rate. A bond may offer investors a period of **call protection** during which the bond is not callable.

call risk
Possibility of a bond being called back before maturity.

call protection
Period during which a bond is not callable.

LIQUIDITY RISK

As we discussed in Chapter 5, some bonds trade in poor secondary markets, so the spreads between their respective bid prices and ask prices (prices at which a dealer would buy or sell the bond, respectively, in response to a customer order) could be quite high. It may be difficult for investors to sell certain bonds before maturity for anything approaching their true values. **Liquidity risk** is a special problem for small municipal bond issues.

liquidity risk
Possibility of not being able to sell a bond before maturity at a price approaching the bond's true value.

FOREIGN EXCHANGE RISK

In recent years, many U.S. investors have been attracted to bonds issued by foreign governments and corporations; many foreign issuers' bonds have offered yields well above those offered by domestic bonds. Many foreign bonds are denominated in foreign currencies, however, so their returns depend on both interest rates and foreign exchange rates. For example, a bond denominated in British pounds (£) may have a par value of £1,000 and a coupon rate of 10 percent. (It pays annual interest of £100.) If the exchange rate between the dollar and the pound ($/£) when the bond is purchased is $1.50 per pound, the bond would cost $1,500 and pay $150 per year in interest. However, if the dollar were to gain strength relative to the pound and the $/£ exchange rate declines to $1.20 per pound, the bond's £100 in annual interest would translate into only $120. Even if everything else remained the same, the bondholder loses $30 a year from the U.S. dollar's increasing strength relative to the British pound. This is foreign exchange risk.

Bond Valuation

So far, we have examined the reasons for buying bonds as well as the general risks investors take when they buy bonds. In this section, we turn to a detailed discussion of bond valuation. Your understanding of bond valuation is critical to your understanding of the general risk/return profile of bonds, as well as how to select and evaluate individual bonds.

BASICS OF BOND PRICING

face value
Amount paid at maturity, also called the par value.

coupon rate
Amount of interest paid each year.

time to maturity
Number of periods before the bond matures. Also called term to maturity.

promised return
Interest rate used to discount a bond's cash flows.

The price of a bond depends on the values of four variables: (1) **face value** (F, also called *par value*), (2) **coupon rate** (CR), (3) **time to maturity** (T), and (4) **promised return.** For a noncallable, default-free bond, the first three variables are fixed at issue. These first three variables also determine the cash flows associated with a bond. The fourth variable, the promised return, is also the bond's required rate of return, the interest rate used to discount its cash flows to determine its present value. Given these four variables, we can calculate the present value of the bond's cash flows, which, added up, equals the bond's price, P_b.

For example, a ten-year bond ($T = 10$) has a 6 percent coupon rate (CR) and a $1,000 face value, F. The promised, or required, return (r) equals 8 percent per annum. The bond's price can be calculated in two steps.

Step 1

Calculate cash flows. The coupon payment (or interest payment per year in dollars), C, equals

$$C = CR \times F \tag{9.1}$$

In our example, 6 percent times $1,000 equals $60. The final cash flow at maturity equals $1,000, the face value, which is repaid in ten years.

Step 2

Calculate the present value of these cash flows to find bond value, P_b.

$$
\begin{aligned}
P_b &= PV \text{ of coupon payments} + PV \text{ of face value} \\
&= \$60(P/A;8\%; 10) + \$1{,}000(P/F; 8\%; 10) \\
&= \$60(6.7101) + \$1{,}000(0.4632) \\
&= \$865.81 \text{ (rounded to the nearest penny)}^3
\end{aligned}
\tag{9.2}
$$

Semiannual Coupons

Equation 9.2 assumes that the bond pays coupon interest annually. The vast majority of bonds actually make coupon payments every six months. To accommodate the semiannual coupon, the bond-pricing equation (Equation 9.2) needs three modifications. The first is to divide the annual coupon by 2. This represents the coupon payment per six-month period. The second change is to divide the required rate of return by 2, and the third is to multiply the time to maturity by 2. For the example above, Equation 9.2 becomes

$$
\begin{aligned}
P_b &= \$30(P/A; 4.0\%;20) + \$1{,}000(P/F; 4.0\%; 20) \\
&= \$30(13.5903) + \$1{,}000(0.4564) \\
&= \$864.11^4
\end{aligned}
\tag{9.3}
$$

Accrued Interest

Someone who buys a bond between coupon payment dates must pay the seller, in addition to the bond's price, the **accrued interest** since the last coupon payment date. When the bond makes its next coupon payment, the new owner receives the entire amount. Virtually all bonds accrue interest daily and pay every six months.

Say, for example, that a bond with an 8 percent coupon pays coupon interest on February 1 and August 1. Assuming a 360-day year and a face value of $1,000, this bond accrues about $0.22 per day ($80/360 days per year) in interest. Someone who buys this bond on May 1, 90 days after its last coupon payment, must pay the seller

accrued interest
Amount of interest between the last coupon payment date and today, paid by the buyer to the seller.

---

[3]From now on, the following notation will be used: $(P/A; r \text{ percent}; T)$ represents the present value of an annuity, received for T periods and discounted at r percent. $(P/F; r \text{ percent}; T)$ represents the present value of a single sum, received in T periods and discounted at r percent. Mathematically,

$$
(P/A; r; T) = \sum_{t=1}^{T} \quad \text{and} \quad (P/F; r; T) = (1 + r)^{-T}
$$

[4]Some argue that merely dividing the yield to maturity by 2 when adjusting semiannual coupon payments is not technically correct. This is because you are actually discounting cash flows at an effective rate higher than the stated yield to maturity, thus understating the "true" price of the bond. This issue has been analyzed and debated in detail elsewhere. See, for example, Frank Fabozzi, *Bond Markets, Analysis and Strategies*, 3rd ed. (Englewood Cliffs, NJ: Prentice-Hall, 1996, pp. 39–42); and especially, James Lindley et al., "A Measurement of the Errors in Intra-period Compounding and Bond Valuation, *The Financial Review* (February 1987), pp. 33–51.

about $20.00 in accrued interest ($0.22 times 90). When the bond makes its next coupon payment, on August 1, the new owner receives the entire six-month (180-day) coupon of about $40.

Accrued interest may seem like a trivial issue, but it does slightly affect bond price. One reason for this goes back to a basic rule of present value. Continuing the above example, the new owner pays $20 today (May 1) and receives back the $20 in three months (on August 1, when the bond makes its next coupon payment). Because this money has a time value, the $20 received on August 1 is worth less than the $20 paid on the purchase date. Furthermore, buying the bond on May 1 instead of on its last coupon payment date (February 1) entitles the new owner to receive the first coupon payment in three months rather than six months.

Adding accrued interest, the basic bond valuation equation, assuming semiannual coupons, becomes

$$P_b = \frac{c}{2} \sum_{t=1}^{2T} \frac{1}{(1 + r/2)^v (1 + r/2)^{t-1}} + \frac{F}{(1 + r/2)^v (1 + r/2)^{2T-1}} \tag{9.4}$$

where v is the days until the next coupon divided by the number of days in the six-month period, and $r/2$ is the appropriate semiannual rate of interest. Accrued interest is added to the bond's price. Although Equation 9.4 looks confusing, it is not as bad as it seems. Let's look at an example.

Maintaining the same example bond we have been using throughout this section (face value of $1,000, term of ten years, 6 percent annual coupon, and 8 percent annual required rate of return—4 percent per six months), assume that you buy the bond exactly three months after its last coupon payment and exactly three months before it makes its next coupon payment (so, $v = 0.5$). Now, compare the prices of the bond with and without accrued interest. The relevant numbers are summarized below:

	Without Accrued Interest	With Accrued Interest
Maturity	Exactly ten years	Nine years and nine months
Number of coupons	20	20
First coupon received	In exactly six months	In three months
Price of bond	$864.11	$881.22

You still receive 20 coupon payments of $30, but now the bond matures in nine years and nine months. The bond's price now equals $881.22 (*plus* $15 in accrued interest). The bond's price is about $17 higher than it is without accrued interest for two reasons. First, the bond matures three months sooner, and second, the owner receives the first coupon payment in three months rather than six months.

Yield to Maturity

We can interpret the continuing bond example as follows: What rate of return would an investor earn by buying a bond today for $864.11, receiving $30 every six months for ten years (a total of 20 payments), and receiving the bond's face value, $1,000, at the end of ten years? The answer is 8 percent per annum. The return on a bond, held to maturity, is referred to as the *yield to maturity*. This is a new name for the promised return, discussed earlier.

yield to maturity
Another name for the promised return on a bond.

A bond's **yield to maturity** represents the market's current assessment of the rate the bond ought to pay given current market conditions. However, the coupon rate represents the market's assessment of the rate the bond should pay at the time of issue. As a result, yield to maturity can be higher or lower than the coupon rate and will change over time as market conditions change.

From another perspective, the yield to maturity is the interest rate that equates the present value of a bond's cash flows to its current price. Technically, a bond's price determines its yield to maturity, not vice versa. Based on the price of a bond and its coupon rate, face value, and maturity, we can compute its yield to maturity. Let's consider a simple example. The market offers a bond today for $1,100. It has a coupon rate of 7.0 percent and a face value of $1,000, and it matures in 20 years. Assume semiannual coupons and that the bond made a coupon payment today (eliminating accrued interest). The bond pricing equation is

$$\$1,100 = \$35(P/A; r/2; 40) + \$1,000(P/F; r/2; 40)$$

Find $r/2$ (the semiannual discount rate) and r (the effective annual rate or yield to maturity). In the dark ages when the authors went to school, this was a fairly tedious task that made use of present value tables and trial and error. These days, financial calculators and PCs have taken over this work. Still, you need to understand what the yield to maturity means and why it is an important number.

Relationship between Coupon Rate and Yield to Maturity

The relationship between a bond's coupon rate (CR) and yield to maturity (YTM) can be stated as follows:

1. If $P_b = F$, then $YTM = CR$.
2. If $P_b < F$, then $YTM > CR$.
3. If $P_b > F$, then $YTM < CR$.

Let's build an intuitive understanding of the relationship between CR and YTM. If the bond's price, P_b, equals its face value, F, then YTM equals CR. Why? Because the bond price already equals its face value (a known cash flow at maturity, assuming a default-free bond), its only return comes in the form of coupon payments. Thus, the yield on this investment if held to maturity (YTM) must exactly equal the return generated from the coupon payments, which is, of course, the coupon rate (CR).

A bond selling below its face value ($1,000) is called a **discount bond.** The total return on a discount bond comes from two cash flows: the coupon payments and the certain payment of the bond's face value at maturity. Thus, yield to maturity is greater than coupon rate because the bond's price appreciation will add value, over and above the return generated by the coupon payments.

A bond selling for more than its face value is called a **premium bond.** For a premium bond, the relationship between yield to maturity and coupon rate is the exact opposite from that for a discount bond. In this case, the certain depreciation of the bond price to its face value reduces the yield to maturity below the coupon rate.

discount bond
A bond selling for less than its face value.

premium bond
A bond selling for more than its face value.

Current Yield

Quotes of a bond price printed in the financial press (as discussed in Appendix A) often state the **current yield** on the bond. The current yield is simply the coupon rate divided by the bond's price (stated as a percentage of face value). For example, the bond we have been using has a price of $864.11 (or 86.411 percent of par) and a

current yield
Coupon rate divided by the bond's price.

coupon rate of 6 percent. Therefore, this bond has a current yield of about 6.9 percent (6 percent divided by 86.411). Notice that the current yield is more than the yield to maturity.

Yield to Call

yield to call
Return on a bond if called.

A call provision may lead a bond investor to calculate another measure of return, the **yield to call.** Basically, this analysis asks the following question: If a bond bought today is called by the issuer at some point in the future, before maturity, what return should the owner expect to earn? An answer to this question requires two modifications to the basic bond pricing equation. First, substitute the call price for the bond's face value, and second, substitute the call date for the maturity date. Assume a twenty-year bond with a current price of $975, a coupon rate of 6.5 percent, and a face value of $1,000. Also, assume the bond is callable in fifteen years at a price of $1,065. Ignoring any accrued interest, the yield to call would be the discount rate that equates $975 to the present value of $65 per year (or $32.50 per six months) for fifteen years, plus $1,065 received at the end of fifteen years. Not surprisingly, the yield to call exceeds the yield to maturity in this example (7.03 percent versus 6.73 percent).

ACTUAL RETURN VERSUS YIELD TO MATURITY

Suppose that you buy the bond discussed in the prior section (6 percent coupon, annual coupon payments, ten-year maturity, face value of $1,000, current price of $865.81, and yield to maturity of 8 percent).[5] You hold the bond for the entire ten-year period, and the issuer pays all interest and principal when due. This investment actually earns 8 percent per annum, right? Not always! Even if you hold a bond until maturity and the issuer does not default, your *actual rate of return* may differ from the promised return (the yield to maturity) when the bond was first purchased. We referred to this variation as reinvestment risk earlier in the chapter. The yield to maturity, or promised rate of return, assumes reinvestment of the coupon payments at the yield to maturity. If the reinvested coupon payments earn a rate other than the yield to maturity, your actual return differs from the promised return.

Having bought the example bond for $865.81 (again, ignoring accrued interest), you hold it to maturity, spending the coupon payments when received. How much cash did the bond actually pay over its ten-year life? You received $1,600 (10 coupon payments of $60 each plus the face value of $1,000). Because the coupon payments were not reinvested, the future value of all the cash received from the bond at maturity (after five years) also equals $1,600. Remember from the basic time-value of money discussion, if we know the present and future values of an investment, and the length of time it is held, we can calculate the **actual rate of return** using the following formula:

actual rate of return
The rate that is effectively or actually earned on the bond investment.

$$ARR = \left[\frac{FV}{PV}\right]^{1/n} - 1 \qquad (9.5)$$

---

[5]We are assuming no accrued interest.

where *ARR* is the actual rate of return, *FV* is the future value of all cash flows on the liquidation date, *PV* is the present value (or price), and *n* is the length of time the investment is held. Using our example, $FV = \$1,600$, $PV = \$865.81$, and $n = 10$. Substituting these values into Equation 9.5 gives an actual rate return of 6.33 percent. (This is also called the *effective annual rate.*) That rate is less than the yield to maturity (and a promised rate of return of 8 percent).

Now, change the example slightly. Assume that, instead of spending the coupon payments, you deposit them in a bank account that pays 3 percent per annum. The new value of the bond investment at the end of ten years equals $1,687.83; the extra $87.83 is interest earned on interest (the return from the reinvested coupons). Equation 9.5 gives an actual rate of return of 6.90 percent (effective annual rate). That is still less than the yield to maturity but higher than not reinvesting coupons at all (for a reinvestment rate of 0 percent).

Now, assume that you can reinvest the bond's coupons in an account that pays 9 percent per annum. Under this assumption, the future value of cash flows in ten years equals $1,911.58 and the actual rate of return equals 8.24 percent.

By now it should be clear: Reinvesting a bond's coupon payments at a higher rate increases the bond's actual rate of return. If the coupons are reinvested at a rate lower (or higher) than the yield to maturity, the actual rate of return will be lower (or higher) than the yield to maturity, or promised rate of return. Of course, this still assumes that the bond is held to maturity and the issuer does not default. Exhibit 9.3 illustrates the relationship between the reinvestment rate and the actual rate of return for the example bond. Notice that the actual rate of return equals the promised rate of return only when the reinvestment rate equals the yield to maturity.

The relationship between reinvestment rates and actual rates of return illustrate that bond investors can be hurt by falling interest rates as well as rising interest rates. Interest rate risk, therefore, reflects the risks associated with interest rates changing (whether upward or downward) during the time an investor owns any bond.

We have more to say about this later in Chapter 10, but here is a simple example that shows how interest rate changes can dramatically affect your bond investment.

Now suppose you buy the ten-year 6 percent coupon bond with a yield to maturity of 8 percent for $865.81. Shortly thereafter the yield to maturity declines to 6 percent. What is the price of the bond now? Knowing that the bond $CR = YTM$, we can deduce that P_b must equal its face value or $1,000, given the relationship between *CR* and *YTM* discussed earlier. If you can sell the bond for $1,060 today, what is your actual rate of return (*ARR*)? It is:

$$ARR = \left[\frac{\$1,060}{\$865.81} \right]^{1/1} - 1 = 22.4\%$$

Twenty-two percent is a far cry from 8 percent or 6 percent! As we found out earlier, changes in interest rates can work for you (or against you). If you can forecast the correct directional change in interest rates, it can work for you. (We'll discuss these and other strategies in the next chapter.) For now, we'll present five bond pricing theorems that will help you understand the impact of term to maturity and coupon on bond prices.

Let's review what we have learned about bond valuation up to this point. The price **RECAP** of a bond is the present value of future cash flows—called coupon payments—plus the present value of the amount received at maturity—called the par value—discounted at the required rate of return—called the yield to maturity.

Exhibit 9.3 ✦ REINVESTMENT RATE AND THE ACTUAL RATE OF RETURN FOR A BOND

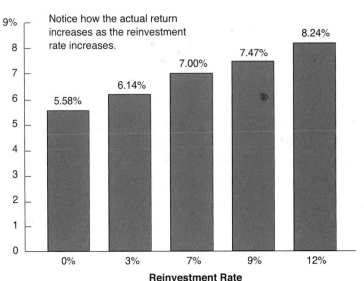

Consider a seven-year bond, with a 7 percent coupon and a face value of $1,000. If this bond has a yield to maturity of 10.0 percent and no accrued interest,

1. Find the bond's price, assuming annual coupon payments.
2. Find the bond's price, assuming semiannual coupon payments.
3. Find the bond's price, assuming it matures in six years and three months and coupons are paid semiannually.
4. Find the bond's yield to call, assuming it can be called in exactly five years at a price of $1,070. (Assume annual coupons.)

Five Bond Pricing Theorems

In this section, we review five well-known bond pricing theorems that attempt to explain various mathematical relationships between bond prices and interest rates. These theorems are important for understanding bond investing. They also provide an important link between understanding bond valuation and interest rate risk.

Before we discuss the bond pricing theorems, let's make two things clear. First, if interest rates are generally rising (or falling), the yield to maturity on every existing bond will rise (or fall). Think about it this way, if the yield on a newly issued five-year Treasury note increased from 6 percent to 6.5 percent, what would happen to the yield on already issued Treasury securities that mature in five years? Obviously, market forces would push their yields upward as well, probably to about 6.5 percent.

Second, yields on short-term and long-term bonds can move in different directions for short periods of time. For example, during the summer of 1993, the yield on Treasury bills (T-bills), which are essentially short-term bonds, rose slightly, whereas the yield on long-term T-bonds fell substantially. With these preliminaries out of the way, let's look at the five bond pricing theorems.

1. BOND PRICES MOVE INVERSELY TO CHANGES IN INTEREST RATES

This first theorem comes from a basic valuation principle: as interest rates rise, bond prices fall (and vice versa). The reason, of course, is that bond investors discount fixed future cash flows at higher interest rates, and higher discount rates give lower present values. This is shown in Exhibit 9.4, which illustrates the various prices of a bond with a thirty-year maturity and a 6 percent coupon, assuming a yield to maturity between 4 percent and 12 percent. For example, at a yield to maturity of 4 percent per annum, the bond has a price of $1,345.84. To increase the bond's yield to maturity to 7 percent, the market would drive its price down to $875.90.

2. LONGER MATURITY MAKES A BOND PRICE MORE SENSITIVE TO INTEREST RATES

The best way to illustrate this pricing relationship is with an example. Consider several bonds, each of which has a coupon rate of 8 percent, a current yield to maturity of 8 percent, and a face value of $1,000. One bond matures in five years, another in ten years, still another in fifteen years, and so forth. How much will the price of each bond change if the market yield to maturity falls from 8 percent to 6 percent? The answer indicates each bond's price sensitivity. We already know that the price of each bond will rise, but will they all rise by the same amount? The answer is *no*. Exhibit 9.5 shows the percentage price changes for all the bonds. Clearly, longer maturities bring greater percentage price increases. (Remember, other than maturity, all the bonds are identical, with initial prices of $1,000.) For example, the five-year bond increases in price from $1,000 to $1,085, or about 8.5 percent. By contrast, the thirty-year bond increases in price from $1,000 to $1,277, or about 27.7 percent.

3. PRICE SENSITIVITY INCREASES WITH MATURITY AT A DECREASING RATE

Take another look at Exhibit 9.5. When the yield to maturity on the bonds falls from 8 percent to 6 percent, the five-year bond increases in price by about $85, the ten-year bond increases in price by about $149, and the fifteen-year bond increases in price by about $196. The ten-year bond is more price sensitive than the five-year bond, and the fifteen-year bond is more price sensitive than the ten-year bond. However, the difference in sensitivity between the fifteen-year and ten-year bonds is *less* than the difference in price sensitivity between the ten-year and five-year bonds ($47 versus $64).

4. LOWER COUPON RATES INCREASE PRICE SENSITIVITY

Again, this theorem is easiest to illustrate using an example. Assume a series of bonds, each having a ten-year maturity, face values of $1,000, and current yields to maturity of 8 percent. The bonds differ only in their coupon rates. One bond has a coupon rate of 4 percent, another has a coupon rate of 6 percent, another has a coupon rate of 8 percent, and so forth. Let's assume the yield to maturity on all the bonds falls from 8 percent to 6 percent. Exhibit 9.6 shows that the prices of all the bonds rise, with the low-coupon bonds rising the most. For example, the price of the 4-percent bond increases from $728 to $851 (16.9 percent) whereas the price of the 12-percent bond increases from $1,272 to $1,446 (13.7 percent).

Exhibit 9.4 ✦ BOND PRICE VERSUS YIELD TO MATURITY

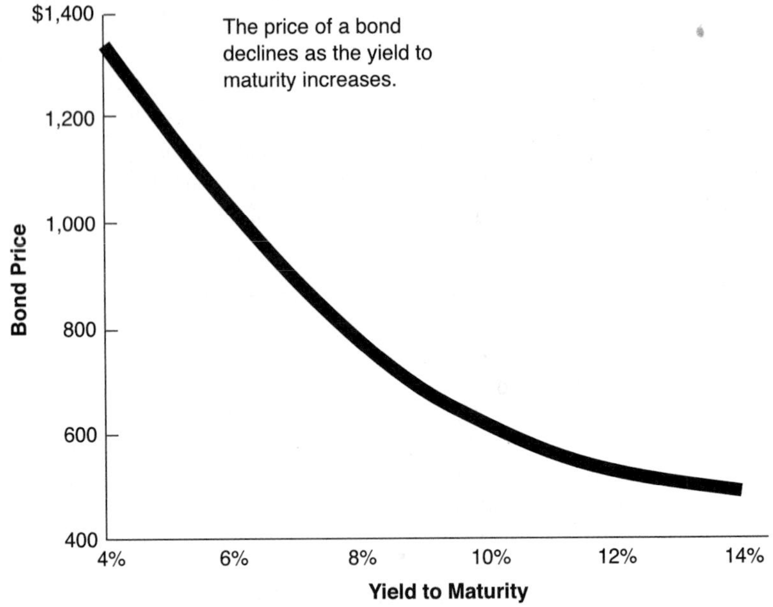

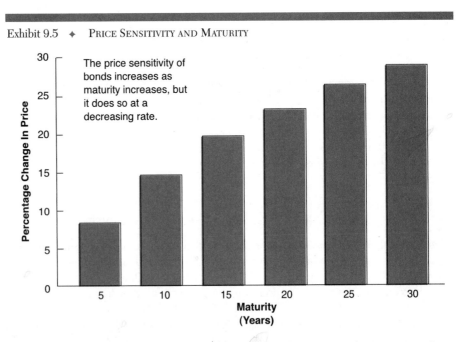

The price of a bond declines as the yield to maturity increases.

NOTE: *The bond has a coupon rate of 6 percent, a maturity of 30 years, and a face value of $1,000.*

Exhibit 9.5 ✦ PRICE SENSITIVITY AND MATURITY

The price sensitivity of bonds increases as maturity increases, but it does so at a decreasing rate.

NOTE: *All bonds have coupon rates of 8 percent and face values of $1,000; price changes assume a drop in the yield to maturity from 8 percent to 6 percent.*

Exhibit 9.6 ✦ PRICE SENSITIVITY AND COUPON RATE

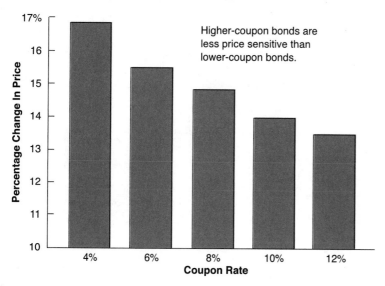

Higher-coupon bonds are less price sensitive than lower-coupon bonds.

NOTE: All bonds have maturities of ten years, and face values of $1,000; price changes assume a drop in yield to maturity from 8 percent to 6 percent.

5. A PRICE INCREASE CAUSED BY A YIELD DECREASE EXCEEDS A PRICE DECREASE CAUSED BY A SIMILAR YIELD INCREASE

Consider a bond with a coupon rate of 8 percent, a maturity of ten years, a face value of $1,000, and suppose its yield to maturity is initially 8 percent. Basic bond valuation confirms that because the yield to maturity equals the coupon rate, the bond is currently selling for its face value. What would happen to the bond's price if its yield to maturity were to fall from 8 percent to 6 percent or rise from 8 percent to 10 percent? The results are shown in Exhibit 9.7. If the bond's yield increases from 8 percent to 10 percent, its price falls by about 12.5 percent. By contrast, if the bond's yield decreases from 8 percent to 6 percent, its price increases by about 14.9 percent.

Assessing Interest Rate Risk

So far, we have discussed bond investment characteristics, including the general risks investors take when they buy bonds and how bonds are valued. In this section we take a more detailed look at how to evaluate the most important risk to a bondholder: interest rate risk. Much of this material flows directly from the bond valuation principles we examined in the prior section.

At this point, it might be useful to summarize what we already know about interest rate risk. As interest rates move up and down, the prices of all bonds change as well. Furthermore, some bonds are more price sensitive than others. Bonds with low coupon rates, for example, are more price sensitive than similar bonds with high coupon rates. Therefore, some bonds expose investors to more interest rate risk (that is, are more price sensitive) than other bonds.

Exhibit 9.7 ✦ PRICE CHANGES FOR INCREASE AND DECREASE IN YIELD

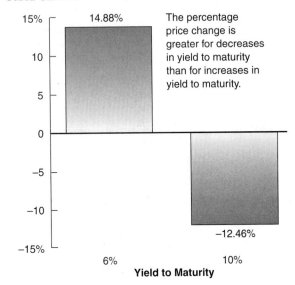

NOTE: Bonds has a coupon rate of 8 percent, a maturity of ten years, and initially yield to maturity is 8 percent.

Although the bond pricing theorems are important for understanding bond investing, each assumes that various factors remain constant while only the one under examination varies. When we try to compare various bonds' price sensitivity levels, these theorems may provide only limited insight. Consider the following two bonds:

Bond A: Coupon = 10%, maturity = twenty years

Bond B: Coupon = 6%, maturity = ten years

Assume that both bonds have the same yield to maturity and face value. Which bond is more price sensitive? So far, we really cannot say. Bond A has the longer maturity, which, according to theorem 2, makes it more price sensitive. However, bond A also has a higher coupon, which, according to theorem 4, makes it less price sensitive. We need some sort of measure by which to compare the price sensitivity of various bonds, regardless of individual coupons and maturities. This measure is called *duration*.

DURATION

duration
Amount of time before the "average" dollar is repaid; a measure of interest rate risk.

The concept of bond duration was formalized by Frederick Macaulay in 1938.[6] **Duration** provides a measure of price sensitivity, and thus interest rate risk, that takes

_____

[6]Frederick Macaulay, *Some Theoretical Problems Suggested by the Movements of Interest Rates, Bond Yields, and Stock Prices in the United States since 1856* (New York: Columbia University Press, 1938).

into account three important factors: coupon rate, time to maturity, and yield to maturity. A longer duration characterizes a more price-sensitive bond.

Technically, duration summarizes the effective maturity of a bond, measuring when an investor receives the average promised cash flow from the bond. More intuitively, duration measures the number of periods required to *recover* the bond's price. As an example, consider a zero-coupon bond with a maturity of five years. Because it pays only one cash flow, at maturity in five years, the average cash flow is received in five years. Therefore, the bond has a duration of five years.

Finding the duration for a bond with a coupon rate not equal to zero is somewhat more complicated. For any bond, duration (D) is calculated as follows:

$$D = \frac{\sum_{t=1}^{T} t(CF_t)(1 + r)^{-t}}{P_b} \qquad (9.6)$$

where CF_t is the cash flow received in period t, T is the number of periods, and r is the appropriate yield to maturity (also adjusted for semiannual coupons if needed). If the bond pays interest semiannually, Equation 9.6 will state D in half-year periods. To restate duration in years, divide D by 2. Let's look at an example.

Exhibit 9.8 details the duration calculation for the familiar bond with a face value of $1,000, a coupon rate of 6 percent, a term of ten years, a yield to maturity of 8 percent (4.0 percent per half-year), and a price of $864.11. The process to calculate duration consists of five steps:

1. List the cash flow received in each period (t). This is column 2 in Exhibit 9.8.
2. Multiply the cash flow (column 2) by the period (the number in column 1). The result, $t \times CF_t$ is shown in column 3.
3. Find the present value of the amount in column 3. This involves multiplying column 3 by the present-value factors shown in column 4. The result is shown in column 5.
4. Sum column 5. In Exhibit 9.8, the sum of column 5 is equal to 12,882.68.
5. Divide the sum by the bond's current price. In the example, 12,882.68 is divided by $864.11. This is the duration of the bond in half-years. Dividing by 2 gives the duration of the bond in years, 7.45.

An investor would receive the bond's average cash flow in about seven years. It should come as no surprise that the duration is relatively close to the bond's maturity, ten years, because the single largest cash flow, the face value, and the final six months' interest ($1,030) arrive when the bond matures.

Investors often look at the ratio $D/(1 + r)$. This measure is referred to as **modified duration.** The above bond's modified duration is equal to $7.45/1.08 = 6.90$. Modified duration reflects the approximate percentage change in price for a given change in yield to maturity.

As mentioned earlier, duration takes into account three important bond pricing factors (maturity, coupon rate, and yield to maturity). The relationship of duration to all three is summed up in three general statements:

1. A longer maturity gives a longer duration, holding the other two factors constant.
2. A higher coupon rate gives a shorter duration, holding the other two factors constant.
3. A higher yield to maturity gives a shorter duration, holding the other two factors constant.

modified duration
Duration divided by the yield to maturity; approximate percentage change in price for a given change in yield to maturity.

The first two statements are fairly intuitive. Bonds with longer maturities spread out their periodic cash flows over longer periods of time. In addition, they take longer

Exhibit 9.8 ✦ EXAMPLE OF DURATION CALCULATION

Basic information

Coupon	6%
Maturity	ten years
Face Value	$1,000
YTM	8%
Bond price	$864.11

Col. 1 Period (t)	Col. 2 Cash Flow (t)	Col. 3 $\times CF$	Col. 4 PV Factor	Col. 5 Col. 3 $\times$ Col. 4
1	$30	30	0.9615	28.85
2	$30	60	0.9246	55.48
3	$30	90	0.8890	80.01
4	$30	120	0.8548	102.58
5	$30	150	0.8219	123.29
6	$30	180	0.7903	142.25
7	$30	210	0.7599	159.58
8	$30	240	0.7307	175.37
9	$30	270	0.7026	189.70
10	$30	300	0.6756	202.68
11	$30	330	0.6496	214.37
12	$30	360	0.6246	224.86
13	$30	390	0.6006	234.23
14	$30	420	0.5775	242.55
15	$30	450	0.5553	249.89
16	$30	480	0.5339	256.27
17	$30	510	0.5134	261.83
18	$30	540	0.4936	266.54
19	$30	570	0.4746	270.52
20	$1030	20,600	0.4564	9,401.84

	Sum	12,882.68
	Sum/Bond price	14.909
	Duration	7.45 years

to return their face values to investors. Bonds with higher coupon rates have larger intermediate cash flows (those prior to maturity) so it takes less time to regain the average dollar.

Exhibits 9.9 and 9.10 illustrate the relationships between duration, maturity, and coupon rates. Exhibit 9.9 shows the durations of four bonds, all with coupon rates of 8 percent and yields to maturity of 6 percent; the bonds have maturities of 5, 10, 20, and 30 years. The positive relationship between duration and maturity is shown clearly. For example, the ten-year bond has a duration of 7.29 years, whereas the thirty-year bond has a duration of 13.56 years.

Exhibit 9.10 shows the negative relationship between coupon rate and duration. All five bonds have maturities of ten years and yields to maturity of 8 percent. Notice that the 4 percent coupon bond has a duration of almost eight years whereas the 12 percent coupon bond has a duration of about 6.5 years.

Exhibit 9.9 ✦ RELATIONSHIP BETWEEN DURATION AND MATURITY

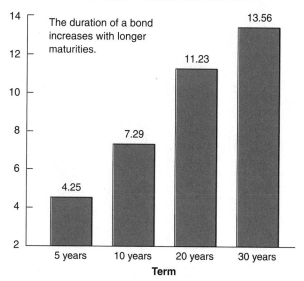

NOTE: *All bonds have coupon rates of 8 percent and yields to maturity of 6 percent.*

Exhibit 9.10 ✦ RELATIONSHIP BETWEEN DURATION AND COUPON RATE

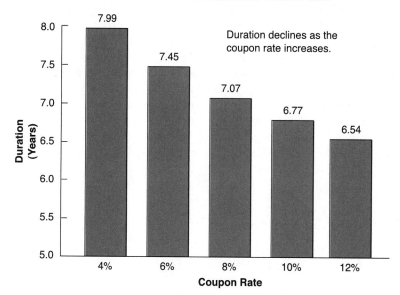

NOTE: *All bonds have terms of ten years and yields to maturity of 8 percent.*

The relationship between duration and yield to maturity is illustrated in Exhibit 9.11. All the bonds have equal coupon rates (8 percent) and maturities (ten years). Because their yields differ, so do their durations. The bond that has a yield to maturity of 4 percent, for example, has a duration of 7.5 years compared with about 6.6 years for the bond with a yield to maturity of 12 percent.

Exhibit 9.11 ✦ RELATIONSHIP BETWEEN DURATION AND COUPON RATE

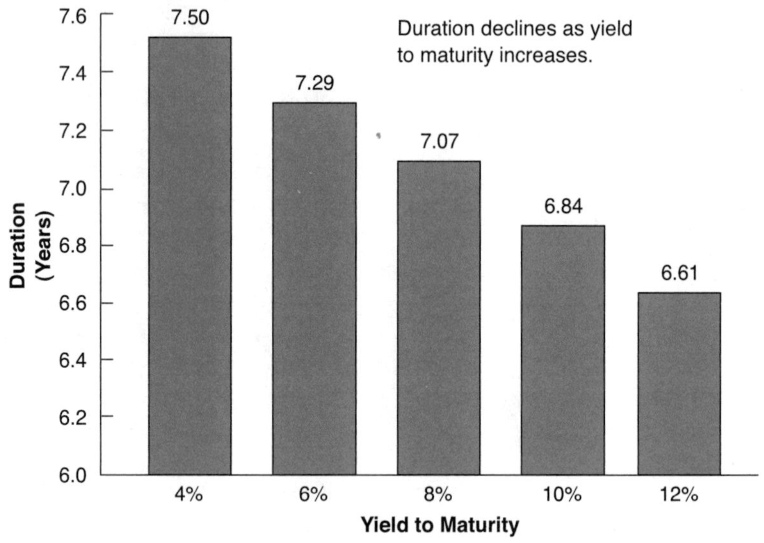

NOTE: All bonds have terms of ten years and coupon rates of 8 percent.

The relationship between yield to maturity and duration is probably less intuitive than the relationships between coupon rates or maturity and duration. Assume a bond has an 8 percent coupon rate and a ten-year maturity as in Exhibit 9.11. A dramatic example would be if interest rates rise from 4 percent to 12 percent, its price will decline. Because you pay less for the bond, the relative recovery years shorten as the coupon that is recovered becomes relatively more significant. Restating that, as the bond prices decline, current yields rise from 6 percent ($80/$1324) to 10 percent ($80/$774). So, the relative significance of coupon increases as interest rates rise, and hence duration decreases.[7] The relationship between duration and yield is important to understanding the uses, and limitations, of duration as a precise measure of price sensitivity and, thus, interest rate risk.

Duration and Price Sensitivity

The prior section explained how to compute duration and the relationship between duration and the three factors that determine bond prices. These discussions lead to

[7]A more technical explanation is as follows: The inverse relationship between yield to maturity and duration results from the nonlinear relationship between the bond's interest rate and its present value. Take another look at Exhibit 9.4. Notice that the relationship between yield to maturity and price is more a convex curve than a straight line. How does this affect duration? Duration measures the slope of a straight line tangent to each point along that curve. As a bond moves up or down the curve, the slope of the line changes. For example, moving down the curve (that is, as yield to maturity increases) implies a decreasing slope of the line.

the obvious conclusion that a longer duration indicates greater price sensitivity, for a given change in yield. This suggests one use of duration: to compare the price sensitivity levels of two bonds regardless of their individual coupon rates and maturities.

As an example, reconsider the two bonds that we tried to compare earlier:

Bond A: Coupon rate = 10 percent, maturity = twenty years, YTM = 8 percent

Bond B: Coupon rate = 6 percent, maturity = ten years, YTM = 8 percent

Before the concept of duration was introduced, we could not say, unequivocally, that one was more price sensitive than the other. Duration more accurately measures this important relationship. The duration of bond A is 9.87 years and the duration of bond B is 7.45 years. Therefore, if yields rise by a given amount (say, from 8 percent to 8.5 percent), the prices of both bonds will fall, but bond A's price will fall by a greater amount. Therefore, bond A has more interest rate risk than bond B. This feature, by itself, makes duration a useful tool for bond investors.

Duration and Price Changes

Can this comparison become any more specific, however? It can, to a point. It has been shown that the price change for a bond, given a change in yield to maturity, can be approximated by the following equation:

$$\Delta P \approx - D\left[\Delta(1 + r)/(1 + r)\right]P_b \tag{9.7}$$

where ΔP is the change in price, D is the bond's duration, $\Delta(1 + r)/(1 + r)$ is the percentage change in the yield to maturity, and P_b is the current price of the bond. Consider the two bonds above, A and B, and assume the yield to maturity on both increases from 8 percent to 8.5 percent. Their approximate price changes can be calculated as follows:

$$\text{Bond A: } \Delta P \approx - 9.87[0.005/(1 + .08)]\,(\$119.79)$$
$$\approx - \$5.47 \text{ (per \$100 face value)}$$
$$\text{Bond B: } \Delta P \approx - 7.45[0.005/(1 + .08)]\,(\$86.41)$$
$$\approx - \$2.98 \text{ (per \$100 face value)}$$

Why is this only an approximate price change? The reason goes back to our discussion in the prior section: As a bond's yield to maturity changes, so does its duration. Duration is a measure of price sensitivity, but only a *point* measure. A greater change in yield to maturity gives a less precise statement of price change calculated using duration. This is sometimes referred to as *duration tracking error.*

Even if duration gives only approximate price changes, it is still a useful measure of interest rate risk. As shown in the Investment Insights box, duration is an important key to assessing the safety of a bond mutual fund.

What have we learned about interest rate risk? First, interest rate risk can be described as a bond's price sensitivity to a change in its yield to maturity. Second, we determined that all bonds expose investors to interest rate risk, although some have more risk than others. Third, we demonstrated the usefulness of a summary measure of price sensitivity (duration).

RECAP

INVESTMENT INSIGHTS

HOW TO APPLY DURATION

In 1994, the Federal Reserve's raising of interest rates several times made bond investors nervous. However, at such times brave investors should hold off from the decision to bail out or jump in until they've looked over their bond's duration.

Equation 9.6, by which we make that analysis, looks complicated, but it's not so hard to interpret. Technically speaking, duration measures the number of years required to recover the average cash flows from the bond investment. It's a mathematical calculation of how long a bond must be held to actually realize the stated yield to maturity given the price you've paid for the bond.

True, the duration formula can be used to link market interest rate changes to bond price changes. Duration can be used to directly link the change in market interest rates to the percentage change in bond price. That is, it can serve as an approximate measure of bond volatility.

Suppose a bond fund has 7.5 years of duration. That is, for a one-percent change in the market interest rate, this bond will experience a 7.5-percent change in its price. If the interest rate goes up one percent for the market, the bond's price will decline by 7.5 percent. Of course, the reverse is true if interest rates decline. So, duration allows an average investor to measure a bond fund's sensitivity to interest rate increases and decreases, and can provide an early warning of dangers ahead.

Most investors realize that long-term bonds are more sensitive to a given change in interest rates than are short-term bonds. Likewise, the longer-term bonds have longer durations than shorter-term bonds. The relationship allows the investor to quantify the approximate gain (or loss) due to interest rate changes. Generally, if you think interest rates will continue to rise, the shorter-duration bonds are better, and when you expect interest rates to head downward, longer-duration bonds are better for investors holding bonds in a long position.

Morningstar now publishes duration figures in its biweekly reports on corporate-general bond funds, corporate-high-quality bond funds and government funds, says Mr. Rekenthaler, editor of Morningstar Mutual Funds, Inc, a publication that tracks mutual fund performance. They also plan to publish duration calculations for the bond portions of hybrid funds, balanced funds and asset-allocation funds that invest in both bonds and common stocks. Unfortunately, Morningstar doesn't provide durations for municipal and international bond funds because the numbers are more difficult to obtain.

Source: The Wall Street Journal, *April 6, 1994, pC1.*

Consider a bond with a coupon rate of 7 percent, a maturity of five years, a face value of $1,000, and a yield to maturity of 7 percent (assume annual coupon payments and no accrued interest).

5. Find the bond's duration and modified duration.
6. Find the approximate price change if the bond's yield to maturity falls from 7 percent to 6.5 percent.

Credit Risk

In this section, we examine the other major risk bond investors face, the risk of not receiving promised cash flows in a timely fashion—credit or default risk. Although all bonds feature interest rate risk, some expose investors to zero credit risk. These are bonds issued by the U.S. Treasury. (Remember, because the Treasury owns the only legal financial printing press, it can always print money to pay its bills.) Bonds issued by corporations and municipalities all have varying degrees of credit risk. Some of these bonds are almost as safe as Treasuries, whereas others are far more speculative. In this section, we discuss how to evaluate credit risk. We also take a detailed look at

Exhibit 9.12   ✦   General Description of Bond Ratings

Description of Potential Credit Risk	Standard & Poor's Rating	Moody's Rating
Capacity to pay interest and repay principal is extremely strong.	AAA	Aaa
Very strong capacity to pay interest and repay principal; only slightly less safe than debt rated triple A.	AA	Aa
Strong capacity to pay interest and repay principal, though somewhat susceptible to adverse changes in financial and economic conditions.	A	A
Adequate capacity to pay interest and repay principal, though more susceptible to adverse changes in economic and financial conditions.	BBB	Baa
Speculative; faces ongoing uncertainties or exposure to adverse conditions that could cause inability to pay interest or repay principal.	BB	Ba
Vulnerable to default, but currently can meet interest and principal obligations.	B	B
Currently vulnerable to default and dependent on favorable conditions to meet obligations.	CCC	Caa
More vulnerable to default and highly speculative.	CC	Ca
Extremely speculative, poor prospects for attaining any real investment standing.	C	C
Currently in default.	DDD or below	—

an actual bond default to see how it affected issuers and investors. First, let's examine **bond ratings**—perhaps the most common tool for assessing credit risk.

bond ratings
Independent assessments of bond credit risk.

BOND RATINGS

Most, although not all publicly traded corporate and municipal bonds are rated by independent investment information services. The two best-known rating agencies are Moody's and S&P. Exhibit 9.12 presents a brief description of Moody's and S&P bond ratings. In addition to those letter ratings, Moody's will occasionally assign a number to a bond rating to indicate where a bond ranks within its rating category. For example, a bond with a rating of A1 is considered of slightly higher quality than a bond with a rating of A3. S&P sometimes adds a plus ($+$) or minus ($-$) to a letter rating to show relative standing within a rating category.

Moody's and S&P rate bonds similarly. Both rate bonds primarily on the issuer's ability to make required principal and interest payments in a timely fashion. Bonds that receive the highest rating (Aaa or AAA), for example, are considered to have virtually no credit risk, regardless of the economic environment. An issuer whose bond receives a middle rating (say, Baa or BBB) is considered to have adequate capacity to make interest and principal payments, but that capacity may be adversely affected by

investment-grade bonds
Bonds with ratings of BBB or greater

speculative-grade (junk) bonds
Bonds with ratings below BBB.

deteriorating economic conditions. Both Moody's and S&P divide bonds into two general categories based on their ratings: **investment-grade bonds** (Baa/BBB-rated issues or above) and **speculative-grade, or junk bonds** (Ba/BB-rated issues, or below).[8]

Moody's and S&P rate newly issued bonds and update their ratings on existing bonds. Both companies publish lists of bonds whose ratings are under review. S&P's publication, for example, is called *Credit Watch*.

Determinants of Bond Ratings

Why do some bonds receive higher ratings than other bonds? As we indicated, Moody's and S&P base a bond rating primarily on the issuer's ability to make required principal and interest payments in a timely fashion. Not surprisingly, the financial characteristics of issuers with high ratings differ from those with lower ratings. For example, a corporate issuer with an Aaa/AAA rating should be stronger financially than a corporation with a Baa/BBB rating. You can see an illustration of this in Exhibit 9.13, which breaks down three-year median values of selected financial ratios by S&P rating category. (These data refer to corporate issuers only.) The data show that higher-rated corporations are, on average, less levered and more profitable, and they have greater capacity to cover fixed financial charges.

In addition to the issuer's financial characteristics, both Moody's and S&P examine other factors when determining bond ratings. These include the nature of the bond, its specific provisions, and the protection it affords creditors in the event of bankruptcy. S&P, for example, assigns a rating of BB to a corporation's subordinated debt if its senior debt has a BBB rating. As another example, a municipal bond that is insured will generally receive an Aaa/AAA rating regardless of other characteristics.

Bond Ratings and Default Rates

Bond ratings raise several important questions. Perhaps the most important is whether bond ratings predict default reasonably well. In other words, has the historical default rate been higher for bonds with lower ratings? Available evidence indicates yes. For example, Exhibit 9.14 lists one-year and ten-year default rates for corporate bonds between 1970 and 1990, broken down by original bond ratings.

Notice in Figure 9.14 that less than one-half of 1 percent of bonds originally rated Aaa defaulted within ten years of issue. (None defaulted within one year of issue.) By contrast, slightly over 8 percent of bonds originally rated B defaulted within one year of issue, and almost one-quarter defaulted within ten years of issue. In addition, notice the dramatic difference in the historical default rates between investment grade bonds (Baa and above) and speculative grade, or junk, bonds (Ba and B). For example, the ten-year default rate for bonds rated Baa was less than 4 percent compared with a ten-year default rate of more than 11 percent for bonds rated Ba.

Another way of assessing the effectiveness of bond ratings is to see whether (and how) they have changed prior to default. We would expect to see bond ratings falling well before issuers actually defaulted, as issuers' financial conditions deteriorate. This appears to be the case. Exhibit 9.15 lists the distribution of original ratings on 556

---

[8]Some institutional investors are prohibited from buying speculative grade bonds.

Exhibit 9.13 ✦ Median Financial Ratios by S&P Rating Category

Rating Category	Fixed-Charge Coverage Ratio	Cash Flow to Long-Term Debt	Long-Term Debt to Capital
AAA	7.48	3.09	8.85%
AA	4.43	1.18	18.88
A	2.93	0.75	24.46
BBB	2.30	0.46	31.54
BB	2.04	0.27	42.52

Source: Debt Rating Criteria, *Standard & Poor's, 1986, p. 51.*

Exhibit 9.14 ✦ Historical Default Rates for Corporate Bonds: 1970–90

Original Rating	Default Rates One Year from Issue	Default Rates Ten Years from Issue
AAA	0.00%	0.37%
Aa	0.04	0.65
A	0.01	0.99
Baa	0.17	3.78
Ba	1.80	11.29
B	8.08	24.17

Source: J. S. Fons and A. E. Kimball, "Corporate Bond Defaults and Default Rates," Journal of Fixed Income, *June 1991, pp. 36-47.*

corporate bond issues that eventually defaulted between 1970 and 1991, as well as the rating distributions one year and six months before actual default.

Only about one-quarter of the 556 corporate issues that actually defaulted between 1970 and 1991 were originally classified as investment grade. (Five bonds were even initially rated AAA.) The rest were originally classified as junk bonds. The most common original bond rating was B. The data suggest that as default approached, the average rating did indeed decline. One year before default, more than half the bonds were rated B, CCC, or CC, whereas less than 10 percent were still classified as investment grade. Finally, six months before reaching default status, less than 8 percent of the bonds carried investment-grade ratings whereas almost 90 percent were rated B or below.

GRAHAM AND DODD ON CREDIT RISK AND BOND SELECTION

Although bond ratings are useful tools for assessing credit risk, they are not perfect predictors. Further, many bonds are not even rated. Potential bond investors often must look beyond bond ratings to evaluate the specific characteristics of issues and issuers. In addition to being the fathers of modern stock analysis, Graham and Dodd also had a lot to say about bond investing.[9]

---

[9]See, S. Cottle, et. al., *Graham & Dodd's Security Analysis,* 5th ed. (New York: McGraw-Hill, 1998), pp.40–482.

Exhibit 9.15 ✦ S&P Rating Distributions of Defaulting Bond Issues

Rating Category	Rating when Issued	Rating Prior to Reaching Default Status	
		One-Year Prior to Default	Six Months Prior to Default
AAA	0.9%	0.0%	0.0%
AA	3.4	0.0	0.0
A	10.8	0.4	7.3
BB	10.6	9.8	5.9
B	47.8	49.4	40.4
CCC	14.6	28.4	40.2
CC	0.7	2.1	5.1
C	0.0	0.6	0.6

Note: The table shows the distribution of bond ratings at the time of issue, one year prior to default, and six months prior to default. For example, almost 48 percent of bonds that eventually defaulted were rated B when issued; almost half of bonds that eventually defaulted were rated B one year prior to reaching default status.

Source: E. I. Altman, "Revisiting the High-Yield Bond Market," Financial Management, Summer 1992, p. 85.

Graham and Dodd argued that bond investors should focus on avoiding losses. Therefore, bond selection is "primarily a negative art. . . . [I]t is a process of exclusion and rejection, rather than [of] search and acceptance."[10] To meet this objective, Graham and Dodd established a set of qualitative and quantitative standards of safety. After reviewing these standards, it is probably reasonable to say that Graham and Dodd would not be big fans of junk bonds!

Graham and Dodd's qualitative standards include stability, issuer size, and issue terms. They argue that more stable companies with better interest coverage ratios and profitability over several business cycles are better credit risks. For example, a company whose interest coverage ratio stays around 3.03 over several business cycles is a better credit risk than one whose interest coverage ranges from, say, 1.5 × to 4.5 × depending on the economic environment. Larger issuers, according to Graham and Dodd, are safer than smaller issuers. Indeed, the historical default rate is higher for smaller issuers (measured in terms of total assets) than for larger issuers. Finally, the terms of the issue are also important. Shorter maturities, more secure types of securities (for example, mortgage bonds), and protective provisions make for safer bonds. For example, Graham and Dodd believed that bonds with sinking funds are better, safer investments compared with bonds without sinking funds.[11]

---

[10]Ibid, p. 441.

[11]A sinking fund is a provision that requires the issuer to retire—by calling—a fixed percentage of bonds each year, over a specified period, before maturity. In essence, a sinking fund shortens the effective maturity of a bond issue and also stretches the repayment of principal over several years. Bonds with sinking funds tend to have lower yields compared with similar bonds without sinking funds.

Exhibit 9.16 ✦ Graham and Dodd's Standards for Safety: Investment Grade Bonds

1. Retained earnings equal to 40 percent of assets, except in capital-intensive businesses, where 25 percent may be adequate.
2. Positive trends in growth and profitability relative to trends in the economy and in the company's industry.
3. Reasonable stability of earning power, with no or infrequent loss years.
4. A minimum size of $50 million as measured by the five-year average market value of the borrower's net worth.
5. Reasonable protection against excessive dilution of the priority of claim on earning power.
6. Net current assets equal to 100 percent of total long-term debt.
7. A working capital ratio of at least 1.75:1.
8. A quick ratio of 1:1.
9. An equity cushion of 200 percent of total debt as measured by the five-year average of the market value of the borrower's net worth.
10. Interest charges earned an average of five times before taxes for industrials and three times for public utilities, with a poorest-year minimum of twice.
11. Total debt service coverage averaging twice and not below once in the poorest year.

Source: S. Cottle et al. *Graham and Dodd's Security Analysis,* 5th ed. (New York: McGraw-Hill, 1988), p. 465. *Reproduced with permission of McGraw-Hill.*

In addition to these qualitative standards, Graham and Dodd also list 11 minimum quantitative standards for investment-grade bonds. They believed, for example, that issuers of investment-grade bonds should have net total current assets (current assets minus current liabilities) equal to at least 100 percent of outstanding long-term debt. We reprint this list in Exhibit 9.16. Unfortunately, no information describes how Graham and Dodd came up with these standards. In addition, these standards are quite strict; many companies with investment-grade bond ratings probably fail to meet them.

See the Investment Insights box on page 234 for a discussion of the demise of Washington Public Power Supply Systems (WPPSS,—often referred to in the financial press as "Whoops"). In the early 1980s, WPPSS provided a prime example of a company defaulting and the rating agencies falling behind in their assessment of the company's financial conditions and default risk. Many investors paid a price for relying on others to do their homework.

Risk and Required Returns for Bonds

Throughout this text, we have discussed the notion that risk and return are related; riskier investments must promise higher returns. Therefore, we would expect to see bond investors demanding higher promised returns on higher-risk bonds. Given that bonds expose investors to several different types of risk, we can relate the promised (required or expected) return on a bond to several factors, as follows:

$$r = f(i, \Delta p, ir, rr, dr, cr, lr, fxr) \tag{9.8}$$

where i is the **real rate of interest,** Δp is the expected rate of inflation over the bond's term, ir is interest rate risk, rr is reinvestment risk, dr is default (credit)

real rate of interest
Rate of interest in the absence of inflation or any risk premium.

INVESTMENT INSIGHTS

ANATOMY OF A DEFAULT

On July 23, 1983, the Washington Public Power Supply System (WPPSS, often referred to in the press as "Whoops") defaulted on approximately $2.25 billion in bonds. The default was the largest municipal bond default in U.S. history, about twice as large as the next largest such default—Orange County, California, in 1994. The WPPSS default was caused by problems associated with two partially completed nuclear power plants in Washington state. Financial problems (for example, cost overruns), regulatory factors, and market forces such as slower growth in demand for electric power led to project cancellations and bond default.

The default had been expected for several months, although the exact timing took the financial markets somewhat by surprise. The market price of WPPSS bonds collapsed; some of the defaulted bonds were trading for as little as 8.5 cents on the dollar. In response to the default, a series of class action federal and state lawsuits were filed on behalf of WPPSS bondholders. The state lawsuits were eventually dismissed. In late 1988, more than five years after WPPSS defaulted, the federal lawsuit plaintiffs (the bondholders) and defendants (the State of Washington, more than 100 utilities, securities firms, and plant contractors) reached a preliminary settlement. The settlement called for payment of approximately $750 million to the plaintiffs. In October 1990, a federal court approved the allocation of these funds to individual bondholders, and final payment was made in September 1992. Bondholders received about 45 cents on the dollar after legal expenses were paid.

Investors can learn several important lessons from the WPPSS default. First, large, well-known bond issues can go into default. The WPPSS bonds were originally rated A by S&P and A1 by Moody's, both investment-grade ratings. Even 18 months before default, the WPPSS bonds still carried an A rating. Not until about eight months before default did S&P drop the WPPSS bonds below investment grade. At the time of actual default, the bonds were rated B.

A second lesson to be learned is that default is costly to bond investors. Although they settled the lawsuit for a record amount and recovered far more than most investors do in defaults, investors received less than half the face value of their bonds. In addition, more than nine years passed before settlement, and of course, investors received nothing during that time. The bottom line of the WPPSS story is that bond investors ignore credit risk at their peril.

risk, *cr* is call risk, *lr* is liquidity risk, and *fxr* is foreign exchange risk. As each risk factor rises (or falls), the promised return on a bond also rises (or falls).

The first two factors in Equation 9.8 (*i* and Δp) make up the required return on a risk-free bond. (The closest thing to a truly risk-free security is a short-term T-bill.) The other seven factors can be thought of as compensation (or risk premiums) for investing in bonds that expose investors to various types of risk. For some bonds, certain risk premiums may be zero (or close to zero). For example, T-bonds have no credit risk, thus investors can demand no risk premium to the bonds' required returns to compensate investors for credit risk. However, T-bonds do expose investors to other types of risk (for example, interest rate risk), and thus those risk premiums will be added to the bonds' promised returns.

Equation 9.8 represents only a general model of the determinants of bond yields and is difficult to quantify. Nevertheless, the model can give some insight into the determinants of bond yields. Now let's take a more detailed look at the relationship between bond yields and two important factors: maturity and credit risk.

term structure of interest rate (yield curve)
Relationship between maturity and bond yields.

BOND YIELDS AND MATURITY

The relationship between bond yields and maturity often is referred to as the **term structure of interest rates,** or **yield curve.** The yield curve shows the relationship between yield and maturity for a group of bonds that are similar in other respects. U.S. Treasury securities are often used to represent the yield curve because all are free of default risk and have excellent secondary markets.

Although the yield curve raises several important and interesting questions, for our purposes in this chapter we will examine only two: What is the expected shape of the yield curve? Does the shape of the yield curve change over time?

Based on our discussion in this chapter, one could argue that the normal shape of the yield curve should be upward sloping. In other words, as the term to maturity increases, so should the yield. There are several reasons for this. We have seen that a longer-maturity bond exposes the investor to greater interest rate risk (holding other factors constant). Also, as one holds a bond longer, the probability of unfavorable changes in interest rates rises. Thus, one could argue that longer-term bonds expose investors to greater amounts of reinvestment risk. Furthermore, longer-term bonds also expose investors to greater amounts of purchasing power risk. After all, it is easier to forecast inflation for next year than to forecast inflation for the next 30 years. Investors who bought bonds back in the 1950s never expected the inflation of the 1970s.

All of this, added up, suggests that, all things being equal, investors would rather own short-term bonds than long-term bonds; investors require inducements (in the form of higher yields) to purchase longer-term bonds. Therefore, the normal shape of the yield curve should be positive. The evidence does indeed suggest that the yield curve is normally upward-sloping. But does it always slope upward? No.

Exhibit 9.17 shows the general shape of the Treasury yield curve between 1966 and 1999. To simplify the shape, the figure shows the yield spread between three-month T-bills and long-term T-bonds (with at least ten years to maturity). A yield spread is the difference in yield between the two instruments. For example, if the yield on three-month T-bills is 4.30 percent and the yield on long-term T-bonds is 7.00 percent, the yield spread (bonds minus bills) is 2.70 percent. If the yield spread is positive, the yield curve slopes upward. Notice that the shape of the yield curve has changed from time to time.

The yield spread between three-month bills and long-term bonds has generally been positive over this time period (indicating an upward-sloping yield curve). However, the slope has been much steeper in some years than other years. In 1992, for example, the spread was more than 4 percent, whereas in 1990 it had been 1.24 percent. In some years, the yield spread has been virtually zero. In 1970, for example, the yield spread was about 0.1 percent. A yield spread close to zero defines a flat yield curve. In other years, yields on T-bills have actually exceeded yields on long-term T-bonds. In 1981, for example, T-bills were yielding almost 2 percent more than long-term bonds. A negative yield spread defines an inverted (that is, downward-sloping) yield curve.

What do differently shaped yield curves mean? We discuss several interesting theories of the yield curve in the next chapter. Each theory has several implications for active and passive bond portfolio management strategies. We discuss these in Chapter 10 as well.

BOND YIELDS AND CREDIT RISK

Just as interest rates have a term structure, they also have a risk structure that takes into account differences in bond yields across bonds with different degrees of credit risk. In general, of course, bonds with higher credit risk always have higher yields.

Exhibit 9.17 ✦ Yᴇʟᴅ Sᴘʀᴇᴀᴅ ʙᴇᴛᴡᴇᴇɴ T-Bᴏɴᴅs ᴀɴᴅ T-Bɪʟʟs

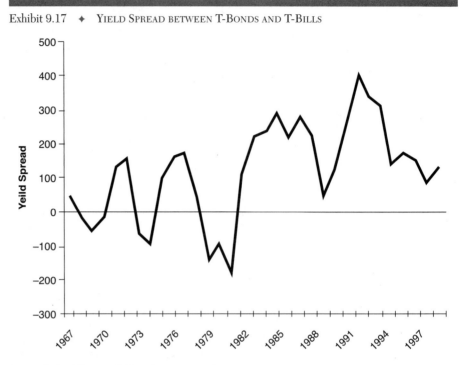

Source: Federal Reserve Bulletin *(various issues).*

However, the yield spreads between bonds of varying credit risk do not remain constant over time. The risk structure of interest rates changes from time to time. As an example, look at Exhibit 9.18, which shows two yield spreads (Aaa corporates minus long-term T-bonds, and Baa corporates minus Aaa corporates) between 1968 and 1999.

Both yield spreads were positive throughout this thirty-year period; the yield spread between Aaa corporates and T-bonds, as well as the spread between Baa corporates and Aaa corporates, averaged about 1 percent. However, both spreads show a good deal of variation around their averages. In 1992, for example, the spread between Aaa corporates and long-term T-bonds was less than one-half of 1 percent (0.48 percent). By contrast, in 1985 the spread was almost 2 percent. During this thirty-year period, the yield spread between Baa and Aaa corporates has been as low as 0.38 percent (1968) and as high as 2.32 percent (1982).

Several theories try to explain the risk structure of interest rates. One popular theory suggests that yield spreads widen and narrow in response to economic expectations. If investors are pessimistic about the economy, yield spreads widen; if investors are optimistic, spreads narrow. Apparently, the argument goes, investors are more quality conscious in a poor economic environment than they are in a good environment. Investors are willing to hold lower-quality bonds in a poor economy but require higher credit-risk premiums.

We have learned quite a bit about bonds in this chapter. We know how to value bonds, measure interest rate risk, and assess credit risk. In the next chapter, we examine passive and active bond-management strategies.

Exhibit 9.18 ✦ Quality Yield Spreads in the U.S. Capital Markets

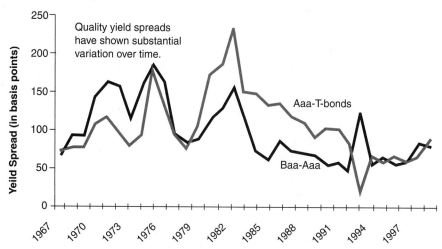

Source: Federal Reserve Bulletin (*various issues*).

Chapter Summary

1. **Why are bonds viable investment alternatives?**
   Bonds are viable investment alternatives because they provide the best source of consistent income. Bonds can also help to diversify a stock portfolio and can produce substantial capital gains. Some bonds offer tax advantages as well.

2. **What risks do bond investors face?**
   Investing in bonds is not without risk. Bond investors are exposed to interest rate risk, credit risk, purchasing power risk, reinvestment risk, liquidity risk, and foreign exchange risk. Bonds vary substantially in terms of risk, and not all bonds expose to every type of risk. T-bonds, for example, have no credit risk.

3. **How are bonds priced?**
   The price of a bond is the present value of future coupon payments plus the present value of the amount to be returned at maturity—called the par or face value—discounted at the yield to maturity. If the bond pays coupon interest twice a year—which most bonds do—an adjustment is necessary to find the price of the bond. If the bond is purchased between the dates when coupon interest is paid, the buyer owes the seller accrued interest. This also affects the bond's price. If coupon payments are reinvested at a rate other than the yield to maturity, the actual return on the bond will differ from the bond's yield to maturity.

4. **What are the basic bond pricing theorems?**
   There are five basic bond pricing theorems. First, bond prices move inversely within interest rates. Second, the price sensitivity of bonds, with respect to changes in interest rates, increases as maturity increases. Third, the price sensitivity of bonds with respect to maturity increases at a decreasing rate. Fourth, bonds with lower coupon rates are more price sensitive compared with bonds with higher coupon rates. Fifth, a price increase caused by a yield decrease exceeds a price decrease caused by a similar yield increase.

5. **How can interest rate risk be measured?**
   Interest rate risk is defined as the price sensitivity of a bond to a given change in interest rates. The most widely used summary measure of interest rate risk is duration.

Duration is defined as the length of time before the average dollar is repaid to the investor. The longer the duration of a bond, the more price sensitive it is. A bond's duration is positively related to its maturity but negatively related to its coupon rate and yield to maturity.

6. How can credit risk be evaluated?

Bonds vary widely in terms of credit risk. One way of assessing credit risk to look at the bond's rating—most corporate and municipal bonds are rated by S&P, Moody's, or both. The higher the rating, the lower the amount of credit risk. Although not perfect, bond ratings are fairly accurate predictors of credit risk. Graham and Dodd suggested some qualitative and quantitative standards for evaluating credit risk, arguing that safety of principal was the most important consideration.

7. How are bond risk and required return related?

The expected, or promised, return on a bond is a function of the real rate of interest plus compensation for the expected rate of inflation. To this, investors add a risk premium that reflects, when applicable, credit risk, interest rate risk, liquidity risk, and foreign exchange risk. The yield curve—the relationship between long- and short-term bond yields—has generally sloped upward. However, at times the yield curve has been flat or even sloped downward. Likewise, the yield spreads between bonds of varying credit risk have varied substantially over time.

Mini Case

This mini-case provides opportunities to practice basic principles of bond valuation. Use the bond data below to answer the following questions:

Coupon rate = 4 percent
Yield to maturity = 6 percent
Face value = $1,000
Maturity = 5 years

1. Assuming annual coupon payments, and maturity in exactly five years, find the price of this bond.
2. Assuming semiannual coupon payments, maturity in exactly five years, and a yield to maturity of 6 percent, find the price of this bond.
3. Why are the prices you found in questions 1 and 2 different?
4. Now, assume that the bond matures in exactly four years and three months. (Also, assume semiannual coupons and an effective annual yield to maturity of 6 percent.) Find the bond's price. How much accrued interest could a buyer owe?
5. Go back to the assumptions in b. If you were to buy the bond today and hold it until maturity, and the issuer did not default, would the actual annual rate of return always be equal to 6 percent? What would the actual rate of return be if you spent the coupon payments?

Review Questions and Problems

1. List some of the reasons investors should consider buying bonds. Elaborate on one reason you listed.
2. What risks are associated with investing in bonds? To which type(s) of risk are all bond investors exposed?
3. List the variables you need to know to find the price of a bond. What is *yield to maturity?*

4. Determine the price of a bond with a 4 percent coupon rate, maturing in ten years, and a yield to maturity of 6 percent.
   a. Assume annual interest payments and no accrued interest.
   b. Assume semiannual interest payments and no accrued interest.

5. Find the price of a bond with a 6 percent coupon rate, maturing in ten years, and yielding 8 percent.
   a. Assume annual interest payments and no accrued interest.
   b. Assume semiannual interest payment and no accrued interest.

6. Determine the price of a bond with a 5 percent coupon rate, maturing in five years, with a yield to maturity of 4 percent.
   a. Assume annual interest payments and no accrued interest.
   b. Assume semiannual interest payments and no accrued interest.

7. Find the price of a bond with zero coupon payments, maturing in ten years, with a yield to maturity of 6 percent.
   a. Assume annual interest payments.
   b. Assume semiannual interest payments.

8. Find the price of a zero coupon bond, maturing in 20 years, with a yield to maturity of 8 percent.
   a. Assume annual interest payments.
   b. Assume semiannual interest payments.

9. Define *accrued interest*. Using the information in question 4, find the price of the bond, assuming the bond matured in exactly fourteen years and nine months.

10. What is the price of a three-year, 6 percent coupon bond yielding 6 percent if the bond matures in two years and eight months and interest is accrued and paid semiannually?

11. What is the price of a three-year, 4 percent coupon bond yielding 6 percent if the bond matures in two years and eight months and interest is accrued and paid semiannually?

12. What is the price of a 6 percent coupon, five-year bond yielding 8 percent if the bond matures in four years ten months and interest is accrued and paid semiannually?

13. Assume a bond has a current price of $1,100, a face value of $1,000, a coupon rate of 8 percent, and exactly ten years to maturity (assume annual coupon payments). Find the bond's yield to maturity. If this bond is callable in exactly eight years at $1,080, what is the yield to call?

14. A ten-year bond is priced at $851.25, and its coupon rate equals 4 percent per annum. Assuming semiannual coupon payments and a $1,000 face value, what is its yield to maturity?

15. A bond matures in 20 years and is priced at $548.60. Its annual coupon rate equals 6 percent, paid semiannually, and it has a face value of $1,000. What is its yield to maturity?

16. A zero coupon bond matures in ten years and is priced at $508.34. If it has a $1,000 face value, what is its yield to maturity?

17. If you were to buy a ten-year, 7 percent coupon bond today for its face value of $1,000, what would your actual rate of return be if you reinvested the coupon payments at 8 percent?
   a. Assume you would hold the bond to maturity and the bond would pay interest once a year.

18. Why is the actual rate of return always equal to the yield to maturity for a zero coupon bond (assuming it is held to maturity and the issuer does not default)?

19. A 6 percent coupon bond has five years to maturity. If coupon is paid annually and reinvested at 7 percent over the five years, what is the actual rate of return?

20. A 4 percent coupon bond matures in ten years and its yield to maturity is 7 percent. If coupon is paid annually and the coupons are reinvested at 5 percent for the next ten years, what is the actual rate of return?

21. Suppose you purchased a ten-year, 5 percent coupon bond with a yield of 7 percent.
    a. What is the bond price?
    b. Two years later, its market yield declines to 6 percent. What is its price two years later?
    c. If you collect two coupon payments and reinvest them at 6 percent and sell the bond, what is your actual rate of return?
22. Suppose you purchased a ten-year, 5 percent coupon bond with a yield of 7 percent.
    a. What is the bond price?
    b. Two years later, its market yield declines to 6 percent. What is its price two years later?
    c. If you collect two coupon payments and reinvest them at 6 percent and sell the bond, what is your actual rate of return?
23. List the five basic bond pricing theorems. How do these theorems relate to interest rate risk?
24. Define *duration*. How does duration relate to interest rate risk?
25. Calculate the duration of a 6 percent coupon, three-year bond yielding 6 percent and interest is paid annually with no accrued interest.
26. Find the duration of a 2 percent coupon, three-year bond yielding 6 percent with interest paid annually and no accrued interest.
27. Assume a bond has a duration of 4.5 years, a current price of $1,000, and a yield to maturity of 7 percent. If the bond's yield to maturity declines from 7 percent to 6.5 percent, how much will the price of the bond increase? What will happen to the bond's duration?
28. Suppose a bond has a duration of 7.62 years, with a current price of $865.806, and a 8 percent yield to maturity. If the bond's yield increases to 8.3 percent, how much will the bond price decrease? What will happen to its duration?
29. What is duration tracking error? What causes it?
30. What are the major issues associated with the use of bond ratings? How well do bond ratings predict actual default rates?
31. According to Graham and Dodd, what should the investor's most important criterion be in selecting bonds? What did they look at when assessing the risk of a bond?
32. Explain the relationship between risk and required return for a bond. Why do bonds generally have positive relationships between maturity and required return?
33. Define *risk structure of interest rates*. Has it remained constant over time? Why or why not?

CFA Questions

1. CFA Level I Examination, 1992
   A bond analyst is looking at a 20-year, AA-rated corporate bond. The bond is non-callable and carries a coupon of 7.5 percent. The analyst computes both the standard yield to maturity and horizon return for the bond, which are as follows:

   Yield to maturity: 8 percent
   Horizon return: 8.96 percent

   Assuming the bond is held to maturity, explain why these two measures of return differ.

CRITICAL THINKING EXERCISE

1. This exercise requires computer work. Open the Bond 1 worksheet in the Data.xls file on the data disk. It contains the data you will need to answer the following questions. You can do this problem by hand, but it is easier to set it up on a spreadsheet.

   a.   Find the bond's duration.

   b.   Assume that the bond's yield to maturity increases from 7.25 percent to 7.75 percent. Find the estimated price change using duration.

   c.   Assume that the bond's yield to maturity decreases from 7.25 percent to 6.5 percent. What will happen to the bond's duration? Why?

   d.   If this bond had a coupon rate of 8.0 percent (not 6.5 percent), a maturity of ten years, a yield to maturity of 7.25 percent, and a face value of $1,000, find the duration.

2.   This exercise requires computer work and library/Internet research. Open the Wal-Mart worksheet in the Data workbook. The worksheet contains financial information on Wal-Mart Stores, Inc. In addition, obtain Wal-Mart's most recent annual report. Your library may have a copy; if not, Wal-Mart's most recent annual report may be obtained from Wal-Mart's web site (www.wal-mart.com) or from the SEC's Edgar database (www.sec.gov/edgar).

   a.   How many of the Graham and Dodd standards for investment grade bonds—listed in Exhibit 9.16 on page 223—does Wal-Mart appear to meet. Would Graham and Dodd, if they were alive, consider Wal-Mart's bonds to be "investment grade"?

   b.   Exhibit 9.12—on page 229—lists median financial ratios by S&P rating category. Based on these medians, what rating would you assign Wal-Mart's bonds? What are the bonds actually rated? What might account for any differences?

MANAGING BOND PORTFOLIOS

PREVIOUSLY . . .

We discussed how bonds are valued and how to assess the two major risks bond investors face: interest rate risk and credit risk.

IN THIS CHAPTER . . .

We continue our examination of bonds with discussions of bond market volatility and the term structure of interest rates. We describe passive and active bond-management strategies as well as interest rate swaps.

TO COME . . .

In the next chapter, we move beyond stocks and bonds to more exotic investments, derivative securities, beginning with options.

Chapter Objectives

After reading Chapter 10 you should be able to answer the following questions:

1. What has happened to the volatility of bond prices?
2. How does the term structure of interest rates affect bond investors?
3. What are some active bond-management strategies?
4. What is passive bond portfolio management?
5. What are interest rate swaps?

Bond investors had a wild ride during the first half of the 1980s. In 1979, yields on long-term U.S. Treasury bonds (T-bonds) broke the 10 percent psychological barrier for the first time in history. Even though rates had been rising quite steadily for several years, the bond market was not especially volatile. Day-to-day (or month-to-month) swings in bond prices and yields were relatively mild. During 1978, for example, the range between the highest and lowest yields on long-term T-bonds was less than 1 percent. That changed abruptly in late 1979.

Between September 1979 and March 1980, yields on T-bonds shot up from about 9 percent to more than 12 percent. Bond yields then changed direction and proceeded to fall by more than 2 percent between March and June 1980. Just as quickly, bond yields again reversed direction and rose sharply, peaking at just more than 15 percent in September 1981. Next, bond yields fell sharply again, falling as low as 10 percent in 1982. T-bond yields started up again, reaching almost 14 percent in June 1984, only to fall sharply again for about the next two years, dropping to as low as 7.3 percent in late 1986.

This volatility shattered, perhaps for many years, the image of bonds as staid, conservative securities that investors could safely buy and hold. The major lesson of the volatile bond market of the 1980s, we believe, is the importance of bond portfolio management. Careful management is essential. The investor wants to take advantage of anticipated changes in interest rates to boost returns or to protect the value of the portfolio from adverse changes in interest rates.

In Chapter 9, we discussed bond valuation principles and the major risks facing bond investors, especially interest rate risk and credit risk. Although investors must never disregard credit risk and must always carefully evaluate the creditworthiness of individual bond issuers and issues, the major risk to which *all* bond investors are exposed is changing interest rates. This chapter explores bond portfolio management techniques, building on the material we discussed in Chapter 9.

Brief History of Bond Market Volatility

Back in the days, say, twenty-five years ago, when bonds were considered dull, almost boring, securities, investors bought bonds for regular income, usually with the intention of holding them to maturity. Investors worried about credit risk, of course, but the risk of not receiving interest and principal when due could be minimized by careful selection and analysis of individual issuers. This was an era when interest rates, and thus bond prices, changed little from month to month. In fact, interest rates often changed little from year to year.

Exhibit 10.1 illustrates this stability. It shows the annual range of yields on long-term U.S. T-bonds (those with maturities in excess of 10 years) between 1948 and 1999. Notice that from 1948 to the early 1970s, the annual difference, or *range*, between the high and low yields on T-bonds was generally quite small. Between 1948 and 1972, it averaged less than 0.6 percent and exceeded 1 percent in only 4 of the 25 years. During the last twenty years shown in Exhibit 10.1 (1977–99), however, the range between the annual high and low yields on T-bonds averaged more than 1.8 percent. The range exceeded 1 percent in 18 of the 23 years, and in 7 of the 23 years, it exceeded 2 percent.

As interest rates have become more volatile, so too have bond returns. This seems reasonable because bond prices and interest rates are inversely related; as interest rates move up, bond prices fall, and vice versa. Bond holding period returns, therefore, are also inversely related to changes in interest rates.

Exhibit 10.2 shows total returns on long-term T-bonds between 1926 and 1995. The figure vividly illustrates the increasing volatility of bond returns over time. With the exception of a few years, bond returns were relatively stable until the late 1960s. By the late 1970s and early 1980s, substantial swings in bond returns became common. (The insert in Exhibit 10.2 shows the returns for 1979 to 1981.)

Exhibit 10.1 ◆ RANGE OF LONG-TERM TREASURY BONDS' ANNUAL YIELDS: 1948–99

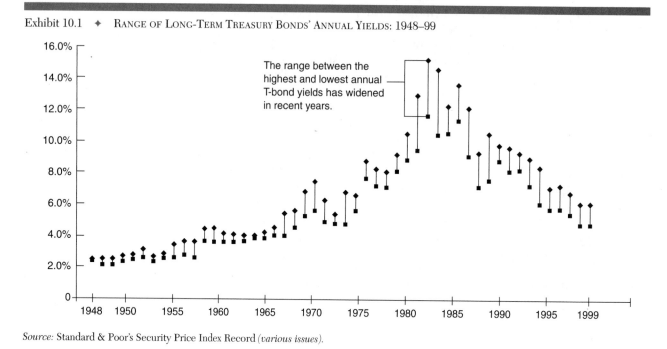

The range between the highest and lowest annual T-bond yields has widened in recent years.

Source: Standard & Poor's Security Price Index Record *(various issues).*

COMPARING STOCK MARKET AND BOND MARKET VOLATILITY

The increase in bond market volatility over the past twenty years raises the question of how bond market volatility compares with that of the stock market. Exhibit 10.3 shows the annualized standard deviations of monthly returns by year for stocks and T-bonds between 1926 and 1996.

Stocks were clearly volatile during the beginning of the period, especially before 1940. The stock market settled down somewhat during the 1940s and 1950s, and although volatility has increased somewhat since the mid-1970s, with the exception of a few years (most notably, 1987), it has not approached the frantic variability of the 1920s and 1930s.

However, Exhibit 10.3 confirms prior evidence on increasing bond market volatility. Further, since the mid-1960s, the bond market has frequently changed almost as erratically as the stock market. In the early 1980s, bond market volatility briefly exceeded stock market volatility.

IMPACT OF BOND MARKET VOLATILITY ON INVESTORS

It is difficult to know exactly what caused the bond market to become more volatile during the past twenty years. Both inflation and institutional changes in the bond market probably contributed. Further, although some evidence suggests that the bond market may have regained some of its former stability during the past couple of years, questions still cloud any prediction of how volatile the bond market will be in the future. Whatever the causes of volatility swings, and whatever the outlook, bond market volatility affects both active and passive investors.

Exhibit 10.2   ✦   MONTHLY RETURNS ON LONG-TERM TREASURY BONDS

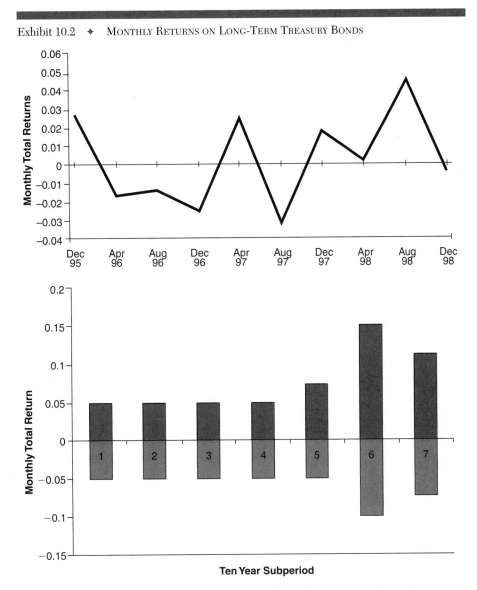

Note: *Subperiod 1: 1926–1935; Subperiod 2: 1936–1945; Subperiod 3: 1946-1955; Subperiod 4: 1956–1965; Subperiod 5: 1966–1975; Subperiod 6: 1976–1985; Subperiod 7: 1986–1995*

The most obvious impact of increased volatility in the bond market is the potential for actively managed bond portfolios to profit from anticipated changes in interest rates. Volatility also increases the potential for losses, however. We assess the potential to increase risk-adjusted profits through active bond portfolio management later in this chapter.

How does volatility affect passive investors? Remember from Chapter 9 that bonds have set face (or par) values. Barring default, a bond will eventually mature and return its par value, regardless of its price in the secondary market before maturity. Why should a passive (buy-and-hold) bond investor care about volatility? The short answer is that increased volatility increases the various risks associated with changes

Exhibit 10.3 ✦ BOND MARKET AND STOCK MARKET VOLATILITY

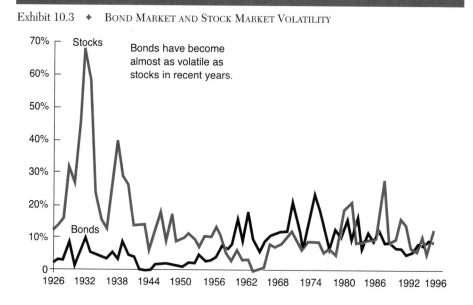

in interest rates, and these risks affect *all* bond investors. For example, increased volatility makes it more difficult to accurately predict an actual rate of return when purchasing a bond. Increased volatility in the bond market, therefore, increases the importance of strategies designed to minimize the risks associated with changes in interest rates. We discuss some of these strategies later in this chapter.

Analyzing the Yield Curve

To structure a sound bond portfolio, passive and active investors alike must understand the relationship between yield and maturity. This knowledge helps the portfolio manager determine the appropriate mix of bond durations in a portfolio. Understanding the relationship between yield and maturity can also indicate when to adjust the average duration of the portfolio. As discussed in Chapter 9, adjusting the average duration of the bond portfolio will alter its sensitivity to changes in interest rates. Making the correct adjustments can dramatically improve the risk and return characteristics of any bond portfolio.

The *term structure of interest rates,* or *yield curve,* is an important tool by which to evaluate the relationship between yield and maturity; a great deal of important information about interest rates lies embedded in the yield curve. To better comprehend this information, the investor must understand the nature of the term structure of interest rates, and this understanding begins with a review of the various theories of the yield curve.

WHAT IS THE YIELD CURVE?

In Chapter 9, we briefly defined the yield curve when discussing the historical relationship between yield and maturity. Recall that the yield curve graphs the relationship between maturity and yield for a group of bonds that are similar in every

Exhibit 10.4 ✦ U.S. Treasury Securities Yield Curve

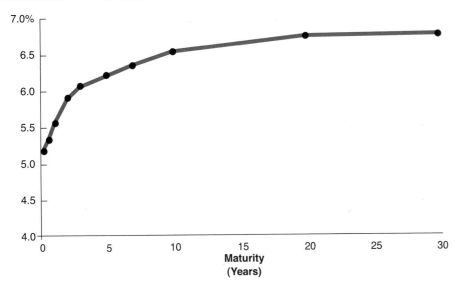

Source: Federal Reserve Bulletin.

respect other than maturity. Because Treasury securities all have similar default risk, call provisions, and tax status, they are usually used to construct the market term structure of interest rates. Further, yields on Treasury securities often serve as benchmarks for determining yields on non-T-bonds. Therefore, analysis of the Treasury yield curve can provide insight into the relationship between yield and maturity of non-T-bonds, as well.

Exhibit 10.4 shows a T-bond yield curve based on yields as of the end of 1999. Notice the classic upward slope, which indicates that yields on short-term Treasuries are lower than yields on long-term Treasuries. As we discussed in Chapter 9, short-term yields are generally lower than long-term yields, but not always. Variations in this relationship have given yield curves a variety of shapes. Occasionally, as in early 1989, the yield curve has been flat, meaning that short-term and long-term yields were roughly the same. At other times, the yield curve has had a hump, as in late 1989 and early 1990; this means that, as maturities increased, yields rose and then fell. In a few cases (most notably, 1981 and 1982), the yield curve has actually been inverted; long-term Treasuries yielded less than short-term Treasuries.

Changes in the yield curve's slope, and even its shape, over short periods of time give rise to several questions. What do the different shapes mean? Does the yield curve contain information about future interest rates? The various theories of the yield curve, which we discuss shortly, address these questions. To fully understand these theories, however, one must understand *forward rates* and how to calculate them.

IMPLIED FORWARD RATES

A **spot rate** of interest is today's prevailing yield on a bond with a particular maturity; a **forward rate** is the expected rate on a bond with a particular maturity at some point in the future (that is, tomorrow's projected spot rate). For example, the current

spot rate
Prevailing yield on a bond with a particular maturity today.

forward rate
Expected rate on a bond with a particular maturity at some point in the future.

yield on a one-year bond is a spot rate; the expected rate on a one-year bond, one year from today is a forward rate. If forward rates are *implied* by current spot rates, knowing current spot rates would allow the bond investor to calculate forward rates.

Suppose that someone wants to make a two-year bond investment. This investor must choose between two alternatives:

✦ Alternative A: Buy a two-year Treasury security
✦ Alternative B: Buy a one-year Treasury security today and another one-year security one year from today

Further, assume indifference between the two alternatives if they produce the same expected dollar return. The one that could produce a higher dollar return would, of course, be preferred. The spot rates are the current market yields on one-year and two-year Treasuries. Knowing these spot rates, can one find the forward rate on a one-year Treasury, one year from today (that is, the rate that would make one indifferent between alternatives A and B)?

The answer depends partly on the timing of interest payments. The example assumes that all the example bonds are pure discount, or zero coupon bonds. Coupon payments would not change the basic relationships we are about to discuss, but they would complicate the mathematics of the relationships between spot and forward rates.

Given the assumption that all bonds are pure discount bonds, we can express the relationship between the two alternatives mathematically. To be indifferent between alternatives A and B, the following relationship must hold:

$$(1 + R_2)^2 = (1 + R_1)(1 + {}_1r_1) \tag{10.1}$$

where R_2 is the spot rate on a two-year bond, R_1 is the spot rate on a one-year bond, and ${}_1r_r$ is the forward rate on a one-year bond, one year from today.[1] To solve for the forward rate implied by the spot rates, manipulate Equation 10.1 as follows:

$$_1r_1 = \frac{(1 + R_2)^2}{(1 + R_1)} - 1 \tag{10.2}$$

For example, if the spot rate on a one-year bond is 4.50 percent and the spot rate on a two-year bond is 4.75 percent, the implied forward rate on a one-year bond one year from today is

$$(1.0475)^2/(1.0450) - 1 = 5.00 \text{ percent}$$

We can also write this relationship as

$$(1.0475)^2 = (1.0450) \text{ X } (1.0500)$$

Thus, buying two consecutive one-year bonds with spot rates of 4.50 percent and 5.00 percent would produce the same total return as buying a single two-year bond at 4.75 percent per annum.

---

[1] In general, R_n is the spot rate on an n-year bond, and $_tr_n$ is the forward rate on an n-year bond t years from today.

Now, let's extend the example to a three-year investment. Four alternative investment combinations are listed, along with their expected return formulas, in Exhibit 10.5. To be indifferent between these four alternatives, all four would have to have the same expected return. Therefore, we can find the forward rates implied by the spot rates calculated from Exhibit 10.5.

To illustrate this, assume that the spot rate on a one-year bond is 4.5 percent, the spot rate on a two-year bond is 4.75 percent, and the spot rate on a three-year bond is 5 percent. As before, assume that all bonds are pure discount bonds. The formula for finding an implied forward rate (the general form of Equation 10.2) is

$$t r_n = \left[\frac{(1 + R_{n+t})^{n+t}}{(1 + R_t)^t} \right]^{1/n} - 1 \qquad (10.3)$$

where t is the number of years from today and n is the bond's time to maturity.

Plugging the assumed spot rates into Equation 10.3 gives the implied forward rates shown below:

$$_1 r_1 = (1.0475)^2/(1.045) - 1 = 5.00\%$$
$$_2 r_1 = (1.05)^3/(1.0475)^2 - 1 = 5.50\%$$
$$_1 r_2 = [(1.05)^3/(1.045)]^{1/2} - 1 = 5.25\%$$

Locking in Future Returns

Computing forward rates from spot rates implies that investors can lock in future rates of return. To illustrate this, compute the market values of discount T-bonds with one-year and two-year maturities. Using the spot rates from the prior example, their prices would be

One-year bond price (per $100) = $100/(1.045) = $95.69
Two-year bond price (per $100) = $100/(1.0475)^2 = $91.14

To lock in the return on a one-year bond one year from today, an investor would sell short the one-year bond today and purchase some multiple of the two-year bond today to return the initial cash outlay to zero. Exhibit 10.6 details the effects of this strategy. If these bonds are risk-free, this strategy locks in a 5 percent return on a one-year bond one year from today.[2]

The potential to lock in future rates suggests a close interrelationship between spot rates and implied forward rates with a yield curve of any shape. One can think of all market interest rates as consisting of explicitly known spot rates, as well as implied forward rates.[3] The interrelationship between spot and forward rates suggests a potential to use implied forward rates to *forecast* future spot rates. Thus, the shape of

---

[2] We should note that borrowing the present value of $100 would be equivalent to a short sale if the loan's interest rate matched the yield on a one-year T-bond. Obviously, it would be difficult for most small, individual investors to sell T-bonds short. However, some large institutional investors and most government bond dealers routinely sell T-bonds short. These investors can also borrow money at rates close to what the government pays.

[3] We can think of a discount bond's yield to maturity as being equal to the geometric average of many shorter-term implied forward rates. For example, the spot rate, R_n, equals

$$R_n = [(1 + R_1)(1 + {_1 r_1})(1 + {_2 r_1}) \dots (1 + {_{n-1} r_1})]^{1/n} - 1$$

Exhibit 10.5   ✦   ALTERNATIVE THREE-YEAR INVESTMENTS

Alternative	Expected Return Formula
One three-year bond	$(1 + R_3)^3$
Three one-year bonds	$(1 + R_1)(1 + {}_1r_1)(1 + {}_2r_1)$
One two-year bond and one one-year bond	$(1 + R_2)^2(1 + {}_2r_1)$
One one-year bond and one two-year bond	$(1 + R_1)^1(1 + {}_1r_2)^2$

Note: ${}_1r_1$ is the forward rate on a one-year bond, one year from today; ${}_2r_1$ is the forward rate on a one-year bond, two years from today; ${}_1r_2$ is the forward rate on a two-year bond, one year from today.

Exhibit 10.6   ✦   LOCKING IN A FUTURE RETURN

	Cash Flow		
	Year 0	Year 1	Year 2
Sell short a single one-year bond	+$95.69	($100)	—
Buy 1.05 two-year bonds	($95.69)	—	+$105
Total cash flow	$0.00	($100)	+$105
One-year return, one year from today = ($105 − $100)/$100 = 5 percent			

the yield curve may indeed give clues about the future direction of interest rates. This is the basic issue addressed by the various theories of the yield curve, as discussed in the next section.

THEORIES OF THE YIELD CURVE

Three general theories seek to explain the shape of the yield curve: the *pure expectations theory*, the *liquidity preference theory*, and the *market segmentation theory*. Each theory draws different conclusions about the interrelationships between spot and forward rates and, as a result, the amount of information contained in the yield curve.

Pure Expectations Theory

pure expectations theory
Forward rates are unbiased estimates of expected future spot rates.

The **pure expectations theory** holds that forward rates are unbiased estimates of expected future spot rates.[4] It is based on the assumption that many, if not all, investors

---

[4]The pure expectations theory does not imply that forward rates always perfectly forecast future spot rates, only that they give unbiased forecasts, which means that forecasts are not consistently too high or too low.

are indifferent between various combinations of maturities that add up to the same term. Investors choose the combination that offers the highest expected return, eliminating any differences in returns between combinations. Going back to the investments shown in Exhibit 10.5, the pure expectations theory says that investors are indifferent between any of those three-year investment combinations. The theory states that all four combinations must offer the same expected rate of return.

If the pure expectations theory is correct, the shape of the current yield curve reveals investors' expectations for the future direction of interest rates. An upward-sloping curve indicates that investors expect rates to rise. In other words, they think that the spot rate on a one-year bond will be higher one year from today than it is today. However, a flat curve suggests that investors expect rates to remain about the same. An inverted curve indicates that investors expect rates to fall.

In addition to the shape of the yield curve, changes in its slope are also important indicators of the market's expectations concerning future spot rates, according to the pure expectations theory. For example, if the slope of the yield curve becomes less steep, the theory says that investors expect smaller magnitudes for future interest rate changes, whether upward or downward.

Liquidity Preference Theory

The **liquidity preference theory** holds that forward rates are good predictors of future rates, but they do not provide unbiased projections because, all things being equal, investors prefer short-term bonds to long-term bonds. Investors will hold longer-term bonds only in exchange for a liquidity premium.

liquidity preference theory
Forward rates are not unbiased projections of future spot rates because, all things being equal, investors prefer short-term bonds to long-term bonds.

Going back to the alternative three-year investment combinations in Exhibit 10.5, the liquidity preference theory states that investors would rather hold three one-year bonds than one three-year bond. Therefore, the expected return from three one-year bonds should be lower than the return from one three-year bond. In equation form, the following would suggest a liquidity preference:

$$(1 + R_3)^2 > (1 + R_1)(1 + {}_1r_1)(1 + {}_2r_1)$$

If the liquidity preference theory is correct, the yield curve should generally slope upward. Further, according to the liquidity preference theory, forward rates should consistently overestimate future spot rates. That is, if the yield curve is upward-sloping, the forward rate on a one-year bond one year from today will be, on average, higher than the current spot rate on a one-year bond. However, depending on the size of the liquidity preference, the actual spot rate on a one-year bond one year from today may be the same, or even lower, than the current spot rate on a one-year bond.

Market Segmentation Theory

The **market segmentation theory** argues that forward rates have essentially no relationship with future spot rates. The reason, according to the theory, is that bonds with different maturities are not substitutes for each other. Some issuers wish to borrow short term and some wish to borrow long term. Short-term borrowers will not borrow long-term, and vice versa. Similarly, some investors prefer short-term bonds, and some prefer long-term bonds. Long-term investors do not see short-term bonds as substitutes, and vice versa. Going back to Exhibit 10.5, market segmentation theory

market segmentation theory
Forward rates are essentially unrelated to future spot rates because bonds with different maturities are not substitutes for each other.

denies that the four alternative three-year investment combinations are substitutes for each other, regardless of their expected returns. One group of investors will buy one-year bonds and a different group of investors will buy three-year bonds.

Therefore, the market segmentation theory argues, spot rates for different bonds are determined solely by interactions of supply and demand with maturity categories. If the market segmentation theory is correct, the shape and slope of the yield curve reveal nothing about the future direction of interest rates. This theory sees implied forward rates as poor forecasts of future spot rates. If, for example, the upward slope of the yield curve becomes steeper, the change means only that supply and demand conditions in either the short or long ends of the bond market have changed.

EMPIRICAL EVIDENCE OF YIELD CURVE RELATIONSHIPS

Some evidence, both anecdotal and scientific, supports all three theories of the yield curve.[5] Some evidence suggests, for example, that implied forward rates forecast future spot rates reasonably well, supporting the pure expectations theory. Supporters of the pure expectations theory note that inverted yield curves have generally occurred during recessions, when current interest rates are high, but declining future interest rates are likely. However, a great deal of evidence finds that forward rates have little value as forecasts of future spot rates. Upward-sloping yield curves are common, but they do not necessarily give way to rising interest rates. For example, in June 1992 the yield curve sloped sharply upward, yet interest rates continued to generally decline throughout the rest of 1992 and much of 1993.

Evidence also gives somewhat ambiguous signals about liquidity preference theory. The typical upward slope of the yield curve is often cited as evidence of a liquidity preference that leads investors, as a group, to prefer short-term bonds to long-term bonds. Average annual yields on Treasury bills (T-bills), for example, have exceeded yields on long-term T-bonds only seven times since 1948. Yet other scientific evidence implies that if a liquidity premium exists, it is not large and is probably limited to short-term bonds.

Evidence of Market Segmentation

The market segmentation theory is difficult to believe in its purest form. Can the markets for long-term bonds and short-term bonds be *completely* separate from one another? Corporations and governments issue both long-term and short-term bonds. Further, many investors seem willing to own varying mixes of maturities, adjusting the average maturities of their bond portfolios as market conditions change. In addition, if the bond market were segmented enough to sever any relationship between current spot rates, forward rates, and future spot rates, the differences could create substantial arbitrage opportunities.

Nevertheless, some evidence supports the contention that shifts in supply and demand conditions can affect the shape and slope of the yield curve. For example, in the early 1980s the municipal yield curve was far steeper than the Treasury yield curve. One study attributed this difference, in large part, to a supply-and-demand imbalance

---

[5]This evidence is reviewed in several sources. See, for example, James Van Horne, *Financial market Rates and Flows* (Englewood Cliffs, NJ: Prentice-Hall, 1993, pp. 108–16).

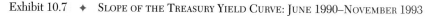

Exhibit 10.7 ✦ SLOPE OF THE TREASURY YIELD CURVE: JUNE 1990–NOVEMBER 1993

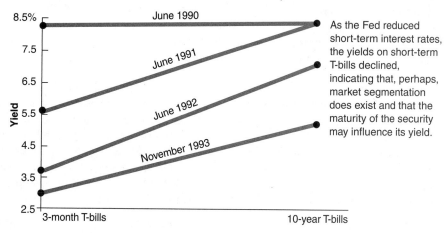

As the Fed reduced short-term interest rates, the yields on short-term T-bills declined, indicating that, perhaps, market segmentation does exist and that the maturity of the security may influence its yield.

Source: Federal Reserve Bulletin (*various issues*).

in the municipal bond market.[6] In the early 1980s, tax-exempt money market funds had grown rapidly. As a result of this heavy demand, the study concluded, yields on tax-exempt money market instruments were "artificially" depressed.

Anecdotal evidence of market segmentation can also be seen in the slope of the Treasury yield curve during the early 1990s. From the middle of 1990 through the middle of 1992, the Federal Reserve began pushing short-term interest rates lower in an attempt to stimulate economic activity. The federal funds rate, for example, fell from 8.29 percent to 3.25 percent between June 1990 and June 1992. The effect of this change on the Treasury yield curve appears in Exhibit 10.7. It shows the spread between three-month T-bills and ten-year T-bonds at various points in time between June 1990 and November 1993.

In June 1990, this Treasury yield curve was essentially flat; the spread between ten-year bonds and three-month bills was only 0.06 percent. As the Fed pushed short-term rates downward, the yield on T-bills fell rapidly from more than 8.2 percent in June 1990 to 5.6 percent in June 1991 and to 3.7 percent in June 1992. The yield on ten-year Treasuries also fell but not nearly as far, from 8.28 percent in June 1991 to 7.26 percent in June 1992. The difference in changes between long-term and short-term rates made the yield curve steeper. The spread between short-term and long-term Treasuries reached record levels in 1991 to 1992. Only in 1993 did the yield on longer-term Treasuries come down and the slope of the yield curve start to become less steep. In November 1993, for example, the spread between ten-year T-bonds and T-bills was 2.50 percent, down from 3.56 percent in June 1992.

One explanation for this behavior is that investors kept long-term rates high due to worries about future inflation and, therefore, higher interest rates. (They may have thought the Fed was easing too much and risking overstimulating the economy.) Investors may also have worried that the federal budget deficit (which set records

---

[6]See David Kidwell and Timothy Koch, "Market Segmentation and the Term Structure of Municipal Yields," *Journal of Money, Credit & Banking* (Spring 1983), pp. 40–55.

throughout the early 1990s) would cause heavy demand for funds by the Treasury. This could alter supply-and-demand factors in the long-term portion of the bond market, influencing the slope of the Treasury yield curve in the early 1990s. Is this evidence of market segmentation? It is hard to say, but in any case, actions by the Federal Reserve to lower interest rates in the early 1990s took an unusually long time to affect the long-term portion of the bond market.

RECAP   Up to this point, we have discussed the slope and shape of the yield curve and important information it may contain for all types of bond investors. These effects are critical regardless of whether the pure expectations, liquidity preference, or market segmentation theory (or a combination of the three) best explains the yield curve. Changes in the slope and shape of the yield curve may forecast future spot interest rates, changes in the size of the liquidity premium, and changes in supply and demand conditions in various segments of the bond market. All bond investors should pay close attention to these implications of the yield curve.

1.   Assume that the one-year spot rate is 5.30 percent, the two-year spot rate is 5.97 percent, and the three-year spot rate is 6.10 percent. Calculate the forward rate on a one-year bond one year from today. Calculate the forward rate on a two-year bond one year from today.

2.   Show how an investor could theoretically "lock in" the rate on a one-year bond two years from today.

Actively Managing Bond Portfolios

Investors can manage their portfolios actively or passively or use strategies that have both passive and active elements. All active strategies require the investor to specify expectations about variables that determine the performance of the assets in the portfolio. For a stock portfolio, important variables include company earnings, dividends, and risk. For a bond portfolio, the investor must estimate interest rates, interest rate volatility, yield curves, and yield spreads. (An estimate of foreign exchange rates should guide any transaction in bonds denominated in a foreign currency.)

Most active bond strategies involve *swaps* in which the investor buys one set of bonds with certain characteristics while selling another set of bonds with different characteristics. Swaps are based on expectations regarding future interest rates, yield spreads, and so forth. Passive portfolio strategies, by contrast, require little attention to expectations. They make no real attempt to forecast the variables that determine the performance of a portfolio's assets. These strategies generally follow buy-and-hold decision rules. The investor buys a well-diversified portfolio and holds those securities, making few if any changes regardless of either current or expected market conditions. In one popular passive portfolio strategy, indexing, the investor tries simply to replicate the performance of a well-known predetermined market index.

In this section, we examine several active bond portfolio strategies. (The next section addresses more passive strategies.) We also try to assess how well active bond-management strategies actually work. Active strategies can be classified as

1.   Interest rate expectations strategies
2.   Yield curve strategies
3.   Yield spread strategies
4.   Foreign exchange strategies
5.   Individual bond selection strategies

Exhibit 10.8   ◆   IMPACT OF ADJUSTING DURATION ON PRICE APPRECIATION OF A
                          BOND PORTFOLIO

Basic Data

Average coupon rate = 7 percent
Average maturity = 10 years
Current average yield to maturity = 7 percent
Current market value = $500,000
Current duration = 7.36 years
New yield to maturity = 6 percent

Duration	Approximate Price Change	Percentage Change
7.36	$34,393	6.88%
7.50	35,047	7.01
8.00	37,383	7.48
8.50	39,720	7.94
9.00	42,056	8.41

Of course, specific strategies can span these categories. For example, we observed in Chapter 9 that changes in interest rates and changes in yield spreads are often interrelated. Therefore, bond strategies based on expected changes in interest rates may also evaluate expected changes in yield spreads.

INTEREST RATE EXPECTATIONS STRATEGIES

We know that as interest rates rise (or fall), bond prices fall (or rise). We also know that certain bonds are more price-sensitive than others and that duration measures the relative price sensitivity of bonds. These premises suggest a fairly basic bond portfolio strategy: lengthen or shorten the average duration of the bond portfolio based on expectations for future interest rates. If rates are expected to fall (or rise), try to lengthen (or shorten) the average duration of the portfolio. One can increase the duration of a bond portfolio by swapping bonds with high coupon rates and short maturities for bonds with low coupon rates and longer maturities. Of course, the opposite swap would shorten the portfolio's duration.

As an example, assume that a bond portfolio has a current market value of $500,000, an average coupon rate of 7 percent, an average yield to maturity of 7 percent, and an average maturity of ten years. These characteristics give the bond portfolio an average duration of about 7.36 years. Suppose that interest rates are about to fall, dropping the average yield to maturity of the bonds in the portfolio from 7 percent to 6 percent. Exhibit 10.8 shows that, without any adjustment to the portfolio's duration, its market value would increase by approximately $34,393 (or 6.88 percent). However, lengthening the duration of the portfolio would cause a larger increase in the portfolio's value. If the portfolio's duration could be increased from 7.36 years to, say, 8 years, the portfolio would increase in value by approximately $37,383 (or 7.48 percent). The change in duration caused about a $3,000 difference in return. If the duration could be increased to nine years, the portfolio's value would increase by approximately $42,056 (or 8.41 percent). Of course, this strategy brings the risk of inaccurate expectations. If interest rates rise as the duration of the portfolio becomes longer, the price decline will be greater than if no change had been made.

Riding the Yield Curve (Horizon Analysis)

Another strategy based on interest rate expectations is sometimes called riding the yield curve. If the yield curve is upward-sloping and expectations predict that neither the shape nor the slope of the yield curve will change over the investment horizon, yields on specific bonds will fall as they ride the yield curve downward (that is, as they approach maturity).

As an example, assume that the current yield on a one-year bond is 4.5 percent and the yield on a two-year bond is 5 percent. If both bonds are discount bonds, the price of a one-year bond is $95.69 and the price of the two-year bond is $90.70. An investor with a one-year investment horizon could buy the one-year bond and earn 4.5 percent. Expectations for stable rates in a year could lead the investor to ride the yield curve by buying the two-year bond and selling it after one year, when it would have one year left to maturity and be priced as a one-year bond. If rates remained unchanged, the two-year bond would sell for $95.69, generating a one-year return of 5.5 percent [($95.69 − $90.70)/$90.70].

Someone who rides the yield curve hopes, of course, that a rising yield curve does not portend rising interest rates, as predicted by the pure expectations theory. If the pure expectations theory is correct, the one-year return from the strategy we just described would be only 4.5 percent.[7] Riding the yield curve should not produce consistently higher returns, therefore, if the pure expectations theory is correct (that is, forward rates are reasonably accurate predictors of future spot rates).

YIELD CURVE STRATEGIES

As we observed earlier in this chapter, historically both the shape and slope of the yield curve have shifted over time. Changes in the shape and slope of the yield curve create several possible trading strategies.[8]

Before we review some yield curve strategies, let's describe the types of changes to the yield curve that have been observed historically. Exhibit 10.9 illustrates three types of changes:

1. *Parallel shifts.* Yields rise or fall over all maturities. The slope of the yield curve remains essentially unchanged as the entire curve moves either up or down.
2. *Changes in slope.* The slope of the yield curve gets either flatter or steeper. A flatter yield curve means that short-term yields rise more than intermediate-term yields, which in turn rise more than long-term yields. A steeper yield curve means the exact opposite; short-term yields decline by more than intermediate-term yields, which decline by more than long-term yields.

---

[7]If the spot rate on a one-year bond is 4.5 percent and the spot rate on a two-year bond is 5 percent, the forward rate on a one-year bond one year from today would be 5.5 percent. According to the pure expectations theory, this is the best unbiased forecast of the spot rate on a one-year bond one year from now. If the rate in one year on a one-year bond did equal 5.5 percent, the price of the original two-year bond would be $94.78 in one year. The one-year return would then equal 4.5 percent.

[8]These strategies are discussed in detail in Frank Fabozzi, *Bond Markets, Analysis & Strategies,* 2nd ed. (Englewood Cliffs, NJ: Prentice-Hall, 1993, pp. 490–95); or Frank Jones, "Yield Curve Strategies," *Journal of Fixed Income* (September 1991), pp. 43–51.

Exhibit 10.9 ✦ TYPES OF YIELD CURVE SHIFTS

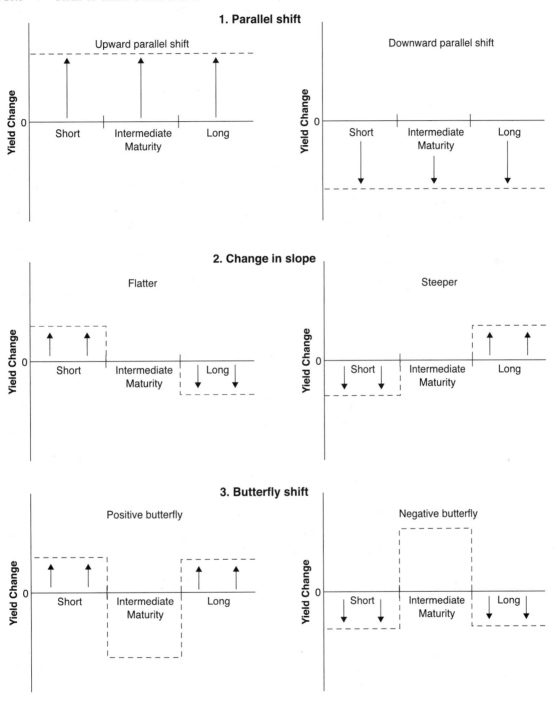

Source: Frank Fabozzi, Bond Markets, Analysis & Strategies, *2nd ed. (Englewood Cliffs, N.J.: Prentice-Hall, 1993). p. 496. Adapted by permission of Prentice-Hall, Inc.*

3.   *Butterfly shifts.* This is a change in the "humpedness" of the yield curve. In a positive butterfly shift, long-term and short-term yields rise more than intermediate-term yields. In a negative butterfly shift, long-term and short-term yields fall more than intermediate-term yields.

Historically, parallel shifts and changes in slope are responsible for the vast majority of observed changes to the yield curve. Furthermore, history shows a high degree of correlation between parallel shifts and changes in slope. Rising yields are often associated with flatter slopes, and falling yields often accompany steeper slopes.

Optimal Yield Curve Strategies

An expected parallel shift in the yield curve, with no other changes, implies probable success for a simple strategy of adjusting the average duration of the portfolio in the opposite direction of the expected change in interest rates. However, a parallel shift combined with some sort of change in slope implies somewhat more complex bond portfolio strategies. Let's look at an example.

Exhibit 10.10 lists yields and prices on three hypothetical discount securities—one short-term, one intermediate-term, and one long-term—assuming a flat yield curve. Based on these inputs, the table outlines optimal yield curve strategies for four scenarios of different parallel shifts and changes in slope. The table states one-year holding period returns, given each scenario's relative yield curve change. The optimal strategy is the one that produces the highest one-year holding period return.

In scenario 1, the yield curve has a parallel downward shift of 0.5 percent, but at the same time, the slope gets steeper by the same amount. The optimal bond to own is the intermediate-term bond, which produces the highest one-year holding period return, 9.05 percent. In scenario 2, the yield curve shifts upward 0.5 percent while the slope gets steeper by the same amount. In this case, the short-term bond produces the highest one-year return of the three, 6 percent. If the yield curve shifts downward by 0.5 percent and the slope gets flatter by the same amount (scenario 3), the long-term bond is optimal, producing a one-year holding period return of 21.04 percent. Finally, if the yield curve has an upward, parallel shift of 0.5 percent, while the slope gets flatter (scenario 4), the long-term bond again produces the highest one-year holding period return of the three, 6 percent.

Depending on the relative change in the yield curve, the optimal strategy is sometimes to hold a short-term bond, sometimes to hold an intermediate-term bond, and sometimes to hold a long-term bond. The optimal yield curve strategies are summarized in Exhibit 10.11.

YIELD SPREAD STRATEGIES

Yield spread strategies involve altering the contents of the bond portfolio to capitalize on existing yield spreads or expected changes in yield spreads. As we discussed in Chapter 9, a yield spread measures the difference in yields between bonds of different qualities. We also observed in the prior chapter that quality-based yield spreads widen and narrow at various points in time. Further, yield spreads often are related to interest rate levels. Yield spreads tend to increase (or decrease) when interest rates are rising (or falling) and tend to be at their maximums (or minimums) when interest rates are historically high (or low). As a result, expectations regarding yield spreads relate closely to expectations regarding interest rates.

Exhibit 10.10 ✦ Examples of Optimal Yield Curve Strategies

1. Price and Yield Data

Bond	Maturity	Yield	Price
Short term	2 years	6.00%	$89.00
Intermediate term	7 years	6.00	$66.51
Long term	15 years	6.00	$41.73

2. Optimal One-Year Strategies, Given Expected Yield Curve Changes

Scenario	Change in Yield Curve		Optimal Bond to Hold	Yield in One Year (%)	Price in One Year	One-Year Return (%)
	Parallel Shift	Change in Slope				
1	Down	Steeper	Intermediate term	5.50%	$72.52	9.05%
2	Up	Steeper	Short term	6.00	94.34	6.00
3	Down	Flatter	Long term	5.00	50.51	21.04
4	Up	Flatter	Long term	6.00	44.23	6.00

Note: All bonds are assumed to be zero coupon bonds. Both parallel shifts and slope changes are ± 50 basis points (0.5 percent). The new short-term yield is 6 percent + parallel shift − slope change; the new intermediate-term yield is 6 percent + parallel shift; the new long-term bond yield is 6 percent + parallel shift + slope change.

However, rising interest rates may also foreshadow an improving economy. As the economy improves, investors may see less risk in lower-quality bonds and become more willing to buy them. Consequently, yield spreads may continue to narrow even as interest rates, in general, rise.

A simple yield spread strategy is a **pure yield pick up swap.** In this strategy, the bond investor swaps lower-yielding bonds for higher-yielding bonds with roughly similar maturities to earn a higher return. At the end of 1996, for example, AA-rated corporate bonds were yielding more than 0.5 percent more than long-term T-bonds (7.29 percent versus 6.75 percent). Someone might swap Treasuries for AAA corporates in an attempt to earn the higher term premium associated with the higher-yielding bonds. This strategy implicitly assumes that neither interest rates nor yield spreads will change significantly over the expected holding period.

Other yield spread strategies are designed to capitalize on expected changes in yield spreads. As we observed in Chapter 9, yield spreads between bonds with varying quality levels tend to be at their maximums when interest rates are at their maximums. This tends to occur right after a peak in economic activity. The usual explanation for this phenomenon is that the risk of default rises in a declining economy. Consequently, investors demand higher premiums to hold non-T-bonds. The reverse is true during an economic expansion. Therefore, as the economic outlook improves, the yield spread between T-bonds and non-T-bonds should start to narrow. In such a situation, the optimal strategy is to swap high-quality bonds for lower-quality bonds if interest rates are expected to remain the same, or even decline, with narrowing yield spreads.

pure yield pick up swap
Swapping lower-yielding bonds for higher-yielding bonds with roughly similar maturities to earn a higher return.

Exhibit 10.11 ✦ Optimal Yield Curve Strategies for Parallel Shift and Change in Slope of the Yield Curve

Parallel Shift in the Yield Curve

Change in the Slope of the Yield Curve	Decrease	No Change	Increase
Steeper	Long-term or Intermediate-term bonds (A less steep curve relative to the yield decrease favors long-term bonds).	Intermediate-term bonds	Short-term
None	Long-term bonds	Long-term bonds	Short-term bonds
Flatter	Long-term bonds	Long-term bonds	Short-term or long-term bonds (A flatter curve relative to the yield increase favors long-term bonds.)

Source: Adapted from Exhibit 20-6 in Frank Fabozzi, Bond Markets, Analysis & Strategies, *2nd ed. (Englewood Cliffs, N.J.: Prentice-Hall, 1993). p. 499.*

Exhibit 10.12 details a hypothetical example. Assume the current yield on fifteen-year Treasuries is 7.5 percent and the yield on ten-year AAA corporates is 8.75 percent (giving us yield spread of 1.25 percent). As interest rates generally decline over the next year, the yield spread between Treasuries and AAA corporates should decline to about 0.75 percent. Both bonds are expected to earn impressive one-year returns, but the AAA corporate bond is expected to earn a higher return (39.6 percent compared with 29.8 percent) due to the decline in the yield spread between Treasuries and AAA corporates.

Another scenario involves narrowing yield spreads during a general rise in interest rates. As we noted earlier, interest rates could rise due to an improving economy, even as yield spreads continue to narrow. In this scenario, an investor might consider making two changes to a bond portfolio: swapping Treasuries and other high-quality bonds for lower-quality bonds, and at the same time reducing the portfolio's average duration.

Tax Swaps

Market forces create yield spreads based on characteristics other than quality level. One of these spreads compares the yield on taxable bonds to that on tax-exempt bonds.

Over the past 30 years, high-quality (AAA-rated or AA-rated) municipal bonds have yielded about 86 percent of the yield on T-bonds with similar maturities on average. (The difference arises because the interest from municipal bonds is exempt from federal income taxes.) That ratio has varied substantially, though. For example, it was more than 90 percent in 1986 and less than 80 percent in the late 1970s. A taxable investor who thinks that the ratio between municipal and Treasury yields is too high might switch from Treasuries to municipals, and vice versa. Further, if an

Exhibit 10.12 ✦ Illustration of a Yield Spread Strategy

	Treasury	AAA Corporate
Term (years)	15	15
Initial yield	7.50%	8.75%
Initial price	$33.80	$28.42
Expected yield	6.50%	7.00%
Expected price	$41.41	$38.78
Holding period return	22.51%	36.45%

Note: Both bonds are assumed to be zero coupon bonds.

investor's marginal federal tax rate goes up (or down), the attractiveness of municipal bonds relative to T-bonds goes up (or down).

For example, consider an investor in a 28 percent federal marginal tax bracket. (This person pays $0.28 in additional taxes on every additional dollar of income.) Also, assume that AAA-rated corporate bonds are currently yielding 7 percent and AAA-rated municipal bonds with similar durations are yielding 4.8 percent. To compare these yields, one must adjust for the fact that interest from municipal bonds is not subject to federal income tax. The municipal bond's taxable equivalent yield of 6.67 percent (4.8% divided by [1-28%]) is less than the yield on corporate bonds. If all other factors are the same, the investor is better off holding corporate bonds rather than municipal bonds.

Now, assume that interest rates in general decline; AAA corporates are now yielding 6 percent and AAA municipals are yielding 4.5 percent. The marginal tax rate remains at 28 percent, but the investor is now better off holding municipal bonds because they have a higher taxable equivalent yield than corporate bonds (6.25 percent versus 6 percent).

FOREIGN EXCHANGE STRATEGIES

As we discussed in Chapter 9, bonds denominated in foreign currencies expose investors to foreign exchange risk, because the coupon payments must be translated back into dollars. Expected changes in foreign interest and exchange rates create some possible bond-trading strategies. Several of these strategies are illustrated in Exhibit 10.13.

One simple strategy is based on the expectation of no significant changes in foreign exchange rates. Investors switch to bonds denominated in foreign currencies if they offer higher yields. This is scenario A in Exhibit 10.13. The investor buys the Canadian government bond because of its higher yield compared with the U.S. government bond.

Another profitable opportunity is created if the investor expects Canadian interest rates to decline, with no change in the exchange rate. In scenario B, Canadian rates decline by 50 basis points to 7.25 percent. The one-year return, in U.S. dollars, is about 12.4 percent.

More complicated strategies are based on expected changes in the exchange rate between the Canadian and U.S. dollars. If the investor expects the Canadian dollar to get stronger relative to the U.S. dollar (rising from, say, US$/C$=0.75 to

Exhibit 10.13 ✦ FOREIGN EXCHANGE STRATEGIES

Basic Information (Canadian Government Bond)

Term (year)	10
Initial yield	7.75%
Price (C$)	47.41
Initial FX rate (US$/C$)	0.775
Price (US$)	36.74

	Scenario				
One Year Hence	A	B	C	D	E
Yield	7.75%	7.25%	7.75%	7.25%	7.25%
Price (C$)	51.08	53.26	51.08	53.26	53.26
One-year return (C$)	7.75%	12.36%	7.75%	12.36%	12.36%
FX rate (US$/C$)	0.775	0.775	0.800	0.800	0.750
Price (US$)	39.59	41.28	40.86	42.61	39.95
One-year return (US$)	7.75%	12.36%	11.23%	15.98%	8.73%

Note: The Canadian government bond is assumed to be a zero coupon bond. Assume a 10-year U.S. government bond is yielding 6.75 percent.

US$/C$=0.80), the one-year return is larger when measured in U.S. dollars than in Canadian dollars (scenario C). The best of all possible worlds for the U.S. investor would be scenario D in which Canadian interest rates decline and the Canadian dollar strengthens relative to the U.S. dollar.

Strategies based on foreign exchange rates can be tricky, however. They can also be risky. The main reason is that interest rates are a major determinant of foreign exchange rates. If Canadian interest rates decline, relative to U.S. interest rates, it is also possible that the Canadian dollar will actually lose value relative to the U.S. dollar. Take a look at scenario E in Exhibit 10.13. Notice that the decline in the value of the Canadian dollar creates a situation in which the one-year return measured in U.S. dollars is substantially less than the one-year return measured in Canadian dollars.

INDIVIDUAL BOND SELECTION STRATEGIES

Individual bond selection strategies seek to uncover individual bonds that are undervalued for some reason. Once the market recognizes that these bonds are undervalued, their prices should rise (as their yields decline), providing a high rate of return. Individual bond selection techniques really look for one of two situations: (1) a bond with a higher yield than other similar bonds (for example, those with the same maturity or bond rating), and (2) a bond for which credit analysis suggests a rating improvement. Let's look at an example.

In the early 1990s, Chrysler was struggling financially. Some observers even speculated about whether the company could survive. As its financial woes mounted, Chrysler's bond rating fell. In July 1990, Standard & Poor's (S&P) and Moody's dropped Chrysler's bond rating below investment grade. Chrysler bonds fell sharply in price as a result of the downgrade, but some investors thought that the market overreacted. They may have been right. As Chrysler's fortunes improved, so did the prices of Chrysler bonds. Between August 1990 and December 1993, for example, the price of Chrysler's 10.95 percent, 2017 debentures rose from 86 percent of par value to more than 120 percent of par value, an increase of more than 41 percent.

Guilt by Association

We refer to a situation in which an entire class of securities is affected by problems of a few individual securities in the class as guilt by association. One can argue that this is another case in which the market overreacts. A good example of this affected high-yield corporate bonds (junk bonds) from 1989 through 1991.

As you probably remember, junk bonds are bonds rated below investment grade (below BBB or Baa). These issues became popular during the 1980s to finance acquisitions, leveraged buyouts, and so forth. By the end of the 1980s, many junk bond issuers faced financial trouble. Several major defaults rocked the junk bond market (notably, the 1990 defaults of Campeau Corporation and Southland Corporation). As a result, prices of all junk bonds were mauled. By April 1990, the average yield on B-rated corporate bonds was more than 8 percent higher than the average yield on T-bonds, setting a record.

Some analysts thought that the market had punished all junk bonds too severely, especially those that carried only moderate credit risk. They started to recommend selected junk bonds.[9] Prices of higher-quality junk bonds soon started to recover. In fact, over the three-year period ending on December 31, 1993, mutual funds that invested in junk bonds had an average annual return of 24.2 percent, compared with 11.7 percent for all taxable bond funds.

Passively Managing Bond Portfolios

Active bond portfolio management strategies attempt to profit from anticipated changes in such variables as interest rates and yield spreads by buying and selling bonds. Passive strategies are more concerned with controlling the risk of a bond portfolio. Passive bond-management strategies fall into two broad categories. **Indexing strategies** are designed to replicate the performance of broad market indexes. The second type of strategies, commonly referred to as **immunization strategies,** are designed to reduce the risks associated with fluctuations in interest rates.

indexing strategies
Strategies designed to replicate the performance of broad market indexes.

immunization strategies
Strategies designed to reduce the risks associated with fluctuations in interest rates.

INDEXING BOND PORTFOLIOS

As we have discussed before, indexing is perhaps the ultimate in a passive investment strategy. Indexing has become a popular choice among bond investors in recent years.[10] The amount of pension money currently invested in bond index funds is more than $100 billion. The Vanguard Bond Fund, an indexed bond mutual fund, currently has more than $5 billion in net assets.

---

[9]See, for example, "Why You Should Buy Junk Now," *Forbes,* April 30, 1990, pp. 440–41.

[10]The issues associated with indexing bond portfolios are discussed in detail in Sharmin Mosavar-Rahmani, *Bond Index Funds* (Chicago: Probus, 1991).

Investors have two basic rationales for indexing bond portfolios. First, indexing tacitly recognizes the extreme difficulty of an active bond investor consistently outperforming the overall market. Second, indexing reduces transaction costs and management expenses compared with actively managed portfolios. For example, a typical pension fund pays advisory fees between 0.15 percent and 0.5 percent per year for active management of a bond portfolio compared with between 0.01 percent and 0.2 percent for an index fund.

This is not to say, however, that indexing has no drawbacks. For one thing, indexing restricts the investor to the sectors of the bond market that the index tracks, even though attractive opportunities may exist in other sectors. Further, indexing does not ensure that sufficient funds will be available at a specific point in time to meet a predetermined liability. This is a common problem for institutional investors such as life insurance companies and pension funds. Other passive bond-management strategies are designed to ensure that future liabilities are fully funded.

Choosing an Index

One of the most important decisions to make when indexing a portfolio is choosing the appropriate index. The most popular index for stock index funds is the S&P 500, although some index funds track broader indexes such as the Wilshire 5,000. Bond index funds may try to replicate the domestic taxable bond market by tracking one of three indexes: the Salomon BIG Index, the Lehman Brothers Aggregate Index, or the Merrill Lynch Domestic Master Index. Each index contains more than 4,500 different bond issues, with a total market value in excess of $3 trillion. Investors who wish to replicate the performance of a specific sector of the bond market (for example, Treasuries, municipals, or foreign bond markets) can choose among several indexes. Examples include the Moody's Bond Buyer Index, a municipal bond index, and the Salomon World Government Bond Index.

Three criteria should guide the choice of an index. First, the index should match the investor's risk tolerance. For example, an investor who wants to eliminate any exposure to credit risk should avoid indexes that include corporate bonds. The second criterion is the investor's set of objectives and goals. An investor who has a short-term investment horizon may find some indexes more appropriate than others. The final criterion is regulatory constraints. Some institutional investors are restricted to investment grade bonds. These investors would have to avoid any indexes that included below-investment-grade bonds.

Indexing Methodologies

Indexing methodologies are more difficult for bond portfolios than for stocks. For one thing, bond indexes contain thousands of individual bond issues. Purchasing each individual bond in proportion to its market value may be difficult, especially because many bonds are thinly traded. In addition, rebalancing presents more of a problem with bond index funds than with stock index funds. Most indexes drop individual bonds once their times to maturity fall below six months or one year. Thus, new bonds are constantly being added to the index, and the index fund must be rebalanced each time. Also, the portfolio manager must decide what to do with all the interest income when it is received.

Several indexing methodologies are available. The most common, the stratified sampling or cell approach, stratifies the bond market into several subclasses based on

Exhibit 10.14 ✦ Stratification of Treasury Securities into Cells

	Type of Security		
Maturity	Notes	Bonds	Total Percentages
1 to 5 years	99%	1%	57%
5 to 10 years	94	6	19
10 to 20 years	0	100	5
More than 20 years	0	100	19
Total percentages	78	22	100

Note: Composition of the market as of June 30, 1996. Excludes Treasury bills and other Treasury securities with times to maturity of less than one year.

criteria such as credit risk, maturity, and issuer.[11] The resulting cells are considered to consist of reasonably homogeneous groups, from which the index selects a sample.

Let's illustrate this approach using a simple example. To design a bond portfolio that is tied to a Treasury index consisting of all U.S. Treasury securities with times to maturity in excess of one year, first divide the Treasury market by maturity. Next, stratify each maturity class by type of security, bonds or notes. As you may recall from Chapter 3, the only difference between bonds and notes, other than maturity when issued, is the fact that some bonds are callable starting five years from their maturity dates. The resulting cells are shown in Exhibit 10.14.

The bottom row shows the breakdown between notes and bonds. Because 78 percent of outstanding Treasuries with more than one year remaining before maturity are notes and 22 percent are bonds, 78 percent of the entire portfolio should consist of notes and 22 percent should consist of bonds. The last column shows the general breakdown of the portfolio by maturity. For example, 19 percent of the portfolio should consist of Treasuries with maturities between five and ten years. The other cells show the breakdown between notes and bonds within each maturity group. The group of securities with maturities between five and ten years should be broken down as 94 percent notes and 6 percent bonds.

Tracking Error

Tracking error is one way of assessing how well an index fund replicates the performance of its benchmark index. Tracking error simply measures the difference between the total return of the portfolio and that of the index. This measure is usually calculated monthly. A Salomon Brothers study found that portfolios indexed to broad bond market indexes (for example, Salomon's BIG Index) had the lowest tracking errors.[12] Portfolios indexed to specific sectors of the bond market (for example, corporate bonds) had the highest tracking errors. Further, indexing a larger portfolio generally leads to smaller tracking error.

tracking error
One way of assessing how well an index fund replicates the performance of its benchmark index.

---

[11]Other indexing methodologies are discussed in Fabozzi, Frank, *Bond Markets*, pp. 518–22.

[12]Reported in Fabozzi, *Bond Markets*, pp. 522–23.

IMMUNIZATION

In contrast to indexing, bond investors use immunization to reduce a portfolio's exposure to the risks associated with changing interest rates. As we discussed in Chapter 9, bond investors are exposed to both interest rate and reinvestment risk. As interest rates rise, bond prices fall. At the same time, however, bond investors can reinvest coupon payments at higher rates, earning more interest on interest. When interest rates fall, bond prices rise, but investors are forced to reinvest coupon payments at lower rates. Therefore, both rising and falling interest rates can hurt bond investors.

Although it is probably impossible to totally eliminate these risks, careful immunization can substantially reduce them. The specific immunization strategy an investor chooses will depend on the risk from which the portfolio needs protection.[13] Let's examine three immunization strategies.

Target Date Immunization

target date immunization
Technique designed to ensure that an investor has sufficient funds available at a point in time to meet a single liability.

Target date immunization seeks to ensure that an investor has sufficient funds available at a point in time to meet a single liability. It does this by setting the duration of the bond portfolio equal to the horizon date (that is, the point in time when the single liability will fall due). This protects the future value of the portfolio from fluctuations in interest rates between the current date and the horizon date. Let's illustrate target date immunization with a simple example.

A pension fund manager determines that the fund will need $10 million in ten years to meet obligations to retiring employees. The current yield to maturity on ten-year bonds is 6.9 percent. Therefore, to have $10 million in ten years, the pension fund needs to invest $5,131,247 (the present value of $10 million discounted at 6.9 percent for ten years). The pension fund manager decides to invest the money in bonds, leaving the three choices listed in Exhibit 10.15. For simplicity, assume that all three bonds have the same yield to maturity, pay interest annually, and are free of credit and call risk.

Does it matter which bond the pension fund buys? Absolutely! Exhibit 10.16 shows the future values of the cash flows after ten years for the bonds under three different interest rate scenarios. The future value of each cash flow is made up of the price of the bond after ten years (in the case of bonds B and C) or the face value (in the case of bond A), the coupon payments, and interest on the coupon payments.

The optimum choice depends on what happens to interest rates. If rates stay exactly the same (6.9 percent), all three bond alternatives will produce exactly $10 million in ten years. However, if rates fall from 6.9 percent to 5.9 percent, bond A fails to produce sufficient cash flows. If rates rise from 6.9 percent to 7.9 percent, bond C fails to produce sufficient cash flows. The durations of bonds A and C are either longer or shorter than ten years. Only bond B, which has a duration close to the horizon date of ten years, produces about $10 million regardless of whether interest rates rise or fall. Exhibit 10.16 details the calculation of the future value of bond B's cash

---

[13]In practice, immunization strategies can become more complicated than what we are about to describe. See, for example, Fabozzi, *Bond Markets,* pp. 511–49. Furthermore, see Chapter 16 for a discussion of how financial futures can reduce interest rate risk.

Exhibit 10.15 ✦ THREE BONDS FOR FUNDING A FUTURE LIABILITY

Bond	Term (years)	Coupon Rate	Yield to Maturity	Duration (years)	Price (per $100 par value)
A	10	10.0%	6.9%	7.08	$121.87
B	16	7.5	6.9	10.00	105.71
C	25	5.0	6.9	13.40	77.66

Note: Bonds pay interest annually.

Exhibit 10.16 ✦ TARGET DATE IMMUNIZATION

Rate of Interest	Future Value of Cash Flow in 10 Years (per bond)			Value of Bonds in 10 Years ($ millions)		
	Bond A	Bond B	Bond C	Bond A	Bond B	Bond C
5.90%	$231.19	$206.29	$156.80	$ 9.73	$10.01	$10.36
6.90	237.51	206.00	151.34	10.00	10.00	10.00
7.90	244.18	206.28	147.11	10.38	10.01	9.72

Details of Calculations of Future Value of Cash Flows in 10 Years for Bond B

Interest Rate	Coupon Payments	Interest on Coupon Payments	Price in 10 Years	Total Cash Flow (Per bond)
5.90%	$75.00	$23.39	$107.89	$206.29
6.90	75.00	28.14	102.87	206.00
7.90	75.00	33.13	98.15	206.28

Notes: Number of bonds purchased with initial investment of $5,131,247 are 42,103 (bond A), 48,543 (bond B), and 66,076 (bond C). Future value of cash flows equals coupon payments, interest on coupons (reinvested at the rate of interest shown), and the face value of bonds (bond A) or the prices of the bonds (bonds B and C).

flows. If rates fall, the decline in interest on coupon income is exactly offset by a higher price in Year 10, and rising interest on interest compensates exactly for a lower price if rates rise. To summarize, then, if interest rates fall and the average duration of the bond portfolio fails to reach the target date, the portfolio will fail to produce the needed cash flow. However, if interest rates rise and the average duration of the bond portfolio runs past the target date, the portfolio will fail to produce the needed cash flow. Only if the duration of the portfolio is equal to the period before the target date will the portfolio produce the needed cash flow.

Two comments should be made about target date immunization. First, buying a zero coupon bond that matures on the horizon date will produce sufficient cash flows regardless of interest rates. Remember, a zero coupon bond has a duration equal to its maturity. In practice, however, such a zero coupon bond may not be available. Second, duration changes as interest rates change, as you may recall from Chapter 9. As

Exhibit 10.17 ◆ ILLUSTRATION OF A DEDICATED PORTFOLIO

	Year	Beginning Obligation	Cash Flow from Bonds	Remaining Obligation
Step 1	1	$ 5,000,000	$ 500,000	$4,500,000
Bond A	2	5,000,000	500,000	4,500,000
	3	10,000,000	500,000	9,500,000
	4	10,000,000	500,000	9,500,000
	5	10,500,000	10,500,000	0
Step 2	1	$ 4,500,000	$ 452,381	$4,047,619
Bond B	2	4,500,000	452,381	4,047,619
	3	9,500,000	9,500,000	9,047,619
	4	9,500,000	9,500,000	0
Step 3	1	$ 4,047,619	$ 430,839	$3,616,780
Bond C	2	4,047,619	430,839	$3,616,780
	3	9,047,619	9,047,619	0
Step 4	1	$ 3,616,780	$ 172,228	$3,444,552
Bond D	2	$ 3,616,780	3,616,780	0
Step 5	1	$ 3,444,552	$ 3,444,552	$ 0
Bond E				

Summary

Bond	Amount Purchased	Maturity
A	$10,000,000	5 years
B	9,047,619	4 years
C	8,616,780	3 years
D	3,444,552	2 years
E	3,280,526	1 year

Note: All bonds have coupon rates of 5 percent, sell at par, and pay interest annually.

a result, if interest rates change significantly, it may be necessary to rebalance the bond portfolio to bring the duration back into line with the horizon date.

Cash-Flow Matching and Multiperiod Immunization.

Many investors need to fund a series of obligations over a period of time. One multi-period strategy is to purchase a series of bonds (either zero coupon or coupon bonds) with durations equal to the horizon date of each obligation. In essence, this strategy extends target date immunization. An alternative strategy is to construct a **dedicated portfolio.** Such a portfolio is designed to generate sufficient cash flow in each period to match the series of obligations the investor faces. The portfolio manager selects a bond with a maturity that matches the last liability and produces sufficient cash flow at maturity to meet this obligation. The coupons from this bond, paid prior to maturity, reduce the other obligations. Next, the portfolio manager selects a second bond with a maturity equal to the next to last obligation that produces sufficient cash flow at maturity to meet this reduced obligation. The portfolio manager continues to go backward in time until all periodic obligations are fully funded. An example of a dedicated portfolio is shown in Exhibit 10.17.

dedicated portfolio
Portfolio designed to generate sufficient cash flow each period to match a series of obligations faced by an investor.

Exhibit 10.18 ✦ Net Worth Immunization

		Amount	Average Interest ($000)	Duration Rate (years)
Original balance sheet	Assets	$10,000	6.5%	7.5
	Liabilities	9,000	5.50	1.5
	Net worth	$ 1,000		

		New Amount	Change	
Rates rise by 2.0 percent	Assets	$8,592	($1,408)	
	Liabilities	8,744	(256)	
	Net worth	$ (153)	(1,153)	

		Amount ($000)	Average Interest Rate	Duration (years)
Net worth immunization	Assets	$10,000	6.5%	4.5
	Liabilities	9,000	5.50	5.0
	Net worth	1,000		

		New Amount	Change	
Rates rise by 2.0 percent	Assets	$9,155	($845)	
	Liabilities	8,147	(853)	
	Net worth	$1,008	8	

Net Worth Immunization

Many depository institutions, such as commercial banks, must compensate for natural mismatches between the average durations of their assets (loans and securities) and the average durations of their liabilities (mainly deposits). Because the average duration of assets is longer than the average duration of liabilities for the typical bank, when interest rates rise, the market value of its assets will fall by more than the market value of its liabilities. As a result, the bank's net worth will fall.[14]

This is illustrated in Exhibit 10.18. The hypothetical bank has total assets of $10 million, total liabilities of $9 million, and a net worth of $1 million. The average duration of the bank's assets is 7.5 years whereas the average duration of its liabilities is 1.5 years. Notice what happens if interest rates rise by 2 percent; the bank's net worth drops from $1 million to −$153,000. **Net worth immunization** is an attempt to narrow the gap between the average duration of a depository institution's assets and the average duration of its liabilities. (We discuss how a bank can do this in the next

net worth immunization
Process designed to narrow the gap between the average duration of a depository institution's assets and the average duration of its liabilities.

___

[14]A bank's net worth is commonly referred to as *capital*. The typical bank has capital equal to between 5 and 10 percent of its assets.

section.) If the average durations of the bank's assets and liabilities could be equated to one another, the institution's net worth would be immunized from increases in interest rates.[15] This is also illustrated in Exhibit 10.18. Notice that if the average duration of the bank's assets is 4.5 years and the average duration of its liabilities is 5.0 years, a 2 percent increase in interest rates has no material effect on the bank's net worth. That is because the decrease in the value of the bank's assets is offset by the decrease in the value of its liabilities.

Interest Rate Swap

interest rate swap
Agreement between two parties to exchange a series of interest payments over a specified period of time.

In an **interest rate swap,** two parties agree to exchange a series of interest payments. Interest rate swaps first emerged in the early 1980s as a way of controlling interest rate and foreign exchange risk. Although the exact size of the swap market is hard to determine precisely, some estimates place the total value of these transactions as high as $2.5 *trillion.* The typical interest rate swap involves two parties that face opposite types of interest rate risk or foreign exchange risk. A third party, a large bank or investment banking firm, usually acts as an intermediary between the two parties. Let's look at an example of a simple interest rate swap.

EXAMPLE OF AN INTEREST RATE SWAP

Assume that a bank has $100 million in ten-year loans outstanding that carry an average annual interest rate of 8 percent. The loans charge simple interest only, so the borrowers make annual interest payments of $8 million. The bank finances these loans by issuing one-year certificates of deposit that pay interest equal to the yield on one-year T-bills plus 0.5 percent. On the other side, assume that an insurance company has sold $100 million worth of 6.5 percent annuities. The insurance company pays simple interest on the annuities once a year, and it invests the proceeds from the sale of the annuities in a floating-rate security. The security's rate is adjusted annually to equal the yield on one-year T-bills plus 1 percent. The bank and the insurance company face opposite types of interest rate risk. If rates rise, the bank suffers; if rates fall, the insurance company suffers. As we discussed in the prior section, the duration of the bank's assets is greater than that of its liabilities. Therefore, if rates rise, the value of the bank's assets falls by more than the value of its liabilities.

To manage their respective risks, the bank and the insurance company decide to do an interest rate swap, with a third party acting as the intermediary. The bank agrees to pay 6.6 percent annually in exchange for the yield on a one-year T-bill. The insurance company agrees to pay the yield on a one-year T-bill in

---

[15]Unless the value of the bank's assets equals the value of its liabilities, the average duration of assets should be less than the average duration of liabilities for new worth to be immunized. Durations should be equated as follows. Let A be the value of the bank's assets, L the value of its liabilities, D_A the duration of its assets, and D_L the duration of its liabilities. To immunize the bank's net worth, AD_A should be set equal to AD_t.

Exhibit 10.19 ✦ Effects of an Interest Rate Swap

Year	One Year T-bill Yield	Bank			Insurance Company		
		Receive	Pay	Net (%)	Receive	Pay	Net (%)
1	4.5%	12.5%	11.6%	0.9%	11.8%	11.0%	0.8%
2	5.0	13.0	12.1	0.9	12.3	11.5	0.8
3	5.5	13.5	12.6	0.9	12.8	12.0	0.8
4	6.0	14.0	13.1	0.9	13.3	12.5	0.8
5	5.0	13.0	12.1	0.9	12.3	11.5	0.8
6	4.0	12.0	11.1	0.9	11.3	10.5	0.8
7	3.0	11.0	10.1	0.9	10.3	9.5	0.8
8	4.0	12.0	11.1	0.9	11.3	10.5	0.8
9	4.0	12.0	11.1	0.9	11.3	10.5	0.8
10	4.0	12.0	11.1	0.9	11.3	10.5	0.8

Note: Each year the bank receives 8 percent and the one-year T-bill yield, and pays the one-year T-bill yield plus 0.5 percent and 6.6 percent. Each year the insurance company receives the one-year T-bill yield plus 1.0 percent and 6.3 percent, and pays 6.5 percent and the one-year T-bill yield.

exchange for a set payment of 6.3 percent. The annual cash flows for both parties are shown below:

	Receives	Pays	Net
Bank	1. 8 percent 2. One-year T-bill yield	1. T-bill yield + 0.5 percent 2. 6.6 percent	0.9 percent
Insurance company	1. T-bill yield + 1 percent 2. 6.3 percent	1. 6.5 percent 2. T-bill yield	0.8 percent

The swap has the effect of paying both parties the same spread each year regardless of whether interest rates rise or fall. This is illustrated in Exhibit 10.19. The exhibit assumes that interest rates first rise and then fall. Notice that the bank makes 0.9 percent each year and the insurance company makes 0.8 percent each year, regardless of what happens to interest rates.

Chapter Summary

1. What has happened to the volatility of bond prices?
   Over the past few years, the volatility of bond prices has sharply increased. Changes in interest rates are more frequent and more pronounced today than they were 20 years ago. In fact, over the past 20 years or so, bond volatility has on occasion even exceeded stock price volatility. Volatility in the bond market creates opportunities for active bond investors and increases the importance of strategies passive bond investors use to minimize the risks associated with changes in interest rates.

2. How does the term structure of interest rates affect bond investors?

The term structure of interest rates shows the relationship between yield and maturity for a similar class of bonds—usually T-bonds are used to construct the term structure. Theorists have explored the possibility that future spot rates are implied by current spot rates and the possibility of locking in future returns. The three major theories of the yield curve are the pure expectations theory, the liquidity preference theory, and the market segmentation theory. Changes in the slope and shape of the yield curve may forecast future spot rates, changes in the liquidity premium, and changes in supply and demand conditions.

3. What are some active bond-management strategies?

Most active bond-management strategies involve swaps: buying one set of bonds with one set of characteristics—such as long durations—while selling another set of bonds with the opposite characteristics. Some examples of active strategies include those based on interest rate expectations, those based on expected changes in the yield curve, strategies based on changes in yield spreads, those based on changes in foreign exchange rates, and individual bond selection strategies.

4. What is passive management?

Passive bond-management strategies are concerned with controlling the risk of a bond portfolio. Examples of passive strategies include indexing, in which a bond portfolio is designed merely to replicate the performance of a broad bond index, and immunization, in which the investor attempts to reduce the amount of interest rate risk to which the portfolio is exposed. Two immunization techniques are target date immunization and cash flow matching. In both cases, the portfolio produces desired future cash flows regardless of changes in interest rates. Financial institutions attempt to immunize their net worth by matching the duration of assets with the duration of liabilities.

5. What are interest rate swaps?

An interest rate swap is an agreement by which two parties agree to exchange a series of interest payments. Interest rate swaps are designed to control interest rate and foreign exchange risk. The typical interest rate swap involves two parties that face opposite types of interest rate or foreign exchange risk, or both. A correctly managed swap guarantees both parties certain cash flows over a period of time.

Mini Case 1

With the following information, you can practice computing implied forward rates from actual spot rates and further understand the various theories of the yield curve. The following yields were quoted on pure-discount U.S. Treasury securities.

Term	Yield
3 months	5.20%
6 months	5.33
1 year	5.55
2 years	5.90
3 years	6.06
4 years	6.13
5 years	6.22
6 years	6.30
7 years	6.36

1. Compute as many implied forward rates from these spot rates as you can.
2. How would each of the three theories of the yield curve interpret the relationship between the forward rates calculated in question 1 and the current spot rates?

3. Show what is meant by riding the yield curve. Show why riding the yield curve would not work if the pure expectations hypothesis were correct.

Mini Case 2

In this mini-case you will learn to construct a dedicated bond portfolio. Use the following information to put together a dedicated bond portfolio. Assume that no zero coupon bonds are available and that all bonds listed sell at par, pay interest once a year, and are free of default and call risks. Round to the nearest dollar.

Year (maturity)	Obligation	Coupon Rate on Bond
1	$20,000,000	4.5%
2	25,000,000	5.0
3	25,000,000	5.5
4	40,000,000	6.0
5	53,000,000	6.0

Review Questions and Problems

1. Explain why all bond investors should be concerned about increased bond market volatility. Cite some specific examples of how bond investors can respond to increased volatility in the market.
2. Define the *term structure of interest rates.* Why are Treasury securities often used to measure the term structure?
3. Assume that a one-year discount bond currently yields 4 percent and a two-year discount bond currently yields 4.25 percent. Find the implied forward rate on a one-year bond one year from today. Show how to lock in that rate today.
4. Assume that a one-year discount bond currently yields 5 percent and a two-year discount bond currently yields 5.5 percent. Find the implied forward rate on a one-year bond one year from today. Show how to lock in that rate today.
5. Explain the differences between the pure expectations theory, the liquidity preference theory, and the market segmentation theory. What would constitute evidence of market segmentation?
6. What is the basic goal of active bond portfolio-management strategies? List several categories of active bond strategies.
7. What is meant by *riding the yield curve?* Would riding the yield curve work if the pure expectations theory of the yield curve were correct?
8. List the three types of changes in the yield curve that have been observed historically. For each kind of shift, what is the optimal yield curve strategy?
9. What is the general idea behind yield spread strategies? Why are yield spread strategies and interest rate strategies often interrelated?
10. Assume the current yield on a BBB-rated ten-year bond is 8.5 percent and the current yield on a ten-year T-bond is 6.5 percent (assume both bonds are pure discount bonds and have face values of $1,000). Also, assume you believe that the yield on the T-bond will fall to 6 percent over the next year and the yield spread between the BBB bond and the T-bond will narrow from 2 percent to 1.5 percent. Calculate the one-year holding period return for both bonds, assuming your expectations are correct. What type of strategy is this?
11. Assume that Congress has just cut the top marginal tax rate on individuals. What would you expect to happen to the yield spread between taxable and tax-exempt bonds? Why?
12. Give two examples of foreign exchange strategies. Why are foreign exchange strategies so potentially risky?

13. Assume that one year ago you purchased a five-year British government bond (the bond is denominated in British pounds, has a face value of £1,000, and is a pure discount bond). At that time, the bond had a yield of 6 percent and the exchange rate ($ per £) was $1.20. Today, one year later, you sold the bond. The yield has fallen to 5.5 percent and the exchange rate is now $1.10. Compute your one-year holding period return in both pounds and dollars. Why are the two different?

14. Why has bond indexing become so popular? What are some important decisions an investor must make when indexing a bond portfolio?

15. What is rebalancing? Why is rebalancing more difficult with bond portfolios than with stock portfolios?

16. What is target date immunization? Show how zero coupon bonds can solve target date immunization problems.

Use the data in the table below to answer questions 17–26.

Congratulations, you have just won the $30-million lottery! You are considering investing the funds in bonds, and you will consider hedging using target date immunization or maximizing your return. You will invest for 4.54 years then liquidate to move to Tahiti. You have narrowed your investment choices to four bonds outlined below.

Bond	Coupon Rate	Yield to Maturity	Term (years)	Duration
E	5%	5%	7 years	6.07
F	5	5	2 years	
G	5	5	5 .0 years	4.54
H	0	5	4.54 years	

Note: Assume that interest payments are made annually and ignore accrued interest. Conduct analysis on one bond even though you will be investing $30 million.

17. What is bond F's duration?

18. What is bond H's duration?

19. What is the price of bond H?

20. If you decide to hedge using target date immunization, will bond E achieve it? Explain your answer by including a discussion on the type of risk that will be greater if you fail to achieve immunization.

21. If you decide to hedge using target date immunization, will bond F achieve it? Explain your answer by including a discussion on the type of risk that will be greater if you fail to achieve immunization.

22. If you decide to hedge using target date immunization, will bond G achieve it? Explain your answer by including a discussion on the type of risk that will be greater if you fail to achieve immunization

23. If you decide to hedge using target date immunization, will bond H achieve it? Explain your answer by including a discussion on the type of risk that will be greater if you fail to achieve immunization.

24. Suppose instead of hedging using target date immunization, you decide to maximize your return. If you anticipate an increase in market interest rates from the current 5 percent to 6 percent, which bond is most desirable? Explain your choice.

25. If interest rates do increase from 5 percent to 6 percent a month after you invest, what is the impact on the bond F's price?

26. Calculate the annual rate of return (ARR) over the 4.54-year investment period for bond F. Assume that you will purchase a 6 percent coupon, four-year bond selling at par value when bond F matures.

27. How can an investor solve a multiperiod immunization problem? Explain how a dedicated portfolio works.

28. Assume that a bank currently has $50 million in assets (with an average duration of five years and an average interest rate of 7.5 percent) and $45 million in liabilities (with an average duration of one year and an average interest rate of 5 percent). If interest rates rise by 2 percent, to what risk are the bank's shareholders exposed? How could the bank immunize the shareholders' investment from adverse changes in interest rates?

29. Two British companies each want to borrow £20 million for five years. Company A has been offered a 9 percent fixed-rate loan or a variable-rate loan with the interest rate equal to LIBOR plus 0.5 percent. Company B has been offered either an 8 percent fixed-rate loan or a variable-rate loan with the interest rate equal to LIBOR plus 0.5 percent. Due to the composition of their assets, Company A would prefer a fixed-rate loan, whereas Company B would prefer a variable rate loan. Construct an interest rate swap that benefits both parties.

30. Two Japanese companies each want to borrow 100 million yen for five years. Company J has been offered a 5 percent fixed-rate loan or a variable-rate loan with the interest rate equal to LIBOR plus 0.5 percent. Company K has been offered either a 4 percent fixed-rate loan or a variable-rate loan with the interest rate equal to LIBOR plus 0.5 percent. Due to the composition of their assets, Company J would prefer a fixed-rate loan, whereas Company K would prefer a variable-rate loan. Construct an interest rate swap that benefits both parties.

CFA Questions

1. CFA Level III Examination, 1991
   Global Foundation has recently hired Strategic Allocation Associates (SAA) to review and make recommendations concerning allocation of its $5 billion endowment portfolio. Global has indicated an interest in introducing a structured approach (in which structured management is broadly defined as indexing, immunization, dedication, etc.) to at least a portion of the fund's fixed-income component.

   After analysis of Global's current asset mix, investment objectives, international exposure, and cash flow data, SAA has recommended that the overall asset mix be 50 percent equity, 5 percent real estate, and 45 percent fixed-income securities. Within the fixed-income component, SAA has further recommended the following allocation:

   50 percent structured management
   40 percent specialty active management (20 percent market timing, 10 percent high-yield, 10 percent arbitrage)
   10 percent nondollar/international active management.

   Global's investment committee has asked you, as a senior partner in SAA, to address several issues. Compare structured management with active management, with specific focus on *each* of the following aspects: predictability of return, level of returns, and cash flow characteristics.

   a. Explain the potential impact on the active managers' strategies and freedoms of action resulting from the introduction of a structured portfolio component.
   b. Compare the stratified sampling approach to bond index construction with an optimization approach. Briefly discuss the strengths and weaknesses of each index construction technique with specific consideration of convexity and changes in yield.

CRITICAL THINKING EXERCISES

1. This exercise requires computer work. Open Bond 2 worksheet in the Data workbook. It gives yields and prices for pure discount bonds with maturities of 1, 7, and

20 years. Classify the 1-year bond as a short-term bond, the 7-year bond as an intermediate-term bond, and the 20-year bond as a long-term bond. The anticipated holding period is one year. Given the following scenarios, determine which bond is optimal.

a. All yields remain constant

b. All yields rise by 1 percent.

c. All yields fall by 1 percent.

d. Yields on long-term bonds fall by 1.5 percent, yields on intermediate-term bonds fall by 0.75 percent, and yields on short-term bonds fall by 0.25 percent.

e. Yields on long-term bonds rise by 1 percent, yields in intermediate-term bonds rise by 1.25 percent, and yields on short-term bonds rise by 1.5 percent.

f. Yields on long-term bonds fall by 1 percent, yields on intermediate-term bonds fall by 1.5 percent, and yields on short-term bonds fall by 2 percent.

2. This exercise requires computer work. Open the Bond 3 worksheet in the Data workbook and use the data provided to answer the following questions:

a. A pension fund will need $10 million in exactly five years. Given current yields, how much will the pension fund have to invest today?

b. Given the choices available, which bond should the pension fund buy? Why?

c. Would your answer to part b change if the fund manager believed that interest rates might rise or fall during the next five years?

d. Show what would happen if (1) interest rates were to rise immediately by 1.5 percent after the bonds were purchased and remain at that level for the rest of the five-year period, or (2) interest rates were to fall immediately by 1.5 percent after the bonds were purchased and remain at that level for the rest of the five-year period.

e. Should the pension fund make any changes to the bond portfolio if rates were either to rise or fall during the five-year period?

3. This exercise requires library research. Find five bonds that have been upgraded by the rating agencies recently (either corporate or municipal bonds). Obtain price and yield information for the bonds six months before the upgrade and six months after it. In addition, obtain yield information from some relevant index for either corporate or municipal bonds. What happened to the bond prices and yields before and after the upgrade announcement? How did the spreads between the yields for your sample bonds and the index yield change? Did they widen or narrow? Had you purchased these bonds six months before the upgrade announcement, approximately how much higher would your return have been compared with the performance of the broad market index? (Hint: S&P's monthly *Bond Guide* is a good source of upgrade, price, and yield information.)

Part 4

Principles

of

Security

Analysis

PART IV IS DEVOTED TO A DETAILED DISCUSSION OF THE FUNDAMENTAL ANALYSIS AND VALUATION OF COMMON STOCKS COMMONLY REFERRED TO AS SECURITY ANALYSIS. THE GOAL OF SECURITY ANALYSIS IS TO DETERMINE WHETHER THE PRICE OF A COMMON STOCK REFLECTS ITS INTRINSIC VALUE. THE PROCESS OF SECURITY ANALYSIS HAS OFTEN BEEN DESCRIBED A SORT OF INVERTED TRIANGLE, AS THE ANALYSIS MOVES FROM THE GENERAL TO THE SPECIFIC. WE START WITH ECONOMIC ANALYSIS, THEN MOVE TO INDUSTRY ANALYSIS, AND THEN MOVE TO COMPANY ANALYSIS. WE THEN CONSIDER SEVERAL STOCK VALUATION MODELS WHICH TIE THE PROCESS TOGETHER. THE OVERALL PURPOSE OF OUR REVIEW OF SECURITY ANALYSIS IS TO SHOW HOW ANALYSTS ARRIVE AT ESTIMATES OF THE VARIABLES THAT APPEAR TO DETERMINE THE VALUE OF COMMON STOCKS. WE WILL SEE THAT THE ANALYST HAS TO CONSIDER BOTH QUANTIFIABLE AND NON-QUANTIFIABLE FACTORS AND ISSUES, MAKING BOTH SUBJECTIVE AND OBJECTIVE JUDGMENTS CONCERNING THE RELATIONSHIP BETWEEN A STOCK'S PRICE AND ITS INTRINSIC VALUE.

ECONOMIC AND INDUSTRY ANALYSIS

PREVIOUSLY . . .

In the prior two chapters, we described the investment characteristics of fixed-income securities and some strategies involving bonds.

IN THIS CHAPTER . . .

We examine the two macro-components of security analysis: economic and industry analysis. All stocks are to some extent affected by these macrofactors. Stock prices, in general, and interest rates are strongly related to the business cycle. Economic variables also affect the fortunes of industries. Regardless of the overall market, variations in industry performance should be expected.

TO COME . . .

In the next two chapters, we discuss company analysis, beginning with qualitative factors and historical financial data.

Chapter Objectives

After reading Chapter 11, you should be able to answer the following questions:

1. Why are economic and industry analysis important?
2. How do investment decisions relate to the business cycle?
3. How are economic forecasts made?
4. How are industries classified?
5. What are the important components of an industry analysis?
6. What are the framework and some techniques used in industry analysis?

In Chapter 8, we briefly discussed the basic steps for analyzing a common stock. *Security analysis,* or *fundamental analysis,* can be thought of as a three-step process describing an inverted triangle, with the analyst moving from the general to the specific. He or she begins with economic analysis and works to determine where the domestic and international economies are headed (expansion or recession), as well as the outlook for important economic variables such as inflation and interest rates. The analyst also considers whether the overall economic outlook appears favorable or unfavorable for stocks.

After assessing the economic environment, the analyst completes an industry analysis. Is the company's industry in a growth phase or a mature phase? Is the industry subject to rapid technological change? Are demographic trends favorable or unfavorable for the industry? Are industry production costs rising more quickly or more slowly than the overall inflation rate? Is the industry subject to substantial government regulation? These are examples of questions an analyst might ask when examining a company's industry.

Following a review of economic and industry factors, the analyst examines the specific company in detail, looking at both quantitative and qualitative issues. We begin our detailed look at security analysis in this chapter with an examination of economic and industry analysis to assess the company's macroenvironment, which strongly influences common stock valuation.

The Importance of Economic and Industry Analysis

We begin our look at macroanalysis of securities by asking a simple question: just how important are economic and industry factors in the valuation of individual common stocks? We believe that both are highly important, although neither economic or industry analysis can substitute for a careful examination of a specific company. History is replete with examples of poor stock performance despite favorable economic environments for stocks and good industry characteristics. The reverse situation (a good stock in poor economic and industry conditions) has occasionally occurred as well. Economic and industry analysis should complement and enhance the analyst's examination of a specific company, not replace it.

Economic analysis is important simply because stock prices have a strong positive relationship with overall economic performance. Since 1949, according to the National Bureau of Economic Research, the U.S. economy has passed through eight economic expansions and eight recessions. During the eight expansions, stock prices, as measured by the Standard & Poor's (S&P) 500, rose an average of 87.8 percent. By contrast, during the eight recessions, stock prices *fell* by an average of 18.2 percent. Not surprisingly, a stronger expansion (or contraction) in economic activity generally produces a larger increase (or decrease) in stock prices. We have more to say about the relationship between stock prices and economic activity later in the chapter.

The same positive relationship between economic performance and stock prices exists in other countries as well. For example, Britain experienced a recession between mid-1990 and late 1991; its real gross domestic product (GDP), stated in constant dollars, removing the effects of inflation, declined by approximately 2.6 percent. The associated decline in British stock prices (measured by the Financial Times 100 index) was slightly more than 16 percent.

It is important to note that over the duration of a bull or bear market, performance levels among various industry groups often show substantial differences. For example, between March 1978 and November 1980 the S&P 500 gained about 53 percent. Auto stocks, however, lost more than one-quarter of their value during the same period. Between October 1983 and July 1984, the S&P 500 dropped by about 10 percent; shares of oil companies rose by 10 percent. Performance of the overall market, along with selected industry groups, during recent years is illustrated in Exhibit 11.1.

The data in Exhibit 11.1 illustrate that regardless of how well the overall market performs, we can expect to see disparate performance among various industry groups. In 1998, for example, semiconductor manufacturers gained more than 65 percent while money center banks gained less than 5 percent. So, even if the economic outlook for stocks in general is favorable, the outlook for some industry groups may not be. Therefore, the analyst must examine the industry as well as the economy.

Macro-analysis is also important because it is naive to assume that the fortunes of individual companies, and thus their stocks' performance, are not somehow tied to the prospects for the overall economy and the industries within which those companies operate. No company operates in a vacuum. For example, as we noted in Chapter 9, one variable that determines the intrinsic value of a common stock is the expected growth in earnings. Without any economic or industry information, could you come up with a reasonable estimate of the expected growth rate in earnings? Probably not, because most companies' future earnings are heavily influenced by economic and industry conditions.

Business Cycles and Investment Decisions

Having established the importance of an examination of economic and industry factors in the evaluation of individual stocks, we now turn to a discussion of the relationship between business cycles and investment decisions. First of all, what is a **business cycle?** Long-term economic growth in the United States (and in other developed, market-oriented countries) has exhibited nonperiodic but recurrent sequences of expansions and contractions (recessions) around the long-term, secular trend. Economists refer to these sequences as business cycles.

business cycle
Nonperiodic recurrent sequences of expansions and contractions around long-term economic growth.

Since the end of World War II, the United States has experienced eight complete business cycles (measured from trough to trough). By comparison, Canada has experienced twelve complete business cycles since 1948, and Britain, France, Germany, and Japan have each experienced seven complete business cycles during the same period. The average business cycle in the United States since 1949 has lasted 62 months (slightly more than five years).

It is important to note, however, that no two business cycles have been exactly alike. The longest complete postwar business cycle lasted 117 months (between February 1961 and November 1970), whereas the shortest lasted only 28 months (between July 1980 and November 1982). During the postwar era, U.S. expansion periods ranged from 12 to 110 months, whereas contractions ranged between 6 and 16 months.[1] During the average postwar expansion, real GDP increased by 5.1 percent per year, with a range between 4 percent and 7.3 percent. The average contraction saw real GDP decline by about 2.5 percent per year, with a range between -0.1 percent and –4.4 percent per year.

BUSINESS CYCLES AND STOCK PRICES

As we discussed earlier, stock prices and economic activity are closely related; economic expansions are generally associated with rising stock prices, and contractions are usually associated with falling stock prices. However, stock prices and economic

---

[1]The longest economic expansion in postwar history began in November 1990 and continues still.

Exhibit 11.1 ✦ Performance of the S&P 500 and Selected Industry Groups: 1994–98

Year	S&P 500	Auto Manufacturers	Major Pharmaceutical Manufacturers	Money Center Banks	Semiconductor Manufacturers
1994	−1.5%	7.2%	8.0%	−8.6%	11.2%
1995	34.1	5.6	51.0	50.2	54.4
1996	22.3	19.6	22.5	37.7	98.5
1997	28.7	10.8	46.6	36.1	7.2
1998	26.7	10.8	40.8	5.0	65.5

Source: Standard & Poor's.

activity are not *coincident;* they do not occur at the same time. Rather, stock prices tend to lead overall economic activity, typically by several months, in all developed, market-oriented economies. Stock prices could fall even when the economy was still expanding, and they could rise in a recession.

Exhibit 11.2 illustrates the leading relationship between stock prices and economic activity in the United States. During expansions, stocks prices (measured by the S&P 500) have on average peaked almost six months before economic activity. Stock prices, on average, have bottomed out roughly five months before the ends of recessions. Note, however, that the leading relationship between stock prices and economic activity has been far from consistent. Stock prices have peaked anywhere between 1 and 13 months before peaks in economic activity. In 1980, stock prices did not actually peak until *after* the economic contraction had begun. The data in Exhibit 11.2 also suggest that the length of the lead time between the peak in stock prices and the peak in economic activity is getting shorter.

To further complicate the relationship, many large declines in stock prices have not led into recessions. The most recent example of this is the 1987 market break. Between August and December of 1987, the S&P 500 dropped by more than 27 percent, yet no recession followed in either 1988 or 1989. In fact, real U.S. GDP grew by more than 7 percent during both years. However, in far fewer cases large increases in stock prices have failed to presage economic expansions.

Why do stock prices tend to lead economic activity? One explanation is that an increase or decrease in stock prices is a self-fulfilling prophecy. Some economists argue that stock price reversals affect consumer and business confidence, and thus spending decisions. A sharp decline in stock prices, for example, may lead to less consumer spending, depressing economic activity. Other economists dismiss the notion that major stock price reversals are the main cause of changes in the direction of economic activity. The Investment History box on page 284 examines whether or not the 1929 Stock Market Crash *caused* the Great Depression. Contrary to popular belief, the answer appears to be no.

Another explanation is that the variables that drive stock prices (for example, earnings, dividends, and interest rates) are based more on *expected* business conditions than on current conditions. Stock investors may be responding to what they think is going to happen rather than what is currently happening. Further, some of the fundamental factors that determine stock prices, such as companies' profit margins

Exhibit 11.2 ✦ Turning Points in the Business Cycle and U.S. Stock Prices: 1949–91

S&P	GDP	Lead (months)
A. Peaks		
January 1953	July 1953	6
July 1956	August 1957	13
July 1959	April 1960	9
December 1968	December 1969	12
December 1972	November 1973	11
February 1980	January 1980	−1
April 1981	July 1981	3
June 1990	July 1990	1
Average		**5.8**
B. Troughs		
June 1949	October 1949	4
September 1953	May 1954	8
December 1957	April 1958	4
October 1960	February 1961	4
June 1970	November 1970	5
September 1974	March 1975	5
April 1980	July 1980	3
July 1982	December 1982	5
October 1990	March 1991	5
Average		**4.8**

Source: Survey of Current Business, *various issues.*

and earnings, also tend to lead overall economic activity.

Stock Prices and Inflation

Stock investors constantly watch for signs of change in the rate of inflation. Any increase in inflation, actual or expected, is considered bad for the overall stock market. (The reverse is also true, lower inflation lifts stocks.) For one thing, rising inflation normally means rising interest rates. Rising interest rates, in turn, tend to depress stock prices, because the required rate of return on a stock moves up and down with general market interest rates.

Exhibit 11.3 shows the relationship between stock returns and inflation. The annual total return from the S&P 500 is shown along with the annual inflation rate between 1968 and 1998. Although the data indicate a generally inverse relationship between stock returns and inflation, it appears that changes in inflation, rather than a particular inflation rate, are more strongly associated with stock market performance.

You must be careful, of course, when interpreting the relationship between stock prices and inflation. Inflation tends to be at its highest around economic peaks and at its lowest around economic troughs. Because stock prices generally lead economic activity, it is not surprising to see falling stock prices and rising inflation in anticipation of an economic peak and subsequent contraction.

DID THE 1929 GREAT STOCK MARKET CRASH CAUSE THE GREAT DEPRESSION?

Two of the most significant events in the history of the twentieth century were the Great Stock Market crash of 1929, which ended one of the great stock market bubbles in history, and the Great Depression, which lasted from the end of the 1920s to the beginning of World War II. Popular history suggests that the stock market crash was a cause of the depression. But, was it really? Before we answer the question, let's review the Great Crash of 1929.

Stock prices, measured by the Dow Jones Industrial Average, almost tripled between late 1920 and the end of 1927. This increase could be characterized as more a standard bull market than a speculative bubble. The increase was generally orderly and was backed by favorable economic fundamentals (inflation, interest rates, and corporate profits).

Sometime during 1928, however, the bull market became a true speculative bubble. After a fairly quiet winter, during which prices actually fell slightly, stock prices began to rise sharply. During the second half of 1928 alone, the Dow increased about 42 percent as trading volume soared. By the end of 1928, the frenzy was in full force.

By almost any measure, 1929 is perhaps the most remarkable and most infamous year in stock market history. The Dow added another 27 percent between early January and September 3, when the bubble finally reached its zenith. Trading was often frantic with wild daily price swings—both up and down. Trading volume set records almost every day, even during the normally slow summer months.

Finally the end came. On September 5, 1929, respected financial adviser Roger Babson, repeated a prediction that a stock market crash was coming. Stocks suffered a sharp sell off that day (this became known as the *Babson Break*). Stocks recovered somewhat and started to drift over the next few weeks, though the market had more down days than up days. The bubble finally ruptured on October 28 and 29. Stock prices dropped in an almost linear fashion. Some individual stocks fell by $5 to $10 per share on each subsequent trade. The Dow lost more than 23 percent, and the dreams of many, along with billions of dollars, were suddenly wiped out.

The 1929 crash was only the beginning of a prolonged slide in stock prices. The next three years, 1930, 1931, and 1932, were among the worst in history for stocks. The Dow lost almost 90 percent of its value between September 3,

1929, and July 8, 1932. Trading volume also evaporated as stocks were shunned. It took the Dow over 25 years to fully recover from the Great Crash. The record established on September 3, 1929, wasn't broken until November 23, 1954.

Back to the original question: did the Great Crash cause the Great Depression? According to many economists and historians, probably not. They note that less than 3 million Americans—out of a population of over 110 million—owned any stocks whatsoever in 1929. Further, substantial evidence indicates that the U.S. economy was already well into a recession by fall of 1929. Industrial production was falling, interest rates were rising, and corporate profits were declining. In fact, according to historians, the weather actually played a bigger role than the stock market. Several years of severe drought in the Midwest devastated the farm economy—which in those days formed a much more significant part of the U.S. economy than it is now. Farmers couldn't repay loans to banks, leading to bank runs and eventually to a general banking panic. Depositors lost billions of dollars as banks failed. The collapse of the banking system pushed an already weakening economy into depression. In the end, the Great Crash was more likely *caused* by the coming Depression, than a *cause* of the Depression.

Overall Market and the Performance Levels of Industry Groups

If the overall stock market tends to lead economic activity, what relationship do specific industry groups have to the economy? The evidence suggests that certain industry groups tend do better during the early phases of bull markets, whereas other groups often do better during the later stages. Historical data suggest that cyclical stocks of credit and consumer-goods firms (for example, home-building companies and automobile manufacturers) generally outperform the overall market early in bull

Exhibit 11.3 ✦ STOCK RETURNS VERSUS INFLATION

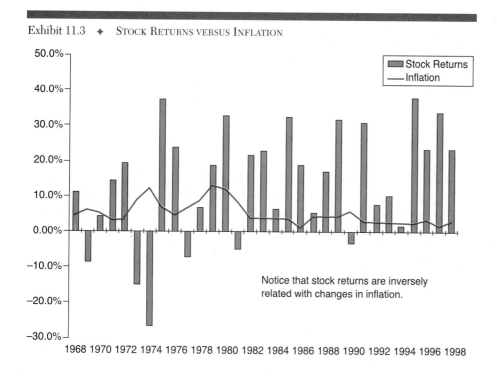

markets. Energy stocks, defensive consumer-goods stocks such as food companies, and utilities exhibit the market's best relative performance late in bear markets. Growth stocks of consumer-goods companies (for example, cosmetics, soft drinks, and pharmaceutical stocks) often outperform the market late in bull markets. Remember to interpret this, and all other studies of past performance, with caution; just because these relationships were true historically does not mean that they will be true in the future.

BUSINESS CYCLES AND INTEREST RATES

Even though no two business cycles are alike, interest rates and business cycles are clearly related. Generally, interest rates rise during economic expansions and fall during economic contractions. During the 1975 to 1980 economic expansion, for example, the yield on three-month Treasury bills (T-bills) rose 634 basis points. In comparison, during the 1981-82 recession, yields on three-month T-bills fell by 654 basis points.

One reason for the relationship between business cycles and interest rates, of course, is inflation. Actual and expected future rates of inflation tend to rise during economic expansions and fall during economic contractions. As actual inflation and inflationary expectations rise, so do interest rates.

In past business cycles, however, both inflation rates and interest rates have tended to rise (and fall) more sharply in the later stages of economic expansions (and contractions). For example, during the first two quarters of the 1975-79 expansion (April through September 1975), the annual rate of inflation was about 7.3 percent.

T-bill yields increased by about 80 basis points between April and October 1975. By contrast, during the last two quarters of the expansion (July through December 1979), the annual rate of inflation was more than 12.5 percent, and T-bill yields increased by more than 300 basis points.

In addition, both inflation and interest rates have often continued to increase or decline for several additional quarters following turning points in economic activity. For example, the rate of inflation remained essentially constant during the first two and one-half years of the 1983-90 expansion.

Aside from inflation, interest rate changes relate to economic activity in another way. The demand for loanable funds by businesses and households rises during expansions and falls during recessions. To illustrate this, Exhibit 11.4 shows the change in a real rate of interest before and during postwar recessions.

As expected, the real rate of interest rose, with one exception, during the four quarters preceding each peak in economic activity. During all postwar recessions, real interest rates have declined. Prior to the 1990-91 recession, for example, the real rate of interest rose by 75 basis points. During the recession itself, real interest rates dropped by almost 300 basis points.

Business Cycles and Yield Spreads

As we noted in the prior section on bonds, a *yield spread* is the difference in yield between any two fixed-income securities. Evidence from past business cycles suggests that yield spreads (based on both credit risk and maturity) often widen and narrow in response to changes in economic activity.

This is illustrated in Exhibit 11.5, which shows the relationship between turning points in economic activity (both peaks and troughs) and the yield spreads between BBB-rated corporate bonds and Treasury bonds (T-bonds) and between T-bonds and T-bills. The spread between T-bonds and T-bills forms part of what is known as the *yield curve*.

The data show that the yield spread between BBB-rated corporate bonds and T-bonds tends to be wider at the ends of contractions and narrower at the ends of expansions. This suggests that bond investors become more quality-conscious during recessions. Investors may be worried that corporations are more likely to default on bonds during economic contractions.

The data presented in Exhibit 11.5 show that the spread between T-bonds and T-bills is generally narrower at peaks in economic activity and wider at troughs. Notice that at some economic peaks, the yield on T-bills actually exceeded the yield on T-bonds. (This is referred to as an *inverted yield curve.*) One explanation for this pattern is that investors expect interest rates to fall at economic peaks or rise at troughs. Another explanation suggests that short-term rates are influenced by expected short-term inflation, whereas long-term rates are influenced by expected long-term inflation. Inverted yield curves have normally coincided with high rates of both inflation and interest. Investors may believe, therefore, that the *average* rate of inflation may be higher in the short run than in the long run.

INVESTMENT TIMING IMPLICATIONS

The relationships between business cycles, stocks prices, and interest rates discussed in the past few pages have several possible implications for investment timing. The

Exhibit 11.4 ✦ Changes in Real Rates of Interest before and during Recessions[a]

Recession	Prerecession Period[b]	During Recession
1953–1954	−0.55%	−0.99%
1957–1958	+1.05	−0.30
1960–1961	+1.90	−0.03
1969–1970	+1.82	−1.50
1973–1975	+0.64	−1.50
1980	+4.57	−5.68
1981–1982	+7.96	−3.69
1990–1991	+0.75	−2.99

[a]Figures are changes in real interest rates over the designed intervals. Real interest rates are defined as the rate on 90-day commercial paper minus a four-quarter average of current and past inflation as measured by the GDP deflator.

[b]The four quarters preceding the peak in economic activity.

Source: Survey of Current Business, *various issues.*

Investment Insights box on page 289 provides some general investment advice for both stock and bond investors at various points in the business cycle.

For example, in anticipation of an economic upturn, and the related increase in stock prices, a stock investor should generally allocate a greater share of a portfolio to cyclical stocks, especially those with high betas. (The higher the beta, the more a stock should increase relative to the overall market.) On the other hand, a bond investor should continue to lengthen bond maturity within the portfolio and should shift some funds from high-quality bonds (for example, T-bonds) to lower-quality bonds given that the yield spread between high-quality and lower-quality bonds is beginning to narrow.

Economic Forecasting

The discussion in the prior section strongly suggests that an ability to forecast eco-

Economic Forecasting

in most industries depend on assumptions concerning future economic activity.

Economic forecasting has two general objectives. The first is to foresee turning points in the business cycle (peaks and troughs), and the second is to provide estimates of specific economic variables such as the growth rate in real GDP, inflation, interest rates, unemployment, and personal income. Even if no recession looms, an investor still needs an idea about whether the economy is likely to grow slowly or rapidly.

The two general approaches to economic forecasting can be roughly classified as qualitative and quantitative forecasting. In a *qualitative forecast,* the economist looks at a variety of economic data and makes a subjective assessment about the economic outlook. A *quantitative forecast* is derived from *econometric models.* Of course, the

Exhibit 11.5 ✦ TURNING POINTS IN THE U.S. ECONOMY AND YIELD SPREADS

Date	Turning Point	BBB, Absolute	T-Bonds, Relative	T-Bonds, Absolute	T-Bonds, Relative
		Yield Spreads			
October 1949	Trough	120	0.55	114	1.09
July 1953	Peak	88	0.29	88	0.42
May 1954	Trough	101	0.40	173	2.21
August 1957	Peak	143	0.39	28	0.08
April 1958	Trough	203	0.73	166	1.48
April 1960	Peak	117	0.28	93	0.29
February 1961	Trough	144	0.38	137	0.57
December 1969	Peak	181	0.26	−86	−0.11
November 1970	Trough	287	0.44	122	0.23
November 1973	Peak	262	0.44	−195	−0.25
March 1975	Trough	144	0.18	236	0.41
January 1980	Peak	158	0.15	−151	−0.13
July 1980	Trough	190	0.19	208	0.26
July 1981	Peak	237	0.18	−119	−0.08
December 1982	Trough	276	0.26	251	0.31
July 1990	Peak	173	0.20	98	0.13
March 1991	Trough	164	0.19	257	0.43

Note: BBB refers to BBB rated corporate bonds: T-Bond refers to Treasury bonds with maturities in excess of 15 years; T-Bill refers to 90-day Treasury bills. Absolute yield spreads are stated in basis points. Relative yield spreads are equal to absolute yield spreads divided by the yields on T-bonds (or T-bills).

Source: Survey of Current Business, *various issues.*

two approaches are not mutually exclusive. Many experienced economic forecasters blend the two perspectives.

QUALITATIVE FORECASTS

As we just mentioned, a qualitative forecast results draws on subjective analysis of economic data. For example, an economist might observe an increase in the number of new household formations in the United States. She might conclude that this is a good sign for future economic growth, because it is likely that an increase in household formations will boost consumer spending on new homes, appliances, furniture, and such. Qualitative forecasts often rely on two techniques: leading indicators and anticipation surveys.

Leading Indicators

A fairly simple approach to economic forecasting is to follow the behavior of specific variables that historically have been indicators, or barometers, of future economic activity. Some economists, for example, carefully examine monetary indicators such as money supply data because they believe future economic growth is more a function

INVESTMENT INSIGHTS

BUSINESS CYCLES AND INVESTMENT TIMING

Stage of the Business Cycle	Stock Investors	Bond Investors
Late recession to trough	1. End of bear market, beginning of bull market 2. Begin to shift portfolio toward high-quality cyclical stocks.	1. Interest rates falling, yield spreads at their widest 2. Continue to lengthen the average maturity (or duration) of a bond portfolio; switch some funds into lower-quality bonds.
Early expansion	1. Early-to-middle bull market 2. Continue to move funds into cyclical growth stocks; buy other cyclical stocks and stock with high betas.	1. Yield spreads beginning to narrow, interest rates still falling. 2. Continue to lengthen the average maturity of the portfolio and switch to lower-quality bonds.
Middle expansion	1. Middle-to-late bull market 2. Slowly lower the portfolio's beta and build cash reserves by taking profits.	1. Interest rates bottoming out and may begin rising, yield spreads continuing to narrow. 2. Start to decrease the average maturity of the portfolio; continue the movement into lower-quality bonds.
Late expansion to peak	1. End of bull market, beginning of bear market 2. Take profits in cyclical stocks, build cash reserves, and reduce portfolio beta; slowly begin buying defensive stocks and utilities.	1. Interest rates rising, yield spreads at their narrowest. 2. Start to move funds toward quality bonds; continue to reduce the average maturity of the portfolio.
Early recession	1. Early-to-middle bear market 2. Begin to shift cash into defensive stocks, utilities, and high-quality, noncyclical growth stocks.	1. Yield spreads widening, interest rates still rising. 2. Hold short-term, high-quality bonds.
Middle recession	1. Middle-to-late bear market 2. Start to take profits in utilities and defensive stocks.	1. Interest rates peaking, and may begin falling, yield spreads continuing to widen. 2. Begin to lengthen the average maturity of the portfolio.

of monetary conditions than anything else. Sometimes, economists combine several indicators into a leading indicator index, the best known of which is the **Index of Leading Indicators,** published by the Conference Board.

Exhibit 11.6 ◆ COMPONENTS OF THE INDEX OF LEADING INDICATORS

Components	Direction Prior to *Trough* in Economic Activity	Direction Prior to *Peak* in Economic Activity
1. Average weekly hours, manufacturing	Up	Down
2. Average weekly initial claims for unemployment insurance	Down	Up
3. Manufacturers' new orders for consumer goods and materials	Up	Down
4. Vendor performance (slower deliveries index)	Down	Up
5. Contracts and orders for plant and equipment (constant dollars)	Up	Down
6. New, private housing units authorized by local building permits (index)	Up	Down
7. Stock prices (S&P 500 index)	Up	Down
8. Money supply (M2)	Up	Down
9. Consumer expectations (index)	Up	Down
10. Yield spread between 10-year Treasury Bond to Federal Funds	Up	Down

index of leading indicators *Well-known combination of 10 economic measures, all of which tend to lead overall economic activity.*

The index combines 10 economic measures, all of which have historically led overall economic activity. Each month the index rises, falls, or remains unchanged. Analysts look for any clear reversal in the *direction* of the index. If the index reaches a certain level and then clearly declines, that is a signal of an impending peak in economic activity (and subsequent recession). However, if the index falls to a certain level and then starts to increase, that is a signal of an impending trough in economic activity (and subsequent expansion).

The index of leading indicators currently has 10 components, listed in Exhibit 11.6 along with the expected direction (up or down) of each component preceding an economic peak or trough. Note that the S&P 500 is one of the components of the leading index. As we have seen, it should rise before an economic trough and fall before an economic peak. Because stock prices are a component of the index of leading indicators, any use of the index to forecast stock prices based on future economic activity can cause conflicts. Changes in stock prices may be driving changes in the overall index, so you might be using changes in stock prices to forecast changes in stock prices!

Anticipation Surveys

Another qualitative economic forecasting method examines surveys that attempt to measure the future economic behavior businesses, consumers, and government agencies. These are commonly referred to as **anticipation surveys.**

Because consumer spending is such a large component of U.S. GDP (approximately 67 percent), many economists examine surveys that measure consumer confidence. This is based on the notion that the more confident consumers are about their current and future economic situation, the more money they will spend, especially on big ticket items such as homes and automobiles. The more consumers spend, the faster the economy grows. You may have noticed that the Consumer Expectations Index—a widely followed anticipation survey—is one component of the index of leading indicators. It is worth noting that the major difference between anticipation surveys and other leading indicators is that anticipation surveys measure *planned* activity, whereas other leading indicators—such as building permits and unemployment claims—measure actual activity. Higher consumer confidence does not always translate into increased consumer spending and increased economic activity.

anticipation surveys
Surveys that attempt to measure the future economic behavior of business and consumers.

ECONOMETRIC MODEL BUILDING

Econometric models apply mathematical and statistical techniques to economic forecasting. These models are the principal tools of the quantitative economist. Although anticipation surveys and leading indicators provide fairly simple forecasts, econometric models provide perhaps the most complex. This most scientific approach to economic forecasting requires the user to specify the precise interrelationships between a variety of economic variables to come up with a model.

econometric models
Applications of mathematical and statistical techniques to economic forecasting.

Econometric models predict the direction of future economic activity and also its duration and magnitude. Instead of a general forecast (for example, sluggish growth in real GDP), an econometric model yields a precise number (for example, next year real GDP will grow by 2.5 percent). The accuracy of this precise forecast depends, of course, on the quality of the input data and validity of the assumptions made by the model builder.

A variety of private and public organizations build econometric models and use them to produce econometric forecasts. Several of the better-known models have been developed by Chase Econometrics, DRI (Data Resources, Inc.), GE, the University of Michigan, and the University of Pennsylvania (Wharton School of Business). These models are extremely complex and contain many equations and dozens of variables. Their forecasts are widely reported in the financial press.

IMPLICATIONS FOR INVESTORS

Economic forecasters, as a group, are not revered for their accuracy. Research backs up that opinion. One study looked at the twenty-year track records of 111 forecasters in predicting the following year's change in real gross national product (GNP).[2] The group, on average, overestimated the change in real GNP in eight of the twenty years

---

[2]Victor Zarnowitz, *Business Cycles* (Chicago: University of Chicago Press, 1992).

by an average error of 0.5 percent. They underestimated the following year's growth rate in nine of the twenty years by an average error of 1.2 percent. In three years, the group missed turning points by an average error of 2.8 percent. This group of forecasters was especially bad at predicting recessions.

Why Is Economic Forecasting Difficult?

If economists have a poor record forecasting future economic activity, the next question is, why? In Chapter 8, we saw that security analysts show little accuracy in forecasting future earnings of companies. Many of the same explanations for their shortcomings apply to economic forecasts.

First, all forecasting is difficult, and forecasting economic activity is probably more difficult than forecasting earnings. It is difficult to obtain good, accurate, and timely data on the U.S. economy. Government economic statistics are constantly revised, and many are considered misleading if not downright inaccurate. Aside from data problems, the U.S. economy is an extremely complex system interrelated with an even more complex system, the global economy.

Second, random shocks on economic activity—such as severe weather events—have both significant and unpredictable impact. For example, a colder than normal winter can affect everything from oil prices to retail sales.

Third, most economic forecasting models are derived from historic data. Such information gives few clues about major structural or secular changes in the economy (for example, the impact of technology on productivity and corporate profits).

Critics argue that economic forecasters tend toward too much respect for momentum; they believe that the next business cycle will look like the last business cycle, when, in fact, major secular changes may cause significant alterations. Finally, human psychology may play a role. Economic forecasters, like securities analysts, may be reluctant to forecast bad news and to make a forecast that differs substantially from those made by colleagues.

Using Economic Forecasts

In view of such poor accuracy, how should investors use economic forecasts? Carefully, of course, and always bearing in mind that even if specific numbers are not always accurate, the commentary behind the numbers may be valuable. Important questions to ask include how economists come up with their forecasts and what variables they consider. *Why* forecasters think that the economy will grow slowly next year, for example, could be useful to investors. Investors should ask why economists believe that inflation and interest rates are likely to rise or fall or why the dollar is likely to grow stronger against most other currencies. A good economic forecast will address these types of questions, and smart investors will attend to the answers. Like securities analysts, general directions implied by economist forecasts may provide much more insight than their specific forecasts of, say, next year's GDP growth rate or inflation.

For example, let's say that you follow the auto industry or are interested in one of the auto stocks. As you might expect, auto sales relate closely to personal income. Higher personal income usually means higher auto sales. Assume an economist tells you that she believes that growth in disposable personal income will accelerate over the next few years.[3] If you believe her reasoning makes sense, this is valuable information because it suggests a good environment for increasing auto sales. Whether her specific forecast of personal income growth ends up 0.5 percent too high or too low is much less important.

Industry Analysis

Having completed an economic analysis, it's time to address the next step in the security analysis process: industry analysis. We begin with a discussion of how to define and classify industries, the classifications upon which industry statistics rely.

DEFINING AND CLASSIFYING INDUSTRIES

In a broad sense, an *industry* might be considered a community that shares common interests that distinguish it from other communities. The dictionary defines an industry as "a distinct group of productive or profit-making enterprises." Although this definition seems straightforward, the work of classifying industries can be difficult and the results somewhat ambiguous. Further complications can arise in assigning specific companies to particular industries.

There are several simple ways to classify industries. One obvious method is to classify industries by product or service (for example, the chemical industry, the airline industry, or the restaurant industry). Another simple way of classifying industries is based on their reactions to the business cycle. A **cyclical industry** is one whose performance tends to relate positively to economic activity. Examples of cyclical industries include auto makers, home builders, and paper companies. A **defensive industry** is one whose performance tends to be relatively insensitive to economic activity, despite some cyclical ups and downs. Examples of defensive industries include electric and gas utilities and the pharmaceutical industry. A **growth industry** is characterized by rapid growth in sales and earnings, often independent of the business cycle. Examples of growth industries during the 1990s included biotechnology and semiconductors.

Several nongovernment organizations have industrial classification systems based on product (good or service) and business cycle characteristics. Two examples are Dow Jones and Standard & Poor's. Both divide companies initially into major industry groups, as Exhibit 11.7 shows. They subdivide each major industry group into secondary groups. As you can see, Dow Jones divides companies into 9 major groups, whereas S&P divides them initially into 24 major groups. Exhibit 11.7 also breaks down the Dow Jones energy group and the S&P fuel group into their various subdivisions. The two systems differ substantially. Dow Jones, for example, includes pipeline companies as part of its energy industry, whereas S&P includes them as part of its utility industry. Investors should be aware of such differences in industry classifications.

These classification systems often define industries by grouping somewhat diverse firms. Take the airline industry as an example. Both Dow Jones and S&P put all airlines into one subgroup. Although each company in the industry provides the same

cyclical industry
Industry whose performance tends to be positively related to economic activity.

defensive industry
Industry whose performance tends to be relatively insensitive to economic activity.

growth industry
Industry characterized by rapid growth in sales, often independent of the business cycle.

---

[3]Disposable personal income is personal income after taxes.

Exhibit 11.7 ✦ Industry Classification Systems

	Dow Jones	Standard & Poor's
A. Major Groups	1. Basic materials	1. Aerospace
	2. Conglomerates	2. Automotive
	3. Consumer cyclical	3. Banks
	4. Consumer noncyclical	4. Chemicals
	5. Energy	5. Conglomerates
	6. Financial services	6. Consumer products
	7. Industrial	7. Containers and packaging
	8. Technology	8. Discount and fashion retailers
	9. Utilities	9. Electrical and electronics
		10. Food
		11. Fuel
		12. Health care
		13. Housing and real estate
		14. Leisure-time industries
		15. Manufacturing
		16. Metals and mining
		17. Nonbank financial
		18. Office equipment and computers
		19. Paper and forest products
		20. Publishing and broadcasting
		21. Service industries
		22. Telecommunications
		23. Transportation
		24. Utilities and power
	Group 5 (Energy)	Group 11 (Fuel)
B. Subdivision	a. Coal	a. Coal
	b. Oil (drilling)	b. Oil and gas
	c. Oil (integrated majors)	c. Petroleum services
	d. Oil (secondary)	
	e. Oilfield equipment	
	f. Pipelines[a]	

[a]In S&P's classification system, most pipeline companies are included in utilities and power (major group), oil and gas transmission (secondary group).

Source: Dow Jones & Company; Standard & Poor's.

service, flying people from point A to point B, grouping them masks differences among domestic airlines such as Southwest, with only domestic routes; domestic airlines such as Delta, with both domestic and international routes; and foreign airlines such as British Airways. Although this is a remarkably diverse group, all the companies in this industry are affected by some of the same general factors such as the price of jet fuel.

Standard Industry Classification System

In an attempt to organize the massive amount of economic data it collects, the federal government developed the Standard Industry Classification (SIC) system. The classification covers all organizations and is updated about every ten years to reflect the economy's changing industrial organization.

The SIC system classifies from the general to the specific by initially grouping all organizations into 11 divisions identified by one-digit SIC codes. It subdivides each division into major groups, each with its two-digit SIC code. It further subdivides each major group into smaller groups with three-digit codes and, finally, into detailed groups with four-digit codes. Companies with the same four-digit SIC are considered a homogeneous industry group.

Although useful to the industry analyst, the SIC system is not perfect. Many divisions and subdivisions are arbitrary, and they can rapidly become outdated. Further, even though many four-digit industry groups are homogeneous, some notable exceptions arise. For example, all airlines fall into a single four-digit industry group.

The point is, to preserve analysis quality, be careful in considering any industry classification system. It is easy, for example, to inadvertently compare a specific company's data with averages for the wrong industry. We'll consider this issue further in the next chapter.

COMPONENTS OF INDUSTRY ANALYSIS

In a nutshell, industry analysis has two general objectives: to determine the long-term secular trend of the industry, and to ascertain the industry's cyclical pattern around its long-term secular trend. To meet these general objectives, a thorough industry analysis must consider several issues, both quantitative and qualitative. The following list includes brief discussions of eight of the most pertinent issues. The more qualitative issues are listed first.

1. *Competitive Structure of the Industry.* The analyst should start by listing all the companies that operate in the industry (both domestically and globally if appropriate). It may also be useful to determine how many are publicly traded, how many are privately owned or owned by other companies, and perhaps, how many are government owned. The analyst should consider some further questions: Which companies have the largest market shares? Have their market shares been rising or falling (that is, has the industry become more or less concentrated) during the past few years? Has the number of competitors risen or fallen in recent years?

    [handwritten: largest market share?]

2. *Permanence.* In this age of rapid changes in technology and major demographic trends, industry permanence has become an important issue. Could technological changes, for example, make an industry obsolete in a short period of time? Yes. Ice companies were among the most established and profitable companies in the United States until a single technological change, introduction of GE's electric refrigerator in 1927, doomed them.

    [handwritten: Technological changes that could affect industry.]

3. *Vulnerability to External Shocks.* How vulnerable is the profitability and performance of an industry to some dramatic economic, political, or natural event? As an example, consider what happened to the airline industry during the Persian Gulf crisis of 1990-91. When Iraq invaded Kuwait on August 2, 1990, fear gripped the world oil market. The price of crude oil soared, and along with it the price of jet fuel. Between July and October 1990, the price of jet fuel more than doubled (from $.553 to $1.158 per gallon). Because each penny increase in the price of jet fuel costs U.S. airlines approximately $150 million per year, this increase devastated airlines' profitability. During the second quarter of 1990, U.S. airlines had an after-tax profit of $503 million; the industry lost $218 million in the third quarter, and $3,647 million in the fourth quarter. If airlines want to continue operating, they have little choice but to pay the going rate for jet fuel, over which they have little control.

    [handwritten: Oil prices ↑ in Gulf War, cost to airlines ↑]

4. *Regulatory and Tax Conditions: Government Relations.* The analyst should determine whether an industry is subject to any special or unusual government regulation at either the federal or state level. The electric utility industry, for example, is subject to much more government regulation than the typical industry. Some industries' foreign operations experience more regulation in other countries than do their operations in the United States.

   Tax issues require consideration. The key question is whether the industry is subject to any special tax treatment with either positive or negative effects. The oil and gas industry, for example, has traditionally had special tax treatment compared with most industries, ranging from oil depletion allowances to windfall profits taxes. The analyst should also keep an eye on emerging federal legislation that may have a special impact on an industry

5. *Labor Conditions.* The key questions concerning labor conditions deal mostly with unions, including what percentage of the work force is unionized and whether that percentage is rising or falling. The industry's overall relationship with the unions is important as well. Further, even if the industry's work force is not heavily unionized, the analyst still must check for unusual labor conditions. For example, does the industry have a difficult time finding and retaining workers? Does it have an unusually high number of workers' compensation claims? The airline industry has been historically troubled by labor problems (both union and nonunion).

6. *Historical Record of Revenue, Earnings, and Dividends.* The analyst should compile a historical record of industry revenue, earnings, and dividends over at least two complete business cycles. This review should look for obvious patterns and trends. Have industry revenue and earnings been growing at above-average rates? Have industry earnings been growing more quickly or slowly than industry revenues? Do patterns in revenue and earnings suggest that the industry is cyclical? What percentage of industry earnings are paid in dividends? Has this percentage changed over time? The historical record can help answer these types of questions.

   The analyst should also examine the industry's cost structure. Obviously, if earnings have risen faster than revenue, the industry's costs, as a percentage of revenue, are falling. However, the analyst needs to determine the relationship between fixed and variable costs (operating leverage) as well. High operating leverage means that a given increase in revenue can translate to a still larger increase in operating profits. The airline industry has a high fixed-cost component; it costs about the same for an airline to operate regardless of whether its load factor (the percentage of seats filled with paying passengers) is 50 percent or 80 percent.

7. *Financial and Financing Issues.* What does the industry's balance sheet look like, and how has it changed over the past few years? The analyst should evaluate how much leverage is common in the industry, how asset-intensive its operations are (the ratio of revenues to assets), and so forth. If an industry must make substantial capital investments in the near future, how much money will it have to raise externally?

8. *Industry Stock Price Valuation.* Finally, the analyst must consider how investors have historically valued the industry's stocks, although, once again, the past is no guarantee of the future. For example, does the industry price/earnings (P/E) ratio typically exceed that of the overall market? Has the industry's P/E ratio changed in recent years? How does the P/E ratio compare with the industry earnings growth rate? A stock's P/E multiple should generally have a positive relationship with its expected earnings growth rate. However, historically some industries have sold for higher P/E multiples than other industries, which could not be explained by differences in their expected earnings growth rates. Current investor favorites often have higher than average P/E ratios.

   The analyst should also assess industry stock performance, measured by price appreciation as well as total returns, relative to an appropriate broad market average.

Exhibit 11.8 ✦ INDUSTRY LIFE CYCLE

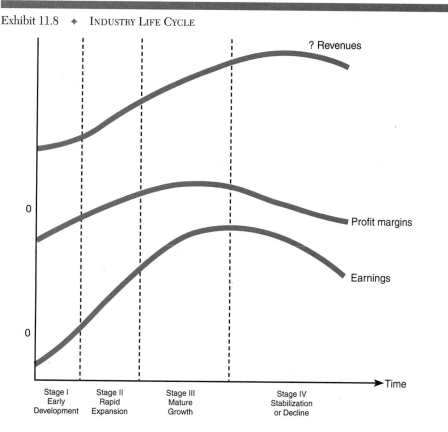

Source: Cohen et al., Investment Analysis and Portfolio Management, *Fifth Ed. Irwin © 1987, p. 376.*

As we saw in Exhibit 11.1, substantial variation in price performance among various industry groups exists regardless of the overall direction of the market.

INDUSTRY LIFE CYCLES

The **industry life cycle theory** provides a framework in which to understand many of the pertinent issues we have just discussed. This theory argues that every industry goes through a life cycle that consists of four stages: birth, growth, mature growth, and stabilization/decline. These stages are illustrated in Exhibit 11.8. Gauging an industry's position in its life cycle may help the analyst gain some important insight into the industry's investment potential.

Before we briefly describe each phase of the industry life cycle, remember that this is a general theory; the life cycles of specific industries differ substantially. For one thing, the speed at which industries move from phase to phase varies. Some industries, for example, stay in a mature growth phase much longer than others. Transitions from phase to phase may be subtle and gradual, and some industries even appear to skip entire phases. Also, technological changes can sometimes cause a mature industry to revert back to a growth industry. In the early 1900s, for example, the oil industry was considered mature, perhaps even declining. Oil was used primarily to

industry life cycle theory
Theory that posits that all industries go through a life cycle consisting of birth, growth, mature growth, and stabilization phases.

light lamps, and the development of electric lighting was eroding demand. The advent of the automobile and the internal combustion engine suddenly launched the oil industry into a major new growth phase.

The oil industry example also illustrates that the industry life cycle is not always a one-way progression. Industries can go backward as well as forward in their life cycles. For another example, consider the aluminum industry. In the 1930s, aluminum appeared to be a dying industry; production was falling rapidly, both in absolute terms and relative to overall industrial production. During the early 1940s, the trend reversed; aluminum production rose much faster than overall industrial production to supply the burgeoning aircraft industry during World War II. Between 1939 and 1945, U.S. industrial production rose 60 percent while aluminum production rose 110 percent. As aircraft production slowed after the end of World War II, aluminum production again started to fall. The aluminum industry entered another phase of rapid growth between 1950 and 1974. The index of aluminum production rose more than 579 percent compared with a 170 percent increase in the index of overall industrial production. Since 1974, the aluminum industry has exhibited characteristics of a mature industry and has grown at about the same rate as the overall economy. With these comments in mind, let's look at each phase in the industry life cycle.

Birth Phase

Industries often are born to exploit a major technical advancement or the invention of some new product. The development of the internal combustion engine, for example, helped give birth to the automobile industry. Infant industries often exhibit several important characteristics. Costs are high, product quality is uneven, sales growth is erratic, and profitability is low. (The industry may actually lose money for most, if not all, of the birth phase.) Birth-phase industries are often highly competitive and dynamic, with many companies entering and exiting.

The birth phase is perhaps the riskiest stage for stock investors, although the rewards can be substantial. A stock investor in an infant industry bets on two things: that the industry and its new good or service will survive infancy (some do not) and that a specific company will be among the survivors.

Growth Phase

The growth phase is typified by a faster industry sales growth rate than the overall economy. Further, industry sales may be less vulnerable to a cyclical downturn in the overall economy compared with more mature industries. As the industry is growing, the quality of its product (either a good or a service) usually improves. Prices often fall, either in absolute or relative terms.[4] Costs tend to fall as production becomes more efficient and capital investment requirements decline. Industry profitability improves as well. During the growth phase, more companies exit the industry than enter it. A few companies tend to grab the lion's share of the industry's growth.

---

[4]A relative price decline could mean one of two things: either the price of the product—or service—rises slower than the rate of inflation or the quality of the product improves relative to the price increase.

Many analysts consider the growth phase the best time to invest in an industry. The product has proven itself, and profits are growing rapidly. Stock investors should generally stick with industry leaders, because they are more likely to prosper. Also, investors should not expect substantial cash dividends. Further, some industries have failed to make the transition from a short period of very rapid growth to a longer period of slower, more sustainable growth to reach the next phase.[5]

Mature Growth Phase

During the mature growth phase, the sales growth rate starts to slow and industry performance may become more cyclical. Product demand starts to near its saturation point, and the industry may begin to face inroads from newer products competing for the same basic market. The competitive structure of the industry is generally quite stable; few companies either enter or exit the industry. In addition, large barriers to entry may have developed. As the industry matures, increasing demand by reducing prices or improving quality becomes more difficult. Companies put more effort into gaining market share in mature industries. Capital investment requirements have fallen to relatively low levels and profits tend to be high. This is often the most profitable stage in the industry life cycle.

This phase imposes lower risk on investors than the rapid growth phase, especially if investors stick to the industry leaders. Even though growth is slowing, profits are high and above-average dividend yields are likely. Investors should not become complacent, however. If growth slows too much, for example, future profits could diminish as competitors start to aggressively cut prices to boost their market shares.

Stabilization or Decline Phase

A mature growth phase can last a long time, and an industry nearing the end of its mature growth phase may begin to grow more rapidly due to technological or demographic changes. Emerging global markets may help pump new life into mature industries. Barring those changes, however, a typical industry eventually reaches a stabilization or decline phase.

Conditions in this last phase are difficult to generalize. In the stabilization or decline phase, industry sales may continue to grow, but more slowly than the overall economy. Alternatively, sales may stabilize to meet replacement demand, which neither increases nor decreases. However, sales may actually start to fall in absolute terms and the industry may eventually disappear. Profitability generally follows the trend in sales.

This can be a difficult phase for investors. If the industry is stable, some companies may be good investments. These stocks may have less risk and pay higher dividends than the average stock. However, as a general rule, most investors should probably avoid declining industries. These companies often have falling profits and deteriorating balance sheets. Further, companies in declining industries face strong temptations to embark on ill-conceived, poorly planned diversification efforts to

---

[5]According to economists, one common reason some growth industries burn out is failure within the industry to develop follow-up products or services that build naturally on the initial success of the initial product or service.

restore growth. These ventures often end up hurting shareholders even more. However, analysts should always carefully monitor declining industries for, as history has shown, their fortunes can rapidly improve due to external factors. (Remember what the automobile did for the oil industry and what growth spurts in aircraft production did for the aluminum industry.)

Analyzing Industry Data

So far in our examination of industry analysis, we have discussed what the analyst ought to look for and what type of information concerning the industry he or she should obtain. At this point, we turn our attention to ways investors can analyze this information to further evaluate an industry.

END-USE ANALYSIS

end-use (product-demand) analysis
Technique that attempts to identify the source(s) of demand for an industry's products or services.

An important tool is **end-use (product-demand) analysis,** in which the analyst attempts to identify the source of demand for the industry's product and, in the process, to uncover relationships that help explain demand. Understanding these relationships will likely help the analyst make more accurate forecasts of future industry revenues and earnings. One approach is to analyze who uses the industry's product and how the demand for the product is likely to change for each user.

As an example, let's briefly look at the semiconductor industry. Who uses semiconductors? Obviously the major user is the personal computer industry (40 percent of semiconductors go into personal computers), but the telecommunications, electronics, defense, and automotive industries use semiconductors as well. Exhibit 11.9 illustrates the consumption of semiconductors, by type of product, in a recent year.

What does Exhibit 11.9 tell us about the outlook for semiconductor sales? According to industry analysts, the two largest users of semiconductors—personal computers and consumer products—are expected to show above-average growth for the next five to ten years. In addition, the value of semiconductors, as a percentage of the price of these products, should increase. Taken together, industry analysts are forecasting that semiconductor sales will approach $300 billion by 2005, up from approximately $125 billion today.

RATIO ANALYSIS

ratio analysis
Dividing industry data by aggregate economic data over a period of time and examining the result for trends.

Industry **ratio analysis** involves dividing industry data by aggregate economic data over a period of time. The movement, or lack of movement, in a ratio may suggest some important characteristics of the industry. Let's look at two examples.

Exhibit 11.10 illustrates the ratio of the auto production index to the overall industrial production index between 1968 and 1999. A ratio equal to 100 would mean that the two production indexes were the same. A rising ratio over time would suggest growth in the auto industry. However, a falling ratio over time would suggest decline. Exhibit 11.10 shows no obvious upward or downward trend, suggesting that the auto industry is a mature cyclical industry. Notice, however, that the ratio between auto production and overall industrial production falls sharply before and during recessions (the shaded areas in Exhibit 11.10) and rises sharply early in economic expansions. This suggests that, although the auto industry is cyclical in nature, it is more volatile than the overall economy, especially around turning points in economic activity.

Exhibit 11.9 ✦ WORLDWIDE SEMICONDUCTOR CONSUMPTION BY TYPE OF PRODUCT

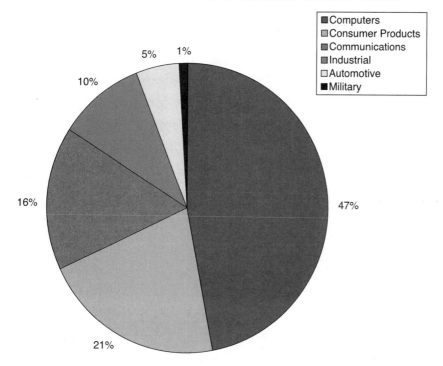

■ Computers
□ Consumer Products
■ Communications
▨ Industrial
□ Automotive
■ Military

Source: Adapted from Standard & Poor's, Industry Survey (Electronics), *May 9, 1996, p. E17.*

Another example is shown in Exhibit 11.11, which shows the ratio of the growth rates in semiconductor sales and auto sales, both relative to the growth rate in GDP. The chart clearly shows that the semiconductor industry is a growth industry; between 1988 and 1998 the growth in semiconductor sales was almost five times overall economic growth. However, the auto industry, with its ratio at or near 100, is more of a cyclical/mature industry. Auto sales rose only slightly relative to overall economic activity.

REGRESSION AND CORRELATION ANALYSIS

Statistics offers two useful and fairly simple techniques for analyzing demand and other industry data: **regression analysis** and **correlation analysis.**[6] Both techniques help quantify many important relationships. As you may remember from statistics, bi-variate regression (regression with two variables) is a mathematical process that fits a line to a series of points on an *XY* scatter diagram. *Y* is the dependent

regression analysis
A statistical technique that determines the relationship between two or more variables.

correlation analysis
A statistical technique that determines the degree to which two variables are related to one another.

---

[6]A multitude of technical issues surround the use of correlation and regression analyses but are beyond the scope of our text. We suggest that you consult a standard statistics or econometrics textbook.

Exhibit 11.10 ✦ RATIO OF AUTO PRODUCTION TO OVERALL INDUSTRIAL PRODUCTION: 1967–99

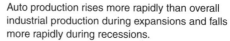

Auto production rises more rapidly than overall industrial production during expansions and falls more rapidly during recessions.

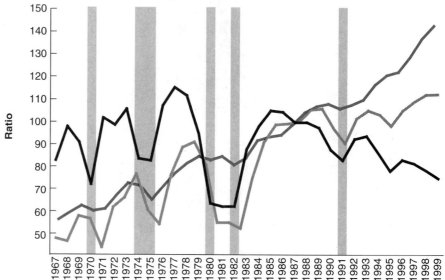

Note: Shaded areas indicated recessions.

Source: Survey of Current Business, *various issues.*

variable, and X is the independent variable. The model states that Y is a function of X (for example, the level of industry sales is a function of GDP). Correlation analysis evaluates the strength of the relationship between X and Y.

Exhibit 11.12 shows an XY scatter diagram. The X axis measures disposable personal income and the Y axis measures auto sales. The regression line is also shown. In equation form, the regression line can be expressed as

$$\text{Auto sales} = 8.749 + 0.043(\text{Income}), R^2 = 0.967$$

The value of Y on the regression line is the predicted value of Y, for a given level of X.

The regression equation helps the analyst to forecast next year's auto sales, based on the expected growth in personal income. Assume, for example, that personal income next year is expected to increase to \$6,100 billion. Based on the regression equation, auto sales should equal $8.749 + 0.043(6,100) = \$271$ billion.

Notice that most of the dots in Exhibit 11.12 fall close to the regression line, meaning that the actual and predicted values for annual auto sales match fairly closely. This suggests a strong relationship between personal income and auto sales. The R^2 statistic measures the strength of this relationship more precisely. It ranges from 0 to 1, and a R^2 close to 1 indicates a stronger statistical relationship between X and Y.

Does this strong historical relationship allow the analyst to rely on the forecast of \$271 billion for next year's auto sales? Yes, and no.

Exhibit 11.11 ✦ RATIO OF SEMICONDUCTOR AND AUTO SALES GROWTH TO GDP GROWTH

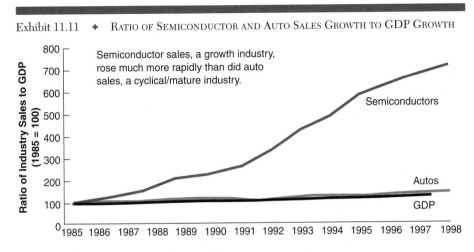

Source: Standard & Poor's, Survey of Current Business.

Exhibit 11.12 ✦ AUTO SALES AND DISPOSABLE PERSONAL INCOME

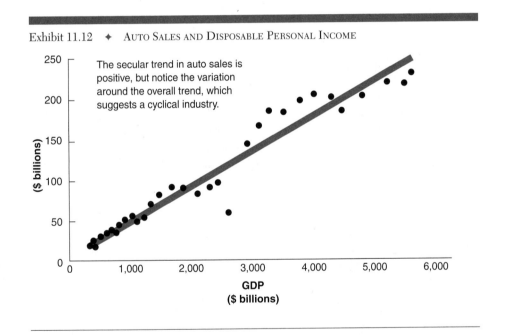

Exhibit 11.12 shows the secular trend in auto sales in relation to the trend in GDP. Both have increased at about the same rate as the overall economy. Notice that Exhibit 11.12 also shows the cyclical variation of auto sales around the secular trend. Remember from Exhibit 11.10, however, that the auto industry tends to be more volatile than the overall economy. Therefore, auto sales tend to be above the secular trend during periods of strong economic growth, especially when the economy is coming out of a recession. Auto sales tend to be below the secular trend during periods of slow economic growth, especially when the economy is entering a recession.

As a result, the forecast produced by the regression equation is a good starting point. The analyst might want to adjust the forecast upward or downward, depending

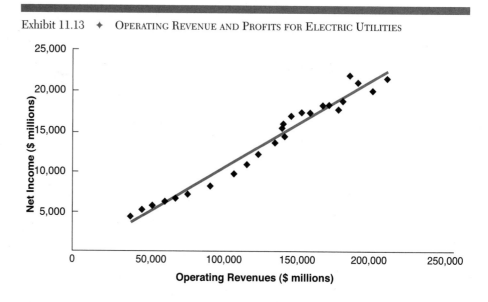

Exhibit 11.13 ✦ OPERATING REVENUE AND PROFITS FOR ELECTRIC UTILITIES

on several factors. For example, if he or she feels that economic growth will be below normal next year, perhaps giving early signs of recession, the analyst should probably lower his or her forecast below the secular trend.

Regression and correlation analysis can help an industry analyst explore many other relationships. One important relationship is that between industry revenue and industry profits. Exhibit 11.13 shows another XY scatter diagram for the electric utility industry for a recent twenty-five-year period. The X axis measures operating revenue, and the Y axis measures profits. Clearly, a strong positive relationship exists between industry revenue and profits. The regression equation equals

$$\text{Profits} = -747.773 + 0.112(\text{Revenues}), R^2 = 0.970.$$

As before, the regression equation can help the analyst forecast. For example, assume that utility revenues are expected to be $230 billion next year. Using the regression equation, we can forecast industry profits of about $25 billion. The high R^2 indicates that the forecast may be fairly reliable.

Finally, let's look at a relationship in which regression and correlation have a different use. Exhibit 11.14 shows the relationship between operating revenues and operating profits for the airline industry over a recent forty-year period. The diagram indicates only a weak relationship between the two series. The estimated regression equation is

$$\text{Operating profits} = -387.071 + 0.043(\text{Operating revenues}), R^2 = 0.373.$$

Although the slope coefficient is positive, indicating that an increase in operating revenues is associated with an increase in operating profits, the low R^2 suggests that the relationship between the two variables is weak. Consequently, the regression equation may be of little use as a forecasting tool. It also suggests that airlines cannot necessarily become more profitable merely by increasing their revenues.

The security analysis must begin by analyzing a variety of economic and industry factors. Although these analyses can provide important insight, the process must

Exhibit 11.14 ✦ OPERATING REVENUES AND OPERATING PROFITS FOR THE AIRLINE
INDUSTRY

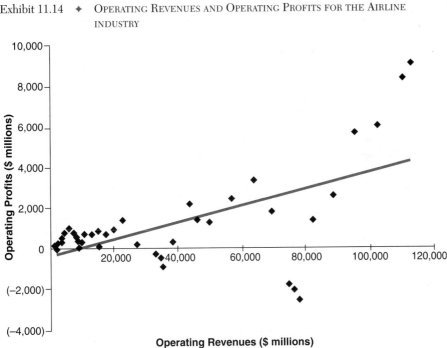

continue with a thorough company analysis. We turn to company analysis in the
next chapter.

Chapter Summary

1. Why are economic and industry analysis important?
   No stock can be valued in a vacuum; all stocks are affected by economic and industry conditions. Stock prices and interest rates are closely related to the business
   cycle. Economic conditions can greatly affect industries. Regardless of the general
   direction of stock prices, substantial variation in performance among industry groups
   is common.

2. How do investment decisions relate to the business cycle?
   Stock prices relate positively to economic growth. Historically, stock prices have led
   the business cycle. In addition, certain industries tend to perform best during different phases of the business cycle. Interest rates also relate positively to the business cycle. Yield spreads tend to be at their highest right before a recession and narrowest
   right before an expansion.

3. How are economic forecasts made?
   Economists make qualitative and quantitative forecasts of future economic activity.
   Qualitative forecasts are general and descriptive in nature and often rely on leading
   indicators and sentiment indicators. Quantitative forecasts are designed to come up
   with specific estimates of future economic activity and are based on mathematical
   models. Although economic forecasting is difficult, and economists have poor
   track records, economic forecasts still can contain a great deal of useful information
   for investors.

4. How are industries classified?

    Industries can be classified in terms of the products or services they produce or their relationship to the business cycle. Several governmental and nongovernmental organizations classify industries. Industry classifications, however, are arbitrary and can be misleading. Further, it can be difficult to place a specific company within a particular industry.

5. What are the important components of an industry analysis?

    The analyst should consider the competitive structure of the industry, its permanence, its vulnerability to external shocks, regulatory and tax considerations, labor conditions, its record of earnings and dividends, various financial and financing issues, and how the industry stocks have been historically valued.

6. What are the framework and some techniques used in industry analysis?

    The industry life cycle approach provides a framework for understanding many of the important issues with respect to industry analysis. According to the life cycle approach, industries go through phases (birth, rapid growth, mature growth, and stabilization). Technological or external changes can cause phases to repeat. Some major techniques used in industry analysis include end-use analysis, ratio analysis, correlation analysis, and regression analysis.

Mini Case

This mini-case will help you practice interpreting actual industry data. Open the Electric Utility worksheet in the Data Workbook. The worksheet contains annual operating and financial data for the electric utility industry. Using these data and some of the techniques discussed in the chapter, answer the following questions.

1. Compute the ratio of utility production to overall industrial production for each year given and graph the result. Compare this graph with the one shown in Exhibit 11.10. What conclusions concerning the utility industry can you draw from this exercise?

2. Graph the relationship between industry revenue and GDP. Regress industry revenue onto GDP (treat industry revenue as the Y variable and GDP as the X variable). How strong is the relationship between GDP and industry revenue?

3. Assume you have a forecast that nominal GDP will grow by 6 percent next year. Using the regression equation you just estimated, forecast industry revenue. Based on your results, would you modify this forecast? Why or why not?

4. Assume you are satisfied with the forecast of industry revenue you obtained in the prior question. Can you now come up with a reasonable estimate of industry profits for next year?

Review Questions and Problems

1. In general terms, why are economic and industry analysis important when evaluating specific common stocks? Do economic and industry conditions influence some stocks more than others?

2. Why does inflation typically increase toward the end of an economic expansion and fall toward the end of a contraction? How does inflation affect stock prices?

3. Why do stock prices lead the business cycle? Cite a example where a large decline in stock prices was not followed by a recession.

4. What factors explain the relationship between interest rates and the business cycle? When, during the business cycle, have the sharpest declines in interest rates occurred?

5. Define the term *yield spread*. Why do yield spreads based on maturity and quality tend to rise and fall during the business cycle?

6. Why is economic forecasting important? What are the two objectives of economic forecasts?

7. What are the two general approaches to economic forecasting? How do the forecasts of future economic activity produced by the two approaches differ?

8. What is an anticipation survey? Why is consumer confidence considered such an important leading indicator of future economic activity?

9. List three components of the index of leading indicators. Identify the direction in each indicator prior to a peak in economic activity.

10. Discuss the various ways industries can be classified. What issues affect an analyst's use of industry classifications?

11. List the major components of an industry analysis. What is meant by the term *permanence?*

12. What are the four stages (or phases) of the industry life cycle? Give several examples of industries that experienced renewed growth due to external changes.

13. What are some characteristics of the mature growth phase? Why is this phase generally the most profitable for investors?

14. Define end-use analysis and ratio analysis. If the ratio of an industry's production index to the overall index of industrial production has remained constant over time, what kind of industry is it?

15. Assume you regress industry sales onto GDP. You come up with following estimated regression equation:

$$\text{Sales (\$ billions)} = 1.753 + 0.014\text{GDP (\$ billions)}, R^2 = 0.98.$$

What kind of industry do you think this is? If GDP next year is expected to be $8,250 billion, forecast industry sales. How much confidence do you have in this forecast?

CFA Questions

1. (Level III, 1995). Identify and briefly describe two methods or approaches used by economists to develop expectations of future inflation.

2. (Level II, 1993). You are presented with the regression shown in the table relating the number of new passenger automobiles produced in the U.S. (in millions) to three variables: auto loan interest rates, national employment, and an index of automobile gasoline prices. You know that some standard regression statistics are missing from the table.

Variable	Coefficient Estimate	Standard Error
Intercept	2.28	0.57
Interest rate	−0.02	0.02
Gas price	0.26	0.13
Employment	0.02	0.01

a. Identify four regression statistics or measures missing from the table that you should consider as you interpret this regression.

b. Explain how each of the four regression statistics or measures identified in your answer to Part *a* can be helpful in interpreting the regression results.

c. Determine which one of four parameters shown in the table is least statistically significant. Show your work.

d. Calculate the forecast for auto production using the table and the forecast values shown below. Show your work.

Interest rate	9.00%
Gas price	$1.19 per gallon
Employment	120.2 million

CRITICAL THINKING EXERCISE

This exercise requires both computer work and library research. Open the Industry worksheet in the Data Workbook. The worksheet contains data for four industries—chemicals, department stores, pharmaceuticals, and railroads—along with some economic data. Using the data and the techniques described in the chapter, determine the life cycle phase of each industry. Which of these industries appear to be cyclical, if any? Assuming you had a good forecast for next year's GDP, for which industry could you come up with the best forecast?

Go to the library and read the most recent Standard & Poor's or Value Line report on each industry. How does S&P and Value Line classify each industry? Other than GDP, what economic and other external factors do you think affect the prospects for each industry?

THE INTERNET INVESTOR

1. As a service to clients, discount broker Charles Schwab offers commentary from various experts on a different industry each week. Visit the Schwab web site (www.schwab.com) and read this week's industry commentary. Write a brief report summarizing the expert's opinion of the industry.

2. Each week Merrill Lynch posts on its web site economic commentary from members of its staff (www.ml.com). Read the current economic commentary. Which events does Merrill Lynch believe will have the biggest impact on investors? Does the commentary reflect qualitative or quantitative economic forecasting?

3. Using one of the various Internet search engines (such as Yahoo!, www.yahoo.com, or Northern Lights, www.nlsearch.com) find sites that provide economic data (both historical and current) for the United States and other countries. Visit several of the sites and prepare a brief report.

COMPANY ANALYSIS: THE HISTORICAL RECORD

PREVIOUSLY . . .

We described economic and industry analysis, the two macro-factors in security analysis.

IN THIS CHAPTER . . .

We review the components of company analysis and discuss how to evaluate the historical record, including the quality of the company's management, its competitive position, and its financial statements.

TO COME . . .

We describe how to forecast a company's future earnings and how to assess the investment potential of its common stock.

Chapter Objectives

After reading Chapter 12, you should be able to answer the following questions:

1. What are the components of a company analysis report?
2. How do analysts evaluate the quality of a company's management?
3. How do analysts evaluate a company's competitive position within its industry?
4. What is financial statement analysis?

In Chapter 8 we briefly told part of the tale of Sunbeam, manufacturer of small household appliances. In the summer of 1996, the company hired "Chainsaw" Al Dunlap as its new CEO. Dunlap, a noted turnaround specialist, immediately began slashing costs, revamping product lines, and firing hundreds of workers. Dunlap's magic appeared to work. In 1996 Sunbeam reported a net loss in excess of $228 million. The next year, 1997, it reported a profit of more than $109 million. Sunbeam's stock price soared from about $12 a share when Dunlap was hired to more than $50 a share by the end of 1997. Quite a turnaround for Sunbeam. Or was it?

Although most investors and analysts cheered the news of Sunbeam's apparent dramatic turnaround, a few uncovered some troubling signs by more closely analyzing Sunbeam's financial statements. For example, although sales rose by 19 percent between 1996 and 1997, accounts receivable rose by 36 percent and inventory rose by 58 percent. Accounts receivable and inventory turnover both slowed dramatically. Big buildups of both accounts receivable and especially inventory can suggest potential problems. Another area of concern was the company's cash flow situation. Sunbeam's actual cash flow—the actual cash the company's operations were generating—fell from $14.2 million in 1996 to *minus* 8.2 million in 1997. In other words, the company spent more cash during 1997 than it collected.

Then, Sunbeam released its first quarter results for 1998 and stunned many on Wall Street by reporting a loss. Not only that, but sales actually fell by 5 percent from first-quarter 1997. However, accounts receivable soared by 90 percent and inventory more than doubled. On the other side of the balance sheet, accounts payable—money Sunbeam owed, mostly to vendors—rose by a staggering 94 percent. One analyst concluded that Sunbeam appeared to be stuck with lots of inventory it couldn't sell, receivables it hadn't collected, and bills it wouldn't pay. Some speculated that Sunbeam secretly encouraged speed-up purchases by big customers to lift its 1997 results. Analysts immediately cut their ratings and investors headed for the exits. By August 1998, Sunbeam's high-flying stock had lost more than 80 percent of its value.

The Sunbeam saga illustrates some of the kinds of information that a careful analysis of a company's historical record, specifically its financial statements can yield. This chapter is the first of two devoted to company analysis and describes how to assess a company's historical record, both qualitative and quantitative factors.

Overview of Company Analysis

Investors buy common stock hoping to earn a satisfactory rate of return in relationship to the risk they assume when buying the stock. One key to determining whether a stock can produce the desired rate of return is its current price. A stock's attractiveness depends on the answer to this question: Is the stock correctly priced today? As we'll see more formally in Chapter 14, the correct price of a stock is essentially the present value of expected future cash flows—dividends and an expected future price. Because no one knows with certainty either the timing or the level of future cash flows, investors must rely on estimates.

Future earnings are probably the most important determinant of a company's future dividend stream and stock price. Because it pays dividends from earnings, higher future earnings often translate into higher future dividends. In addition, independent of the impact on future dividends, higher future earnings usually mean higher future stock prices. In a nutshell, then, *the major goal of company analysis is to forecast the quantity and quality of future earnings.* A thorough company analysis report will consider any item that may materially affect future earnings.

According to the fathers of modern security analysis, Benjamin Graham and David Dodd, the typically company analysis report is divided into four parts:

1. A description of the company's business and properties, including some historical data and details about senior management.
2. Financial material that includes capitalization, a record of earnings and dividends for several complete business cycles, a flow of funds analysis, and an analysis of recent balance sheets and income statements.

3. Past stock price history and volume data.
4. Prospects for the company in the form of projected future financial statements and analysis of the investment merits of the security.

To give you an idea what a real company analysis report looks like, from a real investment firm, we've included a report on Home Depot from an A. G. Edwards analyst on the data disk in the Microsoft *Word* file Home Depot Report.) The generally favorable report contains most of the elements listed by Graham and Dodd. It focuses heavily on the major issues facing Home Depot and an assessment of the company's growth strategy.

In summary, the Home Depot analysis and guidance from Graham and Dodd suggest four general issues that a security analysis report should address: (1) the quality of the company's management, (2) the competitive position of the company within its industry, (3) an analysis of the company's financial statements, and (4) its future financial performance. We'll consider the first three issues in this chapter; the fourth issue, which is probably the most difficult, will be left to Chapter 13.

Assessing the Quality of Management

Some experts believe that the quality of a company's management may be the single most important influence on its future profitability and overall success. A company can have strong financial statements, for example, and yet be overly bureaucratic and incapable of responding quickly to changing business conditions. It's also important to note that management changes can also have a significant impact on stock prices. As an example, examine the chart shown in Exhibit 12.1, which shows the daily trading range and trading volume for Sunbeam between the beginning of June and the end of August 1996. Your eye probably goes to the middle of the chart (July 7). On that day Sunbeam announced that it had hired Al Dunlap as its CEO. The stock price rose by more than 50 percent on heavy volume (almost 8 million shares). As we've noted, however, Dunlap's hiring didn't *quite* work out the way Sunbeam had hoped!

How do you tell if a company is well run? In order to assess management quality, the analyst must first understand the nature of management.

THE NATURE OF MANAGEMENT

One leading expert defines management as follows:

> Management is the attainment of organizational goals in an effective and efficient manner through planning, organizing, leading, and controlling organizational resources.[1]

This general definition of management conveys two important ideas. First, managers are responsible for meeting various organizational objectives both effectively and efficiently. Second, management includes four basic functions: planning, organizing, leading, and controlling. The management process of deploying resources to achieve organizational objectives (that is, promoting organizational performance), within the

---

[1] Richard Daft, *Management,* 5th ed. (Ft. Worth: Harcourt, 2000), p. 8.

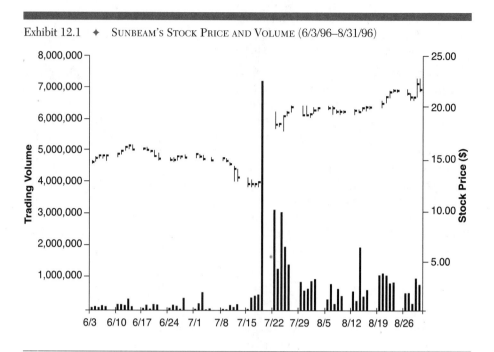

Exhibit 12.1 ✦ SUNBEAM'S STOCK PRICE AND VOLUME (6/3/96–8/31/96)

context of the four basic functions is illustrated in Exhibit 12.2. Let's elaborate on both parts of the definition.

The first part of the definition of management deals with **organizational performance.** Managers are ultimately responsible for applying company resources effectively and efficiently to accomplish the company's goals. *Effectiveness* is defined as the degree to which the company achieves its goals; *efficiency* is defined as the amount of resources required to produce a certain level of output of a good or service.

The second part of the general definition lists four functions. The **planning function** involves setting future goals for the organization and identifying the tasks and resources necessary to obtain those goals. The **organizing function** assigns various parts of the organization and allocates resources within the organization. The **leading function** involves the motivation of employees to achieve the goals of the organization. And the **controlling function** is concerned with monitoring performance, keeping the organization moving toward its goals, and correcting deficiencies.

What skills must managers possess? Experts identify three essential types of managerial skills: technical, conceptual, and human skills. *Technical skills* involve knowledge and mastery of such disciplines as engineering, manufacturing, computer information systems, or finance. *Conceptual skills* involve the ability to think and plan, to see the company as a whole as well as the relationships among its parts. Finally, *human skills* involve the ability to work with and through other people. Some important human skills include leadership, motivation, communication, and conflict resolution.

EVALUATING MANAGEMENT

Determining the quality of management is neither easy nor totally objective. In a nutshell, the fundamental issue is how well the company's management performs the four basic functions. Of course, this analysis cannot stop with an assessment of how

organizational performance
Effective and efficient application of company resources to achieve company goals.

planning function
Setting future goals for the organization and determining the resources needed to meet these goals.

organizing function
Assigning tasks to the various parts of the organization and allocating resources within the organization.

leading function
Motivating employees to achieve the goals of the organization.

controlling function
Monitoring performance, keeping the organization moving toward its goals and correcting deficiencies.

Exhibit 12.2   ✦   MANAGEMENT PROCESS

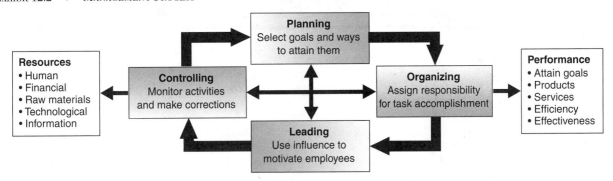

Source: Figure from Richard L. Daft, Management, 4th ed., © 1997, 1994, 1991, 1988, Dryden Press, reproduced by permission of the publisher.

well management has performed in the past; it must extend to likely future performance, as well.

Although many experienced investors have trouble defining good management, they often know it when they see it. The Investment Insights box on page 314 describes the basic tenants used by legendary investor Warren Buffett to evaluate management.

To give you an idea of how investors can assess the quality of management, here are some questions to ask:

1. *What are the age and experience characteristics of senior management?* Information on senior management appears in the company's annual report. These descriptions generally include ages, current titles, and brief biographic sketches of each individual. Experts look for a senior management group with some depth of experience. At the same time, the group should exhibit some diversity in terms of age, length of service with the company, and background. Homogeneity of senior management may have been a source of some of GM's management problems during the 1980s.[2] It's also important to consider likely successors to current leaders, especially if the company bears the stamp of one or two individuals. When Jack Welch announced on November 1, 1999, his intention to retire as CEO of General Electric in 2001, the stock price dropped by more than 5 percent as nervous investors wondered who would replace him. Much of the credit for GE's success during the 1980s and '90s has been given to Jack Welch.

2. *How effective is the company's strategic planning?* Management experts suggest that strategic planning may be the single most important function of senior management because success or failure of this work determines much of the future prosperity of the company. Therefore, the effectiveness of the company's strategic planning efforts can reveal a great deal about the overall quality of a company's management. A good analyst will question whether a company's strategic planning is identifiable, consistent, and feasible. Example of companies often cited for their superior strategic planning include Dell Computer, General Electric, and Johnson & Johnson.

3. *Has the company developed and followed a sound marketing strategy?* An investor's analysis should not discount the importance of a clear, well-planned marketing strategy. To prosper, every company must satisfy consumer demands. An investor should evaluate how well the company has delineated its target market (or markets) and how

[2]Maryann Keller, *Rude Awakening* (New York: Morrow, 1989).

INVESTMENT INSIGHTS

WARREN BUFFET ON MANAGEMENT

The highest complement legendary investor Warren Buffett can pay the management of a company is that they always act as though they were owners, not just managers. To help Buffet assesses the quality of a company's management, he starts by asking three simple questions:

1. **Is management rational?** According to Buffet, rational managers never lose sight of the fact that their primary goal is to increase shareholder value. Consider a company in the mature phase of its life cycle. The company's operations are generating positive cash flow, but, if reinvested, the excess cash earns below-average returns.

Management can do three things with the excess cash. It can reinvest it (and continue to earn below-average returns), it can buy growth (in the form of an acquisition), or it can return the excess cash to shareholders. Buffett argues that the rational thing for managers to do is to return cash to shareholders.

2. **Is management candid?** Candor on the part of managers means reporting financial results clearly and completely and not hiding behind legal, though somewhat dubious, accounting rules. He admires managers who are willing to discuss mistakes and other failures honestly and openly.

3. **Does management resist the institutional imperative?** The "institutional imperative," accord-

ing to Buffet, is the lemming-like tendency of managers to imitate the behavior of their peers, even if their peers make irrational, even stupid, decisions. Evidence of an institutional imperative include

- resisting any changes in the company's current direction;
- spending excess cash on any project or acquisition that comes along, regardless of their merits;
- adopting any of the CEO's business cravings;
- mindlessly following the behavior of peer companies in such areas as acquisitions, divestitures, or executive compensation, whether or not the behavior makes any sense.

well the company combines the four marketing-mix variables (distribution, price, product, and promotion).

4. *Has the company effectively and nimbly adapted to changes in the external environment?* The contemporary business environment is marked by rapid and sometimes unpredictable changes. How well a company anticipates and reacts to changes in its external business environment depends on the quality of its management. Think of the Internet. Which retailers appear to have understood the growing importance of the Internet and have adapted their business strategies accordingly?

5. *Has management maintained, or improved, the company's overall competitive position?* We'll discuss this in depth in the next section, but at least maintaining, and hopefully improving, a company's competitive position is a prime responsibility of management. Well-run companies strive to maintain or improve the competitive positions of all their various business units.

6. *Has the company grown in an organized, sustainable manner?* History is replete with examples of companies that have grown too quickly, outstripping their financial and managerial resources.

7. *Has the company been financed adequately and appropriately?* The quality of management is often reflected in the company's financial statements. As a general rule, better-run companies have better-looking financials than poorly run companies.

8. *Does the company have good relations with employees?* Managers cannot achieve goals by themselves; they must be able to motivate and lead employees. As a general rule, well-run companies have better employee relationships than poorly run companies.

9. *What is the company's public image?* Does a company's public image convey a positive or negative image? Well-run companies understand the importance of public image, though management should never neglect other responsibilities while cultivating a positive public image.

10. *How effective is the company's board of directors?* Well-run companies generally have effective boards of directors. An effective board is one that links CEO pay to specific performance goals, pays retainers to directors in the form of company stock, requires directors to own stock, is elected annually, and contains a majority of members who are not company insiders.

Competitive Position

As we saw in Chapter 11, one task of the industry analyst is to determine the industry's competitive structure. This will shed some light on where the industry currently stands in its life cycle. The company analyst must then assess the competitive position of the specific company within the industry. Initially, this requires answers to two questions.

First, why is the company's competitive position important? A firm's competitive position in its industry will clearly influence its future quality (or riskiness) and quantity of earnings. Simply put, an industry leader or dominant company should produce higher and more consistent future earnings than a company in a weak competitive position. This should be true at any stage of the industry life cycle. For example, if the industry is starting to show signs of stabilization, or even decline, the leading companies may be the only ones that survive for any length of time. Further, how well a company maintains its competitive position over time may reveal a great deal about the quality of its management.

The second question that drives competitive-position analysis is whether or not one should *always* restrict investment choices to industry leaders. This is a difficult question to answer. One theme we emphasize throughout this text, remember, is that investors can rely on few absolutes. An industry may seem attractive, but a company that's not an industry leader may have the most attractive valuation, such as price/earnings (P/E) ratio. This fact, coupled with others, may confirm the decision to invest in the nonleading company.

Nevertheless, *all other things being equal,* leading companies offer lower-risk investment prospects than nonleading companies. Companies that have established dominant positions in their respective industries have proved that they can meet the competition. They have built high market shares for their products and services and demonstrated the ability to lead their industries. Further, these companies have demonstrated the ability to make money; they could not have achieved their dominant positions without operating profitably.

This generalization requires another important caveat: *never* assume that a company will continue to maintain its competitive position within its industry. Although many companies establish dominance and leadership and never lose them, history provides many examples of leading companies that have lost their dominant positions for a variety of reasons.

EVALUATING A COMPANY'S COMPETITIVE POSITION

The discussion of the importance of the company's competitive position raises the question of how to ascertain whether a specific company enjoys a strong competitive position within its industry. In some cases, this could be a fairly straightforward, even easy, task; in others, it is more arduous.

Many companies operate in several different industries. Johnson & Johnson, for example, makes hundreds of different products, from prescription drugs to disposable contact lenses to baby shampoo. Should the analyst evaluate the competitive position of the company in *every* industry in which it operates? Probably, but experienced analysts concentrate their efforts on the industries that provide the largest shares of overall company revenue and earnings. With respect for these complexities, let's now review the forces that determine the competitive position of a company. (One of the critical thinking exercises at the end of the chapter asks you to assess the competitive position of an actual company.)

Revenues or Sales

In general, size is a good guide to competitive position. Historically, at least, higher annual sales or revenue often follow success at meeting the competition. Size alone does not guarantee continuing dominance in the future, however. A better indicator may be the *growth rate* in sales, relative to the industry. The leading company may not necessarily be the largest, but the fastest-growing compared with its competitors.

Profitability

How profitable is the company, especially as compared with the industry? Analysts measure profitability not just in dollars but also by such variables as profit margin and return on equity. This analysis should also determine whether the company is becoming more or less profitable compared with the industry. As a general rule, a more profitable company, especially as compared with its industry, has a better competitive position.

Product Line

A longer and broader product line, compared with the industry, generally indicates a more competitive position. (The term *product* includes both goods and services.) Strong marketing and financial reasons drive a company to increase the length and breadth of its product line. These include expanding growth opportunities, optimizing company resources, increasing the company's importance in the market, and exploiting the product life cycle. Failure to increase the length and breadth of a company's product mix can have severe negative consequences.

New Products and Product Innovation

Another sign of a strongly competitive company is its ability to introduce new products (or improved versions of existing products) more rapidly than its competitors, to take advantage of changes in demand or technology.

Operating Efficiency

Industry leaders, especially those that will be dominant in the future, usually produce goods and services more efficiently than their competitors. Low-cost producers, companies that produce the same quality good or service more cheaply than competitors, are considered more efficient. These firms are more likely to build strong competitive positions within their respective industries.

Pricing

Pricing is an important component of any marketing strategy. Dominant companies tend to follow certain pricing practices, depending on the industry. For example, a **price leader** may hold the dominant competitive position, especially in a mature growth industry. A simple example will illustrate the meaning of price leadership. If company A is the price leader in its industry, all its competitors match its decision to raise (or lower) its prices. However, if a competitor raises (or lowers) its prices, competition will correct the price change unless A makes the same change. Pricing and operating efficiency are often related. A company that is a price leader is often a low-cost producer, as well.

price leader
A company that sets prices in an industry.

Patents and Technology

Many companies have established dominant positions in various industries by exploiting patents and proprietary technologies. Once the patent expires or the technology evolves, however, the company's dominant position in the industry becomes less secure.

Analyzing Financial Statements

After evaluating a company's competitive position within its industry, the analyst will perform a detailed analysis of the company's financial statements. As you probably remember from your introductory accounting and finance classes, the three major financial statements are the balance sheet, the income statement, and the statement of cash flows. Examples of all three statements are shown in Exhibit 12.3.[3]

One issue investors confront when analyzing financial statements is whether or not the numbers are reliable. (We touched on this issue briefly in Chapter 9 when discussing why analysts occasionally blow calls.) Most financial statements do adequately represent a company's financial position, but the numbers can be manipulated to make the company's financial position appear better. Further, some accounting rules give managers wide latitude in reporting certain activities. And, remember some financial statement numbers don't represent cash flows. In rare cases, managers of some companies have gone beyond acceptable manipulation of their financial statements. The Investment History box on page 320 relates how some companies may have manipulated their earnings in the past.

FINANCIAL RATIOS

Financial ratios are one of the most widely used tools for analyzing a company's financial statements. Ratios show relationships between, or within, financial

---

[3]If you need to review the major financial statements and how they relate to one another, consult any basic accounting textbook.

Exhibit 12.3 ✦ THREE MAJOR FINANCIAL STATEMENTS

The Home Depot	Fiscal Year ending January 31		
Income Statement ($ millions)	1999	1998	1997
Sales	30,219.0	24,156.0	19,535.5
Cost of Goods Sold	21,241.0	17,092.0	13,869.1
Gross Profit	8,978.0	7,064.0	5,666.4
Selling, General, and Administrative Expense	5,944.0	4,765.0	3,900.4
Operating Income Before Depreciation	3,034.0	2,299.0	1,766.0
Depreciation and Amortization	373.0	283.0	232.3
Operating Profit	2,661.0	2,016.0	1,533.7
Interest Expense	68.0	61.0	39.4
Nonoperating Income/Expense	61.0	63.0	48.9
Special Items	—	(104.0)	—
Pretax Income	2,654.0	1,914.0	1,543.1
Total Income Taxes	1,040.0	738.0	597.0
Net Income	1,614.0	1,160.0	937.7
Savings due to Common Stock Equivalents	—	—	8.0
Adjusted Net Income	1,614.0	1,160.0	945.7
Earnings per share	1.10	0.80	0.65
Dividends Per Share	0.12	0.09	0.08
Closing price per share	60.50	30.25	16.50
Balance Sheet ($ millions)			
ASSETS			
Cash & Equivalents	62.0	174.0	558.4
Net Receivables	469.0	556.0	388.4
Inventories	4,293.0	3,602.0	2,708.3
Prepaid Expenses	0.0	0.0	0.0
Other Current Assets	109.0	128.0	54.2
Total Current Assets	4,933.0	4,460.0	3,709.4
Net Plant, Property & Equipment	8,160.0	6,509.0	5,437.0
Other Investments	41.0	42.0	48.0
Intangibles	268.0	0.0	0.0
Other Assets	63.0	218.0	147.3
TOTAL ASSETS	13,465.0	11,229.0	9,341.7
LIABILITIES			
Long Term Debt Due In One Year	14.0	8.0	2.5
Accounts Payable	1,586.0	1,358.0	1,089.7
Taxes Payable	100.0	105.0	48.7
Accrued Expenses	981.0	842.0	571.9
Other Current Liabilities	176.0	143.0	129.3
Total Current Liabilities	2,857.0	2,456.0	1,842.1
Long Term Debt	1,566.0	1,303.0	1,246.6
Deferred Taxes	85.0	78.0	66.0
Minority Interest	9.0	116.0	97.8
Other Liabilities	208.0	178.0	134.0

Exhibit 12.3 ✦ THREE MAJOR FINANCIAL STATEMENTS *(CONTINUED)*

Balance Sheet ($ millions)

	Fiscal Year Ending January 31		
	1999	1998	1997
TOTAL LIABILITIES	4,725.0	4,131.0	3,386.5
TOTAL EQUITY	8,740.0	7,098.0	5,955.2
TOTAL LIABILITIES & EQUITY	13,465.0	11,229.0	9,341.7
Shares outstanding (millions)	1,475.5	1,464.2	1,441.5

Cash Flow Statement ($ millions)

	1999	1998	1997
Cash Flow from Operations			
Net Income (loss)	1,614.0	1,160.0	937.7
Depreciation and Amortization	373.0	283.0	232.3
Deferred Income Taxes	7.0	(28.0)	28.8
(Increase) Decrease in Working Capital	(77.0)	(386.0)	(98.7)
Net Cash from Operations	1,917.0	1,029.0	1,100.1
Cash Flow from Investing Activities			
(Increase) Decrease in Fixed Assets	(2,275.0)	(1,396.0)	(1,173.2)
(Increase) Decrease in Short Term Investments	4.0	425.0	(334.4)
Net Cash from Investing Activities	(2,271.0)	(971.0)	(1,507.6)
Cash Flow from Financing Activities			
Increase (Decrease) in Long Term Debt	238.0	(25.0)	470.2
Increase (Decrease) in Common Stock	167.0	122.0	104.5
Payment of Cash Dividends	(168.0)	(139.0)	(110.2)
Other Financing Charges, Net	11.0	10.0	35.5
Net Cash from Financing Activities	248.0	(32.0)	500.0
Effect of Exchange Rate Changes	(4.0)	–	0.2
Net Change in Cash and Equivalents	(110.0)	26.0	92.7

statements. Financial ratios help identify a company's strengths or weaknesses, or highlight areas in need of further investigation.

In your introductory finance class you likely discussed how the various financial ratios are calculated. Financial ratios for companies are typically divided into five general categories: liquidity ratios, asset efficiency (or activity) ratios, leverage and coverage ratios, profitability ratios, and ratios based on market values. Exhibit 12.4 lists the major financial ratios and shows how they're calculated.[4]

---

[4]It is not uncommon to see some small differences in how certain analysts calculate particular ratios. The key, however, is consistency.

COOKING THE BOOKS

One reason security analysts have such a difficult time forecasting earnings is the impact of creative accounting practices. History is full of examples of companies that have used creative accounting to produce dubious earnings reports.

One of the best examples, detailed by Andrew Tobias in his book *The Funny Money Game,* was National Student Marketing. Never heard of it? Well, investors back in the late 1960s knew all about National Student Marketing, one of the great concept stocks of all time. National Student Marketing (NSM) was started by flashy entrepreneur Cortess Randell as a company that would market services to college-age students. NSM grew primarily by acquisition; buying up small companies that sold everything from records to airfare discount cards. Randell was something of a showman and held Wall Street spellbound as he promoted the company almost nonstop. Investors believed his increasingly optimistic earnings projections. After all, youth was in, and this company would soon have a huge share of the youth-oriented market. At its peak in 1969, NSM was selling for a lofty 110 times reported earnings.

The trouble for investors was that NSM's earnings figures were the result of substantial manipulation. For example, in 1969 the company made generous use of "deferred new-product development and start-up costs." These are monies the company actually spent during the year but did not charge against 1969 revenues. Even more amazing, NSM also counted *unearned* revenues. It included almost $4 million in the form of earnings from companies who had generally agreed to be acquired by NSM, but whose acquisitions had yet to be completed.

Like all financial houses of cards, NSM eventually collapsed. A brief bear market in 1970 took care of NSM, as well as several other notable concept companies. A series of investigations by security regulators didn't help. By the end of 1970, NSM had lost more than 98 percent of its value. Cortess Randell pleaded guilty to stock fraud and served several months in prison.

Earnings manipulation continues today. One area of concern for investors are all the special charges many companies routinely take. These charges are often called "restructuring charges" and result from plant closures, divestitures, large layoffs, and the like. They can be substantial. In 1998, Motorola, for example, took a $2 billion restructuring charge, almost as much as it earned in both 1996 and 1997 combined. Some of these charges may be legitimate, but often they are merely a device to manipulate earnings. In 1999, then–SEC Chairman Arthur Levitt, complained that companies were taking "big baths" now to make future earnings look even better.

The SEC prodded the Financial Accounting Standards Board (FASB) to tighten the rules regarding special charges. The SEC also released a report in November 1999 laying out the current accounting rules, with details and examples, with the goal of making restructuring charges smaller and less common.

Liquidity Ratios

liquidity ratios
Ratios that measure a company's ability to meet its short-term obligations.

Liquidity ratios measure a company's *liquidity*—that is, whether it has sufficient liquid assets to meet its short-term obligations. A liquid asset is defined as an asset that can be quickly converted into cash at a price close to the asset's "true" value. Short-term obligations normally are defined as current liabilities. Three liquidity ratios are the current ratio, the quick ratio, and the cash ratio.

Activity Ratios

activity (asset management) ratios
Ratios that measure how effectively and efficiently a company is using its assets.

The second group of ratios, **activity** or **asset management ratios,** measure how effectively and efficiently a company uses its assets to generate revenues or sales. In general, the more efficiently and effectively a company uses its assets, the stronger it is financially. The six principal activity ratios are inventory turnover, accounts receivable turnover, fixed asset turnover, and total asset turnover.

Leverage and Coverage Ratios

Leverage ratios measure the extent to which companies rely on borrowed funds to finance their operations. **Coverage ratios** measure the company's ability to pay its debts. Companies that rely more on borrowed funds are more **leveraged.** Now, the effect of leverage can be both positive and negative. Companies use debt financing to raise capital without existing shareholders giving away some of their control. And, debt financing is cheaper than equity financing—for one thing, interest is tax deductible. Further, leverage can magnify a small increase in operating income into a larger return to shareholders.

Although some leverage can be beneficial, too much leverage can be dangerous. Leverage not only magnifies increases in operating income into larger returns to shareholders, it also magnifies *decreases* in operating income into smaller returns to shareholders. In extreme cases, too much leverage can lead to financial distress and even bankruptcy. The major leverage and coverage ratios are the debt ratio, the ratio of long-term-debt to liabilities, and times interest earned.

leverage ratios
Ratios that measure the extent to which a company relies on borrowed money.

coverage ratios
Ratios that measure a company's ability to repay its debts.

leveraged
The degree to which a company is relying on borrowed money.

Profitability Ratios

Profitability ratios measure how much money a company is earning. The two groups of profitability ratios are profit margins and returns. The principal profitability ratios are gross profit margin, operating profit margin, net profit margin, return on assets, return on equity, earnings growth rate, and the retention rate.

profitability ratios
Ratios that measure how much money the company is making.

Market Value Ratios

Most ratios are based solely on book values, meaning based on numbers that come directly from a company's financial reports. Ratios based on market values give some indication of how investors view a company—both its performance history and its future prospects. Some market-value-based ratios include the price-to-earnings ratio, the price-to-book-value ratio, the dividend yield, and the total return to shareholders.

Interrelationship Among Ratios

As you may have already observed, many of the financial ratios interrelate with one another. Companies with lots of inventory, for example, may have relatively high current ratios, yet low inventory turnover and total asset turnover ratios. A company with a relatively high amount of financial leverage will likely have a high debt ratio and a low times interest earned ratio. Interrelationships are especially important to a company's profitability. A company's profitability is affected by liquidity, asset efficiency, and leverage.

BREAKING DOWN ROE: THE DuPONT FORMULA

Several years ago, analysts working for DuPont devised a method of breaking down *return on equity (ROE)* into various components. Doing this allows the analyst to determine what factors are driving profitability. Breaking down return on equity also allows the analyst to better identify strengths, weaknesses, and areas in need of further investigation.

Exhibit 12.4 ✦ MAJOR FINANCIAL RATIOS

	How Calculated	Home Depot Example (1999)

I. Liquidity Ratios

$$\text{Current ratio} = \frac{\text{Current assets}}{\text{Current liabilities}}$$

$4{,}933.0/2{,}857.0 = 1.73$

$$\text{Quick ratio} = \frac{\text{Current assets} - \text{Inventory}}{\text{Current liabilities}}$$

$(4{,}933.0 - 4{,}293.0)/2{,}857.0 = 0.22$

$$\text{Cash ratio} = \frac{\text{Cash and marketable securities}}{\text{Current liabilities}}$$

$62.0/2{,}857.0 = 0.02$

II. Activity Ratios

$$\text{Inventory turnover} = \frac{\text{Sales}}{\text{Average inventory}}$$

$30{,}219.0/[(4{,}293.0 + 3{,}602.0)/2] = 5.38$

$$\text{Accounts receivable turnover} = \frac{\text{Sales}}{\text{Average accounts receivable}}$$

$30{,}219.0/[(469.0 + 556.0)/2] = 58.96$

$$\text{Fixed-asset turnover} = \frac{\text{Sales}}{\text{Average net fixed assets}}$$

$30{,}219.0/[(8{,}160.0 + 6{,}509.0)/2] = 4.12$

$$\text{Total asset turnover} = \frac{\text{Sales}}{\text{Average total assets}}$$

$30{,}219.0/[(13{,}465.0 + 11{,}229.0)/2] = 2.45$

III. Leverage & Coverage Ratios

$$\text{Debt ratio} = \frac{\text{Total liabilities}}{\text{Total assets}}$$

$4{,}725.0/13{,}465.0 = 35.1\%$

$$\text{Long-term debt to equity} = \frac{\text{Long-term debt}}{\text{Shareholders equity}}$$

$1{,}566.0/8{,}740.0 = 17.9\%$

$$\text{Times interest earned} = \frac{\text{Earnings before interest and taxes}}{\text{Interest}}$$

$2{,}661.0/68.0 = 39.13$

IV. Profitability Ratios

$$\text{Gross profit margin} = \frac{\text{Gross profit}}{\text{Sales}}$$

$8{,}978.0/30{,}219.0 = 29.7\%$

$$\text{Operating profit margin} = \frac{\text{Operating profit}}{\text{Sales}}$$

$2{,}661.0/30{,}219.0 = 8.8\%$

$$\text{Net profit margin} = \frac{\text{Net income}}{\text{Sales}}$$

$1{,}614.0/30{,}219.0 = 5.3\%$

$$\text{Return on assets} = \frac{\text{Net income}}{\text{Average total assets}}$$

$1{,}614.0/[(13{,}465.0 + 11{,}229.0)/2] = 12.0\%$

$$\text{Return on equity} = \frac{\text{Net income}}{\text{Average shareholders equity}}$$

$1{,}614.0/[(8{,}740.0 + 7{,}098.0)/2] = 20.4\%$

Earnings growth rate = Percent change in earnings per share

$(1.10 - 0.80)/0.80 = 38.4\%$

Exhibit 12.4 ✦ MAJOR FINANCIAL RATIOS (*CONTINUED*)

	How Calculated	Home Depot Example (1999)
Retention rate = $\dfrac{1 - \text{Dividends per share}}{\text{Earnings per share}}$		$1 - (0.12/1.10) = 89.5\%$

V. Market Value Ratios

	How Calculated	Home Depot Example (1999)
Price-to-earnings ratio = $\dfrac{\text{Market Price}}{\text{Earnings per share}}$		$60.50/1.10 = 55.0$
Market-to-book value ratio = $\dfrac{\text{Market price}}{\text{Book value per share}}$		$60.50/(8{,}740.0/1{,}475.5) = 10.2$
Dividend yield = $\dfrac{\text{Dividends per share}}{\text{Price per share}}$		$0.12/60.50 = 0.2\%$
Total return to shareholders = $\dfrac{\text{Change in price} + \text{Dividends}}{\text{Prior's year price}}$		$(60.50 - 30.25 = 0.12)/30.25 = 100.4\%$

As a first step, the **DuPont Formula** breaks ROE into the following three components:

$$\text{Return equity (ROE)} = \frac{\text{Net income}}{\text{Average Equity}} = \frac{\text{Sales}}{\text{Average Assets}} \times \frac{\text{Net income}}{\text{Sales}} \times \frac{\text{Assets}}{\text{Average Equity}}$$

DuPont formula
A way of breaking down return on equity into its various components.

You should recognize the first two components: asset turnover and the net profit margin. If you multiply them together, you have return on assets (Net income divided by average assets), or ROA.

The third component of the DuPont formula, assets/average equity, is merely another measure of leverage. The higher the ratio, also called the *equity multiplier,* the more levered the company. If the company has any liabilities at all, the equity multiplier will be greater than one. Therefore, ROE—the return to shareholders—will be greater than return on assets. For example, if the equity multiplier is 2, and return on assets is 8 percent, ROE will be 16 percent. This is the effect of leverage on a company's profitability.

Exhibit 12.5 breaks down ROE for Home Depot. What drives the company's profitability? Home Depot's main driver appears to be asset turnover—the company generates almost $2.50 in revenue for each dollar invested in assets. The company is only modestly levered, and its net profit margin is not unusually high.

INTERPRETING FINANCIAL RATIOS

By themselves, financial ratios are little more than numbers. To be meaningful, ratios must be compared to some sort of a benchmark. A benchmark can be established by looking at the same ratio over a number of years and by comparing a company's ratios to industry (or competitor) averages. In the first case, you're looking for obvious trends, and in the second you're looking for company ratios that appear out of line

Exhibit 12.5 ◆ ROE BREAKDOWN FOR HOME DEPOT

	Fiscal Year Ending January 31				
ROE Breakdown	1999	1998	1997	1996	1995
Sales/Average assets ×	2.45	2.35	2.34	2.36	2.38
Net income/Sales ×	5.3%	4.8%	4.8%	4.7%	5.0%
Average assets/Average equity =	1.56	1.58	1.53	1.56	1.67
Return on equity	20.4%	17.8%	17.3%	17.4%	20.0%

with industry (or competitor) averages. Once the analyst uncovers a trend in a particular ratio, or a ratio that appears out of line with industry (or competitor) averages, the analyst must dig further to determine the underlying cause.

TREND ANALYSIS

Analysts examine the same set of ratios over a number of years to look for obvious trends. If a trend is identified, the next step is to determine the cause (or causes) of the trend and whether the trend suggests a strength or weakness. Let's look at three examples.

Home Depot

Exhibit 12.6 lists several ratios for Home Depot for a recent five-year period. What general conclusions can we draw from the data?

1. The company's profit margins are rising, albeit slowly. The gross margin rose from 29 percent to almost 30 percent, and the net margin rose from less than 5 percent to almost 5.5 percent. Given the narrow margins prevalent in most of the retailing industry, any increase in profit margins is a positive sign. Other measures of profitability—such as return on assets and return on equity—also rose slightly but steadily; another positive trend.

2. Home Depot is relying less on borrowed money. The debt ratio fell from more than 40 percent to about 35 percent. Interest coverage—times interest earned—rose. Investors often disagree whether declining leverage is positive or negative. Warren Buffet, among others, views declining leverage as positive.

3. Asset turnover improved slightly, rising from 2.38 to 2.45. At the same time, however, inventory turnover actually fell somewhat. A slowdown in inventory turnover can indicate a developing problem with inventory management, something the analyst should monitor.

4. Home Depot is not awash in liquidity. Because most of the company's current assets consist of inventory, the quick ratio is substantially less than the current ratio. The cash ratio is smaller still. Both the quick ratio and cash ratios declined slightly. Does the company have enough liquidity? In order to answer that question, the analyst would have to probe the company's cash management system and its sources of short-term emergency funding (for example, bank lines of credit or commercial paper).

5. The company's earnings have generally grown quite rapidly from year to year. The five-year annualized growth rate in earnings is more than 25 percent. Further, the company pays out little of its earnings in the form of cash dividends to shareholders. (The low dividend payout is also reflected by the low dividend yield.) A high retention rate is not uncommon in fast-growing companies.

Exhibit 12.6 ✦ SELECTED RATIOS FOR HOME DEPOT

Ratio	Fiscal Year Ending January 31				
	1999	1998	1997	1996	1995
Current ratio	1.73	1.82	2.01	1.89	1.76
Quick ratio	0.22	0.35	0.54	0.35	0.32
Cash ratio	0.02	0.07	0.30	0.08	0.05
Inventory turnover	5.38	5.42	5.67	5.60	5.82
Accounts receivable turnover	58.96	51.16	54.74	51.77	53.02
Fixed-asset turnover	4.12	4.04	3.95	3.94	4.33
Total asset turnover	2.45	2.35	2.34	2.36	2.38
Total debt to total assets	35.1%	36.8%	36.3%	32.2%	40.4%
Times interest earned	39.13	33.05	38.93	47.36	18.45
Gross profit margin	29.7%	29.2%	29.0%	28.9%	29.0%
Operating profit margin	8.8%	8.3%	7.9%	7.6%	7.9%
Net profit margin	5.3%	4.8%	4.8%	4.7%	5.0%
Return on assets	12.0%	10.3%	10.1%	10.0%	10.9%
Return on equity	20.4%	17.8%	17.3%	17.4%	20.0%
Earnings growth rate	38.4%	22.9%	26.0%	16.7%	30.7%
Retention rate	89.5%	88.1%	88.1%	87.7%	88.6%
Price-to-earnings ratio	55.0	38.1	25.5	29.9	35.4
Market-to-book value	10.2	6.2	4.0	4.4	6.2
Dividend yield	0.2%	0.3%	0.5%	0.4%	0.3%
Total return to shareholders	100.4%	83.9%	8.1%	−1.2%	20.3%

6. Returns to investors have been impressive. A thousand dollars invested in Home Depot stock at the beginning of the period shown would have been worth almost $4,300 by the end of the period. Investors have responded by bidding up the price to earnings, and price to book value ratios.

Albertson's

Another example of trend analysis is shown in Exhibit 12.7. The return on equity for a recent five-year period is broken down into its three components for grocery retailer Albertson's. What trends, if any, are evident from these data?

For one, Albertson's ROE has fallen steadily in recent years, from 26 percent to slightly less than 22 percent—not a huge decline, but nevertheless an obvious trend. Leverage has declined slightly (the equity multiplier fell from 2.25 to 2.19), and the net profit margin has remained about the same. But the main culprit appears to be asset turnover, which fell from 3.44 to 2.80. Although an asset turnover of 2.80 is still high, the analyst needs to investigate further and determine *why* asset turnover fell. Slower inventory turnover? An expansion into nonfood retailing? Ambitious expansion program—building new stores and remodeling old ones? An acquisition that has yet to bear fruit? The point is, the reasons behind the decline may be ominous or they may not be. The ratios alone can't tell you.

Sunbeam

Finally, let's revisit Sunbeam briefly. As we've noted, two trends that alarmed a few analysts prior to the bombshell Sunbeam dropped in 1998 were a steady decline in

Exhibit 12.7 ✦ ROE BREAKDOWN FOR ALBERTSON'S

ROE breakdown	Fiscal Year Ending January 31				
	1999	1998	1997	1996	1995
Asset turnover ×	2.80	2.96	3.11	3.24	3.44
Net margin ×	3.5%	3.5%	3.6%	3.7%	3.4%
Equity multiplier =	2.19	2.13	2.11	2.13	2.25
Return on equity	21.7%	22.2%	23.5%	25.5%	26.0%

both receivables and inventory turnover. The chart in Exhibit 12.8 shows the company's quarterly receivables and inventory turnover during the five quarters preceding the first quarter of 1998. As you can see, both ratios, especially the inventory turnover, declined sharply. Inventory turnover fell from a respectable 1.7 times per quarter (6.8 times per year) to 0.4 times per quarter (1.6 times per year).

INDUSTRY COMPARISONS

Trends in ratios can yield some information about a company, but comparing a company's ratios to industry averages may provide additional insight into the company being analyzed. One year's worth of comparisons are rarely sufficient. Good financial analysis tradecraft suggests that the analyst compare the company's ratios over several years to the industry averages over the same period of time. Before proceeding, however, three points must be made about industry comparisons:

First, different industries have different average ratios. Exhibit 12.9 lists several additional ratios for five companies in five different industries. Notice the substantial differences. Compare leverage ratios, for example: Duke Energy has more than 85 cents in long-term debt for each dollar in equity. By contrast, Nike has less than 10 cents in long-term debt for each dollar in equity. Electric and gas utilities such as Duke Energy rely much more heavily on long-term debt as a source of capital than do most industries.

Another obvious difference between industries is asset turnover. Gap Stores generates almost two dollars in sales for each dollar it has invested in assets. By contrast, Southwest Airlines generates only 90 cents in revenue for each dollar invested in assets. This difference shouldn't surprise you. Airlines are an asset-intensive business, and aircraft are expensive assets.

Second, many industries are far from homogeneous. For example, an apparel retailer such as Gap Stores differs significantly from a grocery/pharmacy retailer such as Albertson's. Not surprisingly, some of their financial ratios are quite different, as shown in Exhibit 12.10. Gap Stores has higher liquidity ratios (current and quick) and higher profit margins (both gross and net). On the other hand, Albertson's turns its inventory much faster and has a higher total asset turnover. None of these differences should come as a surprise; the Gap sells primarily casual clothing while Albertson's sells mostly grocery items.

Finally, many companies operate in several different industries. General Electric makes everything from light bulbs to jet engines. The giant company also owns a broadcasting network (NBC) and has a huge financial services division. The results of an industry comparison may hold less value for a company such as GE than for a company that operates in one well-defined industry.

Exhibit 12.8 ✦ QUARTERLY RECEIVABLES AND INVENTORY TURNOVER FOR SUNBEAM

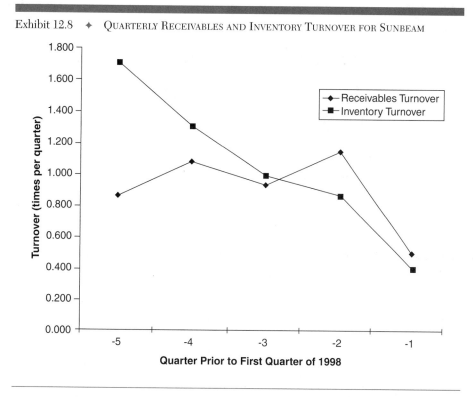

Exhibit 12.9 ✦ INDUSTRY DIFFERENCES IN SELECTED FINANCIAL RATIOS

	Company				
Ratio	American Home Products	Duke Energy	Gap Stores	Nike	Southwest Airlines
Current Ratio	1.68	1.13	1.85	2.05	0.93
Fixed-Asset Turnover	3.30	1.04	4.77	9.96	1.11
Asset Turnover	0.68	0.68	1.95	1.71	0.90
Debt Ratio	60.7%	66.6%	52.5%	41.1%	52.7%
Long-Term Debt/Equity	61.6%	85.2%	31.3%	9.4%	31.3%
Net Profit Margin	14.4%	5.5%	8.2%	8.7%	8.3%
Return on Equity	25.0%	11.2%	33.7%	25.2%	15.8%

With all of this in mind, let's compare two pairs of companies that operate in similar industries. We'll compare Home Depot to Lowe's (its largest competitor), and Bristol Myers Squibb to Merck (both large pharmaceutical companies).

Home Depot versus Lowe's

Exhibit 12.11 lists several financial ratios for both companies over a recent three-year period. A review of the ratios leads to the following conclusions:

Exhibit 12.10 ◆ COMPARING THE RATIOS OF TWO RETAILERS

Ratio	Albertson's	Gap Stores
Current ratio	1.28	1.85
Quick ratio	0.25	1.11
Inventory turnover	11.23 times	8.88 times
Total asset turnover	2.80 times	1.95 times
Debt to total assets	54.0%	52.5%
Long-term debt to equity	46.7%	33.7%
Gross profit margin	28.7%	38.3%
Net profit margin	3.5%	8.2%

Exhibit 12.11 ◆ HOME DEPOT VERSUS LOWE'S

| | 1999 | | 1998 | | 1997 | |
| | Home | | Home | | Home | |
Ratio	Depot	Lowe's	Depot	Lowe's	Depot	Lowe's
Current ratio	1.73	1.46	1.82	1.46	2.01	1.37
Quick ratio	0.22	0.27	0.35	0.27	0.54	0.18
Inventory turnover	5.38	4.69	5.42	4.49	5.67	4.44
Fixed-asset turnover	4.12	3.69	4.04	3.69	3.95	3.95
Total asset turnover	2.45	2.12	2.35	2.10	2.34	2.15
Debt ratio	35.1%	50.6%	36.8%	50.2%	36.3%	50.0%
Times interest earned	39.13	7.64	33.05	7.65	38.93	7.72
Gross profit margin	29.7%	26.9%	29.2%	26.5%	29.0%	25.9%
Net profit margin	5.3%	3.9%	4.8%	3.5%	4.8%	3.4%
Return on assets	12.0%	8.3%	10.3%	7.4%	10.1%	7.3%
Return on equity	20.4%	16.8%	17.8%	14.8%	17.3%	15.1%
Earnings growth	38.4%	33.7%	22.9%	17.8%	26.0%	23.4%
Price-to-earnings ratio	55.0	42.6	38.1	24.7	25.5	19.0
Market -to-book value	10.2	6.6	6.2	3.4	4.0	2.6
Return to shareholders	100.4%	131.1%	83.9%	53.3%	8.1%	7.1%

1. Home Depot has better activity ratios. It turns its inventory faster than Lowe's and generates more in sales from each dollar invested in fixed assets and total assets. However, Home Depot's inventory turnover is falling, and Lowe's inventory turnover is rising slightly.

2. Home Depot is less levered than Lowe's. Lowe's has a higher debt ratio and a lower times interest earned ratio compared with Home Depot. In addition, Home Depot's debt ratio is falling, whereas Lowe's debt ratio has remained about the same.

3. Home Depot is more profitable. It has higher profit margins, a higher return on assets, and a higher return on equity. It should be noted that the profitability of both companies has improved over the period shown.

4. Although the gap between Home Depot and Lowe's appears to have narrowed somewhat in recent years, Home Depot has better-looking financials. Overall, both companies appear to be doing quite well.

Exhibit 12.12   ✦   Bristol Myers Squibb versus Merck

| Ratio | 1998 | | 1997 | | 1996 | |
	Bristol Myers	Merck	Bristol Myers	Merck	Bristol Myers	Merck
Current ratio	1.51	1.69	1.54	1.48	1.49	1.60
Inventory turnover	2.31	5.55	2.23	4.38	2.21	4.38
Accounts receivable turnover	5.93	8.61	5.94	8.55	6.02	7.70
Total asset turnover	1.17	0.93	1.13	0.94	1.05	0.82
Debt ratio	53.5%	60.0%	52.0%	50.0%	55.0%	50.0%
Long-term debt to equity	18.0%	25.2%	17.7%	10.7%	14.7%	9.7%
Operating profit margin	28.0%	23.7%	26.6%	24.0%	26.2%	25.1%
Net profit margin	17.2%	19.5%	19.2%	19.5%	18.9%	19.6%
Return on equity	41.7%	41.0%	44.4%	36.6%	43.4%	32.4%
Earnings growth rate	13.7%	15.1%	13.4%	20.0%	57.8%	18.5%
Price-to-earnings ratio	48.8	32.0	29.2	27.0	15.3	23.9

Bristol Myers Squibb versus Merck

Exhibit 12.12 compares selected ratios for Bristol Myers Squibb with those of Merck. Both companies have generally impressive-looking financials. Both companies are profitable, having high returns on equity and corresponding returns to shareholders. Both companies have about the same amount of leverage, though Merck relies more on long-term debt than does Bristol Myers. In 1998 Merck's long-term debt-to-equity ratio was about 25 percent compared to 18 percent for Bristol Myers.

The only major difference between the two companies lies in the various turnover ratios. Notice that Merck turns its receivables and inventory much faster than does Bristol Myers. In 1998, for example, Merck's inventory turnover was more than twice that of Bristol Myers. Yet Merck's total asset turnover ratio was lower than Bristol Myers' during each of the three years shown. What could explain this? The answer lies further down the balance sheet of each company. At the end of 1998 Merck had total assets of about $31.9 billion. Of that amount, more than $8 billion (about 25 percent) were listed as "intangible." Further, intangible assets rose by more than $1.5 billion between 1997 and 1998. By contrast, only about 10 percent of Bristol Myers' $16.3 billion assets consisted of intangible assets at the end of 1998. Intangible assets actually declined for Bristol Myers between 1997 and 1998. The bottom line is that more intangible assets generally mean slower asset turnover.[5]

---

[5]Some analysts compute asset turnover ratio based only on tangible assets. If we subtracted intangible assets from both Bristol Myers and Merck and recomputed their asset turnover ratios, the results for 1998 would be 1.30 and 1.26, respectively.

Intangible assets consist of goodwill and the value of patents.[6] Both Bristol Myers and Merck sell drugs that still have patent protection. Merck, however, introduced several major new drugs during 1998. Thus, we're not surprised to see a large increase in intangible assets for Merck between 1997 and 1998.

A review of a company's historical record—both financial and nonfinancial—is an important component of a company analysis report. We're not finished with company analysis, however, for we still have to forecast future financial performance in order to fully assess the investment potential of a company's common stock.

Chapter Summary

1. What are the major goal and the components of a company analysis report?
    The major goal of company analysis is to forecast the quality and quantity of future earnings. Four general issues are addressed: (1) quality of management; (2) the company's competitive position within its industry; (3) strengths and weaknesses in the company's financial statements; and (4) the company's future financial performance.
2. How do analysts evaluate the quality of a company's management?
    Management—the effective and efficient attainment of organizational goals—consists of four functions: planning, organizing, leading, and controlling. Assessing management quality can be both difficult and subjective. Analysts look for an experienced management team, good strategic planning and marketing, appropriate financing, sustainable growth, a good public image, and an effective board of directors.
3. How do analysts evaluate the competitive position of a company within its industry?
    Leading companies have several important characteristics. They usually are among the largest companies in an industry and are growing faster than the industry as a whole. Leading companies are more profitable or are becoming more profitable than the industry. A longer and broader product line often indicates a more competitive position, as does the company's ability to introduce new products faster than competitors. Leading companies usually also are the most efficient, exhibit price leadership, and may have the advantage of proprietary technology or patents.
4. What is financial statement analysis?
    Financial statement analysis involves a careful evaluation of a company's financial statements. Financial ratios are among the most important tools for assessing the strengths and weaknesses of a company. The five categories of ratios are liquidity, activity, leverage and coverage, profitability, and ratios based on market values. In and of themselves ratios are just numbers. To be meaningful they must be compared across time, to industry averages or both.

Mini Case

In this mini-case you will practice calculating and interpreting financial ratios. Open the Wal-Mart worksheet in the Data Workbook. Using the data, perform the following exercises:

1. Calculate all the ratios listed in Exhibit 12.4.

---

[6]Under purchase accounting rules, if a company acquires another company, any difference between the value of the assets acquired and the price paid goes on the acquiring company's balance sheet as goodwill. Goodwill and other intangible assets are "amortized" over a set period of time and are a charge on the income statement, similar to depreciation.

2. Break down return on equity into its three components. From where does Wal-Mart's high ROE come?
3. List any major trends the ratios and the ROE breakdown reveal.

Review Questions and Problems

1. What is the major goal of company analysis? What type of information does the typical company report contain?
2. The general definition of management contains two important ideas. What are they? Give an example of each idea in practice.
3. What are the four functions of management? Give a brief example of each function.
4. List some of the important questions to ask when evaluating management. When looking at the characteristics of senior management, what do you want to see?
5. List some aspects you might examine when analyzing the competitive position of a company. Should an investor always limit his or her investments to leading companies?
6. What are the five categories of financial ratios?
7. Use the following ratios to fill in the balance sheet and income statement. All dollar values are in millions.

Current ratio	1.75
Quick ratio	1.00
Gross profit margin	30%
Net profit margin	5%
Accounts receivable turnover	10 ×
Long-term debt to equity	50%
Total asset turnover	1.50
Times interest earned	5.00
Return on equity	15%

Cash and equivalents	$20.0	Current liabilities	
Accounts receivable		Long term debt	
Inventory		Equity	
Total current assets		Total liabilities & equity	
Net fixed assets			
Total assets			

Sales	
Cost of goods sold	
Selling, administrative, and general expenses	
Depreciation	$15.0
Interest	
Earnings before taxes	
Income taxes	$ 5.0
Net income	$15.0

8. A company has a current ratio of 2.00 and a quick ratio of 1.50. If the company has current liabilities of $25 million, how much inventory does it have?
9. A company's return on equity is 30 percent and its net profit margin is 5 percent. It has $300 million in assets and $150 million in equity. What is the company's return on assets and asset turnover? What are the company's total sales?
10. Using the information provided in the prior question, break down the company's return on equity into its three components. Which of the three appears to be driving ROE?

11. Assume the company would like to reduce its assets-to-equity ratio from 2 to 1.75. What would have to happen to asset turnover and/or net profit margin if the company were to maintain the same ROE?

12. Why must the analyst establish benchmarks when interpreting financial ratios? Why is it often so difficult to compare a company's ratios to industry averages?

13. Assume you observed that a company's gross profit margin has been declining steadily for the past few quarters, whereas its net profit margin has remained about the same. Explain how these two trends could occur simultaneously.

14. You observe that a company's current ratio has been declining steadily. Before you conclude that the company's liquidity is deteriorating, what other data should you examine?

15. Below are data for two companies that operate in the same industry. Break down ROE for each company. How are the two companies different? What would you want to investigate next?

	Total Assets	Shareholders' Equity	Sales	Net Income
Company A	$ 350	$ 150	$1,200	$ 40
Company B	$5,500	$2,500	$6,500	$375

Note: ($ millions)

CFA Questions

1. Level II (1993). In reviewing the financial statements of the Graceland Rock Company, you note that net income increased and cash flow from operations decreased from 1991 to 1992.
   a. Explain how net income could increase for Graceland Rock Company while cash flow from operations decreased. Your answer must include three illustrative examples.
   b. Explain why cash flow from operations may be a good indicator of a firm's quality of earnings.

2. Level I (1994). A corporation wants to increase its current ratio from the present level of 1.5 before it ends its fiscal year. The action having the desired effect is:
   a. delaying the next payroll.
   b. writing down impaired assets.
   c. paying current payables from cash.
   d. selling current marketable securities for cash at their book value.

3. Level I (1994). A firm has net sales of $3,000, cash expenses (including taxes) of $1,400, and depreciation of $500. If accounts receivable increase over the period by $400, cash flow from operations equals:
   a. $1,200.
   b. $1,600.
   c. $1,700.
   d. $2,100.

CRITICAL THINKING EXERCISES

1. This exercise requires computer work. Open the Airline worksheet in the Data Workbook. The worksheet contains financial and operating data for Southwest Airlines, US Airways, and the airline industry. Use the data to answer the following questions.
   a. What is your overall assessment of the competitive position of both airlines? On what do you base your conclusion?

    b. . What information other than that presented in the worksheet would you request to further assess the competitive position of both airlines?

2. This exercise requires library/Internet research. According to retail analysts, below are some relevant questions to ask concerning the corporate strategy of any retailer. Considering these questions, read what Value Line, Standard & Poor's, and other investment firms have to say about the following retailers: Home Depot, Nordstrom's, and Wal-Mart. Based on what you know about each retailer, do you agree with the investment firms? Why or why not?

    a.   Has the retailer stayed on top of major demographic and economic trends?

    b.   In what category of retailing is the company? Does it appear to be diversified?

    c.   Where are the company's key regional markets? Are those markets strong or weak economically?

    d.   How strong is the competition relative to the company?

    e.   How does the company position itself in terms of price, value, quality, and service? Where does it make trade-offs between price, value, quality, and service?

    f.   How many stores does the company plan to open? Has its past growth been orderly and well managed?

3. This exercise requires computer work. Open the Sneaker worksheet in the Data Workbook. The worksheet contains financial data for Nike and Reebok over a recent six-year period. Use the data to perform the following exercises.

    a.   Calculate all the ratios listed in Exhibit 12.4 for both Nike and Reebok for the past five years.

    b.   Break down ROE for both companies for the past five years.

    c.   Discuss your findings. Describe what drives ROE for both companies and which company appears to be the strongest financially.

THE INTERNET INVESTOR

1. Pick a company whose stock is publicly traded. Using one of the major search engines, as well some of the major investment oriented web sites, find out as much as you can about the company's senior management, including information on the composition of the board of directors and executive compensation.

2. Visit the web site listed below. Look around the site and prepare a brief report as to the financial information the site contains.

        www.sec.gov/edgar

3. Most companies now include recent financial reports as part of their web sites. Visit the three web sites listed below. Review their financial reports. From the prospective of an investor, which site did you prefer and why?

        www.southwest.com
        www.johnsonandjohnson.com
        www.microsoft.com

COMPANY ANALYSIS: LOOKING FORWARD

PREVIOUSLY . . .

We listed the elements contained in a company analysis report and considered how to assess and analyze a company's current financial position.

IN THIS CHAPTER . . .

We describe various methods for forecasting future earnings, including both simple and more complex models. We also consider estimating some other variables important in determining the intrinsic value of a common stock.

TO COME . . .

Our discussion of security analysis concludes in the next chapter with a description of the major stock valuation models.

Chapter Objectives

After reading Chapter 13, you should be able to answer the following questions:

1. What long-term relationship exists between earnings and stock prices?
2. How are earnings calculated?
3. What are the simple quantitative methods for forecasting earnings?
4. How are business models used to forecast earnings?
5. What are some other financial variables the analyst must estimate?

After the market closed on December 10, 1999, copier and printer maker Xerox Corporation announced that its fourth quarter earnings could drop as much as 40 percent lower than analyst estimates. The company cited a range of factors, including weak sales and reorganization costs. When the markets opened for trading on December 13, Xerox's stock promptly dropped by more than 20 percent on extremely heavy volume as many analysts cut their earnings forecasts. By contrast, on December 9, 1999, silicon chip maker National Semiconductor announced quarterly earnings several cents above analyst expectations. The stock rose by more than 10 percent, also on heavy volume.

These two announcements, and the stock price reactions to them, are not uncommon. Announced earnings are often higher or lower than analyst expectations. Further, considerable evidence—both anecdotal and scientific—suggests that stock prices react significantly to current earnings and expected future earnings. Consequently, the ability to forecast earnings and the factors that drive earnings can greatly improve the security analysis process.

In this chapter we'll examine how analysts forecast the future. We'll review some of the evidence concerning the relationship between earnings and stock prices, the major forecasting techniques, including business models, and other variables the analyst must estimate. In the next chapter, we present several stock valuation models that help find the intrinsic value of a stock.

Earnings and Stock Prices

As we noted in Chapter 3, in the long-run, stock prices follow earnings. Let's revisit this issue in more detail. Anecdotal evidence abounds. For example, over the past forty years stock prices have increased by more than 21.5 times, as measured by the S&P 500. Corporate profits also rose by more than 21 times over the past forty years.

A long-term relationship between earnings and stock prices exists for individual stocks as well. Exhibit 13.1 presents two charts showing the relationship between stock prices and earnings. Although the correlations aren't perfect, stock prices generally rose along with earnings. For example, Merck's earnings rose at an average compound rate of 15.8 percent per year, and its stock price rose at an average annual compound rate of 22.6 percent. Notice also from Exhibit 13.1 that the faster earnings rose, the faster the stock price rose. Gap's earnings increased an average annual compound rate of 28.8 percent in the same year that its stock price rose by more than 37 percent.

Scientific evidence shows a strong relationship between stock prices and earnings.[1] Early studies arrayed stocks by both earnings and prices over varying periods of time. These studies found a strong association between the two arrays. The strength of the association increased over longer and longer time periods. More recent studies have found that perfect earnings forecasts—in other words, knowing actual earnings at the beginning of a period—results in substantial returns. All in all, most research has concluded that earnings and earnings growth rates explain much of the variation in stock returns over time.

Other research has focused on the relationship between earnings announcements and stock price reactions.[2] Generally, these studies find that announcements of higher than expected actual earnings result in significant positive returns around the announcement date. Likewise, lower actual earnings result in negative returns. Many of these studies also find that the positive or negative reaction continues for several months following the announcement.

---

[1]This research is detailed in Samuel Stewart, "Forecasting Corporation Earnings," in *The Financial Analyst's Handbook,* 2nd ed., ed. Sumner Levine (Homewood, Illinois: Richard D. Irwin, 1989), pp. 532–64.

[2]*Ebit.*

Exhibit 13.1 ✦ RELATIONSHIP BETWEEN EARNINGS AND STOCK PRICES FOR TWO COMPANIES

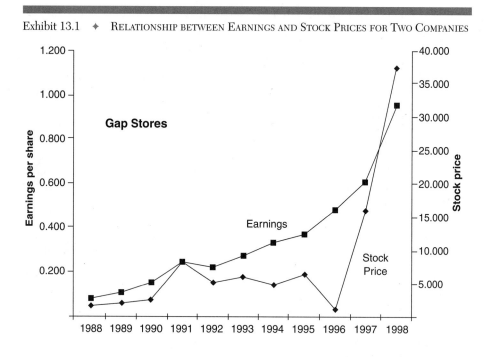

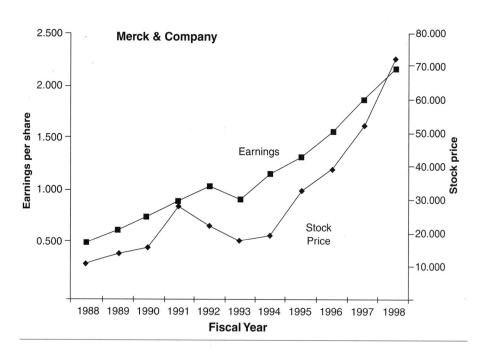

Although the evidence shows a strong relationship, at least in the long run, between earnings and stock prices, history is replete with situations where earnings appear not to matter. Some recent examples include biotech stocks in the early 1990s

and Internet stocks in the late 1990s. The Investment History box on page 338 describes what has happened when earnings failed to follow stock prices.

Earnings and Earnings Forecasts

As you remember from accounting, *earnings per share (EPS)* equal a company's net income divided by the number of outstanding shares. Alas, for many real companies, it's not that simple.

MEASURING EARNINGS PER SHARE

Exhibit 13.2 shows several measures of earnings per share for Xerox Corporation for a recent five-year period. These measures differ because each measure of earnings per share has a different numerator and/or denominator. Let's define each measure shown in the exhibit.

Each of the first three measures of earnings per share have the same denominator but different numerators. **Basic earnings per share from total operations** equals net income divided the number of shares outstanding.[3] **Basic earnings per share from continuing operations** equals net income from only continuing operations divided by the number of outstanding shares. **Basic earnings per share from discontinued operations** equals net income from only discontinued operations divided by the number of outstanding shares. Companies undergoing substantial restructurings often report large (both positive and negative) EPS from discontinued operations. For example, in the 1995 fiscal year, Xerox reported basic EPS from continuing operations of $1.73. At the same time it reported basic EPS from discontinued operations of −$2.48. Thus, the company reported a loss for the year of $0.75 per share.

The next three measures have the same numerator as their basic counterpart, but have a different denominator. So-called **diluted measures** of earnings per share use a figure for the number of outstanding shares assuming employee stock options, convertibles, and warrants are converted into new shares of common stock.[4] Because the number of outstanding shares on a fully diluted basis is more than the basic number of shares outstanding, diluted measures of earnings per share are always lower than basic measures of earnings per share. Depending on the company, the difference between diluted and basic earnings can be quite substantial. For example, for the fiscal year ending June 30, 1999, Microsoft reported basic earnings per share of $1.54. By contrast, diluted earnings per share were only $1.42—almost 10 percent lower than basic EPS. Over the years, Microsoft has relied on stock options as an important component of total employee compensation.

basic earnings per share (EPS) from total operations
Net income divided by the number of outstanding shares.

basic earnings per share (EPS) from continuing operations
Net income from only continuing operations divided by the number of outstanding shares.

basic earnings per share (EPS) from discontinued operations
Net income from only discontinued operations divided by the number of outstanding shares.

diluted measures
Calculations of earnings per share (EPS) that use a figure from the number of outstanding shares assuming employee stock options, warrants, and convertibles are converted into new shares of common stock.

---

[3]The number of outstanding shares is calculated using a weighting procedure established by The Financial Accounting Standards. The weighting procedure takes into account the number of shares issued or redeemed during the fiscal year.

[4]The exact method used to find the number of outstanding shares on a fully diluted basis is complicated. Consult an intermediate accounting text for additional details.

WHEN STOCK PRICES AND EARNINGS DIVERGE

Speculative bubbles are part of investment history. During a speculative bubble earnings and stock prices tend to diverge sharply as prices shoot skyward only to eventually come crashing back to earth. New issues from companies in hot, new industries or technologies are especially bubble prone. Biotechnology has provided some excellent examples.

Biotech companies develop new drugs through genetic engineering. When biotech companies first made their appearance on the investment scene in the early 1980s, investors became so enthralled with biotech that they often forgot that, as with all new technologies, these companies would need a great deal of time, not to mention lots of capital, to develop new, profitable products. And, there were no guarantees of success. Needless to say, biotech stocks have seen several bubbles.

Of all the biotech bubbles, the one that took place in the early 1990s was probably the most spectacular. Shares of Amgen—considered the most profitable and best-managed biotech company— rose more than fourfold in a matter of months between the end of 1989 and the middle of 1992. At its peak in 1992, the stock was selling for 104 times earnings. But the run-up in Amgen stock was nothing compared to other biotech stocks. Shares of a tiny company called Immune Response rose from $2 a share to $63 a share, giving the company a market value of more than $1 billion; not bad for a company with only $4.3 million in revenues.

As with all bubbles, investors finally came to the conclusion that, even if these companies met all their potential and more, they could never earn enough money to justify their stratospheric valuations. The selling began, and the bubble soon burst. By 1993, Amgen had lost 60 percent of its value, and Immune Response had dropped by more than 85 percent.

The table below gives some mind-blowing examples of recent valuations of several Internet stocks. Yahoo, for example, recently had a price-to-sales ratio of almost 300 and a market value in excess of $125 billion. By contrast, Hewlett Packard, a company with more than $40 billion in sales, was selling for a mere 35 times *earnings* and had a market value of less than $120 billion. But at least Yahoo! is making money; most Internet companies aren't. Amazon.com, for example, has a market value of almost $31 billion. Pretty impressive, considering the fact that the company has never made any money. In fact, its losses have gone up every year of its existence. Are earnings passé for companies operating in the new economy? Can Internet stocks defy the laws of financial gravity?

We don't think so. Undoubtedly, the Internet is becoming a big deal. Many Internet companies are well positioned to exploit its explosive growth, and, in the process, earn a great deal of money. Trouble is, not all will survive in that incredibly competitive environment. Years and years will pass before the survivors' earnings catch up with their current stock valuations. Although the past is never a guarantee of the future, the current Internet stock situation looks an awful lot like a classic speculative bubble. And bubbles have always eventually broken.

RECENT VALUATIONS OF INTERNET STOCKS

Stock	Market Value	Price to Sales	Earnings per Share	Price to Earnings
Amazon.com	$31 billion	25 ×	−$1.38	N/A
eBay	$18 billion	113 ×	$0.08	1,763 ×
Inktomi	$10 billion	128 ×	−$0.24	N/A
Red Hat	$16 billion	1,450 ×	−$0.01	N/A
Yahoo!	$125 billion	288 ×	$0.25	1,900 ×

EARNINGS FORECASTS

consensus forecast
Average of forecasts made by analysts following a stock.

Most large Wall Street brokerage and investment firms employ analysts to follow specific stocks. One of their jobs is to forecast earnings. Several investment information services—such as First Call, IBES, and Zach's—compile earnings forecasts made by analysts. They develop **consensus forecasts** for individual stocks, which is essentially the forecast average, as well the range of forecasts made by the analysts.

Exhibit 13.2 ✦ VARIOUS MEASURES OF EARNINGS PER SHARE FOR XEROX CORPORATION

	Year ending December 31			
	1998	1997	1996	1995
Basic EPS	$0.53	$2.16	$1.78	−$0.75
EPS from discontinued operations	−0.29	0.00	0.00	−2.48
EPS from continuing operations	0.82	2.16	1.78	1.73
Fully diluted EPS	0.52	2.02	1.66	−0.81
Fully diluted EPS from discontinued operations	−0.28	0.00	0.00	−2.48
Fully diluted EPS from continuing operations	0.80	2.02	1.66	1.61

Source: Xerox Annual Reports

Consensus Forecasts

One such example is shown in Exhibit 13.3. It shows the range of earnings forecasts, and the consensus forecasts for Motorola and Southwest Airlines for the next two fiscal years. For the fiscal year ending on December 31, 2000, the 32 analysts who follow Motorola forecast earnings ranging from a low of $2.94 a share to a high of $3.40 a share. The consensus, or average, forecast is $3.10 a share. By contrast, the 15 analysts who follow Southwest Airlines forecast earnings for the 2000 fiscal year (which ends on December 31, 2000) ranging from $0.87 to $1.10 a share. The average forecast is $1.03.

The range of earnings forecasts is often a measure of the degree of uncertainty surrounding forecasts. In that sense, analysts appear more certain about Motorola, for which the range is about 15 percent of the average, than they do about Southwest, for which the range of forecasts is about 25 percent of the average).

Earnings Surprises

Investment information services also report so-called **earnings surprises**—earnings that turn out higher or lower than analyst forecasts. Exhibit 13.4 lists quarterly earnings surprises for software maker Oracle Corporation for a recent five-quarter period. As you can see, the analysts correctly forecast Oracle's earnings in only one of the quarters shown. In the other four quarters, analysts ended up underestimating Oracle's earnings by as much as 18 percent. As we briefly discussed in Chapter 8, some studies have concluded that analysts have little forecasting ability. On the other hand, some studies have concluded that analyst forecasts are reasonably accurate.[5]

earnings surprises
Actual earnings higher or lower than the consensus forecast.

Management Forecasts

In addition to analysts' forecasts, management make forecasts, too. Given that managers have access to information not generally available to outside analysts, it is not surprising that management forecasts show greater accuracy than do analyst forecasts.

---

[5]Samuel Stewart, "Forecasting Corporate Earnings," pp. 535–36.

Exhibit 13.3 ✦ EARNINGS FORECASTS FOR MOTOROLA AND SOUTHWEST AIRLINES

		Quarter Ending		Year Ending	
		12/99	3/00	12/99	12/00
Motorola	Consensus	$0.81	$0.59	$2.06	$3.10
	Number of Forecasts	26	14	33	32
	High	0.89	0.63	2.20	3.40
	Low	0.79	0.55	1.90	2.94
Southwest Airlines	Consensus	$0.18	$0.21	$0.90	$1.03
	Number of Forecasts	13	3	15	15
	High	0.20	0.22	0.96	1.10
	Low	0.17	0.20	0.87	0.87

Source: Zach's

Exhibit 13.4 ✦ EARNINGS SURPRISES FOR ORACLE CORPORATION

	Quarter Ending				
	11/99	8/99	5/99	2/99	11/98
Consensus	$0.22	$0.16	$0.32	$0.19	$0.16
Actual	0.26	0.16	0.36	0.20	0.19
Difference	0.04	0.00	0.04	0.01	0.03
Percent	18.2%	0.0%	12.5%	5.3%	16.7%

Source: Zach's

In fact, in the early 1970s the SEC considered a rule that would require companies to disclose management forecasts. The rule was never implemented. However, it is now common practice for managers to discuss their forecasts publicly with analysts who, in turn, disseminate the information to clients and the public.

Forecasting Earnings

Having discussed the relationship between stock prices and earnings, how we measure earnings, and how analysts and managers forecast earnings, we now turn to a discussion of the techniques used to forecast earnings. We'll start by distinguishing between the various approaches to forecasting earnings.

APPROACHES TO FORECASTING EARNINGS

In Chapter 11 we described the difference between qualitative and quantitative economic forecasts. The same difference applies to earnings forecasts. Quantitative forecasts rely on an explicit statistical or mathematical model. On the other hand, qualitative forecasts rely on subjective judgments made by the analyst without direct reference to any statistical or mathematical model. Some analysts' and managers' earnings forecasts are more qualitative in nature, others are more quantitative. In reality, however, most forecasters mix the two techniques. They may use a quantitative model to arrive at a preliminary earnings forecast, which is then "tweaked" using the analysts' judgment.

Another distinction we can draw is between bottom-up forecasts and top-down forecasts. In a **bottom-up forecast,** the analyst starts by studying the relationship between earnings and firm-specific variables. For example, the analyst might ask whether or not earnings are rising or falling relative to sales. In a **top-down forecast,** the analyst begins by studying the relationship between earnings and various economic and industry variables. For example, the analyst might consider the relationship between oil prices and earnings.

bottom-up forecast
A forecast where the analyst begins by studying the relationship between earnings and firm-specific variables such as sales.

top-down forecast
A forecast where the analyst begins by studying the relationship between earnings and economic or industry variables.

Certain companies in particular industries may benefit more from a particular type of forecast. For instance, top-down forecasting may be more appropriate for companies that operate in cyclical industries—such as auto makers and home builders. Although top-down and bottom-up forecasts are not mutually exclusive, most analysts tend to focus on one approach over the other. Warren Buffet and Peter Lynch, for example, both use primarily a bottom-up approach to forecasting earnings and picking stocks.

TREND-BASED FORECASTS

Having reviewed the different approaches to forecasting, let's now turn our attention to some simple techniques used to forecast earnings. Perhaps the simplest forecasting technique is one that merely extrapolates a trend in the data. The chart in Exhibit 13.5 shows Southwest's earnings for 1988 through 1998. As you can see, Southwest earnings generally grew over the period shown, but the growth was somewhat erratic. Using these data, we can extrapolate the trend and come up with a forecast of 1999 earnings for Southwest Airlines.[6]

You can extrapolate a trend in one of two ways. First, you can find the average compound growth rate. Second, you can estimate a simple regression model.

Finding the average compound growth rate involves solving the following equation:

$$g = \left(\frac{EPS_n}{EPS_0}\right)^{1/n} - 1,$$

where EPS_n is earnings at the end of the period, EPS_0 is earnings at the beginning of the period, and n is the number of years. In our example, Southwest earned $0.12 per share in 1988 and $0.87 per share in 1998. From the end of 1988 to the end of 1998 is ten years. Thus, the average compound growth rate is

$$g = (0.87/0.12)^{1/10} - 1 = 21.9\%.$$

---

[6]We're going to use Southwest as our forecasting example throughout. A Critical Thinking Exercise at the end of the chapter asks you to compare Southwest's actual 1999 earnings to our various forecasts.

Exhibit 13.5 ✦ EARNINGS PER SHARE FOR SOUTHWEST AIRLINES

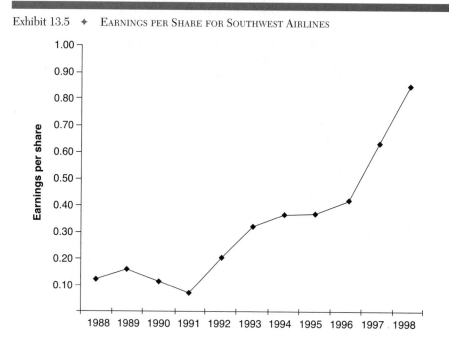

If Southwest's earnings grow at 21.9 percent in 1999, its 1999 earnings will equal

$$(1.219) \times \$0.87 = \$1.06.$$

The other method for extrapolating a trend is to estimate the following simple regression equation:

$$EPS_t = a + b(Year_t).$$

Earnings are the dependent variable, and year is the independent variable. The parameters a and b are the estimated intercept and slope. Using the data shown in Exhibit 13.5, we come up with this regression equation:

$$EPS_t = -133.498 + .067(Year_t).$$

Plugging in 1999 as our year produces the following estimate of earnings:

$$EPS_{1999} = -133.498 + .067(1999) = \$0.74.$$

Comparing the two trend-based forecasts reveals two obvious points. First, the two forecasts are significantly different—the forecast that uses the compound growth rate is quite a bit higher than the regression forecast ($1.06 versus $0.74). Second, the regression forecast of 1999 earnings is actually less than the actual earnings for 1998. The regression forecast is not likely to be particularly accurate.

You can see the problem with the regression forecast by looking at the chart shown in Exhibit 13.6. Notice that although earnings generally increased, they increased in a nonlinear fashion. The regression forecast fits a line to the data. As a

Exhibit 13.6 ✦ EARNINGS REGRESSION

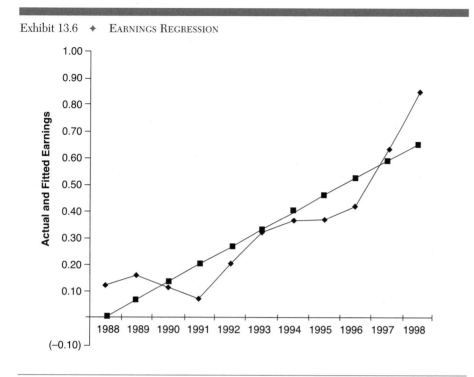

result, in this example the regression line underestimates earnings during the beginning and end of the period and overestimates midperiod earnings.

Although trend-based forecasts are in some cases highly accurate, they tell the analyst little about how a company makes money, and what causes earnings to rise or fall. The answers to these and other questions are important to assessing a stock's investment potential. Consequently, analysts rely on more sophisticated techniques when estimating earnings. Most build business models, which we'll discuss in the next section.

So far, we've discussed two earnings estimation techniques that involve extrapolating the historical trend. Below are eleven years of earnings for Merck. Use these data to answer the following questions.

RECAP

Fiscal Year	Earnings
1988	0.508
1989	0.630
1990	0.760
1991	0.915
1992	1.060
1993	0.935
1994	1.190
1995	1.350
1996	1.600
1997	1.915
1998	2.205

1. Estimate 1999 earnings by finding the average compound growth rate.
2. Estimate 1999 earnings using a trend-based regression equation.
3. Of the two forecasts, which do you believe may be the more accurate? Explain your answer.

BUSINESS MODELS

business model
A model of how a company operates and makes money.

A **business model** is merely a model of how a company operates and makes money. A business model will generate a pro forma income statement and an estimate of earnings. It also can provide much more detailed insight for the analyst. A business model provides a detailed breakdown of revenues and expenses and identifies the key drivers of profitability. This helps the analyst fine tune the forecast and adjust it to changes in the company's operating and financial environment. The typical business model consists of both qualitative and quantitative elements and can take a top-down approach, a bottom-up approach, or a combination of the two.

The easiest way to understand how to build and use a business model is to go through a detailed example. Let's build a business model for Southwest Airlines in order to estimate 1999 earnings and to give you a feel for the kinds of information analysts must understand to properly do their jobs.

Exhibit 13.7 presents income statements and selected operating statistics for Southwest Airlines for a five-year period (1994 through 1998). Mark this page; we'll be referring to Exhibit 13.7 frequently.

Understanding the Business

In order to build a business model you must first have a broad understanding of the business. Airlines are actually relatively simple businesses to understand. They generate most of their revenues in the form of fares by flying passengers from point A to point B. In the process of operating, airlines incur a variety of expenses—labor, fuel, and so on. For the airline to make money, the cost of transporting passengers must be less than what the passengers pay in fares.

According to the 1998 income statement, Southwest collected almost $4 billion in passenger fares. This amounted to more than 95 percent of its total revenues for the year (charter and freight operations generated the balance). The company's operating expenses amounted to almost $3.5 billion. Southwest had operating income of more than $680 million and net income of more than $430 million. It earned 87 cents per share.

Now, we must define some operating terms. An *available seat mile (ASM)* is one seat flying one mile. It's a measure of capacity. A *revenue passenger mile (RPM)* is one fare-paying passenger being transported one mile. The load factor is the percentage of seats filled with fare-paying passengers, which equals revenue passenger miles divided by available seat miles. *Revenue passenger yield* is what Southwest collects in fares from each passenger per mile flown. We can calculate revenue passenger yield by dividing the average fare by the average trip length.

Total Revenues

Armed with some basic understanding of the airline business, we now turn our attention to estimating passenger revenue. Coming up with an estimate of passenger

Exhibit 13.7 ✦ INCOME STATEMENT AND SELECTED OPERATING STATISTICS FOR SOUTHWEST AIRLINES

Income Statement	1998	1997	1996	1995	1994
Passenger revenues ($000s)	3,963,781	3,639,193	3,269,238	2,760,756	2,497,765
Freight revenues	98,500	94,758	80,005	65,825	54,419
Charter and other revenues	101,699	82,870	56,927	46,170	39,749
Total revenue	4,163,980	3,816,821	3,406,170	2,872,751	2,591,933
Operating expenses	3,480,369	3,292,585	3,055,335	2,559,220	2,275,224
Operating income	683,611	524,236	350,835	313,531	316,709
Other expenses (income) net	(21,501)	7,280	9,473	8,391	17,186
Income before taxes	705,112	516,956	341,362	305,140	299,523
Income taxes	271,681	199,184	134,025	122,514	120,192
Net income	433,431	317,772	207,337	182,626	179,331
Operating Statistics					
Revenue passenger miles (000s)	31,419,110	28,355,169	27,083,483	23,327,804	21,611,266
Available seat miles (000s)	47,543,515	44,487,496	40,727,495	36,180,001	32,123,974
Load factor	66.1%	63.7%	66.5%	64.5%	67.3%
Passenger revenue yield (cents per RPM)	12.62	12.83	12.07	11.83	11.56
Operating expenses (cents per ASM)	7.32	7.40	7.50	7.07	7.08
Average fuel cost (cents per gallon)	45.67	62.46	65.47	55.22	53.92
Average passenger fare ($)	75.38	72.21	65.88	61.64	58.44
Average trip length (miles)	597	563	546	521	506

revenues requires that we estimate four variables: available seat miles, load factor, average trip length, and average fare.

As we mentioned, available seat miles are a measure of capacity. Airlines tend to add capacity in a predictable manner. Although Southwest has been among the fastest-growing airlines, its growth rate has slowed in recent years to about 8 to 10 percent per year. Let's assume ASMs grew by 8 percent during 1999 to about 51.3 billion.

During the past eleven years, the load factor has averaged about 67 percent. Let's assume 1999 is an average year. Multiplying the load factor by our estimate of ASMs produces an estimate of about 35 billion revenue passenger miles.

As Southwest has expanded from regional airline to national airline, the average trip length has lengthened each year over the last five years. We can extrapolate this trend to an average trip length estimate of about 625 miles in 1999. As for fares, airline fares—even Southwest's—are generally rising. Coupled with the increase in the average length of each trip (longer trips usually mean higher fares), we'll estimate an average fare for 1999 of $80. Dividing the average trip length into the average fare ($80/625) gives us an estimate of revenue passenger yield of 12.8 cents per RPM.

To find passenger revenue we multiply RPMs by revenue passenger yield; our estimate of 1999 passenger revenue is about $4.4 billion. Because passenger revenue is assumed to be 95 percent of total revenue, we divide the estimate of passenger revenue by .95 to come up with an estimate of total revenue. The final result is an estimate of 1999 revenues of almost $4.8 billion. The details of the revenue calculation are shown in Exhibit 13.8.

Exhibit 13.8 ◆ DETAILS OF REVENUE ESTIMATE

Total revenues = Passenger revenues/.95	$4,635,283 = $4,403,518/.95
Passenger revenues = Revenue passenger yield × Revenue passenger miles	$4,403,518 = 34,402,487 × $0.1280
Revenue passenger yield = Average fare/Average trip length	$0.1280 = $80/625
Revenue passenger miles = Available seat miles × Load factor	34,402,487 = 51,346,996 × .67

Operating Expenses and Operating Profit

A breakdown of operating expenses for the past three years is shown in Exhibit 13.9. Ignoring the catch-all "other" category, the two largest operating expenses are employee wages and jet fuel. Combined, they make up about half of total operating expenses.

Note two important points concerning airline operating costs: First, most airline operating expenses are fixed costs rather than variable costs. In other words, operating expenses are more a function of available seat miles (capacity) than revenue passenger miles. An airline pays about the same to operate a schedule regardless of the number of passengers flown and, therefore, the amount of revenue collected.[7]

Second, most operating expenses have risen at about the same rate as available seat miles. The one exception is the amount spent on fuel. As the price of oil has fluctuated, so has the amount spent on jet fuel. For example, even though ASMs rose by more than 3.5 billion in 1998, the amount Southwest spent on jet fuel actually declined by more than $100 million because the average cost of jet fuel declined by more than 25 percent.

Taken together, these two observations suggest that the rise and fall in jet fuel prices may significantly influence the variation in operating costs per ASM. The chart in Exhibit 13.10 provides some evidence of the relationship between jet fuel prices and operating expenses. Over the 11 years shown, operating expenses tended to rise when jet fuel prices rose and vice-versa.

What about 1999? Oil prices are rising, and so is the cost of jet fuel. A 10 percent average price increase for jet fuel between 1998 and 1999 would not be surprising. Based on the historical relationship shown in Exhibit 13.10, a 10 percent increase in the price of jet fuel would raise operating costs per ASM by about 2.5 percent to 7.5 cents.

Multiplying 7.5 cents by our estimate of 51.3 billion ASMs give us an estimate of about $3.85 billion in operating expenses. Subtracting operating expenses from revenues of $4.64 billion yields an estimated $784 million in 1999 operating income.

Net Income and Earnings per Share

Hang in there, this example is almost complete. Looking at Exhibit 13.8, historically net income has consistently equaled about 60 percent of operating income. Assuming

---

[7]Airlines have a high degree of what we call *operating leverage,* meaning a one percent increase in revenue leads to a more than one percent increase in operating profits.

Exhibit 13.9 ✦ BREAKDOWN OF OPERATING EXPENSES

Operating Expense	1998		1997		1996	
	$000s	Percent	$000s	Percent	$000s	Percent
Salaries, wages, and benefits	1,285,942	36.9%	1,136,542	34.5%	999,719	32.7%
Fuel and oil	388,348	11.2	494,952	15.0	484,673	15.9
Maintenance	302,431	8.7	256,501	7.8	253,521	8.3
Agency commissions	157,766	4.5	157,211	4.8	140,940	4.6
Aircraft rentals	202,160	5.8	201,954	6.1	190,663	6.2
Landing fees and airport leases	214,907	6.2	203,845	6.2	187,600	6.1
Depreciation	225,212	6.5	195,568	5.9	183,470	6.0
Other	703,603	20.2	646,012	19.6	614,749	20.1
Total	3,480,369	100.0	3,292,585	100.0	3,055,335	100.0

nothing unusual occurs in 1999, $784 million in operating income translates into slightly more than $470 million net income, or about $0.93 per share. (Southwest has about 505 million shares of common stock outstanding.)

We've covered a lot of ground, so let's summarize how we reached a 1999 earnings estimate of 93 cents a share. (More details are shown in Exhibit 13.11.) We estimated that available seat miles would increase by 8 percent to 51.3 billion. Multiplying ASMs by the load factor, 67 percent, gives us revenue passenger miles of 35 billion. A combination of slightly higher fares and a slightly longer average trip length gives us a revenue passenger yield of 12.8 cents per RPM. Multiplying revenue passenger yield by RPMs produces passenger revenue $4.4 billion. Dividing passenger revenue by .95 gives us total revenue of $4.6 billion.

Multiplying ASMs by 7.5 cents (operating costs per ASM) equals operating expenses of $3.85 billion. Subtracting operating expenses from total revenue equals operating income of $784 million. Multiplying operating income by .6 equals net income of $470 million. Dividing net income by 505 million equals earnings per share of 93 cents.

SENSITIVITY ANALYSIS

Our business model forecast of 1999 earnings of 93 cents per share is on the high end of analyst forecasts. What could go wrong with our forecast? Plenty. First, we made more than a few assumptions, and our assumptions can be wrong. Instead of increasing by 10 percent, jet fuel might increase by 15 percent. Fares might average $75 rather than $80.

Testing the sensitivity of your forecast to changes in your assumptions will help you identify the key drivers in your forecast. These are the variables to which you should play close attention. If key drivers show evidence of changing more or less than expected, you can adjust your forecast appropriately.

Sensitivity analysis is one technique for identifying the key drivers. The process is to list each of your variables and then change them one at a time by some fixed percentage, keeping the other variables constant. Note which change has the greatest impact on your forecast.

As an example, let's go back to our Southwest business model forecast. For the sake of simplicity, we'll test the sensitivity of our forecast to changes in the following

Exhibit 13.10 ✦ Operating Costs and the Cost of Jet Fuel

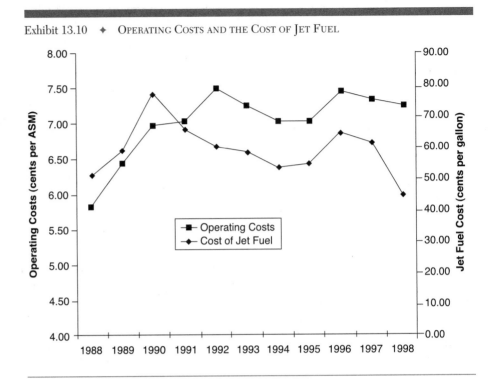

variables: growth rate in ASMs, load factor, average fare, and operating costs per ASM. Below are our original estimates and the revised estimates:

Variable	Original Estimate	Revised Estimate
Growth rate in ASMs	8 percent	7.6 percent
Load factor	67 percent	63.65 percent
Average fare	$80	$76
Operating costs per ASM	7.5 cents	7.875 cents

Note that all the revised estimates are 5 percent higher or lower than the original estimate and are revised in such a way as to lower earnings per share.

The results of the sensitivity analysis are shown below. As you can see, the sensitivity of the earnings forecast varies substantially from variable to variable. For example, a slower growth in ASMs has little impact on earnings per share. If ASMs grow by 7.6 percent rather than 8 percent, earnings decline by less than a penny a share. On the other hand, even a small change in any of the other three variables has major impact on earnings. For example, if the average fare is $76 rather than $80, earnings per share decline by almost one-third. Even a decline in the average fare of a dollar reduces earnings per share by more than 8 cents.

Original forecast	93.2 cents per share
Slower growth in ASMs	92.9 cents per share
Lower load factor	65.6 cents per share
Lower average fare	65.6 cents per share
Higher operating costs per ASM	70.3 cents per share

Exhibit 13.11 ✦ Details of Earnings Calculation

Earnings per share = Net income/Number of outstanding shares	$0.932 = $470,555/505,000
Net income = .60 × Operating income	$470,555 = .60 × $784,258
Operating income = Revenues − Operating expenses	$784,258 = $4,635,283 − $3,851,025
Operating expenses = Available seat miles × Operating expenses per ASM	$3,851,025 = 51,346,996 × $0.075

The sensitivity analysis also identifies some challenges facing airline management. In order to boost earnings, fares must rise more than expenses. In other words, the spread between revenue passenger yield and operating expenses must widen. However, higher fares often mean fewer passengers and lower load factors. In a highly competitive environment, where fare wars are common, airlines must make up for lower revenue passenger yields by cutting costs (which is difficult) or increasing load factors. If they can't, earnings will suffer. Therefore, any current or potential investor in any airline stock must pay careful attention to variables such as load factors, average fares, and fuel costs.

RECAP

Use the Southwest business model to reestimate 1999 earnings. Assume the following (use original estimates for other variables):

4. Average fare increases to $80.50.
5. Operating costs increase to 7.55 cents per ASM.
6. Average fare decreases to $78 *and* the load factor increases to 70 percent.

Forecasting Other Financial Variables

In addition to earnings, the analyst may wish to forecast several other financial variables. Three of these include common stock dividends, after-tax cash flow, and the required rate of return.

DIVIDENDS

Once the analyst arrives at a forecast of earnings, forecasting dividends is relatively straightforward. Most companies that pay common stock dividends—not all companies do—follow reasonably predictable dividend policies. Companies that pay dividends often aim to pay out a certain percentage of earnings in dividends, so that as earnings increase, dividends will tend to increase as well. If you covered dividend policy in your introductory finance class you may remember that dividends are more stable from year to year than earnings, and most companies are reluctant to cut dividends, even if earnings decline.

Let's go back to Southwest Airlines. As you saw in Exhibit 13.9, Southwest pays out only a small fraction of its earnings in dividends. In 1998, for example, the company earned 87 cents a share but paid out only 2 cents a share in dividends (rounded to the nearest penny). Over the prior ten-year period (1989-97), Southwest paid out

Exhibit 13.12   ✦   EARNINGS AND DIVIDENDS FOR MERCK

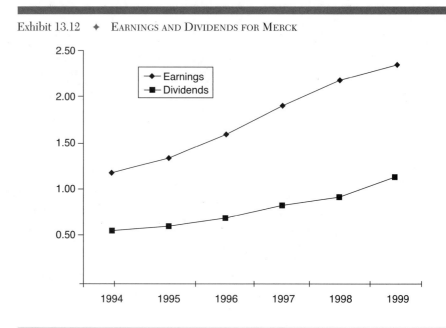

only a penny per share in dividends. Dividend appear likely to remain near 2 cents per share for the near future, regardless of earnings.

Turning to another example, Exhibit 13.12 shows earnings and dividends for drug maker Merck for a recent six-year period. Over the period shown, Merck's earnings and dividends rose pretty steadily each year, averaging about 15 percent annually. Furthermore, Merck paid out an average of about 45 percent of its earnings in dividends. If 2000 earnings rose by about 15 percent, we might expect 2000 dividends of about $1.33 per share.

CASH FLOW

Some analysts believe that a better measure of profitability than earnings is after-tax cash flow. These analysts see a pattern of rising cash flow as more interesting than a pattern of rising earnings. After all, the company uses cash, not earnings, to pay bills, buy back shares, or make capital investments. Year to year, earnings and cash flow can differ significantly for two main reasons. First, accounting rules give companies some leeway when it comes to reporting incomes and expenses. Second, certain expenses—most notably depreciation—don't represent real bills that must be paid.

Measuring After-Tax cash flow

The conventional measure of cash flow subtracts preferred stock dividends (if any) from net income, and adds depreciation and other noncash expenses (as given in the income statement). Dividing after-tax cash flow by the number of outstanding shares produces cash flow per share.

free cash flow
Cash flow from operations minus common stock dividends and minus capital expenditures.

Another term, **free cash flow** is generally defined as cash flow from operations (as reported in the statement of cash flows) minus capital expenditures minus common stock dividends.[8] Opinions differ, however, as to whether free cash flow is any more meaningful than more conventional cash flow measures in measuring how much money a company is actually making. Common stock dividends are optional, and most companies can survive reduced capital spending for a period of time.

Regardless of which measure you use, estimating cash flow requires that you first estimate earnings. Depending on the cash flow measure you use, you next estimate depreciation, the change in working capital, cash dividends, and capital expenditures.

Let's go back to Southwest Airlines and estimate 1999 cash flow using the conventional measure of cash flow (net income plus depreciation). In the prior section we used the business model to estimate a 1999 net income of $470.5 million. What about depreciation? For Southwest, depreciation is fairly easy to estimate because historically depreciation expenses have risen at about the same rate as available seat miles. Because we assumed that ASMs would increase by 8 percent in 1999, we can assume that depreciation expenses will also increase by 8 percent to $243.2 million. Adding back depreciation of $243.2 million to net income of $470.5 million gives us an estimated 1999 after-tax cash flow of $713.7 million, or about $1.41 per share.

REQUIRED RETURN

A final variable analysts often estimate is the required return on a stock. One of the foundations of finance is that risk and return are positively related—higher-risk investments must offer higher expected returns. As we discussed in Chapter 2, the required return on any investment equals the nominal return on a risk-free investment (a combination of the real return and compensation for expected inflation) plus a risk premium.

One method of estimating the required return for common stocks is to use the so-called capital asset pricing model (or CAPM). The CAPM model states that the required return on a stock equals

$$\text{Risk free rate} + \text{Beta(Market risk premium)}.$$

Beta is a measure of a stock's risk—the higher a stock's beta, the greater the risk. By definition the overall stock market has a beta of 1. The *market risk premium* is the required return on the overall market minus the risk-free rate.

CAPM comes from modern portfolio theory, which we'll discuss starting in Chapter 17. For now, a simple example of how analysts use CAPM will suffice. First, we must estimate three variables: beta, the risk-free rate, and the market risk premium. Assume that Southwest Airlines has a beta of 1.4 (we'll describe how to estimate betas in Chapter 18). Typically, the yield on short-term Treasury bills is used as a proxy for the risk-free rate. Currently, it's about 5 percent. Historically, the difference between the return on stocks and the return on T-bills has averaged about 8.5 percent per year. This is often used as a proxy for the market risk premium. However, as the Investment Insights box on page 352 points out, many today argue that stocks are no riskier than bonds. Thus the market risk premium many investors use may be

---

[8]Cash flow from operations generally equals net income plus depreciation (and other noncash expenses) minus the change in working capital. An increase in working capital is considered a use of cash, and a decrease in working capital is considered a source of cash.

INVESTMENT INSIGHTS

ARE STOCKS REALLY RISKIER THAN BONDS?

Conventional wisdom says that stocks are riskier investments than bonds. Consequently, in order to persuade investors to buy stocks instead of bonds, stocks must promise higher returns. As a result, a so-called risk premium should be built into the required return on stocks.

Although still a minority, a growing number of academics and professionals—let's call them revisionists—are beginning to question conventional wisdom regarding stock risk relative to that of bonds. Some even go so far as to argue that stocks are no riskier than bonds, and in fact may be less risky. Although we're not quite ready to fully endorse the revisionist viewpoint, it's important to understand their argument.

Revisionists argue that conventional wisdom is based on the short-term volatility of stocks. Indeed, over short periods of time stock prices are highly volatile—even the most casual observer of the financial markets knows this. For example, if you reviewed the monthly returns from stocks since the mid-1920s, you'd observe that stocks returns were positive only about 53 percent of the time. You'd also note that, on an annual basis, the standard deviation of stock returns is more than twice the standard

deviation of bond returns. Therefore, based on these observations, a substantial risk premium must be offered to induce investors to buy stocks. In fact, since the mid-1920s stock returns have exceeded bond returns by about 8.5 percent per year. Conventional wisdom concludes that 8.5 percent, or thereabouts, is the "proper" equity risk premium.

According to the revisionists, the standard equity risk premium is too high because stocks are much less risky if one looks beyond short-term volatility. Again, historical returns reveal that much of the short-term volatility in stock returns disappears over longer and longer holding periods. Since the mid-1920s, stocks have risen in only about three out of four years—so investors stood a one in four chance of losing money. Not great odds. On the other hand, over rolling five-year periods since the mid-1920s, stock investors earned money 90 percent of the time. And over rolling twenty-year periods, stocks have earned money every time. Further, as the length of the holding period increases, the annualized standard deviation of stock returns falls sharply. In fact, for holding periods of ten years or longer, the annualized standard deviation of stock returns is actually less than the annualized standard deviation of

bond returns. By taking a longer-term perspective, revisionists argue, stocks aren't any riskier than bonds. Therefore, the equity risk premium ought to be closer to zero.

What does all the fuss over the correct size of the equity risk premium mean to investors? It could mean a great deal. It could mean that even though the Dow more than tripled during the 1990s, a historic buying opportunity awaits. According to economists James Glassman and Kevin Hassett, in their book *Dow 36,000*, the equity risk premium is too high. Consequently, stocks are still substantially undervalued, despite the huge gains in stock prices since the early 1980s. They believe that investors are slowly beginning to recognize the fact that stocks aren't as risky as they once believed. As investor perceptions of stock risk changes, Glassman and Hassett suggest, the price investors will pay for stocks rises. Stock prices will continue to rise, they conclude, until the expected return from stocks is no higher than the expected return from bonds. Based on their calculations, the "fair" value of stocks is at least three times higher than today's prices.

Are Glassman, Hassett, and the other revisionists right? That's a question investors must answer for themselves.

too large. Nevertheless, for purposes of this example we'll stick with 8.5 percent as a proxy for the market risk premium.

Putting it all together, the required return for Southwest Airlines is equal to

$$5 \text{ percent} + 1.4(8.5 \text{ percent}) = 16.9 \text{ percent}.$$

How the required return is actually used to value stocks is a topic we'll discuss in the next chapter.

In this chapter we've discussed the importance of estimating earnings when analyzing the investment potential of common stocks. We also described several methods for estimating earnings. The next chapter presents stock valuation models and ties together all the material on security analysis.

Chapter Summary

1. What long-term relationship exists between earnings and stock prices?

   The evidence strongly suggests that, in the long run, a positive relationship exists between earnings and stock prices. Most research has concluded that earnings and the growth rate in earnings explain much of the variation in stock returns over time. Further, studies show that announcements of higher than expected actual earnings result in significant positive returns around the announcement date. Lower actual earnings result in significant negative returns around the announcement date.

2. How are earnings calculated?

   The several measures of earnings per share include basic earnings from total operations, basic earnings from continuing operations, and basic earnings from discontinued operations. In addition, companies report diluted measures of earnings—earnings that assume convertibles, warrants, and employee stock options are converted into new shares of common stock.

   Most large Wall Street brokerage and investment firms employ analysts who follow specific stocks and forecast earnings. Consensus forecasts are the forecast average. The range of earnings forecasts is often a measure of the degree uncertainty surrounding forecasts.

3. What are the simple quantitative methods for forecasting earnings?

   Analysts use several approaches to earnings forecasting. Quantitative forecasts rely on a explicit statistical or mathematical model. Qualitative forecasts rely on subjective judgments made by the analyst without direct reference to any statistical or mathematical model. Bottom-up forecasts begin by determining the relationship between earnings and firm-specific variables. Top-down forecasts begin by determining the relationship between earnings and economic and industry variables. Some simple quantitative methods for forecasting earnings involve extrapolating the trend in historical earnings. Two ways of doing this are calculating the average growth rate and estimating a trend based regression.

4. How are business models used to forecast earnings?

   Most analysts forecast earnings by building a business model of the company. A business model shows how a company operates and makes money. A business model will generate a pro forma income statement and an estimate of earnings. At the same time, however, a business model provides much more insight into both revenues and expenses, and helps the analyst identify the key drivers of profitability. The analyst can fine tune his or her forecast and adjust it to changes in a company's operating and financial environment.

5. What are some other financial variables the analyst must estimate?

   In addition to earnings, analysts estimate three other financial variables: dividends, after-tax cash flow, and the required rate of return. Dividend forecasts often are derived from earnings forecasts. Forecasting dividends is a less daunting task than forecasting earnings because companies tend to follow identifiable dividend policies that rarely change from year to year. Some analysts believe cash flow, not earnings, is the better measure of how much money a company is really making. The most conventional measure of cash flow is net income minus preferred stock dividends (if any), with depreciation (and any other non-cash expenses) added back. The required rate of return is the return a stock should earn, given its risk. A common way of estimating the required rate of return is to use the capital-asset pricing model.

Review Questions and Problems

1. What is the general relationship between earnings and stock prices? Research has concluded that what two variables explain major portions of the variation in stock returns?

2. Explain the difference between basic earnings per share and diluted measures of earnings per share. Why is one never lower than the other?

3. What do we mean by a *consensus earnings forecast*? Of what interest is the range of earnings forecasts?

4. What is the difference between a top-down and a bottom-up approach to earnings? Give some examples of industries where a top-down approach might be more appropriate than a bottom-up approach.

5. What is a trend-based earnings forecast? What are the limitations of trend-based forecasts?

6. Below are eleven years of earnings data for Home Depot. Use these data to find the average compound growth rate and an estimate of earnings for next year.

Year	Earnings
1	0.07
2	0.11
3	0.15
4	0.20
5	0.27
6	0.34
7	0.44
8	0.51
9	0.65
10	0.80
11	1.10

7. Using the data given in the prior question, estimate a simple regression where earnings is the dependent variable and time is the independent variable. Use the regression to forecast earnings for next year.

8. Explain a business model. Why do most analysts build business models when forecasting earnings?

9. Why do some analysts believe cash flow, and not earnings, is a better measure of a company's true profitability? Explain the difference between the conventional measure of cash flow and free cash flow.

10. What is a company's required rate of return? If a company has a beta of .95, a risk-free rate of 5 percent, and market risk premium of 8 percent, what is the company's required rate of return?

CRITICAL THINKING EXERCISES

1. This exercise requires computer work. Open the Home Depot worksheet in the Data workbook. The worksheet contains 11 years of financial and operating data for the company. Use the data to answer the following questions.

   a. Estimate 2001 earnings by extrapolating the trend in the data. Critique your forecasts. In other words, are they of any value?

   b. Build a business model for Home Depot and use the model to estimate 2001 earnings. Clearly state and justify your assumptions.

   c. Test the sensitivity of your business model-based earnings forecast. Which appear to be the key drivers to profitability?

2. This exercise requires both computer work and library/Internet research. In the chapter, we built a business model for Southwest Airlines and used the model to estimate 1999 earnings. Research actual 1999 earnings (compile both financial and operating statistics) and compare our forecast to the actual earnings. Where did we go wrong?

3. This exercise requires both computer work and library/Internet research. Use the business model we built for Southwest Airlines in the chapter to forecast 2001 earnings. (Obtain relevant financial and operating statistics for 1999 and 2000.) Clearly state and justify your assumptions.

THE INTERNET INVESTOR

1. Search one of the investment-oriented web sites (such as quote.yahoo.com or www.quicken.com) for a recent major earnings surprise, one where the difference between the actual and consensus forecast was at least 10 percent. What did the analysts appear to miss?

2. Go to the following web site: investor.msn.com. Click on the section entitled "analyst info." Look up information on consensus forecasts for next year's earnings, the range of forecasts, and earnings surprises for the following companies: Amgen, Cisco Systems, Delta Airlines, DuPont, FPL Group, Lucent Technologies, Procter and Gamble, and Waste Management.

   a. Which company generated the most agreement among analysts over forecasts for next year's earnings? The least agreement? How do you explain so much agreement for one company and so much less for another?

   b. Which company has had the most earnings surprises in recent quarters? Were the surprises positive or negative?

   c. Click on the section entitled "ratings." Do the earnings forecasts correspond with how analysts rate the stocks (strong buy, buy, hold, etc.)? Why or why not?

3. Management often provide an earnings forecast in the annual report to shareholders. Today most companies place copies of their annual reports on their web sites. Visit the web site of a well-known company. Read the most recent annual report, specifically the opinion of management concerning future earnings. Compare management's forecast to analyst forecasts.

FUNDAMENTALS OF COMMON STOCK VALUATION

PREVIOUSLY . . .

We discussed how to analyze various financial aspects of a company with the general expectation that a financially sound company is a "good" investment. The chapter included many factors that may help an investor assess the value of a company and how it may affect its common stock.

IN THIS CHAPTER . . .

We describe methods to value common stocks so that you can make better investment decisions. By understanding the underlying process, investors can better estimate a stock's fundamental value and determine whether it is a good investment. The chapter gives conceptual and practical discussions and a step-by-step process to estimate a fundamental value for American Home Products, a manufacturer of prescription drugs such as Advil, Anacin, Dimetapp, Robitussin, and others.

TO COME . . .

As you gain experience in common stock investing, you may become interested in another avenue of investment—derivative securities. We discuss the risks and rewards associated with these speculative investment securities known as options and futures.

Chapter Objectives

After reading Chapter 14, you should be able to answer the following questions:

1. What is intrinsic value?
2. What is the Dividend Discount Model (DDM)?
3. What is the Earnings Model (EM)?
4. How does an investor conduct fundamental analysis on a company stock?
5. How can an investor value a stock with nonconstant growth?
6. How is the market-to-book ratio used for investment purposes?
7. What are the pros and cons of using the price/earnings multiple, also called the P/E ratio?

How does an investor determine a common stock's fundamental value? Suppose we call the fundamental value a stock's *true value.* How would you determine it? To illustrate how difficult it may be to estimate a common stock's true value, let's consider IBM, a company whose stock price or its market value has changed significantly since its restructuring in 1993.

In late 1993, under the helm of new CEO Louis Gerstner, IBM underwent a major restructuring to increase its stock price from its historical low of about $40 per share. By 1996, IBM common stock traded in the $83 to $135 per share range. Although its value appeared to have risen from its low, it is difficult to determine IBM's true value? Recall from Chapter 7 that the market prices stocks efficiently and fairly so the market value (or price) should be relatively close to its true value. This means IBM's intrinsic value was closer to $100 than $40 in 1996.

Although this may be an unusual example of a company making drastic changes and thereby increasing its intrinsic value, it illustrates that the company's true value can be an elusive number. Therefore, it is helpful to develop a conceptual understanding of instrinsic value so that we can determine what IBM's true value may be.

The true value of a stock is called its *intrinsic value*. We'll give the term a more complete definition soon, but for now let us understand that intrinsic value is important because the investor can base a relatively simple strategy on it. The investor would buy the stock if its market price were less than its intrinsic value and sell it, or sell it short, if its market price were more than its intrinsic value. In an efficient market, the market price should eventually match the intrinsic value, allowing an investor to profit by buying stocks at less than their intrinsic values, because their market prices should rise to match their intrinsic values. Conversely, selling short stocks whose market prices exceed their intrinsic values should generate profits as the market prices fall to the intrinsic values. This basic strategy focuses on finding securities whose prices are inconsistent with their intrinsic values.

We start this chapter with an intuitive discussion of intrinsic value, after which we discuss quantitative models the analyst uses to determine intrinsic values. We begin with the basic Dividend Discount Model (DDM), which implies that a stock's value is simply the present value of its expected future dividends. Next, we turn to the Earnings Model (EM), which posits that stock prices are a function, not only of expected future dividends but also of the growth of earnings due to companies' investment opportunities. The Earnings Model allows us to closely examine the real meanings of the widely used terms *growth company* and *growth stock*. Finally, we review two common measures of stock values, the market-to-book ratio (MV/BV) and the price/earnings ratio (P/E) ratio. This discussion highlights possible pitfalls of buying stocks that only appear to be cheap.

Intrinsic Value

Back in Chapter 8 we described the major differences between technical and fundamental analysis. Briefly, *technical analysis* is based on the belief that past patterns in security prices can be reliable support for predicting future price patterns. By contrast, *fundamental analysis* is based on the notion that every security has an intrinsic value determined by future expectations about the company.

Our earlier characterization of intrinsic value as the true value of a security gives little insight in estimating it. The **intrinsic value** of a stock is defined as the fundamental economic value of the issuing company's equity.[1] A simple, intuitive generalization of what creates value of a stock can clarify our definition.

intrinsic value
Fundamental economic value of issuing company's equity; rationally reflects all relevant publicly available information and, perhaps, privately available information.

---

[1]Economic value is calculated as the present value of a series of cash flows. Later in the chapter we review sources of cash flows.

A company produces goods and services, which it sells. We refer to these products as *projects* or *investment opportunities* of the company. For example, Ford projects produce goods such as cars and trucks, and Walt Disney's projects provide services such as entertainment and relaxation from its films and theme parks. Both firms undertake projects to generate sales. The money left over from sales revenues after paying taxes and other expenses is the company's net profit or earnings. These earnings are the cash returns to the stockholders for investing in the equity of the company. Conceptually, then, the fundamental economic value of a stock is the economic value of these projects, or the present value of the cash returns to stockholders who invest in the company's equity.

Although we admit that this definition ignores other aspects of company operations, a fundamental quantifiable economic value (or intrinsic value) is in essence the present value of the expected future earnings that its investment opportunities will generate. Based on some assumptions we discuss later, the intrinsic value of a common stock also equals the present value of the company's future dividends.

In this chapter, we present four models by which to estimate the intrinsic value of a common stock. These models are simplified generalizations and may be difficult to apply to all common stocks. However, although the model might yield only a rough estimate in some cases, the process still builds important insights into the factors that determine stock prices in the real world.

Dividend Discount Model (DDM)

If any generalization is safe, we can surely say that most investors purchase common stocks with expectations of making profits from their investments. More specifically, though, profits come in two forms: periodic cash dividend payments and capital appreciation from selling the stock at a price higher than the purchase price. How can an investor evaluate the expected profit from an investment? Even when investors do not bother with formal, systematic value determinations, most at least informally assess intrinsic value. Suppose for a moment that someone can travel forward 20 years (to Year 20) and find that a common stock will sell for $18 per share and pay an annual dividend of $1 per share. If that person requires a 16 percent return on the stock (that is, if the required rate of return on stock, ER_s, is 0.16), in Year 19 that investor would be willing to pay

$$V_{s19} = \frac{\$1.00 + \$18.00}{(1 + 0.16)} = \$16.38$$

where V_{s19} is defined as the intrinsic value of the stock in Year 19.

In symbols, this looks like

$$V_{s19} = \frac{DIV_{20} + V_{s20}}{(1 + ER_s)} \tag{14.1}$$

In Year 19, the intrinsic price of the stock just equals the present value of its Year 20 cash flow, $16.38 at a 16 percent required return. Stated differently, if someone pays $16.38 for the stock in Year 19 and expects cash flows over the next year of $19.00, the investment will earn an expected return, ER_s, of 16 percent (0.16).

Suppose that this time traveler decides instead to invest in Year 18 to earn cash flows equal to the sum of Year 19 and Year 20 dividends (DIV_{19} and DIV_{20}) plus the selling price of the stock in Year 20 (V_{s20}). This investor would be willing to pay

$$V_{s19} = \frac{DIV_{19}}{(1 + ER_s)} + \frac{DIV_{20} + V_{s20}}{(1 + ER_s)^2} \qquad (14.2)$$

Assuming dividends in Years 19 and 20 equal to $1 and an expected year 20 price of $18,

$$V_{s18} = \frac{\$1.00}{(1 + 0.16)} + \frac{\$1.00 + \$18.00}{(1 + 0.16)^2} = \$14.98$$

The stock's present value in Year 18 is less than its value in Year 19. Although it pays an extra dollar in dividends in Year 19, the cash flow from the dividend and expected selling price ($19) occurs a year later, in Year 20, and the present value of $19 is less two years earlier, in Year 18, than one year earlier, in Year 19.

This pattern continues as the traveler returns back from Year 17 through Year 1, and finally, to Year 0, today. To invest at Year 0, using the same logic, the investor would be willing to pay

$$V_{s0} = \frac{DIV_1}{(1 + ER_s)} + \frac{DIV_2}{(1 + ER_s)^2} + \cdots + \frac{DIV_{19}}{(1 + ER_s)^{19}} + \frac{DIV_{20} + V_{s20}}{(1 + ER_s)^{20}} \qquad (14.3)$$

Inserting values for expected dividends of $1 per year from Year 1 to Year 20, a Year 20 selling price of $18, and a required return of 16 percent, the value of the stock today equals

$$V_{s0} = \frac{\$1.00}{(1 + 0.16)} + \frac{\$1.00}{(1 + 0.16)^2} + \cdots + \frac{\$1.00}{(1 + 0.16)^{19}} + \frac{\$1.00 + \$18.00}{(1 + 0.16)^{20}} = \$6.85$$

Would the Year 18 valuation of $V_{s18} = \$14.98$ give the same value, V_{s0}, today? Yes, it would! Recall that V_{s18} is the present value of cash flows from Year 19 and Year 20 (Equation 14.2). You merely substitute V_{s18} ($14.98) for the present value of DIV_{19}, DIV_{20}, plus V_{20}.

$$V_{s0} = \frac{\$1.00}{(1 + 0.16)} + \frac{\$1.00}{(1 + 0.16)^2} + \cdots + \frac{\$1.00}{(1 + 0.16)^{17}} + \frac{\$1.00 + \$14.98}{(1 + 0.16)^{18}} = \$6.85$$

Two Implications

Two major implications stem from these numerical examples.

Implication 1.

The Year 18 price, V_{s18}, in the above example is a present value of the Year 20 future dividends and future price, V_{s20}. This implies that the investment holding period is irrelevant for determining the intrinsic value. If you sell it in Year 20 or Year 18, its intrinsic value today still equals $6.85.

Implication 2.

The present value of a selling price far in the future, such as Year 20 (V_{s20} = $18), is small. (The present value of $18 in Year 20 equals only $0.925.) This implication allows us to ignore the future price (which is virtually impossible to predict) because its impact on the intrinsic value is negligible.

GENERAL DIVIDEND DISCOUNT MODEL

dividend discount model (DDM)
Method of evaluating the intrinsic value of a stock based on the present value of expected dividends.

Now, suppose the investor travels past Year 20 to an indefinite point in the future, Year N. The general **Dividend Discount Model (DDM)** formula equals

$$V_{s0} = \sum_{t=1}^{N} \frac{DIV_t}{(1 + ER_s)^t} + \frac{V_{sN}}{(1 + ER_s)^N} \tag{14.4}$$

Remember from Implication 2 that the present value of the price in Year N, V_{sN}, can be ignored because it is virtually equal to zero. This allows the model to approximate the above equation by

$$V_{s0} \approx \sum_{t=1}^{N} \frac{DIV_t}{(1 + ER_s)^t} \tag{14.5}$$

If the dividends remain at $1 per year, the present value calculation is simple using a table of the present value of an annuity. However, if the expected dividends differ for each year, it can be a horrendous task without the aid of a financial calculator. Fortunately, a simpler formula can accommodate dividends that are expected to grow at a constant rate, g.

Let's define the future dividend stream relative to the current dividend as follows:

$$DIV_1 = DIV_0 (1 + g)$$
$$DIV_2 = DIV_0 (1 + g)^2$$
$$\vdots$$
$$DIV_N = DIV_0 (1 + g)^N$$

The general formula of Equation 14.5 can be rewritten to allow for growth in the dividends at a constant rate, g:

$$V_{s0} = \frac{DIV_0 (1 + g)}{(1 + ER_s)} + \frac{DIV_0 (1 + g)^2}{(1 + ER_s)^2} + \cdots + \frac{DIV_0 (1 + g)^N}{(1 + ER_s)^N} \tag{14.6}$$

A constant-growth sequence such as Equation 14.6 converges to

$$V_{s0} = \frac{DIV_0 (1 + g)}{(ER_s - g)} \text{ or } \frac{DIV_1}{(ER_s - g)} \tag{14.7}$$

This DDM assumes a constant growth rate and that $ER_s > g$. For practical purposes, we use Equation 14.7 exclusively to avoid the difficulty, if not impossibility,

Exhibit 14.1 ✦ GENERAL RULE FOR FUNDAMENTAL ANALYSIS

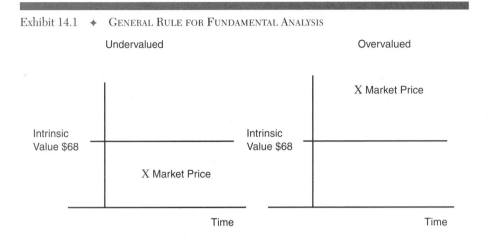

of accurately estimating future dividends for every year. We almost always assume that firms' dividends will grow at a constant rate.

Let's go through an example for American Home Products (AHP), a manufacturer of prescription drugs.[2] Suppose that AHP pays a current annual dividend of $0.91 per share, which should grow at a constant annual rate of 12 percent indefinitely. Also, analysts estimate the company's required return, ER_s, at 13.5 percent. Using Equation 14.7, AHP's intrinsic value is approximately $68:

$$V_{s0} = \frac{\$0.91\,(1 + 0.12)}{(0.135 - 0.12)} = \$68$$

How does a fundamental analyst use this information? To compare the intrinsic value, V_{s0}, with the stock's market price, suppose that on December 6, 2000, AHP is trading at about $50 9/16. Comparing the intrinsic value of $68 with the market price of $50 9/16 (or $50.5625), AHP appears *undervalued.* It is a bargain buy at $50.5625 because it is likely to increase to the fundamental economic value of $68.

The general rules for fundamental analysis prescribe trading strategies when a stock's market price differs from its intrinsic value. The two diagrams in Exhibit 14.1 depict the two possibilities. The horizontal line represents the intrinsic value ($68) and the *Xs* indicate market prices greater than or less than the intrinsic value. A market price less than the intrinsic value (V_{s0}) indicates an **undervalued** security. A market price greater than the intrinsic value indicates an **overvalued** security.

The development of the DDM implies that stock prices are valued by the dividends of the company alone. This seems implicit in Implication 1 above. But how can an analyst value stocks that pay no dividends? We'll accommodate this situation later when we discuss the P/E ratio. First, let's discuss the earnings model, which is important to valuing a stock's intrinsic value whether it pays dividends or not.

undervalued
The market price of a stock is less than the intrinsic value; the stock should be purchased.

overvalued
The market price of a stock is greater than the intrinsic value; the stock should be sold or not purchased.

---

[2]Here we provide the numbers and go through the calculation; in a later section we'll explain how to estimate each variable.

Earnings Model (EM)

earnings model (EM)
Method of estimating intrinsic value of common stock by estimating the present value of earnings for future investment opportunities, including reinvested earnings or retained earnings.

The **Earnings Model (EM)** is another way to estimate the intrinsic value of a common stock. It derives the intrinsic value by dividing the earnings generated by the firm's future investment opportunities into two parts: (1) earnings that the firm pays out as cash dividends and (2) earnings that the firm reinvests to fund future investment opportunities. The EM also serves two purposes other than estimating an intrinsic value:

1. It can identify the underlying factors for a growth company's success.
2. It can contrast a growth company with a growth stock.

In fact, we could argue that future dividends are part of future earnings. Generally speaking, investors value expected dividend streams because those payments represent the return on their investments, but future dividend streams stem from future earnings, or profits, of the company. The EM takes this notion further, demonstrating that future earnings exist only because of investment opportunities, and increases in future earnings will exist if future investment opportunities exist. The EM also adds another dimension to the analysis by clarifying the concept of growth companies; it provides five implications about growth companies and contrasts a growth company and a growth stock. Through the EM, we will shed some light on these elusive terms.

EARNINGS MODEL FORMULA

The general formula for the EM is

$$V_{s0} = \frac{EPS_1}{ER_s} + \frac{EPS_1}{ER_s}\left[\frac{g - ER_s(b)}{ER_s - g}\right] \tag{14.8}$$

where EPS_1 is the expected earnings per share, ER_s is the required rate of return or the expected return, g is the expected constant annual growth rate, and b is the retention rate, or $(1 - \text{dividend payout ratio})$.

Equation 14.8 can be viewed as having two parts: the no-growth term defined by EPS_1/ER_s and the growth term defined by

$$\frac{EPS_1}{ER_s}\left[\frac{g - ER_s(b)}{ER_s - g}\right]$$

The no-growth term represents the present value of the company's flagship product, whereas the growth term represents the present values of the firm's other future investment opportunities. These growth opportunities are expected to grow at a constant rate, g.

Perhaps it is easiest to grasp the model by reviewing an example and tying it to the formula. We use data from AHP to show how the model works.

AMERICAN HOME PRODUCTS: AN EARNINGS MODEL EXAMPLE

No-Growth Term

Suppose that AHP is expecting earnings per share (EPS_1) of $2 next year and that it anticipates no growth as it continues to produce only the pain relief medication Advil, promising shareholders all the profits.[3] The last condition sets the company's dividends per share equal to its earnings per share $(DIV_1 = EPS_1 = \$2.00$ per share). If AHP's profits remain at \$2 per share forever and the shareholders require a return of 13.5 percent (ER_s), the present value (PV) of the stock equals \$2 times the present value of an annuity factor for 13.5 percent in perpetuity.[4] This gives the present value of the stock as \$14.815 per share. It is the amount that investors should pay for AHP's stock if its future growth rate equals zero.

This value can also be calculated by the no-growth term of the EM:

$$PV \text{ of no growth term} = \frac{EPS_1}{ER_s} = \frac{\$2.00}{0.135} = \$14.815$$

PVGO

Now suppose that the company starts up innovative new projects that it expects to fuel growth at a constant rate. Let's explore how to determine the value of the constant-growth term.

Constant-Growth Term

Now, suppose that AHP decides to branch out from Advil to cold medicine (both in high demand). Investors expect these investments to return 23 percent to stockholders (in other words, expected **return on equity,** ROE_1 is 23 percent), and AHP chooses to invest some of the company's current earnings for the new venture. AHP expects to pay \$0.95 per share (DIV_1) as dividends and to retain \$1.05 per share (or retained earnings, RE_1). The company will pay 47.5 percent of its earnings as dividends (0.95/2.00); that is its **dividend payout ratio.** Conversely, AHP's **retention ratio,** b, is 52.5 percent (1.05/2.00). This drop in dividends may seem disturbing, but actually AHP is reinvesting 52.5 percent of its current earnings to provide current stockholders with greater future earnings.

We can use this idea to define the growth rate, g, as

$$g = ROE_1 \times b \tag{14.9}$$

where ROE_1 is the *expected* return on equity and b is the retention rate. (Remember that the ROE_1 should be the firm's *expected* return on equity in the future, not a historical value based on past projects.)[5] Equation 14.9 gives the company's growth rate because the additional earnings plowed back into the company are expected to generate a return on the stockholders' investment equal to ROE_1. So, if additional investments are made with retained earnings (b) and these investments earn a 23 percent return, the stockholders' future earnings will increase by 23 percent of the retained earnings invested, or 0.23 of b. Because b equals 52.5 percent, AHP's earnings will grow at the rate equal to 23 percent of 52.5 percent or 12 percent. This explains why the general formula for the growth rate is $(ROE_1 \times b)$.

Now, let's return to AHP's new venture. AHP retains \$1.05 per share and invests it in Robitussin cold medicine. Assuming that sales generate an expected return of 23

return on equity (ROE)
Return on investment for equity or common stock holder defined as net profits after taxes/common stockholder equity.

dividend payout ratio
Portion of earnings paid as dividend or defined as dividends per share/earnings per share.

retention ratio
Portion of earnings retained in the company or defined as retained earnings/earnings per share.

---

[3] Assume these numbers are given to you by your assistant; we'll discuss where to find them later.

[4] The PV of annuity factor at interest rate i for perpetuity equals $1/i$. For this example, it is $1/0.135 = 7.4074$.

[5] We'll address other caveats in the discussion of fundamental analysis.

percent (ROE_1), the venture's earnings per share come to $0.2415 (23% × $1.05). At the company's required return of 13.5 percent, the net present value (NPV) of this venture to stockholders is $0.739 per share.[6] This says that the Robitussin investment should add $0.739 to the stock price in Year 1. We must discount this Year 1 value to find its Year 0 or current value:

$$NPV_1/(1 + ER_s) = \$0.739/(1 + 0.135) = \$0.651$$

This return from the cold medicine business is also reflected in AHP's earnings per share in Year 2. AHP's Year 1 earnings will increase to $2.2415 per share ($2.00 from the Advil business and $0.2415 from the Robitussin business).

Now, suppose this growth orientation continues in Year 2. Instead of being satisfied with these medications, AHP decides to develop Sonata, an insomnia drug. Again, it will retain 52.5 percent of Year 2 earnings (0.525 × $2.2415, or $1.177 per share) and invest these funds in expanding its Sonata drug. At the same 23 percent return on this investment, AHP increases the value of the stock by $0.828 per share in Year 2; this is the net present value for the insomnia drug in Year 2.[7] Again, to determine the Year 0 value, we must discount the Year 2 value:

$$NPV_2/(1 + ER_s)^2 = \$0.828/(1 + 1.135)^2 = \$0.643$$

The second term back in Equation 14.8 summarizes the present values of all the firm's future growth opportunities ($PVGO$) or the NPVs of the Robitussin, Sonata, and other new discoveries. $PVGO$ is defined to equal the sum of the NPVs of each investment opportunity over the years, or

$$PVGO = \frac{NPV_1}{(1 + ER_s)} + \frac{NPV_2}{(1 + ER_s)^2} + \frac{NPV_3}{(1 + ER_s)^3} + \cdots$$

Because each NPV follows a sequence of constant growth rate equaled to g, it can be rewritten to resemble the growth term in Equation 14.8, or

$$PVGO = \frac{EPS_1}{ER_s}\left[\frac{g - ER_s(b)}{ER_s - g}\right]$$

Combining the present value of the firm's continuing growth opportunities, $PVGO$, with its no-growth term, we have Equation 14.8:

$$V_{s0} = \frac{EPS_1}{ER_s} + \frac{EPS_1}{ER_s}\left[\frac{g - ER_s(b)}{ER_s - g}\right]$$

Equation 14.8 can be further simplified to

$$PVGO = \qquad V_{s0} = \frac{EPS_1}{ER_s}\left[1 + \left(\frac{g - ER_s(b)}{ER_s - g}\right)\right] \tag{14.10}$$

[6]$NPV_1 = [\$0.2415/0.135] - \$1.05 = \$0.739$.

[7]Retained earnings from Year 2 equals $1.177, and the investment is expected to provide a 23 percent return. The cash flow per year equals 0.23 × $1.177 = $0.271. Assuming the investment will continue to perpetuity, the PV of annuity factor is 1/0.135 and $NPV_2 = [\$0.271/0.135] - \$1.177 = \$0.828$.

Using Equation 14.10, AHP's intrinsic value equals

$$V_{s0} = \frac{\$2.00}{0.135}\left[1 + \left(\frac{0.12 - (0.135)(0.525)}{0.135 - 0.12}\right)\right] = \$63.33$$

Exhibit 14.2 summarizes the results. If AHP can continuously find other investment opportunities that earn 23 percent, it can sustain this 12 percent growth rate per year and the intrinsic value of its stock should equal about $63 to $68 or the mid-60s.

Exhibit 14.3 depicts the cash AHP generates and the marginal value of its stock as it accepts positive-NPV investments. The figure begins with the no-growth case, which features constant earnings of $2.00 and a *NPV* of $14.815. Notice that each subsequent investment opportunity adds value to the company's common stock. For example, the Robitussin investment opportunity adds $0.651 per share to the stock price today, and the Sonata investment adds another $0.643 per share to the current stock value. Additionally, each investment adds to the firm's earnings per share, which increases at a constant-growth rate of 12 percent, or $2.00 to $2.2415 to $2.509, and so forth. One vertical axis indicates the marginal value each investment adds to AHP's stock price. Each horizontal step indicates another marginal investment, and the steps climb indefinitely into the future at a *constant-growth* rate, g, or 12 percent. Each year, new projects increase the stock's value by 12 percent from $0.739 ($NPV_1$) to $0.828 ($NPV_2$), and so forth, indefinitely.[8] Notice that both the earnings per share and the marginal value of the stock increase at the constant rate of 12 percent. These growth opportunities, *PVGO*, plus the no-growth term, $[EPS_1/ER_s]$ equals about $63 for AHP.

Now we can conduct our fundamental analysis, as we did with the DDM. The rule is the same: if intrinsic value exceeds the market price, the stock is undervalued; if intrinsic value falls to less than the market price, it is overvalued. Given that AHP's intrinsic value equals $63 and it has a market price of $50.5625, the stock is undervalued, and we would invest.

Recall that at the beginning of the section on the EM, we stated that the model serves two purposes other than intrinsic value estimations. It can identify the underlying factors for a growth company's success, and it can contrast a growth company with a growth stock.

IMPLICATIONS FOR GROWTH COMPANIES

The EM example showed that in general, company earnings growth leads to increasing intrinsic value. Given such is the case, let's discuss how a **growth company** earns a higher intrinsic value that would make it a potentially good investment.

Focus on the second term, or the growth term, of Equation 14.8. Because EPS_1 and ER_s are expected to be positive, notice that the growth term is positive only if $[g - ER_s(b)]$ is positive.[9] This means that g must be greater than $ER_s b$. Becau g equals ROE_1 times b, $ROE_1(b)$ exceeds $ER_s(b)$ only if ROE_1 exceeds ER_s. This say that a growth company must have a return on equity greater than the return require

growth company
Company whose net present value of future investm͠ᵗ opportuͫ…

---

[8]The numbers may differ slightly from equation results due to rounding.

[9]The growth term can be negative if g is less than $(ER_s \times b)$. see Implication 3, following.

Exhibit 14.2 ✦ SUMMARY OF THE AMERICAN HOME PRODUCTS EXAMPLE

EPS_1 = $2.00
DIV_1 = $.95   Dividend Payout Ratio = $0.95/$2.00 = 47.5 percent
RE_1 = $1.05   Retention Ratio = b = $1.05/$2.00 = 52.5 percent
ER_s = 0.135

No Growth Company Value:

Value of AHP if growth equals zero and all earnings are paid out as dividends.
PV = $2.00/0.135 = $14.815

Present Value of Growth Opportunities (PVGO):

ROE_1 = 0.23
Growth rate, $g = ROE_1 \times b = 0.23 \times 0.525 = 12$ percent
$NPV_1 = [\$0.2415/0.135] - \$1.05 = \$0.739$
$\qquad PV[NPV_1] = \$0.739/(1 + .0135) = \$0.651$
$NPV_2 = [\$0.271/0.135] - \$1.177 = \$0.828$
$\qquad PV[NPV_2] = \$0.828/(1 + 0.135)_2 = \$0.643$

Intrinsic Value:

$$V_{s0} = \frac{\$2.00}{0.135}\left[1 + \left(\frac{0.12 - (0.135)(0.525)}{0.135 - 0.12}\right)\right] = \$63.33$$

Exhibit 14.3 ✦ GRAPHICAL SUMMARY OF THE AHP EXAMPLE

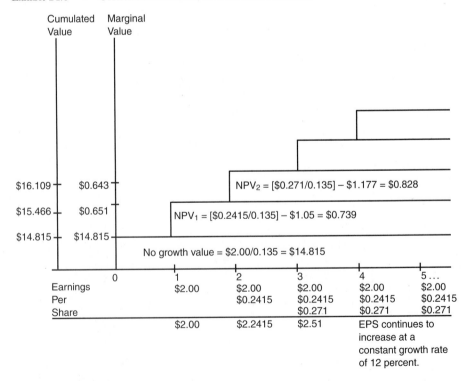

by stockholders.[10] Five implications of this relationship can help investors identify the characteristics of a growth company.

Implication 1.

Not every expanding company is a growth company. Suppose that a stockbroker informs you that General Motors (GM) is expanding extensively, building new warehouses and factories. Is GM a growth company? Its accounting data show growth in the form of increasing fixed assets. However, an astute investor should ask, "What is the company's return on these investments?" Expanding assets do not necessarily constitute growth; the return generated by the increased asset investment is critical. Only if a company's return exceeds the required return does it constitute a growth company.

Implication 2.

Earning positive returns is not enough! Even if the company's investments earn an overall rate of return equal to the return required by stockholders, it is not a growth company. Again, it must exceed the required return, or 13.5 percent for AHP.

Implication 3.

If the company's investments earn a positive overall rate of return less than the required rate of return, it is not a positive growth company but a *negative* growth company. In fact, if g is less than $ER_s(b)$, the stock has a negative growth rate. The stock's *PVGO* will be negative, indicating that company projects decrease the stock's value instead of adding value.

Implication 4.

Retaining profits ($b > 0$) by itself does not constitute growth. Again, the return generated by the invested funds determines whether a firm is a growth company.

Implication 5.

If a company cannot find any investments with returns (ROE_1) greater than the return that stockholders require (ER_s), it can maximize stockholder value by increasing cash dividends instead of retaining earnings to finance negative *NPV* projects.

Now that we understand what constitutes a growth company, let's determine the difference between a growth company and a growth stock. Although these terms seem synonymous, they are not.

Contrasting a Growth Company with a Growth Stock

As defined above, a growth company is a company that undertakes positive *NPV* projects that increase its stock value. Generally, a growth company's stock tends to appreciate as shown by the EM example. However, some exceptions arise. For example, if investors overestimate growth opportunities for a company and bid up its stock's market price based on these rosy expectations, even a growth company may become

---

[10]Actually, an economically more meaningful term for ROE_1 is the *internal rate of return, IRR,* or the rate of return on investment. If we substitute *IRR* for ROE_1, we have $IRR > ER_s$. This is the IRR decision rule for evaluating capital budgeting projects in corporate finance.

overvalued. Technical analysts may also bid up market prices based on some per-ceived buy signal. As investors realize that they may have overestimated the com-pany's opportunities, its excessive market price will decline. That's not to say that the market was wrong; the investors are simply adjusting to the economic value of the company as new information emerges.

Initial public offerings (IPOs) tend to follow this pattern. Snapple, the producer of natural fruit juices and iced tea, is an example of a growth company for which in-vestors overestimated growth. After it went public in December 1992 at $20 per share, its stock price soared. On June 16, 1993, an article in the *Wall Street Journal* mentioned Snapple in a discussion of the most overpriced stocks in the market. At that time, Snapple's P/E ratio was 256 times (a huge multiple, as we discuss later) at a market price of $62.25. The *Journal* article reported money managers' opinion that Snapple's intrinsic value based on its growth opportunities could not justify its $62.25 price. After all, the article reasoned, PepsiCo and Coca-Cola Company could easily enter the bottled iced tea market and burst Snapple's bubble. The article must have led the market to realize that expectations were too rosy, because Snapple's stock price fell to $37.75 by June 30, 1993. Snapple was acquired by Quaker Oats in 1994 for $1.7 billion. In 1997 Quaker Oats quit trying to make a go at it and sold Snapple for only $300 million![11]

growth stock
An undervalued stock or one with a market price less than its intrinsic value; it is expected to earn superior returns compared with other stocks with similar risk.

A **growth stock** is one that is currently undervalued enough to drive its return above those of other stocks at the same risk level. Shares in a growth company do not necessarily constitute a growth stock. For example, a company can be a growth com-pany because PVGO > 0, but it could be overpriced and so not a growth stock.

Alternatively, a stock can be a growth stock although the company is not a growth company. Investors may ignore a stable, unglamorous company, undervaluing its stock to the point that it offers superior returns relative to other stocks at the same risk level, assuming that the efficient market eventually recognizes its intrinsic value.

In most cases, however, we expect a growth company to be a growth stock. Our AHP example typifies a growth company that is also a growth stock because its posi-tive PVGO and the stock is currently undervalued. This says that the stock is a growth company and a good investment; the value of the investment still depends on how much it costs and returns! Someone who buys AHP at $50.5625 will earn a higher re-turn than on other stocks with the same risk because AHP's market price should rise to its economic value of about $63. The moral of all this may be that the difference between real and false growth stocks often is not obvious. Instead of assuming that a company with a positive PVGO (a growth company) is a good investment, always take that last step and compare the stock's intrinsic value with its market price to make sure it is undervalued before chasing those abnormal profits! (This may be a good time to review our discussion of company analysis in Chapter 11.)

The two stock valuation models, the DDM and the EM, are just more formal ways of evaluating common stocks relative to their trading prices. An investor may suggest that AHP is a good investment with ample growth opportunities because AHP may discover many more medical drugs and hence it is currently undervalued. This investor is informally assessing the economic value relative to its traded price.

The Investment Insights box on page 369 reinforces the importance of earn-ings growth in evaluating stock performance. The article discusses the increase in

---

[11]*Wall Street Journal*, July 25, 1997, p. B4:6.

INVESTMENT INSIGHTS

0:00   0:00

THE EFFECT OF EARNINGS ON STOCK PRICES

Earnings and revenue announcements are key factors that drive stock prices; most investors recognize that such announcements are specifically results of investment opportunities of the company. For example, on November 19, 1999, news about Hewlett-Packard (HP)'s increased revenues prompted the Nasdaq Composite Index to hit its twelfth record close in 15 trading days and also pushed the Dow Jones Industrial Average above 11,000.[1] Though much of the increase in the indexes resulted from general euphoria that HP's good news would transfer to other technology stocks, the driving force was earnings announcements. HP announced that its fourth-quarter revenue growth was strong, and its stock increase due to this good news resulted in more than half of the Dow Jones Industrial Average increase of 1.40 percent in one day, closing at 11,035.70.

On more sobering note, on November 23, 1999, an analyst at Credit Suisse First Boston recommended selling four bank stocks, Bank One, J.P. Morgan, Citigroup, and Chase Manhattan.[2] The analyst, Michael Mayo, says he wanted to call "a spade a spade" despite criticisms from his bank stock investors. Although he received heated reactions from traders of those firms, he believes his recommendations were justified. In November 1999 Mayo said bank earnings were of "poor quality" and that banks were "struggling to make their earnings targets and at some point they will start missing their estimates, and the prices will tank." His analysis revealed that bank earnings were currently inflated due to unusual gains on operations from venture capital earnings and, as these accounting extraordinary gains leveled out, their earnings would tumble. Additionally, any rate hikes would add to the troubled bottom-line earnings of banks.

To add an epilogue, on December 15, 1999, an article appeared in the *Wall Street Journal* discussing the affect of rate increases on bank stocks.[3] It seems many bank stocks were affected by shortfalls in earnings. U.S. Bancorp, a Minneapolis-based lender, announced fourth-quarter earnings would fall short of analyst expectations by about 11 percent due to rising interest rates. U.S. Bancorp stock fell 33 percent, from about $90 in early December to $63 by mid-December. Whether Mr. Mayo's call on bank stocks was warranted or not, Chase Manhattan and J.P. Morgan have both experienced a continuing decline in their stock prices, though, not anywhere near the severity experienced by regional smaller banks like U.S. Bancorp.

[1] "Tech Stocks, Sparked by H-P, Push Blue Chips Past 11,000 Once Again," *Wall Street Journal*, November 19, 1999, pp. C1 & C10.

[2] "Bearish Call on Banks Lands Analyst in Doghouse," *Wall Street Journal*, November 23, 1999, pp. C1 & C4.

[3] "Rate Boosts Hit Home for Regional Banks," *Wall Street Journal*, December 15, 1999. p. C1-C2.

Hewlett-Packard stock value when strong revenue and earnings growth were expected. On the flip side, it commented on expectations that bank stocks would suffer earnings growth due to interest rate increases and nonsustainable extraordinary earnings gains. It is important to note that *expected* earnings declines are sufficient to cause stock price declines. Of course, if the expectations are not realized, prices will probably reverse back to current levels.

RECAP

Most investors believe that a stock has an intrinsic value and that, in an efficient market, the stock price will converge to that value. We have described two models, the DDM and the EM, by which to determine a stock's intrinsic value. A sound investment decision should rely on a careful study of a company's financials (as discussed in Chapter 13), investment growth opportunities, and an estimate of its intrinsic value. The analyst also should compare the stock's intrinsic value with its market price to identify any undervalued (or growth) stocks. This step is important because no one should ever assume that a growth company is always a growth stock.

1. Johnson & Johnson (JNJ), the drug company, expects dividends to equal $1.12 next year and its earnings per share is expected to be $3.40. If the company's growth rate is estimated at 14 percent and its required return is 15 percent, what is JNJ's intrinsic value?
2. JNJ is currently trading for $102. Is JNJ an overvalued or undervalued stock? Explain.
3. If JNJ's expected ROE equals 22 percent, is JNJ a growth company? Explain why.
4. Is JNJ a growth stock? Explain why.

Fundamental Analysis in Practice

Value Line is one of many sources of information on which to base an estimate of an intrinsic value for AHP. We used many numbers to explain the two valuation models; Now let's go back to illustrate the calculation of those numbers.

Exhibit 14.4 reprints the one-page Value Line summary on AHP. Given these data, we assume that today is December 31, 1999, and that AHP's earnings, and therefore its future dividend streams, can be estimated by a constant-growth rate, g. Recall the DDM formula:

$$V_{s0} = \frac{DIV_0 (1 + g)}{ER_s - g} \tag{14.11}$$

The following are three basic steps in the process to estimate the intrinsic value of a common stock.

STEP 1: ESTIMATE GROWTH, g

Here we will describe three ways to estimate a firm's growth rate. Because the growth rate is such an important component of the estimate of intrinsic value, we use all three methods to gather as much information as possible. At the end, however, we must settle on one growth estimate.

A. Estimate a Historical Growth Trend for Dividends per Share

Using some historical time period that best illustrates the stock's expected growth in dividends, estimate an average growth rate. The analyst must, of course, decide which period best represents *future* earnings for AHP—not an easy task. Once a historical trend is designated as the best representation of future earnings, the analysis proceeds to estimate AHP's geometric average growth rate, g.

Suppose that the time period from December 31, 1994, to December 31, 1999, best represents the company's expected future dividend growth. Dividends declared per share (Value Line abbreviates this as "Div'ds Dec'd per sh") were $0.74 in 1994 and $0.91 in 1999. Find the growth rate, g, using a compounded future value formula that would make $0.74 compound over five years to equal $0.91:

$$\$0.74(1 + g)^5 = \$0.91$$
$$(1 + g)^5 = 1.2297$$
$$g = 4.22 \text{ percent}$$

Exhibit 14.4 ✦ VALUE LINE REPORT FOR AMERICAN HOME PRODUCTS (AHP)

AMER. HOME PROD. NYSE-AHP

| RECENT PRICE | 59 | P/E RATIO | 31.6 | (Trailing: 33.3 Median: 17.0) | RELATIVE P/E RATIO | 2.25 | DIV'D YLD | 1.6% | VALUE LINE |

| | | | High: | 13.7 | 13.8 | 21.6 | 21.1 | 17.3 | 16.8 | 25.0 | 33.3 | 42.4 | 58.8 | 70.3 | 60.0 | Target Price Range 2003 2004 2005 |
| TIMELINESS 3 Raised 4/28/00 | | | Low: | 10.0 | 10.8 | 11.6 | 15.8 | 13.9 | 13.8 | 15.4 | 23.5 | 28.5 | 37.8 | 36.5 | 39.4 | |

SAFETY 2 Lowered 10/29/99
TECHNICAL 3 Raised 3/10/00
BETA 1.10 (1.00 = Market)

LEGENDS
— 16.5 x "Cash Flow" p sh
.... Relative Price Strength
2-for-1 split 5/90
2-for-1 split 5/96
2-for-1 split 5/98
Options: Yes
Shaded area indicates recession

2003-05 PROJECTIONS
	Price	Gain	Ann'l Total Return
High	85	(+45%)	11%
Low	65	(+10%)	4%

Insider Decisions
	J	J	A	S	O	N	D	J	F
to Buy	0	0	0	0	0	0	0	0	0
Options	0	0	0	0	0	0	0	0	0
to Sell	0	0	0	0	0	0	0	0	0

Institutional Decisions
	2Q1999	3Q1999	4Q1999
to Buy	414	405	407
to Sell	481	502	455
Hld's(000)	885096	879460	871131

Percent shares traded 6.0 4.0 2.0

% TOT. RETURN 3/00
	THIS STOCK	VL ARITH. INDEX
1 yr.	-16.1	19.5
3 yr.	89.7	56.0
5 yr.	240.0	121.2

1984	1985	1986	1987	1988	1989	1990	1991	1992	1993	1994	1995	1996	1997	1998	1999	2000	2001	© VALUE LINE PUB., INC.	03-05
3.69	3.88	4.15	4.33	4.71	5.40	5.39	5.61	6.29	6.69	7.30	10.66	11.01	10.91	10.26	10.39	10.55	11.00	Sales per sh	17.30
.62	.67	.74	.82	.92	1.02	1.07	1.22	1.26	1.38	1.49	1.61	1.99	1.96	2.35	2.08	2.20	2.55	"Cash Flow" per sh	4.10
.53	.59	.64	.72	.80	.88	.92	1.09	1.09	1.18	1.24	1.10	1.48	1.67	1.80	1.77	1.90	2.20	Earnings per sh A	3.55
.33	.36	.39	.42	.45	.49	.54	.60	.67	.72	.74	.76	.78	.83	.87	.91	.95	1.00	Div'ds Decl'd per sh B■	1.25
.12	.15	.17	.24	.29	.20	.20	.18	.34	.42	.38	.51	.51	.64	.62	.77	.80	.80	Cap'l Spending per sh	.85
1.72	1.90	2.01	2.18	2.55	1.58	2.13	2.61	2.85	3.12	3.46	4.42	5.44	6.29	7.33	4.77	5.40	6.35	Book Value per sh C	11.80
1216.0	1207.1	1186.0	1161.8	1168.9	1250.1	1256.1	1262.5	1252.2	1241.3	1228.6	1254.8	1280.0	1300.8	1312.4	1303.9	1295.00	1288.00	Common Shs Outst'g D	1280.00
12.1	12.7	15.7	14.5	12.2	13.5	13.6	14.6	16.9	13.5	12.1	17.9	19.1	21.3	27.4	30.4	Bold figures are		Avg Ann'l P/E Ratio	21.0
1.13	1.03	1.06	.97	1.01	1.02	1.01	.93	1.02	.80	.79	1.20	1.20	1.23	1.43	1.74	Value Line estimates		Relative P/E Ratio	1.40
5.1%	4.9%	3.9%	4.0%	4.6%	4.1%	4.3%	3.8%	3.6%	4.5%	4.9%	3.8%	2.8%	2.3%	1.8%	1.7%			Avg Ann'l Div'd Yield	1.7%

CAPITAL STRUCTURE as of 12/31/99
Total Debt $5581.1 mill. Due in 5 Yrs $2245.0 mill.
LT Debt $3668.6 mill. LT Interest $210.0 mill.
(LT interest earned: 16.4x; Total interest coverage: 15.9x) (37% of Cap'l)

Pension Liability None
Pfd Stock $.1 mill. Pfd Div'd $.05 mill.
24,241 shs. ($2.50 par) callable at $60 ea. cv. into 36.0 com. shs. (Less than 1% of Cap'l)

Common Stock 1,303,916,000 shs. (63% of Cap'l)
MARKET CAP: $76.9 billion (Large Cap)

	6775	7079	7873	8304	8966	13376	14088	14196	13463	13550	13635	14200	Sales ($mill)	22100
	25.0%	26.6%	26.9%	26.9%	27.7%	23.9%	26.6%	25.6%	27.0%	25.6%	26.5%	28.0%	Operating Margin	30.0%
	179.8	167.2	210.2	241.1	306.2	679.2	658.0	394.3	371.1	386.0	400	420	Depreciation ($mill)	700
	1159.5	1375.3	1370.7	1469.3	1528.3	1337.5	1883.4	2160.1	2714.8	2319.9	2460	2840	Net Profit ($mill)	4545
	24.2%	21.9%	29.5%	26.3%	24.7%	36.2%	31.6%	27.9%	30.9%	27.1%	30.0%	30.0%	Income Tax Rate	30.0%
	17.1%	19.4%	17.4%	17.7%	17.1%	10.0%	10.0%	13.4%	15.2%	20.2%	18.0%	20.0%	Net Profit Margin	20.5%
	2797.4	2849.0	3059.4	3223.3	3203.2	3429.8	3132.8	3034.3	3744.9	2627.9	2615	2930	Working Cap'l ($mill)	3500
	776.6	104.7	601.9	859.3	9973.2	7808.8	6020.6	5031.9	3853.2	3668.6	2560	2560	Long-Term Debt ($mill)	3000
	2675.2	3300.6	3562.6	3876.5	5543.0	6962.1	8175.3	9614.8	6214.7	6990	8140	Shr. Equity ($mill)	15075
	35.5%	40.5%	33.3%	31.4%	12.8%	11.9%	16.1%	17.2%	20.9%	24.5%	26.5%	27.0%	Return on Total Cap'l	25.5%
	43.3%	41.7%	38.5%	37.9%	35.9%	24.1%	27.1%	26.4%	28.2%	37.3%	35.0%	35.0%	Return on Shr. Equity	30.0%
	18.1%	19.0%	15.1%	15.0%	14.7%	7.3%	12.8%	13.3%	16.3%	18.3%	17.5%	19.0%	Retained to Com Eq	19.5%
	58%	54%	61%	60%	59%	70%	53%	50%	42%	51%	50%	45%	All Div'ds to Net Prof	35%

CURRENT POSITION ($MILL.)
	1997	1998	12/31/99
Cash Assets	1099.7	1301.5	2413.3
Receivables	2843.1	3276.6	3280.3
Inventory (FIFO)	2412.4	2237.9	2244.8
Other	1006.1	1139.6	1799.7
Current Assets	7361.3	7955.6	9738.1
Accts Payable	794.3	681.0	757.8
Debt Due	89.0	79.7	1912.5
Other	3443.7	3450.0	4439.9
Current Liab.	4327.0	4210.7	7110.2

ANNUAL RATES
of change (per sh)	Past 10 Yrs.	Past 5 Yrs.	Est'd '97-'99 to '03-'05
Sales	8.0%	9.5%	8.5%
"Cash Flow"	9.0%	9.0%	11.5%
Earnings	8.0%	8.5%	12.5%
Dividends	7.0%	4.5%	6.0%
Book Value	11.5%	14.5%	11.5%

QUARTERLY SALES ($ mill.)
Calendar	Mar.31	Jun.30	Sep.30	Dec.31	Full Year
1997	3603	3499	3481	3613	14196
1998	3667	3342	3224	3230	13463
1999	3443	3319	3321	3467	13550
2000	3336	3350	3400	3549	13635
2001	3550	3550	3550	3550	14200

EARNINGS PER SHARE A
Calendar	Mar.31	Jun.30	Sep.30	Dec.31	Full Year
1997	.45	.36	.43	.43	1.67
1998	.50	.40	.46	.44	1.80
1999	.50	.34	.48	.45	1.77
2000	.49	.45	.48	.48	1.90
2001	.55	.50	.60	.55	2.20

QUARTERLY DIVIDENDS PAID B■
Calendar	Mar.31	Jun.30	Sep.30	Dec.31	Full Year
1996	.192	.192	.192	.205	.78
1997	.2055	.205	.205	.215	.83
1998	.215	.215	.215	.225	.87
1999	.225	.225	.225	.230	.91
2000	.230				

BUSINESS:
American Home Products Corporation is a leading manufacturer of prescription, over-the-counter, and proprietary drugs (infant formulas, cold remedies). Important product names include *Advil, Anacin, Dimetapp, Dristan, Norplant, Orudis, Premarin, Robitussin, Naprelan, Rapamune.* Acquired A.H. Robins, '89; American Cyanamid, '94; Genetics Institute, '96; Solvay S.A., '97; Solgar Vitamin and Herb Co., '98. Divested household products unit, '90. Food unit, '97. Medical devices business, '98. Int'l business: 43% of sales. '99 dep. rate: 5.5%. Estimated plant age: 10 yrs. Has 51,656 employees; 62,482 common stockholders. Chairman: J.R. Stafford. Inc.: DE. Address: Five Giralda Farms, Madison, NJ 07940. Tel.: 973-660-5000. Internet: www.ahp.com.

American Home Products' proposed merger with Warner-Lambert was unsuccessful. We attribute this mainly to the fact that arch-rival Pfizer's takeover bid was some 20% higher than AHP's. On a speculative note, we think the rising tide of lawsuits surrounding the company's diet drugs, *Redux* and *Pondimin*, may have also dampened the merger's chances somewhat. In any event, AHP received a $1.8 billion break-up fee from Warner-Lambert (which was used to reduce debt).

Meanwhile, the company recently announced it would sell its Cyanamid Agricultural Products business to BASF for $3.8 billion in cash plus the assumption of certain liabilities. Though AHP would give up around 13% of annual revenues, we think the strategy makes sense, given that the operation had been struggling for a while, due largely to heavy competition and lower worldwide demand for grain. We estimate that the transaction would be dilutive to 2000 share net by between $0.03 and $0.05, but our figures will not reflect this until the deal closes (expected on June 30th). Proceeds from the divestiture could be used for debt reduc-

tion, share repurchases, or to help fund AHP's proposed $4.75 billion national settlement for its two diet drugs.

The company's long-term prospects look bright. AHP is a leading provider of a broad array of commonly used prescription drugs, nutritionals, vaccines, and over-the-counter medications. Moreover, with significant foreign operations, we think it has tremendous upside earnings potential. Another plus for the company is its promising drug-development pipeline, which may greatly bolster results in the coming years.

These good-quality shares have rebounded nicely over the past few months, partly reflecting, we believe, the market's approval of AHP's sale of its agricultural products business. Another factor that may be driving the stock is indications that the diet-drug settlement case may be resolved soon. Nevertheless, the sharp run-up in price has greatly diminished the equity's 3- to 5-year appreciation potential. And for the coming year, AHP shares are ranked only average for relative price performance.

Frederick L. Harris, III *April 28, 2000*

(A) Primary egs. thru 1996, basic after. Next egs. report due late July. Excl. nonrec. gains (losses): '84, 2¢; '86, 5¢; '90, 12¢; '92, 36¢; '94, 22¢; '95, 57¢; '97, (9¢); '98, 25¢; '99,

($2.71)'; '00, 85¢. Excl. loss from discontinued ops.: '00, $1.13. Incl. restruct. charge: '95, 19¢. (B) Next dividend meeting about July 20th. Next ex date about Aug. 10th. Dividend pay-

ment dates: March 1, June 1, Sept. 1, Dec. 1. ■ Dividend reinvestment plan available.
(C) Incl. intang. In '99: $7725.0 mill., $5.92/sh.
(D) In millions, adjusted for splits.

Company's Financial Strength	A+
Stock's Price Stability	60
Price Growth Persistence	75
Earnings Predictability	85

Extrapolating from the historical dividend growth trend, the future growth rate should equals only 4.22 percent.

B. Estimate a Historical Growth Trend for Earnings per Share

Using the same method over the same period, the earnings per share grew from $0.51 in 1986 to $1.83 in 1996. Thus, g equals

$$\$1.24(1 + g)^5 = \$1.80$$
$$(1 + g)^5 = 1.4516$$
$$g = 7.74 \text{ percent}$$

Extrapolating from AHP's historical earnings trend, its estimated growth rate equals 7.74 percent.

C. Earnings Model Growth Definition

Finally, the growth definition in the EM (Equation 14.9) can give an estimate of AHP's growth rate. Notice that AHP has preferred stock outstanding; this analysis should focus on ROE for common equity only. Calculate ROE by subtracting preferred dividends from net profits after taxes and by subtracting preferred stocks outstanding from net worth. Also to find expected ROE, ROE_1, use the year 2000 estimates.[12] AHP's net profits equal $2,615 million, and its net worth equals $11,440 million, whereas preferred dividends equal only $0.05 million and preferred stock outstanding equals only $0.1 million.[13] Because the amount of preferred stock outstanding is so minimal for AHP, it can probably be ignored, but we will go through the calculations. If we were to ignore it, ROE_1 could be obtained from Value Line under the definition of "Return on Shr. Equity." ROE_1 can be calculated as follows:

$$ROE_1 = \frac{\$2615 - \$0.05}{\$11440 - \$0.10} - 0.2286 = 23 \text{ percent}$$

The common stock dividend payout ratio has already been calculated as

$$\text{Dividend payout ratio} = \frac{DIV_1}{EPS_1} = \frac{\$0.95}{\$2.00} = 0.475$$

Now, AHP's growth, using Equation 14.9, is

$$\begin{aligned} g &= ROE_1 \times b \\ &= ROE_1 \times (1 - \text{Dividend payout ratio}) \\ &= 0.23 \times (1 - .475) \\ &= 12.0 \text{ percent} \end{aligned}$$

This definition of growth gives an estimate of the expected growth rate equal to 12.0 percent.

---

[12]Remember that today is the last day in 1999, and that 2000 data will provide expected return on equity (ROE_1) one year from today.

[13]We assume AHP's preferred stock outstanding and dividends remain constant between 1999 and 2000.

STEP 2: ESTIMATE ER_s

Using the capital asset pricing model (CAPM), we can estimate the required return on AHP stock.[14] The CAPM states

$$ER_s = RF + \beta(ER_M - RF) \tag{14.12}$$

The risk-free rate, RF, found in the *Wall Street Journal*, quotes Treasury bond yields at 4 percent annually. The yield spread for the market return, $(ER_M - RF)$, is estimated at approximately 8.6 percent by using the results of historical spreads documented by Ibbotson Associates. Beta, a relative risk measure, found in Value Line, equals 1.10 for AHP.

Based on these numbers, AHP's expected return equals

$$ER_s = 0.04 + 1.10[.086] = 0.1346 = 13.5 \text{ percent}$$

STEP 3: ESTIMATE DIV_1 OR $DIV_0 (1 + g)$

Multiply AHP's dividends per share declared for the current year-end by $(1 + g)$ to obtain DIV_1. An alternative method is to multiply EPS_1 by the dividend payout ratio.

To find DIV_1 in this way, we must set a growth rate that is appropriate for AHP. Because Equation 14.9 attempts to capture expected growth (instead of historical growth), it probably gives the best estimate. This means that DIV_1 equals

$$DIV_1 = DIV_0 (1 + g) = \$0.91(1 + 0.12) = \$1.0192$$

Given the estimates from the three steps and using Equation 14.11,

$$V_{s0} = \frac{DIV_0 (1 + g)}{ER_s - g} = \frac{\$0.91(1 + 0.12)}{0.135 - 0.12} = \$68$$

Alternatively, using EM (Equation 14.10) to estimate AHP's intrinsic value, we have

$$V_{s0} = \frac{\$2.00}{0.135} \left[1 + \left(\frac{0.12 - (0.135)(0.525)}{0.135 - 0.12} \right) \right] = \$63.33$$

These estimates indicate that AHP's intrinsic value is approximately in the mid-$60s per share. Compared with the recent price of $50.5625, the fundamental analyst would say that the stock is undervalued and recommend purchasing it.

Given reasonably efficient markets, and assuming that other market participants agree with our assessment and assumptions, AHP should increase to the mid-$60s range. Before you call your broker, however, consider some caveats.

CAVEATS FOR THE DIVIDEND DISCOUNT MODEL

"Assuming that other market participants agree with our assessment" expresses an important assumption called **homogeneous expectations.** Without this condition, we cannot guarantee that the stock price will converge to the intrinsic value. If other investors have different expectations about AHP, they should arrive at different intrinsic values and different investment decisions, even if they use the same DDM formula.

homogeneous expectations
Assumption about the investors in the market having the same future expectations about a stock.

---

[14]The CAPM is discussed in detail in Chapter 18. The equation attempts to measure an investor's required rate of return for a given stock beta risk relative to the overall market risk.

Further, the DDM is very sensitive to the estimates of the growth rate and the required return on stock ER_s. For example, decreasing the estimate of AHP's growth rate by 1 percent to 11 percent would drop the stock's intrinsic value to $40.40 instead of $63.00. That is a $22.60 difference for a one percentage point difference in the growth estimate. This change would make AHP appear overvalued, not undervalued.

Another variable is equally difficult to estimate: the yield spread between the market portfolio and the risk-free rate, or $(ER_M - RF)$. Ibbotson Associates estimates the yield spread for common stocks between 1926 to 1993 at 8.6 percent, but a yield spread estimate over a shorter period would fall to between 5 and 6 percent. Using a 6 percent yield spread and a 11 percent growth rate results in an intrinsic value estimate for AHP of $-$252.525. This leads to our third caveat: be wary of unreasonable numbers. An intrinsic value can never be negative! It does not make sense to estimate that AHP has negative economic value. In fact, when $g > ER_s$, stop and use another method to calculate intrinsic value because the constant growth assumption is violated!

This warning ties in with the earlier problem with the growth variable. Besides being very sensitive to the growth estimate, the DDM uses an ROE_1 value in the growth estimate that comes from accounting relationships, not a market value or an economic value. This value may not accurately reflect the stock's true expected return on investment. A more meaningful number may be the internal rate of return (IRR) on the firm's investment projects, but that number is not publicly available. (Review footnote 11) Use ROE_1 only with great caution. Again, if the final intrinsic value estimate is unreasonable, be suspicious of ROE_1 or growth estimate.

A final caveat. If a company does not pay dividends, it does not mean its intrinsic value equals zero as the DDM seems to suggest. Unfortunately, the EM cannot be used to estimate an intrinsic value for a company that pays no dividends. Under a later section where P/E ratios are discussed, a modified method is introduced to overcome the zero dividend problem. This alternative method also works well for stocks with $g > ER_s$.

These caveats also apply to the EM, and the moral is the same. An investor needs to carefully study a company's investment opportunities before attempting to estimate its intrinsic value to determine whether the stock might be overvalued or undervalued.

RECAP We analyzed AHP's intrinsic value using the DDM and the EM. Once we determined an intrinsic value, we compared it with the stock's market price. If market price is less than the intrinsic value, the stock is considered undervalued. If market price is greater than the intrinsic value, the stock is overvalued. In this way, fundamental analysis provides a decision rule to buy or sell. Suppose Johnson & Johnson (JNJ) financial data are given below.

	1994	1999	Est. 2000
EPS	$1.56	$2.15	$2.45
DIV	0.57	1.12	1.25
ROE			0.22
Div payout			0.37
Beta	1.22		
Market price	$102		

5. Estimate the historical growth trend for dividends per share for the five year period.
6. Estimate the historical growth trend for earnings per share for the five year period.
7. Estimate growth rate using Equation 14.9, $g = ROE_1 \times (1 - \text{dividend payout ratio})$.
8. Estimate ER_s via the CAPM or Equation 14.12, if the risk-free rate equals 0.04 and the market risk premium equals 0.086.
9. Estimate JNJ's intrinsic value.
10. Is the stock overvalued or undervalued? Explain.

Fundamental analysis clarifies the old adage "Buy low, sell high." The analysis answers the equally old question, how low is low? When market price falls below the intrinsic value, it is time to buy. How high is high? When market price is greater than the intrinsic value, it is high enough to sell. The decision rule is an old one, but finding intrinsic value in a rational, logical way adds credibility to fundamental analysis.

This process has worked when dividends or earnings grow at nearly a constant rate, g. Suppose, however, that dividends and earnings do not follow a constant-growth rate. Even worse, what if growth is greater than the required return on a stock? Notice in Equation 14.11 that V_{s0} is negative if g is greater than ER_s, but in a rational world, stocks can never have negative values.[15] The next section discusses a nonconstant-growth model that allows for variation in the growth rate, even to exceed the required return in some years.

Nonconstant-Growth Model

Here we will modify the DDM to apply it to stocks with different growth rates over various years, including growth rates that exceed expected returns. First, let's discuss whether a stock's growth rate *can* be greater than its required rate of return. Suppose a stock's expected growth rate is 20 percent and the return required by stockholders, ER_s, equals 15 percent. Corporate finance often defines the required rate of return as

$$ER_s = \text{Dividend yield} + \text{Growth rate}$$

assuming a *constant-growth* rate. Based on the formula, a stock cannot grow at a constant rate higher than ER_s for an indefinite period because growth is a component of the expected, or required, rate of return, ER_s. Constant higher growth would, therefore, drive the expected return higher as well. Eventually, then, the growth rate must fall below the required rate of return. Stated differently, growth cannot exceed the required return forever (that is, the growth rate must be nonconstant). This implies that two growth phases must exist: (1) a phase with a nonconstant-growth rate, g, higher than the required return, and (2) a phase with a constant-growth rate, g, less than the required return. Let's see how we can apply a model with a two-phase growth rate.

STEP 1: DETERMINE THE VALUE FOR THE NONCONSTANT-GROWTH PHASE

Suppose that a company is expected to grow at a nonconstant rate of 20 percent for four years and then to grow at a lower rate of 10 percent indefinitely. If the current

---

[15]A negative value says that you would pay me to take the stock from you. Rarely does someone pay to give up something, except for garbage, perhaps.

dividend per share is $2, we can determine the future dividend stream up to Year 4 in the following way:

Year	Dividend per Share
1	$2.00(1 + 0.20) = $2.40
2	2.00(1 + 0.20)² = 2.88
3	2.00(1 + 0.20)³ = 3.46
4	2.00(1 + 0.20)⁴ = 4.15

Because the stock's intrinsic value is the present value of its future dividend stream, we can find the present value of each dividend for the nonconstant-growth period. If stockholders' required rate of return equals 15 percent, each of these future dividends has a present value of

Year	Dividend per Share	Present Value Factor at 15 Percent	Present Value
1	$2.40	0.8696	$2.087
2	2.88	0.7561	2.178
3	3.46	0.6575	2.275
4	4.15	0.5718	2.373
		Total present value of nonconstant-growth dividend stream:	$8.913

A timeline illustrates the cash flows from the nonconstant-growth phase, each cash flow's present value, and the sum of those present values.[16]

TIMELINE FOR NONCONSTANT-GROWTH CASH FLOWS

0	1	2	3	4	5
	$2.40	$2.88	$3.46	$4.15	.....

PV
$2.087 ←
2.178 ←
2.275 ←
2.373 ←
$8.913

Therefore, the present value of the stock in its nonconstant-growth phase equals $8.913.

STEP 2: DETERMINE THE VALUE FOR THE CONSTANT-GROWTH PHASE

Now, let's examine the second phase when the stock's growth falls back to a constant rate. For a moment, suppose we jump forward to Year 4, after which the stock is expected to grow at 10 percent annually with a required rate of return of 15 percent; using the DDM, we can estimate a value for the stock during this period. Treating Year 4 as Year 0, DIV_4 ($4.15) replaces DIV_{s0} and

$$V_{s4} = \frac{DIV_4(1 + g)}{ER_s - g} = \frac{\$4.15(1 + 0.10)}{0.15 - 0.10} = \$91.30$$

---

[16]Timelines are often used in corporate finance to display present value problems. See, for example, Eugene Brigham, *Fundamentals of Financial Management*, 8th ed., Fort Worth, TX: Dryden, 1998.

Recall that this is a Year 4 value. To really find the present value of this future value at Year 0, we must multiply the future value by the present value factor for 15 percent:

$$\$91.30/(1 + 0.15)^4 = \$91.30(0.5718) = \$52.205$$

The timeline below illustrates how the present value of each constant-growth cash flow at Year 4 becomes one cash flow, V_{s4}, for which we find the present value at Year 0:

TIMELINE OF CONSTANT-GROWTH CASH FLOWS

0	1	2	3	4	5	6
				\$4.15	\$4.15(1 + g)	\$4.15(1 + g)^2
				0	1	2

$$V_{s4} = \frac{DIV_0(1 + g)}{ER_s - g}$$

$$V_{s4} = \frac{\$4.15(1 + 0.10)}{0.15 - 0.10}$$

$$V_{s4} = \$91.30$$

PV of constant-growth phase

$$= \frac{V_{s4}}{(1 + ER_s)^4}$$

$$= \frac{\$91.30}{(1 + 0.15)^4}$$

$$= \$52.205$$

Therefore, the value of the stock in its constant-growth rate phase equals \$52.205.

STEP 3: CALCULATE THE INTRINSIC VALUE OF THE TWO-PHASE NONCONSTANT-GROWTH STOCK

Finally, combine the present value of future dividends from the nonconstant-growth phase with the present value of future dividends from the constant-growth phase:

$$V_{s0} = [PV \text{ of nonconstant-growth phase}] + [PV \text{ of constant-growth phase}]$$
$$= [\$8.913] + [\$52.205]$$
$$= \$61.12$$

GENERAL FORMULA FOR THE NONCONSTANT-GROWTH MODEL

The general formula for the two-phase growth model assumes that the constant-phase growth rate remains the same indefinitely and that it is less than the required rate of return, ER_s:

$$V_{s0} = \sum_{t=1}^{T} \frac{DIV_0(1 + g_n)^t}{(1 + ER_s)^t} + \frac{DIV_0(1 + g_n)(1 + g_c)}{ER_s - g_c}\left[\frac{1}{(1 + ER_s)^T}\right] \qquad (14.13)$$

where DIV_{s0} is the current dividend per share, g_n is the nonconstant-growth rate, g_c is the constant-growth rate when g_n is less than ER_s, ER_s is the required rate of return, and T is the number of years that the stock grows at the nonconstant-growth rate.

The model can be extended to three or more phases as long as the last phase is a constant-growth phase. The example below shows how to extend to three different growth rates.

THREE-PHASE NONCONSTANT-GROWTH MODEL

Suppose that a firm's current dividend of $2 is expected to grow at 20 percent for the first two years, then to decline to 10 percent for the next three years, and finally to settle at an 8 percent constant rate thereafter. The timeline below illustrates the process, which closely resembles the two-phase model:

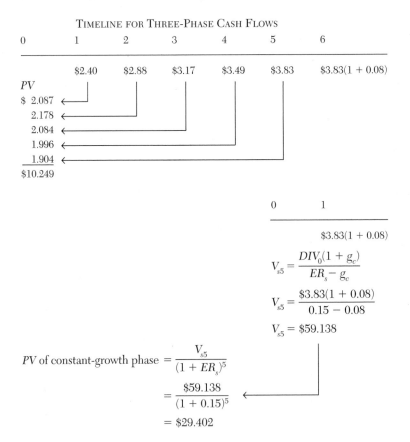

TIMELINE FOR THREE-PHASE CASH FLOWS

0	1	2	3	4	5	6
	$2.40	$2.88	$3.17	$3.49	$3.83	$3.83(1 + 0.08)

PV
$2.087
2.178
2.084
1.996
1.904
$10.249

0	1
	$3.83(1 + 0.08)

$$V_{s5} = \frac{DIV_0(1 + g_c)}{ER_s - g_c}$$

$$V_{s5} = \frac{\$3.83(1 + 0.08)}{0.15 - 0.08}$$

$$V_{s5} = \$59.138$$

$$PV \text{ of constant-growth phase} = \frac{V_{s5}}{(1 + ER_s)^5}$$

$$= \frac{\$59.138}{(1 + 0.15)^5}$$

$$= \$29.402$$

First, the timeline shows the present value of the nonconstant-growth phase, including both the 20 percent growth phase and the 10 percent growth phase (step 1); this equals $10.249. It next shows the present value of the constant-growth phase (step 2), $29.402. Finally, it combines the two nonconstant-growth phase values with the constant-growth phase value to find the intrinsic value: $10.249 + $29.402 = $39.651.

Notice that it does not matter how many different nonconstant-growth rates a stock has. This process finds the present value of each cash flow separately in step 1.

ESTIMATING THE NONCONSTANT AND CONSTANT-GROWTH RATES

Now, let's briefly discuss how we can estimate these growth rates. The nonconstant-growth rate for Year 1 can be estimated using Equation 14.9:

$$g = ROE_1 \times b$$

Value Line reports usually provide estimates of companies' return on equity and dividend payout ratios for the following year in bold type. Remember, the retention rate, b, equals (1 − dividend payout ratio). How long will the company grow at the super-growth rate? Again, that is difficult to estimate, but four to five years is a good approximation.

Value Line can provide data for next year, but how do you estimate a constant-growth rate for a stock several years from today? This is more difficult. One suggestion is to enter an industry average ROE into Equation 14.9 and assume that the stock will approximate the return of the average industry firm when it can no longer grow at a nonconstant rate. Value Line provides industry data, as do other sources.[17]

The two-phase model may more accurately value a high-growth company than a constant-growth DDM could. For example, Dole Foods Co., Inc., the well-known pineapple and fruit juice company, is expected to grow at 19.6 percent based on its ROE_1 and its retention rate (23% × 0.85); however, Value Line expects the foods industry overall to grow at 10 percent. Dole Foods would have trouble sustaining a 19.6 percent growth rate indefinitely while its industry was growing at 10 percent. The two-phase model should give a better value for a high-growth company such as Dole Foods.

RECAP

We examine a valuation process for a nonconstant-growth stock when growth is greater than required rate of return. We apply a modified, two-phase DDM with two growth rates, a nonconstant-growth rate, g_n, that was greater than the required rate of return and a constant-growth rate, g_c, that was less than the required rate of return.

11. Suppose that Dole Foods Co., Inc., is expected to grow at 20 percent for five years, after which its growth rate will decline to a constant rate of 10 percent. If Dole Foods' current dividends per share are $0.70, what is its intrinsic value?

Now, we turn to a third method that investors use to find undervalued stocks. It has become increasingly popular due to recommendations by some researchers.[18]

Relative Valuation Techniques

Market-to-Book Ratio

Another valuation method based on the **market-to-book ratio (MV/BV)** has become popular in recent years as a way to find undervalued stocks. The ratio is defined as

$$MV/BV = \frac{\text{Total market value of stock}}{\text{Total assets} - \text{Total debt} - \text{Preferred stock}} \quad (14.14)$$

where MV, the total market value of the stock equals the stock's market price per share multiplied by the number of shares outstanding, and BV, the company's total

market-to-book ratio (MV/BV)
Market price per share/book value per share; stocks with low MV/BV (MV/BV < 1) are considered good potential investments.

---

[17]Other sources are the *Standard & Poor's Industry Survey* and the Standard & Poor's Statistical Service.

[18]Eugene Fama and Kenneth French, "The Cross-Section of Expected Stock Returns," *Journal of Finance*, June 1992, pp. 427–66.

assets minus total debt minus preferred stock, measures the book value of common equity or common stock.

If the company does absolutely nothing to generate sales, the market value of its stock should approximately equal its book value. *Book value* measures the equity value of the firm if it were to sell all its assets and pay off all its debts and preferred stock at the values on its balance sheet. Book value presumably gives the company's value, assuming it were to stop operating and liquidate. When the company does nothing, market value equals book value and the ratio MV/BV equals 1.0.

This means that if MV/BV is less than 1.0, someone could profit by buying enough shares of the stock to gain a controlling interest in the company and sell its assets for book value. For example, suppose that a company has a ratio of MV/BV equal to 0.8. This ratio says that the stock is selling for $0.80 per share for every $1.00 of its equity's book value. Someone might buy up all the shares at $0.80, take control of the company, and liquidate it for $1.00 per share, making $0.20 per share on the investment, a 20 percent return. During the mergermania of the 1980s, corporate raiders such as T. Boone Pickens became well known for this strategy.

An investor who has smaller financial means could still reason that the stock was undervalued because its shares should be worth at least its book value. In an efficient market, investors would force management to take action so that the ratio comes closer to 1.0. The stockholders may even replace the old management with a more efficient group or create incentives for them to make better investment decisions (positive net present value investments).

Based on this kind of scenario, the MV/BV ratio strategy directs investors to buy stocks of firms that have low MV/BV ratios. A company turnaround should, it is hoped, raise the stock's market value at least to its book value.

What type of stock has an MV/BV ratio greater than 1.0 or market value greater than book value? Growth companies, such as those discussed in the section on the EM, for one. Investors may bid up market value above book value because the value generated by the firm's investment opportunities is greater than its liquidated value. The ratio above 1.0 suggests that the firm is actually earning positive returns on its investments (positive net present values), raising its value above that of a similar company doing nothing (which would be worth its book value).

Remember from the discussion of the EM, however, that shares in growth companies do not necessarily represent growth stocks. To invest in growth stocks, one must find stocks that are undervalued (with market values less than their intrinsic values) to earn returns superior to those of other stocks with the same risk level.

BEWARE OF MV/BV

Unfortunately, the MV/BV ratio cannot distinguish between the overvalued stocks with MV/BV greater than 1.0 and undervalued growth stocks with MV/BV greater than 1.0. Stated differently, because market value is the market price, not intrinsic value, MV/BV can be greater than 1.0 in two cases: (1) MV/BV greater than 1.0 with market value greater than intrinsic value (an overvalued stock) and (2) MV/BV greater than 1.0 with market value less than intrinsic value (undervalued growth stock). Investors want to find the second type, not the first.

Another danger with MV/BV is that the book value may differ from the company's true liquidation value. Even if market value is less than book value, liquidation may not generate cash equal to book value. Book value is just an accounting number and may not reflect all the market forces that determine the firm's liquidation value.

For example, Value Line reported AHP's book value per share as $8.30 in 1999, when its stock was trading for approximately $50.00 (MV/BV equals 6.02). Because MV/BV is greater than 1.0, AHP is considered a growth company. We also consider it a growth stock, because it was undervalued when we compared its market value with its intrinsic value. Again, do not lose sight of the importance of examining the stock to determine the company's investment opportunities and the returns they may generate in the future, rather than blindly applying a ratio-based decision rule that has seemed to work in the past. After careful analysis, compare the stock's market price with its estimated intrinsic value to determine whether it is undervalued. The MV/BV ratio may be part of a good initial sorting process to find potential good investments but do not stop there; do the fundamental analysis described above.

Besides the MV/BV ratio, another ratio is popular with investors who hunt for undervalued stocks. It is called the P/E ratio.

Price/Earnings Ratio

The **price/earnings ratio,** more often referred to as the P/E ratio, is a commonly used measure to which investors refer when searching for potential investments. However, many pitfalls complicate fundamental valuation using the P/E ratio. This section starts with a discussion of how an investor may view the P/E ratio and then delves into some of the underlying problems.

The P/E ratio is defined as

$$\text{P/E ratio} = \frac{\text{Market price per share}}{\text{Earnings per share}} \qquad (14.15)$$

price/earnings ratio (P/E) Market price per share/earnings per share. Some investors buy low-P/E stocks because they believe low P/E stocks are cheap; others buy high-P/E stocks because they believe these stocks are popular.

INTERPRETING P/E RATIOS

Given the definition above, how would an investor interpret P/E to make an investment decision? Suppose two firms, Apple and IBM, have P/E ratios of 10 and 15. An investor might interpret the P/E of 10 as indicating that the stock is selling for 10 times the company's earnings; that is, the stock price per share is 10 times the company's earnings per share (usually written as 10X). They often view the ratios as a unit-pricing scale. Apple's P/E of 10X means that the market values the stock at $10 per $1 of company earnings, whereas it values IBM at $15 per $1 of earnings. This resembles grocery shopping, in which ground chuck may sell for $2.50 per pound whereas sirloin steak sells for $3.75 per pound. Both IBM and sirloin steak appear more expensive.[19] An investor may reason that Apple can provide the same dollar of earnings more cheaply than IBM, hence the stock may appear more attractive. This investor believes that the low P/E stock pays a greater return because it cost less for the same $1 of earnings.

Another investor may reason that the market values IBM's $1 in earnings at $15 whereas it values Apple's $1 at only $10; therefore the market considers IBM more valuable and more likely to rise in price. This investor may purchase IBM stock. As Exhibit 14.5 indicates, both types of investors are right. Unfortunately, not all stocks beat the Standard & Poor's (S&P) 500 Index or the market benchmark all the time.

---

[19]Of course, we in no way imply that Apple is analogous to ground chuck and IBM to sirloin steak.

Exhibit 14.5 ✦ HOLDING PERIOD RETURN FOR LOW P/E AND HIGH P/E
STOCKS FROM 1986 TO 1996 AND 1991 TO 1996

Holding Period Return (HPR) from September 1986 to September 1996

Low P/E Stock	P/E	HPR	High P/E Stock	P/E	HPR
1. Storage Technology	3.7	37.1%	1. VICORP Restaurant	89.5	−17.6%
2. Long Island Lighting	4.2	151.4	2. Handy & Harman	85.0	30.4
3. DeBeers Consolidated	4.6	506.5	3. MCI Communications	85.0	212.4
4. McDermott International	4.7	53.0	4. Rouse Company	66.7	72.9
5. Chrysler	5.1	195.4	5. Butler International	63.3	150.0
6. Ford Motor	5.6	465.8	6. Lamson & Sessions	62.0	180.0
7. United Illuminating	6.2	75.4	7. Coherent, Inc.	60.0	166.7
8. CalFed Bancorp	6.3	−74.9	8. Comcast Corp.	60.0	493.6
9. GlenFed, Inc.	6.4	449.0	9. Homestake Mining	60.0	48.4
10. Great Western Financial	6.7	146.7	10. Hudson's Bay Company	59.5	2.1
			S&P 500 Index	—	246.5

Holding Period Return (HPR) from September 1991 to September 1996

Low P/E Stock	P/E	HPR	High P/E Stock	P/E	HPR
1. Salomon	4.3	95.1%	1. Noranda	90.0	113.3%
2. KLM Dutch	4.6	72.4	2. Media General	84.0	838.7
3. Travelers	4.7	732.0	3. LADD Furniture	73.3	−4.3
4. Telefoia Eso	5.9	165.3	4. Fieldcrest Cannon	64.0	93.4
5. Provident Life	5.5	147.5	5. Coherent, Inc.	63.6	164.3
6. Paine Webber	6.0	211.5	6. Telephone & Data	63.3	186.0
7. Safeguard Scientific	6.0	1500.0	7. ALZA Corp. 'A'	62.9	63.6
8. Aetna	6.2	264.6	8. New York Times	62.9	262.1
9. Fremont General	6.3	201.8	9. Playboy Enterprises	61.7	252.5
10. Pioneer Financial Services	6.6	303.2	10. Ampco-Pittsburgh	61.0	134.0
			S&P 500 Index	—	77.7

Exhibit 14.5 shows a sample of low-P/E and high-P/E stocks, in which the P/E ratios were calculated in 1986 and 1991, respectively. The stocks were tracked until 1996, and the exhibit shows the results of the total holding period returns for the low-P/E and high-P/E stocks. Several firms with low P/E ratios earned handsome returns from 1986 to 1996 and also from 1991 to 1996; however, many failed to earn as much as the S&P 500 Index over the same period. Firms such as DeBeers Consolidated, the diamond company, earned a 506.5 percent return in ten years. Ford Motor (465.8 percent) and Glendale Federal, Inc. (449.0 percent) both have tremendous returns over the ten-year period; however, several companies did not exceed the S&P 500 Index return of 246.5 percent. The five-year period had 9 out of 10 stocks outperform the S&P 500 Index return of 77.7 percent. Of the nine stocks, Safeguard Scientific (1500.0 percent) and Travelers (732.0 percent) had the highest returns, followed by Pioneer Financial Services (303.2 percent), Aetna Insurance Company (264.6 percent), Paine Webber (211.5 percent), and Fremont General (201.8 percent).

How did the high-P/E stocks fare? Again, the results show that high-P/E stocks did not always outperform the market (S&P 500 Index). Only one company, Comcast Corp., outperformed the S&P, with a 493.6 percent return, whereas the rest fell short. During the five-year period, high-P/E stocks fared better. Noranda (113.3 percent), Media General (838.7 percent), Fieldcrest Cannon (93.4 percent), Coherent, Inc. (164.3 percent), Telephone & Data (186.0 percent), New York Times (262.1 percent), Playboy Enterprises (252.5 percent), and Ampco-Pittsburgh (134.0 percent) outperformed the S&P 500 Index return.

Exhibit 14.5 suggests that buyers of high-P/E stocks may be buying high-demand glamour stocks. Unfortunately, glamour stocks of today may quickly become unglamorous. Further, buying at a stock's peak price increases the danger of buying overvalued investments. Clearly, P/E alone is not a good basis for choosing stocks.

The P/E ratio may have other uses, though. Can we use P/E to conduct fundamental analysis?

DETERMINING VALUE FROM P/E

A quick way of approximating a stock's value is to multiply its P/E ratio by its expected earnings per share, EPS_1:

$$V_{s0} = (\text{P/E ratio}) \times (EPS_1) \tag{14.16}$$

For AHP, this calculation would equal

$$V_{s0} = 26.8 \times \$2.00 = \$53.60$$

Does this quick estimate approximate AHP's intrinsic value? It does not, because the P/E ratio was calculated using market price per share, just like the MV/BV ratio. As you see, a value based on a P/E ratio may ignore many factors that an intrinsic value estimate must incorporate.

Let's carefully examine some of the factors that P/E-based fundamental analysis may ignore. First, the DDM can give a theoretical definition of P/E:

$$V_{s0} = \frac{DIV_1}{ER_s - g}$$

Dividing both sides of the equation by EPS_1 gives

$$\text{P/E ratio} = V_{s0}/EPS_1 = \frac{DIV_1/EPS_1}{ER_s - g} \tag{14.17}$$

This equation is a theoretical definition of the P/E ratio, substituting intrinsic value for price. It implies that the P/E ratio consists of three components:

1. DIV_1/EPS_1, the dividend payout ratio for next year's dividends and earnings
2. ER_s, the required rate of return by investors
3. g, the expected growth rate

Now, let's examine the effects of these components on the P/E ratio. Suppose that someone believes that a high P/E indicates a better investment selection and devises a strategy to buy common stocks with high P/E ratios. What factors might he look for to ensure he has made a sound investment decision when using P/E?

1. Suppose the P/E is high because the company truly has exceptional growth opportunities (that is, a high expected g leads to a high P/E). If P/E is high due to strong growth opportunities, the stock may be a reasonable investment. This is analogous to a growth company with a high intrinsic value based on high expected growth.

    Suppose the P/E ratio is high because an inexperienced analyst ignored the level of risk inherent in ER_s. The future stream of expected earnings per share of IBM is probably less risky than the future stream of expected earnings per share for Apple. In this case, P/E would be high only because the novice (in ignorance) calculated the value based on IBM's required rate of return, ER_s, rather than Apple's required rate of return, assuming that the two computer firms have similar required rates of return. Using the rate of return of a stable company as the expected return for a riskier company leads the calculated P/E ratio to overstate the true P/E.

2. Most analysts calculate a P/E ratio by dividing a stock's price per share by the firm's current earnings per share (EPS_{s0}). As our formula shows, the calculation should instead reflect expected earnings per share (EPS_1). For a firm with rising earnings, a P/E based on current earnings per share will overstate the true P/E ratio.

3. Finally, an expected earnings per share close to zero can give a large calculated P/E ratio. In fact, as expected earnings per share approaches zero, the P/E ratio approaches infinity. As an example, if a company has estimated expected earnings per share of $0.01 and a price per share of only $1, its P/E ratio equals 100 times.

After examining each component separately, we can draw the following conclusion: A P/E, high because of exceptional growth potential, may be a good reason to invest. A P/E high because the calculation included the wrong expected return for the company's risk level, cannot support a decision to invest. P/E also can deceive the investor if it fails to reflect expected earnings or if it reflects small earnings per share.

LOW-P/E STOCKS

Many of the problems we discussed for high-P/E stocks also apply to low-P/E stocks. However, proponents of the low-P/E investment strategy believe that such stocks are the best investments because they are cheap. For example, Graham and Dodd suggest that for "value" investing one should never buy a stock with a P/E higher than 12.

This strategy resembles contrarian investing (discussed in Chapter 7), which advocates buying last year's worst-performing stocks. Contrarians look for low P/Es because other investors have shunned the stocks, believing that low P/Es indicate likely candidates for undervalued stocks. Recall that Chapter 7 discussed results from several studies that examined low-P/E stocks. Generally, these stocks have seemed to earn excess returns in the past, and the studies indicate that they earn superior returns. However, researchers continue to explore why low P/Es seem to indicate consistently strong performance. The relationship has been linked to the small-firm effect, which implies strong growth in companies with low market values, and the January effect, because much of the performance advantage of small firms has occurred in January. Still, no final judgment has been passed. Like the MV/BV ratio, P/E analysis may be a good initial sorting method to identify candidates for more thorough fundamental analysis. A sound investment decision still requires detailed research about the company.

IMPLICATIONS FOR INVESTORS

The foremost problem with P/E analysis arises from basing fundamental analysis on Equation 14.15, which calculates price based on market value. Instead, Equation 14.17, which substitutes intrinsic value for price, gives a more accurate representation of company value. The best use of P/E comes from comparing values calculated by Equations 14.15 and 14.17 rather than comparing P/Es of different companies. This point helps clarify three problems with P/E-based investing.

1. It is dangerous to compare two companies' P/Es. Instead, the analyst should compare a company's intrinsic value to its market value. Comparing P/Es of two firms could ignore critical differences between them.
2. Some investors avoid high-P/E stocks because the statistic makes them look too expensive. A high P/E does not always mean that a stock is too expensive. Again, compare a company's P/E calculated from its market price (Equation 14.15) to that calculated from its intrinsic value (Equation 14.17). This comparison may make a high-P/E stock look like a bargain!
3. Similarly, some investors believe that all low-P/E stocks are cheap and likely to be undervalued. Wise investors do not rely on this likelihood; they make direct comparisons of market prices with intrinsic values. The proper comparison may reveal that a lower-P/E stock is not so cheap.

At the risk of sounding like a broken record, if a company's investment opportunities offer solid potential, it is a growth company and its shares may be a growth stock. You can identify a growth stock by comparing Equation 14.15 with Equation 14.17. If the P/E ratio is used correctly, it leads to the same investment decisions as the EM or the DDM. Given the potential of P/Es to mislead, most investors should use the EM or the DDM to perform a fundamental analysis. It is the same analysis and gives much more straightforward results.

TWO ALTERNATIVE USES FOR P/E

Those who must use P/E ratio as a way to make investment decisions could try Charles Holt's approach. Holt has developed a formula that provides a different perspective on the use of P/E ratios.[20] Instead of calculating a P/E ratio and investing based on whether it is low or high, Holt's method analyzes the stock's current growth rate and its stated P/E ratio. His formula determines the number of years the stock must grow at its current growth rate to justify the stated P/E ratio.

For example, suppose that a stock's stated P/E is 25 and its current growth rate is 20 percent, whereas the stock market's growth rate is 8 percent. If Equation 14.18 yields 21, the stock must grow at 20 percent for 21 years to justify the 25X P/E. Could this stock really grow at 20 percent for 21 years when the general market is growing at 8 percent? An alternative interpretation suggests that someone who pays 25 times the stock's earnings must hold it for 21 years to recover the investment. This method puts the company's P/E ratio in a different perspective.

---

[20]Charles Holt, "The Influence of Growth Duration on Share Prices," *Journal of Finance*, September 1962.

The formula is

$$t \text{ (in years)} = \frac{\ln[(P/E_g)/(P/Es)]}{\ln\left[\dfrac{(1 + g_g + d_g)}{(1 + g_s + d_s)}\right]} \tag{14.18}$$

where P/E_g is the P/E ratio for a growth stock, P/E_s is the P/E ratio for a stock market index (for example, the S&P 500), g_g is the growth rate of a growth stock, g_s is the growth rate of a stock market index, d_g is the dividend yield of a growth stock, and d_s is the dividend yield of a stock market index.

The Investment Insights box illustrates this alternative use of P/E for Planet Hollywood, the restaurant featuring Hollywood stars and movie memorabilia. In six months, Planet Hollywood's stock price soared from its IPO in April 1996 of $18 to $27.875, which produced a truly incredible P/E of 62 times estimated 1996 earnings of $0.45 per share. Other well-known companies had much lower P/Es that year, for example, Coca Cola (P/E 37) and McDonald's (P/E 21). First, notice that Planet Hollywood's earnings per share were relatively small, which elevated the P/E. Second, as one analyst noted, such a high P/E ratio is not sustainable even if earnings were to meet expectations. The analyst concluded that the earnings must beat the expectation in order to justify such high P/E and that the investor would realize no addition capital appreciation if the stock were purchased at this high P/E level. This interpretation is similar to the alternative use of P/E.

Let's use the appropriate numbers provided in Exhibit 14.6 for Planet Hollywood (g) and the S&P 500 Index (s) to find the number of years (t) Planet Hollywood must grow at 20 percent to justify its current P/E of 62 times.

$$t \text{ (in years)} = \frac{\ln[62/20]}{\ln\left[\dfrac{(1 + 0.40 + 0.0)}{(1 + 0.15 + 0.05)}\right]} = 7.34 \text{ years}$$

Accordingly, Planet Hollywood would have had to grow at 40 percent in order to meet analyst expectations and to maintain their high P/E ratio. As noted in the box, Planet Hollywood failed to meet these expectations and filed bankruptcy in September 1999. The firm reorganized under a new symbol, PLHYA, and traded at about $4 per share, but by December 1999 its stock price plummeted to $0.06 per share. This is a good example, though one of the most severe cases, of what happens to stock prices when companies fail to meet earnings growth already impounded in the stock price.

Interpreting Holt's method of P/E, Planet Hollywood must grow at the rate of 40 percent for almost seven and a half years to justify a P/E ratio of 62 times. What are the chances that any company can maintain a growth rate of 40 percent per year for seven years when the stock market is growing at 15 percent? If this seems unlikely, it raises questions about the reasonableness of the P/E ratio. Perhaps the P/E ratio is high because the calculation ignores risk. Perhaps the stock is simply overvalued.

A second alternative use of P/E is to value companies that currently pay no dividends. Most high technology companies that have recently been popular investment choices fall under this category. Consider a company's forecasted earnings per share

INVESTMENT INSIGHTS

PLANET HOLLYWOOD'S ASTRONOMICAL P/E RATIO

Travel back in time to late 1996. The suspect in our story is Planet Hollywood, the restaurant featuring Hollywood stars and movie memorabilia. Planet Hollywood is a new publicly traded stock with phenomenal P/E ratio, but analysts reviewing the company seem to doubt whether it can sustain its growth rate to support such a high P/E. They interpret the incredible P/E ratio similar to the alternative method of P/E by Holt. In just six months, Planet Hollywood's stock price soared from its April 1996 IPO of $18 to $27.875, which gives it a P/E ratio of 62 times estimated earnings of $0.45 per share. This is considered astounding because other global well-established companies have much lower P/E ratios, for example Coca Cola (P/E 37) and McDonald's (P/E 21). Let's conduct an investigation into whether a 62 times P/E is justifiable for Planet Hollywood.

First, notice that its earnings per share is relatively small and its P/E large. Second, analysts from a Boston money management company state that Planet Hollywood must meet and exceed analysts forecasts of earnings estimates to justify this high P/E multiple, an interpretation similar to the alternative use of P/E by Holt. Holt's interpretation states that Planet Hollywood must sustain its super-growth rate for almost 7.5 years in order to justify paying this

high P/E ratio. Our final analysis of Planet Hollywood is that the P/E ratio is too high or that the stock is overvalued because it cannot sustain the 40 percent growth rate as in the past six months.

Traveling back to our own time, we scan old financial news to discover that our analysis was on target. In September 1999, Planet Hollywood filed bankruptcy. They definitely could not maintain such a phenomenal growth rate of earnings nor justify the high P/E ratio. The chart below shows what happens to stock prices that do not meet analyst

expectations and ones that have already impounded the phenomenal growth and cannot meet it. Planet Hollywood reorganized after filing bankruptcy and traded under the symbol PLHYA. It opened at about $4 per share, but by early January 2000, the stock was trading at about $0.06 per share.

Source: Some of the information came from "P/E Reaches Stars at Planet Hollywood," by staff reports of the Wall Street Journal, *Robert McGough and Eleena de Lisser,* Wall Street Journal, *October 1996, p. C1.*

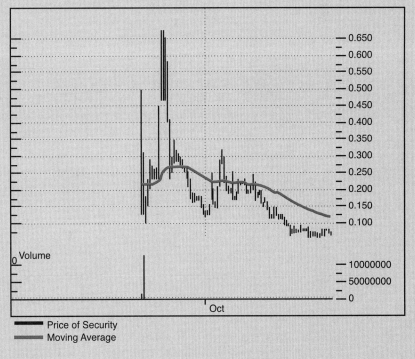

and P/E, usually provided by analysts and in investment reports. Suppose these forecasts are for three years in the future (or Year 3). Multiply the forecasted P/E and the forecasted earnings per share to obtain price for Year 3, P_3. To estimate an intrinsic value, V_{s0}, calculate the present value of P_3 using a risk-adjusted required return,

Exhibit 14.6 ✦ EFFECT OF P/E RATIO WHEN MEASURED IN t YEARS

Company	P/E Ratio (P/E)	Growth Rate (g)	Dividend yield (d)
Planet Hollywood (g)	62X	40%	0%
S&P 500 Index (s)	20X	15	5

ER_s. (ER_s) can be calculated using CAPM, as discussed in a previous section of this chapter. The intrinsic value, V_{s0}, of a stock that pays no dividends equals

$$V_{s0} = P_3/(1 + ER_s)^3 \qquad (14.19)$$

This method allows us to incorporate risk (ER_s) and expectations about the company's future earnings.

For example, Value Line forecasts Microsoft, the software company, earnings at $3 per share in 2002 and its P/E ratio at 35 times.[21] This gives a $105 (35 times $3) price for 2002 or P_3. Discounting at Microsoft's required return (ER_s equals .15), its intrinsic value is estimated at $107. Now, you can decide whether Microsoft is undervalued or overvalued by comparing its intrinsic value with the market price for Microsoft.

RECAP "If the shoe fits, wear it!" All kinds of investors, novices and money managers alike, follow this advice and use the MV/BV and P/E ratios to make investment decisions simply because they seem to work. Research studies have shown stocks with low MV/BV and low P/E ratios tend to earn superior returns, and practical investors say, "If it works, use it."

12. Johnson & Johnson's market price equals $102, and its expected earnings per share equals $3.40. What is JNJ's P/E ratio?

13. If JNJ's book value per share equals $12.50, what is its MV/BV ratio at a market price of $102?

Many money managers use criteria such as P/Es below 14 times, MV/BV ratios below 1.5 times, and price/sales per share ratios below 1.0 to define bargain stocks. Using those criteria, in 1996, they seem to favor issues such as Cyprus Amax Minerals, a company that mines copper and other minerals; American Building Maintenance, a janitorial company for office buildings; and Russ Berrie, a toy and gift marketer. Comments about American Building Maintenance, stating that the company's "fundamentals are decent," as well as the fact that their P/E is only 12 times relate closely to the discussion in this chapter. Another money manager commented that, at $20, Kmart was "dirt cheap." Perhaps her estimate of Kmart's intrinsic value was in the high 20s.

These money managers used terms similar to ours. They used low P/E and MV/BV ratios as part of initial sorting processes to find stocks that were likely to be undervalued, but they did not stop there. Most money managers continue to examine

---

[21]Microsoft earnings per share and P/E estimates are obtained from Value Line, December 1999.

the fundamentals and the growth opportunities for these companies to see if the stocks still look undervalued based on those assessments. When they use terms such as *dirt cheap* or *a little expensive* or *realistic target*, they seem to have estimated intrinsic values for these stocks and compared them with market prices before making investment decisions.

Implications for Investors Using Fundamental Analysis

We have learned some ways to determine whether or not to invest in certain stocks. One way is to calculate an intrinsic value. If the company has had and will continue to have relatively constant earnings growth, use either the DDM or the EM. If the company is currently experiencing extraordinarily high growth, use the nonconstant-growth model. And finally, if a company pays no dividends, use the P/E method described in that section. If a company is a new issue (an IPO) or has declining earnings, an investor cannot rely on these methods but must dig deeply into qualitative information about the company's future investment opportunities. Remember the implications pointed out in the EM section. That is, the return on investment must exceed the required return, ER_s, before it adds value to the company stock. Once the intrinsic value is estimated, an investor must compare this value with the stock's market price. If the intrinsic value is greater than the market price, the stock is undervalued and an attractive investment. If the intrinsic value is less than the market price, the stock is overvalued, suggesting a decision to sell any currently owned shares or perhaps to sell short. Of course this final decision is made after considering all other factors and growth opportunities for the company as described in Chapters 11 through 13 as well as in this chapter. Fundamental analysis is a combination of intrinsic valuation and company analysis in the context of the economy and industry.

Investors have found shortcut methods for fundamental analysis. Two popular methods rely on MV/BV and P/E ratios. These two ratios have some conceptual shortcomings but have been proven effective analytical tools. They can underlie an effective initial sorting process to identify stocks that are likely to be undervalued. The ratio-based strategy calls for buying stocks with low MV/BV or low P/E ratios because those tend to be undervalued, relatively cheap issues. The analysis should not stop with just finding low-P/E stocks or low-MV/BV stocks; based on the DDM or the EM, further analysis should confirm undervaluation by comparing a stock's intrinsic value with its market price. Analyzing and studying a company's future investment opportunities increase the odds of finding undervalued, or growth, stocks. This analysis of the company's fundamental economic value must evaluate *future* opportunities and separate true growth opportunities from fluff.

Gap Stores is a good example of a company that has been a growth company and growth stock. The firm sells quality casual clothing, especially jeans, with growth opportunities nationwide. If you had invested in 100 shares when Gap went public in 1976 for $18 per share, those shares would have been worth $46,725 at the stock's peak in 1987. The firm's earnings grew from $0.08 per share in 1977 to $0.49 in 1987 (an average growth rate of 20 percent per year).

Gap Stores *was* a good investment in the 1980s, but did it continue to please investors in the late 1990s? The company continued to expand, opening new stores and updating its assortment of clothing. With expansion, sales rose by 19 percent in 1996 and capital expenditure for 1996 were close to $350 million, including 175 to 200 new stores, 30 to 40 units and some store remodeling. The biggest sales growth has materialized in its newest venture, Old Navy Clothing, introduced in 1993. Old Navy Clothing became profitable in 1996, and with its value-priced clothing and lower operating costs, it is becoming a larger portion of Gap's business. In February 2000 Gap Stores reported that sales grew 27 percent in the fourth quarter of 1999 and profits increased 32 percent. Their biggest expansion ever was announced for 2000, expecting to add 660 stores. They also introduced Gap Body, a toiletries and lingerie store, in mid-1998 in New Jersey and expects to open 40 to 60 more in 2000. In addition, the company is expanding internationally in Europe and Asia. Indeed, it still seems to be a growth company. Is it a growth stock? As always, the bottom line is that a "good" investment's market price must be lower than its intrinsic value. By early 2000 Gap Stores stock was trading at about $43 adjusting for a recent stock split.

Next we will explore an even more exciting area of investment—derivative securities—better known as options and futures. With excitement usually comes greater risk, and the next chapters will discuss risks involved in derivative securities. Once you develop a better understanding of the risks, you may find that options and futures can be used for hedging as well as speculative purposes. Studying Chapters 15 and 16 may open up other investment avenues.

Chapter Summary

1. What is intrinsic value?
   The intrinsic value of a common stock is its fundamental economic value. Fundamental analysts try to determine the intrinsic value of a stock by evaluating the future dividend payments and growth opportunities of the company. This chapter discusses the methods by which an investor may estimate an intrinsic value for a company's common stock.

2. What is the Dividend Discount Model?
   The DDM is one method by which to estimate a common stock's intrinsic value. The model defines common stock value as the present value of the stock's future dividend stream and its future value. A constant dividend growth model can be used if company dividend growth is estimated at an average constant rate, g.

3. What is the Earnings Model?
   The EM is another method by which to estimate a common stock's intrinsic value. The model assumes that a company's earnings grow at a constant rate, g, and defines common stock value as the present value of the future earnings stream of the company. It also shows that the future earnings stream is generated by the firm's future growth opportunities. We discussed some implications stemming from the EM, and we differentiated a growth company from a growth stock.

4. How does an investor conduct fundamental analysis on a company stock?
   Once an intrinsic value is calculated using the models described above, the analyst can assess whether the stock is an attractive investment. Intrinsic value is a benchmark value to which the analyst compares the stock's market price. If the market price is less than the intrinsic value, the stock is undervalued and an attractive investment; if the traded price is greater than the intrinsic value, the stock is overvalued and should be avoided.

5. How can an investor analyze a stock with nonconstant growth?
   When growth is greater than required rate of return, the DDM and EM break down. Nonconstant-growth stocks with growth greater than required rate of return require a modified two-phase DDM. This method combines an estimate of a nonconstant-growth rate and a constant-growth rate to calculate the present value of dividends using the appropriate growth rates for each period of time.

6. How do investors use the MV/BV ratio?

Exhibit 14.7   ◆   WRIGLEY (WWY) COMPANY DATA SHEET

	1994	1999
EPS	$1.73	$2.65
DIV	$0.90	$1.38

Wrigley has no preferred stock issue. Beta equals 0.95.

	1999	2000
Return on Shr Equity	23%	23%
All Div'ds to Net Profits	50	49

The MV/BV ratio, defined as the market value of the stock divided by its book value, is another way to determine whether a stock is undervalued. The market value of a stock should at least equal its book value because that is the value of the firm's assets after its liabilities are satisfied. If the MV/BV ratio equals 1.0, market value equals book value. If the ratio is less than 1.0, the stock's price is depressed below the book value and it may be undervalued because, if the company is liquidated (assets sold and liabilities paid off), an investor may make an excess positive return. Investing in low-MV/BV stocks is a popular investment criterion.

7. What are the pros and cons of using the price/earnings multiple?
Using the DDM, four components make up the P/E ratio. Whatever the P/E, only if the firm has solid growth opportunities is the stock a good investment. However, P/E ratios do not account for the risk of the stock, is misleading if earnings per share is close to zero, and generally most P/Es are improperly calculated using the current earnings per share instead of the forecasted earnings per share. The DDM or EM could provide the same conclusion, without the potential problems of P/E. The chapter offers an alternative use of P/E that may not be as misleading.

Mini Case 1

This mini-case will help you practice applying fundamental analysis on a company. Exhibit 14.7 provides financial information for Wrigley (WWY). Suppose this is the end of 1999 and you are estimating Wrigley's intrinsic value.

a. Estimate WWY's expected long-run growth rate using the dividend trend, the earnings trend, and Equation 14.9.
b. Estimated WWY's required rate of return using the CAPM, with the risk-free rate at 4 percent and Ibbotson & Associates' market risk premium estimate of 8.6 percent.
c. Estimate DIV_1, using equation $DIV_0 (1 + g)$.
d. Estimate WWY's intrinsic value using the DDM.
e. Estimate WWY's intrinsic value using the EM.
f. Is WWY overvalued or undervalued if its market price is $83? What investment decision would you make on WWY?
g. What other information would you consider before making this investment decision? (HINT: Review Chapters 11 through 13).

Mini Case 2

This mini-case will help you apply the alternative P/E method from Equation 14.18 and learn to interpret it.

	P/E ratio	Growth rate	Dividend yield
Netscape	120X	85.0%	0%
S&P 500 Index	20X	10.0	5.0

a. Apply Holt's model to determine the number of years that Netscape must grow at 55 percent to justify its current P/E ratio. The S&P information was obtained from the S&P Statistical Service.

b. Research and find out what happened to Netscape stock in 1998.

Review Questions and Problems

1. What is a stock's intrinsic value, and how do fundamental analysts use this figure?

2. Suppose that a stock's expected dividends are $1.50 per year for the next ten years and its expected price in Year 10 is $65. The required rate of return equals 0.12.
   a. What is the price of the stock in Year 5?
   b. What is the price of the stock today using the future value of $65?
   c. Determine the price of the stock today based on the stock price for Year 5.
   d. What can you conclude about your answers in questions b and c? Explain.

3. Suppose that a stock's expected dividends are $2 per year for the next ten years and its expected price in Year 10 is $85. The required rate of return equals 0.17.
   a. What is the price of the stock in Year 3?
   b. What is the price of the stock today using the future value of $85?
   c. Determine the price of the stock today based on the stock price for Year 3.
   d. What can you conclude about your answers in questions b and c? Explain.

4. Suppose that a stock's expected dividends are $1 per year for the next 15 years and its expected price in Year 15 is $125. The required rate of return equals 0.14.
   a. What is the price of the stock in Year 10?
   b. What is the price of the stock today using the future value of $125?
   c. Determine the price of the stock today based on the stock price for Year 10.
   d. What can you conclude about your answers in questions b and c? Explain.

5. Suppose that stock A's current dividends per share are $1.55 and you expect it to grow at a 15 percent annual rate for the next five years. Also, you speculate that it will sell for $95 five years from now. You would like to earn 18 percent on this investment.
   a. How much are you willing to pay for the stock today?
   b. Suppose it is selling for $42.50 today. Would you buy the stock or not? Explain.

6. Suppose PepsiCo's expected price in Year 2002 is $50 and the company expects to pay dividends of $2.25 in 2000, $2.50 in 2001, and $2.75 in 2002.
   a. If today is the end of 1998, what is PepsiCo's intrinsic value if ER_S equals 15 percent?
   b. If PepsiCo is selling for $45 today, is it undervalued or overvalued based on its intrinsic value? Would you invest in Pepsi stock?

7. Suppose Coca Cola's expected price in 2002 is $75 and the company expects to pay dividends of $.92 in 2000, $1.10 in 2001, and $1.30 in 2002.
   a. If today is the end of 1998, what is Coke's intrinsic value if ER_S equals 16 percent?
   b. Applying fundamental analysis to Coca Cola, would you invest in its stock if it were selling for $65 today? Explain.

8. Suppose that stock W's expected dividends equal $1.65 and it is expected to grow annually at 9 percent for an indefinite period.
   a. If the required rate of return is 12 percent, what is the stock's intrinsic value?
   b. If stock W's price today were $56.50, would you invest or not? Explain.

9. Suppose that stock Z's expected dividends equal $2.50 and it is expected to grow annually at 12 percent for an indefinite period.

     a.   If the required rate of return is 16 percent, what is the stock's intrinsic value?

     b.   If stock Z's price today were $75.50, would you invest or not? Explain.

10.   Stock X is currently trading at $29.50. Its current dividends per share equal $1.25, and this amount is expected to double in ten years.

     a.   What is stock X's growth rate?

     b.   If you have a 12 percent required return on stock X, what is its intrinsic value?

     c.   Is it overvalued or undervalued? Explain.

11.   Stock ABC is currently trading at $42.50. Its current dividends per share equal $0.50, and this amount is expected to triple in ten years.

     a.   What is stock X's growth rate?

     b.   If required return on stock X equals 0.13, what is its intrinsic value?

     c.   Is it overvalued or undervalued? Explain.

12.   Stock DOG is currently trading at $85. Its current dividends per share equal $2.50, and this amount is expected to triple in 15 years.

     a.   What is stock DOG's growth rate?

     b.   If required return on the stock equals 0.18, what is its intrinsic value?

     c.   Is it overvalued or undervalued? Explain.

13.   Gunhoe Company expects its return on equity to equal 25 percent and expects to pay 40 percent of profits as dividends. Its current dividends are $2, and the investors require a 18 percent return.

     a.   What is Gunhoe's expected growth rate?

     b.   What is Gunhoe's intrinsic value?

     c.   If its market price is $73.50, would you invest in Gunhoe stock? Explain.

14.   Why is it incorrect to say that a stock's intrinsic value is equal to the present value of its earnings per share?

15.   State the equation for an intrinsic value based on the EM. Based on the EM, how does one define the term *growth company*? (Hint: When is present value of growth opportunities positive?)

16.   Using the concept developed in the EM, comment on the following statement made by a tipster: "WXY Corp. is purchasing a lot ($250 million) of machines and warehouses right now. They must be expanding, and so they must be a growth stock. I would strongly recommend that you buy 200,000 shares today."

17.   General Form has been investing in several projects this last month, but the stock price has not moved at all. A puzzled stockbroker asks, "Is the market stupid?" Explain the possible reasons for the stable stock price by referring to the EM.

18.   For what reasons can a company's P/E ratio be high? Why is this ratio not an accurate measure of a good investment?

19.   Explain how a low MV/BV ratio could contribute to a good investment strategy.

20.   Corie Kobb plans to invest in common stocks for a period of 12 years, after which she will sell out and buy a lifetime room-and-board membership in a retirement home. She believes that Odell Mines is currently, but temporarily, undervalued by the market. Kobb expects Odell Mines' current earnings per share and dividend to double in the next 12 years. Odell Mines' last dividend was $2, and its stock currently sells for $45 a share.

     a.   To estimate Odell Mines' expected return, Kobb finds that the U.S. Treasury bill rate is at 4 percent, whereas the S&P 500 Index has a 14 percent rate of return. Also, the stock's beta estimate is 0.6. Estimate Odell Mines' required rate of return.

     b.   If Corie Kobb wants to earn a 10 percent return, would she buy the stock?

     c.   If Corie Kobb purchases Odell Mines for $45 per share, what rate will she earn?

21.   MaDonna plans to invest in common stocks for a period of 15 years, after which she will sell out and retire. She believes that stock XYZ is currently, but temporarily, undervalued by the market. MaDonna expects XYZ's current earnings per share of

$5.00 to increase to $35.69 in the next 15 years. XYZ's current dividend was $1.25, and its stock currently sells for $50 a share.

a. To estimate XYZ's expected return, MaDonna finds that the U.S. Treasury bill rate is at 5 percent, and the S&P 500 Index has a 14 percent expected rate of return. Also, the stock's beta estimate is 1.3. Estimate XYZ's required return.

b. If MaDonna wants to earn a 16.7 percent return, would she buy the stock?

c. If MaDonna purchases XYZ for $50 per share, what rate will she earn?

22. Stock ABC is considered a growth stock with a nonconstant-growth rate of 25 percent for the next five years, followed by 15 percent sustainable annual growth thereafter. ABC's current dividends per share are $1.10, and its required rate of return is 18 percent. Calculate its intrinsic value.

23. Stock CAT is considered a growth stock with a nonconstant-growth rate of 20 percent for the next five years, followed by 14 percent sustainable annual growth thereafter. CAT's current dividends per share are $2, and its required rate of return is 16 percent. Calculate its intrinsic value.

24. Boston Chicken (ticker symbol BOST) went public in 1993 and pays no dividends to its stockholders. An analyst forecasts its earnings per share to equal $2.60 in three years with a P/E ratio of 25 times.

a. Estimate Boston Chicken's forecasted price three years from now, given that the analysts' forecasts are accurate.

b. If the market risk premium equals 0.086, the U.S. Treasury bill yields 5 percent, and the analyst estimates BOST's beta at 1.55, what is Boston Chicken's required return?

c. What is Boston Chicken's intrinsic value?

d. If Boston Chicken is currently selling for $35 per share, is it a good investment? Explain.

25. Cisco Systems went public in 1990 and pays no dividends to its stockholders. Analysts' forecasts estimate that Cisco's earnings per share will equal $2.10 in three years, and its expected P/E ratio will be 35 times.

a. Estimate Cisco's forecasted price three years from now if the analyst forecasts are accurate.

b. If the market risk premium equals 0.086, the U.S. Treasury bill yields 5 percent, and the analyst estimates Cisco's beta to equal 1.65, what is Cisco's required return?

c. What is Cisco's intrinsic value?

d. If Cisco is currently trading for $54 per share, is it a good investment? Explain.

26. Papa John International (ticker symbol is PIZZA) went public in 1993 at $13 per share, and the stock currently pays no dividends. Analysts' forecasts estimate that Papa John's earnings per share will equal $2.10 in three years and its expected P/E ratio will be 30 times.

a. What product does Papa John produce and sell?

b. Estimate Papa John's forecasted price three years from now if the analysts' forecasts are accurate.

c. If the market risk premium equals 0.086, the U.S. Treasury bill yields 5 percent, and the analyst estimates Papa John's beta to equal 1.80, what is PIZZA's required return?

d. What is Papa John's intrinsic value?

e. If Papa John is currently trading for $47 per share, is it a good investment? Explain.

27. Go-Tek Company is expecting its return on equity to equal 15 percent and expects to pay 20 percent of profits as dividends. Its current dividends are $1, and the investors require a 16 percent return.

a. What is Go-Tek's expected growth rate?

    b.   What is Go-Tek's intrinsic value?

    c.   If its market price were $30, would you invest in Go-Tek stock? Explain.

    d.   What is Go-Tek's earnings per share if the dividend payout ratio is currently 20 percent?

    e.   What is Go-Tek's intrinsic value if it pays all the company's earnings per share as dividends?

    f.   Assuming that the return on equity remains constant at 15 percent, what should the management do to increase the intrinsic value?

28. Silly-Con Valley Company is expecting its return on equity to equal 18 percent and expects to pay 10 percent of profits as dividends. Its current dividends are $2, and the investors require a 20 percent return.

    a.   What is Silly-Con's expected growth rate?

    b.   What is Silly-Con's intrinsic value?

    c.   If its market price were $60, would you invest in Silly-Con stock? Explain.

    d.   What are Silly-Con's earnings per share if the dividend payout ratio is currently 10 percent?

    e.   What is Silly-Con's intrinsic value if it pays all the company's earnings per share as dividends?

    f.   Assuming that the return on equity remains constant at 18 percent, what should the management do to increase the intrinsic value?

    g.   What conclusion about dividend policy can you draw from this problem?

29. ZAP, Inc.'s expected dividends are $2.50 per share, and its expected earnings per share are $10. The required rate of return, ER_s, for ZAP equals 0.18, and the expected return on equity is 0.20.

    a.   What is the ZAP's growth rate?

    b.   Calculate the intrinsic value of the stock using the EM.

    c.   Suppose the *Wall Street Journal* reports that ZAP is trading at $85. Using fundamental analysis, would you buy the stock? Why?

    d.   Using the EM and the present value of growth opportunities term, determine if the stock is a growth company.

    e.   Is stock ZAP a growth stock?

30. SpiderWeb, an Internet company, expects dividends to equal $1.50 per share and its expected earnings per share at $5.00. The required rate of return for the stock equals 0.13, and the expected return on equity is 0.12.

    a.   What is SpiderWeb's growth rate?

    b.   Calculate the intrinsic value of the stock using the EM.

    c.   Suppose the *Wall Street Journal* reports that the stock is trading at $35. Using fundamental analysis, would you buy the stock? Why?

    d.   Using the EM and the present value of growth opportunities term, determine if the stock is a growth company.

    e.   Suppose your client comments that this stock has a growth rate that is greater than zero, so it should be a growth stock. Is he or she right? If so, how would you support his or her comment, and if not, how would you explain his or her error?

31. HPT's current dividends are $1.00 per share, expected to increase to $3.7072 in ten years. The required rate of return for the stock equals 0.16, and the expected dividend payout ratio equals 20 percent.

    a.   Calculate HPT's growth rate.

    b.   What is HPT's current earnings per share?

    c.   Calculate the intrinsic value of HPT using the EM.

    d.   Suppose the *Wall Street Journal* reports that the stock is trading at $55. Using fundamental analysis, would you buy the stock? Why?

    e.   Using the EM and the present value of growth opportunities term, determine if the stock is a growth company.

32. MICK, an entertainment company, reported current earnings per share to equal $10 per share, and expects earnings to double in ten years. It currently pays 25 percent of earnings as dividends. The required rate of return for the stock equals 0.10.
    a. What is MICK's growth rate?
    b. What is MICK's return on equity?
    c. Calculate the intrinsic value of the stock using the EM for MICK.
    d. Suppose the *Wall Street Journal* reports that the stock is trading at $85. Using fundamental analysis, would you buy the stock? Why?
    e. Is MICK a growth company? Explain.
    f. Is MICK a growth stock? Explain.

33. Zoom, Inc., a laser company, expects earnings per share of $20 per share next year, and shareholder equity per share equals $87. The company is expected to pay $5 in dividends next year. The required rate of return for the stock equals 0.19.
    a. What is Zoom, Inc.'s return on equity?
    b. What is Zoom, Inc.'s growth rate?
    c. Calculate the intrinsic value of Zoom, Inc. using the EM.
    d. Suppose the *Wall Street Journal* reports that the stock is trading at $295. Using fundamental analysis, would you buy the stock? Why?
    e. Is it a growth company?
    f. Suppose your client comments that because this stock has a growth rate greater than zero, it should be a growth stock. Is he or she right or not? If so, how would you support his or her comment, and if not, how would you explain his or her error?

CFA Question

1. (Level I, 1993) Mulroney recalled from her CFA studies that the constant-growth discounted dividend model (DDM) was one way to arrive at a valuation for a company's common stock. She collected current dividend and stock price data for Eastover and Southampton, shown in the table below.

	Current share Price	Current dividend per share	1992 EPS Estimate	Current Book Value per share
Eastover (EO)	$28	$1.20	$1.60	$17.32
Southampton (SHC)	48	1.08	3.00	32.21
S&P 500	415	12.00	20.54	159.83

a. Using 11 percent as the required rate of return (that is discount rate) and a projected growth rate of 8 percent, **compute** a constant-growth DDM value for Eastover's stock and **compare** the computed value for Eastover to its stock price indicated in the table. **Show** calculations.

Mulroney's supervisor commented that a two-stage DDM may be more appropriate for companies such as Eastover and Southampton. Mulroney believes that Eastover and Southampton could grow more rapidly over the next three years and then settle in at a lower but sustainable rate of growth beyond 1994. Her estimates are indicated in the table below.

PROJECTED GROWTH RATES

	Next 3 Years (1992, 1993, 1994)	Growth Beyond 1994
Eastover (EO)	12%	8%
Southampton (SHC)	13	7

b. Using 11 percent as the required rate of return, **compute** the two-stage DDM value of Eastover's stock and **compare** that value to its stock price indicated in the table for Part A. **Show** calculations.

c. **Discuss** *two* advantages and *three* disadvantages of using a constant-growth DDM. **Briefly discuss** how the two-stage DDM improves upon the constant-growth DDM.

2. (Level I, 1993) In addition to the discounted dividend model (DDM) approach, Mulroney decided to look at the price/earnings ratio and price/book ratio, relative to the S&P 500, for both Eastover and Southampton. Mulroney elected to perform this analysis using 1987–91 data and current data.

   a. Using the data from the above tables and the table below, **compute** *both* the current and the five-year (1987–91) average relative price/earnings ratios and relative price/book ratios for Eastover and Southampton.

   b. **Discuss** *each* company's current relative price/earnings ratio as compared to its five-year relative price/earnings ratio and *each* company's current relative price/book ratio as compared to its five-year average relative price/book ratio.

	1986	1987	1988	1989	1990	1991	5-Year Average (1987–91)
Average P/E							
Eastover Co. (EO)	18.9X	14.2	9.9	18.6	12.3	27.8	
Southampton (SCH)	16.6X	9.9	9.0	7.0	13.2	20.6	
S&P 500	15.8X	16.0	11.1	13.9	15.6	19.2	15.2
Average price/book							
Eastover Co. (EO)	1.6X	1.8	1.5	1.6	1.2	1.5	
Southampton (SCH)	1.1X	1.1	1.1	1.2	1.0	1.1	
S&P 500	1.8X	2.1	1.9	2.2	2.1	2.3	2.1

   c. Briefly discuss *one* disadvantage for *each* of the relative price/earnings and relative price/book approaches to valuation.

3. (Level I, 1988) You decide to apply the constant growth dividend discount model $[P_0 = D_1/(k-g)]$ to Tennant's most recent financial data to develop a suggested market value for the company's stock.

   Calculate a value for Tennant common stock by applying the constant growth dividend discount model based on Tennant's 1987 operating and balance sheet data. Assume that an investor's required rate of return is a five percentage point premium over the current risk-free rate of return of 7 percent.

TENNANT COMPANY
SELECTED HISTORIC OPERATING AND BALANCE SHEET DATA (000)
AS OF DECEMBER 31

	1975	1981	1987
After-tax income	$ 4,429	$ 9,603	$ 9,818
Total assets	$33,848	$63,555	$106,098
Total common stockholder equity	27,722	46,593	69,516
Long-term debt	6	532	2,480
Earnings per share	$0.78	$1.78	$1.85
Dividend per share	0.28	0.72	0.96
Book value per share	4.55	8.63	13.07

CRITICAL THINKING EXERCISES

1. At the library, find information on fast-food restaurant chain McDonald's, and conduct a fundamental analysis. If necessary, use the nonconstant-growth model instead of the DDM. Is McDonald's stock overvalued or undervalued? Carefully justify your answer with information to back your analysis.

2. Repeat the fundamental analysis conducted in mini-case 1 on Wrigley with more recent Value Line data. Do you concur with the analysis conducted in the mini-case? Justify your answer.

3. Using Value Line or a similar source, find the ten stocks with the highest P/E ratios and the ten with the lowest P/E ratios as of December 31, 1989. Also, find their stock prices at the end of 1989. Find today's stock prices for these 20 stocks. Calculate returns for the ten low-P/E stocks and the ten high-P/E stocks. (Remember to include dividends paid from 1987 to today.) Next, calculate an arithmetic mean return for each group of low P/Es and high P/Es. Does this return confirm or refute the contention that low-P/E stocks outperform high-P/E stocks?

4. Using Value Line again, find the ten stocks, as of December 31, 1989, with the highest and lowest MV/BV ratios. Find today's stock prices for these 20 stocks. Repeat the same process of calculating returns for each group. Discuss your results. What is your conclusion?

THE INTERNET INVESTOR

1. Visit a brokerage firm web site that offers news about a recent company earnings announcement (for either the quarter or the year). Determine the effect of any difference between forecasted earnings and actual earnings on the stock price. Discuss factors that may have affected the difference in forecasted and actual earnings.

2. Visit a brokerage firm or security analysis firm web site and find a company analysis report produced by an analyst. What factors does the analyst mention that are consistent with the models discussed in this chapter? What factors aren't consistent with the factors mentioned in the models discussed in this chapter? Discuss which factors are important and why.

3. Find a stock that interests you and follow its news releases from one of the Internet sites. Usually a brokerage firm web site will provide news releases that may influence the firm. Find the intraday prices for the day and determine whether the stock prices react appropriately to the news releases. Does the stock movement lag or lead the news release?

Part 5

Derivative Securities

IN THE NEXT TWO CHAPTERS, WE DESCRIBE SO-CALLED DERIVATIVE SECURITIES, OPTIONS AND FUTURES. THEY ARE CALLED DERIVATIVE SECURITIES BECAUSE THE OPTIONS AND FUTURES DERIVE THEIR VALUE FROM OTHER SECURITIES. IN PART BECAUSE OPTIONS AND FUTURES LINK CLOSELY TO THE STOCK AND BOND MARKETS, IT IS IMPORTANT TO UNDERSTAND THE BASICS OF DERIVATIVE SECURITIES, EVEN IF YOU NEVER PARTICIPATE IN OPTIONS AND FUTURES MARKETS. FOR ONE THING, OPTIONS AND FUTURES ARE CLOSELY LINKED TO THE STOCK AND BOND MARKETS.

FUNDAMENTALS OF OPTIONS

PREVIOUSLY . . .

In the prior three chapters, we described the investment characteristics of common stock and some strategies involving stock investing. Security analysis taught us that by understanding and analyzing the company, we could make a sound investment decision in the company's common stock.

IN THIS CHAPTER . . .

We discuss the fundamentals of options, one of two major types of derivative securities. The pricing of options and investment strategies using options are described. In addition, we examine other securities that involve options.

TO COME . . .

In the next chapter, we continue our coverage of derivative securities by examining futures contracts.

Chapter Objectives

1. What are the basic characteristics of option contracts?
2. What is the value of an option at expiration?
3. What are some common option-trading strategies?
4. How are options valued?
5. What other securities resemble options?

Assume that a few years ago you bought shares of Oracle stock for $15. Today, Oracle is selling for about $75. You are still optimistic about the company's long-run prospects but worry about a short-term price decline. You wonder if you can somehow protect most of your profits while still holding on to your stock.

Alternatively, let's assume you have decided that Yahoo's stock price will rise sharply over the next few months. The trouble is that, at $404 a share, you are not sure you want to commit $40,400 to buy 100 shares. Can you make money in Yahoo stock without having to buy the stock?

Here's one last scenario to consider. You have watched shares of Microsoft rise sharply over the past few months mainly in response to a proposed antitrust case settlement with the Justice Department. You have decided that Microsoft will be volatile until the settlement and, at least in the short term, its stock price will fall. You could sell Microsoft stock short, to take advantage of your expectation, but you believe short sales are too risky. You want another way to profit if Microsoft's stock price does fall.

By trading options, you can accomplish all three of these investment objectives. You could buy a put option to protect your Oracle profits; buy a call option to profit if Yahoo's stock takes off; and buy a put option to profit if Microsoft's stock price falls.

In this chapter, we discuss the fundamentals of options. Options differ greatly from more traditional investments such as stocks and bonds and confront investors with a unique set of risks. At the same time, however, options offer investors unique opportunities, examples of which we outlined above. Options are not for everyone, but they play an important role in the contemporary investment world.

Basic Characteristics of Option Contracts

exercise (strike) price
Price at which stock is bought or sold if an option is exercised.

expiration date
Date the option expires; usually the third Friday of the month indicated.

call option
An option to buy.

put option
An option to sell.

in-the-money
If the stock price exceeds the exercise price of a call option.

out-of-the-money
If the stock price is less than the call option's exercise price.

at-the-money
If the stock price equals the call option's exercise price.

derivative security
Security whose value derives from another security.

An *option contract* gives the buyer, or holder, the right, but not the obligation, to buy or sell a stated number of shares of common stock (usually 100 shares) at a specified price (called the **exercise** or **strike price**) until a specified point in time (called the **expiration date**).[1] An option to buy stock is a **call option;** an option to sell stock is a **put option.** Let's look at an example of each.

On December 15, 1999, a call option on IBM stock with an exercise price of 110 that would expire in January 2000 was selling for 6 1/2. On the same day, a put option on IBM with the same exercise price and expiration date was selling for 7 1/8. Owning the call option gives the holder the right *to buy* 100 shares of IBM at $110 per share until January 21, 2000. Owning the put option gives the holder the right *to sell* 100 shares of IBM at $110 per share until January 21, 2000. The price of the call option was $650 (6 1/2 times 100) and the price of the put option was $712.50 (7 1/8 times 100). IBM stock closed on December 15, 1999, at 109 per share. If a call option has a stock price higher than the exercise price, it is said to be **in-the-money.** If a call option has an stock price less than the exercise price, it is **out-of-the-money.** If a put option's stock price is less than the exercise price, the put is in-the-money. If the put option's stock price is greater than the exercise price, the put is out-of-the-money. If, by chance, the exercise price of an option, either a call or a put, is equal to the stock price, the option is **at-the-money.** Notice that the IBM call is out-of-the-money (stock price equals $109 and exercise price is $110), and the IBM put is in-the-money.

An option is considered a **derivative security** because its value derives from another security (that is, the underlying stock). Because a call is an option to buy at a set price, holding all other factors constant, its price should move in the same direction as the price of the stock; the price of a put, because it is an option to sell, should move in the opposite direction from the price of the stock.

Investors may buy call options when they expect the price of a particular stock, such as IBM, to rise over a short period of time. However, investors may buy put options when they believe that the price of the underlying stock will fall over a short

---

[1]Almost all options are protected from stock splits and stock dividends. If the underlying stock splits, say, 2 for 1, the exercise price of the options will automatically be halved.

period of time. A buyer can decide whether the option is worthwhile by calculating the premium on the option. The **premium** can be defined as the "break-even" dollar increase (or decrease) in the stock price for the option to be profitable.

The premium on a call option is the call price minus the stock price plus the exercise price. For the 110 January IBM call, the premium equals

$$\$6.50 - \$109 + \$110 = \$7.50$$

This premium reflects the one-dollar deficit in the IBM call, meaning it is out-of-the-money by a dollar plus the market price on the call contract cost of $6.50, making the premium $7.50. So, for the buyer of the call to begin making a profit, IBM stock must increase past the break-even point of $7.50.

The premium on a put option is defined as the put price minus the exercise price plus the stock price. For the 110 January IBM put, the premium equals

$$\$7.125 - \$110 + \$109 = \$6.125$$

Again, this premium indicates the dollar amount by which IBM stock must decrease before the buyer of the put can begin making a profit. Because the put is in-the-money by one dollar, the break-even amount drops by one dollar. However, the buyer paid $6.125 more than the profits that can accrue from the put option, making $6.125 the premium beyond the put option value.

Options create some tricky situations. The option holder has the right to buy or sell stock at a set price for a set period of time. The option holder is said to have a **long position.** If the option is *exercised* (that is, if the holder actually buys or sells the stock), from whom does she buy the stock or to whom does she sell it? The answer is the seller of the option. In other words, the call option seller agrees to sell stock at a fixed price for a fixed period of time to the call option buyer at the buyer's discretion. Likewise, the put option seller agrees to buy stock at a fixed price for a fixed period of time from the put option buyer, again at that buyer's discretion. Selling an option often is referred to as **writing an option;** the option writer is said to have a **short position.** It is important to remember that in options every long position *must* have a short position.

Why would anyone write an option and accept an uncertain obligation? The writer does this in exchange for the price of the call. The call writer receives the amount paid by the call buyer and agrees to assume the risk of delivering the stock when "called." The put writer also receives the put price, which is paid by the put buyer. The writer assumes the risk of taking the stock from the buyer when the stock is "put" on him.

Options traders often use the terms *intrinsic value* and *time value* when referring to options. The intrinsic value of a call option equals either zero if the option is out-of-the-money or the difference between the stock price and exercise price if the option is in-the-money. The intrinsic value of a put option equals either zero if the option is out-of-the-money or the difference between the exercise price and stock price if the option is in-the-money. The time value of an option is defined as the difference between the price of the option and its intrinsic value. If the option is in-the-money, the time value equals the premium. The use of the term *time value* is unfortunate because the difference between an option's price and intrinsic value, like the size of the option's premium, is a function of more than the time until expiration. We'll explore this issue in more depth later in the chapter when we discuss option pricing models.

premium
Call price minus the current stock price plus the exercise price.

long position
Position held by the buyer of the option.

writing an option
Selling an option.

short position
Position held by the writer of the option.

Exhibit 15.1   ✦   SUMMARY OF RIGHTS AND OBLIGATIONS OF IBM OPTIONS BUYERS AND
SELLERS

Type of Option	Long Position (Buyer)	Short Position (Writer)
110 January call	Has the right but no obligation to buy 100 shares of IBM stock at $110 per share until January 21, 2000.	Is obligated to sell 100 shares of IBM stock at $110 per share until January 21, 2000, if the option is exercised.
110 January put	Has the right but no obligation to sell 100 shares of IBM stock at $110 per share until January 21, 2000.	Is obligated to buy 100 shares of IBM at $110 until January 21, 2000, if the option is exercised.

The general reason an investor writes an option is to capture the price of the option. In our earlier IBM example, someone might write the call option expecting that IBM's stock would rise little between early January and mid-January. Similarly, someone might write the put option, betting that IBM's stock would not fall too far over the same period. In an option writer's ideal situation, the option expires unexercised. The buyer of the IBM call option would allow it to expire unexercised if IBM were trading at less than $110 per share on January 21. The buyer of the IBM put option would allow it to expire unexercised if the stock were trading at more than $110 per share on January 21. Exhibit 15.1 summarizes the rights and obligations of the long and short positions for the IBM call and put option contracts.

Now that we have defined option contracts and explained the rights and obligations of both parties, let's discuss how option contracts are traded.

OPTION TRADING

An investor can trade options much like stocks and bonds, by giving a market order or a limit order for a specific option to a broker. The broker then transmits the order to the exchange, where the option is traded and the order is executed. Note, however, that most brokerage firms have restrictions on option trading by clients. Most, for example, handle option trades only for clients who have large holdings of cash or other liquid assets in their accounts.

Before 1973, options traded only on the over-the-counter (OTC) markets. The OTC markets allowed investors to determine the terms of each contract, such as the strike price, expiration date, and number of shares. Transaction costs for these individualized contracts were quite high, and trades were infrequent after the initial transaction.

In 1973, the Chicago Board Options Exchange (CBOE) was formed as the first organized option exchange. Since then, most options trading has occurred on organized exchanges. By 1989, options were traded on five U.S. exchanges, including the CBOE, American Stock Exchange (AMEX), Philadelphia Stock Exchange (PB), Pacific Stock Exchange (PC), and New York Stock Exchange (NYSE).

Options also trade actively on several foreign stock exchanges. Three of the largest option markets outside the United States are located in London, Tokyo, and Toronto.

The organized exchanges provide significant advantages over OTC option trading. Five important ones are listed below:

1. *Standardized Contracts.* The strike price on a modern option is standardized, as is the expiration date (the close of business on the third Friday of the stated month). Strike prices usually are stated in $5 increments, although larger increments are likely for stocks priced at more than $100 and increments as low as $2.50 are possible for stocks priced at less than $30 per share. New call option contracts with new strike prices are written as a stock's price exceeds currently available strike prices.

2. *Increased Liquidity.* Trading on organized exchanges allows buyers and sellers to exchange option contracts at any time.

3. *More Comprehensive Disclosure and Surveillance Rules.* Organized exchanges impose relatively strict trading, disclosure, and monitoring procedures. They also keep a market flowing smoothly.

4. *Guaranteed Clearing of Contracts.* The Option Clearing Corporation (OCC), clearinghouse for options trading, is jointly owned by the exchanges where options are traded. The OCC basically acts as a guarantor of each options trade to ensure that all parties meet their contractual obligations. Because option traders need not be concerned with the creditworthiness of other participants, the OCC helps create liquidity in the options market. The OCC acts as an agent between the buyer and the seller (or writer) of an option. Once the buyer and seller agree on a price (through orders executed by their brokers), the OCC writes and sells to the option buyer while it buys the contract from the seller. Because all options investors contract with the OCC, it guarantees that all contracts are fulfilled. Also, the OCC is responsible to fulfill any exercised options contract. If a call option is exercised, the OCC arranges for a member firm to randomly select a client who has written (or sold) a call to deliver 100 shares of the specified common stock at the strike price. If a put option is exercised, the OCC arranges for a member firm to randomly select a client who has written a put to purchase 100 shares of the specified common stock at the strike price.

5. *Lower Transaction Costs.* Brokerage fees for options traded on organized exchanges are substantially less than fees required for OTC trading. The lower costs reflect increased trading activity (which simplifies making a market), and the OCC relieves brokers of many functions, as discussed above.

Option Price Quotations

Exhibit 15.2 provides a listing of option price quotes from the *Wall Street Journal* for December 15, 1999. Let's examine IBM call and put options. IBM has options expiring in December, January, and April. At each expiration date, individual option contracts have several strike prices, ranging from $85 to $140.

The first column in the *Wall Street Journal* quotes provides the company name with its closing stock price for that day below. The second column lists option strike prices, and the third column lists expiration months. (Remember, virtually all options expire on the third Friday of the month.) The next two columns list the volume of call options traded and the last transacted price per share. (Multiply by 100 for the dollar price of the option contract.) The last two columns list the volume of put options traded and the last transacted price for the put. A dotted line means that no such option contract exists or none was traded.

As you look through option price quotations in the *Wall Street Journal* or other financial publications, two questions may come to mind. First, why do some stocks underlie more options with different strike prices and expiration dates than others? The

Exhibit 15.2 ✦ OPTION PRICE QUOTES FROM THE *WALL STREET JOURNAL*

Option/Strike	Exp.	Call Vol.	Call Last	Put Vol.	Put Last
Chiron 35	Dec	622	1	...	...
CienaCp 70	Dec	538	2¼	234	3⅛
Cisco 80	Dec	764	18⅜	20	1/16
97 15/16 80	Jan	288	19½	593	13/16
97 15/16 80	Apr	631	23¾	26	3¼
97 15/16 85	Dec	1196	13½	35	1/16
97 15/16 85	Jan	626	15⅜	1193	1¾
97 15/16 90	Jan	1312	11½	570	2 15/16
97 15/16 95	Dec	630	3¾	855	⅝
97 15/16 95	Jan	168	8⅛	1128	4¾
97 15/16 100	Dec	3009	15/16	722	2⅞
97 15/16 100	Jan	886	5½	79	6⅞
97 15/16 105	Jan	1608	3½	46	9½
97 15/16 110	Jan	846	2¼	...	...
Citigrp 50	Dec	2185	3¾	828	⅛
53½ 50	Jan	447	5⅛	1080	1¼
53½ 55	Dec	4314	⅜	1605	1¾
53½ 55	Jan	725	2¼	450	3⅜
53½ 55	Mar	2736	4	106	4½
53½ 55	Jun	1539	5¾	1005	5¾
53½ 60	Dec	1244	1/16	20	6⅜
53½ 60	Jan	582	¾	1	6¼
53½ 60	Mar	873	2	...	...
53½ 70	Jun	1112	1½	...	...
CitrixSys 80	Dec	450	29	...	...
Coke 60	Dec	186	1 13/16	414	7/16
61¼ 60	Jan	130	3⅜	972	2
61¼ 80	Jan	4	⅛	500	18½
ColumEn 60	Feb	1010	3½	...	...
57½ 65	Feb	950	1¼	...	...
CmpUSA 7½	May	1535	11/16	500	2
Compaq 22½	Dec	393	2¾	90	1/16
25⅛ 25	Dec	3426	½	1335	7/16
25⅛ 25	Jan	2361	2	310	1⅝
25⅛ 27½	Dec	551	1/16	31	2 11/16
25⅛ 27½	Jan	619	1	34	3¼
25⅛ 30	Jan	844	½	20	5½
25⅛ 37½	Jul	806	15/16	...	...
CompSc 75	Mar	108	11½	505	4⅞
Cmpuwr 35	Dec	2643	⅞	65	13/16
ConAgr 25	Dec	...	...	1012	3½
ConcCm 17½	Feb	530	4	32	3¼
Conexnt 75	Dec	454	¼	...	...
Cnseco 17½	May	941	3⅜	32	2 5/16
CypSem 25	Jun	...	...	500	3½
Davox 20	Jan	500	5	...	...
DayHud 75	Jan	664	2½	3	6¼

Option/Strike	Exp.	Call Vol.	Call Last	Put Vol.	Put Last
DellCptr 40	Dec	518	1⅝	1546	7/16
41 1/16 40	Jan	1021	3½	533	2
IntgDv 30	Jan	1671	⅞	...	...
Intel 55	Jan	32	18⅞	433	7/16
72 13/16 65	Jan	467	9¾	275	1⅞
72 13/16 70	Dec	2658	3⅛	2001	½
72 13/16 70	Jan	428	6½	801	3½
72 13/16 70	Apr	398	10⅛	80	6¼
72 13/16 75	Dec	2047	7/16	6541	3⅛
72 13/16 75	Jan	4685	3¾	864	6
72 13/16 75	Apr	694	7¾	82	8⅜
72 13/16 80	Dec	456	1/16	564	7⅛
72 13/16 80	Jan	1199	2¼	498	9
72 13/16 85	Dec	590	1/16	3	12
72 13/16 85	Jan	409	1⅜	43	12½
72 13/16 90	Jan	533	⅝	100	17⅞
72 13/16 90	Apr	510	2⅞	95	18⅝
72 13/16 95	Jan	432	⅜	10	21½
Intelligrp 17½	Jan	520	8¾	...	...
IntrDig 22½	Jan	536	3⅛	...	...
19⅜ 25	Jan	880	2½	17	7½
IntrCm 25	Dec	2500	7½	...	...
31⅜ 30	Jan	4010	5	...	...
I B M 80	Jan	...	...	1210	⅜
109 85	Jan	3	24	784	9/16
109 90	Jan	305	19⅞	809	1
109 95	Jan	149	15¾	422	1¾
109 100	Dec	186	8⅝	939	⅛
109 105	Dec	438	4	1661	9/16
109 105	Jan	391	9⅛	456	4¾
109 110	Dec	2159	1½	1206	2⅛
109 110	Jan	930	6½	179	7⅛
109 110	Apr	447	11¼	120	10¼
109 115	Dec	1264	5/16	169	6½
109 115	Jan	535	4⅛	172	10¼
109 120	Dec	438	1/16	148	11⅝
109 120	Jan	1329	2⅞	160	13¾
109 125	Jan	1136	2⅛	...	...
109 130	Jan	827	1¼	...	...
109 140	Apr	441	2 11/16	...	...
IntFibcm 10	May	417	1 11/16	60	2 9/16
IntlSpdw 60	Jan	...	...	505	5⅝
IntVceBr 17½	Dec	548	1 13/16	...	...
18 15/16 17½	Apr	1019	5⅜	...	...
18 15/16 20	Jan	556	2 9/16	...	...
JDS Uniph 110	Dec	418	13½	2	¼
219⅞ 130	Dec	2237	3⅞	470	13

Source: Wall Street Journal, *Wednesday, December 25, 1999, p. C16.*

answer to that is rather simple. The exchange, say, the CBOE, determines the number of option contracts available. Its decision is based on investor interest and the volatility of the stock. In general, more investor interest in a stock and a more volatile price lead the exchange to create more options.

A second common question is why do some option prices seem out of line, either too high or too low? Remember that each price printed reflects the price of the last transaction; it is not a current bid or ask price. The fact that a call option last traded for 6 1/2 does not mean that anyone could buy or sell for 6 1/2 now if the stock price has changed substantially. Also, keep in mind that many options listed are not actively traded. (Look at the volume figures.)

OPTIONS ON OTHER SECURITIES

During the 1980s, many exchanges began to offer options on stock indexes such as the Standard & Poor's (S&P) 100 and Value Line Index. Options on industry indexes, foreign currencies, and commodity and financial futures also became available. We'll discuss the index options and foreign currency options here, leaving options on financial futures for Chapter 16.

Index Options

An **index option** is a call or put based on a stock market index such as the S&P 100, S&P 500, Value Line Index, or Major Market Index. The S&P 100 Index is a value-weighted average of the 100 largest stocks in the S&P 500. The Major Market Index is an average—weighted by price—of 20 large-firm stocks, most of which are also included in the Dow Jones Industrial Average sample. The Value Line Index is an arithmetic (equally weighted) average of approximately 1,700 stocks. Examples of index option price quotations appear in Exhibit 15.3.

> **index option**
> *Call or put option based on a stock market index.*

Unlike stock options, exercise of an index option does not require the writer to deliver the securities that comprise the index; instead, a cash settlement takes place. The writer pays, in cash, the difference between the strike price of the option and the value of the index at the time of exercise, multiplied by a fixed number. The multiplier for S&P 100 options is 100. For example, suppose that you were to write a call option on the S&P 100 Index with a January 2000 expiration and a strike price of 620. Now, assume that the buyer exercised the option when the index equaled 758. You, the writer, would owe the option buyer $13,800, composed of 758 (the index value when the option was exercised) minus 620 (the option's exercise price) multiplied by 100. More recently, foreign stock index options have been introduced into U.S. options markets. Options are available on such foreign stock indexes as the Financial Times 100 and the Japan Index (a composite index of most major Japanese stocks).

Foreign Currency Options

A currency option gives the holder the right to buy or sell a specified quantity of foreign currency for a specified amount of U.S. dollars. Contracts are quoted in cents or fractions of a cent per unit of foreign currency. Foreign currency options are traded on the PB and the CBOE.

Long-Term Options

In 1994, the CBOE initiated trading in long-term options, called LEAPS®. These long-term call and put options are similar to standard call and put options except that they have expiration dates of up to two years from the date of issue. LEAPS® are available on both individual stocks and major stock indexes.

Option Value at Expiration

In this section, we discuss how to find the values of call and put options at expiration. This allows the investor to determine the profit or loss, at expiration, from the four basic option trades (buying a call option, writing a call option, buying a put option, and writing a put option). Before we get to this, however, we need to define some symbols.

Exhibit 15.3 ✦ PRICE QUOTES FOR INDEX OPTIONS

Strike		Vol.	Last	Chg.	Int.
S & P 100 INDEX(OEX)					
Mar	540 p	10	1½	...	147
Jan	550 c	8	213¼	+ 24¼	14
Jan	550 p	1,250	¼	...	3,019
Jan	560 p	107	5/16	...	798
Feb	560 p	110	1	...	32
Jan	580 p	161	7/16	− 1/16	344
Feb	580 p	29	1¼	...	151
Dec	600 c	11	160	− 7	17
Jan	600 c	5	163¾	− 3	428
Jan	600 p	100	⅝	...	2,529
Feb	600 c	1	171	− 4	1
Feb	600 p	125	2	+ 3/16	289
Dec	610 c	8	150	+ 9	14
Jan	610 c	5	154	+ 8	31
Jan	610 p	155	13/16	+ 1/16	591
Jan	620 c	9	144	− 1	98
Jan	620 p	110	1⅛	+ ⅜	2,146
Feb	620 p	1	2⅞	+ 5/16	137
Mar	620 p	1	4½	+ ¼	199
Jan	630 p	100	1¼	+ ¼	1,403
Jan	640 p	133	1½	+ ¼	1,052
Feb	640 p	305	3¾	− ¼	201
Dec	650 c	5	112¼	− 2¼	53
Dec	650 p	20	1/16	...	2,533
Jan	650 p	131	2¼	+ ⅝	3,056
Dec	660 c	12	103	− 4⅛	539
Dec	660 p	17	1/16	...	4,683
Jan	660 p	130	2½	+ ½	2,348
Feb	660 p	7	5½	+ ¾	247
Mar	660 c	1	119	+ 2	59
Dec	665 c	12	98	+ 4	174
Dec	665 p	12	1/16	...	3,777
Dec	670 c	14	94	+ 1¼	491
Dec	670 p	20	1/16	...	4,588
Jan	670 c	10	99¼	+ 2¼	232
Jan	670 p	8	3	+ ⅝	688
Feb	670 p	30	6¾	+ 1	93
Dec	680 c	61	78⅞	− 2⅝	957
Dec	680 p	71	1/16	...	8,380
Jan	680 c	8	90	+ 2½	1,789
Jan	680 p	41	3⅜	+ 7/16	3,091
Feb	680 p	8	6¾	+ ½	238
Mar	680 p	41	10½	− ¼	1,571
Dec	685 c	10	77	+ 1	419
Dec	685 p	30	1/16	...	3,185
Dec	690 c	63	74	− 3	1,241
Dec	690 p	353	1/16	...	4,446
Jan	690 c	10	79	− 4⅜	1,459
Jan	690 p	23	4¾	+ 1	1,836
Feb	690 p	10	7⅞	+ ⅝	1,850
Jan	695 c	10	77	+ 33½	2
Jan	695 p	2,522	5⅜	+ 1¼	544

Source: Wall Street Journal, *December 15, 1999, p. C16.*

The value, or price, of a call option at a point in time is denoted by C_T. The value of a put option is denoted by P_T. The value of the underlying stock is denoted by S. We define the exercise price of the option as E and the time left until the option's expiration as T. At the expiration date, T equals 0.

VALUING CALLS AND PUTS AT EXPIRATION

Let's assume that a time traveler can return to a point in time right before the January 2000 IBM options expired. This would be a few minutes before the markets closed on January 21, 2000. How much would this person expect the January call and put options to be worth? (Remember the exercise price is $110, so E equals 110) The answer, of course, depends on the price of IBM's stock. Let's start with the call option.

Call Option Value at Expiration

Assume IBM's common stock was trading for $120 per share moments before the market closed on January 21, 2000. How much would the 110 January call be worth? The answer is $10. To see why, consider what would happen if the option were selling for $7. One could then buy the option contract for $700, exercise it immediately to buy IBM for $110 per share, and then sell the IBM shares on the NYSE for $120 per share. The profit, ignoring commissions, would be $300, and this return would be risk-free. This is an example of arbitrage, the simultaneous purchase and sale of two different securities to make a guaranteed profit.

Now, what would happen if IBM's stock were trading for $100 per share moments before the 110 January call was about to expire? The call would be worthless $(C = 0)$. After all, would you pay *anything* for an option to immediately buy a stock at $110 per share when it was selling for $100 in the stock market?

These examples illustrate that valuing a call option at expiration is fairly simple. It is equal to zero if the option is about to expire out-of-the-money $(S \leq E)$; the value of the call is equal to the stock price minus the exercise price $(S - E)$ if the call is about to expire in-the-money. More formally, the value of a call option at expiration equals

$$C_T = \text{Max}\,(0, S - E), \text{ where } T = 0$$
$$C_T = 0, \text{ if } S \leq E \quad\quad (15.1)$$
$$C_T = (S - E), \text{ if } S > E$$

Put Option Value at Expiration

Similar logic leads to a value for a put option at expiration. Let's use the 110 January IBM put option. Right before the put option expires on January 21, 2000, suppose that IBM's common stock is selling for either $120 per share or $100 per share.

If IBM were selling for $120 per share, the put option would be worthless; it would be about to expire out-of-the-money. No one would pay anything for an option that would allow the holder to immediately sell IBM at $110 per share when one could get $120 per share in the stock market.

However, if IBM were trading at $100 per share right before the put option expired, it would have a value of $10. If it were selling for less than $10, arbitrageurs could buy the option, buy the stock, and exercise the option (in essence selling the stock at $110 when its market price was $100).

Putting the example into a more general form, the value of a put option at expiration is equal to zero if the option is about to expire out-of-the-money $(S \geq E)$ or $E - S$ if the put option is about to expire in-the-money $(S < E)$. More formally, the value of a put option at expiration equals

$$P_T = \text{Max}(0, E - S), \text{ where } T=0$$
$$P_T = 0, \text{ if } S \geq E \quad\quad (15.2)$$
$$P_T = (E - S), \text{ if } S < E$$

CALCULATING THE PROFIT AND LOSS FROM AN OPTION

Knowing the value of call and put options at expiration allows one to calculate the profit or loss from the four basic option trades (buying a call, writing a call, buying a put, and writing a put). Example calculations will use the two familiar IBM options; the 110 January call was selling for 6 1/2 (the buyer paid $650 to the writer) about four weeks before expiration, and the 110 January put was selling for 7 1/8 (the buyer paid $712.50 to the writer) four weeks before expiration in January 2000.

Buying a Call Option

The profit from buying the call option depends, of course, on the price of IBM's stock at expiration. Exhibit 15.4 shows the profit or loss from buying the 110 January call, with a purchase price of $650, for various stock prices. The data are graphed in Exhibit 15.5. At a stock price of 110 or below, the call expires out-of-the-money and worthless; the buyer loses $650. However, at a stock price greater than 110, the buyer's profit or loss equals

$$[(S - E) - 6.5] \times 100$$

For example, at a stock price of 120, the buyer's profit equals

$$[(\$120 - \$110) - \$6.5] \times 100 = \$350$$

In general, then, the profit or loss from buying a call option is

$$\text{Profit (Loss)} = (C), \text{ if } S \leq E \text{ when } T = 0$$
$$= [(S - E) - C] \times 100, \text{ if } S > E \text{ when } T = 0$$

where C is the price paid for the call option.[2]

Before we go any further, we should make two additional points. First, in reality, most option buyers do not exercise their options when they decide to take profits in cash unless they actually want to buy or sell the underlying stock. Buyers simply sell their options on the appropriate markets. Exercising an option entails additional transactions, and thus additional transaction costs. For example, exercising a call to cash in option profits requires the holder to sell the shares of stock acquired by exercising the option. The profit from selling the option will be the same, before transaction costs, as that from exercising the option and selling the stock. This is simply because many investors in the market pay virtually no transaction costs. Their low-cost trades help to eliminate any arbitrage profits.

Second, the example shown in Exhibit 15.4 helps illustrate the derivative nature of options. Options derive their values from the values of the underlying stocks (IBM in the example). Notice how the value of the call option at expiration increases exactly as much as the stock price once the call option is in-the-money ($S > E$).

Writing a Call Option

The profit or loss from writing the 110 January IBM call is also shown in Exhibit 15.4 for various stock prices. Exhibit 15.5 shows clearly that the profit or loss for the option writer is the exact opposite of the profit or loss for the option buyer. This an important

---

[2]Now that you understand how call profits are calculated, it's easier to remember it as (S-E-C).

Exhibit 15.4 ✦ PROFIT (LOSS) FROM BUYING OR WRITING A 110 IBM CALL OPTION

Stock Price at Expiration ($T = 0$)	Value of Call Option	Profit (Loss)[a]	
		Buyer	Writer (Seller)
$ 85.00	$ 0.00	$ (650)	$ 650
90.00	0.00	(650)	650
95.00	0.00	(650)	650
100.00	0.00	(650)	650
105.00	0.00	(650)	650
E = 110	0.00	(650)	650
115	5.00	(150)	150
120	10.00	350	(350)
125	15.00	850	(850)
130	20.00	1,350	(1,350)
135	25.00	1,850	(1,850)

[a]Initial price of the option is $650 and the exercise price equals $110.

Exhibit 15.5 ✦ PROFIT (LOSS) FROM BUYING OR WRITING A 110 JANUARY IBM CALL OPTION AT EXPIRATION

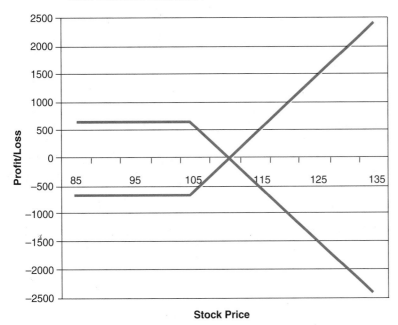

characteristic of option trading: it is a **zero sum game**—for someone to make a dollar, someone else must lose a dollar. In the example, at a stock price of 110, the option buyer loses $650 and the writer of the option makes $650.

zero sum game
Investment in which for someone to make a dollar, someone else must lose a dollar.

Buying a Put Option

Exhibit 15.6 shows the profit or loss from buying the 110 IBM January put at $7.125 for various stock prices at expiration. (Exhibit 15.7 shows the data in graph form.) If IBM stock is selling for 110 or higher just before the put option expires, the option is worthless. (It is about to expire out-of-the-money.) The buyer of the option loses $712.50. However, if IBM is selling for less than 110 just before the put option expires, it is about to expire in-the-money. The profit or loss equals the difference between the exercise price ($E = 110$) and the stock price, minus $7.125, multiplied by 100. For example, at a stock price of 100, the profit from the put option is

$$[(\$110 - \$100) - \$7.125] \times 100 = \$287.50$$

In general, then, the profit or loss from buying a put equals

$$\text{Profit (Loss)} = (P), \text{ if } S \geq E, \text{ where } T = 0$$
$$= [(E - S) - P] \times 100, \text{ if } S < E \text{ when } T = 0$$

where P is the price paid for the put option.[3]

Writing a Put Option

The profit or loss from writing the 110 January IBM put for $712.50 is also shown in Exhibit 15.6 for various stock prices at expiration. Exhibit 15.7 illustrates that the profit or loss from writing the put is the exact opposite of the profit or loss from buying the same put option. Put option trading is also a zero sum game. If IBM is trading for $100 per share right before the 110 January put option expires, the buyer of the option has made $287.50 and the writer of the option has lost $287.50.

Common Option-Trading Strategies

In this section, we review some of the unique risks and opportunities of options along with common option-trading strategies.[4] Some of these strategies involve positions in options alone (either calls or puts), whereas others combine option positions with positions in the underlying stocks. Throughout this discussion, we illustrate these strategies using various January 2000 IBM options and IBM's common stock. The options, their prices, and the stock price are shown below:

Security	Price[a]
IBM common stock	$109
105 January call	9 1/8
115 January call	4 1/8
105 January put	4 3/4
115 January put	10 1/4

[a]Quotes from *Wall Street Journal,* December 15, 1999.

---

[3]Again, after developing an understanding of the profits, it's easier to remember it as (E-S-P).

[4]Traders use many more option strategies than we discuss in this section. See, for example, Don Chance, *An Introduction to Options & Futures,* 3rd ed. (Fort Worth, TX: Dryden, 1995, pp. 197–236).

Exhibit 15.6 ✦ Profit (Loss) from Buying or Writing a 110 January IBM Put Option

Stock Price at Expiration ($T = 0$)	Value of Put Option	Profit (Loss)[a]	
		Buyer	Writer (Seller)
$85.00	$25.00	$1,787.50	$(1,787.50)
90.00	20.00	1,287.50	(1,287.50)
95.00	15.00	787.50	(787.50)
100.00	10.00	287.50	(287.50)
105.00	5.00	(212.50)	212.50
E = 110	0.00	(712.50)	712.50
115	0.00	(712.50)	712.50
120	0.00	(712.50)	712.50
125	0.00	(712.50)	712.50
130	0.00	(712.50)	712.50
135	0.00	(712.50)	712.50

[a]Initial price of the option is $712.50 and the exercise price equals $110.

SOME UNIQUE RISKS AND OPPORTUNITIES OF OPTIONS

Option trading offers investors some unique opportunities. Options, as we see in the next section, can be used to *hedge*—reduce the risk of—stock positions. At the same time, however, option trading exposes investors to substantial unique risks. An obvious risk of options is the need to be right not only about the direction of a move in a stock's price but also about its timing. Someone who believes the S&P 100 will decline by a certain percentage over the next few months may buy a put option that expires in three months. Even if that person is right and stocks do decline, she may still be wrong about when. The decline may begin in four months, after the three-month put option expires. Another risk unique to options is the fact that options trading is a zero sum game; for someone to make money, someone else has to lose the same amount. Still, options do offer investors attractive features.

One of the most potentially attractive features of call options is their inherent leverage. Buying a call option is similar to buying a stock on margin. To illustrate this inherent leverage, compare the holding period returns from buying IBM stock and buying the 115 January call. Exhibit 15.8 is a graph of the returns, assuming various stock prices at the call option's expiration date. If you had guessed right and IBM rose in price between December and January 2000, you would have been better off buying the call option rather than the stock itself. For example, had IBM moved from 109 to 125, the return from owning the stock would have been about 15 percent (ignoring transaction costs). However, owning the 115 January call option would have given a return of more than 142 percent.

As an aside, many cases of insider trading have involved options rather than stocks. Some famous insider trading cases in the 1980s, more often than not, involved buying call options. The reason comes from the inherent leverage of call options. Those who knew that the price of a stock was going to rise could generate far higher profits from the same dollar investment in the options market than in the stock market.

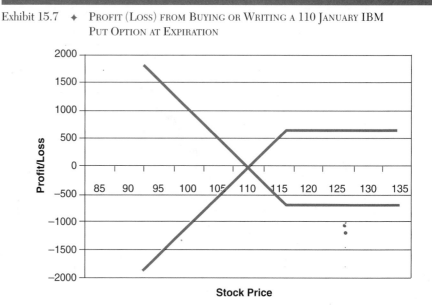

Exhibit 15.7 ✦ PROFIT (LOSS) FROM BUYING OR WRITING A 110 JANUARY IBM PUT OPTION AT EXPIRATION

The trouble with leverage, of course, is that it is a double-edged sword. Take another look at Exhibit 15.8. Had IBM's stock stayed at about 109 or even fallen, the call option owner would have been worse off than the stockholder. For example, had IBM's stock declined from 110 to 100 between December and January 2000, the stock's return would have been about −9 percent. However, the option's return would have been −100 percent. The option would have expired out-of-the-money and been worthless.

Put options offer investors unique opportunities as well. They give investors the opportunity to speculate on the prices of specific stocks or on specific stock indexes, declining over short periods of time. Remember, as we discussed in Chapter 3, investors can sell a stock short (selling borrowed shares and buying them back later, it is hoped at a lower price). Short sellers often face restrictions. An investor may find it easier to speculate on price declines using put options rather than short sales.

Finally, consider the unique risk associated with writing options; the potential gain is limited, whereas the potential loss is almost unlimited. In Exhibit 15.8, the maximum gain from writing the 110 January call would have been the price on the option, $650. However, if IBM's stock had soared over the next four weeks, the potential loss would have been much higher. Had IBM been trading at $120 per share in mid-January, the call option writer would have lost $350 per option contract. Only experienced option traders who can afford to risk substantial capital should consider writing options.

STRATEGIES INVOLVING ONE OPTION CONTRACT

We have already seen the profit and loss associated with buying and writing call and put options as shown in Exhibits 15.4 through 15.7. By now, you should have a pretty good idea of what investors expect when they buy and write call and put options; they buy call options to speculate on the price of a stock rising over a short period of time,

Exhibit 15.8 ✦ HOLDING PERIOD RETURN FROM IBM COMMON STOCK
AND A 115 IBM CALL OPTION

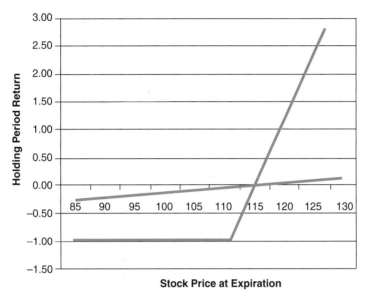

and they buy put options to speculate on the price of a stock falling over a short period of time. An investor who writes an option attempts to capture the option's price,
hoping that it expires out-of-the-money.

Buying and writing call and put options involves more than just choosing an underlying stock on which to trade options. One must also decide which call or put to
buy or write. Go back to Exhibits 15.2 and 15.3 for a moment; look at all the options
available for specific stocks or indexes. Deciding which option to buy or write often
depends on a trade-off between risk and return. Generally, an option further out-of-
the-money, with a shorter time until expiration, or both has a greater potential return
and greater risk for the option buyer. The option writer takes more risk on an option
with a strike price close to the stock's price, with a longer time until expiration, or
both. Let's illustrate this with an example.

Let's say you believed that IBM's stock price would rise sharply between early
December and mid-January 2000. This would support a decision to buy a January call
option. The next question is, which strike price should the option have? The inherent
risk/return trade-off is shown in Exhibit 15.9. The figure shows the holding period return for the 105 January call and the 115 January call between early January and the
options' expiration date in mid-January.

The call option with the higher exercise price would cost less (4 1/8 versus 9 1/8),
and its leverage potential would be greater. For example, if the price of IBM were to
rise to 125 at about the options' expiration date, the 115 call would produce a return
in excess of 142 percent, whereas the 105 call would produce a return of about 119
percent. (This, and all the examples that follow, ignores transaction costs.) At the same
time, however, the 115 call is riskier than the 105 call. Assume that IBM's stock rises
only slightly from 109 to 115 between early November and mid-January. The 105 call
would produce a return of about 9.6 percent. The 115 call, however, would expire
at-the-money, returning a *negative* 100 percent.

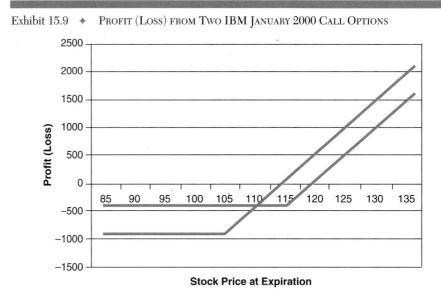

Exhibit 15.9 ✦ Profit (Loss) from Two IBM January 2000 Call Options

STRADDLES

straddle

Buying both a call and a put with the same exercise price and the same expiration date.

A **straddle** involves buying both a call and a put with the same exercise price and the same expiration date. A straddle is essentially a bet on the volatility of the underlying stock. However, a *reverse straddle* involves writing both a call and a put with the same exercise price and the same expiration date. Not surprisingly, a reverse straddle is a bet against volatility in the underlying stock.

Assume that a trader believed in early January 2000 that one of two things was going to happen to IBM by mid-January: either the stock would continue to rise sharply (because Y2K was not a problem) or would fall sharply due to Y2K problems. In a straddle, the trader would buy both the 110 January call (for 6 1/2) and the 110 January put (for 7 1/8). The profit or loss from this straddle is illustrated in Exhibit 15.10.

For the straddle to be profitable, the stock price would have to move substantially in one direction or the other. At the expiration date, stock price of about 95 and less, or about 125 and more, the straddle is profitable. The straddle buyer would have suffered if IBM had remained at around 110 through mid-January.

Exhibit 15.10 also illustrates the profit and loss from a reverse straddle. This trade combined writing the 110 January call and 110 January put. The strategy works if IBM's common stock remains about 110 until mid-January. Like writing a call or a put individually, a wrong guess exposes the option writer to an almost unlimited potential loss.

SPREADS

spread

Buying one option and writing another on the same underlying stock.

A **spread** involves purchasing one option and writing another on the same underlying stock. The options differ only in terms of one parameter, usually either exercise price or expiration date. The most common type of spread is a money spread.[5]

---

[5]In addition to money spreads, option traders can construct calendar spreads, butterfly spreads, and box spreads. See Chance, *Introduction to Options*, pp. 208–17.

Exhibit 15.10 ✦ PROFIT OR LOSS FROM BUYING OR WRITING A STRADDLE

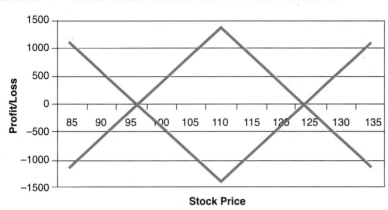

Money Spreads

A money spread involves the purchase of one call or put option and the sale of another. The options have the same expiration date but different exercise prices. Money spreads are often referred to as either *bull spreads* or *bear spreads,* because they constitute bets on whether underlying stocks' prices will rise or fall over a short period of time.

Exhibit 15.11 illustrates both a bull spread and a bear spread. In the bull spread, one buys the 105 January call and writes the 115 January call. In general, a bull spread involves buying the call with the lower exercise price, E_1, while writing the call with the higher exercise price, E_2. In the bear spread, one writes the 105 January call and buys the 115 January call. Notice the limits on how much one can make or lose with either spread. The bear spread, for example, has a maximum profit of $500 and a maximum loss of $500. (It is only by coincidence that the profits and losses are equal).

Bull and bear spreads can also be constructed with put options. A bear spread would involve buying the put with the higher exercise price, E_2, while writing the put with the lower exercise price, E_1. A bull spread would combine writing the put with the higher exercise price, E_2, while buying the put with the lower exercise price, E_1.

Why Trade Spreads?

As you probably have already guessed, a bull spread using call options is a substitute for simply buying a call option, whereas a bear spread using call options is a substitute for writing a call option. The advantage of a bull spread over buying a call option is that smaller upward movements in the price of the underlying stock will produce higher profits. For example, if IBM had moved from about 109 in December to 115 in mid-January, the bull spread shown in Figure 15.11 would have produced a profit of $500. By contrast, simply buying the 105 January call would have produced a profit of only $87.50 because of the huge price of the 105 call (9 1/8). By selling the 115 call, you defray the cost of the 105 call. The disadvantage of the bull spread is that it would limit the maximum profit to $500, regardless of how high IBM's stock price were to climb.

Exhibit 15.11 ✦ Profit or Loss from a Bull Spread or Bear Spread

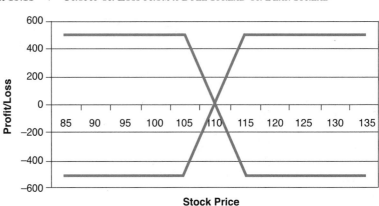

The advantage of a bear spread over simply writing a call option is obvious: limited downside risk. Remember, simply writing a call option exposes one to unlimited potential loss. The bear spread shown in Exhibit 15.11 would limit the potential loss to $500, regardless of how high IBM's stock price were to climb. Although a bear spread does sacrifice some upside potential, most experienced option traders speculate on price declines by using spreads rather than simply writing individual call options.

COMBINING OPTION AND STOCK POSITIONS

Another common use of options is to combine them with positions in underlying stocks. These combined positions are often called hedges; the option is used to reduce the risk of the stock position. Let's look at three common techniques that combine options and stock: writing covered calls, buying protective puts, and covering short sales.

Writing Covered Calls

covered call
Writing a call option on stock the investor already owns.

Writing a **covered call** involves writing a call option on a stock already owned by the investor. Investors write covered calls for two basic reasons: to increase income from the stock (because the writer of an option receives the option premium) and to reduce the downside risk of the stock. Optimism about a stock's long-term prospects does not eliminate worry about it in the short term.

Assume someone bought IBM at 110 and, at the same time, wrote a 110 January call option, perhaps thinking that IBM's stock price should increase in the long run, despite concern that it may not rise over the short term due to anticipated Y2K problems. The profit and loss from this combination is shown in Exhibit 15.12. Note that this is an unusual position. In reality, few investors would buy a stock and immediately write a call option on it. They are more likely to write call options on stocks they have owned for some time.

As shown in Exhibit 15.12, if IBM's stock had declined slightly from 110 to 105 between December and mid-January 2000, the covered call would have been more

Exhibit 15.12 ✦ Profit (Loss) from a Covered Call on IBM

Stock Price at Expiration ($T = 0$)	Profit (Loss)		
	Call	Stock	Covered Call
$ 85	$ 650	($2,500)	($1,850)
90	650	(2,000)	(1,350)
95	650	(1,500)	(850)
100	650	(1,000)	(350)
105	650	(500)	150
110	650	0	650
115	150	500	650
120	(350)	1000	650
125	(850)	1500	650
130	(1,350)	2000	650
135	(1,850)	2500	650

profitable than simply owning the stock. At the same time, had IBM declined in price, the profit from writing the call would have offset some of the loss from the stock position. (The losses in the stock are only paper losses, of course; they become real cash losses only if the stock is actually sold.)

Protective Puts

A **protective put** is another common combined stock option position in which an investor buys put options on stock he or she already owns. The rationale for a protective put is straightforward: it reduces some of the downside risk associated with owning stocks, either by guaranteeing a sale price or offsetting losses on the stock with profits on the put. Protective puts can be thought of as a kind of insurance.

Exhibit 15.13 assumes that an investor purchased 100 shares of IBM stock in November 1999 for $100 a share and has watched the stock rise sharply in price. The investor worries about the stock falling in the near term. So, she decides to protect some of the profit by buying a 110 January put for 7 1/8. Notice that even if IBM's stock price collapses, the investor has "locked in" a profit of $287.50.

Buying a protective put requires careful attention to the strike price of the option. A higher strike price lowers the risk, but at the same time, a higher strike price also increases the cost of the put. This decision resembles the choice of a deductible on auto insurance: a higher deductible reduces the cost of the auto insurance, but it increases the loss from an accident.

protective put
Buying a put option on stock the investor already owns.

Covered Short Sales

A **covered short sale** is similar to a protective put: the option provides insurance. In a covered short sale, the investor combines a short position in a stock with a long position in a call option. Remember, a short sale represents a bet on a drop in the price of a stock, allowing the investor to buy back borrowed shares at a lower price. The risk of a short sale is the potential loss if the stock price does not drop. The call option reduces some of this risk.

covered short sale
Buying a call option on stock the investor has shorted.

Exhibit 15.13   ✦   PROFIT (LOSS) FROM BUYING A PROTECTIVE PUT ON IBM STOCK

Stock Price at Expiration ($T = 0$)	Put	Stock	Protective Put
$ 85	$1,787.50	($1,500)	$ 287.50
90	128.50	(1,000)	287.50
95	787.50	(500)	287.50
100	287.50	0	287.50
105	(212.50)	500	287.50
110	(712.50)	1,000	287.50
115	(712.50)	1,500	787.50
120	(712.50)	2,000	1,287.50
125	(712.50)	2,500	1,787.50
130	(712.50)	3,000	2,287.50
135	(712.50)	3,500	2,787.50

For example, assume that in early January 2000, anticipating Y2K problems, you are convinced IBM's stock will fall sharply over the next few weeks. You decide to short the stock at 110 and, at the same time, buy the 110 January call for 6 1/2 in December 1999. The results are shown in Exhibit 15.14.

The exhibit shows clearly how owning the call option greatly reduces the risk of the short sale. For example, if IBM were to soar to $125 per share by mid-January, the combined position would lose only $650, compared with a $1,500 loss for a simple short sale without the call option. Of course, like all insurance, buying the call would reduce some of the short sale's profits if IBM were to fall in price.

Pricing Options

Up to now, we have discussed how to determine the value of an option at expiration, and we have used this knowledge to examine the profit and loss potentials of several common option-trading strategies. This section explores the factors that affect the value of an option before expiration. These factors help explain why some options are worth more than others and why option prices rise and fall. They also help us to understand the most widely used option pricing model.

DETERMINANTS OF OPTION VALUES

The fundamental value of an option before expiration is affected by six factors: (1) the price of the underlying stock, (2) the exercise price, (3) the length of time until expiration, (4) the volatility of the underlying stock, (5) the level of interest rates, and (6) the amount of dividends the underlying stock pays between now and the expiration date. Let's discuss each of these factors.

Price of the Underlying Stock

As the price of the underlying stock rises the value of a call option rises. As the stock price falls, the call option falls. The reverse is true for a put option; the value of a put rises as the stock falls in price. The put value falls as the stock value rises.

Exhibit 15.14 ◆ PROFIT (LOSS) FROM A COVERED SHORT SALE ON IBM

Stock Price at Expiration ($T = 0$)	Buy a Call	Sell Short on the Stock	Covered Short Sale
$ 85	($650)	$ 2,500	$1,850
90	(650)	2,000	1,350
95	(650)	1,500	850
100	(650)	1,000	350
105	(650)	500	(150)
110	(650)	0	(650)
115	(150)	(500)	(650)
120	350	(1,000)	(650)
125	850	(1,500)	(650)
130	1,350	(2,000)	(650)
135	1,850	(2,500)	(650)

Exercise Price

Because a call is an option to buy, a higher exercise price implies a lower value. A put is an option to sell, so a higher exercise price implies a higher value. To verify these relationships, refer back to Exhibit 15.2. Notice that the 105 January call on IBM sold for 9 1/8, whereas the 115 January call sold for 4 1/8. The 105 January put sold for 4 3/4, whereas the 115 January put sold for 10 1/4.

Time until Expiration

Referring again to Exhibit 15.2, what relationship do you see between the value of IBM options and their times until expiration? The relationship, for both calls and puts, is positive; a longer time until expiration implies a higher price. For example, the 120 December 1999 call traded for 1/16 whereas the 120 January 2000 call traded for 2 7/8.

Why do we see this positive relationship between option price and time until expiration? The answer is simply that a longer time until expiration increases the probability that an option will become in-the-money before it expires.

Earlier in this chapter, we defined an option's premium. For a call, the premium is equal to the price of the option plus the exercise price minus the current stock price. For a put, the premium equals the price of the option plus the current stock price minus the exercise price. If the price of the underlying stock were to remain constant, the option's premium should diminish as the expiration date gets closer.

Volatility of the Underlying Stock

An option buyer's loss is limited to the price of the option. However, the potential profit is almost unlimited. As a result, the stock price at expiration is irrelevant if the option expires out-of-the-money. For example, someone who bought the 115 January call for 4 1/8 would not have cared whether IBM sold for 120 or 115 in mid-January. In both cases, the option would have expired out-of-the-money and the owner would have lost $412.50. However, IBM's stock price would become critical if the option were about to expire in-the-money.

This means that more volatility in the underlying stock makes an option more valuable. Increased volatility increases the odds that the option will expire in-the-money. This is true for both call and put options.

One way of gauging the volatility of the underlying stock is to compare the premiums investors are willing to pay for options on particular stocks. For example, recently AT&T was trading for 55 1/4. At the same time, a 55 January 2000 call option was trading for 3. The option had a premium of 3 − 55 1/4 + 55 = 2 3/4. On the same day, Amazon.com was trading for 95 5/8 and a 100 January 2000 call was trading for 11 1/2. The Amazon.com option had a premium of 11 1/2 − 95 5/8 + 100 = 15 7/8. Conventional wisdom suggests that Amazon.com's common stock is more volatile in price than is AT&T's common stock.[6]

Level of Interest Rates

As interest rates rise, the value of a call option increases, while the value of a put option decreases. This may initially seem puzzling, but the reason is quite straightforward. As interest rates rise, the present value of the exercise price falls. To exercise a call option, the owner must pay something (the exercise price); therefore, as the present value of this price falls, the value of the call option should rise. The reverse, of course, is true for a put option.

Dividends

We mentioned earlier that options are protected from stock splits and stock dividends. If a stock splits two for one, for example, the exercise price of all options will automatically be halved. Options are not, however, protected from cash dividends. Now, you may also remember that when a stock goes ex-dividend, its price falls because the buyer is no longer entitled to the current dividend. A larger cash dividend (as a percentage of the stock price) implies a greater price decline. What does this mean for the price of an option?

If the underlying stock pays dividends between the option's purchase and its expiration date, the dividend payment and the resulting price drop on the ex-dividend date will tend to decrease the value of a call option and increase the value of a put option. A larger dividend causes a greater price decrease in a call option or increase in a put option.

Exhibit 15.15 summarizes the relationships between these six factors and the value of an option before expiration. Although the material that follows is somewhat more difficult than what we have covered up to this point, understanding the relationships summarized in the exhibit will help you understand why some options are worth more than others and why option prices increase or decrease over time. This is important knowledge if you wish to successfully trade options.

BLACK-SCHOLES OPTION-PRICING MODEL[7]

An option-pricing model developed by Fischer Black and Myron Scholes in 1973 is probably the best-known option-pricing model and is widely used by option traders.[8]

---

[6]Amazon.com's beta was 2.98 and AT&T's beta was about 1.10.

[7]This section can be skipped without any loss of continuity.

[8]Fischer Black and Myron Scholes, "The Pricing of Options and Corporate Liabilities," *Journal of Political Economy* (May-June 1973), pp. 637–59.

Exhibit 15.15 ✦ SIX FACTORS THAT AFFECT THE VALUE OF OPTIONS BEFORE EXPIRATION

Variable	Direction of Change	Impact on the Value of	
		Call Option	Put Option
1. Price of underlying stock	Higher	Increases	Decreases
2. Exercise price	Higher	Decrease	Increases
3. Time until expiration	Longer	Increases	Increases
4. Volatility of underlying stock	Higher	Increases	Increases
5. Interest rates	Higher	Increases	Decreases
6. Dividends	Larger	Decreases	Increases

The model was developed for *European call options.* European options are identical to *American options* except that they can be exercised only on the expiration date.[9] All options traded throughout the world are American options.

The Black-Scholes model makes several important assumptions. It assumes that the risk-free rate and the underlying stock's price volatility remain constant over the life of the option and that the underlying stock pays no dividends. Given these assumptions, the fundamental value of a European call is

$$C = S[N(d_1)] - Ee^{-rT}[N(d_2)]$$

$$d_1 = \frac{\ln(S/E) + \left(r + \frac{\sigma^2}{2}\right)T}{\sigma\sqrt{T}}$$

$$d_2 = d_1 - \sigma\sqrt{T}$$

(15.3)

where C is the fundamental value of the option, S is the current price of the underlying stock, E is the exercise price, T is the time until expiration stated in years (for an option that expires in six months, $T = 0.5$), r is the risk-free rate of interest, σ is the standard deviation of the underlying stock (a measure of volatility), $\ln(S/E)$ is the natural log of S/E, e equals 2.71828 (the base of the natural log function), and $N(d)$ is the probability that a random draw from a standard normal distribution function will be less than d. The term Ee^{-rT} is the present value of the exercise price, assuming continuous compounding. With a little math, the Black-Scholes model, Equation 15.3, can be modified to price European put options.

Loose Interpretation of the Black-Scholes Model

Although the formula looks horrendous, it is comprehensible if you take it step by step. If the price of the stock when the option expires is certain, assuming that $S > E$, the two $N(d)$ terms will be close to 1. This makes Equation 15.3 approach

$$C = S - Ee^{-rT}$$

[9]Mathematically, European options are much simpler to value than American options. However, it can be shown that a rational investor will never exercise a call option before expiration, choosing instead to sell the option. See, Chance, *Introduction to Options,* pp. 80–83 and 94–95.

In English, the call price equals the current stock price minus the present value of the exercise price.

At the other extreme, if the option stands virtually no chance of expiring in-the-money, the two $N(d)$ terms approach zero. The value of the option also approaches zero.

For all the probabilities in between, the Black-Scholes Option-Pricing Model can be loosely interpreted as saying that the value of a call is equal to the expected stock price at expiration minus the present value of the exercise price, both weighted by the probability of the option expiring in-the-money.

Determinants of the Fundamental Value of an Option

Exhibit 15.15 lists the six variables that appear to affect the value of an option. The Black-Scholes model incorporates five of the six. (Remember that it assumes that the underlying stock pays no dividends.) Adjusting the values of these five factors individually in the model increases or decreases the value of the call, exactly as shown in Exhibit 15.15.

For example, increasing the underlying stock's standard deviation, σ in Equation 15.3, while holding all the other variables constant, increases the value of the call option. Familiar information about the intrinsic value of a call option confirms the validity of the Black-Scholes model. (That is always a good feeling.)

Applying the Black-Scholes Model

Let's apply the Black-Scholes model to one of the IBM options we have been using, the 110 January call option. One appealing characteristic of the model is that all its variables but one are easily available from a source such as the *Wall Street Journal.* The current stock price (S), the exercise price (E), the risk-free rate (r), and the time to expiration (T) can be obtained from the financial press. The only variable that must be estimated is the standard deviation of the underlying stock—usually using historical stock returns (continuously compounded).

In early January 2000, the following information could be used to estimate the value of the 110 January IBM call option: $S = 109$, $E = 110$, $T = 36/365 = 0.0986$, and $r = 4.0$ percent. Annualizing the standard deviation of monthly returns from IBM stock for the past 60 months gives us an estimate of $\sigma = .458$.

The first step is to calculate d_1 and d_2. Based on our inputs, $d_2 = 0.0358$ and $d_2 = -0.1080$. The next step is to find the probability that a random draw from a standard normal distribution $N(d_1)$ and (one with a mean of 0 and a standard deviation of 1.0) will be less than 0.0358 and -0.1080, respectively. The answers are $N(d_2) = 0.5143$ and $N(d_2) = 0.4570$. The final step is to fill in the values in Equation 15.3:

$$C = (\$109)[0.5143] - (\$110)(e^{-0.0986(.04)})\,[0.4570]$$
$$= \$5.985$$

Note that we have rounded these numbers, so you may get an answer that is a penny or two different.

The Black-Scholes model gives a price for the call option of $5.985. Its actual market price, as of December 15, 1999, was $6.50. The Black-Scholes model's estimate is pretty close to the market price of the 110 January IBM call. Remember, though, that the prices quoted in the press are past trade prices, not current bid or ask prices.

Arbitrage Strategy Using the Black-Scholes Model

Someone who believes the Black-Scholes model's estimate of the fundamental value of a call option may be able to use a simple arbitrage trading strategy. The Black-Scholes model gave a fundamental value for the IBM call of $5.985 (rounded to $6). Assuming that its market price is $6.50, the Black-Scholes model estimates that the call is overpriced.

An arbitrageur could profit from the overpriced call by buying IBM stock and writing the IBM 110 call. If the Black-Scholes model's price is correct, the call is overpriced, and when the market corrects this mistake, the arbitrageur makes money regardless of whether the stock price rises or falls. How many shares does the arbitrageur buy for every call written—assuming one call controls one share of stock? The answer is 0.5143, the value of $N(d_1)$.[10] Because each call contract is associated with 100 shares of the stock, we multiply the hedge ratio, $N(d_1)$ by 100, or 0.5143 × 100 = 51.43 shares per contract.

Let's illustrate with an example. Suppose the market price of a 85 January call is $5 and its fundamental value from the Black-Scholes model is $4.63. Also, the hedge ratio, $N(d_1)$ is calculated to equal 0.55 and the stock is trading at $85. In the sample trade, buying 550 shares at $85 costs $46,750; writing 1,000 calls at $5.00 generates income of $5,000. The net investment is $41,750. Now, assume that the price either rises to $86 or falls to $84.

If the price rises to 86, the position makes $550 on the stock (550 shares times $1); if the price falls to 84, the stock's value falls by $550. What about the option? The term $N(d_1)$ indicates the change in the price of the option, given a $1 change in the price of the stock. This is not a change in the market price but only a change in the option's fundamental value. Given that $N(d_2)$ is 0.55, if the stock rises to 86, the price of the option should be $5.18 ($4.63 + $0.55). Therefore, the option position will lose only $180 in value (1,000 times $0.18). The net profit from the combined option/stock position is $370.

If the stock falls to 84, the new option price should be $4.08, giving profit on the option position of $920 (1,000 times $0.92). The net profit, should the stock decline in price from the combined option/stock position, is $370, the same profit as the price increase. Remember, this assumes that the market eventually recognizes the fact that the option is priced above its fundamental value and corrects this overpricing.

This is but one example of how the Black-Scholes model could be used in the real world of option trading. Before investing your tuition money for next year based on the Black-Scholes model, note a few caveats about the model:

1. The Black-Scholes model does not consider dividend payments that accrue while the hedged position remains outstanding. Recall from the previous section that a dividend payout decreases a call's price.
2. The model assumes that the risk-free rate, r, and the standard deviation of the stock return are constant over time; they may well vary.
3. The model also assumes that stock prices are continuous, and no sudden extreme jumps occur. From the IBM example, we know that the market can give no guarantee of continuous pricing as new information becomes available.

---

[10] $N(d_1)$ is referred to as the "hedge ratio," meaning that one could construct a risk-free portfolio combining the option and the stock—either buying the option and shorting the stock or writing the option and buying the stock. This portfolio would earn the risk-free rate regardless of whether the stock moved up or down in price.

4. The model also assumes that the hedging process is continuously managed so that hedges remain continuously perfect. Unfortunately, the trades necessary to guarantee this would quickly erode any profits through commission costs.

Like all mathematical models, the Black-Scholes formula approximates the real world and so requires caution. Nevertheless, the model has opened a way to price options and other securities that resemble them. The model is widely used by option traders to identify potentially over- and underpriced options.

Other Securities that Resemble Options

Several securities have features like those of options, allowing investors to buy or sell something at fixed prices for fixed periods of time. Many of the same pricing rules we have discussed up to this point apply to these securities as well. The most common securities with option-like features are convertibles and warrants.

CONVERTIBLE SECURITIES

convertible security
A bond or preferred stock that gives the owner the right to convert the security for a specified number of shares of common stock.

A **convertible security,** either a bond or a preferred stock issue, gives the holder the right to convert the security for a specified number of shares of common stock in the same company that issued the convertible. The prescribed number of shares obtained when the bond or preferred share is tendered for conversion, the **conversion ratio,** is normally fixed for the life of the convertible. For example, a conversion ratio of 20 says that a convertible bond can be exchanged for 20 shares of the company's common stock.

conversion ratio
Number of shares of common stock received if the conversion feature is exercised.

To see how a convertible security resembles a call option, let's look at an example. Starbucks issued a convertible bond with a conversion ratio of 43.01 (meaning that each bond can be exchanged for 43.01 shares of Starbucks common stock), a face value of $1,000, a coupon rate of 4 1/4 percent, and a maturity date of 2002. This bond gives its owner the right to buy 43.01 shares of Starbucks stock (by exchanging the bond) at a *conversion price* of $23.25 per share ($1,000 divided by the conversion ratio) until the bond matures in 2002. Until the owner exercises the option and converts the bond, it pays $42.50 per year in coupon interest.

Valuing a Convertible Security

To value a convertible security, let's consider Starbucks' convertible bond, which had a market price of $1,500. At the same time, Starbucks common stock was trading at $34 per share. Multiplying the current stock price (34) by the conversion ratio (43.01) gives the bond's **conversion value,** $1,462 (rounded to the nearest dollar). In other words, the owner of the convertible could exchange the bond for common stock worth about $1,462.

conversion value
Current stock price multiplied by the conversion ratio.

In option terminology, the Starbucks convertible bond is in-the-money because the stock price, $34, exceeds the conversion price, equivalent to an option's exercise price, of $23.25. Further, the convertible is selling at a premium above its conversion value ($1,500 versus $1,462). Why? As we have discussed, one factor that makes some call options more valuable is the volatility of their underlying stocks. Starbucks has historically been a volatile stock.

Exhibit 15.16 ✦ VALUING A CONVERTIBLE BOND

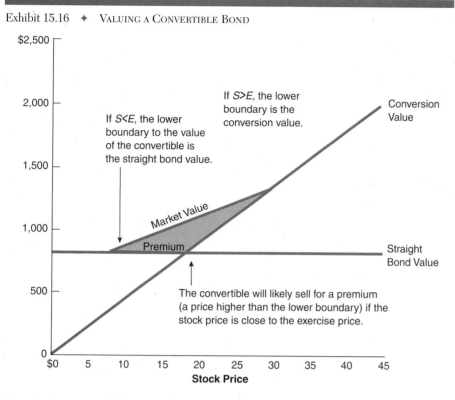

Note: *The above convertible has a conversion ratio of 43.01 and a straight bond value of $782.*

The conversion value, of course, has a linear relationship with the stock price, as Exhibit 15.16 illustrates. Will the conversion value always form the lower boundary to the value of a convertible, regardless of the stock price? No. If the Starbucks convertible had no conversion option, it would simply be a corporate bond with a maturity in 2002 and a coupon rate of 4.25 percent. Presumably, it would be valued as such. This is referred to as the convertible's *straight bond value,* the value of the convertible without the conversion feature.

To estimate the straight bond value, find the price of the bond at the same yield to maturity common for straight bonds with similar maturity and quality characteristics. Straight bonds similar to the Starbucks convertible had yields to maturity of about 10 percent. Therefore, the bond pricing equation developed in Chapter 9 gives the Starbucks convertible a straight bond value of about $782 per $1,000 of par value. The straight bond value is also shown in Exhibit 15.16.

To summarize, the straight bond value is the lower boundary for the value of a convertible if $S < E$. If $S > E$, the lower boundary becomes the conversion value. Will the convertible always sell for a premium over its straight bond value? Not necessarily; it depends on the relationship between the stock price and bond's conversion price. If the convertible is deeply out-of-the-money, it will likely sell for close to its straight bond value. However, if the convertible is deeply in-the-money, it will likely sell for close to its conversion value. For values in between, the convertible will sell for a premium, perhaps a large one, above its straight bond value.

Why Buy Convertibles?

Convertibles can offer investors attractive combinations of the best of both bonds and stocks. They have more upside potential than bonds; as the stock price increases, so does the value of the convertible. However, convertibles provide more downside protection than stocks; they can always be valued as straight bonds. Furthermore, the coupon rate on a convertible usually exceeds the stock's dividend yield by a substantial amount. The Starbucks convertible had a coupon rate of 4.25 percent; Starbucks common stock pays no cash dividends.

Convertibles are not perfect securities, however. For one thing, they tend to be rated lower than straight bonds. (The Starbucks convertible is rated single B.) For another, because of the conversion feature, convertibles have lower coupon rates than similar straight bonds. The investor must give up some current income in exchange for the conversion feature. As a result, when considering a convertible, an investor must evaluate the prospects for the company's common stock.

Another risk is unique to convertibles: almost all convertibles are callable. Issuers may use the call provision to essentially force conversion. Would you, assuming you are a rational investor—and we hope at this point that you are—ever exercise the conversion feature before maturity? No! You would exercise the conversion option only if the convertible were in-the-money. If it is in-the-money, its value will increase dollar for dollar as the stock price increases, and it will still offer the downside protection of a bond and the higher current income from the coupon payments. When the issuing company wants the convertible bond converted into common stock, if it is deeply in-the-money and the call price is well below the market price, the firm will call the bond. Rather than allowing the company to call the bond in exchange for its par value, you would either convert the bond into common stock or sell the bond to someone else who would.

WARRANTS

warrant
A long-term call option issued by a company giving its owner the right to buy a fixed number of shares of stock at a fixed price for a fixed period of time.

A **warrant** is simply a long-term call option issued by a company. It allows the holder to buy a fixed number of shares of stock (usually one warrant buys one share) from the issuing company at a fixed price for a fixed period of time. Warrants usually have lives of between five and 10 years when issued. They are often attached to other securities, such as bonds. Most warrants can be detached and sold in the secondary market. Warrants typically trade, along with the company's stock, on one of the major stock exchanges.

Given the recent stock market boom, warrant issues have virtually disappeared and companies are issuing additional shares of its stock instead. However, Intel's warrant in 1997 serves as an example. The warrant allowed the owner to buy one share of Intel common stock for $41.75. When the warrants expired they were selling for 120 3/4, whereas Intel's common stock was selling for 160.

Valuing a warrant is similar to valuing a call option. The Intel warrant is deeply in-the-money ($S > E$) and is selling for a premium of $2.50 ($120.75 − $160 + $41.75). That may not seem high, but remember that even though Intel has been a volatile stock, the warrant was deeply in-the-money and expired in one year.

Trading strategies for warrants are similar to those for call options. Warrants, like call options, have inherent leverage that allows individuals to speculate on the price of a specific stock moving up over the next few months or years. Warrants can also be used to cover, or hedge, a short sale. The downside of warrants is that they are available on only a limited number of stocks, and they often are not actively traded.

Chapter Summary

1. What are the basic characteristics of option contracts?
   A call option gives the owner the right, but not obligation, to buy shares of stock at a fixed price for a fixed period of time. The owner of a put option has the right, but not obligation, to sell shares of stock at a fixed price for a fixed period of time. Every option bought must have a seller. The seller—or writer—of a call option may be obligated to sell stock at a fixed price; the writer of a put option may be obligated to buy stock at a fixed price.

2. What is the value of an option at expiration?
   The value of a call option at expiration is equal to the maximum of zero or the difference between the stock price and the exercise price. At expiration the value of a put option is equal to the maximum of zero or the difference between the exercise price and the stock price.

3. What are some common option-trading strategies?
   Investors buy options as a way of speculating on short-term price movements in stock or stock indexes. If you believe a stock will rise in price, you might buy a call option. If you believe a stock will fall in price, you might buy a put option. Many option traders trade several options at the same time. A straddle involves buying a call and a put option with the same expiration date and exercise price. It is a bet that the stock price will move substantially in one direction or the other. Another common option trade is a spread—say, buying one call option while selling another with a different exercise price. Spreads are less risky than buying or selling just one option. Options can also be used to reduce the risk of a position in the underlying stock.

4. How are options valued?
   The intrinsic value of an option is a function of six variables: the price of the underlying stock, the exercise price, the time until expiration, the level of short-term interest rates, the volatility of the underlying stock, and the amount of dividends the stock pays before expiration. The Black-Scholes Option Pricing Model explicitly includes five of these six variables—the model assumes the underlying stock pays no dividends.

5. What other securities resemble options?
   A convertible security is a bond or preferred stock that can be converted into common stock, at a fixed price, for a fixed period of time. In essence, a convertible contains a call option and can be valued as such. A warrant is a long-term call option issued by corporations. Warrants often are attached to other security issues. Warrants often trade in the stock markets.

Mini Case 1

This mini-case allows you to practice finding prices, premiums, values at expiration, and profits (losses) for S&P 100 (OEX) options. Use the information below to answer the questions.

Strike Price	Expiration	Call or Put	Price
760	January 2000	Call	43 3/4
760	January 2000	Put	6 3/4
760	February 2000	Call	50 3/4
760	February 2000	Put	13 3/4
770	January 2000	Call	37
770	January 2000	Put	8 3/4

1. When do the options expire? What rights do they give their buyers?
2. Which options are in-the-money? Find the options' premiums. What does *premium* mean?

3. What will the call and put options be worth when they expire?
4. Construct profit and loss graphs for a call option's buyer and writer (you choose the call option).
5. Construct profit and loss graphs for a put option's buyer and writer (you choose the put option).
6. Assume you believe the OEX will rise sharply during the next few days; use the above options to construct a bull spread.

Mini Case 2

This mini-case applies the Black-Scholes Option Pricing Model to an actual call option.

    Stock: America Online (AOL)
    Stock price: 81 1/8
    Exercise price: 85
    Risk-free rate of interest: 4.10 percent
    Expiration: 26 days
    Standard deviation of stock returns: 0.674
    Market price of call: 5 7/8

1. Is the AOL call option in-the-money? What is its intrinsic value? What is its time value?
2. Use the above information and the Black-Scholes model to find the fundamental value of this option.
3. If the fundamental value of the option differs from its market price, explain how to take advantage of this difference.

Review Questions and Problems

1. What is a derivative security? Why are options considered derivative securities?
2. What rights and obligations does an option buyer have? How do these differ from the rights and obligations of the option writer?
3. Explain cash settlement of index options. Give a numerical example.
4. If a put option has a price of $5 and an exercise price of $50 while the underlying stock is selling for $48, is the put option in-the-money? What is its premium?
5. For the put option described in question 4, calculate the profit and loss from holding the option to expiration. How much would the price of the stock have to change for the option buyer to break even?
6. What does it mean when we say call options have inherent leverage? What other risks are unique to options?
7. From the option prices shown in Exhibit 15.2, construct a bull spread using Cisco 95 and 105 January call options. Create a profit/loss table if the stock price equals $85, $90, $95, $100, $105, $110 or $115 at expiration. What is the purpose of a bull spread?
8. From the option prices shown in Exhibit 15.2, construct a bull spread using Cisco 95 and 105 January put options. Create a profit/loss table if the stock price equals $85, $90, $95, $100, $105, $110 or $115 at expiration. What, if any, advantage do you see in using the puts versus the calls to create a bull spread?
9. Using the options quotes shown in Exhibit 15.2, construct a straddle using Cisco 100 January options. Create a profit/loss table if the stock price equals $90, $95, $100, $105, or $110 at expiration. What is the purpose of a straddle?
10. Using the option prices shown in Exhibit 15.2, create a money spread using Intel 70 and 80 January call options, to reflect the expectation that Intel stock prices should

decline. Create a profit/loss table if the stock price equals $60, $65, $70, $75, $80, $85, or $90 at expiration.

11. Using the option prices shown in Exhibit 15.2, create a money spread using Intel 70 and 80 January put options, to reflect the expectation that the price of Intel stock should increase. Create a profit/loss table assuming the stock price equals $60, $65, $70, $75, $80, $85, or $90 at expiration.

12. Suppose you bought an Intel stock at $50 in July and the stock price rose to $85 by November. Assume you want to hold the stock until January for tax purposes, but you are afraid the stock may decline between mid-December and January. How can you protect your profits using a put? Create a profit/loss table assuming that the stock price equals $60, $65, $70, $75, $80, $85, or $90 at expiration.

13. Using Exhibit 15.2 find the intrinsic value of Compaq 25 January call? Is it in-the-money? Explain. What is its time value and its premium?

14. Using Exhibit 15.2, find the intrinsic value of an Intel 75 January put. Is it in-the-money? Explain. What is its time value and its premium?

15. Suppose you bought an Intel stock at $50 six months ago and the stock price has risen around $73 today. You decide to write a covered call on the Intel stock using the 75 January call. Create a profit/loss table for a covered call assuming that the stock price equals $60, $65, $70, $75, $80, $85, or $90 at expiration.

16. Discuss the six factors that affect the value of a call option before expiration. How do these relationships change for the value of a put option before expiration?

17. Give a loose interpretation of the Black-Scholes Option Pricing Model. How realistic are the model's assumptions?

18. Assume a convertible bond with a $1,000 face value is convertible into 25 shares of stock. What is the conversion price? If the stock price is currently $50, how much is the conversion value?

19. What are the major investment advantages of convertibles? What are their drawbacks?

20. What makes a warrant simply a long-term call option? Why might an investor buy a warrant as opposed to the underlying stock?

CFA Questions

1. (Level I, 1993) An at-the-money protective put position (comprised of owning the stock and the put):
   a. Protects against loss at any stock price below the strike price of the put.
   b. Has limited profit potential when the stock price rises.
   c. Returns any increase in the stock's value, dollar for dollar, less the cost of the put.
   d. Provides a pattern of returns similar to a stop-loss order at the current stock price.

2. (Level I, 1993) In the Black-Scholes option valuation formula, an increase in a stock's volatility:
   a. Increases the associated call option value.
   b. Decreases the associated put option value.
   c. Increases or decreases the option value, depending on the level of interest rates.
   d. Does not change either the put or call option value because put-call parity holds.

3. (Level I, 1993) An American option is more valuable than a European option on the same dividend paying stock with the same terms because the:
   a. European option contract is not adjusted for stock splits and stock dividends.
   b. American option can be exercised from date of purchase until expiration, but the European option can be exercised only at expiration.
   c. European option does not conform to the Black-Scholes model and is often mis-priced.

    d. American options are traded on U.S. exchanges, which offer much more volume and liquidity.

4. (Level I, 1988) Which one of the following transactions would be considered a protective strategy?
    a. Sell a call against a stock you sold short.
    b. Buy a call on a stock you own.
    c. Sell a naked put.
    d. Buy a put on a stock you own.

5. (Level I, 1988) Warrants typically:
    a. Are exercisable only by the owner of the attached instrument.
    b. Do not have a secondary trading market.
    c. Are exercisable into 100 shares of the underlying stock.
    d. Provide the investor with financial leverage.

6. (Level I, 1988) Which of the following comparative statements about stock call options and warrants is correct?

		Call Option	Warrant
a.	Issued by a company	No	Yes
b.	Sometimes attached to bonds	Yes	Yes
c.	Often has a maturity of many years	No	No
d.	Is a type of stock option	Yes	No

7. (Level I, 1988) An investor would consider converting a convertible bond into common stock if the bond's
    a. Break-even time exceeds five years.
    b. Conversion value exceeds its market price.
    c. Conversion premium exceeds its yield to maturity.
    d. Yield to maturity equals that on comparable nonconvertible bonds.

CRITICAL THINKING EXERCISES

1. This exercise requires computer work. Contained in the America Online (AOL) worksheet in the Data Workbook are recent prices for AOL options. Using the information contained in the file, perform the following calculations and answer the following questions:
    a. Calculate each option's premium. Why are some premiums larger than others?
    b. Construct a straddle and a reverse straddle using the options that are closest to being at-the-money. Calculate the profit and loss from both at expiration.
    c. Assume that someone believes that the AOL will rise over the next few weeks. Describe some option trades that would take advantage of this anticipated rise in prices. Which would be the most risky? The least risky?
    d. Assume you already own AOL; describe two option strategies that can reduce the risk associated with your stock position.

2. This exercise requires both computer work and library research. In the Black-Scholes worksheet in the Data Workbook are returns for five stocks. Use these returns to compute standard deviations for the series. Using a recent issue of the *Wall Street Journal* or a similar publication, find one call option on each of these five stocks.
    a. Using the standard computed deviations, along with the other input variables from the financial press, calculate the Black-Scholes model's intrinsic value for each.
    b. Comparing the Black-Scholes values to the options' market prices; is either option correctly valued? What could explain differences between the Black-Scholes prices and the market prices?

c. Assume you believe the Black-Scholes model finds the "correct" intrinsic value for call options, describe some option/stock trades you could execute to take advantage of your belief.

3. This exercise requires library research. Potomac Electric Power has a convertible bond issue outstanding that matures in 2015 and has a coupon rate of 7 percent. Answer the following questions about this bond:

a. What are the bond's conversion ratio and conversion price?

b. What is the bond's current conversion value? Is the convertible currently in-the-money or out-of-the-money?

c. If this bond were not convertible, for what price would it sell? (What is its straight bond value?)

d. What is the bond's current market price?

e. How much of a premium is included in the bond's current price? Why does this premium seem relatively small?

THE INTERNET INVESTOR

1. Find a stock with several options written on it. Using a web site that provides stock price quotes and options quotes, chart the daily stock price, one call option contract close to being at-the-money, and one put option contract with the same expiration and exercise over a one month period. What observations can you make from the relationship between stock price, call price, and put price? What do you figure are investor expectations for the stock in question?

2. Using a web site that provides options quotes, track the call option quotes for a non-technology firm and call options quotes for a technology firm. Use at-the-money calls and same expiration dates. What factors described in Exhibit 15.15 do you observe from the data?

3. Using a web site that provides options quotes, chart two call option quotes for a technology stock. Find two calls with the same exercise price but different expirations. What can you conclude from the data? Find two calls with the same expiration but different exercise prices. What can you conclude from these data?

FUTURES CONTRACTS

PREVIOUSLY . . .

We discussed the first major type of derivative security, options. We described not only stock options but other securities that contain options.

IN THIS CHAPTER . . .

We continue our coverage of derivative securities by examining futures contracts. These contracts call for the future delivery of an asset at a price agreed on today. Futures are traded in a variety of underlying assets, everything from corn to stock indexes. They share some characteristics of options but have some important differences.

TO COME . . .

We conclude our journey into the world of investments by discussing modern portfolio theory and diversification, one of the most popular investment process today. All professional investment advisers, technical and fundamental, agree that diversification is the best way to reduce risk.

Chapter Objectives

1. What are futures contracts?
2. How can futures contracts be valued?
3. Who uses futures?
4. What are financial futures?
5. What are options on futures?

Suppose that you are in the market for a new car, so you visit the local dealer who is selling this year's hottest new model. At the dealership, the dealer does not have a car to sell you right now. The dealer will have the model you want in one month. Waiting a month for delivery is actually better for you, because you would like to sell your old car to raise money for the down payment. You and the dealer might enter into a binding contract in which you agree to take delivery of the car in one month at a specified price and the dealer agrees to deliver the car in one month at the same price. This kind of agreement is commonly called a **forward contract.**

forward contract
Contract calling for the future delivery of an asset at a price agreed on today.

Most economic transactions occur in the spot, or cash, market, however, in which the buyer takes delivery of the asset from the seller immediately. As the above example illustrates, the buyer and seller may agree to complete the transaction at some future date. For these individuals, forward contracts offer a way of locking in the price of the asset today and, further, guaranteeing that the transaction will be completed at a future date.

If a forward contract is an agreement between a buyer and seller that stipulates the future delivery of some asset, at a specified price, what is a futures contract? A **futures contract** is simply a highly standardized version of a forward contract. Futures contracts specify standard amounts, delivery dates, and so forth. Unlike forward contracts, futures contracts are marketable and trade on organized exchanges, subject to specific rules.

futures contract
Highly standardized version of a forward contract.

In this chapter, we examine futures contracts, through which people take positions in such assets as Treasury bonds (T-bonds), Japanese yen, soybeans, pork bellies, orange juice, gold, and crude oil. Like options, which we discussed in Chapter 15, futures are considered derivative securities, which means, as you may recall, that their values derive from underlying assets. Also like options, futures are considered speculative in nature; options and futures are inherently more risky than more traditional financial assets such as stocks and bonds. However, as we also saw in Chapter 15, and as we discuss in this chapter, traders use both options and futures to *reduce* the risks associated with stock and bond positions.

What are Futures?

A *futures contract* is a binding legal contract that calls for the future delivery of an asset. The contract specifies the asset to be delivered, the delivery location, the amount to be delivered, the delivery date, and the price. A futures contract has two parties, or *positions:* the long position and the short position. The person who holds the **long position** agrees to accept delivery of the asset, at the terms specified by the contract, and the person who holds the **short position** agrees to deliver the asset, again at the terms specified by the contract. Someone who goes long in July corn at $2.50 per bushel agrees to accept delivery of 5,000 bushels (the size of one corn contract) in July at a price of $2.50 per bushel. It is important to note that for every long position there *must* be a short position.

long position
Person agreeing to take deliver of the asset.

short position
Person agreeing to deliver the asset.

Trading in futures, like that in options, is considered a zero sum game. If someone makes a dollar in a futures position, the person who holds the opposite position must lose a dollar. If the price of a futures contract rises by a certain amount, the wealth of the long position increases by that amount, and the short position's wealth declines by that amount.

Must the holder of the long position take delivery of the corn? Yes, if the position remains open until the delivery date. However, before the actual delivery date he or she can close out the position merely by taking the opposite position in the same contract. For example, someone who is long in July corn can close out the position by going short in July corn. Most futures traders have no intention of taking delivery, or delivering, the assets they trade; the large majority close out their positions before the delivery dates.

An example of a futures contract summary appears in Exhibit 16.1. The exhibit shows the highlights of the futures contract on U.S. T-bonds—one of the most actively traded futures contract. The contract sets specific terms for elements such as size

---

Exhibit 16.1 ✦ CONTRACT HIGHLIGHTS: U.S. TREASURY BOND FUTURES

Size	$1,000,000 face value U.S. Treasury bonds.
Deliverable Grade	U.S. Treasury bonds maturing at least 15 years from date of delivery, if not callable; if callable, not so for at least 15 years from the first day of the delivery month. Coupon based on an 8 percent standard.
Price Quotation	In points ($1,000) and thirty-seconds of a point; for example, 92-16 equals $92^{16}\!/_{32}$.
Minimum Price Fluctuation	One thirty-second of a point, or $31.25 (one tick) per contract.
Daily Trading Limits	3 points ($3,000) per contract above or below the previous day's settlement price.
Months Traded	March, June, September, and December
Trading Hours	7:20 a.m. to 2 p.m. (Chicago time), Monday through Friday. Evening trading hours are 5:20 to 8:05 p.m. (Central Standard time) or 6:20 to 9:05 p.m. (Daylight Savings time), Sunday through Thursday.[a]
Ticker Symbol	US
Last Trading Day	Seven business days prior to the last business day of the month.
Last Delivery Day	Last business day of the month.
Delivery Method	Federal Reserve book entry wire transfer system.

[a]Project A afternoon session hours are 2:30 to 4:30 p.m. (Chicago time), Monday through Thursday, and Project A overnight session hours are from 10 p.m. to 6 a.m., Sunday through Thursday.

Source: Chicago Board of Trade 1997 Specifications. Courtesy of the Chicago Board of Trade.

($100,000 face value), deliverable grade (any T-bond with at least 15 years remaining to call), delivery months (March, June, September, and December), and delivery method (Federal Reserve book entry wire transfer system).

EVOLUTION OF MODERN FUTURES MARKETS

The historical origins of forward and futures contracts go back to ancient civilizations. Evidence indicates that the Greeks and Romans actively traded instruments that we would recognize today as forward contracts. Roman emperors are said to have engaged in active forward contracting to ensure that grain was available during winter.

The origins of modern futures exchanges can be traced to the establishment, in 1848, of the Chicago Board of Trade (CBOT). In the mid-1800s, Chicago was rapidly becoming a major transportation and distribution center for agricultural products, especially grains such as corn and wheat. Farmers shipped their grain to Chicago for sale and distribution eastward along rail and water shipping channels. The problem, of course, is that grain production in the Midwest is seasonal in nature. At harvest time, supplies would soar, often overwhelming the city's storage facilities, and prices would plunge. As supplies diminished through the winter and spring, prices would soar.

To alleviate some of the problems associated with the seasonal nature of grain production, the newly formed CBOT began to offer farmers what were known as *to arrive contracts*. These contracts allowed farmers to deliver their grain at predetermined future dates at prices set in advance of delivery. Financiers soon discovered that these contracts allowed them to speculate on grain prices without having to worry about taking delivery of the grain and storing it. Modern futures trading had begun.

In late 1874, a second futures exchange was established in Chicago. Initially named the Chicago Produce Exchange, it concentrated on futures contracts in meat and livestock. In 1898, the exchange was renamed the Chicago Mercantile Exchange (CME). Also in the late 1800s, the Coffee, Sugar & Cocoa Exchange and the New York Cotton Exchange were formed in New York. Other futures exchanges, both in the United States and the rest of the world, soon followed.

Development of Financial Futures

Before 1972, futures trading was limited to physical commodities such as grains, cotton, and metals. In 1972, the International Monetary Market (IMM), a subsidiary of the CME, was created in response to the 1971 decision by most Western nations to allow their currency exchange rates to fluctuate. The IMM began offering futures contracts on foreign currencies—the first financial futures. This was followed in 1975 by the CBOT's introduction of the first futures contract on an interest-bearing financial instrument, the GNMA mortgage pass-through security. In 1976, the IMM introduced a futures contract on 90-day Treasury bills (T-bills), and in 1977, the CBOT introduced a futures contract on long-term T-bonds that soon became the most successful new contract of all time.

The early 1980s saw the emergence of stock index futures contracts. In 1982, the Kansas City Board of Trade launched a futures contract based on the Value Line Index. This was followed a few months later by the CME's introduction of a futures contract based on the Standard & Poor's (S&P) 500. By the mid-1980s, trading in financial futures exceeded trading in commodity futures.

Today's Futures Exchanges

Approximately 14 exchanges handle futures trading in the United States today. In addition, another 11 major futures exchanges operate in other parts of the world. The two largest futures exchanges are still the two oldest: the CBOT and the CME. Today, these two exchanges accounted for approximately 40 percent of all futures trading worldwide. Several of the fastest-growing futures exchanges, however, are located outside the United States. The Singapore International Monetary Exchange, established only in 1984, has emerged in recent years as a major trading center for financial futures, especially currency futures.

One characteristic of today's futures exchanges, especially those in the United States, is exchange specialization. One exchange tends to dominate trading in a specific asset. Virtually all trading in T-bond and Treasury note (T-note) futures, for example, takes place on the CBOT. The New York Mercantile Exchange dominates trading in petroleum futures. The exchanges compete intensely to introduce new contracts. Once a successful new contract is introduced, the exchange that introduced it will likely develop a near monopoly in trading in that contract.

In the United States, futures trading is regulated by the Commodity Futures Trading Commission (CFTC), rather than the Securities and Exchange Commission (SEC). The CFTC regulates futures on stocks and bonds. Several bills have been introduced in Congress in recent years that would eliminate the CFTC and give regulatory power over futures trading to the SEC.

TYPES OF CONTRACTS

We can initially divide futures contracts into those based on physical commodities and those based on financial instruments. We can divide physical commodities contracts into those based on agricultural products (grains and oilseeds, livestock and meat, and food and fiber) and those based on nonagricultural products (lumber, metals, and petroleum). Financial futures can be divided into three more specific categories: currency futures, stock index futures, and interest rate futures. The major futures contracts traded on U.S. futures exchanges, along with the dominant exchange for each, are listed in Exhibit 16.2.

Requirements for a Viable Futures Market

An asset that develops a viable futures market must have five characteristics: (1) the ability to be standardized, (2) active demand, (3) the ability to be stored for a period of time, (4) relatively high value in proportion to bulk, and (5) relatively high value in proportion to storage and other carrying costs. As an example, consider gold. Gold can be standardized (for example, by purity grades). It is subject to active demand; some 20 million ounces of gold are bought and sold each year. Gold can be stored; it does not deteriorate over time. It is valuable in proportion to its bulk; one pound of gold is worth almost $6,000. Finally, the cost of storing and carrying gold for a period of time is probably less than 5 percent of its value.

MECHANICS OF FUTURES TRADING

As with the world's stock exchanges, futures exchanges have become more and more automated in recent years. Some foreign futures markets conduct all trading via computer systems; in some cases, no trading takes place on the floor of the exchange (similar to trading on the Nasdaq system or the London Stock Exchange).

In the United States, futures markets, particularly the two largest, the CBOT and the CME, still retain much of the traditional futures trading system. In this *open outcry system,* trading takes place on the floor of the exchange, where traders stand in trading pits (each contract is assigned to one pit) and bid against one another. They shout out buy and sell bids and use hand signals to communicate to other traders. Every trader standing in the pit has, at least in theory, an equal chance of trading. Unlike the New York Stock Exchange (NYSE) or Nasdaq, futures exchanges have no specialists or market makers as such. Generally, all traders are allowed to trade all contracts listed on the exchange, although many traders choose to specialize in particular futures contracts.

Who Are the Traders?

All traders must be either members of the exchange or employees of members. Some people trade on the floor by leasing trading privileges from a member. The CBOT, for example, currently has about 3,600 members. Like NYSE seats, memberships are bought and sold. Recently, a CBOT membership sold for about $450,000.

Traders can be grouped into three general categories: commission brokers trade strictly for others; local traders trade strictly for their own, or their firms' accounts;

Exhibit 16.2 ✦ Major Futures Contracts Listed on U.S. Exchanges

Contract	Exchange	Contract	Exchange	Contract	Exchange
Grains and Oilseeds		**Metals & Petroleum**		**Stock Index**	
Corn	CBOT	Copper	COMEX	Nikkei 225	CME
Oats	CBOT	Crude Oil	NYMEX	Major Market Index	CBOT
Soybeans	CBOT	Gold	COMEX	NYSE Index	NYFE
Soybean meal	CBOT	Heating oil	NYMEX	S&P 500	CME
Soybean oil	CBOT	Natural gas	NYMEX	**Interest Rate**	
Wheat	CBOT	Palladium	NYMEX	Eurodollar	CME
Livestock and Meat		Platinum	NYMEX	Municipal bond index	CBOT
Feeder Cattle	CME	Propane	NYMEX	Treasury bills	CME
Hogs	CME	Silver	COMEX	Treasury bonds	CBOT
Live cattle	CME	Unleaded gasoline	NYMEX	Treasury notes (10 yr)	CBOT
Pork bellies	CME	**Foreign Currency**		Treasury notes (5 yr)	CBOT
Food and Fiber		Australian dollar	CME	Treasury notes (2 yr)	CBOT
Cocoa	CSCE	British pound	CME		
Coffee	CSCE	Canadian dollar	CME		
Cotton	NYCTN	German mark	CME		
Domestic sugar	CSCE	Japanese yen	CME		
Orange juice	NYCTN	Swiss franc	CME		
Rice	CRCE				
World sugar	CSCE				

Notes: CBOT is the Chicago Board of Trade; CME is the Chicago Mercantile Exchange (or one of its subsidiaries); COMEX is the Commodity Exchange; CRCE is the Chicago Rice and Coffee Exchange; CSCE is the Coffee, Sugar & Cocoa Exchange; NYCTN is the New York Cotton Exchange; NYFE is the New York Futures Exchange; and NYMEX is the New York Mercantile Exchange.

and dual traders perform both functions, sometimes acting as brokers and sometimes trading for their own accounts.

We can also classify local and dual traders in terms of trading style. Scalpers attempt to profit from small changes in the contract prices; they rarely hold positions open for more than a few minutes. Day traders also attempt to profit from short-term market movements. Although they hold positions much longer than scalpers, they do not hold positions overnight. Finally, position traders hold positions open over much longer periods of time and attempt to profit from longer-term market movements.

Placing an Order

Placing an order to buy or sell a futures contract (go long or go short) is similar to placing an order to buy or sell stocks or bonds. In response to the order, the broker contacts the firm's trading desk on the floor of the exchange. The order is relayed for execution to the firm's floor broker or to a dual trader who handles the firm's orders. After execution, the same chain returns confirmation of the trade. Futures traders can place the same types of orders we discussed in Chapter 3 (market orders, stop-loss orders, limit orders, good until canceled orders, and day orders). Commissions on futures trades vary widely from firm to firm. Some brokerage firms offer no futures trading services for their customers.

Role of the Clearinghouse

A feature unique to the options and futures markets is the clearinghouse, or clearing corporation. Each futures market operates a clearinghouse as a nonprofit corporation owned by members of the exchange. The clearinghouse acts as both an intermediary and guarantor to every trade. The first clearinghouse was organized by the CBOT in 1925.

Any futures trade, as we have noted, requires a short position for every long position, and vice versa. Both parties promise to fulfill certain contractual obligations (deliver, or take delivery, of the asset at the agreed-on price at the agreed-on time). Without a clearinghouse, each party would have to depend on the other party to fulfill his or her contractual obligations. If one party failed to meet obligations, the other party would be left with a worthless claim.

The clearinghouse guarantees that both parties fulfill their contractual obligations by acting as a counterparty in each trade. Let's say Trader W decides to go long in July corn. To do this, Trader W must find someone to go short (Trader X). The clearinghouse would establish a short position in July corn with Trader W, who wants to go long in July corn. At the same time, The clearinghouse would establish a long position in July corn with Trader X.

Margins and Daily Price Limits

settlement price
Price established at the end of each trading day used to calculate trader's margins.

marked to market
Adjusting each trader's margin account by the change in the settlement price.

In a futures transaction, both parties must post margin deposits (either in cash or, in some cases, T-bills).[1] After satisfying this initial margin requirement, they must also meet maintenance margin requirements. The margin, a percentage of the contract's value, acts as a good-faith security deposit. At the end of each trading day, a committee of traders and clearinghouse officials meets to establish a **settlement price** for each contract. Based on that settlement price, each open account is **marked to market** daily. Depending on whether a trader is long or short and whether the current settlement price is higher or lower than the previous day's settlement price, that trader's margin will either rise or fall. Margin transactions are best illustrated with an example.

Assume you take a long position in March crude oil at $24.15 per barrel on February 3. You must post an initial margin of $2,970 and maintain a margin of $2,000.[2] Suppose the position remains open until February 14. Exhibit 16.3 shows the settlement prices and transactions for the margin account during the period between February 3 and February 14. Notice how losses are subtracted from your' account, whereas gains are added to the account.[3] Also note that on February 7, the balance in your' margin account falls below the maintenance requirement, $2,200. You must

---

[1] In stock trading, remember, *margin* is the amount of your money you put up to buy a stock— you borrow the rest. Futures traders do not borrow money.

[2] These are the minimum margins on crude oil futures set by the exchange where they are traded. In reality, most traders would be required to post higher margins, depending on their futures brokerage firm.

[3] Some firms might allow you to withdraw "surplus" margin from the account—that is the amount above the initial margin.

Exhibit 16.3 ✦ DAILY RESETTLEMENT EXAMPLE

On February 3, a trader went long in March crude oil at $24.15 per barrel (1,000-barrel contract). The position remained open until February 14. The trader was required to post an initial margin of $2,970 and maintain a margin of $2,200.

Date	Settlement Price	Daily Mark to Market	Initial Margin Account Balance	Deposit or (Withdrawal)	Ending Margin Account Balance
Feb. 3	$24,150		$0	$2,970	$2,970
Feb. 4	24,250	100	3,070	0	3,070
Feb. 5	24,250	0	3,070	0	3,070
Feb. 6	23,750	(500)	2,570	0	2,570
Feb. 7	23,000	(750)	1,820	1,150	2,970
Feb. 10	22,750	(250)	2,720	0	2,720
Feb. 11	23,500	750	3,470	0	3,470
Feb. 12	23,750	250	3,720	0	3,720
Feb. 13	24,500	750	4,470	0	4,470
Feb. 14	25,000	500	4,970	(4,970)	0

deposit another $1,150 into the account to bring the balance back up to the initial requirement. On February 14, you close out your position by going short in March crude oil at $25 per barrel. You withdraw the amount in the margin account, $4,970. You end up making $850 ($4,970 − $2,970 − $1,150).

Partly because a trader must post only a small percentage of the contract's value as margin, many contracts limit the maximum daily price change (crude oil futures generally have a daily limit of $1.50 per barrel). If the contract price moves up or down by the maximum amount, the contract is said to be **limit up** or **limit down.** Normally, no trading can take place at prices outside the daily price limits. However, the exchanges can, under certain circumstances, increase daily price limits to help ensure orderly markets.

limit up (limit down)
The maximum amounts, high and low, by which the futures price can change during a particular trading day.

Delivery Procedure

As we noted earlier, most traders have no intention of taking delivery, or delivering, the asset on which they trade futures. However, exceptions arise; delivery actually occurs in about 3 percent of T-bond and T-note contracts, for example. Should a trader actually wish to take delivery, or deliver, the asset, he must follow the delivery procedure specified by the contract. In all cases, the short initiates the delivery procedure.

Futures Pricing Primer

In this section we review the pricing of futures contracts, covering two theories of futures pricing. One theory suggests that futures prices and expected spot prices are related, whereas the other theory denies any relationship between futures prices and expected spot prices. Before we discuss these two theories, let's consider several important pricing concepts, beginning with a discussion of how to read futures price quotations in the financial press.

FUTURES PRICE QUOTATIONS

Exhibit 16.4 reproduces a sample set of futures price quotations for one trading day. For example, the first quote refers to a contract on corn futures traded on the CBOT. Prices are quoted in cents per bushel, which means 207 cents is equal to $2.07 per bushel. Delivery dates range from March 2000 to December 2001. The March 2000 contract settled on January 7, 2000, 207 per bushel; it has traded as high as 270 per bushel and as low as 195 1/4 per bushel.

Open Interest

open interest
Number of contracts outstanding at any point in time.

Open interest refers to the number of contracts outstanding at any point in time. Remember, each contract must have both a long and a short position. As of January 7, 2000, traders had taken approximately 216,368 long positions and 216,368 short positions in March 2000 corn. Open interest changes constantly as contracts are traded. To see how transactions affect open interest, take a look at the hypothetical example shown in Exhibit 16.5.

The table's hypothetical futures market has five trading days and five participants. During the first day, A goes long in 10 contracts; B takes the short position. Open interest increases by 10 contracts. During the second trading day, C goes long in 10 contracts; D takes the short position. Open interest increases again by 10 contracts.

Notice what happens, however, on days 3 and 4. Trader B, who went short on day 1, closes out the position by going long in 10 contracts; E takes the short position. This is considered a trade of existing contracts (E replaces B) and has no affect on open interest. The same thing is true on day 4 when D, who went short on day 2, closes out the position (F replaces D). On the last day, E closes out a short position by going long. In the same trade, A also closes out a long position by going short. This trade *decreases* open interest by 10 contracts. At the end of the five-day trading period, only C and F still have open positions, so total open interest equals 10 contracts. As you would expect, open interest increases as the time until delivery gets shorter. Open interest typically peaks a few weeks before the first delivery date and then declines sharply. By the time the first delivery date arrives, open interest is close to zero for some contracts.

BASIS AND SPREADS

The terms *basis* and *spread* receive a great deal of attention in the futures markets. Both are important concepts for understanding futures pricing. In addition, many trading strategies, which we discuss later in the chapter, rely on expected changes to basis or spread, or both. Let's discuss basis first.

basis
Difference between the cash price of an asset and the future price.

Basis is merely the difference between the cash price, or spot price, of an asset and the futures contract price. Basis can be either negative or positive. Basis also can change for futures contracts with different delivery dates. The cash price of an asset can differ depending on location and grade. A properly measured basis should compare the cash price of an asset that matches the specific delivery characteristics of the futures contract as closely as possible.

Exhibit 16.6 shows an example of basis for T-bond futures. The cash price of T-bonds is the price of the 8 percent bond that matures in November 2021. This bond can be delivered in any of the contracts shown in Exhibit 16.6.

Exhibit 16.4 ✦ PRICE QUOTES FOR FUTURES

FUTURES PRICES

Friday, January 7, 2000

Open Interest Reflects Previous Trading Day.

GRAINS AND OILSEEDS

	Open	High	Low	Settle	Change	Lifetime High	Lifetime Low	Open Interest
CORN (CBT) 5,000 bu.; cents per bu.								
Mar	203¼	207¾	202½	207	+ 3¼	270	195¼	216,368
May	210¼	214¼	209¾	214	+ 3¼	261	202½	63,420
July	217	221½	217	220¾	+ 3	278½	209	64,588
Sept	224	228	224	227½	+ 2¾	257	215¾	17,830
Nov	....	....	....	234½	+ 3	245	222½	573
Dec	233¼	237	233	236¾	+ 2¾	279½	225¼	36,634
Mr01	242	245½	241¾	245½	+ 3	246½	233¾	1,112
Dec	254½	256½	254½	256	+ 1	263	246½	1,355
Est vol 42,000; vol Thu 49,216; open int 402,333, +4,062.								
OATS (CBT) 5,000 bu.; cents per bu.								
Mar	109	109½	108¼	109½	+ ½	135	107	7,162
May	114¼	115¼	114	114¾	+ ½	133	112¾	3,029
July	112¾	113¾	112½	113¼	+ ½	124¼	110½	1,700
Sept	....	....	....	117¼	+ ¼	130	115¾	659
Dec	....	....	....	124½	+ ½	135	123	877
Est vol 650; vol Thu 1,707; open int 13,432, +86.								
SOYBEANS (CBT) 5,000 bu.; cents per bu.								
Jan	465½	472	465½	471½	+ 3½	632	415	6,477
Mar	474½	479½	473¼	478¾	+ 3¼	598	423½	64,751
May	483¼	487½	481¼	487	+ 3	554	432	25,563
July	489	494¼	488	493¼	+ 3	647	440	23,827
Aug	491½	494¾	491½	494	+ 4½	541½	441	2,734
Sept	490½	497	490½	495¼	+ 3¼	541	450	715
Nov	498	502¾	496½	502	+ 4	631	453	10,665
Est vol 50,000; vol Thu 52,600; open int 134,773, −812.								
SOYBEAN MEAL (CBT) 100 tons; $ per ton.								
Jan	148.30	149.70	148.00	149.10	....	164.00	123.30	5,135
Mar	149.80	151.20	149.20	150.70	+ .30	162.00	126.30	38,906
May	150.00	151.60	149.70	151.00	....	162.60	127.30	22,808
July	151.70	152.80	151.00	152.50	+ .20	164.20	130.00	17,094
Aug	151.00	152.90	151.00	152.10	+ .30	164.00	131.00	5,854
Sept	152.00	153.00	151.50	152.30	+ .30	164.00	132.00	3,305
Dec	155.50	156.50	155.50	156.00	− .20	169.00	135.50	7,018
Est vol 14,000; vol Thu 26,151; open int 102,269, +537.								
SOYBEAN OIL (CBT) 60,000 lbs.; cents per lb.								
Jan	15.75	15.90	15.72	15.90	+ .18	24.90	15.32	3,193
Mar	16.05	16.23	16.01	16.19	+ .14	23.95	15.58	57,847
May	16.38	16.55	16.32	16.51	+ .13	23.50	15.91	22,840
July	16.70	16.80	16.64	16.80	+ .12	22.30	16.21	20,087
Aug	....	....	....	16.96	+ .16	21.00	16.37	4,628
Sept	16.92	17.05	16.92	17.05	+ .14	21.70	16.52	2,774
Oct	17.17	17.20	17.17	17.20	+ .12	22.25	16.85	3,308
Dec	17.45	17.48	17.42	17.48	+ .10	20.62	16.97	13,617
Est vol 15,000; vol Thu 27,879; open int 129,206, +1,715.								
WHEAT (CBT) 5,000 bu.; cents per bu.								
Mar	248¼	252	246	251¾	+ 3¼	340	236½	84,590
May	258½	263	257¼	262¾	+ 3¼	322	246¾	10,187
July	268	273	267	272½	+ 2¾	347	256¾	24,575
Sept	278½	283	278	283	+ 3¾	335	266½	1,797
Dec	293	298½	293	297¼	+ 2¾	345	280½	4,024
Est vol 18,000; vol Thu 19,643; open int 125,219, +884.								
WHEAT (KC) 5,000 bu.; cents per bu.								
Mar	274	278	273	277¾	+ 2¾	361½	262½	40,233
May	284	289	283¾	289	+ 3¾	340½	272¾	8,815
July	295	299	294¼	299	+ 3¼	366	282	11,821
Sept	308½	308½	308½	308½	+ 3¼	346	291	710
Dec	....	321	318	320½	+ 3½	354	302	791
Est vol 6,288; vol Thu 6,378; open int 62,370, −758.								
WHEAT (MPLS) 5,000 bu.; cents per bu.								
Mar	315	317¾	314¾	317½	+ 1¾	386	312½	11,490
May	323½	327	323½	326¾	+ 2	389	320	5,073
July	332	335	332	334¼	+ 1¾	380	327¼	2,439
Sept	340	341½	340	340¾	+ ¾	385	334½	1,069
Dec	349	351	349	350	+ ½	390	344	324
Est vol 2,798; vol Thu 3,894; open int 20,432, −123.								
CANOLA (WPG) 20 metric tons; Can. $ per ton								
Jan	255.00	256.50	255.00	256.50	+ 1.80	353.50	250.00	356
Mar	258.30	261.30	258.10	260.00	+ 1.50	335.00	254.60	34,780
May	264.30	264.90	264.00	264.50	+ 2.30	306.50	259.00	8,892
July	267.50	269.60	267.50	268.70	+ 2.20	309.00	260.00	9,451
Aug	....	....	....	271.00	+ 2.40	302.50	264.00	450
Sept	....	....	....	272.50	+ 2.50	295.90	271.00	305
Nov	275.00	277.00	275.00	275.70	+ 2.00	315.90	269.00	1,214
Est vol 3,535; vol Thur 7,721; open int 55,448, +326.								
WHEAT (WPG) 20 metric tons; Can. $ per ton								
Mar	128.00	129.50	128.00	129.30	+ 0.80	151.50	126.50	6,410
May	131.50	132.20	131.50	132.20	+ 0.70	141.00	129.50	664
July	133.50	134.50	133.50	134.50	+ 0.80	146.30	132.80	392
Oct	....	....	....	138.30	+ 0.80	141.50	137.00	531
Est vol 200; vol Thur 219; open int 7,997, +224.								
BARLEY-WESTERN (WPG) 20 metric tons; Can. $ per ton								
Mar	111.70	112.50	111.40	112.50	+ 0.60	129.00	111.50	5,401
May	115.00	115.50	114.50	115.50	+ 0.40	125.40	114.60	3,280
July	116.60	117.30	116.60	117.30	+ 0.50	126.60	116.50	1,257
Oct	120.00	121.00	120.00	121.00	+ 0.60	127.90	118.50	4,364
Dec	....	....	....	124.00	+ 1.50	123.50	121.10	404
Est vol 1,000; vol Thur 1,610; open int 14,706, −884.								

	Open	High	Low	Settle	Change	Lifetime High	Lifetime Low	Open Interest
Oct	21.00	21.00	20.90	20.74	+ 0.04	21.58	14.22	12,904
Nov	20.67	20.67	20.39	20.45	+ 0.07	21.15	15.60	9,222
Dec	20.20	20.40	20.10	20.19	+ 0.08	21.00	13.85	36,110
Ja01	19.92	19.95	19.92	19.95	+ 0.10	20.73	14.25	13,421
Feb	19.68	19.70	19.68	19.73	+ 0.13	20.44	14.30	3,751
Mar	19.48	19.48	19.48	19.53	+ 0.15	20.11	14.44	3,433
Apr	....	....	....	19.35	+ 0.17	19.80	15.80	1,479
May	....	....	....	19.18	+ 0.19	19.27	15.80	1,340
June	18.90	19.15	18.90	19.04	+ 0.20	19.62	14.56	10,459
July	....	....	....	18.93	+ 0.21	19.05	19.05	410
Aug	....	....	....	18.84	+ 0.21	18.40	18.40	371
Sept	....	....	....	18.76	+ 0.21	18.98	17.96	2,248
Oct	....	....	....	18.69	+ 0.21	....	....	517
Nov	....	....	....	18.63	+ 0.22	19.05	18.20	393
Dec	18.55	18.55	18.50	18.57	+ 0.23	19.10	14.90	16,620
Ja02	....	....	....	18.51	+ 0.23	....	....	377
Feb	....	....	....	18.45	+ 0.23	....	....	187
Mar	....	....	....	18.40	+ 0.24	18.65	18.45	2,075
June	18.20	18.20	18.20	18.26	+ 0.25	18.98	17.35	1,683
Dec	....	....	....	18.02	+ 0.27	21.38	15.50	4,847
Dc03	....	....	....	17.65	+ 0.27	22.00	15.92	4,792
Dc04	....	....	....	17.53	+ 0.27	19.27	16.35	4,725
Dc05	....	....	....	17.49	+ 0.27	18.40	17.00	686
Est vol 180,853; vol Thu 176,785; open int 511,248, +4,015.								
HEATING OIL NO. 2 (NYM) 42,000 gal; $ per gal.								
Feb	.6600	.6710	.6460	.6475	− .0153	.7070	.3750	51,474
Mar	.6415	.6560	.6285	.6289	− .0139	.6820	.3760	18,691
Apr	.6180	.6220	.6055	.6044	− .0119	.6500	.3760	8,547
May	.5920	.5930	.5830	.5799	− .0094	.6205	.3800	9,090
June	.5690	.5750	.5680	.5619	− .0069	.6000	.3790	6,872
July	.5590	.5665	.5550	.5544	− .0044	.5860	.3890	12,787
Aug	.5525	.5650	.5525	.5519	− .0034	.5860	.3970	4,977
Sept	....	....	....	.5559	− .0029	.5775	.4260	3,810
Oct	....	....	....	.5594	− .0024	.5755	.4717	2,222
Nov	.5700	.5700	.5680	.5634	− .0019	.5925	.4792	1,298
Dec	.5720	.5730	.5720	.5669	− .0019	.5950	.5110	8,908
Ja01	....	....	....	.5684	− .0014	.5965	.5254	2,904
Feb	.5650	.5650	.5650	.5624	− .0009	.5920	.5360	1,215
Mar	....	....	....	.5454	− .0004	.5630	.5250	477
Apr	....	....	....	.5294	+ .0001	.5450	.5140	220
May	....	....	....	.5134	+ .0006	.5380	.5075	190
June	....	....	....	.5009	+ .0006	....	....	125
Est vol 40,656; vol Thu 45,345; open int 133,807, −144.								
GASOLINE-NY Unleaded (NYM) 42,000; $ per gal.								
Feb	.6780	.6910	.6600	.6610	− .0179	.7245	.4090	38,130
Mar	.6770	.6875	.6640	.6651	− .0142	.7150	.4400	17,119
Apr	.7120	.7165	.6960	.6970	− .0120	.7400	.5050	16,274
May	.7050	.7050	.6895	.6900	− .0100	.7270	.5170	6,415
June	.6875	.6875	.6845	.6790	− .0075	.7055	.5510	2,853
July	....	....	....	.6635	− .0045	.6940	.5980	4,356
Sept	....	....	....	.6210	− .0020	.6475	.5980	2,832
Est vol 41,865; vol Thu 45,027; open int 89,550, +2,587								
NATURAL GAS, (NYM) 10,000 MMBtu.; $ per MMBtu's								
Feb	2.195	2.230	2.155	2.173	− .023	3.100	2.125	53,814
Mar	2.230	2.260	2.190	2.221	− .016	2.885	2.119	33,464
Apr	2.260	2.275	2.225	2.246	− .014	2.665	2.015	19,834
May	2.280	2.300	2.260	2.270	− .013	2.595	1.960	14,934
June	2.315	2.320	2.285	2.297	− .012	2.600	2.001	14,087
July	2.345	2.345	2.310	2.323	− .012	2.625	2.005	12,397
Aug	2.370	2.370	2.345	2.349	− .012	2.625	2.005	11,890
Sept	2.385	2.390	2.370	2.370	− .012	2.630	2.100	9,380
Oct	2.410	2.415	2.395	2.395	− .012	2.670	2.100	8,650
Nov	2.545	2.545	2.535	2.530	− .012	2.800	2.240	5,630
Dec	2.680	2.680	2.665	2.660	− .015	2.915	2.380	12,387
Ja01	2.710	2.710	2.690	2.694	− .011	2.945	2.400	6,720
Feb	2.600	2.600	2.595	2.583	− .011	2.825	2.305	4,500
Mar	2.490	2.490	2.490	2.476	− .009	2.687	2.210	4,373
Apr	2.377	2.377	2.377	2.375	− .007	2.560	2.120	4,105
May	2.353	2.353	2.353	2.351	− .007	2.545	2.119	3,946
June	2.367	2.367	2.367	2.365	− .007	2.545	2.095	4,934
July	2.385	2.385	2.379	2.377	− .007	2.552	2.095	5,582
Aug	2.395	2.395	2.392	2.390	− .007	2.560	2.102	2,453
Sept	2.402	2.402	2.402	2.400	− .007	2.571	2.137	1,973
Oct	2.432	2.432	2.432	2.430	− .007	2.605	2.133	2,030
Nov	....	....	....	2.558	− .007	2.745	2.275	2,874
Dec	....	....	....	2.683	− .007	2.895	2.415	3,178
Ja02	....	....	....	2.710	− .007	2.910	2.450	3,034
Feb	....	....	....	2.605	− .007	2.775	2.440	2,252
Mar	....	....	....	2.500	− .007	2.668	2.360	1,927
Apr	....	....	....	2.404	− .007	2.575	2.290	1,130
May	....	....	....	2.383	− .007	2.550	2.350	955
June	....	....	....	2.390	− .007	2.550	2.345	1,709
July	....	....	....	2.396	− .007	2.560	2.365	609
Aug	....	....	....	2.404	− .007	2.565	2.412	854
Sept	....	....	....	2.407	− .007	2.570	2.423	1,116
Oct	....	....	....	2.440	− .007	2.600	2.465	506
Dec	....	....	....	2.700	− .006	2.760	2.720	161
Est vol 52,195; vol Thu 55,558; open int 257,937, +3,199.								
BRENT CRUDE (IPE) 1,000 net bbls.; $ per bbl.								
Feb	23.57	23.98	23.05	23.09	− 0.53	25.90	11.92	49,545
Mar	23.05	23.33	22.62	23.07	− 0.42	24.80	12.18	63,155
Apr	22.35	22.69	22.12	22.39	− 0.19	23.70	14.17	25,921
May	21.70	21.85	21.47	21.70	− 0.15	23.00	14.88	15,289
June	21.13	21.34	20.90	21.09	− 0.12	22.20	12.32	23,372

	Open	High	Low	Settle	Change	Lifetime High	Lifetime Low	Open Interest
Mr01	99.29	99.29	99.27	99.27	− .06	99.54	98.07	8,128
June	99.17	99.17	99.15	99.15	− .05	99.41	98.20	3,417
Sept	99.04	99.04	99.01	99.01	− .05	99.30	98.05	4,357
Dec	....	....	....	98.87	− .04	99.15	97.89	107
Mr02	....	....	....	98.77	....	98.86	97.97	179
Est vol 6,230; vol Thu 1,334; open int 67,977, +624.								
SHORT STERLING (LIFFE)-£500,000; pts of 100%								
Jan	93.80	93.82	93.80	93.81	− .01	94.28	93.80	21,602
Feb	....	....	....	93.66	....	93.92	93.75	130
Mar	93.55	93.56	93.52	93.55	+ .02	95.17	91.96	176,228
June	93.15	93.19	93.14	93.17	+ .03	95.17	92.47	157,737
Sept	92.87	92.94	92.86	92.92	+ .06	95.13	92.86	107,474
Dec	92.66	92.74	92.66	92.72	+ .07	98.80	92.66	69,304
Mr01	92.62	92.68	92.62	92.67	+ .06	95.08	92.62	59,288
June	92.59	92.64	92.58	92.63	+ .06	95.08	92.50	45,372
Sept	92.58	92.63	92.58	92.62	+ .06	95.09	92.41	35,923
Dec	92.56	92.60	92.56	92.58	+ .05	95.07	92.31	20,181
Mr02	92.62	92.66	92.62	92.64	+ .05	95.13	92.34	17,238
June	92.70	92.72	92.70	92.73	+ .05	95.10	92.39	9,351
Sept	92.80	92.80	92.79	92.81	+ .04	95.11	92.38	6,077
Dec	92.84	92.86	92.84	92.86	+ .04	95.11	92.45	4,199
Mr03	....	....	....	93.01	+ .04	94.69	92.49	1,642
June	....	....	....	93.13	+ .04	93.88	92.83	162
Sept	....	....	....	93.21	+ .04	93.56	93.54	470
Est vol 78,164; vol Thu 58,628; open int 732,378, +9,840.								
LONG GILT (LIFFE) (Decimal)-£50,000; pts of 100%								
Mar	109.22	109.75	109.07	109.57	+ .49	115.66	109.07	56,969
Est vol 20,877; vol Thu 18,599; open int 56,969, +3,105.								
3 MONTH EURIBOR (LIFFE) Euro 1,000,000; pts of 100%								
Jan	96.66	96.68	96.66	96.68	+ .03	96.72	96.48	26,558
Feb	96.52	96.52	96.52	96.53	+ .03	96.60	96.52	1,500
Mar	96.36	96.39	96.35	96.38	+ .02	97.38	96.22	334,720
June	95.97	96.03	95.96	96.00	+ .04	97.27	95.90	225,868
Sept	95.68	95.77	95.67	95.74	+ .07	97.16	95.64	184,521
Dec	95.32	95.44	95.31	95.41	+ .10	97.00	93.36	122,372
Mr01	95.21	95.32	95.21	95.30	+ .10	96.96	95.18	84,278
June	95.04	95.16	95.04	95.14	+ .10	96.85	94.98	67,981
Sept	94.90	95.02	94.89	95.00	+ .11	96.75	94.82	54,070
Dec	94.69	94.82	94.69	94.79	+ .12	96.58	92.57	22,312
Mr02	94.66	94.78	94.66	94.75	+ .12	96.48	94.50	16,557
June	94.57	94.65	94.57	94.66	+ .12	96.37	94.40	14,818
Sept	94.49	94.57	94.49	94.58	+ .12	96.25	94.28	10,122
Dec	94.32	94.41	94.31	94.39	+ .11	96.06	94.15	6,280
Mr03	94.26	94.29	94.26	94.35	+ .11	96.01	94.13	2,356
June	94.18	94.18	94.18	94.27	+ .11	95.45	94.02	3,339
Sept	....	....	....	94.21	+ .11	95.15	93.97	3,034
Dec	....	....	....	94.10	+ .11	95.07	94.15	116
Mr04	....	....	....	94.09	+ .11	94.50	94.10	410
June	....	....	....	94.06	+ .11	94.43	94.04	505
Sept	....	....	....	94.00	+ .11	94.40	94.33	660
Est vol 206,261; vol Thu 151,170; open int 1,182,377, +22,969								
3-MONTH EUROSWISS (LIFFE) SFr 1,000,000; pts of 100%								
Mar	97.98	98.02	97.95	97.97	− .02	98.67	97.10	87,263
June	97.55	97.58	97.50	97.55	+ .01	98.51	96.90	39,145
Sept	97.27	97.28	97.20	97.26	+ .01	98.36	96.63	24,461
Dec	96.90	96.91	96.85	96.88	+ .01	98.12	96.30	13,062
Mr01	96.78	96.81	96.78	96.79	+ .01	98.04	96.20	11,789
June	96.58	96.58	96.58	96.59	+ .01	97.47	96.20	2,472
Sept	96.48	96.49	96.48	96.47	+ .01	96.76	95.88	4,690
Dec	96.30	96.32	96.30	96.31	....	96.46	96.30	4,654
Est vol 21,509; vol Thu 19,423; open int 187,536, −213.								
EURO BTP ITALIAN GOVT. BOND (LIFFE) Euro 100,000; pts of 100%								
Mar	101.55	102.59	101.55	102.55	+ 1.05	106.70	101.55	4,062
Est vol 166; vol Thu 683; open int 4,062, +167.								
CANADIAN BANKERS ACCEPTANCE (ME)-C$1,000,000								
Jan	....	....	....	94.80	+ 0.02	94.89	94.69	1,485
Feb	94.64	94.64	94.64	94.64	+ 0.01	94.70	94.63	250
Mar	94.45	94.52	94.38	94.51	+ 0.04	95.55	93.85	119,877
June	94.05	94.11	93.96	94.10	+ 0.06	95.34	93.73	53,023
Sept	93.73	93.79	93.68	93.79	+ 0.05	95.24	93.50	24,404
Dec	93.50	93.56	93.49	93.56	+ 0.05	95.13	93.38	13,773
Mr01	93.35	93.41	93.35	93.41	+ 0.06	95.10	93.27	7,070
June	93.25	93.32	93.25	93.32	+ 0.06	95.07	93.25	5,108
Sept	93.19	93.20	93.19	93.26	+ 0.06	93.73	93.18	1,973
Dec	....	....	....	93.21	+ 0.06	94.74	93.13	425
Mr02	....	....	....	93.16	+ 0.06	94.73	93.30	175
June	....	....	....	93.11	+ 0.06	93.42	93.37	1,675
Sept	....	....	....	93.06	+ 0.06	93.39	93.39	315
Est vol 27,582; vol Thur 27,379; open int 229,553, +4,637								
10 YR. CANADIAN GOVT. BONDS (ME)-C$100,000								
Mar	117.00	117.50	116.50	117.45	+ 0.36	120.80	116.35	32,610
Est vol 3,490; vol Thur 4,254; open int 32,610, +572.								
10 YR.EURO NOTIONAL BOND(MATIF)-Euros 100,000								
Mar	84.19	84.70	84.10	84.63	+ 0.60	87.92	83.82	42,913
Est vol 76,814; vol Thur 116,328; open int 42,913, +5,898.								
3 MONTH EURIBOR (MATIF)-Euros 1,000,000								
Jan	....	....	....	96.67	+ 0.02	96.69	96.66	5,512
Mar	96.36	96.38	96.36	96.37	+ 0.01	97.26	96.36	15,010
June	95.96	96.00	95.96	95.99	+ 0.03	97.14	95.00	6,706

Exhibit 16.5 ✦ HOW TRADING AFFECTS OPEN INTEREST

Trading Day	Number of Contracts Traded	Long Position	Short Position	Change in Open Interest
Day 1	10	Trader A	Trader B	+10
Day 2	10	Trader C	Trader D	+10
Day 3	10	Trader B	Trader E	None
Day 4	10	Trader D	Trader F	None
Day 5	10	Trader E	Trader A	−10

Open interest after Day 5:

	Long Position	Short Position
Trader A	0	0
Trader B	0	0
Trader C	10	0
Trader D	0	0
Trader E	0	0
Trader F	0	10

Note: Total open interest = 10 contracts

Notice that the T-bond basis gets larger (more positive) as the time to delivery lengthens. This indicates that the spot price of T-bonds is higher than the futures price. Does this mean that the futures market expects interest rates to rise and the price of T-bonds to fall? As we see when we discuss the two general theories of futures pricing a little later, the answer to this question could be either yes or no.

Convergence

As the delivery date approaches, it seems natural to expect basis to approach zero. In other words, spot prices and futures prices should show convergence as the time until delivery approaches zero. Will basis always equal zero on the delivery date? The answer is yes, with a couple of qualifications: If the spot and futures prices are for *exactly* the same grade of asset, the same delivery location, and the same delivery size, the basis should be zero on the delivery date.

spread
Difference in prices of two futures contracts.

intracommodity spread
Difference in price between two futures contracts on the same asset but with different delivery dates.

intercommodity spread
Difference in price between two futures contracts on different but related assets.

Spreads

A **spread** is the difference between the prices of two different futures contracts. Traders watch two major types of spreads. An **intracommodity spread** measures the difference in price between two futures contracts on the same asset but with different delivery dates; an example would be the spread between March and June crude oil contracts. An **intercommodity spread** measures the difference in price between two futures contracts on different assets but with the same delivery date. Traders are most interested in intercommodity spreads that involve related, but different, assets. Examples of related assets include heating oil and unleaded gas, corn and soybeans, gold and silver, and T-bills and T-bonds.

Exhibit 16.6 ✦ BASIS OF T-BOND FUTURES

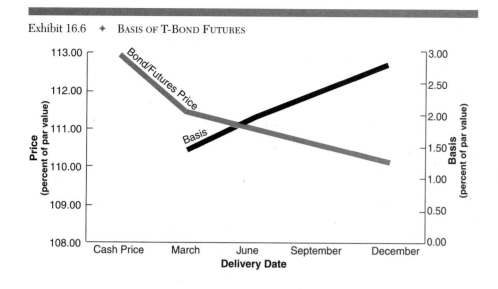

Spreads are important because of the likelihood of strong economic relationships between them. Spreads that become either too narrow or too large may create some profitable trading opportunities. Many of the speculative trading strategies that we review later in the chapter involve trading spreads (that is, buying one contract while selling another).

FUTURES PRICES AND EXPECTED FUTURE SPOT PRICES

With terms defined and a foundation established, we can build two models of futures contract prices. The first general theory of futures pricing argues for a strong relationship between futures prices and expected future spot prices. The presence of speculators in the futures market may seem to guarantee at least a general relationship between the two. For example, assume that 30-day corn futures are selling for $2.75 per bushel while the expected spot price of corn in 30 days is $2.60 per bushel. The speculator could go short in the futures contract, planning to buy corn in the spot market in 30 days at $2.60 and deliver the corn via the futures contract, collecting $2.75 per bushel. In the process, the trader would make $0.15 per bushel.

Should the futures price, with delivery at a specific point in time, merely equal the future spot price expected at the same future point in time? Even if the assets' characteristics in the spot market are identical to those specified in the futures contract, we see several good reasons why the futures price may only approximate the expected future spot price.

One reason is transaction costs. In the example above, say that transaction costs to go short in the futures contract amount to $0.25 per bushel. Now the speculative trade no longer appears profitable because the speculator can net only $2.50 per bushel while paying $2.60 per bushel.

Risk-Bearing Services of Speculators

A more important reason why the futures price may only approximate the expected future spot price comes from the fact that both hedgers and speculators trade in the futures market. A hedger has a position in the asset's cash market and uses futures to reduce the risks associated with this cash position. A speculator has no position in the cash market and seeks merely to profit from anticipated changes in prices. Therefore, hedgers are more risk-averse than speculators. In fact, speculators may be willing to assume some of the risk that hedgers are trying to avoid, if they can expect appropriate returns. This effect on the relationship between futures prices and expected future spot prices is best illustrated graphically.

Exhibit 16.7 illustrates a hypothetical futures market that includes both hedgers and speculators. The figure assumes that hedgers are net short. In other words, the sum of all the positions held by hedgers shows more short positions than long positions. For the market to function, therefore, speculators must be net long. As a futures contract's price declines, speculators should be willing to hold more long positions. At the same time, however, hedgers should be willing to hold fewer short positions.

Now, assume that $S(n)$ is the expected future spot price of some asset n periods from today. If the futures price were to equal $S(n)$, speculators would be willing to hold no position in the futures contract, because their goal is to make money by taking risk. To induce them to hold long positions in the futures, the futures price calling for delivery n periods from today, $F(n)$, must be below the expected spot price. The futures price has to clear the market, so the number of short positions desired by hedgers equals the number of long positions desired by speculators. The figure shows where $F(n)$ falls in the hypothetical market, relative to $S(n)$. S is the number of short positions and L is the number of long positions; S must equal L for the market to clear.

What will happen over time as the delivery date approaches? If the expected future spot price remains unchanged, the futures price must rise, as shown in Exhibit 16.8. This rise in the futures price can be considered the expected return to speculators for assuming some of the risk that hedgers want to avoid. The tendency of futures prices to rise as the delivery date approaches was referred to by the legendary economist John Maynard Keynes as *normal backwardation*.[4]

The reverse can also be true. If hedgers are net long, speculators must be net short. Therefore, for the market to clear, the futures price must be above the expected spot price [that is, $F(n) > S(n)$]. If expected spot prices do not change, the futures price should decline as the delivery date approaches. This is sometimes referred to as *contango*.

FUTURES PRICES AND THE COST OF CARRY

cost of carry
Cost associated with storing an asset until the futures delivery date.

The other major theory of futures pricing argues that the price of a futures contract is merely the current spot price plus the **cost of carry,** the cost associated with storing the asset until the delivery date. In other words,

$$F(n) = S(1 + c) \qquad (16.1)$$

where $F(n)$ is the futures price, S is the spot price, and c is the net cost of carry (expressed as a percentage of the asset's value). The notion of cost of carry can also help to relate the price of a futures contract with a distant delivery date to the price of

---

[4]See John Maynard Keynes, *A Treatise on Money* (London: MacMillan, 1930).

Exhibit 16.7 ◆ FUTURES MARKET WITH BOTH HEDGERS AND SPECULATORS

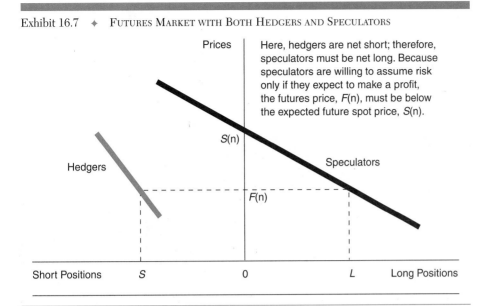

> Here, hedgers are net short; therefore, speculators must be net long. Because speculators are willing to assume risk only if they expect to make a profit, the futures price, $F(n)$, must be below the expected future spot price, $S(n)$.

a contract on the same asset with a nearby delivery date. The price of the distant futures contract must equal the price of the nearby contract plus the cost of carrying the asset between the two delivery dates.

At first glance, this formula appears to establish a relationship between the futures price, the spot price, and the cost of carry; otherwise, arbitrage opportunities would exist. For example, assume that the current spot price of gold is $320 per ounce and a three-month gold futures contract specifies a price of $346 per ounce. If the cost of carry for gold for three months is 5 percent (including storage, insurance, financing, and such), an arbitrageur could profit from these prices, as shown below:

Time	Transaction	Cash Flow
Today	1. Buy gold in the spot market for $320 per ounce.	−$320 per ounce
	2. Short 3-month gold futures for $346.	
Three months hence	3. Pay storage cost (5% per ounce).	−$16 per ounce
	4. Deliver gold to satisfy the futures contract; collect $346 per ounce.	+$346 per ounce
		Net profits = $10 per ounce

This string of transactions would generate a risk-free profit of $10 per ounce. Of course, because other traders can do the same, these prices would not last long. Think about it this way: Who would be willing to sell gold today at $320 per ounce? Who would be willing to go long in a three-month futures contract at $346? Demand should push the spot price of gold upward or the three-month futures price downward, or both.

If futures prices are determined by the cost of carry, the basis may be either positive or negative, depending on whether the cost of carry is positive or negative. For most physical commodities—such as corn and crude oil—we would expect a positive

Exhibit 16.8 ✦ THEORY OF NORMAL BACKWARDATION

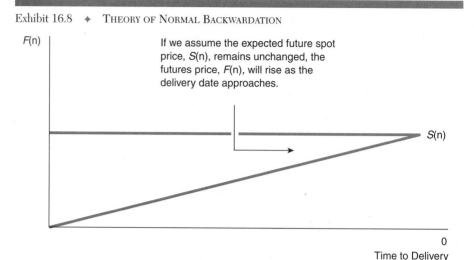

Note: F(n) is the futures price; S(n) is the expected future spot price; 0 is the delivery date, at which time to delivery equals 0.

cost of carry. In other words, it costs something to buy and store the commodities for a period of time. Therefore, if futures prices are related to the cost of carry, the basis for physical commodities should be negative.

What about the positive basis of T-bond futures, shown in Exhibit 16.6? The cost of carry for T-bonds is negative if short-term rates are lower than long-term rates. T-bonds pay coupon interest, even if they are held for only a short period of time, because interest accrues daily between coupon payment dates. If long-term rates exceed short-term rates, which they generally do, the amount of coupon income from T-bonds should exceed the cost of financing the bonds for a short period of time. Let's look at a simple example.

Assume that the price of a six-month T-bond futures contract and the spot price of an 8 percent T-bond are both 100 (or 100 percent of par). If the cost of financing T-bonds for six months equals 6 percent annually, one could profit by buying the bonds and shorting the six-month futures. In six months, the trader would deliver the bonds to satisfy the futures contract. The financing cost is 3 percent (6 percent of 100 divided by 2), so the effective cost is 103 percent (100 + 3). However, besides the 100 percent for the bonds at delivery, the trader also gets six months of coupon interest, 4 percent (8 percent divided by 2). This amounts to a riskless profit of 1 percent per bond (100 + 4 − 100 − 3). As in the prior gold example, this arbitrage situation should not last long in the real futures market.

In the real marketplace, several factors prevent the price of any futures contract from simply equaling the current spot price plus the cost of carry. For one, real-market trades impose transaction costs, which the examples have ignored. For another, characteristics of some assets may limit their storage (for example, orange juice may not last indefinitely in storage).

Restrictions on Short Sales

Perhaps the most important complication to the cost of carry theory is that restrictions on short sales often limit spot market transactions. Think about the gold transaction we discussed earlier. In that example, the following relationship created an arbitrage opportunity:

$$F(n) > S(1 + c)$$

What would happen if the reverse were true: $F(n) < S(1 + c)$. To profit, the arbitrageur would have to go short in the cash market, go long in the futures market, collect the storage cost, take delivery, and cover the short position in the cash market. Could someone really go short in the spot market for gold and collect the storage cost? It is hard to conceive of such a transaction for gold or any physical commodity. Therefore, perhaps Equation 16.1 should be modified to state

$$F(n) \leq S(1 + c)$$

In other words, perhaps $S(1 + c)$ should be considered an upper boundary to the price of a futures contract.

Consider futures on other assets, however, such as T-bonds. Some traders can go short in T-bonds in the cash market; in fact, government bond dealers can go short almost as easily as they can go long. Even if it is possible to go short in the cash market, however, other restrictions limit short sales. The most common restriction is the need to keep some of the proceeds of a short position in a margin account. (This was discussed in Chapter 3.) Consequently, a trader cannot earn a market rate of return on the entire proceeds.

WHICH THEORY OF FUTURES PRICING IS CORRECT?

In our view, both theories are correct in the sense that both help us understand the relationship between current spot prices, expected future spot prices, and futures prices. Expected future spot prices clearly influence futures prices. At the same time, however, cost of carry relationships limit futures prices in relation to spot prices.

Which theory gives the most accurate price for a futures contract may depend on the asset. If trading in a contract faces few restrictions on short sales and hedgers are neither net short nor net long, futures prices are probably more closely related to costs of carry. Treasury note and bond futures probably fit in this group. However, if short sales face major restrictions and if hedgers are clearly net short or net long, futures prices are probably more closely related to expected future spot prices. Cost of carry, however, still restricts futures prices. Most physical assets probably fit more easily into this group.

Uses of Futures Contracts

Having described the basic characteristics of futures contracts and their pricing, we now turn to a discussion of the general uses of futures contracts. We examine both speculative and hedging positions. Let's begin with several speculative positions.

SPECULATING WITH FUTURES

As we have discussed, a speculator is a trader who has no cash position in the asset. She attempts to profit from expected price changes. The most basic speculative position is an outright position in a futures contract. The choice of the position, long or short, depends on the trader's expectations for future movements in the asset's price.

For example, suppose that a speculator decides that gold is currently overvalued because she sees no signs of inflation in most countries, the political situation is stable, the production of gold is well above consumption, and several countries appear to be selling some of their gold reserves. The speculator may decide to go short in June gold at $348 per ounce. The size of the contract is 100 ounces, so the initial value of one contract is $34,800. This requires about a $3,000 margin deposit per contract.

Assume that the expectation is right. In two months, June gold is down to $320 per ounce. The speculator closes out the position by going long in June gold. In essence, she sold gold for $348 per ounce ($34,800 per contract) and bought it back at $320 per ounce ($32,000 per contract). This generated a profit of $28 per ounce ($2,800 per contract). On a $3,000 investment (assuming price changes while the position was open required no margin calls), the return is a rather healthy 93 percent ($2,800/$3,000).

What can go wrong? Lots, of course. Gold prices might defy reason and continue to rise. The trader may correctly perceive gold as overvalued but misjudge the timing of the price correction. If the market does not recognize that gold is overvalued until July, after she closes out the position, the move comes too late. Another potential risk is that gold might rise sharply after the trader goes short, causing a margin call. If she is unwilling or unable to deposit more cash, the position will be closed out. If gold then starts to fall, it is too late.

All of this demonstrates that outright positions in futures are *highly* risky. Also, the potential loss is almost unlimited; one can easily lose much more than the initial margin deposit. Experienced futures traders understand that outright positions are risky, and as a result, most speculate using intracommodity and intercommodity spreads. Because spreads are unlikely to change dramatically, they are far less risky than outright positions. Let's look at some examples of both.

Intracommodity Spreads

As we have discussed, an intracommodity spread is a combination of a long position in one contract with a simultaneous short position in another contract on the same asset with a different delivery date. As an example, assume that today is January 6, 2000, and March 2000 crude oil is selling for $24.15 a barrel and June 2000 crude oil is selling for $22.74 a barrel—the spread is $1.41 a barrel. A speculator believes that oil prices are headed lower over the next month and this will have a more substantial impact on the distant contract than the near-term contract. In other words, the spread between the March and June crude contracts should get wider. He would buy the March contract and sell the June contract. The details are shown in Exhibit 16.9.

Notice that even though the trader lost money on the March contract, he made money on the trade because the spread did what was expected: It got larger. It increased from $1.41 per barrel to $2.01 per barrel.

Intercommodity Spread

An intercommodity spread combines a purchase of one contract with a sale of another; the contracts have the same delivery date, but different, although related,

Exhibit 16.9 ✦ EXAMPLE OF AN INTRACOMMODITY SPREAD

Date	Transaction
January 30	1. Buy March crude oil at $24.15.
	2. Sell June crude oil at $22.74.
February 28	3. Sell March crude oil at $23.80.
	4. Buy June crude oil at $21.79.
Profit (loss)	5. March crude oil: Loss of $0.35 per barrel × 1,000 barrels = ($350) loss.
	6. June crude oil: Profit of $0.95 per barrel × 1,000 barrels = $950 profit.
	Total profit = $600

Exhibit 16.10 ✦ EXAMPLE OF AN INTERCOMMODITY SPREAD

Date	Transaction
January 30	1. Buy March heating oil at 65.28 cents per gallon (42,000-gallon contract).
	2. Sell March unleaded gas at 68.35 cents per gallon (42,000-gallon contract).
February 28	3. Sell March heating oil at 75.28 cents per gallon.
	4. Buy March unleaded gas at 73.35 cents per gallon.
Profit (loss)	5. Profit on March heating oil = 10 cents per gallon × 42,000 gallons = $4,200 profits.
	6. Loss on March unleaded gas = 5 cents. per gallon × 42,000 gallons = ($2,100) loss
	Overall profit = $2,100

assets underlie them. As in an intracommodity spread, the speculator hopes to profit from a change in the spread.

Assume today is January 6, 2000. A trader observes that March heating oil is trading for 65.28 cents per gallon and March unleaded gasoline is trading for 68.35 cents per gallon. She believes that oil companies are about to reduce their production of heating oil while boosting their production of unleaded gasoline. At the same time, she believes that the demand for heating oil will remain high during February and early March. Consequently, the price of heating oil should rise relative to the price of unleaded gasoline. So, she would buy March heating oil and sell March unleaded gasoline. Details of this intercommodity spread are shown in Exhibit 16.10.

Because heating oil became more expensive relative to gasoline, the trader ended up making money. This was true in spite of the fact that the prices of both commodities rose and she lost money on the unleaded gasoline contract.

HEDGING WITH FUTURES

Futures, as you know, can help traders hedge cash positions. Ideally, the hedge should be constructed in such a way that

$$\Delta C + \Delta F = 0 \tag{16.2}$$

where C is the change in the value of the cash position and F is the change in the value of the futures position. No matter what happens to the price of the asset, the overall wealth remains unchanged. In reality, it is hard to construct an ideal hedge, but a careful hedger may be able to come close.

Essentially, constructing a hedge requires a decision about what position to take in the futures market and in what contract (asset, delivery date, and number). The first decision is easy. The position in the futures market should be the *opposite* of the position in the cash market. In other words, if an increase in price in the cash market decreases the trader's wealth, this is a short position in the cash market. Consequently, the trader should go long in the futures market.

Deciding what contract to trade can be straightforward or something of a problem, depending on what asset the hedge must protect. Let's look at an example of both a short hedge and a long hedge.

Short Hedge

short hedge
Short position in the futures market to offset a long position in the cash market.

A farmer may need a classic **short hedge.** Let's say that it is springtime and an Iowa corn farmer has just planted a crop for harvest in late September or early October. The farmer worries that the cash price of corn—currently $2.58 per bushel—will fall between planting and harvest time. Because the farmer is long in the cash market, the hedge requires a short position in the futures market. The farmer anticipates harvesting about 51,000 bushels of corn. Because each futures contract consists of 5,000 bushels, the farmer should short about 10 (51,000/5,000) September corn contracts.

The hedge turns out well, as shown in Exhibit 16.11. The market justified the farmer's worries, as corn fell in price between May and September. Because of the hedge, however, the losses in the cash market were almost totally offset by profits from the futures position.[5] Of course, few actual hedges turn out quite this well, but this example illustrates the logic behind the short hedge.[6]

Long Hedge

long hedge
Long position in the futures market to offset a short position in the cash market.

Now, assume that today is March 1 and in two months a corporate treasurer must make a regular payment of DM100 million to a European supplier. Currently, the exchange rate between the dollar and the mark is DM0.60 per dollar; DM100 million is worth about $60 million. The treasurer worries that the value of the dollar will fall relative to the mark, meaning that the DM/dollar exchange rate will rise.

In essence, the firm is short in the cash market. The appropriate hedge, therefore, is a **long hedge:** Go long in DM in the foreign exchange futures market. Because each DM contract consists of DM125,000, the treasurer should buy 800 June DM contracts (DM100,000,000/DM125,000)—there is no May contract. The relevant information on the long hedge is shown in Exhibit 16.12.

---

[5]You may wonder why the farmer does not just go ahead and deliver corn to satisfy the futures contracts and collect $42.60 per bushel. The major reason is the cost of shipping the corn from the Iowa farm to the delivery location at a major export terminal (for example, New Orleans).

[6]Of course, had the price of corn risen between May and September the farmer would have been better off by not hedging because she ends up losing money in the futures market. However, the purpose of hedging, remember, is not to make money but to reduce risk.

Exhibit 16.11 ✦ EXAMPLE OF A SHORT HEDGE

Date	Transaction
May 1	Short 10 September corn contracts at $2.60 per bushel (5,000 bushels per contract).
September 15	1. Harvest 51,000 bushels of corn, sell in cash market for $2.40 per bushel.
	2. Buy 10 September corn contracts at $2.43 per bushel.
Profit (loss)	3. Cash market: Loss of 18 cents per bushel ($2.58 − $2.40) × 51,000 bushels = $9,180 loss.
	4. Future market: Profit of 17 cents per bushel × 10 contracts × 5,000 bushels = $8,500 profit.
	Overall loss = $680

Had the treasurer not hedged, the rise in the value of the DM relative to the dollar would have cost the company an additional $6 million to meet its May DM100-million obligation. The profits from the long hedge in DM futures reduced this loss to less than $400,000.

Financial Futures: A Closer Look

We have already noted that trading in financial futures currently exceeds, by a wide margin, trading in futures on physical assets. Now, let's take a closer look at financial futures. First, we examine in more detail futures on money market instruments (T-bills and Eurodollars), coupon-bearing instruments (T-bonds and T-notes), and stock indexes. We also look at several ways to use financial futures both to speculate and to hedge.

TREASURY BILL AND EURODOLLAR FUTURES

T-bill and Eurodollar futures are traded on the IMM, which is part of the CME. Both contracts are similar in design, and futures on both T-bills and Eurodollars can be used to speculate on or hedge against short-term movements in interest rates. However, traders must recognize some important differences between the two contracts.

Treasury Bill Futures

T-bill futures have delivery dates in March, June, September, and December. Any T-bill with a maturity of 90, 91, or 92 days at the time of delivery can satisfy the contract. All bills delivered, however, must have the same maturity. The face value of T-bills delivered, per contract, is $1 million. Price quotations are based on the IMM index:

$$IMM = 100\% - DY \qquad (16.3)$$

Exhibit 16.12 ✦ EXAMPLE OF A LONG HEDGE

Date	Transaction
March 1	Buy 800 June DM contracts at $0.5789 per DM (DM125,000 per contract).
May 1	1. Buy DM100 million at a spot rate of $0.66 per DM, cost $66 million.
	2. Sell 800 June DM contracts at $0.6350 per DM.
Profit (loss)	3. Loss in cash market: $0.06 per DM × DM100 million = $6 million loss.
	4. Profit in futures market: $0.0561 per DM × 800 × DM125,000 = $5.61 profit.
	Total loss = ($390,000)

---

where *DY* is the discount yield on 90-day T-bills. (We discussed how to find the discount yield in Chapter 2.) The value of one T-bill contract equals

$$\text{Value of contract} = \$1,000,000 \times [100 - (100\text{-}IMM)(90/360)/100] \qquad (16.4)$$

where *IMM* is the IMM index value.

If the discount yield on T-bills were equal to 5 percent, the IMM index would equal 95. The value of one T-bill contract, with an IMM index of 95, would be

$$\$1,000,000 \times [100 - (100 - 95)(90/360)/100] = \$987,500$$

The minimum price fluctuation in T-bill futures is one basis point (0.01 percent) in the discount yield, which translates to $25 per contract. If 91-day or 92-day bills are delivered, the price of the contract would be adjusted slightly by substituting the correct number of days into Equation 16.4.

Eurodollar Futures

Eurodollar futures are based on Eurodollar bank deposits. As we described in Chapter 2, Eurodollar deposits are time deposits held in foreign banks or their U.S. branches. Even though federal law no longer limits the rates offered by U.S. banks, Eurodollar rates are still higher than comparable U.S. interest rates. This is caused, in part, by lack of deposit insurance on Eurodollar deposits.

The Eurodollar futures contract has a face value of $1 million, and its price is based on the three-month LIBOR (London Interbank Offered Rate), the average interest rate offered by large London banks on Eurodollar deposits. We find the value of a Eurodollar futures contract in the same way as we find the value of a T-bill futures contract (Equations 16.3 and 16.4), with one major exception. Unlike T-bills, Eurodollars are not discount securities; rather, they are add-on instruments. Like most bank deposits, they pay interest on the amount deposited.

The add-on yield is calculated as follows:

$$(\text{Interest/Purchase price}) \times (360/\text{Days to maturity})$$

The IMM index for Eurodollars equals

$$100\% - \text{Add-on yield}$$

The value of one Eurodollar contract is found using Equation 16.4.

The other major difference between T-bill and Eurodollar futures is that Eurodollar futures are **cash settled.** Instead of allowing the short position to deliver an asset, all accounts that remain open on the last trading day are settled in cash at a LIBOR-based rate determined by the CME clearinghouse.

cash settled
No delivery of the asset actually occurs; all open accounts are settled in cash.

TREASURY BOND AND NOTE FUTURES

Futures contracts on T-bonds and T-notes (notes, five-year notes, and two-year notes), all of which are traded on the CBOT, are virtually identical to each other, except for the deliverable instruments they specify. All T-bond and T-note contracts, with the exception of the two-year note contract, are based on securities with $100,000 in par value. (The two-year note's contract size is $200,000.) The prices of all bond and note contracts assume a coupon rate of 6 percent, and prices are stated in 32nds of a percent. If the price of June bond future is stated as 115–08, the decimal price is 115.25 (115 and 8/32), or $115,250 per contract.[7] The minimum price fluctuation is 1/32, or $31.25 per contract. Treasury note and bond futures have delivery dates in March, June, September, and December.

Conversion Factors and Invoice Amount

As we just noted, all T-bond and T-note contracts are priced assuming an 6 percent coupon rate. Because the short position can deliver any Treasury security that meets the maturity requirements specified by the contract, regardless of the coupon rate, invoice amounts are adjusted by so-called conversion factors. The conversion factor is the price of the bond delivered, assuming a par value of $1 and a yield to maturity of 8 percent. Generally, bonds with coupon rates greater than 6 percent have conversion factors greater than 1, whereas bonds with coupon rates less than 6 percent have conversion factors less than 1.

If the short actually delivers securities to the long to fulfill the futures contract, the invoice amount equals

$$\text{(Settlement price as a percentage of par} \times \text{Number of contracts} \times \\ \$100,000 \times \text{Conversion factor)} + \text{Accrued interest}$$

Assume that a short decides to deliver 10 T-bond contracts. The settlement price when the short established the position was 110–16 (110.5 percent of par). The short decides to deliver bonds with a coupon rate of 9 percent and a maturity of exactly 17 years three months. The conversion factor for these bonds is 1.0925, and accrued interest equals $22,500 (three months of interest, at 9 percent per year, on $1 million worth of bonds). The invoice equals

$$1.105 \times 10 \times \$100,000 \times 1.0925 + \$22,500 = \$1,229,712.50$$

---

[7]Like price quotations in the cash market, T-bond and T-note futures prices are quoted in percentages of par value. A price of 11–08 translates into 11.25 percent of par value.

Cheapest to Deliver

One feature unique to T-bond and T-note futures is that some bonds and notes are cheaper to deliver than others because of the way in which conversion factors are computed. Essentially, the method of computing and using conversion factors assumes that all deliverable securities have the same yield to maturity. In reality, of course, they do not. Remember, the short initiates delivery and also chooses the instruments to deliver, assuming that they meet the conditions of the contract. Logically, the short should choose the most advantageous instrument. The instrument that is cheapest to deliver is the one that costs the least compared with the futures price. Let's illustrate this with an example. All the following bonds can be delivered against the March 2000 T-bond futures contract. (Prices and accrued interest as of January 6, 2000.)

	Bond A	Bond B	Bond C	Bond D
Price (per $100 par value)	89.3125	104.25	131.875	145.8125
Accrued interest (per $100 of par value)	2.75	1.5104	2.0573	5.1563
Cash price (per $100 of par value)	92.0625	105.7604	133.9323	150.9688
Conversion factor	.7761	.9274	1.1795	1.3050
Adjusted cash price	118.6220	114.0397	113.5501	115.6849
Futures price	111.4375	111.4375	111.4375	111.4375
Ratio of adjusted cash price to futures price	1.0645	1.0234	1.0190	1.0381

Note: The adjusted cash price equals the cash price of the bond divided by its conversion factor.

The security that is cheapest to deliver has the lowest adjusted-cash-price to futures-price ratio. In our example, bond C is the cheapest to deliver. Determining which instrument is the cheapest to deliver is not difficult. As a result, a futures contract's price should closely match the price of the instrument that is cheapest to deliver as the first delivery date approaches.

STOCK INDEX FUTURES

Stock index futures are contracts based on well-known indexes of common stocks. Today, the most actively traded stock index futures contract, based on the S&P 500, is traded on the CME. Delivery dates are December, March, June, and September. The futures price is quoted in the same manner as the index. The value of one futures contract is the index value multiplied by $500. (An index value of 780 would give one contract a value of $390,000.) Like Eurodollar futures, S&P 500 futures are cash settled.

One feature unique to stock index futures is the lack of any daily limits on price fluctuations, either upward or downward. In theory, a trader could lose an entire margin deposit during one trading day. However, in the wake of the 1987 market break, the futures markets instituted a set of procedures called *circuit breakers*. In periods of extreme stock market volatility, when the index rises or falls by a certain amount, the circuit breakers kick in and trading in stock index futures is suspended.

Program Trading

Stock index futures have faced criticism due to the controversial practice of program trading, computer-assisted trading of large blocks of stock simultaneously with stock index futures. Program trading attempts to take advantage of perceived pricing errors between the stock index (the cash market) and the stock index futures. Let's illustrate program trading with a hypothetical example.

The current index value is 765, and the index futures contract is trading for 795. Between now and the settlement date, in one year, the short-term rate of interest is 6 percent and the dividend yield is 2.5 percent. On the settlement date, the futures price and stock index will converge to the same value. Let's assume the index closes at 765 in one year.

Today, the trader borrows $382,500 (765 × $500) and buys the stocks in the index. Simultaneously, he goes short in the futures at 795. In one year, he sells the index stocks (collecting $382,500), repays the loan (paying $22,950 in interest), and collects the cash dividends ($9,562.50, or 2.5 percent of $382,500). He also closes out the futures position, buying the contract at 765. The profit from the futures trade is $15,000 [(795 − 765) × $500]. Overall, he earns $1,612.50 ($15,000 + $9,562.50 − $22,950). The example assumes that the index is "cheap" relative to the futures. By buying the index and, at the same time, going short in futures, the trader locked in a profit. The position would make money regardless of whether the stock index were to rise or fall in value.

Note two points about the hypothetical example of program trading. First, transaction costs, which we ignored, would be considerable for all but large institutional investors. Second, the trader need not actually borrow the money today to purchase the index stocks. The short-term interest rate of 6 percent could also be considered the opportunity cost associated with tying up $382,500 in capital for a period of time.

As we noted, program trading is controversial. Some critics have blamed the technique for increasing volatility in the stock market. Some have even laid much of the blame for the 1987 market break (Meltdown Monday) on program trading. The evidence that program trading has contributed to stock market volatility or the 1987 market break is, however, ambiguous at best.

SPECULATING AND HEDGING WITH FINANCIAL FUTURES

Financial futures create numerous opportunities to speculate on stock prices, interest rates, changes in the shape of the yield curve, and other market moves. As with all futures, most speculative trades in financial futures involve trading spreads. Financial futures can also be used to create both long and short hedges. A pension fund manager can use financial futures, for example, to hedge against declines in the portfolio's stock or bond prices.

In this section, we look at examples of a speculative trade in financial futures (an intracommodity spread using T-bond futures), a short hedge using T-bond futures, and a long hedge using S&P 500 futures. These are three of dozens of examples of speculative and hedging positions using financial futures.[8]

Intracommodity Spread Example

Assume that today is February 1. Based on economic data, a trader believes that weak economic growth and modest inflation should force interest rates downward in the

---

[8]For more details, see *Treasury Futures for Institutional Investors* (Chicago: Chicago Board of Trade, 1990); and Donald Chance, *An Introduction to Options & Futures*, 3rd ed. (Fort Worth, TX: Dryden, 1995).

Exhibit 16.13 ✦ INTRACOMMODITY SPREAD USING T-BOND FUTURES

Date	March Futures (prices in 32nds)	December Futures (prices in 32nds)	Spread (32nds)
February 1	111–16	110–00	48
March 1	114–00	112–00	64
Profit (loss)	Profit of 2–16 per contract = $2,500 profit	Loss of 2–00 per contract = ($2,000) loss	16 per contract

near future. As interest rates fall, of course, bond prices rise. Although a general decline in interest rates would affect all T-bond futures prices, the prices of futures for near-term delivery should rise more than the prices of futures for distant delivery.[9] The trader decides to buy five March T-bond futures contracts and, at the same time, sell five December T-bond futures. If interest rates were to decline as expected, with the position remaining open until March 1, the results would resemble those in Exhibit 16.13.

The initial spread between the March and December bond contracts was 48/32 ($1,500 per contract). Even though the prices of both contracts rose as rates declined, the June contract rose more in price than the December contract. As a result, the spread between the two contracts widened to 64/32 ($2,000). The trader made 16/32 ($500) per contract, for a total profit of $2,500.

Example of a Short Hedge

On February 1, a pension fund holds $10 million-worth (measured by face value) of the 11 percent T-bond, currently priced at 145.8125 per $100 of par value—current value is $14,581,250. The fund manager is concerned about interest rates rising, and thus bond prices falling, over the next few weeks. To protect the portfolio, the manager constructs a short hedge using March T-bond futures. Because each T-bond futures contract has a face value of $100,000, the fund manager shorts 100 contracts at 111.4375. The market fulfills the fund manager's expectation, and interest rates rise over the next 30 days. By early March, the value of the fund's bonds declines by $90,625. The March futures, however, also fall; the short position produces a profit of $59,375, reducing the overall loss to $31,250. The details are shown in Exhibit 16.14.

Although the futures contracts reduced the fund's cash market loss by almost two-thirds, the fund manager did not construct an optimal hedge. A better tactic would consider that, as rates rise, the cash market instrument would show a greater dollar price change than the dollar change in price in the futures. Consequently, weighting the hedge by the conversion factor would have produced a better result. This is also shown in Exhibit 16.14. Had a weighted hedge been used, the loss would have been reduced to less than $13,000.[10]

---

[9]The reason for this relates to the relationship between bond futures prices and the cost of carry, which, remember, is negative if short-term rates are less than long-term rates. See *Treasury Futures for Institutional Investors*, pp. 70–72.

[10]Weighting strategies can get quite sophisticated, depending on the instrument being hedged. See *Treasury Futures for Institutional Investors*, pp. 37–48.

Exhibit 16.14 ◆ SHORT HEDGE EXAMPLE USING T-BOND FUTURES

A. Unweighted Hedge

	Futures	Cash
February 1	Short 100 March T-bond contracts at 111.4375	Hold $10 million (face value) of 11 percent bonds priced at 145.8125 or $14,581,250
March 2	Buy 100 March T-bond contracts at 110.84375	Hold $10 million of 11 percent bonds priced at 144.90625 or $14,490,625
Profit (loss)	$59,375	($90,625)

B. Weighted Hedge

Face amount of bonds/Contract size × Conversion factor = Number of contracts

$10,000,000/$100,000 × 1.3050 = 131 contracts
Profit on futures = 131 × $593.75 = $77,781.25
Loss in cash market = $90,625
Overall loss = $12,843.75

Example of a Long Hedge

On January 13, a corporate treasurer is reviewing investment plans for the pension fund contribution the company plans to make in March. The $10 million contribution will be invested in a pension fund at the fund's net asset value on the day of the contribution. Currently, the fund's net asset value is $50 per share, so the $10 million contribution would buy 200,000 shares. The treasurer is concerned about stock prices rising before March and decides to construct a long hedge using S&P 500 futures.

After deciding on a March delivery date, the treasurer must determine the number of contracts to buy. Assume that the current price of March S&P 500 futures is 780. This gives a current dollar value of $390,000 per contract (780 × 500). Dividing $390,000 into $10 million (the amount to be invested in March) gives 25.6. This is not the final answer, however. Assume that the pension fund has a beta of 0.95, meaning that, historically at least, the pension fund is about 95 percent as volatile as the overall market. Weighting the hedge by the pension fund's beta gives 24.3 (0.95 × 25.6). Rounding off, the treasurer should buy 24 March S&P 500 futures at 780.

Details of this long hedge are shown in Exhibit 16.15. The table shows the results if stock prices were to rise, as the treasurer feared, between January and March. This would boost March S&P 500 futures by 5 percent, to 819. The price per share of the pension fund rose to $52.25. The loss in the cash market would amount to $450,000 ($2.25 × 200,000), and the profit in the futures market would amount to $468,000 (39 × $500 × 24). In this case, the treasurer ended up making a small profit, $18,000.

Of course, if stock prices were to fall rather than rise, the treasurer would lose money in the futures market and make money in the cash market. Remember, however, that the idea behind hedging is not to make money but rather to reduce the risk associated with a position in the cash market.

Exhibit 16.15 ✦ EXAMPLE OF A LONG HEDGE USING S&P 500 FUTURES

	Futures	Cash
January 13	Go long in 24 March S&P 500 contracts at 780	Will have $10 million for investment in March, current price = $50 per share
March 15	Go short in 24 March S&P 500 contracts at 819	Invest $10 million at $52.25 per share
Profit (loss)	$468,000	($450,000)

Options on Futures

In 1982, the Commodity Futures Trading Commission allowed each futures market to begin trading options on one futures contract. The pilot program proved so successful that options on futures were permanently authorized in 1987. Today, options, both calls and puts, are available on most actively traded futures contracts.

CHARACTERISTICS OF OPTIONS ON FUTURES

By now, you should be familiar with the characteristics of futures contracts. From Chapter 15, you should be familiar with the characteristics of call and put options. Putting them together, you will see how options on futures work. An option on a futures contract gives the holder the right, but not the obligation, to go long (with a call) or short (with a put) in a specific futures contract, at a specific price (the stated exercise price), until some point in the future (the option's expiration date). An option on a futures contract expires the month before the delivery month of the underlying futures contract, so a March 2000 T-bond call option expires in February.

As with all options, an option on a futures contract requires a seller (writer) for every buyer. The writer of a call option can be obligated to establish a short position in the futures, whereas the writer of a put option can be obligated to establish a long position in the futures. The most the buyer of an option on a futures contract can lose is the price he or she paid for the option. However, the option writer faces potentially unlimited losses.

USING OPTIONS ON FUTURES

Almost all trading strategies that use stock options (whether for speculation or hedging) apply to options on futures as well. Much of the discussion in Chapter 15 transfers directly to options on futures. However, it would be useful to examine two basic strategies for options on futures: buying a call option instead of the futures contract, and using a call to protect a short position in the futures contract.

Buying a Call

From Chapter 15 we know that the profit (or loss) from holding a call option on a futures contract until expiration is

$$\text{Profit (Loss)} = \max(0, F - E) - C$$

Exhibit 16.16 ✦ Profit (Loss) from Buying a Call Option on a T-Bond Futures Contract

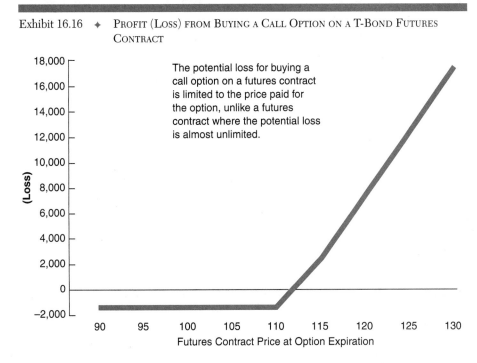

The potential loss for buying a call option on a futures contract is limited to the price paid for the option, unlike a futures contract where the potential loss is almost unlimited.

Note: Option price is 1–22, strike price is 111.

where F is the price of the futures contract at expiration, E is the exercise price, and C is the price paid for the call option. Assume that someone buys a 111 March T-bond call at 1–22 (1 and 22/64, or $1,343.75). The profit or loss from buying one call, at various futures prices, is shown in Exhibit 16.16.

Buying the call can substitute for establishing a long position in the futures. Assume that a trader expects interest rates to decline before the end of February. She could go long in March futures at 111–14 or buy the call option on the March futures contract mentioned earlier ($E = 114$, $C = 1 - 22$). The profits and losses from both strategies, at various prices, are shown in Exhibit 16.17.

If the price of March T-bonds were to fall from 111–14 to 100, the loss from holding the long position in the futures contract would be more than $11,400, compared with $1,343.75 from holding the option on the futures contract. The advantage of buying the call, as opposed to the futures contract, is the limit on the loss to the cost of the option ($1,343.75 in the example). The loss from a futures position is, at least technically, unlimited. Of course, the disadvantage of the call option is that it sacrifices some of the profit should T-bond prices rise as expected.

Using a Call Option to Protect a Short Futures Position

As we have seen, outright futures positions are risky. Consequently, most traders use spreads. An alternative to a spread is to combine an option on a futures contract with a futures position. For example, one could combine a call option with a short futures position. Let's look at an example.

Exhibit 16.17 ✦ BUYING A CALL OPTION VERSUS BUYING A FUTURES CONTRACT PROFIT (LOSS)

Future Price (at option expiration)	Futures	Call Option
90	($21,437.50)	($1,343.75)
95	(16,437.50)	(1,343.75)
100	(11,437.50)	(1,343.75)
105	(6,437.50)	(1,343.75)
110	(1,437.50)	(1,343.75)
115	3,562.50	2,656.25
120	8,562.50	7,656.25
125	13,562.50	12,656.25
130	18,562.50	17,656.25

Note: The price of the futures contract, when the position was established is 111–14. The price of the call option is 1–22.

Exhibit 16.18 ✦ SHORTING A FUTURES CONTRACT AND BUYING A CALL OPTION PROFIT (LOSS)

Future Price (at option expiration)	Futures	Call Option	Total
90	$21,437.50	($1343.75)	$20,093.75
95	16,437.50	(1343.75)	15,093.75
100	11,437.50	(1343.75)	10,093.75
105	6,437.50	(1343.75)	5,093.75
110	1,437.50	(1343.75)	93.75
115	(3,562.50)	2,656.25	(906.25)
120	(8,562.50)	7,656.25	(906.25)
125	(13,562.50)	12,656.25	(906.25)
130	(18,562.50)	17,656.25	(906.25)

Note: The futures contract is shorted at 111–14. The call option is purchased for 1–64.

Assume that you short March T-bonds at 111–14, in expectation of falling bond prices. To protect the position, should prices rise, you also buy a 111 March call at 1–22. The profit and loss from the combination is shown in Exhibit 16.18. Your loss is limited to slightly more than $900, regardless of how high T-bond prices go. However, the combination sacrifices profit should prices fall. The cost of the protection is $1,343.75, the price of the call option.

Chapter Summary

1. What are futures contracts?

   Futures are real contracts that call for the sale of an underlying asset, at a point in the future, at a price agreed on today. Futures contracts have a short position (the party delivering the asset) and a long position (the person taking delivery of the asset). Both parties are required to post margin, which increases with gains and decreases with losses. Futures are available in agricultural commodities, precious metals, petroleum products, foreign currencies, interest-bearing instruments, and stock indexes.

2. How are futures contracts valued?

   Futures traders pay attention not only to the price of the contract but also to the basis—the spread between the cash price and the futures price—and a variety of spreads—both intracommodity and intercommodity. Two general theories apply to futures pricing. The first says that the price of a futures contract relates to the expected future spot price of the asset. The second says that futures prices relate to the current spot price plus the cost of carry. Both theories aid in our understanding of futures pricing.

3. How do traders use futures?

   Traders use futures either to speculate on the price of an asset or used to hedge a cash position. Few successful futures traders trade outright positions, most trade spreads—buying one contract while selling another. Hedgers establish a position in the futures market that is the exact opposite of their position in the cash market. Thus losses in the cash market are offset by gains in the futures market and gains in the cash market are offset by losses in futures. Hedgers use futures not to make money but rather to reduce the risk of their cash positions.

4. What are financial futures?

   Financial futures are currently the most popular type of futures. They are available on T-bills, Eurodollars, T-bonds, T-notes, and stock indexes, to name the most actively traded. Financial futures can be used to speculate on interest rates and stock prices. They can also be used to hedge cash positions in the stock and bond markets.

5. What are options on futures?

   A call option gives the owner the right to establish a long position in the underlying futures at a specific price, and a put option gives the owner the right to establish a short position in the underlying futures at a specific price. Calls and puts can be used as substitutes for futures positions. They can also be used to reduce the risk of outright futures positions.

Mini Case 1

This mini case constructs an intercommodity spread using futures on T-bonds and five-year T-notes. Assume that today is December 1. Between now and early next year, interest rates should fall. Further, the slope of the yield curve should remain essentially unchanged. Today, T-bonds are priced at 111 and five-year T-notes are priced at 107.

a. If interest rates do decline, what will happen to bond and note prices? What should happen to the spread between bonds and notes (both price and yield)?

b. What is the appropriate intercommodity spread if rates should decline and the slope of the yield curve does not change?

c. Assume that rates fall, as expected, and the position closes out with March notes selling for 113 and March bonds selling for 120-16. How much did the intercommodity spread make?

Mini Case 2

This mini case sets up a hedge using a futures contract. Assume that today is January 5. A company will receive payment from its Japanese customers on February 25. The payment will be denominated in Japanese yen and will be equal to ¥10 billion. The current yen-dollar exchange rate is (¥1 − $0.0092). The March yen futures contract (¥12.5 million per contract) is currently trading at 0.0094.

    a.   What change in the value of the dollar relative to the yen should the company be concerned about between now and late February? Explain.

    b.   What is the proper hedge using yen futures?

    c.   Assume that the spot exchange rate equals ¥15 $0.0085 on February 25. On the same day, March yen futures are selling for 0.0083. How much did the company lose in the cash market and how much did it make in the futures market? How well did the hedge work out?

Review Questions and Problems

1.   Describe the characteristics of a futures contract. How does a futures contract differ from a forward contract?

2.   Why is futures trading considered a zero sum game? Who makes money and who loses money if futures decline in price?

3.   Who begins the delivery process? Does a long position have to take delivery of the asset?

4.   What characteristics does an asset require to develop a viable futures market? Why has an active futures market developed in Treasury securities?

5.   Describe the role of the clearinghouse. Why is the clearinghouse so important to the orderly functioning of a futures market?

6.   What is margin in futures trading? What happens at the end of each trading day to a futures margin account?

7.   Assume that a trader goes long in March T-bonds at 114–00 (1140/32). The trader must post $4,000 in initial margin and maintain $3,000 in margin. What would happen to the account if March T-bonds were to settle the next day at 113–16? Would the trader face a margin call?

8.   Describe open interest. Assume that A went short in 10 March T-bonds two weeks ago (B went long). Today, A went long in 5 March T-bonds (C went short). How much would open interest change?

9.   What is basis? Does basis have to equal zero on the delivery date?

10. Explain the differences between intracommodity and intercommodity spreads. Why are spreads important?

11. What is normal backwardation? What does normal backwardation assume about the net position of hedgers?

12. Explain cost of carry. Why is the cost of carry generally negative for T-bond futures? Illustrate with a numerical example.

13. Assume that the spot price of gold is $350 per ounce and the price of a three-month futures contract is $380. What do these prices imply about the cost of carry for gold? If the actual cost of carry were $5 per ounce per month, show how one could profit from these spot and futures prices.

14. What is an outright futures position? Assume you went short in March unleaded gasoline at 65 cents per gallon. How much would you make or lose if you close out your position at 62 cents per gallon?

15. If someone buys March corn and, at the same time, sells March wheat, what type of spread is traded? What does the trader expect to happen to the prices of corn and wheat between now and March?

16. What is the general idea behind hedging? What decisions about futures must the hedger make?

17. What are Eurodollars? Explain the differences between T-bill and Eurodollar futures.

18. What is the conversion factor in T-note and T-bond futures? Why does the conversion factor lead to the notion of the cheapest security to deliver?

19. Use the following information to find the invoice amount on a T-bond futures contract.

Settlement price	115–16
Conversion factor	1.1795
Size of contract	$100,000
Number of contracts	5
Accrued interest	2.0573 per $100

20. What is program trading? If a trader believes that futures are overpriced, relative to the current index, how could he take advantage of this?

21. Assume that a trader is long in T-bonds in the cash market. What is she concerned about in the near term? What position should she establish in the futures market?

22. What are options on futures? Why would someone buy a put option as opposed to establishing a short position in the futures contract? Illustrate with a numerical example. (Assume that T-bonds futures are currently trading for 112 and a 112 put option is trading for 1–16.)

CFA Questions

1. (1991 CFA Exam, Level II) Robert Chen, CFA, is reviewing the characteristics of derivative securities and their use in portfolios.

    Chen is considering the addition of either a short position in stock index futures or a long position in stock index options to an existing well-diversified portfolio of equity securities. **Contrast** the way in which *each* of these *two* alternatives would affect the risk and return of the resulting combined portfolios.

    Four factors affect the value of a futures contract on a stock index. Three of these factors are the current price of the stock index, the time remaining until the contract maturity (delivery) date, and the dividends on the stock index. **Identify** the *fourth* factor and **explain** *how and why* changes in this factor affect the value of the futures contract.

    Six factors affect the value of call options on stocks. Three of these factors are the current price of the stock, the time remaining until the option expires, and the dividend on the stock. **Identify** the other *three* factors and **explain** *how and why* changes in *each* of these three factors affect the value of call options.

CRITICAL THINKING EXERCISES

The following exercise requires computer work. Open the Futures worksheet in the Data workbook. It lists prices of T-bond and T-note futures, along with prices of call and put options on bond and note futures.

a. Assume you believe that interest rates are going to decline over the next few weeks. List some trades—using both futures and options—that you could make to take advantage of your expectation. Assume that you close out your positions after bond yields fall by 75 basis points and note yields fall by 50 basis points. Calculate the profit or loss from each trade you established.

b. Illustrate why an option is less risky than taking an outright position in a futures contract.

c. Construct a bull spread and a bear spread using options. What futures trade(s) would be similar to these option spreads? Illustrate your potential profit or loss from each trade.

THE INTERNET INVESTOR

1. Use a news web site to find out the seasonal supply and demand for a grain commodity. Determine whether it should imply an expected rise or fall in the futures price for that commodity. Find the commodity in the *Wall Street Journal* and discuss whether your expectation was correct or not. Explain your answer.

2. Find any significant news items about a commodity or financial instrument (stock index or interest rate changes). Speculate what activity the news might stimulate and create a speculative position. Now create a scenario that requires a hedged position.

3. Ascertain today's general stock market performance by visiting a web site with stock market information. Speculate impact on the stock index futures. How would you create a hedge using the spot price and the futures price?

Part 6

Modern Portfolio Theory

THE NEXT THREE CHAPTERS DISCUSS MODERN PORTFOLIO THEORY (MPT). TOPICS WILL INCLUDE RISK AVERSION, MEASURING RISK AND RETURN (FOR BOTH INDIVIDUAL SECURITIES AND PORTFOLIOS), EFFICIENT FRONTIERS, THE CAPITAL ASSET PRICING MODEL, ARBITRAGE PRICING, AND HOW TO EVALUATE THE PERFORMANCE OF INVESTMENT PORTFOLIOS. THIS SECTION'S DISCUSSIONS ARE MORE CONCEPTUAL AND THEORETICAL THAN THOSE PRIOR, BUT WE WILL SHOW HOW MODERN PORTFOLIO THEORY CAN PROVIDE INSIGHT INTO MANY REAL-WORLD INVESTMENT SITUATIONS. FOR EXAMPLE, THE CONCEPT OF DIVERSIFICATION, RECOGNIZED AND VALUED BY MOST INVESTMENT PROFESSIONALS, COMES DIRECTLY FROM MPT. MODERN PORTFOLIO THEORY SHOWS HOW DIVERSIFICATION CAN IMPROVE INVESTORS' RISK AND RETURN TRADE-OFFS AND HELPS US UNDERSTAND WHY DIVERSIFICATION WORKS.

RISK AND DIVERSIFICATION

PREVIOUSLY . . .

We discussed derivative securities and how to evaluate risk and returns for options and futures. We learned to hedge by combining options with common stocks as well as combining various future contracts.

IN THIS CHAPTER . . .

Now that you have developed an understanding of bonds, common stocks, options, and futures, you may decide to invest in combinations of these various securities. Because we won't always choose the stellar investments despite conducting every analysis possible, wise investors hedge their bets by not putting "all their eggs in one basket"— by diversifying. The chapter discusses risk and how investors are generally risk averse, as well as how to measure expected returns. Finally, we discuss how to measure portfolio risk and return.

TO COME . . .

If all risk-averse investors are likely to diversify and hold portfolios rather than just one or two stocks, we can develop a model based on that idea. It is called the Capital Asset Pricing Model (CAPM).

Chapter Objectives

1. What is risk aversion, and why are investors, as a group, risk averse?
2. What are the general investment implications of risk aversion?
3. Why is standard deviation a good measure of risk, and how does an investor compute standard deviations for both individual securities and portfolios?
4. What is the impact of security correlations on portfolio risk?
5. What are the benefits of diversification, and how can investors achieve them?
6. What is the meaning of efficient diversification and modern portfolio theory?

Two of the apparent truisms we discussed initially in Chapter 1, and have touched on many times since, were the positive relationship between historical returns and risk and the beneficial effects of investment diversification. Investment instruments that have—at least over the past 65 years or so—exhibited higher rates of return have also shown more variability around their average returns. You may recall from the historical data presented in Chapter 2 that common stocks have, on average, returned more than Treasury bills (T-bills) since 1926 (13.1 percent versus 3.8 percent per year), but stock returns have also shown far more volatility. Therefore, an investor who wants to increase expected returns must be willing to accept higher levels of risk. However, the historical evidence also suggests that owning a group of investment instruments can allow one to beat the risk/return trade-off, at least up to a point. In other words, owning five stocks will generally produce a better risk/return profile over time than owning one stock. Both of these truisms form the basis of modern portfolio and investment theory, as we discuss in more detail in this chapter. We also have in earlier chapters touched frequently on many of this chapter's key ideas. In this chapter, we tie many of these ideas together and more formally develop the concepts of risk and diversification.

Chapter 17 begins with a discussion of risk aversion, why most investors are risk averse, and what risk aversion implies about the long-term relationship between risk and return. The discussion establishes the importance of risk. Next, we turn to measuring risk, including measuring historical versus expected risk, measuring risk for an individual security, and measuring risk for a group of securities (a portfolio). This chapter also includes a detailed discussion of diversification and two types of risk, market risk and firm-specific risk. We examine diversification across securities and the fallacy of time diversification, and we'll also scrutinize naïve versus efficient diversification. A discussion of efficient diversification naturally leads to a discussion of modern portfolio theory, which concludes the chapter.

What is Risk Aversion?

Suppose your state were to begin a new lottery today. For five dollars, you would have an equal chance of losing or winning five dollars. If you play the game, you have a 50/50 chance of coming out five dollars richer or five dollars poorer. The expected payoff is, of course, zero.[1] Would you play this new lottery game? You might answer yes as you are reading this, but if you were playing with real money, you would probably answer no. If you play this lottery, you can actually expect to be worse off. The lottery involves obvious risk (the chance you may come away poorer), with no compensation for that risk. Now, suppose your state offered another new game. For five dollars, you would have an equal chance of winning nothing or winning ten dollars. Knowing the expected payoff is five dollars, would you play the second game? You are much more likely to play the second game than the first, because this second game offers some compensation for the risk involved with playing.

As trivial as these lottery games sound, the two fundamental questions involved (would you play? and why?) are really the same questions all investors must answer when making investment decisions. For example, assume you could buy a T-bill for $1,000, hold it for a year and receive $1,060 (a 6 percent return). As we have pointed out, T-bills are as close to a truly risk-free investment as you can get. Now, also assume that you could invest your $1,000 in shares of a high-risk junk bond fund. In a year, shares of the fund could be worth $1,500 (a 50 percent return), or only $500 (a minus 50 percent return); the expected return is 0 percent. Assuming each outcome has about a 50/50 chance of occurring, which investment would you choose? Most investors would tend to choose T-bills simply because the junk bond fund offers no

---

[1]Remember, the expected payoff is a weighted average of the possible outcomes. In this case, the expected payoff equals 0.50(−$5) + 0.50($5).

compensation for its added risk. In fact, the expected payoff from the fund is less than the almost certain payoff from the T-bill investment ($1,000 versus $1,060). It is hard to imagine any rational investor choosing the junk bond fund investment.

Make some changes to the example, however, and the decision becomes more interesting and ambiguous. Assume that the T-bill still offers an almost certain 6 percent return and the junk bond fund has the same two possible outcomes ($1,500 or $500), but now assume a 75 percent chance that the fund will be worth $1,500 in one year and only a 25 percent chance that it will be worth $500. The expected payoff becomes $1,250 (an expected return of 25 percent). Which would you choose in this situation? It is hard to say. Some investors would choose to invest in the junk bond fund, and others would still choose to invest in T-bills.

Although the above example is obviously simplified, it still serves to illustrate the important concept of **risk aversion,** also discussed in Chapter 2. Most investors appear willing to pay to avoid risky situations. Paying to avoid risk is exactly what we do when we purchase insurance. We pay premiums to shift some or even all of the risk of owning a home, driving a car, and so forth, to the insurance company. To put the notion of risk aversion another way, most of us will voluntarily take risks only if we receive proper compensation for that risk. We measure that proper compensation by expected returns. So, risk aversion is, in turn, related to expected returns.

risk aversion
The notion that people need an incentive to voluntarily accept risk—the risk/return relationship is positive.

RISK AVERSION AND EXPECTED RETURNS

Perhaps the most important implication of risk aversion is that an investment should show a positive relationship between expected returns and risk. As we have seen, risk-averse investors will take risk only in exchange for sufficient compensation (that is, returns). Therefore, higher-risk investments must offer risk-averse investors higher expected rates of return. If a high-risk investment offers an insufficient expected rate of return at a given price, either the price must fall. Now, assume that investors are, as a group, risk neutral. **Risk-neutral investors** would demand no relationship between risk and return. In fact, in a well-functioning market, all investments would have the same expected return, regardless of risk. Arbitrage would quickly eliminate any differences. As far-fetched as that sounds, consider the relationship between risk and return if investors are, as a group, **risk takers.** Because risk takers will pay to take risk, the relationship between expected returns and risk is negative. In other words, high-risk investments must actually offer lower expected returns compared with safer investments!

risk-neutral investor
An investor demands no relationship between risk and return.

risk-taker
An investor is willing to pay to take risk—the risk/return relationship is negative.

If our logical argument fails to convince you that investors are risk averse, reviewing some of the historical evidence on risk and return might. Chapter 2 reviewed the long-term historical performance of the major investment instruments. We found that higher-risk investments have historically, on average, returned more than lower-risk investments. For example, between 1926 and 1999, the return on common stocks in the United States—represented by the Standard & Poor's (S&P) 500—exceeded the return on U.S. T-bills by, on average, about 9.3 percent per year (13.1 percent versus 3.8 percent). By any conventional and reasonable measure, common stocks are more risky than T-bills. Exhibit 17.1 shows the distribution of yearly returns for both investments. Notice how the historical returns from T-bills are clustered together. For example, in 50 out of 74 years, T-bill returns ranged between 0 percent and 5 percent. By comparison, common stock returns have exhibited far more variability. S&P 500 Index stocks earned more than 30 percent in 19 different years and lost more than 10 percent in eight different years, between 1926 and 1999.

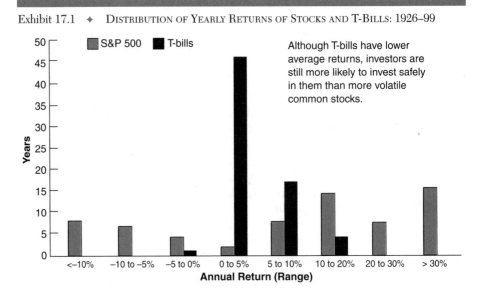

Exhibit 17.1 ◆ DISTRIBUTION OF YEARLY RETURNS OF STOCKS AND T-BILLS: 1926–99

Although T-bills have lower average returns, investors are still more likely to invest safely in them than more volatile common stocks.

RELATIVE RISK AVERSION AND EXPECTED RETURNS

A little earlier we pointed out that some investors are probably more risk averse than others. In other words, investor A may be relatively more risk averse than investor B. What does this imply about the relationship between risk and expected returns? The answer is quite straightforward: relatively more risk aversion increases the expected return investors demand for the same risk level. This is best illustrated with a simple example.

Let's say that investor A is relatively more risk averse than investor B. Exhibit 17.2 shows their hypothetical trade-offs between risk and expected return.[2] Level f represents the expected return from a risk-free asset (for example, a T-bill). As the level of risk increases (say, to level a), the expected return for both investors increases, consistent with the notion of risk aversion. Notice, however, that the expected return for investor A (the more risk-averse investor) increases more (from level f to level y) than the expected return for investor B (from level f to level x). In fact, the risk level would increase all the way to level b before investor B's expected return would reach level y.

The notion of relative risk aversion helps explain why certain investors hold only low-risk assets whereas others hold higher-risk assets. An investor who is relatively more risk averse may think that the compensation for holding, say, stocks, does not justify their added risk. This investor would own mainly T-bills and certificates of deposit (CDs). However, a relatively less risk-averse investor may think the compensation for owning stocks justifies the added risk and thus would hold mainly stocks.

RECAP   We have shown in this section that most investors are probably risk averse, although to varying degrees. Examples showed that investors would avoid a gamble (risk)

---

[2]These are referred to as indifference curves. An investor is indifferent between each point on the curve. In other words, each point (investment) offers an identical risk/return trade-off.

Exhibit 17.2 ✦ RISK AVERSION AND EXPECTED RETURNS

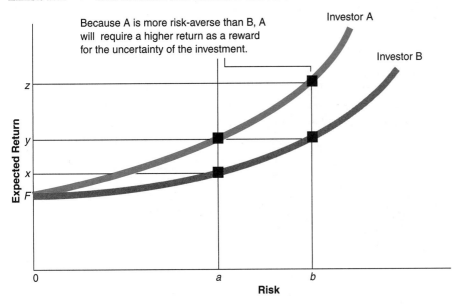

unless its expected payoff (or return) were to exceed that of a sure thing. Clearly, risk and expected return must be closely related. As a result, we can assume that investors will prefer investments with higher expected returns and lower risk. Further, risk aversion is the basis on which we can make statements about investment choices, as you will see in Chapter 18. Given that risk and expected return are among the most striking features of the securities markets, and probably among the most important criteria in investment selection and analysis, the next question naturally becomes, how do we measure risk and expected return?

Measuring Risk and Return: Individual Securities

In this section, we examine four topics: how to measure returns for individual securities, how to measure risk, how to calculate a standard deviation, and how investors can use risk and return measures to make security selections.

HOW TO MEASURE RETURNS

Back in Chapter 2, we discussed how to measure a one-year (or one-period) return for a security. Recall that the holding period return (*HPR*) for a stock i can be calculated as follows:

$$HPR_{i,t} = \frac{P_{i,t} - P_{i,t-1} + CF_{i,t}}{P_{i,t-1}} \text{ or } \frac{P_{i,t} + CF_{i,t}}{P_{i,t-1}} - 1 \qquad (2.1)$$

where $P_{i,t}$ is the price in period t (for example, year t), $P_{i,t-1}$ is the price in period $t-1$, and $CF_{i,t}$ is the cash flow received in period t (dividends for common stock and interest for bonds). In this chapter let's use common stocks as examples with the understanding that the general concept can be applied to all securities. Suppose the closing price of stock i one year ago was \$15, the owner received \$1 in dividends during the year, and today's closing price is \$17. The one-year return equals

$$[(\$17 + \$1)/\$15] - 1 = 20 \text{ percent}$$

Also recall from Chapter 2, that we can measure *ex-ante* expected return, as in the following example. Someone is considering buying stock i today at its current price of \$20 per share. In one year, the investor expects the stock to sell for \$25 per share and pay a \$1 dividend. In this case, the expected return (ER_i) would be measured by

$$ER_i = \frac{P_{i,t+1} - P_{i,t} + DIV_{i,t+1}}{P_{i,t}} \text{ or } \frac{P_{i,t+1} + DIV_{i,t+1}}{P_{i,t}} - 1 \tag{17.1}$$

where $P_{i,t}$ is today's price, $P_{i,t+1}$ is the expected price one period after t (usually one year), and $DIV_{i,t+1}$ is the expected dividend in period $t + 1$.

Using Equation 17.1, we can compute the one-year return:

$$[(\$25 + \$1)/\$20] - 1 = 30 \text{ percent}$$

Now, even though Equations 2.1 and 17.1 are similar, they are different. The first computes an actual one-year return, whereas the second computes an expected one-year return. The expected return is based on a forecast (or guess) of future prices and dividends, and the holding period return is based on actual prices and dividends.

Now, let's take a more sophisticated look at the prior problem to account for several possible future prices. Assume that the investor is uncertain about the stock price one year from today, which may depend on the company's sales growth. (Assume that the dividend will likely be \$1.) The following table represents the possibilities:

Sales Growth Rate	Price One Year from Today	Return
Above average	\$30	55%
Average	25	30
Below average	20	5

Note: *Today's price is \$20 and the returns are computed using Equation 17.1.*

Further assume a probability of each sales growth rate occurring next year. (These are sometimes referred to as *states of nature*.) The firm expects a 30 percent chance of generating above-average growth, a 40 percent chance of average growth, and a 30 percent chance of below-average growth. We can now compute the expected return for stock i a little differently:

$$ER_i = \sum_{s=1}^{S} R_{i,s} \, Pr(s) \tag{17.2}$$

where R is the return for stock i in state s (above-average, average, or below-average sales growth) and $Pr(s)$ is the probability of state s occurring. In our example,

$$ER_i = 0.55(30\%) + 0.30(40\%) + 0.05(30\%) = 30 \text{ percent}$$

Of course, it may be difficult, perhaps almost impossible, to forecast the future states of nature, the probability of each state occurring, and the rate of return from each state.

Why, you may ask, should anyone bother? The answer is that in making an investment decision, an analyst strives to obtain a future return for the stock and to choose the stocks with the highest returns after adjusting for risk. Conceptually, it is important to recognize that investment decisions must rest on the return one expects to earn. It does little good to know what one could have earned (or the historical return); the critical value is the return from investing today, so investors strive to estimate future returns, or **ex-ante returns.**

In most cases, it is easier and more convenient to calculate actual, historical, or **ex-post returns.** The historical equivalent of the expected return, computed using Equation 17.2, is the average (or mean) return over a specified period of time. In Chapter 2, we discussed how to compute an average return from an actual return series. It is worth repeating here. The general formula for calculating a mean return (M_i) for stock i is

$$M_i = \frac{1}{T} \sum_{t=1}^{T} R_{i,t} \qquad (17.3)$$

where T is the number of time periods included in the sample and $R_{i,t}$ is the stock i return for period t (calculated using Equation 2.1).[3] A time period could be a day, a month, or a year. An example of how to calculate a mean return appears in Exhibit 17.4. The ending stock price for American Home Products (AHP) is given, along with the dividend (if any), on a monthly basis from January 1998 through January 2000. The monthly return is computed using Equation 2.1. Summing the monthly returns and dividing by T (number of months, or 24 in this example) completes the calculation. Thus, over the two-year period, AHP had an average monthly return of 0.88 percent.[4]

HOW TO MEASURE RISK

Up to this point, we have discussed risk in a rather intuitive way. We have relied on basic observations and conventional wisdom to distinguish between risk levels of various securities. For example, in Chapter 2, we observed that historical returns on common stocks have exhibited far more variation over time than returns on long-term, high-quality corporate bonds. We have argued that a stock, such as an electric utility stock, that pays a high dividend and grows at a slow predictable rate is probably a less risky investment over time than a cyclical stock (for example, shares of an

ex-ante returns
Forecasted or predicted returns.

ex-post returns
Historical returns.

---

[3]When we use historical returns, we assume each return has a $1/T$ probability of occurring where T is the number of returns. This is analogous to multiplying each return in Equation 17.2 by the probability $1/T$ that return occurring.

[4]In Chapter 2, we saw how to annualize a monthly return. For AHP, if the average monthly return equals 0.88 percent, the annualized return equals

$$[(1 + \text{monthly return})^{12} - 1] = (1.0088)^{12} - 1 = 11.09\%$$

Not a lot, given what you hear about those technology stocks. We'll look at Yahoo later as a comparison.

automobile manufacturer). In other words, the electric utility stock will show less variation in price and returns over most time periods. Although we have yet to precisely define investment risk and discuss how it can (and should) be measured, the term we keep coming back to is *variation,* or *dispersion,* around an average, or expected value. Now, we must develop a risk measure that incorporates these intuitive observations into something more precise, allowing us to make risk comparisons between securities and portfolios.

Exhibit 17. 3 presents some data on returns for S&P 500 Index stock (including both dividends and capital gains) between 1980 and 1999. For each year, the table gives a yearly return along with three common measures of variation (or dispersion) around that average value. The risk measures are based on monthly returns. Each could be used as a risk measure. Let's briefly examine each.

Range

The range is simply the highest value minus the lowest value. In general, a larger range indicates greater risk. For example, during 1988, the monthly return for the S&P 500 index ranged between 4.70 percent and −3.31 percent (for a total of 8.01 percent). By contrast, during 1987, monthly returns ranged between 13.43 percent and −21.52 percent (for a total of 34.95 percent). Stock returns appear to have varied more during 1987 than during 1988.

Number of Negative Outcomes

In Exhibit 17.3, this is the number of months during a year when the monthly return was less than zero.[5] For example, in seven months during 1990 the index generated negative monthly returns. By contrast, it had monthly returns less than zero in only two months during 1980, 1995, and 1996.

Standard Deviation (or Variance)

standard deviation
A statistic measuring the dispersion of a distribution around its mean; a measure of risk.

Standard deviation is a statistical measure of dispersion around the mean (average) of a distribution.[6] A higher standard deviation indicates a greater dispersion, or variation, around the mean. From Exhibit 17.3, the year with the highest standard deviation of monthly returns was 1987 (30.50 percent); 1995 had the lowest standard deviation of monthly returns (1.48 percent). Even though investors seem to think that the market is more volatile today, 1999's standard deviation was 13.13 percent.

From the exhibit, it would not be unreasonable to conclude that all risk measures are equally good. After all, it does seem to show a close relationship between all three measures. Years that show greater variation by one measure tend to show greater variation by the others, and the measures agree on less-variable years as well. Despite this, we will argue that standard deviation is the superior measure of dispersion and

---

[5]Zero need not be the only benchmark. Another could be the number of periods in a given set of periods the index earned less than the return on a low-risk investment such as T-bills or bank CDs.

[6]The variance is the square of the standard deviation. Unlike standard deviation, however, variance has a different unit of measurement from the mean and thus is not as useful for comparisons. If returns are normally distributed, 67 percent of the distribution lies within one standard deviation of the mean (plus and minus); 95 percent of the distribution lies within two standard deviations of the mean.

Exhibit 17.3   ✦   ALTERNATIVE RISK MEASURES

Risk Measures Based on Monthly Returns

Year	Annual Return	Range	Number of Negative Returns	Standard Deviation
1980	32.4%	20.82%	2	18.31%
1981	−4.91	10.82	6	12.89
1982	21.41	17.79	6	19.14
1983	22.51	10.71	4	9.92
1984	6.27	16.59	5	10.01
1985	32.16	10.89	4	12.17
1986	18.47	15.70	4	17.94
1987	5.23	34.95	4	30.50
1988	16.81	8.01	4	10.07
1989	31.49	11.47	4	12.35
1990	−3.17	18.78	7	18.39
1991	30.55	20.49	3	16.00
1992	7.67	7.91	4	6.05
1993	9.99	6.69	4	6.26
1994	−1.54	8.34	5	3.06
1995	34.11	4.60	2	1.48
1996	17.34	11.91	2	10.83
1997	31.01	13.56	3	15.93
1998	26.67	22.61	3	21.48
1999	23.04	9.48	5	13.13

Notes: Standard deviation has been annualized; range is the highest monthly return that year minus the smallest monthly return; and number of negative returns is the number of months during the year with monthly returns less than zero.

Source: CRSP tapes, (University of Chicago, 1998) and Yahoo Stock Index Quotes 2000).

thus security risk. Although range indicates the spread between the highest and lowest values, it says nothing about the distribution of returns in between. For example, how many values are closer to the high than the low? The number of negative returns indicates nothing about the range of the distribution, nor does it say anything about the returns that are greater than zero.

By contrast, the standard deviation provides rather full information about the distribution. For example, if we assume that the stock returns follow a normal distribution (a bell-shaped curve), one standard deviation from the mean accounts for about 67 percent of the possible returns, and two standard deviations from the mean account for 95 percent of the possible returns.

CALCULATING STANDARD DEVIATION

Standard deviation is a statistical measure of the dispersion, or variation, around the expected value, or mean, of a distribution. To illustrate this further, let's go back to the earlier example in which the probability of a firm's sales growth being above average, average, or below average determined the expected return of 30 percent. Although the expected return is 30 percent, actual returns show dispersion around it. We can calculate the standard deviation (SD_i) of this expected future return (ex-ante return):

$$SD_i = \left[\sum_{s=1}^{S} (R_{i,s} - ER_i)^2 \, Pr(s) \right]^{1/2} \qquad (17.4)$$

where $R_{i,s}$ is stock i's return for state s, $Pr(s)$ is the probability of state s occurring, and ER_i is the expected return from the probability distribution.

The example data are provided below:

State of Sales Growth Rate	Probability of State	Return
Above average	30%	55%
Average	40	30
Below average	30	5

To use the formula, first subtract each return from the expected return, ER_i; next square the difference, then multiply by its probability; finally sum the products for each and take the square root:

$(R_{i,s} - ER_i)$	$(R_{i,s} - ER_i)^2$	$(R_{i,s} - ER_i)^2 P(s)$
$(0.55 - 0.30)$	$(0.25)^2 = 0.0625$	$0.0625(0.30) = 0.01875$
$(0.30 - 0.30)$	$(0.00)^2 = 0.0000$	$0.0000(0.40) = 0.00000$
$(0.05 - 0.30)$	$(-0.25)^2 = 0.0625$	$0.0625(0.30) = 0.01875$

$$\text{SUM} = 0.0375$$
$$\text{Standard deviation} = SD_i = \sqrt{0.0375} = 0.1936$$

As for return measures, ex-ante standard deviations, not ex-post values, should guide investment decisions. The decision should depend on the risk expected from investing in the stock. A future, expected, or ex-ante risk is important to assess to decide how risky it will be to invest in this stock.

A historical standard deviation can also be calculated by using known ex-post returns. As we have said, this may seem attractive, because historical returns can be measured more precisely and data on historical returns are more easily accessible. For historical returns, standard deviation equals

$$SD_i = \left[\frac{1}{(T-1)} \sum_{t=1}^{T} (R_{i,t} - M_i)^2 \right]^{1/2} \qquad (17.5)$$

where T is the number of time periods (usually years or months) in a particular sample, $R_{i,t}$ is the return for period t, and M_i is the mean return over the entire sample period.[7] An example of the mechanics of this calculation is presented in Exhibit 17.4. The monthly returns we computed earlier for AHP are given in the first column. The second column gives the difference between each monthly return and the mean (1.07 percent). The third column squares the second column. Then, the third column is summed, divided by $(24 - 1)$ or 23, and the square root taken. The result is a monthly standard deviation of 12.77 percent.[8]

---

[7]Statistical theory suggests that one should divide by n for a population and divide by $(n\text{-}1)$ for a sample. Technically speaking, we should divide by $(n\text{-}1)$ because the return observation set is usually not the population but a sample of historical returns.

[8]Recall from Chapter 2 that the monthly standard deviation can be annualized as follows: multiply the monthly standard deviation, calculated using Equation 17.5, by the square root of 12. In the AHP example, the annualized standard deviation equals 44.24 percent.

Exhibit 17.4 ✦ AMERICAN HOME PRODUCTS (AHP) STOCK RISK CALCULATION

Month t Month, Year	P_t End Price	DIV_t Dividends	1 HPR_t Return	2 $(HPR_t - AM)$	3 $(HPR_t - AM)^2$
Jan. 1998	$46.0481				
Feb. 1998	45.4546	$0.22	−0.0081	−0.0169	0.0003
Mar. 1998	46.2425		0.0173	0.0085	0.0001
Apr. 1998	45.1516		−0.0236	−0.0324	0.0010
May 1998	48.3125	0.22	0.0749	0.0661	0.0044
June 1998	51.75		0.0712	0.0624	0.0039
July 1998	51.50		−0.0048	−0.0136	0.0002
Aug. 1998	51.00	0.22	−0.0054	−0.0142	0.0002
Sept. 1998	52.625		0.0319	0.0231	0.0005
Oct. 1998	48.9275		−0.0703	−0.0791	0.0063
Nov. 1998	64.476	0.22	0.0954	0.0866	0.0075
Dec. 1998	56.375		0.0562	0.0474	0.0022
Jan. 1999	58.6875		0.0410	0.0322	0.0010
Feb. 1999	59.50	0.22	0.0176	0.0088	0.0001
Mar. 1999	65.25		0.0966	0.0878	0.0077
Apr. 1999	61.00		−0.0651	−0.0739	0.0055
May 1999	57.625	0.22	−0.0517	−0.0605	0.0037
June 1999	57.375		−0.0043	−0.0131	0.0002
July 1999	51.00		−0.1111	−0.1199	0.0144
Aug. 1999	41.50	0.22	−0.1820	−0.1908	0.0364
Sept. 1999	41.50		0.0000	−0.0088	0.0001
Oct. 1999	52.25		0.2590	0.2502	0.0626
Nov. 1999	52.00	0.23	−0.0004	−0.0092	0.0001
Dec. 1999	$39.25		−0.2452	−0.2540	0.0645
Jan. 2000	$48.00		0.2229	0.2141	0.0459

SUM = 0.2686

SUM = 0.2112   SUM /$(T - 1)$ = 0.0117

MEAN = 0.0088   ST. DEV. = 0.1081

Note: $HPR = \left[\dfrac{(P_t + DIV_t)}{P_{t-1}}\right] - 1$ and AM is the arithmetic mean of monthly returns.

SECURITY SELECTION

Recall in Chapter 2 we discussed how investors can choose between securities by using the risk and return concepts developed above. For a quick review, consider the following stocks:

Stock	Mean Return	Standard Deviation
A	12%	12%
B	12	10
C	14	12

Clearly, a risk-averse investor would find stock B a superior investment to stock A. B offers the same return (12 percent) but has less risk (a lower standard deviation) than A. Similarly, stock C is a superior investment to stock A. C has the same risk level (a standard deviation of 12 percent) but offers a higher return (14 percent versus 12 percent) than A. In general, we can say that if two securities have the same standard deviation but different expected returns, the security with the higher expected return is superior to the security with the lower expected return. A risk-averse investor will always choose the security with the higher expected return for securities with equal risk. Also, if two securities have identical expected returns but different risk levels, the security with the lower standard deviation is superior to the security with the higher standard deviation. When one investment is clearly superior to another using mean return and standard deviation, it exhibits **mean-variance dominance** or **mean-variance efficient.** In the previous example, B is mean-variance dominant over A.[9]

The selection decision so far has been pretty straightforward. Let's make it more complicated. Which would you prefer, stock B or stock C? B has the smaller standard deviation but also the lower expected return. However, C has the higher expected return but also the higher standard deviation. Now the selection decision is more ambiguous. You may prefer B to C (or C to B for that matter), but you really cannot say that one is superior to the other.

Another statistic related to standard deviation may help to clarify some investment selection decisions: the **coefficient of variation (CV),** which was introduced in Chapter 2. It can be used as a crude assessment of a security's risk/return trade-off. Recall the CV equals the standard deviation divided by the mean (SD/M). Statisticians use CV as a method of scaling standard deviations to account for differences in means. It measures the percentage of risk for every percentage return. Stock F in the table below has 0.67 percent of risk for every 1 percent of return. A lower CV indicates a better risk/return trade-off.

To see how the CV works, let's look at another hypothetical example:

Stock	Mean	Standard Deviation	CV
D	10%	10%	1.00
E	20	20	1.00
F	18	12	0.67

Again, the table gives little basis on which to choose between D and E. They have the same CV and, one could argue, offer the same risk/return trade-off. What about a choice between F and E or F and D? We really cannot say that F is superior to either E or D, but we can say that F offers a better risk/return trade-off (it has a lower CV). Why? Well, F has a lower mean than E (18 percent versus 20 percent), but it has substantially less risk as well (a standard deviation of 12 percent versus a standard deviation of 20 percent). Also, F does have a higher standard deviation than A (12 percent versus 10 percent) but offers a much higher mean return (18 percent versus 10 percent). We can display these results on a return/risk graph such as Exhibit 17.5. The stock that is farthest toward the upper-left corner usually offers the best risk/return trade-off. (See the shaded area in Exhibit 17.5.)

mean-variance dominance or mean-variance efficient
Condition in which a stock or portfolio has the highest expected return for a given risk, or the lowest risk for a given expected return.

coefficient of variation (CV)
Standard deviation divided by the mean; a measure of an investment's risk per return trade-off.

RECAP This section discussed the notion of risk and how to measure it, as well as the concept of ex-ante versus ex-post returns. Conceptually, we would like to measure risk and

---

[9]Variance equals the standard deviation squared (SD^2) and is also used as a risk measure. The relative level of risk between securities remains the same for the two measures, even if their scales differ.

Exhibit 17.5 ✦ Risk/Return Graph for Security Selection

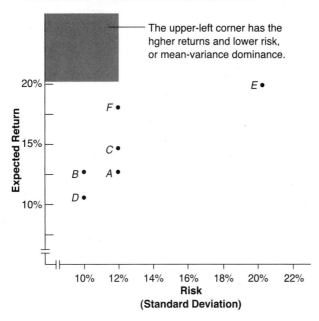

The upper-left corner has the hgher returns and lower risk, or mean-variance dominance.

return ex-ante, but we usually calculate risk and return using ex-post data. We also discussed how the stock selection can be made by using expected returns and standard deviation risk.

America Online (AOL)	1995	1996	1997	1998	1999
HPR_t	167.86%	−11.33%	187.60%	532.15%	100.83%

1. Calculate AOL's ex-post (historical) mean return for the 1991 to 1995 period.
2. Calculate AOL's standard deviation risk.

We have the following stocks' returns, ER_i, and standard deviations, SD_i.

Stock	ER_i	SD_i
X	10%	15%
Y	10	12
Z	18	20

3. Does any one stock dominate another? Explain why?
4. Calculate the CV for stock Y and stock Z. Does one dominate the other? If not, what type of investor would choose Z over Y?

Portfolio Risk and Return

A *portfolio* is simply a group, or collection, of securities. Evaluation of a portfolio broadens beyond the risk and return levels of the individual securities to the risk and return level of the group as a whole. How do we measure portfolio risk and return? Your initial answer might be that a simple combination of the risk and return levels of the individual securities would equal the portfolio risk and return. When it comes to calculating the mean, or expected, return from a portfolio, this answer is correct. The expected ex-ante return for a portfolio is defined as

$$ER_p = \sum_{t=1}^{N} X_i \, ER_i \qquad (17.6a)$$

The mean historical ex-post return from a portfolio is computed as

$$M_p = \sum_{t=1}^{N} X_i \, M_i \qquad (17.6b)$$

where ER_i and M_i are the expected and mean returns from security i and X_i is the percentage of the portfolio invested in security i. An obvious condition of Equations 17.6a and 17.6b is that the sum of the Xs must equal 1.0.[10] Calculating the standard deviation for a portfolio of securities can also be relatively simple. In fact, the formulas presented in the prior section can be used in most cases. For example, the standard deviation of monthly returns shown in Exhibit 17.3 for the S&P 500 Index, which is, of course, a portfolio, was calculated using Equation 17.5. We simply calculated the portfolio return (that is, the return for the S&P 500) for each time period and found the standard deviation of those returns. Calculating portfolio standard deviations becomes more challenging when one must understand the impact of the interrelationships between the returns of the individual securities in the portfolio. We start with the simplest type of portfolio: one with two securities.

STANDARD DEVIATION OF A TWO-SECURITY PORTFOLIO

Let's begin by considering the following hypothetical example of the probability distributions for two individual stocks.

State of the Economy	Probability	Return Stock A	Stock B
Good	0.30	+30%	+ 5%
Normal	0.40	+15	+10
Poor	0.30	+ 0	+15
Expected return		**+15%**	**+10%**
Standard deviation		11.7%	3.9%
Coefficient of variation		0.78	0.39

The expected return for each stock was calculated using Equation 17.2, and the standard deviations were calculated using Equation 17.4. For example, stock A's expected return equals

$$0.30(30\%) + 0.40(15\%) + 0.30(0\%) = 15 \text{ percent}$$

as shown in bold type above.

---

[10]Normally, we would assume that all the Xs must be positive as well, and thus all would have values between zero and one. This assumption is not necessary if the possibility of short sales is allowed. In other words, it is possible that some Xs could be negative while others give a partial sum greater than 1.0.

Assume that company A builds and sells automobiles. The auto maker does better when the economy does better. Assume that company B makes antacids and aspirin, both of which may be in higher demand in a lousy economy. Further, suppose that the investor commits equal proportions of wealth to stocks A and B: 50 percent is invested in A and 50 percent in B. The return distribution for the portfolio of stocks A and B looks like this:

State of the Economy	Probability	Portfolio Return
Good	0.30	17.5%
Normal	0.40	12.5
Poor	0.30	7.5
Portfolio expected return		12.5%
Portfolio standard deviation		3.9%
Portfolio CV		0.31

Notice that the expected return for the portfolio is simply a weighted average of the expected returns for the two stocks individually and is consistent with the result of Equation 17.6b. For example, the portfolio return under the good state of economy equals

$$0.50(30\%) + 0.50(5\%) = 17.5 \text{ percent}$$

The standard deviation, which was calculated using Equation 17.4, is not consistent with Equation 17.6b. In fact, the standard deviation of this portfolio, 3.9 percent, is exactly the same as the standard deviation of stock B (the antacid and aspirin maker) and is considerably less than the standard deviation of stock A (the auto maker), even though half of the portfolio is made up of stock A.[11] Note that the portfolio CV is smaller than either stock A's or stock B's individual CV. How could this be?

The answer lies in the interrelationship between the return distributions for the two stocks. Notice that if the economy performs well, stock A has a higher than expected return and stock B has a lower than expected return. The situation is exactly reversed if the economy performs poorly. Statisticians refer to the interrelationship between probability distributions as **covariance (COV)**. The COV statistics for ex-ante returns, are calculated as follows:

covariance (COV)
Statistical measure of how two stock returns move together; measure of co-movement.

$$COV(A,B) = \sum_{s=1}^{S} (R_{A,s} - ER_A)(R_{B,s} - ER_B)Pr(s) \qquad (17.7)$$

where $R_{A,s}$ and $R_{B,s}$ are the returns for stocks A and B for the various states of the economy, s; ER_A and ER_B are the expected returns for A and B; $Pr(s)$ is the probability of occurrence of state s; and SD_A and SD_B are the standard deviations for stocks A and B.

In the above example, the returns for the two stocks have negative covariance. In other words, as one stock's return gets larger, the other's return gets smaller, and vice versa. The actual covariance between the two stock returns is -0.0045.[12]

---

[11]The portfolio standard deviation is calculated as
$$SD_p = [(0.175 - 0.125)^2(0.30) + (0.125 - 0.125)^2(0.40) + (0.75 - 0.125)^2(0.30)]^{1/2}$$
$$= \sqrt{0.0015^{1/2}} = 0.039 \text{ or } 3.9 \text{ percent}$$

[12]In our example, covariance is calculated as
$$(0.30 - 0.15)(0.05 - 0.10)(0.30) + (0.15 - 0.15)(0.10 - 0.10)(0.40)$$
$$+ (0.00 - 0.15)(0.15 - 0.10)(0.30) = -0.0045$$

The above example has obviously been concocted. Let's look at an example using some historical stock return data. If historical returns are used to calculate the covariance, the equation becomes

$$COV(A,B) = \frac{1}{(T-1)} \sum_{t=1}^{T} [(R_{A,t} - M_A)(R_{B,t} - M_B)] \tag{17.8}$$

where T is the number of time periods (usually annual, quarterly, or monthly returns), $R_{A,t}$ and $R_{B,t}$ are returns over period t for stocks A and B, and M_A and M_B are mean returns for A and B.

correlation coefficient
Statistical measure of co-movement similar to the covariance; scaled to be between −1.0 and +1.0.

Another statistical term that measures the interrelationship between two variables is called the **correlation coefficient** (CORR). It is interpreted just like the covariance, however, the correlation is scaled so that its value can never be lower than −1.0 or higher than +1.0, or −1.0 < CORR(A,B) < +1.0. A positive sign implies that the two stocks generally move together, up or down, and the number between −1.0 to +1.0 conveniently provides the degree to which the two stocks covary.

The equation for the correlation coefficient equals

$$CORR(A,B) = COV(A,B)/SD_A SD_B \tag{17.9}$$

For the example above, the correlation coefficient for stocks A and B equals:

$$CORR(A,B) = (-0.0045/(0.117)(0.039) = -1.0$$

A −1.0 means it is a perfect negative correlation indicating that the two stocks, A and B, move in reverse direction (if one goes up, the other is expected to go down) and in a constant proportional amount. What would these statistics look like for real stocks using ex-post returns?

Exhibit 17.6 presents monthly return data for American Home Products (AHP) and Yahoo (YHOO) from February 1998 to January 2000. At the bottom of each column, the table gives mean monthly returns, standard deviations of returns, and coefficients of variation for both stocks. (All means and standard deviations were calculated using Equations 17.3 and 17.5.) AHP had an average monthly return of 1.07 percent, with a standard deviation of 12.77 percent and a CV of 11.935. YHOO had an average monthly return of 17.48 percent with a standard deviation of 31.79 percent and a CV of 1.818.

Column 4 gives the portfolio return, assuming half of the portfolio is invested in AHP and half in YHOO, for each time period. At the bottom, the table lists the mean, standard deviation, and CV for the portfolio. Notice that the portfolio's average return, 9.18 percent, is exactly a weighted average of the mean returns for AHP and DIS, but the standard deviation, 16.287 percent, is not. It is less than YHOO's standard deviation but slightly higher than AHP's. As in the prior example, the explanation for this lies in the interrelationship between AHP's and YHOO's returns, measured by the covariance or correlation.

We next compute the covariance and correlation between the two sets of returns based on the ex-post return formulas for covariance and correlation (Equations 17.9 and 17.10). The calculation is detailed in Exhibit 17.7. Columns 2 and 3 list the monthly returns for AHP and Yahoo. The fourth and fifth columns list the differences between each return and its respective mean. The sixth column is the product of columns 4 and 5, called the *cross product*. In this case the cross products seem both

Exhibit 17.6 ✦ PORTFOLIO RETURN CALCULATION

1 Month t Month, Year	2 AHP Return	3 Yahoo Return	4 Portfolio Return
Feb. 1998	−0.0081	0.1548	0.0734
Mar. 1998	0.0173	0.2630	0.1402
Apr. 1998	−0.0236	0.2867	0.1315
May 1998	0.0749	−0.0793	−0.0022
June 1998	0.0712	0.4384	0.2548
July 1998	−0.0048	0.1552	0.0752
Aug. 1998	−0.0054	−0.2415	−0.1235
Sept. 1998	0.0319	0.8768	0.4543
Oct. 1998	−0.0703	0.0104	−0.0299
Nov. 1998	−0.0954	0.4674	0.2814
Dec. 1998	0.0562	0.2341	0.1451
Jan. 1999	0.410	0.4951	0.2681
Feb. 1999	0.0176	−0.1334	−0.0579
Mar. 1999	0.0966	0.0969	0.0968
Apr. 1999	−0.0651	0.0375	−0.0138
May 1999	−0.0517	−0.1528	−0.1022
June 1999	−0.0043	0.1639	0.0798
July 1999	−0.1111	−0.2079	−0.1595
Aug. 1999	−0.1820	0.0811	−0.0504
Sept. 1999	0.0000	0.2169	0.1085
Oct. 1999	0.2590	−0.0024	0.1283
Nov. 1999	−0.004	0.1881	0.0939
Dec. 1999	−0.2452	1.0338	0.3943
Jan. 2000	0.2229	−0.1866	0.0182
MEAN =	0.0088	0.1748	0.0918
ST. DEV. =	0.1081	0.3179	0.1554
Coefficient of Variation CV =	12.2359	1.8183	1.6926

positive and negative, but the December 1999 cross product overwhelms the others, resulting in a negative correlation. This means that the two stock returns tend to move in opposite directions; when one goes up, the other goes down. Column 6 is summed and divided by (24–1) or 23, giving the covariance (−0.00563). Dividing the covariance by the product of the two standard deviations gives the correlation coefficient, −0.234. Thus, it appears that the two series of returns generally moved in the opposite direction during 1998 and 1999, although not always.

With these two examples serving as an introduction, let's look at the formula for finding the standard deviation of a two-security portfolio:

$$SD_p = [X_A^2 SD_A^2 + (1 - X_A)^2 SD_B^2 + 2X_A(1 - X_A)COV(A,B)]^{1/2} \qquad (17.10)$$

Remember from Equation 17.9 that

$$CORR(A,B) = COV(A,B)/SD_A SD_B$$

Rearranging terms gives

$$COV(A,B) = SD_A SD_B CORR(A,B)$$

Exhibit 17.7 ✦ COVARIANCE AND CORRELATION CALCULATION

1 Month *t* Month, Year	2 AHP Return	3 Yahoo Return	4 AHP (Ret-AM)	5 Yahoo (Ret-AM)	6 (4)x(5)
Feb. 1998	−0.0081	0.1548	−0.0169	−0.0200	0.0003
Mar. 1998	0.0173	0.2630	0.0085	0.0882	0.0008
Apr. 1998	−0.0236	0.2867	−0.0324	0.1119	−0.0036
May 1998	0.0749	−0.0793	0.0661	−0.2541	−0.0168
June 1998	0.0712	0.4384	0.0624	0.2636	0.0164
July 1998	−0.0048	0.1552	−0.0136	−0.0196	0.0003
Aug. 1998	−0.0054	−0.2415	−0.0142	−0.4163	0.0059
Sept. 1998	0.0319	0.8768	0.0231	0.7020	0.0162
Oct. 1998	−0.0703	0.0104	−0.0791	−0.1644	−0.0130
Nov. 1998	−0.0954	0.4674	0.0866	0.2926	0.0253
Dec. 1998	0.0562	0.2341	0.0474	0.0593	0.0028
Jan. 1999	0.0410	0.4951	0.0322	0.3203	0.0103
Feb. 1999	0.0176	−0.1334	0.0088	−0.3082	−0.0027
Mar. 1999	0.0966	0.0969	0.0878	−0.0779	−0.0068
Apr. 1999	−0.0651	0.0375	−0.0739	−0.1373	0.0102
May 1999	−0.0517	−0.1528	−0.0605	−0.3276	0.198
June 1999	−0.0043	0.1639	−0.0131	−0.0109	0.0001
July 1999	−0.1111	−0.2079	−0.1199	−0.3827	0.0459
Aug. 1999	−0.1820	0.0811	−0.1908	−0.0937	0.0179
Sept. 1999	0.0000	0.2169	−0.0088	0.0421	−0.0004
Oct. 1999	0.2590	−0.0024	0.2502	−0.1772	−0.0444
Nov. 1999	−0.004	0.1881	−0.0092	0.0133	−0.0001
Dec. 1999	−0.2452	1.0338	−0.2540	0.8590	−0.2182
Jan. 2000	0.2229	−0.1866	0.2141	−0.3614	−0.0774
MEAN =	0.0088	0.1748		SUM =	−0.1851
ST. DEV. =	0.1081	0.3179		COV =	−0.008049
				CORR =	−0.234

This gives an alternative formula for the standard deviation of a two-security portfolio:

$$SD_p = [X_A^2 SD_A^2 + (1 - X_A)^2 SD_B^2 + 2X_A(1 - X_A)(SD_A)(SD_B)(CORR(A,B))]^{1/2} \quad (17.11)$$

where X_A is the percentage of the portfolio invested in stock A, and $(1 - X_A)$ is the percentage of the portfolio invested in stock B. From Equation 17.10 you should see that the standard deviation of a two-security portfolio contains three elements: the standard deviation of stock A, the standard deviation of stock B, and the covariance between A and B.

Applying Equation 17.11 to the AHP/Yahoo example, the standard deviation of the portfolio (weighted one-half in AHP and one-half in YHOO) equals

$$SD_p = [(0.25)(0.1277)^2 + (.25)(0.3179)^2 + 2(0.5)(0.5)(0.1277)(0.3179)(−0.139)]^{1/2} = 0.1554$$

This is exactly the number reported in Exhibit 17.6 based on Equation 17.5! We have easier ways to compute the standard deviation of a two-security portfolio, so how useful is Equation 17.11? The most important feature of Equation 17.11 is its ability to explicitly show that the standard deviation of a two-security portfolio is not simply the weighted average of the two individual standard deviations. The two securities' variations with each other must also be taken into account. You can see from Equation 17.11 that if the two securities move in opposite directions and thus have negative covariance and correlation, the standard deviation of the portfolio could be less than the standard deviation of either security individually. The portfolio could easily offer a better risk/return trade-off than the individual securities. It all depends on the correlation between the two sets of returns. We explore this issue in detail next.

CORRELATION AND PORTFOLIO STANDARD DEVIATION

The prior discussion has shown, albeit indirectly, that the correlation between two sets of security returns can have a major impact on the risk of the resulting two-security portfolio. Let's look at the relationship in more depth. The relationship between correlation and portfolio standard deviation is best illustrated with an example.

Consider two securities: Security A has an expected return of 12 percent and a standard deviation of 6 percent, whereas security B has an expected return of 20 percent and a standard deviation of 10 percent. Is one a better investment than the other? Not really. Both securities, for example, have the same CV (CV = 0.50).

Now, combine A and B into a portfolio. The expected portfolio return will be a simple weighted average of the two individual expected returns, or 16 percent, if one-half of the portfolio is invested in A and one-half is invested in B. We also know that the portfolio standard deviation will depend on the covariance, or correlation, between A and B. Let's look at three possible scenarios, summarized in Exhibit 17.8.

Exhibit 17.8, part a assumes that the returns for A and B move together perfectly and in the same direction $[CORR(A,B) = +1.0]$. In other words, the correlation coefficient between A and B equals +1.0. The **investment opportunity set** provides all the possible combinations of A and B and is graphed in Exhibit 17.8a. Moving along the line from point A to point B, the percentage of the portfolio invested in A decreases, whereas the percentage invested in B increases. Portfolio P_1 consists of one-half A and one-half B. Notice that portfolio P_1 has a standard deviation that is a weighted average of those of A and B, 8 percent. Because P_1 has an expected return of 16 percent, it has the same CV as A and B. Does P_1 offer a better risk/return trade-off than either A or B? No. In fact, none of the possible combinations of A and B in this scenario offer a better risk/return trade-off than the two individual stocks. If the correlation between any two stocks equals +1.0, no better risk/return trade-off exists; an investor can increase expected return only by increasing risk.

Now, pick a different stock, C, to pair with A, and assume for simplicity that C's return and risk are the same as B's but its correlation with A equals zero. Suppose returns from A and C move completely independently of each other, or $CORR(A,C) = 0.0$. All the possible combinations of A and C are graphed in Exhibit 17.8b. For example, portfolio P_2 is half A and half C. Portfolio P_2 also has an expected return of 16 percent but a standard deviation of only 5.8 percent, and its CV equals 0.36. One could argue that P_2 offers a better risk/return trade-off because its CV is lower than those of A or C. P_2, for example, has only slightly less risk than A (5.8 percent compared with 6.0 percent) and a much higher expected return (16 percent versus 12 percent).

This potential to obtain a better risk/return trade-off by combining imperfectly correlated securities is called **diversification.** This case shows that any correlation

investment opportunity set
Possible combinations of stocks in a portfolio calculated by varying the percentage holdings in each stock.

diversification
Spreading your investment dollars among several different investments to reduce risk.

Exhibit 17.8 ✦ TWO-SECURITY PORTFOLIO COMBINATIONS WITH VARIOUS CORRELATIONS

a.

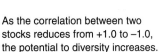

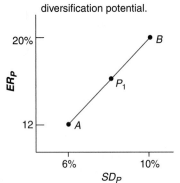

b.

For A and C, a point such as P_2 offers a better risk/return trade-off than A.

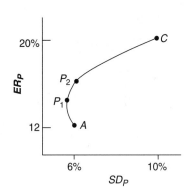

c.

For A and D, with a correlation of −1.0, risk could be reduced to zero (at P_5).

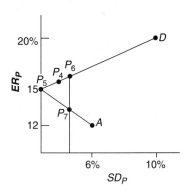

between two stocks less than 1.0 indicates a potential to diversify. Graphically, the range of combinations between two stocks gives a nonlinear (bow-shaped) curve that allows diversification to occur. As Exhibit 17.8b shows, several possible combinations of A and C offer better risk/return trade-offs than either stock alone. A point such as P_3 has the minimum risk for a portfolio combination of A and C. Its expected return equals 14.1 percent (A's is 12.0 percent), and its risk equals 5.1 percent (A's is 6.0 percent). In fact, any combinations of A and C from P_3 to C offer better risk/return trade-offs than combinations between A and P_3. Of course, the choice of the actual portfolio between P_3 to C depends on the amount of risk the investor is willing to take.

As a final scenario, let's assume that the two return series move together perfectly, although in opposite directions. Thus, A and D have perfect negative correlation $[CORR(A,D) = -1.0]$. Again, let us assume that D has the same return and risk as stock B.[13] The investment opportunity set for A and D is shown in Exhibit 17.8c. Portfolio P_4 is half A and half B. Like P_1 and P_2, P_4 has an expected return of 16 percent, but its standard deviation is only 2 percent. Portfolio P_4 offers a better risk/return trade-off than A, and a risk-averse investor would actually prefer it—P_4 has a higher expected return and less risk than does stock A. In fact, a risk-averse investor would not choose any combination of A and D between point A and point P_5 because other combinations offer higher expected returns for the same level of risk, such as P_6 compared with P_7. Furthermore, portfolio P_5 is a combination of A and D (62.5 percent in A and 37.5 percent in D) that reduces the portfolio risk to zero with an expected return of 15.0 percent.

---

[13]In reality, perfect negative correlation is not possible, although negative correlation can be achieved using derivative securities in hedging (see Chapter 15). Generally, securities are positively correlated to each other; negative correlation is rare.

In summary, as the correlation coefficient decreases from $+1.0$ to -1.0, potential diversification benefits grow. Also, notice that diversification improves the risk/return trade-off only if the correlation is less than $+1.0$. Stated differently, as long as the correlation is less than $+1.0$, combinations of securities offer diversification potential.

Another way to see the effect of the correlation coefficient on the portfolio standard deviation (and diversification potential) is to examine Equation 17.11 again. Recall the formula,

$$SD_p = [X_A^2 SD_A^2 + (1 - X_A)^2 SD_B^2 + 2X_A(1 - X_A)(SD_A)(SD_B)(CORR(A,B))]^{1/2} \qquad (17.11)$$

Let's examine the three terms in the formula. The first term, $X_A^2 SD_A^2$, is always positive because both terms are squared, so it will only add to the portfolio risk. Similarly with the second term, $(12X_A)^2 SD_B^2$. The third term, $2(X_A)(1X_A)(SD_A)(SD_B)$ $(CORR(A,B))$, however, can be positive or negative because every term is positive except for the correlation coefficient, $CORR(A,B)$. The correlation coefficient can be negative, which would reduce portfolio risk. In fact, that is what we found in the earlier examples; if the correlation between pairs of stocks was low or negative, it provides the greatest diversification benefit or reduction in portfolio risk.

INVESTMENT OPPORTUNITY SET FOR A TWO-SECURITY PORTFOLIO

An investment opportunity set that identifies the portfolio combinations is fairly easy to define for a two-security portfolio. Apply Equation 17.6b to find M_p and Equation 17.11 to find SD_p, varying the proportions invested in each security (X), as shown in the example below.

Suppose that you have already calculated the mean, M_j, and standard deviation, SD_j, of each security, A and E, and their correlation coefficient, $CORR(A,E) = -0.20$.

Stock	M_i	SD_i
A	12%	6%
E	20	10

Now the investment combinations can be determined by varying the amount invested in A and E in Equations 17.6b and 17.11 (where X_A is the percentage invested in A and X_E is the percentage invested in E). Because the percentages invested must add up to 100 percent, X_E can be written as $(1-X_A)$, and Equations 17.6b and 17.11b can be written as

$$M_p = X_A(M_A) + (1 - X_A)(M_E)$$
$$SD_p = [X_A^2 SD_A^2 + (1 - X_A)^2 SD_E^2 + 2X_A(1 - X_A)(SD_A)(SD_E)(CORR(A,E))]^{1/2}$$

For example, if $X_A = 0.10$ percent, then $(1 - X_A) = 0.90$. Plugging in these percentages,

$$M_p = 0.10(12\%) + (0.90)(20\%) = 19.2 \text{ percent}$$
$$SD_p = [(0.10)2(0.06)^2 + (0.90)(0.10)^2 + 2(0.10)(0.90)(0.06)(0.10)(-0.20)]^{1/2}$$
$$= 8.9 \text{ percent}$$

This calculation represents one point on the M_p versus SD_p graph. To find several more combinations of securities A and E, just change the percentages X_A and

$(1 - X_A)$. Exhibit 17.9 displays several combinations. Graphing the results in the table gives Exhibit 17.10, which resembles the curves in Exhibit 17.8.

minimum variance portfolio
Combination of stocks in a portfolio that gives the lowest portfolio standard deviation risk.

One use of an investment opportunity set might be to find the **minimum variance portfolio**. Using calculus, solve for X_A and E's proportion $(12X_A)$. An investment of X_A in stock A—and $(1 - X_A)$ in stock E—provides the lowest portfolio risk:

$$X_A = \frac{SD_E^2 - SD_A SD_E CORR(A,E)}{SD_A^2 + SD_E^2 - 2(SD_A)(SD_E)CORR(A,E)} \quad (17.12)$$

For our example above, it equals

$$X_A = \frac{(0.10)^2 - (0.06)(0.10)(-0.20)}{(0.06)^2 + (0.10)^2 - 2(0.06)(0.10)(-0.20)} = 0.70$$

The proportion invested in E must equal $(1-X_A)$ because the two securities must add to 100 percent:

$$X_E = (1-X_A) = (1 - 0.70) = 30 \text{ percent}$$

We can also find the portfolio expected return M_p and risk SD_p for the percentage that provides the minimum risk portfolio. Again, using Equations 17.6b and 17.11,

$$M_p = (0.70)(12\%) + (0.30)(20\%) = 14.4 \text{ percent}$$
$$SD_p = [(0.70)^2(0.06)^2 + (0.30)^2(0.10)^2 + 2(0.70)(0.30)(0.06)(0.10)(-0.20)]^{1/2} = 4.6 \text{ percent}$$

Actually, the results in Exhibit 17.9 already showed that the SD_p is lowest with 70 percent in security A and 30 percent in security E. Also, Exhibit 17.10 shows that these percentages are indeed the lowest-risk portfolio combination. By examining the SD_p in Equation 17.11 and Exhibit 17.10, it is clear that the risk can be reduced because SD_p is a nonlinear equation. It is also evident that correlation plays a major role in diversification. It is the only term in Equation 17.11 that contributes to reducing risk.

STANDARD DEVIATION OF AN N-SECURITY PORTFOLIO

Finding the standard deviation of a portfolio that contains more than two securities is a logical extension of what we have discussed so far. Extending Equation 17.11b to N assets creates

$$SD_p = \left[\sum_{i=1}^{N} X_i^2 SD_i^2 + \sum_{i=1}^{N} \sum_{\substack{j=1 \\ i \neq j}}^{N} X_i X_j COV(i,j) \right]^{1/2} \quad (17.13)$$

where X_i is the percentage of the portfolio invested in security i (as before, the X values must sum to 1.0), SD_i is the standard deviation of security i, and $COV(i, j)$ is the covariance between security i and security j.

Now, Equation 17.13 may look horrible at first glance, but it is not as complicated as it seems. Like Equation 17.11, it states that the standard deviation of a portfolio is a function of two elements. The first element is the variances (the squares of the standard deviations) of the individual securities and the second element is the covariances

Exhibit 17.9 ✦ Various Combinations of Securities A and E

X_A	$(1 - X_A)$	M_p	SD_p
0%	100%	20.0%	10.0%
10	90	19.2	8.9
20	80	18.4	7.8
30	70	17.6	6.9
40	60	16.8	6.0
50	50	16.0	5.3
60	40	15.2	4.8
70	30	14.4	4.6
80	20	13.6	4.8
90	10	12.8	5.3
100%	0	12.0	6.0

Note: M_p is the portfolio's mean return and SD_p is the portfolio's standard deviation.

Exhibit 17.10 ✦ Two-Security Portfolio Combinations of Securities A and E

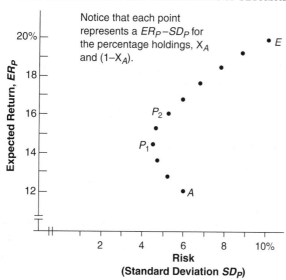

Notice that each point represents a $ER_P - SD_P$ for the percentage holdings, X_A and $(1-X_A)$.

Note: P_1 is 70 percent in Security A and 30 percent in E. It is the minimum-variance portfolio. P_2 is 50 percent in Security A and 50 percent in E.

between each possible pair of securities. The double summation operator ($\Sigma\Sigma$) in the covariance element means that each covariance term appears twice. (Look at the covariance term in Equation 17.11.)

Let's use Equation 17.13 to calculate the standard deviation of a sample multi-stock portfolio. First, if the portfolio contains three securities (A, B, and C), Equation 17.13 becomes

$$SD_p = [X_A^2 SD_A^2 + X_B^2 SD_B^2 + X_C^2 SD_C^2 + 2X_A X_B COV(A,B) \\ + 2X_A X_C COV(A,C) + 2X_B X_C COV(B,C)]^{1/2}$$

(17.14)

Notice that we have three covariance terms because we have three possible pairs of securities (A and B, A and C, B and C).[14]

Suppose we add another stock, Disney, to AHP and Yahoo. The portfolio consisting of one-third AHP, one-third Yahoo, and one-third Disney has a portfolio mean return that equals 1.78 percent. The portfolio's mean return, 1.78 percent, is simply a weighted average of the three stocks' mean returns. The portfolio's standard deviation, calculated using Equation 17.5, equals 11.66 percent. Notice that the portfolio standard deviation is much less than Yahoo's standard deviation, but similar to AHP and Disney's. If the correlation is less than 1.0, which it is for all three pairs of correlations, portfolio has potential to reduce risk. This is the benefit of diversification!

We can also find the portfolio's standard deviation using Equation 17.14. Recall that the covariance between AHP and Yahoo equals −0.007713. (We went through the calculation in Exhibit 17.9.) Using the same procedure, the covariance between AHP and Disney equals 0.001742 and the covariance between Disney and Yahoo equals 0.005501. The respective correlation coefficients equal 0.16 and 0.17, indicating that the returns move together generally but not perfectly. Each stock makes up one-third of the portfolio, and the respective standard deviations are 10.81 percent (AHP), 10.44 percent (Disney), and 31.79 percent (Yahoo). Using Equation 17.14, the portfolio's standard deviation equals, not surprisingly, 11.66 percent. So if you own Internet stocks, it may be wise to diversify by combining with other stocks. It reduces Yahoo's risk while maintaining risk close to Disney's and AHP's.

Again, you may question the value of using Equation 17.13 to find the standard deviation of an N-asset portfolio. We agree that it's a computational device only, it is not that critical to memorize. However, as we have said before, Equation 17.13 illustrates explicitly the impact of security correlation and covariance on portfolio risk. The standard deviation of a portfolio is not simply the weighted average of the standard deviations of the individual securities. The procedure for calculating the standard deviation of a portfolio also provides a good illustration of the concept of diversification.

RECAP

This section discusses how to calculate portfolio return and risk. It also discusses the virtues of diversification and how the correlation coefficient between securities is the key factor to diversification. Diversification by investing in stocks with correlation less than 1.0 reduces the portfolio risk and possibly increases portfolio return.

5.   Using the mean returns, standard deviation, and correlation displayed in Exhibit 17.7 for AHP and Yahoo, calculate the portfolio return if you invest 40 percent in AHP and 60 percent in Yahoo.

6.   Using the information from Exhibit 17.9, calculate the portfolio standard deviation using Equation 17.11a if you invest 40 percent in AHP and 60 percent in Yahoo.

---

[14]The number of possible pairs of securities equals: $N!2!/(N-2)!$, where N is the number of securities. The ! sign means factorial, which mathematically is equal to $(1\times2\times3\times4\times \ldots \times N)$. For example, $4! = (1\times2\times3\times4) = 24$. So, a four-security portfolio would have $24/4 = 6$ covariance terms (each appearing twice); there are six possible pairs of securities. A ten-security portfolio would have 45 covariance terms! (That was an exclamation point, not a factorial.)

Diversification

When we discussed how to calculate the standard deviation of a portfolio in the prior section, we illustrated, albeit indirectly, two important points about diversification. They can be summarized as follows:

1. Diversification can improve the risk/return trade-off if the correlation between individual security returns in the portfolio is less than 1.0 (that is, returns are not perfectly correlated).
2. The benefits of diversification increase as the correlation coefficient gets smaller (that is, approaches -1.0).

The benefits of diversification appear obvious, and they are easy to obtain. Let's now consider how to obtain the benefits of diversification in some realistic investment settings.

DIVERSIFICATION ACROSS SECURITIES

Perhaps the most straightforward way for investors to diversify is by spreading their investment funds across several different securities. We have seen this already, both with manufactured and real return data. For example, we saw that owning two stocks instead of just one can produce a risk/return trade-off that most risk-averse investors would prefer.

The benefits of diversification across securities show clearly in Exhibit 17.11. The data used to generate this graph were taken from the CRSP database. (We discuss the CRSP database in Appendix A.) First, we randomly selected one stock from the CRSP database, then another, creating a portfolio of two stocks, then another to make a three-stock portfolio, and so forth. (All portfolios are equally weighted combinations of the stocks.) We then calculated daily returns for each portfolio. Notice how the portfolio standard deviation generally falls as the number of securities increases. The one-stock portfolio has an annualized standard deviation of 193.6 percent, the two-stock portfolio has an annualized standard deviation of 100.7 percent, and so forth.[15] By contrast, the 20-stock portfolio has a standard deviation of only 15.3 percent.

This occurs simply because returns between pairs of securities are not perfectly correlated. For example, the correlation coefficients between the first stock and the other 19 range from -0.10 to 0.09. Recall that some diversification potential exists so long as the correlation coefficient between two pairs of returns is less than 1.0.

TWO TYPES OF PORTFOLIO RISK

The need to diversify leads to a distinction of two types of risk: **market risk and firm-specific risk**. Let's discuss this further.

Suppose your investment portfolio contains only shares in Yahoo stock. The return on the stock is affected by economic factors such as business cycles, the inflation rate, interest rates, and others (as discussed in Chapter 11), as well as firm-specific factors such as increased competition, managerial policies, and new innovations (as

market risk
Risk inherent in the market such as business cycles, the inflation rate, interest rates, and other economic factors.

firm-specific risk
Risk specifically tied to the company, such as labor contracts or new product development.

---

[15]Assuming T trading days in a year, the annualized standard deviation equals the standard deviation of daily returns multiplied by the square root of T.

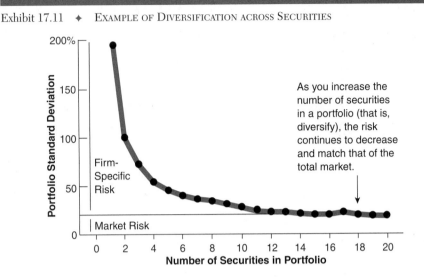

Exhibit 17.11 ✦ EXAMPLE OF DIVERSIFICATION ACROSS SECURITIES

discussed in Chapters 12 and 13). Every stock return is affected by both kinds of factors in varying degrees.

Now, suppose you own two stocks, Yahoo and Disney. Although these stocks are both affected by market-related factors (perhaps not to the same degree), their firm-specific factors may differ. For example, if the weather becomes extremely cold and rainy, sales receipts at Disney's theme parks may suffer, but you may spend more time surfing the Net on Yahoo. The firm-specific factors can lead to offsetting returns between two stocks. Of course, this is the crux of the power of diversification; as the number of stocks in a portfolio increases, the firm-specific risk becomes negligible. However, the market risk related to economic factors affects all stocks, so it cannot be eliminated through diversification. This can also be seen in Exhibit 17.11. As diversification across securities increases, firm-specific risk decreases until the only risk left is the market risk.

The market risk that exists even with diversification is also called systematic risk or nondiversifiable risk. The firm-specific risk that can be eliminated by diversifying is called diversifiable risk or nonsystematic risk. Two important points stem from this discussion: (1) a portfolio of stocks can virtually eliminate firm-specific risk, and (2) the only relevant risk is the market risk when portfolios are held, because the firm-specific risk decreases to virtually zero.

A mathematical example can illustrate the power of diversification. The next section shows that as the number of securities increases, the effect of each company's standard deviation is virtually zero, and the portfolio risk is measured entirely by the covariance between the securities.

MATHEMATICAL EFFECTS OF DIVERSIFICATION

We can mathematically show that the standard deviations of securities have minuscule effects on portfolio standard deviation risk, SD_p, using Equation 17.13:

$$SD_p = \left[\sum_{i=1}^{N} X_i^2 SD_i^2 + \sum_{i=1}^{N} \sum_{\substack{j=1 \\ i \neq j}}^{N} X_i X_j COV(i,j) \right]^{1/2} \tag{17.13}$$

Suppose the standard deviation to avoid the square root sign.

$$SD_p^2 = \sum_{i=1}^{N} X_i^2 SD_i^2 + \sum_{i=1}^{N} \sum_{\substack{j=1 \\ i \neq j}}^{N} X_i X_j SD_i SD_j CORR(i,j)$$

Suppose we create a naïve portfolio in which stocks are randomly chosen and invested in equal proportions. If we have N stocks, each X equals $(1/N)$. The equation becomes

$$SD_p^2 = \frac{1}{N} \sum_{i=1}^{N} \frac{1}{N} SD_i^2 + \sum_{i=1}^{N} \sum_{j=1}^{N} \frac{1}{N^2} COV(i,j)$$

It is difficult to figure out from the formula, but there are N variances (SD_i^2) and $N(N\text{-}1)$ covariances. Now, just for simplicity (and also to make our point), suppose that each SD_i^2 is the same for each stock. This reduces the term to SD^2 (no subscript because they are all the same). Similarly, for the covariances, suppose they all equal COV; then SD_p^2 equals

$$SD_p^2 = \frac{1}{N} SD^2 + \frac{(N-1)}{N} COV$$

Now, we can really see the power of diversification. As the number of stocks (N) increases, $(1/N)$ decreases. When N becomes large, $(1/N)$ becomes virtually equal to zero. This makes the standard deviation of each stock almost irrelevant! Similarly, the covariance term becomes more important as N increases because $(N-1)/N$ approaches 1.0 as N becomes large. Why? Because $(N-1)/N = 1-(1/N) = 1$ as N becomes large. This exercise shows that the standard deviation of stocks has almost no effect on the portfolio risk SD_p^2; this leaves the covariance between stocks as the only important term.

DIVERSIFICATION ACROSS TIME

Go back to Chapter 2 and reexamine Exhibit 2.16. It presents mean annualized total returns from the S&P 500 Index (Large stocks) and an index of long-term U.S. Treasury bonds (T-bonds), between the end of 1925 and the end of 1999, for different assumed holding periods. For one-year holding periods, buying at the beginning of the year and selling at the end of the same year, the S&P 500 produced a mean annualized return of 13.1 percent. However, the data show considerable variation around this mean ($SD = 20.1$ percent and $CV = 1.53$). However, for 25-year holding periods (that is, buying at the beginning of Year 1 and selling at the end of Year 25, reinvesting all dividends along the way), the mean annualized return from the S&P 500 was much less, 11.1 percent, but this return also showed far less variation around the mean ($SD = 2.4$ percent and $CV = 0.21$). In fact, the standard deviation and CV both fall consistently as the length of the holding period increases.

The same pattern is evident, although not as dramatic, for T-bond returns. For one-year holding periods, long-term U.S. T-bonds produced a mean annual return of 5.4 percent, again with a fair amount of variation around the mean ($SD = $ 9.1 percent and $CV = 1.67$). Increasing the holding period to 25 years, however, improves the risk/return profile. The mean annualized rate of return does fall to 4.2 percent, but the standard deviation, and thus the CV, fall even more ($SD = 2.6$ percent and CV = 0.63). As with stock returns, the standard deviation and CV fall consistently as the length of the holding period increases. This phenomenon in which the annualized standard deviation declines as the time horizon increases is called **time diversification**.

Many articles in the financial press attest to the benefits of time diversification. A *Wall Street Journal* article illustrates that longer holding periods have historically lowered the risks associated with stock investing, as Exhibit 2.16 also illustrates.[16] The article shows that if the S&P 500 Index was held for only a one-year period, the stock index return trailed a T-bill investment 40 percent of the time. If the stock index was held for a five-year period, it trailed T-bills 31 percent; however, over a 20-year holding period, the stock index earns a higher return than T-bills 100 percent of the time.

The Investment Insights box on page 497, features a strategy called **dollar-cost averaging** and argues that buying equal dollar amounts of a mutual fund at regular intervals (weekly, monthly, and so on) will help investors "even out" temporary market highs and lows. But, although it may well produce less-variable returns over the long run, dollar-cost averaging still involves risks.

If everything said about time diversification were true, an investor could reduce risk simply by increasing the investment period, a perfect tactic for retirement funds! Unfortunately, time diversification is a fallacy. It is true that the annualized standard deviation falls as the investment time horizon increases based on rates of return. Unfortunately, however, uncertainty compounds as number of years increases. This implies that the total dollar return becomes more uncertain as the investment horizon becomes longer. Stated differently, the annualized standard deviation does not say anything about the total dollar return; as the holding period becomes longer, the risk of the total dollar return becomes greater. Most investors worry about the total dollar return on a retirement fund rather than the decreasing annualized standard deviation, so it is important to note that to feel safer with time diversification is only illusory.

Studies have provided evidence that although the confidence interval round the expected return narrows as investment periods increase over time, the confidence intervalue of the dollar return widens as investment periods increase. That is the standard deviation around the mean decreases over longer investment periods for percentage return distribution, but it increases for dollar return distribution. For example, a one year investment has a spread around the mean of 32 percent (or a spread that ranges from −7 percent to 25 percent) when a one year investment period is simulated. In contrast, a 20 year investment period has a 8 percent spread around the mean (or a spread that ranges from 5 percent to 13 percent) when it is simulated. This illustrates that as the investment period lengthens, the standard deviation (where the spread equals two standard deviations from the mean) decreases. This is time diversification.

---

[16]Karen Slater, "Long Haul Investing: Riding Out the Risk in Stocks," *Wall Street Journal*, December 16, 1991, p. C1.

INVESTMENT INSIGHTS

0:00   0:00

DOLLAR COST AVERAGING HELPS REDUCE MARKET VOLATILITY

If the recent stock market volatility is keeping you up at nights, dollar cost averaging may be the solution. This process requires an equal dollar investment of a stock or mutual fund at regular intervals, usually monthly or quarterly. It avoids investing all your money at one time, perhaps at the peak of the market.

An example may be helpful. Suppose you decide to invest $200 monthly in a mutual fund. A three month investment period might be

Month	Investment	Price per share	# of shares purchased
January	$200	$20	10.0 shares
February	$200	$16	12.5
March	$200	$25	8.0
TOTAL	$600		30.5 shares

The average price over the three month period is $20.33 and you bought 30.5 shares. However, dividing the total dollar invested ($600) by 30.5 shares equals only $19.67. So instead of paying $20.33, your investment cost only $19.67. Dollar cost averaging allows you to buy more shares when the prices are lower and fewer shares when the prices are higher. As a result, the average cost of the shares is lower than the average price during the period. You might say that the method automatically times the market for you; buying more shares when the market is down and less shares at its peak.

Of course you may ask, is there a catch to this simple method? It definitely should not be set on auto-pilot because there is a downside risk. If the fund you chose for dollar cost averaging purpose turns out to be a poor performing mutual fund, this method can't bail you out. Dollar cost averaging does not protect you from losing money. Let's review the earlier example and suppose that the fund prices fall continuously from $20 to $15 to $10 and you have accumulated 43.33 shares by dollar cost averaging over three months. The value of these shares would equal $433.30 at $10 per share, resulting in a loss of $166.70 or a 28 percent decline in investment. If the price continues falling the greater the loss the longer you hold it. So dollar cost averaging does not protect you from a bad investment.

Conversely, if the prices are continuously rising then you would be better off investing everything up front ($600 in our example) instead of dollar cost averaging. However, we never know that the prices won't falter until after the fact. You could not tell before the fact then, of course, it's too late. Given that's the case and that prices are likely to fluctuate over time, dollar cost averaging will work if you invest for the long haul.

Actually many people use this method without knowing it. If you participate in a 401(k) or a profit-sharing retirement fund, you're actually dollar cost averaging, investing a set amount each month Also many mutual fund companies and brokerage firms have a direct deposit program making it easy to dollar cost average.

However, the results are quite different when wealth distributions measured in total dollar returns are examined. The confidence intervals around the dollar returns widens as the investment horizon lengthens. To illustrate, suppose a one year investment has a mean dollar return equal to $1,500 and its spread around the mean ranges from $1,000 to $2,000. In contrast, a 20 year investment period has a mean equal to $4,000 and its spread around the mean ranges from $2,500 to $10,500 which is considerably wider than the one year investment spread. The example shows that as the investment period lengthens, the standard deviation for total dollar returns (measured by the spread) increases and makes longer term investments riskier.

What does all this mean? It means that investors must be careful when using these measures and not lose sight of the objective. To maximize long-term dollar return (perhaps for a retirement fund), one must be aware that risk increases for investments over longer periods, even if the standard deviation of the rate of return decreases. Perhaps a good example is IBM. Many investors considered IBM stock a good retirement investment because it had been a market bellwether for decades, earning the nickname "Big Blue" for its stature as a leader among blue-chip stocks. Suppose you purchased 100 shares of IBM in the early 1980s for about $100 (total investment of $10,000) as a retirement fund. If you had to sell in 1993, its market price was about $45 per share—worth only $4500—not even half of your invested dollars! If you could have waited until the year 2000, that same investment would have been worth about $40,000. So, the first lesson learned is to diversify and not invest in one stock, no matter how sexy the "dot com" name sounds, and the second lesson is to understand that longer investment horizon increases your uncertainty (risk) of its final wealth.

EFFICIENT DIVERSIFICATION

naïve diversification
Technique in which an investor diversifies by randomly selecting securities for the portfolio investment.

Most of the examples of diversification we have discussed up to this point are examples of **naïve diversification.** The stock selection technique we used to produce Exhibit 17.11 is a classic example of naïve diversification: the stocks were added to the portfolio randomly. Although adding additional securities to a portfolio will generally improve its risk/return profile, nothing guarantees that it will produce the best risk/return profile. In other words, naïve diversification will not necessarily maximize return for a given level of risk, nor will it necessarily minimize risk for a given level of return.

efficient diversification
Technique in which an investor diversifies by finding the portfolio combinations that produce the highest return for a given risk or the lowest risk for a given return.

By contrast, **efficient diversification** involves finding the portfolio combinations that produce the best risk/return profiles. It involves the use of mathematical techniques to search through all possible combinations of securities to determine which provide maximum expected returns for given risk levels or which subject the investor to the minimum amount of risk for given levels of return. In the process, all diversifiable risk is eliminated. These mathematical techniques are derived from a body of theory usually referred to as **modern portfolio theory (MPT).**

modern portfolio theory (MPT)
A body of theory that includes the concept of diversification and measures security risk/return via the capital asset pricing model (CAPM).

We can trace the origins of MPT to an article published in 1952 by Harry Markowitz.[17] Markowitz argued that an investor could produce an optimal allocation of securities within a portfolio that would achieve the best possible risk/return trade-off. In other words, one can build a portfolio that minimizes risk for a given level of return or, alternatively, that maximizes expected return for a given level of risk. The basic technique used by Markowitz finds, for a given set of securities, the *efficient frontier*. Portfolios that lie along the efficient frontier offer investors the optimal risk/return combinations; these portfolios are called **mean-variance efficient portfolios.**[18]

mean-variance efficient portfolios
Portfolios that provide the highest return for a given risk or the lowest risk for a given return.

---

[17]See "Portfolio Selection," *Journal of Finance* (March 1952), pp. 77–91. In 1990, Harry Markowitz, Merton Miller, and William Sharpe were awarded the Nobel Prize in economics for their work in developing MPT.

[18]In this text, we measure risk by portfolio standard deviation, SDp, rather than variance, which equals SD_p^2. No major difference exists between the two measures; the numerical value differs, but the relative risk level remains the same between securities or portfolios. To label a portfolio *mean-variance efficient* is the same as labeling it *mean-standard deviation efficient*. We will stick to the conventional phrase here and use *mean-variance efficient*.

Exhibit 17.12 ✦ Efficient Frontier for Three Stocks

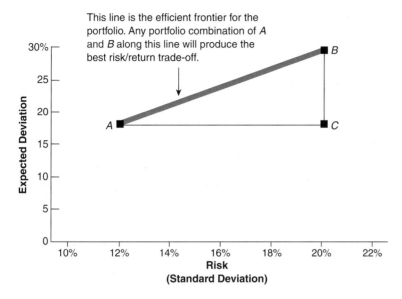

Let's illustrate an efficient frontier by considering a simple example with just three assets (A, B, and C), presented in Exhibit 17.12. Each asset is plotted based on its standard deviation and expected return. Notice that A and C have identical expected returns whereas B and C have identical standard deviations. Clearly, A is superior to C because it has less risk (that is, a lower standard deviation) for the same expected return. By the same token, B clearly offers a superior risk/return trade-off compared with C because it has a higher expected return for the same level of risk.

How can one choose between A and B? Although someone may prefer A to B or vice versa, remember that no one can really say one is better than the other. In this simple example, A and B form endpoints along the efficient frontier.

Assume that a straight line connects A and B. By definition, all the portfolios along that line would be combinations of A and B, and all, including A and B, would maximize expected return for a given risk level and minimize risk for a given expected return. All portfolios that lie along the efficient frontier produce the optimal risk/return trade-offs of all feasible combinations of the securities; at the same time, these efficient portfolios minimize nondiversifiable risk. Thus the Markowitz model allows an investor to reduce the number of feasible combinations under consideration to only those that lie along the efficient frontier, even though hundreds or even thousands of portfolios may remain.

How to Find an Efficient Frontier

The data necessary to find the efficient frontier for a set of securities, using the Markowitz model, consist of three items: the standard deviation of returns for each security, the mean (or expected) return for each security, and the correlation coefficient between returns for each possible pair. The Markowitz model can be used with either ex-ante data or ex-post data.

Exhibit 17.13 ✦ Inputs Needed to Find an Efficient Frontier for Five Securities

Stock	Mean Return	Standard Deviation	Coefficient of Variance
AHP	17.46%	15.59%	0.89
Boeing	32.16	21.76	0.68
Disney	23.99	28.09	1.17
Duke Power	21.76	15.17	0.70
Texaco	22.53	14.59	0.65

Correlation Matrix

Stock	AHP	Boeing	Disney	Duke	Texaco
AHP	1.00				
Boeing	0.49	1.00			
Disney	0.52	0.69	1.00		
Duke Power	0.50	0.38	0.12	1.00	
Texaco	0.25	−0.04	−0.18	0.28	1.00

The Markowitz model involves solving a set of mathematical equations to minimize portfolio standard deviation, subject to a minimum stated expected return. It does this by varying the percentages of the total portfolio invested in the individual securities. Computer software has simplified the work, so finding an efficient frontier is not difficult. Let's look at an example. Exhibit 17.13 lists the data necessary to find an efficient frontier for five stocks: AHP, Boeing, Disney, Duke Power, and Texaco over five years. It gives the mean annualized monthly return and annualized standard deviation for each stock, along with the correlation coefficient for each pair of stocks.

A spreadsheet application (for example, Excel) can be used to identify the efficient frontier shown in Exhibit 17.14. Ten portfolios create different combinations of the five stocks that lie along the efficient frontier; they are plotted along with an equally weighted portfolio of the five stocks. The relevant characteristics of the portfolios (mean returns, standard deviations, and percentages invested in each security) are also presented in Exhibit 17.14. Notice that the equally weighted portfolio does not lie along the efficient frontier.

The 10 that do lie along the efficient frontier vary widely in their makeup. Portfolio 1 is the only one of the 10 that contains AHP (albeit only 7.29 percent). None of the 10 efficient portfolios contain all five stocks. In fact, portfolios 5 through 9 holds only two stocks (Boeing and Texaco). Portfolio 10 is even 100 percent Boeing! Of course, the Markowitz method does not guarantee that all stocks will be included in all, or even any efficient portfolios. The makeup of an efficient portfolio depends on the risk/return characteristics of the individual securities as well as the correlations between them.

By definition, remember, any portfolio that lies along the efficient frontier maximizes return for a given risk level and minimizes risk for a given return. To check this, let's compare the equally weighted portfolio to portfolios that lie along the efficient frontier. The equally weighted portfolio has about the same return as portfolio 2 (23.43 percent versus 23.29 percent) but a higher standard deviation (14.03 percent versus 10.95 percent). Similarly, the equally weighted portfolio has about the same

Exhibit 17.14 ✦ SAMPLE OF SOME PORTFOLIO COMBINATIONS ON THE EFFICIENT FRONTIER FOR THE FIVE SECURITIES

Portfolio	Portfolio Mean Return	Portfolio Standard Deviation	AHP	Boeing	Disney	Duke Power	Texaco
1	22.13%	10.68%	7.29%	0.00%	14.95%	29.49%	48.27%
2	23.29	10.95	0.00	7.38	13.89	26.25	52.86
3	24.31	11.68	0.00	19.20	15.97	18.20	54.86
4	25.49	12.73	0.00	31.02	1.60	10.15	57.23
5	26.53	14.13	0.00	41.93	0.00	0.00	58.07
6	27.57	16.10	0.00	53.54	0.00	0.00	46.46
7	28.78	18.63	0.00	65.16	0.00	0.00	34.84
8	29.84	21.46	0.00	76.77	0.00	0.00	23.23
9	31.07	24.55	0.00	88.39	0.00	0.00	11.61
10	32.16	27.77	0.00	100.00	0.00	0.00	0.00
Equally weighted	23.43	14.03	20.00	20.00	20.00	20.00	20.00

standard deviation as portfolio 5 (14.03 percent versus 14.13 percent) but a lower mean return (23.43 percent versus 26.53 percent). Thus, most risk-averse investors would choose portfolio 2 or portfolio 5 over the equally weighted portfolio, because the efficient portfolios offer superior risk/return trade-offs. We cannot say, however, that risk-averse investors would choose portfolio 2 over portfolio 5 (or vice versa).

This example has considered only five stocks. Could an efficient frontier be computed for all publicly traded stocks? If so, what would its shape look like? The answer to the first question is yes; even though the amount of data required would be enormous, the mathematical process would be the same. As for the shape, most agree that the full-market efficient frontier would look something like Exhibit 17.15. It starts at the minimum risk portfolio and extends upward and to the right.

Implications for Investors

Chapter 17 has taught us that we must invest in several stocks to benefit from diversification. Also, we have learned that a lower correlation (lower than 1.0) between securities gives us greater diversification benefits. However, we have also found that by naïvely or randomly choosing 20 securities, we can achieve most of the benefits of diversification. Of course, many investors lack the capital to invest in many stocks. Perhaps, this is why mutual funds have become so popular. They have created a niche in the investment market by obtaining funds from several investors who may not have the ability to purchase several stocks. Mutual funds pull together resources (funds and talent) so that all investors who purchase mutual funds invest in several stocks via the funds.

In Chapter 18 we'll rely on the notion that risk-averse investors will invest in portfolios with optimal risk/return trade-offs to develop a risk/return relationship for securities. We'll discuss a way to quantify security risk and develop a model called the *Capital Asset Pricing Model (CAPM)* to relate risk to return. You may ask, why is this important to security analysis? Only by quantifying a stock's risk can we determine a

Exhibit 17.15 ✦ FULL-MARKET EFFICIENT FRONTIER

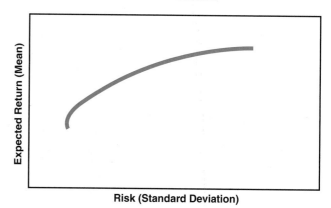

reasonable expected return (via CAPM) for the stock and compare our predicted return with the CAPM required return to decide whether it is a good investment. Chapter 18 also covers security analysis and reveals its similarity to the fundamental analysis discussed in Chapter 14.

Chapter Summary

1. What is risk aversion and why are investors, as a group, risk averse?
   Some simple lottery-type games suggest that most individuals are unlikely to play a risky game unless they receive some compensation for that risk. This is because most individuals probably have utility of wealth functions that increase at decreasing rates. Thus, a typical individual cares less about a $1 increase in wealth than a $1 decrease in wealth.

2. What are the general investment implications of risk aversion?
   The most important implication of risk aversion is that risk becomes a dominant consideration in security selection. As a result, over time, a positive relationship should exist between risk and return. The historical record confirms that higher-risk investments such as common stocks have returned more, on average, than lower-risk investments such as U.S. T-bills.

3. Why is standard deviation a good measure of risk, and how does an investor compute standard deviations for both individual securities and portfolios?
   Among several alternative measures of risk, standard deviation is a good measure because it uses the entire return distribution and because it expresses, in a single statistic, the degree to which two securities have similar return distributions. We saw how to measure standard deviation for both individual securities and groups of securities (portfolios) using either historical return data (ex-post returns) or expected future returns (ex-ante returns). We looked at how to compare securities and portfolios based on their risk/return trade-offs.

4. What is the impact of security correlations on portfolio risk?
   Several examples (with both real and concocted data) suggest that, although the expected (or mean) return for a portfolio is simply the weighted average of expected returns of the individual securities, the standard deviation of a portfolio is not a simple function of individual security's standard deviations. The reason for this lies in the interrelationships (or correlations) between the return distributions of the securities.

5. What are the benefits of diversification, and how can investors achieve them?
    Diversification can help investors achieve better risk/return trade-offs, reducing risk without significantly reducing expected returns. Diversification is possible so long as security returns are not perfectly correlated (their correlation coefficient is less than 1.0). Also, some actual historical data confirm that diversification is not a difficult goal for investors to achieve. Investors can easily diversify by spreading investment funds across several different investments. In doing so, they can eliminate firm-specific or diversifiable risk, leaving only market or systematic risk.

6. What do we mean by efficient diversification and MPT?
    We ended the chapter with a discussion of efficient diversification and the basics of MPT. MPT seeks the combinations of securities that offer optimal risk/return trade-offs, the so-called efficient frontier. An efficient frontier based on a set of five actual stocks verified that all portfolios that lie along the efficient frontier do indeed minimize risk for a given level of return and maximize return for a given level of risk.

Mini Case 1

This case provides practice calculating the mean, standard deviation, and CV, and in selecting stocks for a risk-averse investor.

Open the Stock Returns worksheet in the data workbook. The file contains monthly returns for 100 stocks. Use the data and a spreadsheet or calculator to answer the following questions:

1. What is the mean return for the first five stocks over the entire five-year period?
2. What is the standard deviation for each stock?
3. What is the CV for each stock? Which stock offers the best risk/return trade-off?
4. Graph the results of the five stocks on a risk/return graph (with ER-SD risk). Which one lies the farthest toward the northwest (upper-left) corner? What does that imply?

Mini Case 2

This case creates a two-security investment opportunity set.

Open the Stock Returns worksheet in the data workbook. The file contains monthly returns for 100 stocks. Use the data on Wal-Mart and Amgen to answer the following questions.

1. What are the mean returns and standard deviations for both stocks?
2. What is the correlation coefficient for the pair?
3. Create a table like Exhibit 17.9 and determine the portfolio return and standard deviation for various percentage holdings in Wal-Mart and Amgen. Start with 0 percent as X percent for Wal-Mart and change it by 10 percent increments.
4. Graph the results on an expected return/standard deviation graph.
5. Using the table and graph, find the proportional investment in Wal-Mart and Amgen that has the minimum variance.
6. What are the exact proportions for the minimum variance portfolio?
7. Discuss what proportions you would invest in Wal-Mart and Amgen.

Review Questions and Problems

1. How would you describe a risk-averse investor?
2. What does risk aversion imply about the long-term relationship between risk and return?

3. Suppose you have an option of investing $10,000 in T-bills to earn a guaranteed 4 percent annual return or investing in eBay, which recently went public. Suppose the stock has a 40 percent chance of earning 100 percent in a year and a 60 percent chance of going bankrupt within a year. Which investment would a risk-averse investor choose?

4. Suppose you had invested in three stocks in 1999. Calculate the stocks' holding period returns:

Stock Name	Year-End 1998 Price	1998 Annual Dividends	Year-End 1999 Price
Toys-R-Us	$21.75	$0.00	$36.625
Tootsie Roll	39.625	0.29	36.25
Hewlett-Packard	83.75	0.48	96.00

5. Suppose you invested in the following three stocks during 1999. Calculate the stocks' holding period returns.

Stock Name	Year-End 1998 Price	1998 Annual Dividends	Year-End 1999 Price
Boeing	$78.375	$1.12	$92.875
Texaco	78.50	3.40	96.50
IBM	91.375	1.40	133.25

6. Suppose you had invested in these three stocks during 1999. Calculate holding period returns for the three stocks.

Stock Name	Year-End 1998 Price	1998 Annual Dividends	Year-End 1999 Price
AHP	$26.375	$0.89	$39.25
Duke Power	47.375	2.12	49.00
Disney	30.00	0.26	29.25

7. What is the difference between an actual holding period return and an expected return?

8. Suppose today is year t, last year was $t - 1$, and next year will be $t + 1$. The prices and disbursed cash dividends for a stock for these years are listed below:

Year	Price	Dividend
$t - 1$	$58	$1.00
t	65	1.50
$t + 1$	72	2.00

   a. Calculate the actual holding period return.
   b. Calculate the expected return.

9. Suppose today is year t, last year was $t - 1$, and next year will be $t + 1$. The prices and disbursed cash dividends for a stock for these years are listed below:

Year	Price	Dividend
$t - 1$	$42	$2.00
t	48	2.50
$t + 1$	53	3.00

   a. Calculate the actual holding period return.
   b. Calculate the expected return.

10. The following probabilities are given for each state of the economy and the respective stock returns:

		Returns	
State of Economy	Probability	Anheuser Busch	Toys-R-Us
Good	50%	+10%	+30%
Normal	30	+15	+20
Poor	20	+25	+ 5

a. What is the expected return for each state of the economy for each stock?
b. What is the standard deviation for each stock?
c. What is the portfolio expected return from investing 50 percent in each stock?
d. Calculate the correlation coefficient.
e. What is the portfolio standard deviation for an equally weighted portfolio of Anheuser Busch and Toys-R-Us?

11. The following probabilities are given for each state of the economy and the respective stock returns:

		Returns	
State of Economy	Probability	Johnson & Johnson	Disney
Good	70%	+ 5%	+40%
Normal	20	+12	+25
Poor	10	+20	+ 7

a. What is the expected return for each state of the economy for each stock?
b. What is the standard deviation for each stock?
c. What is the portfolio expected return from investing 50 percent in each stock?
d. Calculate the correlation coefficient.
e. What is the portfolio standard deviation for an equally weighted portfolio of Johnson & Johnson and Disney?

12. Following are five years of returns are given for Pepsi and Hewlett-Packard:

Year	Pepsi	Hewlett-Packard
1	32.22%	80.56%
2	27.24	65.41
3	20.88	11.10
4	29.47	28.14
5	56.70	69.39

a. Calculate the actual mean return for each stock.
b. Suppose someone invests 50 percent in each stock. Calculate the mean return for the portfolio using Equation 17.3 and again using Equation 17.6b.
c. Calculate the correlation coefficient between Pepsi and Hewlett-Packard.
d. If someone invests 50 percent in each stock, calculate the portfolio standard deviation using Equation 17.5 and again using Equation 17.11.

13. Suppose you have decided to invest 20 percent in Pepsi and 70 percent in Hewlett-Packard. Using the data from problem 12, find the portfolio return and standard deviation.

14. Five years of returns are given below for Toys-R-Us and Tootsie Roll:

Year	Toys-R-Us	Tootsie Roll
1	14.82%	21.45%
2	16.20	12.18
3	6.17	−6.24
4	−25.08	−10.18
5	−28.98	33.61

    a.   Calculate the actual mean return for each stock.

    b.   Suppose someone invests 20 percent in Toys-R-Us and 80 percent in Tootsie Roll. Calculate the mean return for the portfolio using Equation 17.3 and again using Equation 17.6b.

    c.   Calculate the correlation coefficient between Toys-R-Us and Tootsie Roll.

    d.   If someone invests 20 percent in Toys-R-Us and 80 percent in Tootsie Roll, calculate the portfolio standard using Equation 17.5 and again using Equation 17.11.

15. Suppose you have decided to invest 10 percent in Toys-R-Us and 90 percent in Tootsie Roll. Using the data from problem 14, calculate the portfolio return and standard deviation.

16. Five years of return data are given for IBM and Texaco:

Year	IBM	Texaco
1	7.21%	9.83%
2	−10.97	10.81
3	13.07	12.72
4	32.17	−2.75
5	25.71	37.43

    a.   Calculate the actual mean return for each stock.

    b.   Suppose someone invests 50 percent in each stock. Calculate the mean return for the portfolio using Equation 17.3 and again using Equation 17.6b.

    c.   Calculate the correlation coefficient between IBM and Texaco.

    d.   If someone invests 50 percent in each stock, calculate the portfolio standard deviation using Equation 17.5 and again using Equation 17.11.

17. Suppose you decide to invest 30 percent in IBM and 70 percent in Texaco. Using the information from problem 16, calculate the portfolio return and standard deviation.

18. Two stocks, A and B, have expected returns of 10 percent and 25 percent with standard deviations of 15 percent and 20 percent, respectively. The correlation coefficient is +0.30. If one invests 40 percent in stock A and 60 percent in B, what are the portfolio expected return and standard deviation?

19. Determine the proportional investment in stocks A and B from question 18 that provides the minimum variance portfolio.

    a.   What is the expected return of the minimum variance portfolio?

    b.   What is the standard deviation of the minimum variance portfolio?

20. Compare the two portfolios in questions 18 and 19. Is one preferred over another? Explain.

21. Two stocks, J and K, have the expected returns of 20 percent and 30 percent with standard deviations of 25 percent and 35 percent, respectively. The correlation coefficient is −0.20. If one invests 30 percent in stock J and 70 percent in stock K, what are the portfolio expected return and standard deviation?

22. Determine the proportional investment in stocks J and K from question 22 that provides the minimum-variance portfolio.

    a.   What is the expected return of the minimum variance portfolio?

    b.   What is the standard deviation of the minimum variance portfolio?

23. Compare the two portfolios from questions 21 and 22. Is one preferred over another? Explain.

24. Suppose the mean returns for two stocks, A and E, are 12 percent and 20 percent and their standard deviations equal 6 percent and 10 percent, respectively, and its correlation coefficient equal to 0.0. Determine the proportional holdings in A and E that would give the minimum variance portfolio. Graph and compare to Exhibit 7.10.

    a.   What is the portfolio's expected return?

    b.   What is the portfolio's standard deviation?

25. Suppose stocks A and E in problem 24 have a correlation coefficient equal to -1.0. Determine the proportional holdings in A and E that would give the minimum variance portfolio.
    a. What is the portfolio's expected return?
    b. What is the portfolio's standard deviation?

26. Suppose that two stocks, X and Y, have the following mean returns and standard deviations. The correlation between the two stocks is -0.50.

Stock	Mean Return	Standard Deviation
X	15%	8%
Y	25	14

    Graph an investment opportunity set for these two stocks.
    a. Estimate the proportions of X and Y that make up the minimum variance portfolio from the graph.
    b. Calculate the proportions of X and Y that make up the minimum variance portfolio using Equation 17.12. How close was your estimate?

27. Suppose that two stocks, L and M, have the following mean returns and standard deviations. The correlation between the two stocks is $+0.15$.

Stock	Mean Return	Standard Deviation
L	13%	15%
M	21	25

    Graph an investment opportunity set for these two stocks.
    a. Estimate the proportions of L and M that make up the minimum variance portfolio from the graph.
    b. Calculate the proportions of L and M that make up the minimum variance portfolio using Equation 17.12.
    c. How close was your estimate?

28. Explain why the correlation coefficients between securities are the key determinants of a portfolio's degree of diversification.

29. Suppose three stocks have the following risk and return characteristics:

Stock	Expected Return	Standard Deviation
X	0.05	0.08
Y	0.12	0.15
Z	0.12	0.15

    The correlations between X and each of the other stocks are

    $$CORR(X,Y) = +0.35$$
    $$CORR(X,Z) = -0.35$$

    a. Based on portfolio theory, which combination, XY or XZ, is expected to have greater diversification benefits? Explain.
    b. Now, graph an investment opportunity set for X and Y versus X and Z.
    c. Do any combinations of XY dominate XZ? If so, show your answer on the investment opportunities on the risk/return graph.

30. Suppose four stocks have the following risk and return characteristics:

Stock	Expected Return	Standard Deviation
A	0.10	0.05
B	0.20	0.10
C	0.20	0.10
D	0.20	0.10

The correlations between A and each of the other stocks are

$$CORR(A,B) = + 1.0$$
$$CORR(A,C) = + 0.50$$
$$CORR(A,D) = - 0.90$$

    a.   Graph an investment opportunity set for A and B, A and C, and A and D by the process described in Chapter 17, page 491. Which combination offers the greatest diversification benefits? Explain.

31. Suppose three stocks have the following risk and return characteristics:

Stock	Expected Return	Standard Deviation
J	0.15	0.15
K	0.35	0.30
L	0.25	0.30

The correlation coefficients between J and each of the other stocks are

$$CORR(J,K) = + 0.05$$
$$CORR(J,L) = - 0.15$$

    a.   Graph the investment opportunity sets for each portfolio, JK and JL. Over what proportional holdings does portfolio JK dominate JL?

    b.   In which, if any combinations of proportional holdings does JL dominates JK? Show your answers on the graph and indicate the approximate proportional holdings for each portfolio.

32. What is the difference between market risk and firm-specific risk? Name two other terms for market risk. Name two other terms for firm-specific risk.

33. Suppose a manager of a fund must decide which of two stocks, B or C, to combine with stock A. The portfolio will hold 50 percent in A and 50 percent in B or C. The stocks' expected returns and risk characteristics are given below:

Stock	Expected Return	Standard Deviation	Coefficient of Variation
A	15%	15%	1.00
B	20	10	0.50
C	20	15	0.75

The correlation coefficient $CORR(A,B)$ is +0.90 and $CORR(A,C)$ equals −0.80. The manager concludes that B has a lower risk (and CV), so it is the obvious choice. Do you agree or disagree? Explain why.

34. Suppose a portfolio manager must decide which of two stocks, D or E, to combine with stock F. The portfolio will hold 40 percent in stock F and 60 percent in D or E. The stocks' expected returns and risk characteristics are given below:

Stock	Expected Return	Standard Deviation	Coefficient of Variation
F	12%	18%	1.50
D	24	30	1.25
E	24	28	1.17

The correlation coefficient $CORR(D,F)$ is +0.50 and $CORR(F,E)$ equals +0.00. The manager concludes that E has a lower risk and CV and so is the obvious choice. Do you agree or disagree? Explain why. Show calculations to support your explanation.

CFA Questions

1. (Level 1, 1992) Given $100,000 to invest, what is the expected risk premium in dollars of investing in equities versus risk-free T-Bills (U.S. Treasury Bills) based on the following table?

Action	Probability	Expected Return
Invest in	0.60	$50,000
Equities	0.40	−$30,000
Invest in		
Risk-free T-bill	1.0	$ 5,000

   a. $13,000
   b. $15,000
   c. $18,000
   d. $20,000

2. (Level 1, 1992) Based on the scenarios below, what is the expected return for a portfolio with the following return profile?

	Market Condition		
	Bear	Normal	Bull
Probability	0.20	0.30	0.50
Rate of return	−25%	10%	24%

   a.   4%
   b.   10%
   c.   20%
   d.   25%

3. (Level 1, 1993) Which one of the following portfolios cannot lie on the efficient frontier as described by Markowitz?

	Portfolio	Expected Return	Standard Deviation
a.	W	9%	21%
b.	X	5	7
c.	Y	15	36
d.	Z	12	15

4. (Level 1, 1994) Portfolio theory as described by Markowitz is most concerned with
   a.   The elimination of systematic risk.
   b.   The effect of diversification on portfolio risk.
   c.   The identification of unsystematic risk.
   d.   Active portfolio management to enhance return.

5. (Level 1, 1988) A portfolio stocks generates a −9 percent return in 1985, a 23 percent return in 1986, and a 17 percent return in 1987. The annualized return (geometric mean) for the entire period is
   e.   7.2 percent
   f.   9.4 percent
   g.   10.3 percent
   h.   none of the above.

6. (Level 1, 1988) Kathy Chronos, CFA, has reduced the holdings of all stocks in her diversified portfolio and purchased money market securities. The risk Chronos is reducing is primarily
   i.   Reinvestment risk.
   j.   Interest rate risk.

     k.   Default risk.

     l.   Systematic risk.

7.   (Level 1, 1988) A correlation matrix is most useful for understanding

     m.   Geometric returns.

     n.   Portfolio diversification.

     o.   Arbitrage pricing theory.

     p.   Skewed distributions.

CRITICAL THINKING EXERCISES

1.   Open the Stock Price worksheet in the data workbook. The file contains month-end prices for Disney, AHP, and Yahoo.

     a.   Create a column to calculate the holding period return for each month, January 1998 to January 2000, for each stock.

     b.   Calculate the mean return and standard deviation using the Excel spreadsheet common =AVERAGE(:) to calculate the mean and =STDEV(:) to calculate the standard deviation for the stock.

     c.   Check to see that your results match the results presented in the file.

     d.   Calculate a portfolio return with one-third proportional holdings in each stock, AHP, Disney, and Yahoo. Create a column to calculate each monthly portfolio return, then calculate the portfolio mean and standard deviation. Now, calculate the portfolio mean and standard using Equations 17.3 and 17.14. Check your results with the results presented in the file.

2.   Open the Stock Returns worksheet in the data workbook. The file contains monthly returns for many stocks. Use the data in the file choose five stocks (together in class) and answer the following questions.

     a.   What are the mean returns, standard deviations, and pair-wise correlation coefficients for the stocks.

     b.   Display the five stocks' mean returns and standard deviation risk on a return-standard deviation risk graph.

     c.   Choose two stocks and discuss your reasons for your choices.

     d.   Create at least 10 portfolio combinations with your 2 stocks by varying the percentages invested in the 2 stocks. Remember, the percentages must sum to 100 percent.

     e.   Which of your 10 portfolios appear to be the most "efficient" compared with the others? Justify your answer.

THE INTERNET INVESTOR

1.   Find an Internet site that provides a chart of stock prices. Choose one Internet stock and one utility stock. Obtain daily stock price quotes for two months.

     a.   Calculate daily holding period periods for each stock.

     b.   Graph a distribution similar to Exhibit 17.1, where the x axis represents holding period returns in increments of 1 percent (that is, 0 percent to 1 percent, 1 percent to 2 percent, and so on) and the y axis represents the number of days the stock return fell in each percentage increments. Create one distribution for the Internet stock and another for the utility stock on the same graph.

     c.   Which stock distribution appear riskier? Explain.

     d.   Calculate range, number of days with negative returns, and standard deviation for each stock. Do these measures agree with your assessment in question c?

     e.   Explain which measure provides more information.

2. Find an Internet site that provides historical monthly stock prices for at least 2 months, starting from the most current month that has ended and going back 24 months. Possible sites are Yahoo (stock quotes), Microsoft Explorer, and AOL.

   a. Obtain closing stock prices (adjust for stock splits) and dividends for three stocks.

   b. Calculate monthly holding period returns, mean, and standard deviation for each stock.

   c. Graph the three stocks on a return-standard deviation risk graph.

   d. Using a spreadsheet, create an investment opportunity set with the three stocks.

   e. What combinations of these stocks would you invest? Explain why.

CAPITAL ASSET PRICING THEORY

PREVIOUSLY . . .

We developed portfolio theory and found that rational risk-averse investors will diversify by holding several securities. Investors can choose from several efficient diversified portfolios, especially those that attain the highest return for the lowest risk on the efficient frontier. However the choice of the risky portfolio is based on investor risk preference.

IN THIS CHAPTER . . .

We discuss a method in which the risky-portfolio choices of all rational risk-averse investors are designated as the market portfolio (portfolio M). Given this premise, we quantify security risk and develop the Capital Asset Pricing Model (CAPM). The CAPM can be used to value securities and conduct security analysis much like the fundamental analysis in Chapter 14.

TO COME . . .

Chapter 19 discusses extensions of the CAPM as well as the arbitrage pricing theory (APT), which is another method for valuing securities. Chapter 20 applies the concepts developed in Chapter 18 to evaluate portfolios or mutual funds.

Chapter Objectives

1. What is the capital market line (CML)?
2. How is the Capital Asset Pricing Model (CAPM) developed?
3. What is the difference between standard deviation and beta risk measures?
4. How can an investor apply the CAPM to security analysis?
5. How do you estimate beta?
6. What is the good news and the bad news about beta?

In Chapter 17, we examined how a portfolio of securities can provide diversification, which offers the potential to reduce risk and increase return. In fact, we established that any rational investor would hold a diversified portfolio instead of one or two securities. This raises the question of how can individual securities be priced when everyone holds combinations of securities? More specifically, you may be wondering how this will help with security selection, as discussed in Chapter 14.

Chapter 17 discussed securities only in the context of a portfolio. However, Chapter 17 developed two important ideas that will link portfolio theory to a security risk/return relationship. It showed that risk-averse investors require higher returns to compensate them for risk. Further, investors who hold well-diversified portfolios eliminate firm-specific risk, so their only relevant risk is the market risk (also referred to as *systematic risk*).

This chapter develops techniques to measure market risk and security risk. By quantifying a security risk measure, we can determine a risk/return relationship for individual securities. The risk/return relationship is specified by the **Capital Asset Pricing Model (CAPM).** It provides an objective way of determining risk and return for each security in the context of portfolio diversification. The general notion presented in CAPM, that investors will accept higher risk only if compensated with higher returns, is also central to modern portfolio theory, as Chapter 17 showed.

capital asset pricing model (CAPM)
Equation that quantifies security risk and defines a risk/return relationship.

Before we embark on a development of the theory, let's discuss the assumptions. These assumptions are necessary to develop a model that provides a linear representation of the risk/return relationship; some assumptions are necessary to make decisions, whereas others just simplify meanings. We admit that these assumptions may be unrealistic, but they help to simplify the model so we can gain some insights on how security risk and return relate. Also, it is important to recognize that the value of the model resides in the insights it provides with respect to the real world and not in the realism of its assumptions. Later, in Chapter 19, we discuss other developments of the model that relax some of the assumptions listed here; for now, however, we start by including all the assumptions to develop the original CAPM.

Assumptions of the Capital Asset Pricing Model

Several assumptions are necessary in developing the capital asset pricing theory:

1. Let us assume that investors have homogeneous expectations. This means that everyone has equal information and the same perceptions about the securities and the market. This assumption is necessary so that everyone will perceive the same efficient frontier otherwise, market equilibrium may not prevail.

2. Frictionless capital markets. This assumption means that no impediments prevent investors from creating their optimal portfolios. It prevents additional costs or constraints (which may vary among investors) from affecting investment decisions to create frictionless markets. These listed restrictions include
   a. No transaction costs, brokerage fees, or bid-ask spread fees exist.
   b. No taxes are payable.
   c. Securities can be divided in any proportions investors choose to optimize their portfolio.
   d. One person's trading activity will not affect prices.

3. Investors are rational and seek to maximize their expected utility functions. This assumption allows us to determine investment choices for a standard group of risk-averse investors.

4. Investment is for one period only. This assumption is important to prevent future investment strategies from affecting today's prices. For example, investment horizons that vary from two years to twenty years may affect investment choices (and prices) today.

5. All investors can borrow or lend at the risk-free rate. This assumption simplifies the risk/return relationship. Without it, the risk/return relationship may be nonlinear.[1]

Efficient Frontier and the Optimal Risky Portfolio

In Chapter 17, we learned that the efficient frontier represents a series of portfolios that provide the highest return for a given risk or the lowest risk for a given expected return. See Exhibit 18.1.

As expected, a security's expected return (ER_s) and standard deviation (SD_s) will be inferior to those at any point on the efficient frontier, and hence any security will lie below the efficient frontier. Although an individual security may lie below the efficient frontier, it may be part of one (or several) of the portfolios on the efficient frontier. It may represent 5 percent of the value of a portfolio and 8 percent of another portfolio that lie on the efficient frontier.

A rational investor will always choose a portfolio that lies on the efficient frontier, but which one? Remember, a portfolio on the efficient frontier has the maximum return for a given risk level, so the answer depends on an individual's preference for risk and return. Earlier, we discussed the investor's risk aversion. This risk/return characteristic can be graphed as a utility function (or indifference curve). Two investors with different utility functions will choose different risky portfolios. Exhibit 18.2 combines the efficient frontier with two investors' utility curves.[2]

Investor A, who is more risk averse, chooses P5, which exposes the portfolio to relatively low risk. Investor B, who is less risk averse, chooses P10, which is riskier but also provides a higher return.[3] This is helpful, but practically speaking, utility curves are difficult to assess. More important, provides no objective portfolio choice. The portfolio chosen (and the percentage invested in each security) will differ depending on the individual's utility curve. For example, investor A's choice of P5 may consist of 2 percent in AHP, whereas investor B's choice of P10 may have 35 percent invested in AHP. Besides, how often have you been asked by your stockbroker to describe your utility function?

Developing the Capital Market Line (CML)

risky portfolio
Any portfolio with total (or standard deviation) risk greater than zero.

To solve this problem, we introduce a risk-free asset, RF. The closest asset to a truly risk-free investment is a short-term U.S. Treasury bill. With a zero standard deviation, or risk, it lies on the y axis. Now, combine RF with a **risky portfolio** such as P_1. Exhibit 18.3 shows the combination between RF and P_1.

The combination of RF and P_1 is also a portfolio, and its expected return, ER_p, using Equation 17.6a, equals

---

[1] Economists and finance academics have a biased expectation that the risk/return relationship should be a linear relationship. Also, only with a linear relationship can we separate personal (utility function) decisions from objective investment decisions. This point will be clearer after we discuss the portfolio separation theorem.

[2] Assumption 3, that investors are rational and maximize their utility functions, allows us to make portfolio choices for investors with different utility functions. Given this assumption, an investor will choose a risky portfolio that maximizes his or her utility function.

[3] Investor A may be a retired, middle-income individual, whereas investor B may be someone wealthy, such as Bill Gates.

Exhibit 18.1 ✦ EFFICIENT FRONTIER

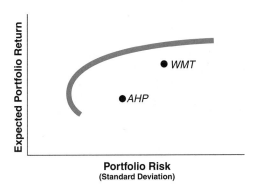

Exhibit 18.2 ✦ EFFICIENT FRONTIER AND UTILITY CURVES FOR INVESTORS A AND B

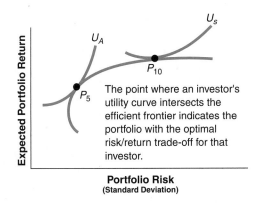

$$ER_p = XER_{P_1} + (1 - X)\, RF \tag{18.1}$$

where X is the proportion of wealth invested in the risky portfolio P_1 and $(1 - X)$ is the proportion invested in the risk-free asset RF. The standard deviation risk of the RF-P_1 combination can be calculated using Equation 17.11:

$$SD_P = [X^2 SD_{P_1}^2 + (1 - X)^2 SD_{RF}^2 + 2X(1 - X)SD_{P_1}SD_{RF}CORR(P1, RF)]^{1/2}$$

The last two terms equal zero because SD_{RF} equals zero. This leaves

$$\begin{aligned} SD_P &= \sqrt{([X]^2 SD_{P_1}^2]^{1/2}} \\ &= (X)SD_{P_1} \end{aligned} \tag{18.2}$$

The standard deviation of the portfolio combination RF-P_1 is linear because the risk-free rate has a zero standard deviation.

Exhibit 18.3 ✦ COMBINATION OF RISK-FREE ASSET RF AND RISKY PORTFOLIOS P1 AND P2

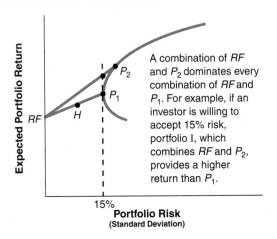

The line between RF and P₁ can be interpreted in the same way as that between two security combinations in Chapter 17. Point RF represents a 100 percent investment in the risk-free asset whereas point P1 represents a 100 percent investment in the risky portfolio P₁. The halfway point, H, represents a 50 percent investment in each. Remember, investors want to maximize their expected returns for a given risk.

As shown in Exhibit 18.3, a combination of RF and P₂ dominates any point on the line created between RF and P₁. For example, suppose an investor is interested in maintaining a 15 percent risk level. He could invest 100 percent in P₁ or, better yet, invest 90 percent in P₂ and 10 percent in RF to reach point I. The P₂ and RF combination has the same 15 percent risk but a higher expected return, ER_p. Being rational, an investor would choose P₂ over P₁.

Of course, why stop there? Other combinations with RF, such as P₃, P₄, and so on, will dominate those before. As shown in Exhibit 18.4, portfolio M, where a tangent line from RF touches the efficient frontier, is the line that dominates any other line that can be drawn from RF to any point on the efficient frontier, even P₁₀. This line from RF to M is called the **capital market line (CML).** The CML identifies all efficient portfolios and surpasses the old (curved) efficient frontier, except at point M. Recall that *efficient* means that it has the highest expected return for a given risk, or the lowest risk for a given expected return. The CML is discussed in more detail later.

Like the earlier examples, the line represents percentage investment in RF and the risky portfolio M. For example, a point halfway between RF and M represents a 50 percent investment in RF and M each. Once an investor has decided on a personally desirable combination of RF and M, she can calculate the expected portfolio return and its expected standard deviation risk by using Equations 18.1 and 18.2.[4] For 50 percent investments in each, the ER_p and SD_p equal

capital market line (CML)
Line that describes the percentage holdings in the risk-free asset and the risky diversified market portfolio.

---

[4]When using Equations 18.1 and 18.2, it is easiest to convert all percentages into decimals and later convert back to percentages if you prefer.

Exhibit 18.4 ✦ COMBINATIONS OF RISK-FREE ASSET RF AND RISKY PORTFOLIO M

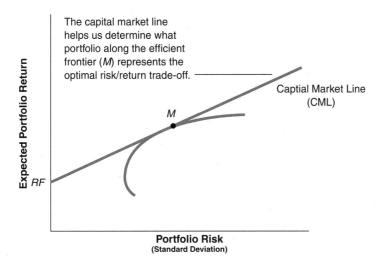

The capital market line helps us determine what portfolio along the efficient frontier (*M*) represents the optimal risk/return trade-off.

Captial Market Line (CML)

M

RF

Expected Portfolio Return

Portfolio Risk
(Standard Deviation)

$$ER_P = (0.50)ER_M + (1 - 0.50)RF \qquad (18.3)$$

$$SD_P = (0.50)SD_{P1} \qquad (18.4)$$

If *RF* equals 6 percent and ER_M equals 16 percent with an 8 percent SD_M, the portfolio expected return, ER_p, is 11 percent and SD_p, is 4 percent.

$$ER_P = (0.50)(0.16) + (1 - 0.50)(0.06) = 0.11 \text{ or } 11 \text{ percent}$$
$$SD_P = (0.50)(0.08) = 0.04 \text{ or } 4 \text{ percent}$$

At point M, 100 percent is invested in risky portfolio M. What about beyond point M? We defer this discussion until later to deal with the significance of the CML to investors who are choosing their optimal risky portfolios.

Remember the utility curves and how we determined which portfolio investors A and B would choose? A chose P_1 and B chose P_{10}. Now, recall from earlier discussions in Chapter 17 that investors gain utility as their utility curves move upward and to the left (toward the northwest). As shown in Exhibit 18.5, investor A's utility increases as the curve moves out from U_A to U'_A. U'_A is tangent to the CML and represents perhaps a 90 percent investment in *RF* and only 10 percent in the risky portfolio M. As we observed earlier, investor A is highly risk averse, choosing between RF and M consistently with his or her conservative utility function. What about investor B?

B also increases his or her utility by moving from U_B to U'_B. B chooses to invest −100 percent in RF and 200 percent in the risky portfolio M. What does it mean to invest a negative percentage in RF? To be beyond M, it means that an investor has borrowed at the risk-free rate RF and invested more than 100 percent in portfolio M. (A negative percentage allocation means borrowing.) In reality, it just means that a person bought on margin or borrowed money to invest more wealth than she has. Investor B is borrowing 100 percent at the risk-free rate and investing twice her wealth (200 percent) in portfolio M. If $100 represents her invested wealth, B borrows an

Exhibit 18.5 ✦ CML AND INDIVIDUAL UTILITY CURVES

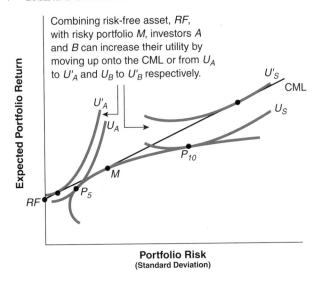

Combining risk-free asset, *RF*, with risky portfolio *M*, investors *A* and *B* can increase their utility by moving up onto the CML or from U_A to U'_A and U_B to U'_B respectively.

borrowing-lending line
Any point to the left of M on the CML implies lending at RF and any point to the right of M on the CML implies borrowing at RF.

additional $100 and invests $200 in M. This example implies a 50 percent margin, borrowing half of what is invested. Investor B is definitely not as risk averse as A and is willing to take more risk for a higher return.

Using the examples of investors A and B and their choices, we can segment the CML between lenders and borrowers. For that reason, the CML is sometimes called the **borrowing–lending line.**[5] The section between RF and M is called the *lending line,* and beyond M, it is called the *borrowing line.* Why? Let's go back to investor A, who invested 90 percent in RF and 10 percent in M. If A invests in RF, he is basically lending money at the risk-free rate. Therefore, by investing 90 percent of his wealth in RF, A is lending 90 percent of his wealth. Investor B, by investing −100 percent of her wealth in RF, is borrowing 100 percent of her wealth at the risk-free rate. Exhibit 18.6 shows how the CML is segmented between lenders and borrowers.

At this point, we have made an important discovery. Both investors A and B will now choose to invest in the risky portfolio M along with the risk-free asset RF. Although they are diametrically different in their risk preferences, both investors will now choose M instead of P1 or P10. Notice that assumption 1 (homogeneous expectations) is critical here. If we allowed investors to lack homogeneous expectations, even with the risk-free asset, investors A and B may perceive different efficient frontiers and choose risky portfolios other than M. Also, assumption 2 (frictionless markets) is necessary because impediments might lead investors to perceive different efficient frontiers based on their tax brackets or transaction fees.

Now, going back to the choice of portfolio M, we have resolved the earlier problem of dealing with utility curves and different risk preferences. It now seems that all

---

[5]This relies on assumption 5, that everyone can borrow at the same rate as they lend, RF; otherwise, the borrowing-lending line would be nonlinear.

Exhibit 18.6 ✦ CML: THE BORROWING-LENDING LINE

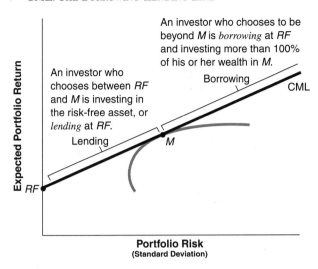

investors will choose the risky portfolio M; not P1, P2, P5, or P10, but M! This is a profound discovery; we can now separate the risky portfolio choice from the subjective individual utility functions. This premise, called the **portfolio separation theorem,** states:

> Individuals choose the risky portfolio independently of their utility functions. All risk-averse investors choose the same risky portfolio regardless of utility functions, then they decide on the combination of RF and the risky portfolio, based on their utility functions.

For example, investors A and B chose portfolio M as their risky portfolio despite their differences in risk aversion because M combined with RF is efficient. (It has the highest expected return for a given risk or the lowest risk for a given expected return.) Once M is chosen, the proportion (X) invested in RF and the balance invested in M depend on risk preference; how much risk is someone willing to take for a higher return? A invested only 10 percent in portfolio M, whereas B invested a whopping 200 percent in M. Note that their portfolio combinations of RF and M will have different ER_p and SD_p values, which can be calculated using Equations 18.1 and 18.2.

The portfolio separation theorem emphasizes the importance of M as the only risky portfolio chosen by *all* investors. Because M is the only risky portfolio, it must include all traded assets from art, stamps, and coins to financial securities. If so, it is appropriate to call it the **market portfolio.** Also, if it contains all traded assets, it must be well diversified.

Furthermore, theoretically, the securities in the market portfolio are value-weights of each security's proportion in the market portfolio. It is calculated as the security's total market value (price per share multiplied by the number of shares outstanding) divided by the total market value of all the securities in M. In practice, however, a proxy such as the Standard & Poor's (S&P) 500 Index, which is considered well diversified, substitutes for the market portfolio.

Finally, the CML that combines RF and M holds an important position, too. It defines all efficient portfolios, which are just combinations of RF and M. It can also

portfolio separation theorem
Allows investors to separate the decision of selecting the risky portfolio from the investor's risk preference (or utility curve).

market portfolio
The only risky portfolio chosen by all risk-averse investors. Because it is demanded by all investors, it must contain all the securities.

be interpreted as a unique linear relationship between standard deviation risk, SD_p, and its expected return, ER_p, for all the RF-M choices for individuals. The equation of the CML equals

$$ER_p = RF + \left[\frac{ER_M - RF}{SD_M} \right] SD_p \tag{18.5}$$

where the y intercept (where the CML crosses the y axis) is RF and the slope equals $(ER_M - RF)/SD_M$. Keep this in mind; it will be an important factor in developing the CAPM.

Now, we have almost reached our goal, to find a model that shows how securities are priced. Recall that it is called the CAPM.

RECAP The CML defines efficient combinations of RF and portfolio M. It defines only one optimal risky portfolio, M; all investors prefer to combine M with the risk-free asset RF. If M is preferred by all rational risk-averse investors, it must be the market portfolio.

1. Suppose you prefer to invest 30 percent in portfolio M and 70 percent in the risk-free asset. If ER_M equals 16 percent and RF equals 6 percent, what is your portfolio's expected return ER_p?
2. For the above portfolio, what is the portfolio risk, SD_p, if SD_M equals 8 percent?

So far, we have only developed the portfolio M and justified why everyone will invest in M. If all rational risk-averse investors prefer only one risky portfolio, M (which is the market portfolio), the risk that each security contributes to M is the only relevant risk for a security. The relevant risk of securities such as AHP, WMT, and DUKE is just what they contribute to M's risk. Exhibit 18.7 shows how all those securities are parts of the market portfolio M; and the next section discusses how to measure their risk, defined as each security's risk contribution to the market portfolio's risk.

Capital Asset Pricing Model

M must contain all tradable securities, as everyone invests only in M, and it must be well diversified. We also know from Chapter 17 that if everyone invests in a well-diversified portfolio, only market risk is relevant. Any firm-specific risk is eliminated purely through portfolio diversification. Because everyone invests in a well-diversified portfolio, M, by determining portfolio M's market risk, investors will know the risk level of their investment. Portfolio M's risk can be written as

$$\text{Portfolio M's risk} = \text{Market risk}$$

Further, because M is the only risky portfolio to consider, the relevant risk for each security is the amount of risk it contributes to M, or the security's market risk, ignoring firm-specific risk. If each security risk is stated as

$$\text{Security risk} = \text{Total risk}$$
$$= \text{Market risk} + \text{Firm-specific risk}$$

Exhibit 18.7 ✦ CML AND INDIVIDUAL SECURITIES

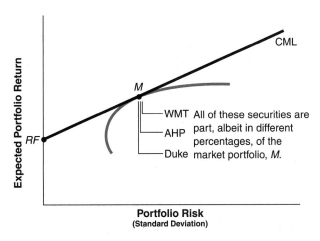

then we could restate portfolio M's market risk as

Portfolio M's risk = (Security 1's market risk + Security 2's market risk
+ …. + Security N's market risk)

We are no longer interested in total risk (or standard deviation) of a security but in its risk contribution to the larger market portfolio.

Also, recall from Chapter 17 that, as the number of securities (N) increases, the security risk, SD, falls virtually to zero; the only relevant risk is the security's covariance with the other securities in a well-diversified portfolio (in this case, the market portfolio M). We need to develop a measure of the security's risk contribution to the market portfolio, which we will call the security's *relative risk measure*.

Developing a Relative Risk Measure

Recall that Equation 17.13 defined the total risk of any portfolio p as

$$SD_p = \left[\sum_{i=1}^{N} X_i^2 SD_i^2 + \sum_{i=1}^{N}\sum_{j=1}^{N} X_i X_j COV(i,j)\right]^{1/2}$$
$$i \neq j$$

Instead of any portfolio, p, we will use Equation 17.13 to define the market portfolio and the risk contribution of security i to M. First, take the square of Equation 17.13 to ignore the square root sign. Rewrite it as

$$SD_p^2 = \sum_{i=1}^{N} X_i^2 SD_i^2 + \sum_{i=1}^{N}\sum_{j=1}^{N} X_i X_j SD_i SD_j CORR(i,j) \tag{18.6}$$
$$i \neq j$$

We will further rewrite Equation 18.6 by separating the summation over i from the summation over j, which adds up all the securities to make portfolio M. Now we can identify security i's contribution to the market portfolio M as

$$SD_M^2 = \sum_{i=1}^{N} X_i \left[X_i SD_i^2 + \sum_{j=1}^{N} X_j SD_i SD_j CORR(i,j) \right] \quad (18.7)$$

Let's examine the term in brackets, which equals the total risk contribution of security i to the market portfolio:

$$\begin{array}{l} \text{Total risk} \\ \text{contribution} \\ \text{of security i} \end{array} = \left[X_i SD_i^2 + \sum_{j=1}^{N} X_j SD_i SD_j CORR(i,j) \right] \quad (18.8)$$

Equation 18.8 represents the total risk contribution of security i to the market portfolio M, in which the first term is $X_i SD_i^2$ and the second term, $X_j SD_i SD_j CORR(i,j)$, equals $X_j COV(i,j)$.[6] The first term measures the contribution of security i's total risk, multiplied by the proportion of security i in M; the second term measures the amount of risk security i contributes *to* security j and security j's proportion in portfolio M. By summing the $COV(i,j)$ over j

$$\left[\sum_{j=1}^{N} X_j COV(i,j) \right]$$

we capture how security i contributes to the risk of each of the other securities that make up the market portfolio M. The two terms together capture the total risk of security i in the market portfolio.

Now, suppose that we want to measure the total risk of security i relative to the market portfolio risk, SD_M^2. Equation 18.8 can be rewritten as

$$\begin{array}{l} \text{Relative risk} \\ \text{contribution} \\ \text{of security i} \end{array} = \frac{\text{Total risk contribution of security i}}{\text{Total risk of market portfolio, M}}$$

$$= \frac{X_i SD_i^2}{SD_M^2} + \frac{\sum_{j=1}^{N} X_j SD_i SD_j CORR(i,j)}{SD_M^2} \quad (18.9)$$

Similar to the portfolio risk equation (Equation 17.13), this equation states that the relative security risk is composed of two types of risk: total risk of security i (SD_i^2) and its correlation (or covariance) with other securities. Because the market portfolio M consists of several thousand securities, each security's contribution, denoted by X_i, is small. This makes $X_i SD_i^2 / SD_M^2$ virtually equal to zero. (Remember, this is the power of diversification discussed in Chapter 17.)

---

[6]Remember that $CORR(i,j)$ is defined as $CORR(i,j) = [COV(i,j)/(SD_i)(SD_j)]$, so we can rearrange terms and have $COV(i,j) = (SD_i)(SD_j)CORR(i,j)$.

This makes the relative risk contribution of security i equal to

$$\text{Relative risk contribution of security i} \approx 0 + \frac{\sum_{j=1}^{N} X_j SD_i SD_j CORR(i,j)}{SD_M^2} \tag{18.10}$$

If the summation is taken over all securities j, it equals the risk of the market portfolio, and Equation 18.10 becomes

$$\text{Relative risk contribution of security i} \approx 0 + \frac{SD_i[SD_M CORR(i,M)]}{SD_M^2}$$

$$\frac{SD_i}{SD_M} CORR(i,M) = \beta_i \tag{18.11}$$

Equation 18.11 says that the relative risk of security i equals security i's total risk relative to the market portfolio risk (SD_i/SD_M) multiplied by security i's risk contribution to the larger portfolio, M, measured by $CORR(i, M)$. This relative risk definition is better known as beta, β_i.

Because $CORR(i, M) = COV(i, M)/SD_i SD_M$, we can also rewrite Equation 18.11 as

$$\text{Relative risk contribution of security i} \approx \frac{COV(i, M)}{SD_M^2} = \beta_i \tag{18.12}$$

This is also another definition of **beta, β,** for security i. The relative risk contribution of security i equals β.

Now, let's determine the beta for the market portfolio M. Using Equation 18.11,

$$\beta_M = \frac{SD_M}{SD_M} CORR(M,M)$$

Any variable must be perfectly correlated with itself, or $CORR(M, M) = +1.0$, so the market portfolio beta, β_M, equals 1.0. Because the market portfolio is a value-weighted average of all the traded securities, it says that an average security risk contribution is equal to 1.0. If security i's beta, β_i, is greater than 1.0, security i's risk contribution is higher than the average security or the market portfolio risk. If β_i, is less than 1.0, its risk contribution is less than the average security or the market portfolio risk. The market portfolio's beta can serve as a reference point for security risk. Let's continue our discussion on beta to obtain an intuitive feel for it and determine how to interpret it.

beta
Measures the security risk or its volatility relative to the market portfolio. If beta is greater than 1.0, the security is riskier than the market.

UNDERSTANDING BETA

This section discusses the meaning and interpretation of beta. We start with a list of four ways to view beta and then discuss the difference between beta and the standard deviation risk (or total risk) of a stock.

1. All security betas are measured relative to the market portfolio beta, which equals 1.0. If a security beta is greater than 1.0, its risk is greater than the market portfolio's risk; if it is less than 1.0, its risk is less than the market portfolio's. The market beta of 1.0 serves as a reference point for security betas.

2. Alternatively, we can interpret a beta greater than 1.0 to mean that the security contributes more than average risk to the well-diversified market portfolio.

3. Also, the numerical value of beta, such as AHP's beta of 0.66, makes implications regarding returns. If the return on the market portfolio changes by 1 percent, AHP's return will move up or down by 0.66 percent. Therefore, high-beta securities returns move more aggressively than the market portfolio, whereas low-beta securities are more conservative. Money managers have created strategies to invest heavily in high-beta stocks in bull markets. Using the same analogy, many will invest in money markets (risk-free assets) or low-beta stocks when they expect bear markets or unpredictable conditions.

4. Finally, because beta is a relative measure, the index used as a proxy for the market portfolio can make a big difference in the beta estimate. For example, if Hewlett-Packard (HP) were measured relative to the Dow Jones Industrial Average (DJIA), it would correlate closely, because the Dow is a price index made up of only 30 stocks including HP. The DJIA hit 11,000 on November 18, 1999, mostly because of a significant jump in HP stock resulting from strong fourth-quarter revenue growth. HP's 22 percent jump accounted for more than half of the DJIA gain.[7] However, if we measure HP's beta relative to the Wilshire 5,000 index, which includes thousands of stocks, HP's beta may show less correlation, and so the beta estimate may be less than one. It's important to know what market index serves as a proxy for the market to measure each security beta.

Two Types of Risk Revisited

Next, let's examine intuitively how to use the beta instead of standard deviation risk. In Chapter 17, we discussed two types of risk: market risk and firm-specific risk. Also, remember that a security's total risk is composed of market risk plus firm-specific risk. Now, we can define the relative market risk for a security as its beta, so the total risk of a security return can be divided into beta and firm-specific risk. Beta is also referred to as the systematic or nondiversifiable risk; it is the component of security risk associated with the market portfolio, M. Alternatively, it is the part of the security's risk that is inherent in the market and the extent to which it moves with the system; hence, this systematic risk cannot be diversified away. By contrast, the firm-specific risk, or risk unique to the firm, can be eliminated simply by holding a well-diversified portfolio such as M; this is diversifiable risk. Often-cited sources of firm-specific risk are labor disputes or negotiations, product tampering (as in the Tylenol and Pepsi episodes), resignations of CEOs, and awards of government contracts.

Now, let's contrast investment decisions made by total risk versus beta. Suppose AHP's total risk, SD_{AHP}, is 10 percent, and Wal-Mart's, SD_{WMT}, equals 15 percent. Assume, for simplicity, that the expected return equals 20 percent for both securities. Based on what we said in Chapter 17, a risk-averse, rational single-security investor would prefer AHP with 10 percent total risk. However, now that the investor can hold a well-diversified portfolio such as M, the total risk is no longer relevant. Only the

---

[7]*Wall Street Journal*, November 19, 1999, pp. C1, C10.

systematic risk (beta) or the risk that the security contributes to the large portfolio M is relevant.[8]

Suppose that total risk can be decomposed as follows for AHP and Wal-Mart:

$$SD_{AHP} = 10 \text{ percent} \quad \begin{cases} \text{Systematic risk} & = \quad 8 \text{ percent} \\ \text{Diversifiable risk} & = \quad 2 \text{ percent} \end{cases}$$

$$SD_{WMT} = 15 \text{ percent} \quad \begin{cases} \text{Systematic risk} & = \quad 4 \text{ percent} \\ \text{Diversifiable risk} & = \quad 11 \text{ percent} \end{cases}$$

Given that the two securities have the same expected return, an investor naively using the total risk measure would incorrectly choose AHP (which has a lower *SD* of 10 percent) when, in fact, Wal-Mart has a lower systematic risk of 4 percent as compared with AHP's 8 percent.

CAPM DERIVATION

Now that we have an intuitive feel for the security's relative risk contribution, β_i, we can develop a risk/return measure for securities. To take that final step to derive the CAPM, let's go back to the investment choice and reiterate some points. Remember, all risk-averse investors will invest in one risky portfolio, M. If so, portfolio M must be the market portfolio consisting of all traded securities. Recall that M is optimal because it lies on the CML and is preferred over all other risky portfolios. Now, what does it take for M to be on the CML? To lie on the CML, it must have the same slope as the CML. From Equation 18.5,

$$\text{Slope of CML} = \frac{(ER_M - RF)}{SD_M}$$

This is interpreted as the market portfolio's ratio of reward $(ER_M - RF)$ to risk (SD_M).

What is the reward-to-risk ratio for a security? Let's first discuss how to measure reward for securities. Then we'll cover risk.

Reward for Investing in a Security

In Chapter 17, we found that risk-averse investors are enticed to invest in risky securities only if they are compensated for risk. Chapter 1 defined this risk/return relationship as

$$ER_i = RF + \text{Risk premium}$$

The compensation for accepting risk equals

$$(ER_i - RF) = \text{Risk premium}$$

---

[8]We use systematic risk, defined as $\beta(SD_M)$, instead of beta because it provides a percentage risk measure comparable with total risk (which also is in percentage terms). Beta is a risk measured relative to the market portfolio, so it is an absolute number and cannot be compared with total risk given as a percentage.

The left side of the equation $(ER_I - RF)$, is the reward for accepting risk. Now, how do we measure security risk?

Security Risk

Recall that security i's risk is only relevant to the extent that it contributes to the market portfolio, M. That risk contribution is beta, β_i, also known as systematic risk and it can also be defined as $\beta_i SD_M$. The term $\beta_i SD_M$ redefines security i's risk contribution to the market portfolio as a percentage rather than an absolute number, like beta. For example, if β_i equals 1.2 and SD_M equals 20 percent, security i's percentage risk contribution equals $\beta_i SD_M$ or $(1.2)(0.20) = 0.24$ or 24 percent. Now, we can define reward-to-risk ratios for a security.

Security's Reward-to-Risk Ratio

Using this definition of the risk contribution of security i, its reward-to-risk ratio can be defined as

$$\text{Security i's reward-to-risk ratio} = \frac{(ER_i - RF)}{\beta_i SD_M}$$

Because security i is part of the larger market portfolio, M, its reward-to-risk ratio must equal M's reward-to-risk ratio from the CML:

$$\frac{(ER_i - RF)}{\beta_i SD_M} = \frac{(ER_M - RF)}{SD_M} \tag{18.13}$$

Why? Remember that $\beta_i SD_M$ is security i's risk contribution to M. As this contribution increases, its reward must increase proportionately; otherwise M's reward-to-risk ratio would change and may no longer be optimal (that is, may no longer lie on the CML).[9] To be in market equilibrium and for M to maintain its optimal position, the reward-to-risk ratio for each security must maintain its proportion of the market portfolio's reward-to-risk ratio.

Risk/Return Relationship

Now that we have determined the relationship between reward-to-risk ratios necessary to maintain an optimal portfolio, M, we can use it to find a security's risk/return relationship. Solve Equation 18.13 for ER_i:

$$ER_i = RF + \beta_i(ER_M - RF) \tag{18.14}$$

---

[9]We use calculus to prove this. If you are interested in a mathematical proof, go to the following references. William Sharpe, "Capital Asset Prices: A Theory of Market Equilibrium," *Journal of Finance* (September 1964); John Lintner, "The Valuation of Risky Assets and the Selection of Risky Investments in Stock Portfolios and Capital Budgeting," *Review of Economics and Statistics* (February 1965); and Jan Mossin, "Equilibrium in a Capital Market," *Econometrica* (October 1966).

Finally, we have developed a risk/return measure for securities such as AHP: the Capital Asset Pricing Model or CAPM. The security risk premium, $\beta_i (ER_M - RF)$, equals the risk contribution to the market portfolio multiplied by the market portfolio's risk premium. This makes sense because we presume that all risk-averse investors will purchase the market portfolio, so all security risk must be measured relative to the market portfolio risk. The CAPM is important because it allows us to quantify the *security's* risk premium and define a linear representation of risk/return relationship for all securities and portfolios. This relationship comes from modern portfolio theory (MPT). It relies on the idea that risk-averse investors will diversify away as much risk as they can; beyond that, expected return increases only with added risk. Because this is the minimum return compensation expected based on the beta risk, we will call it the "required return."

The CAPM (Equation 18.14) can also be displayed graphically. This gives the **security market line (SML),** as displayed in Exhibit 18.8.

Notice that this graph uses beta, as opposed to standard deviation, as a measure of risk. The expected return equals the risk-free rate, RF, at zero beta; it increases as beta increases. The expected return when beta equals 1.0 is the expected return on the market portfolio, ER_M. Because we have two points, RF at zero beta and ER_M at beta 1.0, we can draw a line to obtain the SML. Remember that Equation 18.14, the CAPM formula, creates the SML. To verify this, let's find the equation of the line for the SML.

Recall that the equation of a line equals

$$Y = a + bX$$

where a is the y-intercept of the line, b is its slope, X is the independent variable, and Y is the dependent variable. For the SML, β_i is the independent variable and ER_i is the dependent variable. What are the y-intercept and the slope?

The y-intercept is just the point at which the line crosses the y axis, RF in Exhibit 18.8. Recall that the slope is defined as

$$\frac{\text{Rise}}{\text{Run}} = \frac{\Delta Y}{\Delta X} = \frac{(ER_M - RF)}{(1.0 - 0.0)} = (ER_M - RF)$$

For the SML, the slope equals $(ER_M - RF)$, so the equation of the SML is

$$ER_i = RF + (ER_M - RF)\beta_i$$

This equation for the SML equals Equation 18.14, the CAPM equation. The CML and SML sound similar at first, but in the next section we'll contrast the two lines to clear up this confusion.

DIFFERENCES BETWEEN THE CML AND SML

At this point, we have introduced terms with two similar names, the capital market line (CML) and the security market line (SML). The latter graphs the CAPM equation. Let's contrast the two to avoid any confusion.

The lines differ in two ways. The most obvious is the risk measure; the CML measures risk by standard deviation, or total risk, whereas the SML measures risk by beta to find the security's risk contribution to portfolio M. The second difference is

security market line (SML)
Risk/return relationship for securities and a graphical representation of the CAPM.

Exhibit 18.8   ✦   SECURITY MARKET LINE (SML)

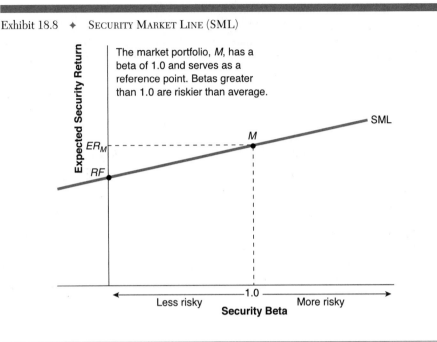

more subtle. The CML graph defines only efficient portfolios, whereas the SML graph defines both efficient and nonefficient portfolios and securities. Let's embellish on these points.

Firm-specific risk or diversifiable risk for portfolios on the CML is virtually zero because the CML contains only well-diversified, efficient portfolios. Even though it measures total risk (by standard deviation), it contains only market risk and almost no firm-specific risk. Also, remember that when the risk-free asset was introduced, all risk-averse investors preferred only one risky portfolio, the market portfolio M. All portfolios on the CML are merely combinations of the risk-free asset and the market portfolio M.

The SML includes all portfolios and securities that lie on and below the CML. Because everyone invests in M, each security (or portfolio) risk is determined as its risk contribution to M. This risk contribution is defined as beta. Every security (or portfolio) on the SML exists only as part of M, and the relevant risk is the security's contribution to M's risk. Again, firm-specific risk is irrelevant to the SML, but for a different reason than the reason it is irrelevant to the CML.

RECAP   The CAPM (or its graph, the SML) provides a risk/return relationship for every security and portfolio. It measures risk as beta, a relative risk contribution to the market portfolio M, because all investors are assumed to hold only M as their risky portfolio choice. The total risk (or standard deviation) of a security is no longer relevant, because the firm-specific part of risk can be diversified away, leaving only beta. The CAPM quantifies the risk premium for securities as $\beta_i(ER_M - RF)$ or the security risk contribution, β_i, multiplied by the market risk premium. The market beta equals 1.0 and serves as a reference point for other security betas. If a security's beta is greater than 1.0, it is riskier than the average security, or the market portfolio; if its beta is less than 1.0, it is less risky than the market.

3. Using Equation 18.11, calculate security i's beta, if the correlation between the security and the market portfolio equals $+0.55$, SD equals 0.06, and SD_M equals 0.35.
4. Given the beta from above, calculate security i's required return, ER_s, using the CAPM (or Equation 18.14) if ER_M equals 0.18 and RF equals 0.03.

Now that you have some insights on the development of the CAPM, let's apply this model to security analysis; this will also promote a better understanding of the SML. The analysis really repeats the fundamental analysis conducted in Chapter 14. The only difference is that the CAPM replaces intrinsic values measured in dollars with expected returns measured in percentages. (We compare the two approaches later.) The next section illustrates how to conduct a security analysis using the CAPM.

CAPM and Security Analysis

Suppose that a U.S. Treasury bond is currently yielding 5 percent and the current traded prices for AHP, Washington Water Power, Wal-Mart, and Echo Mining Co., as of February 2000, are $48.00, $19.00, $57.875, and $22.00, respectively. Let's see how we can conduct security analysis using CAPM. This is also an excellent alternative to value stocks that do not pay dividends.

SECURITY ANALYSIS

Value Line gives recent beta estimates for the four stocks of 1.00, 0.55, 1.25, and -0.20. Also, data from Ibbotson Associates gives an average yield spread between the S&P 500 Index and the U.S. Treasury bill rate of 0.086. Given these data and Equation 18.14, we can estimate the required return for each of the four securities.

$$ER_i = RF + \beta_i(ER_M - RF) \tag{18.14}$$

For AHP (AHP), it equals

$$ER_{AHP} = 0.05 + 1.05\,(0.086) = 0.140$$

For Washington Water Power (WWP), it equals

$$ER_{WWP} = 0.05 + 0.70(0.086) = 0.110$$

For Wal-Mart (WMT), it equals

$$ER_{WMT} = 0.05 + 1.10(0.086) = 0.145$$

For Echo Mining (MN), it equals

$$ER_{MN} = 0.05 + -0.20(0.086) = 0.033$$

Let's find these required returns on an SML graph, Exhibit 18.9. Because the SML is the graph for Equation 18.14 (the CAPM), they must all lie on the SML.[10]

---

[10]If a required return does not lie on the line, redo the calculations for Equation 18.14 or straighten your line. Remember, a required return *must* lie on the SML because the SML and Equation 18.14 (CAPM) are equal.

Exhibit 18.9 ✦ SECURITY MARKET LINE ANALYSIS

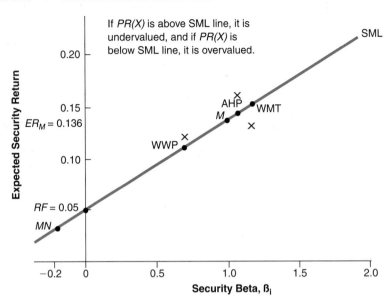

The first three securities, those with positive betas, lie on the SML, and their corresponding required returns are greater than the risk-free rate *RF*. What about Echo Mining Co., with its negative beta? What does it mean to have a negative beta and a corresponding *ER_s* less than *RF*? Although quite unusual, this is certainly possible. A negative beta means that the fund is negatively correlated with the market portfolio. This negative correlation can help to improve diversification benefits for the market portfolio. Remember the ultimate diversification benefit is derived from two assets that are perfectly negatively correlated (*CORR* = −1.0); this can reduce the combined portfolio risk to zero. To achieve this risk reduction, investors are willing to purchase the security even if it earns less than the risk-free rate *RF*.[11]

Next, we calculate the predicted return for each security based on today's price, $P_{i,t}$, a predicted price a year from today, $P_{i,t+1}$, and expected dividends during the coming year, $DIV_{i,t+1}$. Exhibit 18.10 provides the data for the four securities.

Predicted prices and dividends can be estimated by the procedure described in Chapter 13 on company analysis, which presented a procedure to estimate $P_{i,t+1}$ and $DIV_{i,t+1}$ to calculate PR_i. Of course, you may wonder whether every investor will make the same predictions. This is where assumption 1, that all investors have homogeneous expectations, is important. Recall that this assumes that everyone has the same perceptions about securities and the market.

---

[11]Why might gold and other precious metals tend to be negatively correlated with the market portfolio? Typically, when a financial market is in a severe downturn (for example, a war or a depression), financial assets are riskier, sometimes even worthless, and a greater demand for tradable precious goods such as gold results. In Chapter 2, we reviewed evidence that in the 1970s gold did well and stocks did poorly. During the 1980s and 1990s, stocks have on average outperformed gold.

Exhibit 18.10 ✦ PRICES, DIVIDENDS, AND PREDICTED HOLDING PERIOD RETURN

Security Name	Today's Price, $P_{i,t}$	One-Year Predicted Price, $P_{i,t+1}$	Expected Dividends $DIV_{i,t+1}$	Predicted Holding Period Return, PR_i
AHP	$48.00	$54.00	$1.70	0.16
WWP	19.00	20.04	1.24	0.12
WMT	57.875	65.00	0.21	0.13
MN	22.00	22.726	0.00	0.033

Now, this information will allow us to calculate an annual predicted holding period return, PR_i, for security i. A predicted return is calculated as

$$PR_i = (P_{i,t+1} - P_{i,t} + DIV_{i,t+1})/P_{i,t}$$

Predicted returns are calculated for each of the four securities.

$$PR_{AHP} = (\$54.00 - \$48.00 + \$1.70)/\$48.00 = 0.14$$
$$PR_{WWP} = (\$20.04 - \$19.00 + \$1.24)/\$19.00 = 0.12$$
$$PR_{WMT} = (\$65.00 - \$57.875 + \$0.50)/\$57.875 = 0.13$$
$$PR_{MN} = (\$22.726 - \$22.00 + \$0)/\$22.00 = 0.033$$

These predicted holding period returns are graphed onto Exhibit 18.9 with an X at the specified beta for each security. If the X lies above the SML (or $PR_i > ER_i$), the security is undervalued; if the X lies below the SML (or $PR_i < ER_i$), the security is overvalued. See Exhibit 18.9 again: AHP and WWP are undervalued, and WMT is overvalued. Echo Mining is priced as required by the CAPM.

Because the CAPM is an ex-ante (or expectation) model, it provides estimates of an appropriate future return for a given risk from investing today. Comparing this value to an expected return based on current and future market data, PR_i suggests a decision rule. If a security seems likely to have a higher return than its risk level justifies ($PR_i > ER_i$), it is undervalued and a good investment. However, a lower return than its risk would justify ($PR_i < ER_i$) suggests that a security is overvalued and not a good investment.

This analysis should sound familiar. It is just like the intrinsic value method of fundamental analysis. Recall from Chapter 14 that we estimated an intrinsic value of a security and compared it with the traded price. A traded price higher than the intrinsic value characterized an overvalued security; a price lower than the intrinsic value characterized an undervalued security. SML analysis is simply another form of fundamental analysis, using percentage returns instead of dollar values. However, because SML analysis measures predicted returns, it reverses the decision rule. Be careful not to confuse the two rules for SML and intrinsic value analyses! The two analyses and their decision rules are summarized in Exhibit 18.11.

Why do SML and intrinsic value analysis reverse their decision rules? The reason is that we assume that all investors predict the same price a year from now, $P_{i,t+1}$.

Exhibit 18.11 ✦ DECISION RULES FOR FUNDAMENTAL ANALYSIS AND CAPM SECURITY
ANALYSIS

Fundamental Analysis
$V_{s,0}$ is the intrinsic value of security S.
$P_{s,0}$ is the current market price for security S.

CAPM Analysis
ER_s is the expected return according to the CAPM for security S.
PR_s is the predicted return using the predicted market price, $P_{s,t+1}$, expected dividends,
$DIV_{s,t+1}$, and the current price, $P_{s,t}$.

Decision Rules
$P_{s,0} < V_{s,0}$ implies $PR_s > ER_s$; security is undervalued.
$P_{s,0} > V_{s,0}$ implies $PR_s < ER_s$; security is overvalued.

Given this predicted price, SML analysis calculates a predicted holding period return, PR_i. If the return is higher than the required return according to the CAPM, it plots above the line, indicating that an investor can earn more than required. This also means that the investor paid less than required, making the security undervalued and a bargain.

If all investors agree that AHP is undervalued, demand for AHP will rise, driving the current price upward. How high will it rise? It will go up to about $48.86, a price that will allow investors to earn about 14 percent, the required return for the stock's market risk as calculated by the CAPM. Because current price (on which intrinsic value is based) and expected return (on which SML analysis is based) are inversely related, the decision rules are reversed.

The analysis might proceed to find the equilibrium price at which the investor would earn a just return. Solve for the predicted return, PR_i:

$$PR_i = (P_{i,t+1} - P_{i,t} + DIV_{i,t+1})/P_{i,t}$$
$$P_{i,t} = (P_{i,t+1} + DIV_{i,t+1})/(1 + PR_i) \tag{18.15}$$

To set PR_i equal to the CAPM required return, substitute ER_i for PR_i:

$$P_{i,t} = (P_{i,t+1} + DIV_{i,t+1})/(1 + ER_i) \tag{18.16}$$

It does make sense that the current price should just equal the present value of future cash flows, $P_{i,t+1}$ and $DIV_{i,t+1}$. For AHP, this equals

$$P_{AHP} = (\$54 + \$1.70)/(1 + 0.14) = \$48.86$$

So, AHP's current stock price will rise from $48.00 to around $48.86. At that price, AHP stock is at market equilibrium. Now it is neither undervalued nor overvalued but just equaled to its intrinsic value.

All this relies on an accurate beta value. In the next section, we discuss how to estimate beta and introduce two new terms, the *security characteristic line* and the *market model*.

In this section, we learned how to analyze securities using CAPM and predicted returns. This security analysis is analogous to the fundamental analysis discussed in Chapter 14. Using predicted returns, we found that if security i has a predicted return greater than the CAPM required return, its expectation exceeds what is required and it is a good investment. Also, we conclude that its predicted return is greater because you underpaid for the stock or it is undervalued. If security i has a predicted return less than the CAPM required return, its expectation did not meet what is required and it is not a good investment. Alternatively, if its predicted return is less, we can conclude that you overpaid for security i or it is overvalued. It is also effective for valuing stocks that do not pay dividends.

RECAP

5. Suppose stock B has an estimated beta of +1.30. The market expected return equals 0.18 and the risk-free rate equals 0.05. What is stock B's required return via the CAPM.
6. Suppose you predict its price will increase to $90 in one year and dividends are expected to be $4.50 during that year. Stock B is currently trading for $80. What is its predicted return?
7. Is stock B a good investment? Discuss whether the stock is undervalued or overvalued.
8. Display stock B's required return and predicted return on a SML risk/return graph. Carefully label the risk-free rate, market portfolio, and stock B's returns.

Estimating Beta

A beta estimate measures the changes of a security's return relative to the market return. A **security characteristic line** shows this graphically as the relationship between the return on the market portfolio, M, and a security return, $R_{i,t}$. The relationship can be estimated mathematically by a simple linear regression model called the **market model:**

$$R_{i,t} = \alpha_i + \beta_i R_{M,t} + e_{i,t} \tag{18.17}$$

security characteristic line
Defines the relationship between the security return and the market portfolio return.

market model
Simple regression equation used to estimate the relationship between the security return and the market portfolio return.

where α_i is the *y*-intercept estimate of the regression, β_i is the slope estimate for the regression line (also referred to as beta), $R_{M,t}$ is the return on the market portfolio in time t (usually measured in months or years), $R_{i,t}$ is the return on security i in time t, and $e_{i,t}$ is a random error term for the variation of security i's return around the regression line in time t.

Exhibit 18.12 graphs AHP monthly returns for 1991 to 1995. The parameter estimates, using ordinary least squares regression, give this market model equation:

$$R_{AHP,t} = 0.0053 + 0.88R_{M,t} + e_{AHP,t} \tag{18.18}$$

A statistical package estimates , α_i and β_i as 0.0053 and 0.88. The slope coefficient, β_i is the estimate of systematic risk or beta. This confirms beta's role as the measure of volatility relative to the market return. If the market return changes by 1 percent, AHP's return will change by 0.88 percent; this is simply the definition of a slope. Alpha, α_i, also has a special interpretation; however, we reserve its detailed discussion until Chapter 20.

Exhibit 18.12 ✦ REGRESSION ANALYSIS TO ESTIMATE BETA

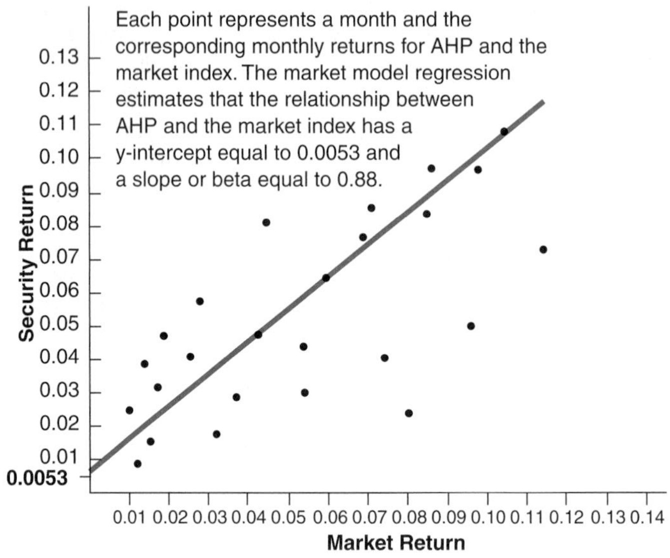

Each point represents a month and the corresponding monthly returns for AHP and the market index. The market model regression estimates that the relationship between AHP and the market index has a y-intercept equal to 0.0053 and a slope or beta equal to 0.88.

INFORMATION SERVICE BETA ESTIMATES

Many financial advisory firms such as Merrill Lynch, Value Line, and others provide estimates of beta. Exhibit 18.13 displays a sample of securities and their betas, estimated by an ordinary least squares regression model. Notice that the utility stocks tend to have betas less than 1.0, the beta of the market portfolio. Because most consumption of gas and electricity is unrelated to market moves, these firms are typically not highly correlated to the market. Duke Power has a 0.11 beta, whereas Washington Water Power has a 0.41 beta. Other betas are about 1.0, and some are much greater than 1.0; Charles Schwab's beta is more than twice the market level at 2.11. It makes sense for Schwab to be more volatile than the market as its business ties closely to trading volume, which tends to be high when the market is doing well. Betas tend to range from -0.9 to almost 4.0. Many high-technology firms have high betas, reflecting their participation in a risky competitive industry. Advanced Micro Devices (2.04) and Hewlett-Packard (1.43) fall in this category. Securities with betas close to 1.0 are Lockheed (0.93), Philip Morris (0.89), Tootsie Roll (0.96), and Wal-Mart (1.07).

CALCULATING BETA: SEPARATING SYSTEMATIC RISK FROM DIVERSIFIABLE RISK

Using the market model, one can calculate systematic risk and diversifiable risk. Recall the market model:

$$R_{i,t} = \alpha_i + \beta_i R_{M,t} + e_{i,t}$$

The variance of this relationship, SD_i^2, would equal

$$SD_i^2 = \beta_i^2 SD_M^2 + SD_e^2$$

Exhibit 18.13 ✦ BETA ESTIMATES FOR SELECT FIRMS

Security	Beta	R-square	Residual Standard Deviation
Abbott Labs	0.71	0.37	0.0520
Advanced Micro Devices	2.04	0.42	0.1346
American Home Products	0.66	0.46	0.1094
Bank of America	1.18	0.29	0.1038
Barnett Banks	1.29	0.43	0.0848
Charles Schwab	2.11	0.44	0.1277
Chrysler	1.45	0.45	0.0908
Duke Power	0.11	0.01	0.0496
Hewlett-Packard	1.43	0.61	0.0652
Johnson & Johnson	0.86	0.52	0.0462
Kmart	1.41	0.69	0.0540
Lockheed	0.93	0.41	0.0637
Occidental Petroleum	0.82	0.42	0.0545
Orion Pictures	1.46	0.15	0.2000
Pennzoil	0.51	0.11	0.0831
Philip Morris	0.89	0.45	0.0561
Ralston Purina	0.58	0.31	0.0495
Tootsie Roll	0.96	0.39	0.0684
Toys-R-Us	1.19	0.54	0.0630
United Airlines	1.35	0.28	0.1238
Wal-Mart	1.07	0.61	0.0499
Washington Water Power	0.41	0.27	0.0380

The previous equation has two terms. The first can be interpreted as a security's correlation with the market portfolio, or its systematic risk; the second term is interpreted as the portion of risk not explained by the independent variable, $R_{M,t}$. This is the firm-specific or diversifiable risk. To simplify the equation, substitute in the definition for beta (Equation 18.11):

$$\beta_i = (SD_i/SD_M)CORR(i,M)$$

This makes β_i^2 equal to

$$\beta_i^2 = (SD_i^2/SD_M^2)(R^2)$$

where $CORR(i,M)^2$ is shortened to R^2. This means that the diversifiable risk, SD_e^2 must equal

$$SD_e^2 = (1 - R^2)SD_i^2$$

This allows one to rewrite the total risk, SD_i^2, as

$$SD_i^2 = R^2(SD_i^2) + (1 - R^2)(SD_i^2)$$

R^2 is equal to $CORR(i,M)^2$ for a simple regression (one independent variable). It ranges from 0.0 to +1.0. As R^2 approaches 1.0, the explanatory power of the independent variable for the dependent variable increases. This indicates how closely the security return correlates to the market return. A higher R^2 indicates a higher predictive power of the market return for the security return; this gauges the reliability of the beta estimate from the regression, helping the analyst to interpret Exhibit 18.13.

Using the beta and R^2 data presented in Exhibit 18.13 and Equation 18.18, one can separate total risk into its systematic and diversifiable components for AHP:

$$SD^2_{AHP} = 0.46(0.054) + (1 - 0.46)(0.054)$$

This can be interpreted to mean that 46 percent of AHP's total risk is systematic risk and 54 percent of total risk is firm-specific or diversifiable risk. The formula provides a convenient way to calculate how much of total risk can be eliminated in a well-diversified portfolio. Furthermore, in regression analysis, R^2 measures the explanatory power of the independent variable ($R_{M,t}$) for the dependent variable ($R_{i,t}$); this indicates how much of the variation of $R_{i,t}$ (denoted by SD^2_{AHP}) is explained by variation in $R_{M,t}$.

Having explained how to estimate beta, we can now show how to interpret its graphic representation, the security characteristic line. This will reduce confusion between the SML and the security characteristic line. They appear similar, but they perform different roles.

DIFFERENCES BETWEEN THE SML AND THE SECURITY CHARACTERISTIC LINE

The most obvious difference is in the variables graphed by the x axis and the y axis. The SML displays required return, ER_i, values for a cross section of securities on the vertical axis and betas on the horizontal axis. It shows the relationship of two variables for many securities. By contrast, the security characteristic line measures a security's returns on the vertical axis and the market portfolio's returns (usually S&P 500 returns) on the horizontal axis, using time series data, which shows the relationship between the security's return and that of the market over time. The slope of the SML equals ($ER_M - RF$), whereas the slope of the security characteristic line equals β_i. The y-intercept of the SML is the risk-free rate, RF, and the y-intercept of the security characteristic line equals α_i. Because the relationships are different, the uses of the lines differ, too.

The security characteristic line is primarily used to determine how a security return correlates to a market index return. The R^2 that results from regressing the security return on the market index return indicates how well the market index return can explain the security return. A higher R^2 indicates greater explanatory power. Its other use is to estimate beta, which is the slope of the security characteristic line.

The SML, by contrast, is used for estimating the required return for a security relative to its risk measured by beta, β_i. The β_i value for the SML comes from the slope estimate of the security characteristic line. The security characteristic line estimates beta, and the SML graphs it. In Chapter 20, we explain how to interpret the slope of the SML as a reward-per-risk measure called the Treynor measure. That chapter shows that the y-intercept of the characteristic line can be interpreted as a reward measure, too.

We conclude this chapter by reviewing some research studies and opinions about beta. What is the practical value of beta, and what are some problems with beta?

Good News and Bad News About BETA

Of course, researchers and practitioners have estimated beta since its discovery and found some good news and some bad news. They have focused on two real issues. One is how well one can estimate beta—a purely statistical question. The other is how well one can predict future betas using past beta estimates. After all, the goal of security analysis is to measure its future systematic (beta) risk to determine what returns to expect.

Researchers and practitioners have found that a single measure of the actual relationship between a security return and the market portfolio return is dubious at best. They have found little correlation between security returns and market portfolio returns, which beta attempts to measure. Exhibit 18.13 listed low R^2 values, which evaluated the explanatory power of the market portfolio's return for a security return. Duke Power, for example, has an R^2 of 0.01, and most are below 0.50. (The maximum is 1.0.) Studies have found that portfolio betas have a much higher correlation with the market portfolio, so portfolio beta estimates may be more reliable than security beta estimates.[12]

The issue of measuring future betas can be addressed by summarizing Marshall Blume's study, "On the Assessment of Risk."[13] He shows that historical betas can be better predictors of future betas for large portfolios, even if they are unreliable for individual securities. His study correlated beta estimates for individual securities from July 1954 to June 1961 with estimates from July 1961 to June 1968. He found correlations for single security beta estimates for the two periods of only 0.60 with an R^2 value of 0.36; if the number of securities in a portfolio increased from one to two, however, the correlation also increased to 0.73 with an R^2 of 0.53. When Blume included 50 securities in a portfolio and estimated its beta over the same two time periods, he found that the correlation increased to 0.98.

Exhibit 18.14 suggests that as the number of securities in a portfolio increases, beta estimates become better predictors of subsequent-period beta estimates. Blume's study may suggest that historical betas are better predictors of future betas for mutual funds. However, other evidence suggests that mutual fund betas change because fund managers deliberately change the risk compositions of their funds. Remember, though, that the risk level must still comply with the portfolio objective, so it should change only within limits.

To summarize, the good news may be that portfolio (and mutual fund) betas are relatively stable. Analysts can use them with some degree of confidence. Be wary of security beta estimates, however.

Academics and practitioners alike seem doubtful as to the value of beta as a risk measure. In a shocking confession, an article by Eugene Fama and Kenneth French states that beta is nearly worthless as an explanation of a stock's relative performance over time. They suggest that strategies based on investing in stocks with low price-to-book ratios and small-capitalization firms produce better long-term performance than

---

[12]For a more complete discussion, see Fischer Black, Michael C. Jensen, and Myron Scholes, "The Capital Asset Pricing Model: Some Empirical Tests," in Michael C. Jensen, ed. *Studies in the Theory of Capital Markets* (New York:Praeger Publishers, 1972).

[13]Marshall Blume, "On the Assessment of Risk," *Journal of Finance* (March 1971), pp. 1–10.

Exhibit 18.14 ✦ CORRELATION OF BETA ESTIMATES FROM ONE TIME PERIOD TO A SUBSEQUENT PERIOD

Number of Securities in Portfolio	Correlation Coefficient[a]	R^{2}[b]
1	0.60	0.36
2	0.73	0.53
4	0.84	0.71
7	0.88	0.77
10	0.92	0.85
20	0.97	0.95
35	0.97	0.95
50	0.98	0.96

[a]The correlation coefficient (CORR) ranges from −1.0 to +1.0 where +1.0 is a perfect correlation in which one variable (past beta) can perfectly predict the other (future beta).

[b]R^2 is the correlation coefficent squared. It has the same interpretation as the correlation but is limited to a range from 0.0 to +1.0.

Source: Marshall Blume, "One the Assessment of Risk" *Journal of Finance* (March 1971), pp. 1–10.

strategies based on beta.[14] The favored strategies basically look for firms selling cheaply compared with the book values of their assets, while avoiding those that sell far above their asset values. Also, firms with smaller market values appear to outperform firms with larger market values.

These findings reduce the analytical value of beta to the point that some favor ignoring it, as discussed in the first Investment Insight feature. In the Investment Insights box on page 539, "Beta is Dead", Mark Hulbert, who follows investments newsletters, almost gleefully announces that "Beta Is Dead." He points out that beta is no longer regarded as sacred, allowing securities analysts to consider other strategies. Hulbert's work is to rank investment strategies; he believes that this task has become more important with the loss of beta.

Although there is merit to ranking performance, Hulbert must be careful not to mislead investors. To say that beta is dead, making his task all the more important, may seem biased. In fact, we must be careful with analysts who dismiss beta too quickly. It still serves a purpose of quantifying risk. Moreover, it is important to remember that ranking past performance provides some information, but what worked during the 1990s may not work in the 2000s. In Chapter 20, we discuss whether a money manager's past performance can predict future performance.

In response to Hulbert, another practitioner, Peter Bernstein, wrote an article, which appears in the second Investment Insights feature on page 540, "If Beta is Dead, Where is the Corpse?". Bernstein cautions readers against totally dismissing beta. He summarizes the implications of Fama and French's study and writes that even if beta may be pronounced dead, it does not invalidate the importance of the risk/return relationship. As we have also emphasized, investors are smart enough to accept riskier investments only in exchange for compensation in the form of higher

---

[14]Eugene Fama and Kenneth French, "The Cross-Section of Expected Stock Returns," *Journal of Finance* (June 1992), pp. 427–446.

INVESTMENT INSIGHTS

BETA IS DEAD

Capital Ideas (Free Press, $24.95), by Peter Bernstein, the founder and first editor of the *Journal of Portfolio Management,* is a fine book and should be read by anyone wanting to understand modern Wall Street. Unfortunately for the book, almost as soon as it came out, the investment theory it highlights became discredited.

The book tells how the capital assets pricing model got its modest beginnings among a few upstart professors, took the rest of academia by storm, won Nobel Prizes for several economists, and in the process became standard operating procedure for institutional investors.

Bernstein's book was in bookstores only a few weeks when a revolutionary study was published by one of the heroes of Bernstein's story, University of Chicago Professor Eugene Fama. Fama and coauthor Professor Kenneth French discovered that beta, a central analytical tool of the capital asset pricing model, is worthless as an explanation of stocks' relative performance over time.

Beta is a scoring system that rates individual stocks according to their volatility. The theory holds that the only way you can beat the market is by buying high-beta stocks—which also means you take a lot of risk. Despite several decades of confident academic assertions to the contrary, Professors Fama and French found that high-beta stocks don't do any better than low-beta stocks.

So far, other than an article by fellow columnist David Dreman (*Forbes,* Mar. 30, 1992), the reaction to Fama and French's study has been remarkably muted, but it means that the foundation of much of Wall Street's research has been yanked away. It leaves finance departments and business schools with the unsavory prospect of teaching theories to their students and then having to concede that those theories are wrong.

All this is reassuring for the individual investor, however. Despite the theoretical anarchy in academia and the cries of anguish from computer jocks whose programs are now pointless, beta's death gives the investor new hope. No longer can market-beating strategies be dismissed on the grounds that they must have incurred above-market risks. No longer can promising approaches be ignored because they don't conform to theoretical orthodoxy.

One of the best illustrations of this need for theoretical humility is the diversity of approaches pursued by the four investment letters that have beaten the market since 1980, when the *Hulbert Financial Digest* began tracking the industry's performance. Not only are their approaches theoretically distinct, some actually contradict each other. But in a world that recognizes more than one road to riches, this need not pose a problem.

For example, in first place since 1980 is Dan Sullivan's *The Chartist,* which utilizes only technical analysis. In second place is the *Value Line Investment Survey,* whose famed ranking system focuses on several different factors, such as price and earnings momentum. In third place is Martin Zweig's *The Zweig Forecast,* which uses a wide variety of technical, fundamental, and monetary indicators. And in fourth place is another Value Line service—*OTC Special Situations Survey,* which utilizes strictly fundamental valuation criteria.

That's pretty interesting, isn't it? Each of the four leading services uses an approach significantly different from the other three.

Or consider the outstanding performance of a newer letter. Editor Louis Navellier was trained in the intricacies of modern portfolio theory, and reportedly stopped short of completing his Ph.D. thesis only because he was impatient to begin applying his academic research to the investment world.

Navellier's success suggests that, even if beta is dead, the trip from gown to town is still worth making. Focusing on over-the-counter stocks, he has achieved a 37 percent compound annual return since the beginning of 1985 (when *HFD* began monitoring his performance), more than doubling the market's annualized total return over the same period. Navellier isn't surprised by Fama's findings. He tells me that his own research found no more than about a 30 percent correlation between a stock's performance and its beta.

How can we make sense of all this? One finance professor remarks that, in the wake of the Fama/French study, his profession today is where Newtonian physics was prior to Einstein: waiting and searching for a theory that makes sense of the markets, recognizing that previous explanations are woefully inadequate.

As a monitor of investment letter performance, perhaps I'm biased, but I believe advisory letters have a valuable role to play. Innovation comes more easily to letter editors than to institutions. And the lesson of Bernstein's book and Fama's research is the need for innovation and keeping an open mind.

Most of the myriad letters out there won't beat the market. That's why it is so crucial to monitor their performance rigorously and objectively, so that we can discover those methods that genuinely have promise. But we're all better off because so many of them are willing to try.

Source: Mark Hulbert, "Beta Is Dead," Forbes, June 22, 1992, p. 239. Reprinted by permission of Forbes Magazine © Forbes Inc., 1992.

INVESTMENT INSIGHTS

IF BETA IS DEAD, WHERE IS THE CORPSE?

After Mark Hulbert's high compliment to my book, *Capital Ideas,* I hope I do not appear ungrateful if I take issue with his conclusions. He invokes the study by Professors Fama and French to assert that "beta's death gives the investor new hope. . . . No longer can market-beating strategies be dismissed on the grounds that they must have incurred above-market risks."

With all due respect, I think Mr. Hulbert may be reading more into the Fama–French study than is there.

The essential message of Fama–French is that long-term average returns are inversely correlated with price/book ratios and the size of a stock's market capitalization. In other words, small stocks do better than big ones, and stocks that sell cheaply relative to book value do better than those that sell at large premiums to book. As these two factors appear to dominate long-run performance, a stock's volatility relative to the market—its beta—loses its significance as a predictor of returns. As beta is often considered the most useful gauge of a stock's riskiness, the traditional linkage between risk and expected return appears to have crumbled. Hence, Mark Hulbert's good cheer.

Yet Fama–French cannot have sundered the relationship between risk and return unless we make the dangerous assumption that all investors are off their trolleys. Investors are not likely to take risks unless they expect returns above what they could expect on riskless

investments. You do not drill for oil if all you can hope for is what a Treasury bill would provide. This requirement for higher returns from riskier investments pervades all investment decisions.

Consequently, investors tend to price riskier assets so that those assets will provide the higher returns demanded. In the long run and on the average, wildcat oil drillers earn more than investors in Treasury bills. When they do not, drilling dries up.

From this follows a second consequence. Predicting return is tough. But if return is related to risk, and if we can somehow measure risk, then risk will give us a guide to the probable rate of return! That upside-down use of the risk–return trade-off is what lent beta its attraction. Fama–French's demonstration that beta is a poor predictor of return is the source of Mr. Hulbert's cry of joy.

Yet beta has been moribund for some time as a predictor of returns, as many types of multifactor models have supplemented the single influence of the market on asset valuation. In addition, the current popularity of small-cap investing and of "value" strategies indicates that the professors were by no means the first to find an interesting road to the mother lode.

Thus, Mr. Hulbert neglects two elements of the Fama–French study. First, there is nothing in the Fama–French story to suggest that risk and return are unrelated. Fama and French focus on expected returns. The issue of whether small-cap and value stocks have outperformed because they are *riskier* than

large companies and growth companies remains unresolved. This anomaly has haunted the Capital Asset Pricing Model, which is based on beta, for many years. But we do know that small companies are riskier than large companies. We also know that stocks do not sell at low prices relative to their assets if a company is prospering and growing. Although quantifying these risks is an elusive task, the Fama–French findings merely suggest that we do not yet have a good handle on calibrating risk.

Second, the implication that small-cap stocks and value stocks will *systematically* outperform after adjustment for risk flies in the face of common sense. The opposite conviction, that large-cap growth stocks would always outperform the market, led many prominent investment managers into Disasterville in the crash of 1974. These notions violate the one overriding lesson of investment theory: Do not put all your eggs in one basket. Tilting in one direction may be acceptable; abandoning diversification is perilous.

Investment is still a process of reading decisions under conditions of uncertainty. Risk is still the dominant consideration for investors. The stock market is still a volatile arena that does not feature free lunches. You makes your choice, but never forget that you pays your money for doing so. There is nothing in Fama and French to contradict any of these truths or to overcome the nastiest truth of them all—that past performance, no matter how impressive, is no guarantee of future returns.

Source: Peter L. Bernstein, "If Beta Is Dead, Where Is the Corpse," Forbes, *July 20, 1992, p. 343. Reprinted by permission of Forbes Magazine © Forbes Inc., 1992.*

returns. (We have called it a *risk premium*.) Based on this premise, Bernstein notes that small-capitalization stocks are riskier, so their stock returns must be higher. Also, stocks of firms with low price-to-book ratios would not sell cheaply if these companies were "prospering and growing"; this suggests that these firms, too, are unusually risky investments.[15] Because risk is an important factor in making investment decisions, even without a perfect measure of risk, one must incorporate some kind of risk measure to allow for these risk/return differences.

As Bernstein says, no one should despair just because beta was found to be less than perfect. It is still helpful in objectively quantifying risk and in recognizing a positive relationship between risk and return. Beta is still used by practitioners and academics alike. Recent developments have pointed out weaknesses, but they have not invalidated the concept that higher risk implies a higher required return. Finally, understanding how risk measures are developed is helpful in discovering an underlying meaning of risk.

The next chapter expands on the CAPM and relaxes some of its assumptions to determine a more general risk/return relationship. Chapter 19 also examines some empirical studies of the CAPM and shortfalls of the studies, and it develops another measure of the risk/return relationship using arbitrage as its driving force.

Implications for Investors

This chapter has developed a risk/return relationship for stocks, Capital Asset Pricing Model (CAPM), which enables investors to quantify risk for a stock and hence to compare the value of a stock to its risk level. We already know that a riskier stock should have a higher required return. Using the CAPM, we conducted fundamental analysis using the required return versus the predicted return. Even though stock betas are relatively unstable, studies have found portfolio betas to be relatively stable over time.

Even if beta measure of risk has its problems, investors recognize that risk must be accounted for when evaluating stocks, and although not perfect, beta is a start. The bottom line is to use beta wisely, knowing it has several problems.

Chapter Summary

1. What is the CML?
   By making a few assumptions about rational investors and capital markets and adding the risk-free asset, we can determine that all investors will choose M as their risky portfolio. The line that starts at the risk-free rate, RF, and extends to M is called the capital market line (CML). It is also called the *lending–borrowing line* because it distinguishes investors that lend and borrow at the risk-free rate, RF.
2. How is the CAPM developed?
   Because all investors will invest in the same risky portfolio, M, we can show that each security risk should be measured by its contribution to the risk of the well-diversified portfolio M. The relative risk contribution of security i to portfolio M is defined by beta, β_i. This allows us to develop a model in which a security's required return, ER_i, equals $RF + \beta_i(ER_M - RF)$.

[15]We discussed this point back in Chapter 14 when we explained the role of the price-to-book ratio in security analysis.

3. What are the differences between the standard deviation and beta risk measures?
   We can now decompose the standard deviation, or total security risk, into two components:(1) systematic or beta risk, and (2) firm-specific or diversifiable risk. Because we assume that all investors hold well-diversified portfolios based on M, we can assume that they eliminate all diversifiable risk. Therefore, the only risk to consider for investment purposes should be the systematic risk.

4. How can an investor apply the CAPM to security analysis?
   First, calculate a security's required return via the CAPM. This is the return that a security should earn, given its beta. Next, calculate the predicted holding period return, PR_i and compare it with the required return estimated from the CAPM, ER_i. If $PR_i > ER_i$, the security is undervalued; if $PR_i < ER_i$, the security is overvalued.

5. How do analysts estimate beta?
   Beta is estimated by a regression estimation process called the ordinary least squares method. The independent variable is the return on a proxy for the market portfolio (usually the S&P 500 Index): the dependent variable is the security's return. The slope of the resulting regression line equals beta.

6. What is the good news and bad news about beta?
   Research has found two items of bad news about beta. Security beta estimates have low explanatory power, and the predictability of a future beta is poor. In fact, some academics and practitioners believe that beta has all but lost its usefulness. The good news is that portfolio beta estimates are relatively reliable predictors of future portfolio betas; for a portfolio of approximately 20 stocks, beta's predictability is approximately 90 percent or better. These news flashes imply that, even if beta's power over the investment community has waned, some risk measure is still necessary to make good investment decisions.

Mini Case 1

This case uses the SML for security analysis. An assistant has compiled the following data from various sources.

Security Name	Today's Price, $P_{i,t}$	Predicted Price After One Year, $P_{i,t+1}$	Expected Dividends $DIV_{i,t+1}$	Risk Measure Beta, β_i
Cisco Systems (CSCO)	$127.50	$153	0	1.50
Hewlett-Packard (HP)	$129.375	$153	1.00	1.30
IBM (IBM)	$115.625	$125	$0.55	1.10

1. What required return does the CAPM give for each security, assuming that the market risk premium equals 0.086 and the US T-bill yield equals 0.05?
2. Graph the SML and place each of the three securities along it.
3. Find the predicted holding period return, PR_i, for each security.
4. Which stocks are overvalued or undervalued? Display the results on the graph from question 2.
5. What will happen to CSCO's price? At what price will it be in equilibrium?
6. What will happen to IBM's price? What is its equilibrium price?

Mini Case 2

In this case you will estimate betas and interpret the market model regression. The 60 monthly returns for 3 stocks, CSCO, HP, and IBM, are available on the data disk.

Open Stock Returns workbook, and using software such as Excel, run a market model regression. Answer the following questions.

1. The market model is

$$R_{i,t} = \alpha_i + \beta_i R_{M,t} + e_{i,t}$$

What are the beta estimates for CSCO, HP, and IBM?
2. Interpret the R^2 values. How do they relate to the correlation coefficient, $CORR(i,M)$?
3. What is the total risk for each security?
4. What can we say about each security's systematic and diversifiable risks?

Review Questions and Problems

1. How do assumptions 1 through 5 help to develop the CAPM? Which assumptions are necessary and which just simplify the model?
2. You choose a risky portfolio, P3, with an expected return of 0.12 and a standard deviation of 0.15. The risk-free rate, RF, equals 0.05. You want to invest 20 percent in RF and 80 percent in P3.
   a. What is the RF - P3 portfolio's expected return?
   b. What is the portfolio's standard deviation?
   c. Draw the CML for portfolio P3.
3. What is the significance of introducing the risk-free asset to the investment opportunity set?
   a. What theorem results from introducing the risk-free asset and what is the significance of the theorem?
   b. What line results from the introduction of the risk-free asset?
   c. What is the significance of portfolio M in the line defined in b?
4. What two types of risk make up the standard deviation of a security return?
   a. Discuss the two types of risk.
   b. Why is only one relevant in the CAPM?
5. You expect UAL (United Airlines) to hit $75 per share with zero expected dividends this year. Its current price is $55.375, and your research sets UAL's beta at 1.25. The market risk premium is 0.086, with Treasury bills yielding 0.06. Is UAL a good investment? Conduct a security analysis using the CAPM and explain your answer.
6. American Airlines (AMR) is expected to hit $95 per share with zero expected dividends this year. Its current price is $88.5, and your research sets AMR's beta at 1.35. The market risk premium is 0.086, with Treasury bills yielding 0.06. Is AMR a good investment? Conduct a security analysis using the CAPM and explain your answer.
7. Display American Airlines' required and predicted returns on a SML graph, include the risk-free asset and the market portfolio on the SML line.
8. Delta Airlines (DAL) is expected to hit $87 per share with $0.20 expected dividends this year. Its current price is $77.5, and your research sets DAL's beta at 1.45. The market risk premium is 0.086, with Treasury bills yielding 0.06. Is DAL a good investment? Conduct a security analysis using the CAPM and explain your answer.
9. Display Delta Airlines required and predicted returns on the SML graph, include the risk-free asset and the market portfolio on the SML line.
10. The correlation coefficient of GM with the market portfolio is +0.80, SD_{GM} is 45 percent, and SD_M is 40 percent. The correlation between Pepsi and the market portfolio is +0.50 and SD_{PEP} is 72 percent.
    a. Calculate separate betas for GM and Pepsi.
    b. Compare the two and explain the results.

c. What factors affect betas, and what can we conclude about how they affect GM and Pepsi's betas?

11. The correlation coefficient of GE with the market portfolio is +0.65, SD_{GE} is 20 percent, and SD_M is 50 percent. The correlation between AT&T and the market is +0.45, and $SD_{AT\&T}$ is +0.60.

    a. Calculate separate betas for GE and AT&T.

    b. Suppose someone says, "Just looking at the correlation, you can tell that GE has a higher beta." Agree or disagree. Explain the differences.

12. You are given the following information about two mutual funds, A and B:

Fund	Current Price	Expected Price	Expected Dividend	Estimated Beta
A	$53.50	$60.00	$2.00	1.10
B	76.75	82.00	1.00	0.80

$(ER_M - RF) = 0.086$ and $RF = 0.02$

    a. Estimate the required returns using the CAPM.

    b. Graph the CAPM's required returns for the market portfolio, the risk-free asset, and the two funds.

    c. Represent the predicted returns on the graph with Xs. Is either fund overvalued or undervalued?

    d. At what current price would the two funds be at equilibrium?

13. You are given information about two stocks below.

Stock	Current Price	Expected Price	Expected Dividend	Estimated Beta
X	$40.50	$53.00	$1.50	1.20
Y	62.75	78.00	0.80	2.20

$(ER_M - RF) = 0.07$ and $RF = 0.03$

    a. Estimate the required returns using the CAPM.

    b. Graph the CAPM's required returns for the market portfolio, the risk-free asset, and the two funds.

    c. Represent the predicted returns on the graph with Xs. Is either fund overvalued or undervalued?

    d. At what current price would the two funds be at equilibrium?

14. You are given information about two stocks below.

Stock	Current Price	Expected Price	Expected Dividend	Estimated Beta
W	$22.50	$26.00	$0.00	1.30
Z	35.00	46.00	0.00	1.50

$(ER_M - RF) = 0.06$ and $RF = 0.04$

    a. Estimate the required returns using the CAPM.

    b. Graph the CAPM's required returns for the market portfolio, the risk-free asset, and the two funds.

    c. Represent the predicted returns on the graph with Xs. Is either fund overvalued or undervalued?

    d. At what current price would the two funds be at equilibrium?

15. You expect stock of firm C to sell for $100 a year from now and to pay a $5 dividend during the year. If the stock's correlation coefficient with portfolio M is +0.40, SD_C = 50 percent, SD_M = 30 percent, RF = 6 percent, and ER_M = 15 percent, at what price should the stock sell today? Explain your results.

16. Firm G's stock is currently trading at $65 and is expected to rise to $80 in a year and expects to pay dividends of $4 during the year. If the stock's correlation coefficient with the market portfolio equals -0.25, SD_G is 0.30, SD_M is 0.40, RF is 0.03, and ER_M equals 0.18, what is the predicted return and the CAPM required return for this stock? Should you invest in firm G's stock? Explain.

17. What is the intrinsic value for firm G from problem 16?
    a. Conduct fundamental analysis and determine whether it is overvalued or undervalued.
    b. Compare results with those found in problem 16.
    c. How are the two methods analogous? Explain.

18. You are interested in estimating IBM's beta. IBM's correlation with the Dow Jones Industrial Average is $+0.85$, and SD_{IBM} equals 40 percent; SD_{DJ} is 20 percent. You also decide to look into the Wilshire 5,000 stock index as a proxy for the market portfolio. SD_W is 25 percent, and its correlation with IBM is $+0.20$.
    a. Calculate IBM's beta with the Dow.
    b. Calculate IBM's beta with the Wilshire 5,000.
    c. Under what conditions would you use the Dow versus the Wilshire index?

19. The Dow's expected return is 30 percent, and Treasury bills are yielding 10 percent. Suppose the expected return of the Wilshire 5,000 is 40 percent. Using the data given here and in question 18, answer the following questions:
    a. Draw an SML with the Dow as the market portfolio.
    b. Draw an SML with the Wilshire 5,000 as the market portfolio on the same graph.
    c. What is the drawback of using the wrong market index?

20. Microsoft's correlation with the Dow (DJIA) equals $+0.55$, whereas its correlation with the Wilshire 5,000 Index is $+0.65$. Microsoft's SD equals 0.60, SD_{DJIA} is 0.20 and the Wilshire SD equals 0.30.
    a. Calculate Microsoft's beta with DJIA.
    b. Calculate Microsoft's beta with the Wilshire 5,000 Index.
    c. Under what condition would you use the beta calculated with the DJIA versus Wilshire 5,000 Index?

21. Suppose the DJIA's expected return equals 18 percent, the U.S. Treasury bill is expected to yield 3 percent, and the Wilshire 5,000 Index's expected return is 20 percent.
    a. Calculate Microsoft's required return using the DJIA and information from problem 20.
    b. Calculate Microsoft's required return using the Wilshire 5,000 Index and information from problem 20.
    c. Suppose Microsoft trades at $184 today and is expected to increase to $169 in one year. Microsoft pays no dividends. What is Microsoft's predicted return?
    d. Conduct security analysis with each market index above.
    e. Discuss possible problems when the wrong index is used.

22. Graph the two SMLs for Microsoft and the predicted return.

23. A security's standard deviation equals 20 percent, and its market model results are summarized below:

$$R_{i,t} = 0.03 + 1.32R_{M,t} + e_{i,t} \quad R^2 = 0.35$$

    a. What is the correlation coefficient between security i and the market portfolio?
    b. What is the security's beta?
    c. What are its systematic and diversifiable risks?

24. Suppose stock J has a total risk of 0.40 and a correlation with the market of $+0.25$. Stock K has a total risk of 0.50 and a correlation with the market of $+0.85$.
    a. What are stock J's systematic and diversifiable risks?

    b.   What are stock K's systematic and diversifiable risks?

    c.   Your client thinks that stock J is less risky and wants to invest in J instead of K along with her diversified mutual fund. What would be your advice to her?

25. Firm XYZ, which invests in precious metals, has a beta of −0.54. What does it mean to have a negative beta? What are its benefits?

26. The following data for McDonald's (MAC), Waste Management (WM), and Abbott Labs (ABT) were compiled for your information:

Stock	Expected Return	Standard Deviation	Systematic Risk	Diversifiable Risk
MAC	0.10	0.122	0.068	0.054
WM	0.20	0.200	−0.005	0.205
ABT	0.05	0.080	0.075	0.005

Correlation coefficients: $CORR(MAC,WM) = -0.60$
$CORR(MAC,ABT) = 0.25$
$CORR(WM,ABT) = 0.05$

    a.   If a client wants to invest equal proportions in only two securities, which two would you recommend? Answer the question without performing any calculations, but based simply on your knowledge about portfolio theory. Explain in words.

    b.   Suppose your client already holds a well-diversified portfolio such as the S&P 500 Index. Which stock would you recommend? Why?

    c.   Your client says that WM is far too risky with a standard deviation of 0.20, especially compared with the other two firms' standard deviations of 0.12 and 0.08. How would you address his concern? Carefully explain, assuming that your client holds a well-diversified portfolio.

27. The following information has been compiled on United Airlines (UAL), Disney (DIS), and Johnson & Johnson (JNJ).

Stock	Expected Return	Standard Deviation	Systematic Risk	Diversifiable Risk
UAL	0.25	0.30	0.20	0.10
DIS	0.15	0.20	0.15	0.05
JNJ	0.30	0.26	−0.02	0.28

Correlation coefficients: $CORR(UAL,DIS) = +0.85$
$CORR(UAL,JNJ) = +0.05$
$CORR(DIS,JNJ) = -0.10$

    a.   Display the three securities on a total risk/return graph.

    b.   If a client wants to invest equal proportions in only two securities, which two would you recommend? Answer the question without performing any calculations, but based simply on your knowledge of portfolio theory. Explain in words.

    c.   Suppose your client already holds a well-diversified portfolio such as the S&P 500 Index. Which stock would you recommend? Why?

    d.   Your client says that JNJ is far too risky with a standard deviation of 0.26, especially compared with Disney's standard deviation of 0.15. How would you address his concern? Carefully explain, assuming that your client holds a well-diversified portfolio.

28. What are the differences between the CML and the SML?

29. What are the differences between SML and the security characteristic line?

✦ CAPITAL ALLOCATION LINE

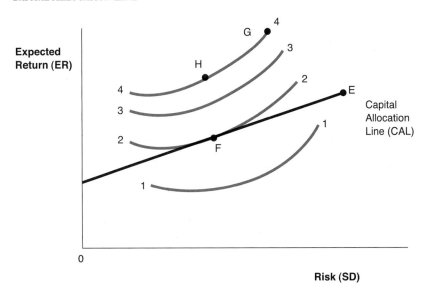

CFA QUESTIONS

(Level 1, 1993) Use the above graph to answer questions 1 and 2.
Expected Return (ER)
Risk (SD)
The Capital Market Line (CML) is also referred to as the Capital Allocation Line (CAL).

1. Which indifference curve represents the greatest level of utility that can be achieved by the investor?
   a. 1
   b. 2
   c. 3
   d. 4
2. Which point designates the optimal portfolio of risky assets?
   a. E
   b. F
   c. G
   d. H
3. (Level 1, 1993) Which one of the following portfolios cannot lie on the efficient frontier as described by Markowitz?

	Portfolio	Expected Return	Standard Deviation
a.	W	9%	21%
b.	X	5	7
c.	Y	15	36
d.	Z	12	15

4. (Level 1, 1993) Portfolio theory as described by Markowitz is most concerned with
   a. the elimination of systematic risk.
   b. the effect of diversification on portfolio risk.

✦ RISK AND RETURN

    c.   the identification of unsystematic risk.

    d.   active portfolio management to enhance return.

5.   (Level 1, 1993) Capital asset pricing theory asserts that portfolio returns are best explained by

    a.   economic factors.

    b.   specific risk.

    c.   systematic risk.

    d.   diversification.

6.   (Level 1, 1988) John Pixel, CFA, has constructed an efficient frontier, shown above, to help him manage his stock portfolio. Pixel's portfolio is indicated by the point P above. Without lending or borrowing, Pixel could change his portfolio and

    a.   both increase returns and reduce risk.

    b.   increase returns.

    c.   reduce risk.

    d.   neither increase returns nor reduce risk.

CRITICAL THINKING EXERCISE

1.   Open the Stock Returns worksheet in the data workbook. The file contains 60 monthly returns for AHP and the S&P 500 Index . Use the LINEST command in Excel and run a regression equation (Equation 18.17) using AHP return as the dependent variable (Y) and the S&P 500 as the independent variable (X). Equation 18.17 is

$$R_{i,t} = \alpha_i + \beta_i R_{M,t} + e_{i,t} \qquad (18.17)$$

The Excel command is

    =LINEST(y variable array, x variable array, TRUE,TRUE). The results for the y-intercept equals α and the slope equals β. How does it compare to results on page 533? Discuss.

2.   Open the Stock Price worksheet in the data workbook. The file contains monthly returns for stocks along with a market index. It also contains Value Line estimates of the current prices, P_t, for the stock, expected earnings per share, EPS_{t+1}, expected dividends per share, DIV_{t+1}, and expected P/E ratios a year from today. Use the data and a spreadsheet program to answer the following questions:

    a.   Using the market model, estimate betas for the 10 stocks.

    b.   If Treasury bills are yielding 0.04 and the market risk premium equals 0.086, estimate the required return for each stock using the CAPM.

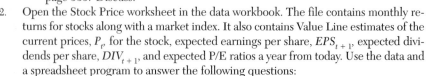

c. Each stock's predicted price, $P_{i,t+1}$, can be calculated by using Equation 8.15 or

$$EPS_{i,t+1} \times P/E_{i,t+1}$$

   using the *EPS* and P/E estimates provided in the far right column of Value Line. Calculate each stock's predicted holding period return for the coming year.
d. Determine which stocks seem overvalued or undervalued. Explain.
e. Using the data provided and the required return calculated from part b, estimate each stock's intrinsic value using Chapter 8's dividend discount model.
f. Determine which stocks are currently overvalued or undervalued. Explain.
g. Show that the results of e and f are consistent and really the same analysis.

THE INTERNET INVESTOR

1. Go to an Internet site with stock prices and dividends and obtain daily and monthly prices and dividends paid for two stocks over a three-year period. Also obtain daily and monthly prices for the S&P 500 Index for the same time period.
    a. Calculate daily returns and monthly returns using the HPR equation for the two stocks and the S&P 500 Index.
    b. Using the LINEST function in Excel, run a market model regression for each stock using the daily returns.
    c. Repeat part b using monthly returns.
    d. Compare the beta estimates for each stock based on monthly and daily returns. What conclusions can you draw from the results?
2. Find an Internet site with net asset values (or prices) for mutual funds. Obtain monthly prices over a five-year period for a mutual fund and the S&P 500 Index.
    a. Calculate monthly returns using the HPR equation for the mutual fund and the S&P 500 Index.
    b. Using the LINEST function in Excel run a market model regression for the mutual fund.
    c. Is the beta risk for the mutual fund close to 1.0? Explain theoretically whether it should be close to 1.0 or not. If it isn't, provide explanation as to why it may not be close to 1.0. (For example, examine the composition of the mutual fund).

EXTENSION OF CAPITAL ASSET PRICING THEORY[1]

PREVIOUSLY . . .

We developed the Capital Asset Pricing Model (CAPM) and its application to security analysis. We presented several views regarding the status of the CAPM, many of which indicated that the CAPM and its beta risk measure was far from perfect.

IN THIS CHAPTER . . .

We examine extensions of the CAPM and several empirical tests of the CAPM including Roll's critique of the CAPM empirical tests. Generally, we conclude that we must use the CAPM and its beta risk with care. This chapter also introduces the arbitrage pricing theory (APT), which is another way to view risk and return. Unfortunately, APT also has its drawbacks in application.

TO COME . . .

Next, we build on portfolio theory and the CAPM developed in Chapters 17 and 18 and develop ways to measure portfolio performance. These performance measures are applied to mutual funds and allow investors to choose the "best" performing mutual fund for their investment.

Chapter Objectives

1. What is the zero-beta portfolio model?
2. What are some results of empirical tests of the Capital Asset Pricing Model?
3. What is Roll's critique of the Capital Asset Pricing Model?
4. What is the arbitrage pricing theory?

We spent quite a bit of time and energy developing the Capital Asset Pricing Model (CAPM) in Chapter 18. The final results can be summarized as follows:

1. Securities are priced in relation to their beta risk levels because all rational investors hold well-diversified portfolios equivalent to the market portfolio.
2. A security's total risk (standard deviation) is composed of two types of risk: beta risk and diversifiable risk.
3. Beta is estimated by a market regression model.

---

[1]This chapter covers advanced material and can be omitted without loss of continuity.

4. Beta estimates can accurately predict future portfolio betas but not individual securities' betas.

In this chapter, we turn to several other issues that can be viewed as extensions, or empirical tests, of the CAPM. Three issues are discussed, grouped under three topics: modifications of the CAPM, empirical tests and critiques of the CAPM, and arbitrage pricing theory (APT).

The first section deals with practical modifications to the CAPM. Recall that Chapter 18 required several restrictive assumptions to derive the CAPM. We discuss the Black's zero-beta model, which drops one particular assumption: that investors can borrow and lend at the risk-free rate.[2] This less restrictive model seems to produce results that conform more closely than those of the CAPM to empirical market performance.

This leads to a discussion of empirical tests of the CAPM and the more robust zero-beta model, followed by a critique of the CAPM. This section outlines the steps required to conduct the empirical tests to develop a clear idea of the procedures adopted by researchers and some appreciation of their tremendous efforts.

In Chapter 18 we discussed some problems with the CAPM; the second section continues that discussion with Roll's critique of the CAPM and its empirical tests.[3] Roll mathematically proves that the CAPM cannot be empirically tested (despite all the tests that researchers have conducted). His critique provides some insights on what researchers can test and what they have actually tested.

Finally, given the state of CAPM, the third section reviews Ross's alternative security pricing model called APT.[4] Ross uses the principle of arbitrage to develop a model with several factors and corresponding betas to price securities. The model's premise states that identical assets (assets of similar risk) must sell at identical prices. Stated differently, it says that each security return can give a price based on a linear combination of factors (or portfolios) that mimic that security's return. If the risk for the security and the linear combination of portfolios are equal, but the returns are not, the market will arbitrage the profits away to set identical prices for all identical assets. The last section of the chapter elaborates on the concept of APT.

Now, let's start with the zero-beta model, a modification of the CAPM.

Modifications of the CAPM

As you may have noted, some of the assumptions required for the CAPM, as stated in Chapter 18, are quite restrictive. One particularly unlikely assumption states that all investors can borrow or lend at the risk-free rate, RF. If investors cannot all borrow at the same risk-free rate, some may choose risky portfolios based on their risk/return preferences (utility curves). This returns asset pricing theory to square one; recall that introducing the risk-free rate separated the objective choice of all investors to invest

---

[2]Fischer Black, "Capital Market Equilibrium with Restricted Borrowing," *Journal of Business* (July 1972), pp. 444–55.

[3]Richard Roll, "A Critique of the Asset Pricing Theory's Tests," *Journal of Financial Economics* (June 1977), pp. 129–76.

[4]Stephen Ross, "Return, Risk, and Arbitrage," in *Risk and Return in Finance*, vol. 1, ed. I. Friend and J. Bicksler (New York: Ballinger, 1976).

in portfolio M from the subjective choices of percentages to invest in the risk-free asset and portfolio M.[5] A common rate at which investors can borrow or lend allows them to adjust these percentages to achieve their own preferred combinations of risk and return. Without the common rate, they must choose different risky portfolios to meet their individual needs.

To address this problem, Black suggests that each investor create a personal combination of the chosen risky portfolio, P, and a portfolio of stocks that is uncorrelated to portfolio P, as shown in Exhibit 19.1. The portfolio that is uncorrelated to P is called the **zero-beta portfolio.** The zero-beta portfolio consists of a combination of securities with a beta equal to zero or with a zero correlation to the chosen risky portfolio P. The expected return of the zero-beta portfolio, $ER[Z(P)]$, is calculated as the weighted average return of all the securities in the portfolio. Notice that each risky portfolio has a different zero-beta portfolio associated with it. For example, consider P_1 and P_2 in Exhibit 19.1. An investor who chooses risky portfolio P_1 will choose $Z(P_1)$ as the uncorrelated zero-beta portfolio with expected return $ER[Z(P_1)]$ and risk $SD[Z(P_1)]$. Notice that $Z(P_1)$ may differ from the risk-free rate. This is a result of dropping the assumption that investors can borrow and lend at the risk-free rate RF.

Black's model has three major implications:

1. Any combination of portfolios on the efficient frontier will also be on the efficient frontier.
2. Any efficient portfolio, such as P_1 or P_2 in Exhibit 19.1, will have associated with it a zero-beta portfolio. The expected return of this zero-beta portfolio is found by the intersection of a tangent line from P_1 or P_2 with the y axis; its standard deviation (SD) is found by drawing a horizontal line from the intersection to the efficient frontier.
3. The expected return of any security i can be expressed as a linear relationship of any two efficient portfolios, such as P_2 and P_1. The relationship is

$$ER_i = ER_{P1} + (ER_{P2} - ER_{P1}) \left[\frac{COV(i,P_2) - COV(P_1,P_2)}{SD^2(P_2) - COV(P_1,P_2)} \right] \qquad (19.1)$$

These implications are sufficient to derive the zero-beta model. To find a market equilibrium risk/return relationship, aggregate the efficient risky portfolio choices of all investors; this becomes the market portfolio. Because any combination of efficient portfolios is itself efficient, the market portfolio identified in this way must be efficient. Into Equation 19.1, substitute the market portfolio M for the risky portfolio P_2 and the market portfolio's zero-beta portfolio $Z(M)$ for P_1. Note also that $COV[M,Z(M)]$ equals 0.0 by definition. By rearranging terms, Equation 19.1 simplifies to

$$ER_i = ER[Z(M)] + \{ER_M - ER[Z(M)]\} \left[\frac{COV(i,M)}{SD_M^2} \right] \qquad (19.2)$$

Recognize that $COV(i,M)/SD_M^2$ is beta, β_i. This gives a revised expression of the risk/return relationship as

$$ER_i = ER[Z(M)] + \beta_i\{ER_M - ER[Z(M)]\} \qquad (19.3)$$

Exhibit 19.2 provides a graphic example of the zero-beta model described by Equation 19.3. Notice that the beta still equals 1.0 for the market portfolio; however,

---

[5]Go back to reread portfolio separation theorem in Chapter 18 for a quick refresher if you need to.

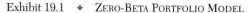

Exhibit 19.1 ✦ Zero-Beta Portfolio Model

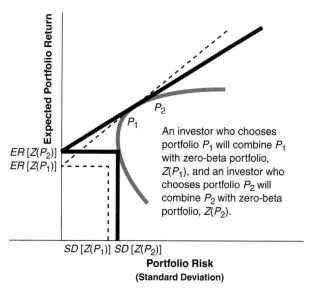

the y-intercept is equal to the expected return for the zero-beta portfolio, $ER[Z(M)]$, and the slope equals $ER_M - ER[Z(M)]$.

This is similar to the CAPM expressed in Equation 18.14. In fact, Equation 19.3 is simply a more general expression of the risk/return relationship.[6] If the CAPM truly defines the relationship between risk and return, empirically, the return on the zero-beta portfolio should equal RF. To determine whether $ER[Z(M)]$ equals RF, first define the market portfolio M, then mathematically solve for the associated zero-beta portfolio. For practitioners, this implies the possibility of a linear risk/return relationship, even if the y-intercept of the equation does not equal the risk-free rate. Simply identify a market index portfolio and mathematically solve for the return on the zero-beta portfolio, which need not equal RF.

In the next section, we outline the procedures by which researchers have empirically tested the CAPM. In that process, they have also tested the zero-beta model simply by determining whether $ER[Z(M)]$ equals RF. If not, a test would support the zero-beta model but not the CAPM.

Empirical Tests and Critique of the CAPM

Empirical Tests

Once a theory is developed, researchers test the model to determine how valid it is. To put it more scientifically, tests evaluate whether the hypothesis implied by the

---

[6]This is usually the case. Relaxing assumptions make a model more general, with the more restrictive model as a subset. Remember, this version of the asset pricing model no longer assumes that all investors can borrow or lend at the risk-free rate, RF.

Exhibit 19.2 ✦ RISK/RETURN RELATIONSHIP FOR ZERO-BETA PORTFOLIO MODEL

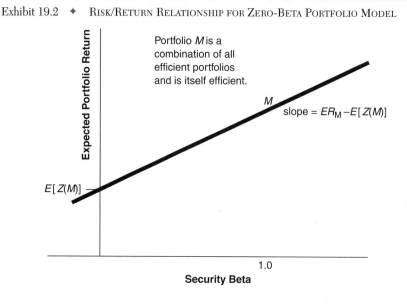

model can be refuted empirically. Before we discuss the procedure for testing the CAPM, let's talk about what is testable about the CAPM.

Unfortunately, along with its apparently unrealistic assumptions, any test of the CAPM must evaluate two implications jointly. That is, if the data contradict the theory, the problem could arise from either of the following two implications, or both:

1. The risk/return relationship is consistent with the data.
2. The market is efficient.

The first implication is straightforward; what about the second? Remember, one of the major requirements of CAPM is that the efficient market prices securities based on all information and that market equilibrium prevails. The second implication of the CAPM is important because empirical testing assumes that securities are at equilibrium; an empirical test cannot tell failure due to a deficient model from failure due to market disequilibrium. If empirical tests find evidence rejecting the CAPM, they could have three consequences: (1) reject the CAPM, (2) label the market inefficient, or (3) both.

Given the evidence provided in Chapter 7 on market efficiency, it may be safe to assume that the market is relatively efficient and proceed with empirical testing. This jump past market efficiency is possible because the testing will consider several hundred *randomly* selected securities, which should eliminate any systematic inefficiencies such as small-firm effects or low price/earnings ratio (P/E) effects.[7] Several

---

[7]Remember that small-firm or low P/E ratio effects can skew results only if securities are sorted by size or P/E.

researchers have conducted empirical tests of the CAPM.[8] The empirical studies have followed a similar series of basic steps. First, a typical test uses the market model in a regression of excess returns for a security i on the excess return for the market portfolio, $(R_{M,t} - RF_t)$ over a 60-month period (**Excess return** is defined as the difference between the risk-free rate and the return on security i or $(R_{i,t} - RF_t)$. This is often called the **first pass regression** because it is the first of two regressions in the CAPM empirical testing procedure. It estimates the beta for each security i. The test must run this regression individually for several hundred securities, with each **time series regression** equal to

$$(R_{i,t} - RF_t) = a_i + b_i(R_{M,t} - RF_t) + e_{i,t} \tag{19.4}$$

Recall from the discussion of the market model that a time series regression compares time-based data (for example, returns over 60 months) for a single variable (for example, $R_{i,t}$). To distinguish between estimated betas and theoretical betas, we use b_i for an estimated beta and β_i for the theoretical beta.

In the second step of a test of the CAPM, the estimated beta values, b_j, serve as independent variables for **cross-sectional regressions,** which regress securities' mean excess returns $M(R_{i,t} - RF_t)$ on their b_j values. This is called the **second pass regression** because it is the second set of regressions run to test the CAPM.

The cross-sectional regression equals

$$M(R_{i,t} - RF_t) = \gamma_0 + \gamma_1 b_i \quad i = 1, 2, 3, \ldots, N \tag{19.5}$$

where N equals the number of securities in the sample, $M(R_{i,t} - RF_t)$ is the mean of the security return minus the risk-free rate (Treasury bill rate) over the entire testing period; b_i is the estimated beta from the first pass regression; γ_0 is the y-intercept of the second pass regression; and γ_1 is the slope of b_i. This is a cross-sectional regression because the regression data consist of several hundred securities' returns regressed on their corresponding beta values, b_i.

We add a second independent variable, SD_e^2, which represents diversifiable or firm-specific risk, to determine whether this factor affects security returns. This gives the following regression:

$$M(R_{i,t} - RF_t) = \gamma_0 + \gamma_1 b_i + \gamma_2 SD_e^2 \tag{19.6}$$

The theoretical CAPM model in Chapter 18 is stated as

$$ER_i = RF + \beta_i(ER_M - RF) \tag{18.4}$$

This can be rewritten as

$$ER_i - RF = \beta_i(ER_M - RF)$$

excess return
Return over and above the required return estimated by the CAPM; actual return minus the CAPM return.

first pass regression
Time series regression used to estimate beta for a security and used for empirically testing the CAPM.

time series regression
Regression analysis using data for variables (stock return versus market index return) over time.

cross-sectional regression
Regression analysis using data at a given time for many stocks.

second pass regression
Method used to empirically test the CAPM, in which the beta estimate from a time series regression is imposed as an independent variable for a second cross-sectional regression.

---

[8]Two of the first empirical studies were J. Lintner, "Security Prices, Risk, and Maximal Gains from Diversification," *Journal of Finance* (December 1965), pp. 587–615; and M. H. Miller and M. Scholes, "Rate of Return in Relation to Risk: A Reexamination of Some Recent Findings," in *Studies in the Theory of Capital Markets*, ed. M. C. Jensen (New York: Praeger, 1972).

If the mean excess return for the security estimates the ex-ante expected excess return for the security, Equation 19.6 equals Equation 18.14. Therefore, if the CAPM correctly describes the risk/return relationship for securities,

$$\gamma_0 = 0 \quad \gamma_1 = (ER_M - RF) \quad \gamma_2 = 0$$

Unfortunately, the empirical results are far from satisfying. Lintner and Miller and Scholes all found that

1. γ_0 was statistically significantly different from zero.
2. γ_1 was statistically significantly less than the mean market portfolio excess return, or $M(R_{M,t} - RF)$.
3. γ_2 was statistically significantly different from zero.

This should not provoke despair, however. Black, Jensen, and Scholes suggested that the poor results could have stemmed from measurement errors for b_i values, which served as independent variables in the second pass regressions.[9] These authors reasoned that measurement errors in the b_i estimates caused biases in the second pass regression and hence reduced the power of the tests. They improved the empirical technique by evaluating security portfolios instead of individual securities in the second pass regressions. The researchers created a three-step procedure to reduce estimation errors and applied the new technique to data from 1931 to 1965.

Step 1.

Based on 60 months of return data (for example, from 1931 to 1935) for each security, estimate a security beta. If the sample includes 600 securities, rank the estimated 600 security betas in descending order. Divide these betas into 10 portfolios and identify the firms that belong in each portfolio.

Step 2.

Estimate betas for the 10 portfolios created in step 1. Conduct the regression on results for a different time period (for example, 1936 to 1940) so that the measurement errors for security betas are independent of any measurement errors in portfolio betas. This is the first pass regression described earlier. Estimating betas for portfolios reduces the variance of the error term or SD_e^2. Stated differently, portfolios are more highly correlated with the market portfolio than with individual securities.

Step 3.

Run the second pass regression on the 10 portfolios' excess returns, averaged over another time period (for example, 1941).

Exhibit 19.3 summarizes the results. Black, Jensen, and Scholes found that the theoretical CAPM relationship understated low betas and overstated high betas over the period from 1931 to 1965. The zero-beta model seemed to fit the data better than the CAPM did, although it failed to give consistent results. The researchers also found

---

[9] F. Black, M. C. Jensen, and M. Scholes, "The Capital Asset Pricing Model: Some Empirical Tests," in *Studies in the Theory of Capital Markets*, ed. M. C. Jensen (New York: Praeger, 1972).

Exhibit 19.3   ✦   EMPIRICAL FINDINGS FOR THE CAPM

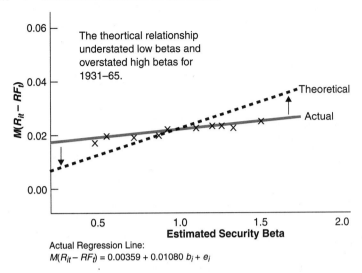

The theortical relationship understated low betas and overstated high betas for 1931–65.

Theoretical

Actual

Estimated Security Beta

Actual Regression Line:
$M(R_{it} - RF_t) = 0.00359 + 0.01080\, b_i + e_i$

Source: F. Black, M. C. Jensen, and M. Scholes, "The Capital Asset Pricing Model: Some Empirical Tests," Studies in the Theory of Capital Markets, *ed. M. C. Jensen (New York: Praeger, 1972).*

that the average zero-beta portfolio return is much greater than the risk-free rate. Undaunted by the poor findings, these authors continue to pursue the modified version of the CAPM, or the zero-beta model.

The major difficulty with this test of the CAPM is the use of ex-post data to evaluate ex-ante returns. Even if the test results are less than perfect, therefore, one could attribute the difference to the fact that historical data do not determine ex-ante results. For example, Black, Jensen, and Scholes split their second pass regression over several subperiods. They found that from April 1957 to December 1965, ex-post data gave a regression line with a slightly negative slope, as displayed in Exhibit 19.4. In reality, of course, a negative risk/return relationship is impossible. Would you invest in a security for which you expected a lower return for greater risk? In an efficient market, investors would sell those securities, forcing their prices to decline until the securities earned returns commensurate with their risk levels. This result emphasizes the fact that expectations (like the weather forecasts) may not match actual results.

We have reviewed some obvious problems revealed by empirical tests of the CAPM. The next section outlines even more damaging evidence from these kinds of empirical tests.

CRITIQUE OF THE CAPM

To add to the chorus of detractors, Richard Roll provides a critique of the CAPM and creates doubt about the value of empirical testing and results of CAPM.[10] His critique can be summarized in six premises.

---

[10]Richard Roll, "A Critique of the Asset Pricing Theory's Tests," *Journal of Financial Economics* (June 1977), pp. 129–76.

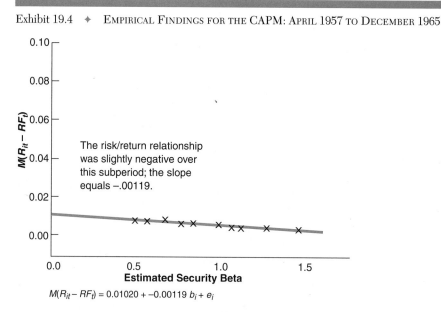

Exhibit 19.4   ✦   EMPIRICAL FINDINGS FOR THE CAPM: APRIL 1957 TO DECEMBER 1965

The risk/return relationship was slightly negative over this subperiod; the slope equals −.00119.

$$M(R_{it} - RF_t) = 0.01020 + {-0.00119}\, b_i + e_i$$

Source: F. Black, M. C. Jensen, and M. Scholes, "The Capital Asset Pricing Model: Some Empirical Tests," Studies in the Theory of Capital Markets, ed. M. C. Jensen (New York: Praeger, 1972).

1. **Limits on Tests.** The only testable implication from the CAPM is whether the market portfolio is mean-variance efficient (that is, whether it lies on the efficient frontier).

2. **Linear Risk/Return Relationship.** If the market portfolio is mean-variance efficient, mathematical relationships require that the beta risk/return relationship (graphed by the security market line, SML) is exactly linear. Once the market portfolio is established as efficient, the second pass regression adds nothing; the relationship must be linear. However, this creates further problems, outlined in the next three premises.

3. **Market Portfolio Composition.** The true composition of the market portfolio is unobservable, so it is impossible to test the first two premises accurately. Conceptually, the true market portfolio should consist of all traded assets, which includes common stocks, bonds, preferred stocks, real estate, art, and any other traded assets. Could professional baseball, basketball, and football players fall under the category of traded assets?

4. **Range of SMLs.** The vast market proxies offer an infinite number of ex-post mean-variance efficient portfolios, each with an SML that tracks an exact linear beta risk/return relationship. Essentially, every efficient portfolio has a different SML. Therefore, each security i has a different beta estimate, based on the efficient portfolio with which it is correlated. Using different sample portfolios as market proxies, even if they are mean-variance efficient, will produce different beta estimates for each security; these differences can be significant. Exhibit 19.5 displays individual SMLs for two different efficient portfolios, P_1 and P_2 (SML_{P1} and SML_{P2}).

5. **Market Efficiency Effects.** In a nutshell, Roll states that using a substitute, such as the Standard & Poor's (S&P) 500 Index, for the market portfolio creates two problems:

   a. Even if the proxy is mean-variance efficient, it does not accurately represent the true market portfolio.

   b. Even if the proxy is not efficient, the true market portfolio may still be efficient.

Exhibit 19.5 ✦ Different Well-Diversified Portfolios and Their
Corresponding SMLs

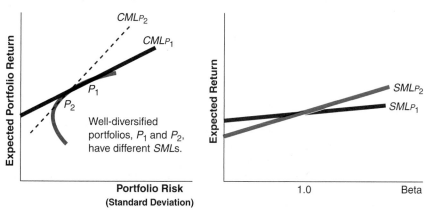

6. **Conflicts between Proxies.** Finally, more confusion may arise when different substitutes for the true market portfolio may be closely correlated, even though some may be efficient and others not. This difference leads to varying conclusions with regard to the beta risk/return relationship. Remember, efficient portfolios give perfectly linear beta risk/return relationships, whereas inefficient portfolios give linear estimates that fail to line up perfectly.

What can we conclude about the empirical test results presented earlier? The empirical tests confirmed only that their substitutes for the market portfolio were not mean-variance efficient. The researchers certainly did a lot of work, but they did not test the CAPM!

Roll convincingly showed that the CAPM is untestable, but this does not make it valueless. The general agreement is that the CAPM has its merits and should be used carefully. Although some controversy remains about its merits, many still regard it as a useful tool. It does provide a theoretical justification for the risk/return relationship, and it does describe a quantifiable measure of risk. Although the CAPM's beta requires cautious use, some will argue that having an inexact quantifiable risk measure is better than having none at all. Peter Bernstein's comments in the Chapter 18 Investment Insight box summarize the consensus; the CAPM is a useful framework in which to see how riskier investments provide higher returns.[11]

While Roll was adding to the demise of the CAPM, Stephen Ross was developing an alternative way to look at asset pricing. His work culminated in the APT, discussed in the following section.

Arbitrage Pricing Theory

Given the theoretical and empirical problems with the CAPM, some researchers have turned to alternative theories to explain asset pricing. Stephen Ross used the old idea

---

[11]The 2nd Investment Insight box reprints Peter Bernstein's article, "If Beta Is Dead, Where Is the Corpse?" in Chapter 18.

of arbitrage to develop another view of asset returns. The resulting *arbitrage pricing theory (APT)* is a way to price securities. Although its final equation seems an extension of the CAPM, its logical development is different. The CAPM stems from utility theory concepts of investor preference for risk and return, whereas APT is built on the principle of arbitrage.

CONCEPT OF ARBITRAGE

arbitrage principle
Process in which an investor buys the lower priced asset and sells the higher priced asset, both similar in risk, and captures the difference as arbitrage profits.

The general **arbitrage principle** states that two identical securities (or goods) should be bought and sold at identical prices. You might also say that if one invests nothing, one should get nothing in return.[12]

Although this sounds pretty straightforward, an example can help illustrate its application to securities. Remember the concept of selling short? Suppose one could borrow a stock with no margin requirements or transaction costs and sell it for $69. The proceeds of the sale could finance a purchase of the stock for $69. This would constitute a zero investment, and it would generate zero profits; for every dollar gained (or lost) in the long position, the investor would lose (or gain) the same amount in the short position. For instance, if the example stock were to rise to $70, the long position would make $1, but the short position would lose $1. This eliminates any possibility of profits from arbitrage. Investing nothing gains nothing.

Now, look at an example that offers arbitrage opportunities but still requires no investment. The theory holds that this situation will disappear quickly as arbitrageurs' trades drive prices toward equilibrium. Suppose that two stocks, A and B, have identical risk levels. If stock A is expected to earn 12 percent and stock B 10 percent, careful trading can create arbitrage profits. Because all investors perceive stocks A and B to have identical risk, an arbitrageur can sell short $100 of B and invest long $100 in A and receive a $2 in arbitrage profits:

	Today	One Year Later
Short position in B	$100	$100(1 + 0.10) = ($110)
Long position in A	($100)	$100(1 + 0.12) = $112
Investment	$ 0	Net profits = $2

Of course, if this is a sure thing, why stop with $100? Arbitrageurs will sell B and buy A to make unlimited profits while investing no money until the prices of stocks A and B reach equality.[13] This is a simple example of arbitrage; now, we discuss how the principle can suggest a model for security prices in the context of developing a single-factor APT.

SINGLE-FACTOR APT

single-factor APT model
Risk/return relationship in which one variable (or factor) is related to the stock return and is used to measure stock risk.

Let's formulate a **single-factor APT model** to describe how arbitrage operates. Suppose that ex-post returns, $R_{i,t}$, are generated according to some stochastic relationship described as

---

[12]This sounds similar to the old adage "nothing ventured, nothing gained" or the slogan from aerobics classes, "no pain, no gain."

[13]Other investors quickly catch onto a scheme like this, and their demand for the stock with the lower price drives prices toward equality. (Academics refer to this as *market equilibrium*.)

$$\tilde{R}_{i,t} = E_{0,t} + \beta_{i,t}\tilde{F}_{1,t} + \tilde{e}_{i,t} \quad \text{for } i = 1, 2, \ldots, N \tag{19.7}$$

where $E_{0,t}$ is the security's expected return if $\beta_{i,t}F_{1,t}$ equals zero; $\tilde{F}_{1,t}$ is a factor (which we will call F1) that affects stock i's ex-post return for year t; $\beta_{i,t}$ is the sensitivity (systematic risk or beta) of stock i to factor F1; $\tilde{e}_{i,t}$ is the firm's stock price movement that is uncorrelated to F1. (This is essentially the firm-specific risk for year t.) $E(\tilde{e}_{i,t})$ is assumed to equal zero.

The F1 factor can be decomposed into two types of factors: (1) a factor expected by investors ($EF_{i,t}$) and (2) an unexpected factor ($\tilde{f}_{1,t}$). Rewrite Equation 19.7 more explicitly:

$$\tilde{R}_{i,t} = E_{0,t} + \beta_{i,t}(EF_{1,t} + \tilde{f}_{1,t}) + \tilde{e}_{i,t} \tag{19.8}$$

where $EF_{1,t}$ is F1's expected effect on stock i's ex-post return for year t and $\tilde{f}_{1,t}$ is the effect of the unanticipated change in stock i's ex-post return, which is also uncorrelated to $e_{i,t}$.

Finally, rewrite Equation 19.8 as

$$\tilde{R}_{i,t} = ER_{i,t} + \beta_{i,t}\tilde{f}_{1,t} + \tilde{e}_{i,t} \tag{19.9}$$

where $ER_{i,t}$ equals stock i's expected return, or $(E_{0,t} + \beta_{i,1}EF_{1,t})$.

An example may help to clarify this relationship between $EF_{1,t}$ and $\tilde{f}_{1,t}$. Suppose that stock i is AHP and factor F1 represents the change in the rate of inflation. If the change in inflation rate is zero, AHP's return is 10 percent ($E_{0,t}$ = percent).

Suppose, however, that everyone believes that inflation will increase by 3 percent ($EF_{1,t}$ is 3 percent.). Because stocks tend to suffer during periods of high inflation, AHP should decline. If AHP's beta relative to the F1 factor equals -1.5, its return is expected to fall by 4.5 percent (-1.5×3 percent) and its expected return, ER_{AHP}, equals 5.5 percent:

$$ER_{AHP} = 10\% + [-1.5(3\%)] = 5.5 \text{ percent}$$

Remember, however, that 3 percent is only a predicted change in F1. If the actual change in the rate of inflation is equal to $+4$ percent, so that $\tilde{f}_{1,t}$ is $+1$ percent, the effect on AHP's actual, realized return is

$$ER_{AHP} = ER_{AHP} + [-1.5(1\%)] = 5.5\% - 1.5\% = 4.0 \text{ percent}$$

The difference between actual and expected inflation causes the actual, realized return ($R_{AHP,t}$) to be 1.5 percent lower than the expected return, ER_{AHP}; the stockholder expects 5.5 percent but realizes only 4.0 percent.

Now, what is $\tilde{e}_{i,t}$, the firm-specific effect on the stock's actual return? The variable $\tilde{e}_{i,t}$ might measure the effects of the hackers shutting down Yahoo's web site for several hours (the incident occurred in February 2000 and affected Yahoo, eBay, and E°Trade) or for AHP litigation on a product that causes side effects. This effect would cause the actual return to differ from ER_{AHP}. Notice the difference between $\tilde{e}_{i,t}$ and $\tilde{f}_{1,t}$. The latter captures the effect of F1 that is not predicted correctly (unexpected inflation), whereas $\tilde{e}_{i,t}$ captures the firm-specific effect, which is not captured by $\tilde{f}_{1,t}$ and is uncorrelated to $\tilde{f}_{1,t}$.

SINGLE-FACTOR APT FOR A WELL-DIVERSIFIED PORTFOLIO

Next, let's discuss the risk/return relationship for a well-diversified portfolio. Start with the same ex-post relationship (Equation 19.9), but modify it for a portfolio:

$$\tilde{R}_{p,t} = ER_{p,t} + \beta_{p1}\tilde{f}_{1,t} + \tilde{e}_{p,t} \tag{19.10}$$

One benefit of diversification is elimination of virtually all firm-specific risk, as described in Chapter 17. Recall from that chapter that the effect of a security's standard deviation, SD_i, on a well-diversified portfolio's standard deviation, SD_p is virtually zero; the only relevant risk is the covariance of each security with the portfolio. Another way of saying this is that the standard deviation of unexpected, $(\tilde{e}_{p,t})$, or firm-specific risk equals zero. Because the expected value of firm-specific risk, $E(\tilde{e}_{p,t})$, equals zero and its standard deviation, $SD(\tilde{e}_{p,t})$, is zero, the actual effect on the portfolio return of $\tilde{e}_{p,t}$ must equal zero for a well-diversified portfolio. The ex-post return relationship for a well-diversified portfolio becomes[14]

$$\tilde{R}_{p,t} = ER_{p,t} + \beta_p \tilde{f}_{1,t} \tag{19.11}$$

Well-diversified portfolio risk equals[15]

$$SD_P^2 = \beta_P^2 SD_{f,1}^2 \quad \text{or} \quad SD_P = \beta_P SD_{f,1}$$

The APT imposes three conditions:

1. No wealth is invested.
2. A portfolio can eliminate firm-specific risk, $\tilde{e}_{p,t}$. (Of course, this is possible by holding a well-diversified portfolio.)
3. If arbitrage opportunities exist, the market can without risk or cost arbitrage the profits to eliminate any discrepancies between any combinations of portfolios or securities at the same risk level.

If these conditions hold, it follows mathematically that portfolio expected return, $ER_{p,t}$, has a linear relationship with beta, β_p

$$ER_{p,t} = E_{0,t} + \beta_p EF_{1,t} \tag{19.12}$$

---

[14]This involves constructing portfolios so that $E(\tilde{e}_{p,t})$ equals zero. Also, remember from statistics that if an expected value is zero and actual values show no deviation from its (standard deviation is zero), then all the values that make up $e_{p,t}$ must be zero.

[15]Portfolio risk can be shown mathematically to equal

$$SD_P = \beta_P SD_{f,1}$$

Recall that

$$SD_P^2 = \beta_P^2 SD_{f,1}^2 + SD_e^2$$

Having established that SD_e^2 is virtually zero for a well-diversified portfolio, then

$$SD_P^2 = \beta_P^2 SD_{f,1}^2$$

Taking the square root gives

$$SD_P = \beta_P SD_{f,1}.$$

An example may be helpful here. The following example shows both the rationale for security return and how the arbitrage process is truly risk-free; the dollar payoff is the same, regardless of any unanticipated changes in the portfolio return. Based on that premise, the example shows that Equation 19.12 follows from the assumptions of the single-factor APT.

Suppose that a single-factor model defines expected and realized returns as

$$\text{Realized return: } \tilde{R}_{p,t} = ER_{p,t} + \beta_p \tilde{f}_{1,t}$$
$$\text{Expected return: } ER_{p,t} = E_{0,t} + \beta_p EF_{1,t}$$

Suppose, also, that three portfolios C, D, and K have expected returns of 14 percent, 16 percent, and 17 percent with $\beta_{p,1}$ (systematic risk) measures of 0.7, 1.7, and 1.2, respectively. So, portfolio K has a systematic risk of 1.2 and an expected return of 17 percent. Investing 50 percent of your wealth in C and 50 percent in D gives a systematic risk of combined portfolio CD as

$$\beta_{CD} = X_c \beta_{C,1} + (1 - X_C)\beta_{D,1} \tag{19.13}$$

where X_C is the proportion invested in portfolio C. For the example,

$$\beta_{CD} = 0.50(0.7) + (1 - 0.50)(1.7) = 1.2$$

Portfolio CD has the same systematic risk as portfolio K; however, its expected return equals 15 percent. Using Equation 17.6a, the portfolio expected return is

$$ER_{CD} = X_C(ER_C) + (1 - X_C)(ER_D)$$
$$= 0.50(0.14) + (1 - 0.50)(0.16) = 0.15 \text{ or } 15 \text{ percent}$$

This example presents an arbitrage opportunity because portfolios K and CD have the same systematic risk ($\beta = 1.2$), but K's expected return is 17 percent, whereas CD's is 15 percent. Arbitrage with no risk and no investment can be constructed by selling short $100 of portfolio CD and using the proceeds to buy $100 of portfolio K. This results in zero investment and zero risk, as displayed in the first part of Exhibit 19.6.

Now, let's see what happens a year from today if the unanticipated change $(\tilde{f}_{1,t})$ equals −3 percent, 0 percent, or 5 percent. Exhibit 19.6 displays the results of the realized dollar payoffs, calculated as

$$\text{Dollar payoff} = INV + INV(ER_{p,t} + \beta_{p,1}\tilde{f}_{1,t}) \tag{19.14}$$

where INV is the dollar amount invested ($100 in the example) and $(ER_{p,t} + \beta_{p,1}\tilde{f}_{1,t})$ is the actual realized return, from Equation 19.11. These results show that the dollar payoffs are exactly the same regardless of the unanticipated changes; whether the model's single factor changes by −3 percent, 0 percent, or 5 percent, the net profits equal $2. This is the meaning of risk-free arbitrage; the technique guarantees a known dollar payoff a year from today, regardless of the unanticipated changes. This allows arbitrageurs to exploit mispricing between portfolios of equal systematic risk until the profits become zero (that is, the portfolios' returns become equal).

Exhibit 19.6 ✦ ARBITRAGING PORTFOLIO K WITH PORTFOLIO CD

A. Investment Today

	Dollar Investment	Systematic Risk
Sell Portfolio CD short:		
Short Portfolio C	$ +50	−0.35
Short Portfolio D	+50	−0.85
Buy Portfolio K	−100	+1.20
Net investment	$ 0	Net risk 0.00

B. One year Later
Unanticipated Changes

Realized Dollar Payoffs

$\tilde{f}_{1,t}$

$$= INV + INV(ER_{p,t} + \beta_{p,1}\tilde{f}_{1,t})$$

Low $\tilde{f}_{1,t}$
C: Dollar payoff =	−{$50 + $50[0.14 + 0.7(−0.03)]}	$−55.95
D: Dollar payoff =	−{$50 + $50[0.16 + 1.7(−0.03)]}	−55.45
K: Dollar payoff =	$100 + $100[0.17 + 1.2(−0.03)]	113.40
Net profits		$ + 2.00

Expected $\tilde{f}_{1,t}$
C: Dollar payoff =	−{$50 + $50[0.14 + 0.7(0)]}	$−57.00
D: Dollar payoff =	−{$50 + $50[0.16 + 1.7(0)]}	−58.00
K: Dollar payoff =	$100 + $100[0.17 + 1.2(0)]	117.00
Net profits		$ + 2.00

High $\tilde{f}_{1,t}$
C: Dollar payoff =	−{$50 + $50[0.14 + 0.7(+0.05)]}	$−58.75
D: Dollar payoff =	−{$50 + $50[0.16 + 1.7(+0.05)]}	−62.25
K: Dollar payoff =	$100 + $100[0.17 + 1.2(+0.05)]	123.00
Net profits		$ + 2.00

This says that the risk caused by the unanticipated changes, $\tilde{f}_{1,t}$, can be eliminated by constructing two portfolios (CD and K) that have offsetting effects; therefore, $\tilde{f}_{1,t}$ is not relevant in pricing security if it can be eliminated with off-setting arbitrage portfolios. This suggests removing $\tilde{f}_{1,t}$ from Equation 19.11:

$$\tilde{R}_{p,t} = ER_{p,t} + \beta_{p,1}\tilde{f}_{1,t}$$

If so, the realized return, $\tilde{R}_{p,t}$ can be best described by the expected return, $ER_{p,t}$. Recall, however, that $ER_{p,t}$ is defined by Equation 19.12 as

$$ER_{p,t} = E_{0,t} + \beta_{p,1} EF_{1,t}$$

This shows intuitively that if one portfolio (K) can be replicated by combinations of other portfolios, its expected return can be described by Equation 19.12.

Let's rework the example of portfolios C, D, and K to develop another intuitive technique to evaluate returns describing the arbitrage process. Suppose the realized returns for portfolio K and portfolio CD are defined by Equation 19.11 as

$$\tilde{R}_{K,t} = ER_{K,t} + \beta_{K,1}\tilde{f}_{1,t} \quad \text{and} \quad \tilde{R}_{CD,t} = ER_{CD,t} + \beta_{CD,1}\tilde{f}_{1,t}$$

Because ER_K equals 0.17 and $\beta_{K,1}$ equals 1.2, rewrite portfolio K's realized return as

$$\tilde{R}_{K,t} = 0.17 + 1.2\,\tilde{f}_{1,t}$$

Portfolio CD's $ER_{CD,t}$ equals 0.15 and its $\beta_{CD,1}$ equals 1.2, and its realized return equals

$$\tilde{R}_{CD,t} = 0.15 + 1.2\,\tilde{f}_{1,t}$$

Because the portfolio combination in CD has the same systematic risk of 1.2 but earns only 15 percent, an arbitrageur will sell CD short and buy portfolio K with the proceeds of the short sale giving a net investment of zero. The results look like this:

Buy portfolio K	$\tilde{R}_{K,t}$	$= (0.17 + 1.2\,\tilde{f}_{1,t})$
Sell short portfolio CD	$-\tilde{R}_{CD,t}$	$= -(0.15 + 1.2\,\tilde{f}_{1,t})$
Arbitrage profits	$(\tilde{R}_{K,t} - \tilde{R}_{CD,t})$	$= +0.02$

The arbitrage generates a 2 percent profit. Notice, also, that the effects of any unanticipated changes, $\tilde{f}_{1,t}$, are offset no matter what that number is: -3 percent, 0 percent, or 5 percent. This says that the arbitrage investment risk is zero. Because all arbitrageurs are guaranteed to realize this profit, they will continue to make these trades until portfolio K's price rises enough to reduce its return to 15 percent.

Generally, if a portfolio (for example, K) with a higher return can be replicated as a combination of other portfolios (for example, C and D), arbitrage profits exist. However, arbitrageurs quickly eliminate this mispricing between portfolios. For that reason, all portfolios with the same systematic risk must lie on the same line, defined by Equation 19.12. Stated differently, portfolios with the same systematic risk must have the same expected return.

The linear relationship for portfolios CD and K may be

$$ER_{p,t} = 0.03 + 1.2(0.10) = 0.15 \text{ or } 15 \text{ percent}$$

This relationship is displayed in Exhibit 19.7.

The risk/return relationship defined by Equation 19.12 needs one last modification. The systematic risk factor in Equation 19.12 can be normalized so that the average $\beta_{p,1}$ equals 1.0. This gives a general normalized risk/return relationship of

$$ER_{p,t} = E_{0,t} + \beta_{p,1}(ER_{1,t} - E_{0,t}) \tag{19.15}$$

where $E_{0,t}$ is the expected return for the portfolio if the systematic risk for the portfolio is zero; $\beta_{p,1}$ is the systematic risk for a portfolio (equal to 1.0 for the average systematic risk for F1); and $(ER_{1,t} - E_{0,t})$ is F1's risk premium.

Exhibit 19.7 ✦ ARBITRAGING PORTFOLIO K USING PORTFOLIO CD

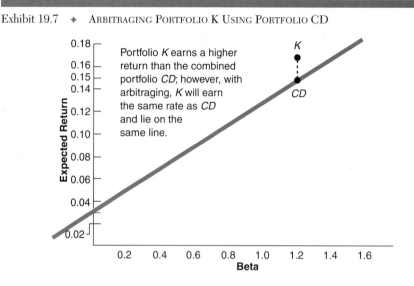

This normalization allows us to interpret APT's measure of systematic risk like the CAPM's beta. If systematic risk is greater than 1.0, the portfolio's systematic risk is higher than the average of all portfolios; if it is less than 1.0, the portfolio is less risky than average. Again, this provides a reference point for factor F1's systematic risk.

Having developed an intuitive feel for arbitrage, we make a leap by induction to apply the principle to valuation of securities. If a well-diversified portfolio can be valued by Equation 19.12, what about individual securities? Each security must also follow Equation 19.12 as long as arbitrageurs can create well-diversified portfolios to mimic a security's extraordinary return. Put differently, if AHP were compensating investors for firm-specific risk such as product tampering [for example, if $SD(e_i) \neq 0$], shrewd investors could create combinations of other stocks in a portfolio that would have the same systematic risk level as AHP. They would sell the portfolio short and buy more AHP, driving AHP's price upward until its return came to equal the portfolio's, or until AHP's $SD(e_i)$ would no longer affect its security return.

Therefore, if a security return could be recreated by a combination of other securities' returns (in a portfolio), no arbitrage profits would remain and all securities would be priced to reflect only the systematic risk associated with the factor. This says that Equation 19.15, which we have applied only to well-diversified portfolios, can be extended to security i's return:

$$ER_{i,t} = E_{0,t} + \beta_{i,1}(ER_{1,t} - E_{0,t}) \quad \text{for } i = 1, 2, \dots, N \quad (19.16)$$

This equation should look vaguely familiar. It resembles the CAPM formula, if some assumptions are made. We see in the next section that the single-factor APT model and the CAPM take on exactly the same form, but we also examine differences between the two processes.

SINGLE-FACTOR APT AND THE CAPM

Because $\beta_{i,1}$ is defined as a security's sensitivity to factor F1, this APT variable has the same definition as beta in the CAPM. Given a single-factor APT model and defining

F1 as the market portfolio M, the term $ER_{1,t} - E_{0,t}$ in Equation 19.16 becomes $ER_{M,t} - RF_t$. Also, if $E_{0,t}$ equals RF, it makes Equation 19.16 equal to

$$ER_i = RF + \beta_{i,M}(ER_M - RF)$$

The term $(ER_M - RF)$ is the market risk premium, and $\beta_{i,M}$ is security i's systematic risk relative to the market portfolio M.

The result is the same formula as the CAPM. However, the process of arriving at the final formula is quite different; the APT model uses the arbitrage principle, whereas the CAPM uses utility theory. Let's discuss how the APT develops the single-factor model.

DEVELOPMENT OF THE SINGLE-FACTOR APT

In Chapter 17, we found that risk-averse investors are enticed to invest in risky securities only if they are compensated for risk. Even in Chapter 1, we defined a risk/return relationship as

$$ER_i = RF + \text{Risk premium}$$

The compensation for accepting risk equals

$$ER_i - RF = \text{Risk premium}$$

The left side of the equation, $ER_i - RF$, is the reward for accepting risk. How can one measure security risk?

Recall from the previous section that systematic risk is the only relevant risk for a well-diversified portfolio because a portfolio diversifies away any firm-specific risk. Therefore, a reward-to-risk ratio for a well-diversified portfolio can be defined as

$$\text{Reward-to-risk ratio} = \frac{(ER_p - RF)}{\beta_p}$$

In market equilibrium, the reward-to-risk ratios for all well-diversified portfolios must be equal, otherwise market forces would arbitrage any profits until they reached equality. In essence, the reward-to-risk ratio must increase proportionately or else arbitrage opportunities, as described earlier, are possible. If so, arbitrageurs will eliminate any discrepancies in portfolios with arbitrage profits. For two well-diversified portfolios, P and Q,

$$\frac{(ER_p - RF)}{\beta_p} = \frac{(ER_Q - RF)}{\beta_Q}$$

Now, what about securities? If securities' returns can be duplicated by combinations of other portfolios, in market equilibrium, they too must have reward-to-risk ratios that equal those of the portfolios. For example, suppose a well-diversified portfolio, M, can combine other securities so that its systematic risk is the same as security i. Their reward-to-risk ratios must equal

$$\frac{(ER_i - RF)}{\beta_i} = \frac{(ER_M - RF)}{\beta_M}$$

If not, arbitrage would drive them into equality. Suppose that security i's reward-to-risk ratio equals 0.8, whereas the ratio of the combination portfolio M equals 0.6.

$$\frac{(ER_M - RF)}{\beta_M} = \frac{(0.12 - 0.06)}{1.0} = 0.6$$

$$\frac{(ER_i - RF)}{\beta_i} = \frac{(0.30 - 0.06)}{0.30} = 0.8$$

Investors who notice that security i has a greater reward-to-risk ratio than portfolio M will purchase security i and sell portfolio M short until the two reward-to-risk ratios become equal. This says simply that as risk increases, reward must increase in the same proportion for every security in the market; otherwise mispricing occurs. However, arbitrage quickly corrects any mispricing to prevent a security from earning a reward out of proportion to its risk.

If securities can be combined into a portfolio that duplicates the return of security i, but with a different reward-to-risk ratio, arbitrage will occur. In the end, most securities and portfolios have a single reward-to-risk ratio:

$$\frac{(ER_j - RF)}{\beta_j} = \frac{(ER_i - RF)}{\beta_i} = \frac{(ER_M - RF)}{\beta_M}$$

In equilibrium, all securities, including portfolios, must have the same reward-to-risk ratio or

$$\frac{(ER_i - RF)}{\beta_i} = \frac{(ER_M - RF)}{\beta_M}$$

Remember that if beta is normalized, the average beta equals 1.0, where the average portfolio is represented by a well-diversified portfolio M. Therefore, the reward-to-risk ratio equals

$$\frac{(ER_i - RF)}{\beta_i} = \frac{(ER_M - RF)}{1.0}$$

Solve for ER_i to determine the risk/return relationship for security i:

$$ER_i = RF + \beta_i(ER_M - RF) \tag{19.17}$$

If portfolio M is defined as the market portfolio, beta, β_i is security i's risk contribution to the market portfolio and $(ER_M - RF)$ is the market risk premium.

You probably recognize Equation 19.17 as the CAPM from Chapter 18; however, the process of developing the formula using APT is different from that in Chapter 18, which used utility theory and the capital market line (CML). The next section outlines the differences between the single-factor APT and the CAPM.

DIFFERENCES BETWEEN THE SINGLE-FACTOR APT AND THE CAPM

Four major differences separate the single-factor APT and the CAPM:

1. The APT is appealing because it relies only on the premise that arbitrage will preclude any mispricing in a rational capital market, maintaining market equilibrium. The CAPM relies on utility theory and risk aversion to develop the risk/return relationship. This gives CAPM a less intuitive basis than the APT.
2. The development of the single-factor APT assumes a well-diversified portfolio that affects returns on individual securities. The APT does not rely on any unobservable market portfolio, as the CAPM does.
3. However, the CAPM does have its strengths. Its development shows that all traded securities will lie on its risk/return line; the APT guarantees that diversified portfolios must lie on the line, but individual securities may diverge somewhat. It recognizes the possibility of small mispricing errors, although it is virtually impossible for most securities to systematically deviate from the APT's risk/return line.
4. Both models have drawbacks that become apparent when conducting empirical tests. The CAPM is not testable because no one can observe the true market portfolio, whereas the APT does not define its factors, nor does it rely on a set number of factors.

Both models have weaknesses and strengths, so it is impossible to say that one model is clearly better. However, both models help the analyst to quantify a risk premium and both define risk/return relationships that are still useful in evaluating securities for investment decisions.

The final step we take is to develop a multifactor APT, which assumes that many factors are significant in explaining security returns. We start with a two-factor APT and generalize to the N-factor APT. In either case, the underlying principle is the same; the only difference is the initial premise that more than one factor can affect an ex-post security return.

APT WITH MULTIPLE FACTORS

The concept of security pricing based on arbitrage can extend to more than one factor. In fact, introduction of several factors says only that security j's return depends on more than one force, so it can be recreated by holding a linear combination of different factors. Using the same arbitrage principle, we show that if a security's return can be mimicked by combining several stocks in a portfolio, no arbitrage profits remain. We begin by extending the single-factor relationship to a two-factor relationship.

Two-Factor APT

A two-factor APT extends the single-factor APT by defining a security's realized returns and expected returns as

$$\text{Realized return:} \quad \tilde{R}_{i,t} = ER_{i,t} + \beta_{i,1}\tilde{f}_{1,t} + \beta_{i,2}\tilde{f}_{2,t} + \tilde{e}_{i,t} \tag{19.18}$$

$$\text{Expected return:} \quad ER_{i,t} = E_{0,t} + \beta_{i,1}EF_{1,t} + \beta_{i,2}EF_{2,t} \tag{19.19}$$

where $E_{0,t}$ is security i's expected return if it is uncorrelated to F1 and F2; EF_1 and EF_2 are the factors' expected effects, based on F1 and F2, respectively; $\tilde{f}_{1,t}$ and $\tilde{f}_{2,t}$ are the effects of unanticipated changes in stock i's ex-post return, which are uncorrelated to $e_{i,t}$ ($\tilde{f}_{1,t}$ and $\tilde{f}_{2,t}$ are also uncorrelated); $\beta_{i,1}$ and $\beta_{i,2}$ are the systematic risk effects of F1 and F2, respectively; finally, $\tilde{e}_{i,t}$ is the firm-specific risk, which is uncorrelated to F1 and F2.

Well-diversified portfolios can eliminate firm-specific risk through diversification, so their realized returns equal

$$\text{Realized return} \qquad \tilde{R}_{p,t} = ER_{p,t} + \beta_{p,1}\tilde{f}_{1,t} + \beta_{p,2}\tilde{f}_{2,t} \qquad (19.20)$$

Again, an example can illustrate that the effects of unanticipated changes $\tilde{f}_{1,t}$ and $\tilde{f}_{2,t}$ are offset in arbitrage, leaving the expected return, $ER_{p,t}$, in a linear relationship with systematic risk, or beta, as defined in Equation 19.19.

Suppose that two portfolios, P and Q, have the following systematic risks to F1 and F2 and expected returns, ER_P and ER_Q:

Portfolio	$\beta_{p,1}$	$\beta_{p,2}$	$ER_{p,t}$
P	0.1	0.1	0.05
Q	0.3	0.6	0.18

Investing 300 percent in portfolio P would give the following risk levels and expect return:

$$\beta_{p,1} = 3(0.1) = 0.3$$
$$\beta_{p,2} = 3(0.2) = 0.6$$
$$ER_{p,t} = 3(0.05) = 0.15$$

Notice that portfolio P's risk levels are now equal to those of portfolio Q, but its return is lower (15 percent versus 18 percent). This suggests a strategy of selling short a dollar of portfolio P for every dollar invested in portfolio Q. This results in the following realized returns for portfolios P and Q:

Realized return for
  investment in portfolio Q $\tilde{R}_{Q,t}$ $= (0.18 + 0.3\tilde{f}_{1,t} + 0.6\tilde{f}_{2,t})$

Realized return for
  short sale of portfolio P $-\tilde{R}_{p,t}$ $= -(0.15 + 0.3\tilde{f}_{1,t} + 0.6\tilde{f}_{2,t})$

$$(\tilde{R}_{Q,t} - \tilde{R}_{P,t}) \quad = +0.03$$

Again, the unanticipated effects, $\tilde{f}_{1,t}$ and $\tilde{f}_{2,t}$, offset each other for well-diversified portfolios, generating a 3 percent arbitrage profit. The arbitrage will continue until the expected returns from the portfolios are equal, so the two-factor APT for a well-diversified portfolio can be described by

$$ER_{p,t} = E_{0,t} + \beta_{p,1}EF_{1,t} + \beta_{p,2}EF_{2,t}$$

This assumes that most securities' returns can be replicated as combinations of other securities or portfolios, so arbitrage profits will be virtually zero for securities, too. If so, security i's expected return can also be written as a linear relationship of the beta risks of the two factors:

$$ER_{i,t} = E_{0,t} + \beta_{i,1}EF_{1,t} + \beta_{i,2}EF_{2,t}$$

As in the single-factor APT, standardizing each beta can set the average beta equal to 1.0 for each factor's beta. The standardized two-factor APT equals

$$ER_{p,t} = E_{0,t} + \beta_{p,1}(EF_{1,t} - E_{0,t}) + \beta_{p,2}(EF_{2,t} - E_{0,t}) \qquad (19.21)$$

where $E_{0,t}$ is the expected return value when all factors equal zero; $(EF_{1,t} - E_{0,t})$ and $(EF_{2,t} - E_{0,t})$ are risk premiums for factors F1 and F2, respectively; $\beta_{i,1}$ and $\beta_{i,2}$ are systematic risks for factors F1 and F2, respectively.

The two-factor APT is derived much like the single-factor APT. The only difference is that it includes more than one factor to describe the realized return.

N-Factor APT

Now, suppose that N factors describe the realized return for a security. Security j's realized return equals

$$\tilde{R}_{j,t} = E_{0,t} + \beta_{j,1}(EF_{1,t} + \tilde{f}_{1,t}) + \beta_{j,2}(EF_{2,t} + \tilde{f}_{2,t}) + \ldots$$
$$+ \beta_{j,N}(EF_{N,t} + \tilde{f}_{N,t}) + \tilde{e}_{j,t}$$

where $k = 1, 2, \ldots, N$ representing the k factors; where the $EF_{k,t}$ terms are the expected values of the k factors in period t. The $\tilde{f}_{k,t}$ terms are the unexpected values of the k factors in period t, $\tilde{e}_{j,t}$ is the firm-specific risk that is uncorrelated to any of the unexpected $f_{j,t}$ values; $\beta_{j,k}$ are the sensitivities or systematic risks associated with each of the k factors; $E_{0,t}$ is the expected return value when each of the N factors equals zero.

First, separate and collect the expected values of all the k factors as one term and the unexpected values as the second term:

$$\tilde{R}_{j,t} = (E_{0,t} + \beta_{j,1}EF_{1,t} + \beta_{j,2}EF_{2,t} + \ldots \beta_{j,N}EF_{N,t})$$
$$+ (\beta_{j,1}\tilde{f}_{1,t} + \beta_{j,2}\tilde{f}_{2,t} + \ldots + \beta_{j,N}\tilde{f}_{N,t}) + \tilde{e}_{j,t} \tag{19.22}$$

Because the first term in parentheses can be defined as the expected return for all the factors that are correlated with security j, make the following substitution:

$$ER_{j,t} = (E_{0,t} + \beta_{j,1}EF_{1,t} + \beta_{j,2}EF_{2,t} + \ldots \beta_{j,N}EF_{N,t})$$

Inserting this into Equation 19.22 gives

$$\tilde{R}_{j,t} = ER_{j,t} + (\beta_{j,1}\tilde{f}_{1,t} + \beta_{j,2}\tilde{f}_{2,t} + \ldots + \beta_{j,N}\tilde{f}_{N,t}) + \tilde{e}_{j,t} \tag{19.23}$$

This formula says that if an expected return on a security can be recreated by factors and their systematic risks are equal (or portfolios of other securities) arbitrageurs will price the two the same, assuming they must pay no transaction costs. This means that the security's realized return must equal its expected return, which is explained by many factors, plus the unanticipated changes of those factors. Therefore, each $\beta_{j,k}$ is composed of two components: the part of security return that is sensitive to and explained by factor $F_{k,t}$ and the part that is sensitive, but not explained by $F_{k,t}$; the second part is captured by a random term, $\tilde{f}_{k,t}$. The unpredictable component can be unexpected factor outcomes ($\tilde{f}_{k,t}$) or unexpected firm-specific events ($\tilde{e}_{j,t}$). If a factor to explain a security return were an industry index, an unanticipated outcome might be a new drug breakthrough; a firm-specific outcome could be a product-tampering episode. Again, if the three conditions outlined for the single-factor APT model hold, virtually no arbitrage opportunities exist, implying the relationship

$$ER_{j,t} = E_{0,t} + \beta_{j,1}(EF_{1,t} - E_{0,t}) + \beta_{j,2}(EF_{2,t} - E_{0,t}) + \ldots$$
$$+ \beta_{j,N}(EF_{N,t} - E_{0,t}) \tag{19.24}$$

where $EF_{k,t} - E_{0,t}$ is the risk premium for the kth factor; $E_{0,t}$ is the expected return value when all N factors equal zero (this value is uncorrelated to all the factors); $\beta_{j,k}$ equals the systematic risk or beta of security j with the kth factor. Also, each factor must be uncorrelated with the other factors (that is, $CORR(F1, F2) = 0.0$). The same relationship must hold for other pairs of factors.

This formula says that each factor, F_k, captures an independently different effect and its sensitivity is measured by its corresponding beta, $\beta_{j,k}$. The only requirement is that the number of factors must be less than the number of securities being evaluated. Researchers have found that three to six factors can eliminate virtually all arbitrage opportunities.[16]

FINAL SYNOPSIS OF APT

multifactor APT model
Risk/return relationship in which many variables (or factors) are related to the stock returns and are used to measure the stock risk.

The **multifactor APT model** is more robust than the CAPM because it allows for several factors that may affect security returns and it avoids the need to identify a true market portfolio. However, it has some empirical problems of its own. The factors are not well defined, so the analyst must empirically attempt to identify the factors significant in describing security returns. This creates two types of problems: (1) the factors may change, depending on the sample of securities used to ascertain them, and (2) factors may change over time.

Researchers have found that increasing the sample size also increases the number of factors that significantly affect security returns. The question of what the factors are is difficult to resolve. Furthermore, the number of factors appears to vary, not only with the sample but with time periods as well.

An alternative strategy is to define factors that appear plausible descriptions of security returns. For example, Chen, Roll, and Ross tested specified factors and found that a large part of a security's return can be explained by four factors: (1) differences between yields to maturity on long-term and short-term Treasury securities, (2) inflation rates, (3) differences between yields to maturity on BB-rated corporate bonds and Treasury bills, and (4) growth of industrial production (or gross national product).[17]

In conclusion, extensive research continues toward determining the appropriate risk measures, but both academics and practitioners agree that risk level is an important component in making good investment decisions.

Implications for Investors

Generally, these extensions of CAPM define risk slightly differently. However, the extensions of CAPM and the APT all tell us that risk is an important component of evaluating investments and that we should account for it by using models or theory helpful in quantifying it. Most investors resort to the CAPM despite its shortcomings to measure risk and allow for other qualitative factors in order to determine the risk level of each investment.

---

[16]Richard Roll and Stephen Ross, "An Empirical Investigation of the Arbitrage Pricing Theory," *Journal of Finance* (December 1980), pp. 1073–1103.

[17]Nai-Fu Chen, Richard Roll, and Stephen Ross, "Economic Forces and the Stock Market," *Journal of Business* (September 1986), pp. 383–404.

![] **Chapter Summary**

1. What is the zero-beta portfolio model?
    The zero-beta portfolio model relaxes the CAPM's assumption that all investors can borrow and lend at the risk-free rate, RF. It results in a similar linear, beta risk/return relationship; however, it replaces the risk-free asset with a zero-beta portfolio, or a stock portfolio that is uncorrelated to the market portfolio.
2. What are some results of empirical tests of the CAPM?
    Empirical findings for the CAPM are less than satisfactory. Major findings indicate that (1) actual beta risk/return relationships are flatter than theory suggests, (2) the y-intercept does not equal the risk-free rate, RF, and (3) the slope for the SML was slightly negative during some periods in 1957 to 1965.
3. What is Roll's critique of the CAPM?
    Roll mathematically proves that the CAPM cannot be empirically tested because any efficient portfolio will have an exactly linear beta risk/return relationship, as described by the CAPM. Unless the analyst can identify an ex-ante market portfolio (which is impossible), no one can test the CAPM. One can test only whether the proxy for the market portfolio is mean-variance efficient.
4. What is the APT?
    The APT is based on the theory that identical assets must be priced exactly the same, otherwise, investors will arbitrage the profits to zero. Ross developed an alternative way of viewing asset pricing based on this principle. His model is more robust than the CAPM and incorporates a formula exactly like the CAPM. However, the process of arriving at the final formula is quite different. (CAPM uses utility theory, and APT uses arbitrage theory.) Also, the APT can include multiple factors.

Review Questions and Problems

1. What assumption of the CAPM is relaxed to develop the zero-beta portfolio model?
2. What are the general results of the empirical tests for the CAPM and zero-beta portfolio model?
3. How would you explain the negative risk/return relationship that is documented for the April 1957 to December 1965 period?
4. What are the premises of Roll's critique of the CAPM?
5. According to Roll, what are the implications of the empirical results provided by Black, Jensen, and Scholes?
6. The chapter example on portfolios CD and K shows the dollar payoffs if $\tilde{f}_{1,t}$ equals −3 percent, 0 percent, and 5 percent. What are the dollar payoffs if $\tilde{f}_{1,t}$ equals −5 percent and 2 percent?
7. The chapter example on portfolios CD and K shows the dollar payoffs if $\tilde{f}_{1,t}$ equals −3 percent, 0 percent, and 5 percent. What are the dollar payoffs if $\tilde{f}_{1,t}$ equals −10 percent and +10 percent?
8. What are the conceptual differences between the single-factor APT and the CAPM?
9. Suppose that one factor affects ex-post realized returns and expected returns. The systematic risk, $\beta_{p,1}$, and expected returns for three well-diversified portfolios, A, B, and X, are given in the table below.

Portfolio	$\beta_{p,1}$	$ER_{p,t}$
A	1.2	0.15
B	0.3	0.06
X	0.9	0.11

    If you invest in portfolio B and in portfolio X, what arbitrage profits can you gain when you hedge the BX portfolio with portfolio A? Create a table similar to Exhibit

19.6. Show the realized dollar payoffs at unanticipated changes of −8 percent and +12 percent.

10. Suppose that two factors affect ex-post realized returns and expected returns. The systematic risks, $\beta_{p,1}$ and $\beta_{p,2}$ and expected returns for two well-diversified portfolios, R and S, are given in the table below.

Portfolio	$\beta_{p,1}$	$\beta_{p,2}$	$ER_{p,t}$
R	0.5	0.3	0.12
S	1.0	0.6	0.09

    a. Write the expected return and systematic risk relationship for portfolios R and S.
    b. Write the realized return and systematic risk relationship for portfolios R and S.
    c. Do these portfolios offer any arbitrage opportunities? If so, how would you construct the arbitrage?

11. Suppose that two factors affect ex-post realized returns and expected returns. The systematic risks, $\beta_{p,1}$ and $\beta_{p,2}$ and expected returns for two well-diversified portfolios, X and Y, are given in the table below.

Portfolio	$\beta_{p,1}$	$\beta_{p,2}$	$ER_{p,t}$
X	0.2	0.4	0.16
Y	0.1	0.2	0.09

    a. Write the expected return and systematic risk relationship for portfolios X and Y.
    b. Write the realized return and systematic risk relationship for portfolios X and Y.
    c. Do these portfolios offer any arbitrage opportunities? If so, how would you construct the arbitrage?

CFA Questions

1. (CFA Exam, Level I, 1993) Research on the CAPM and beta has concluded that
   a. Short-term results may contradict the CAPM.
   b. Estimated betas change over time.
   c. Estimated betas depend on the choice of the market index.
   d. All of the above.
   Explain your answer.
2. (CFA Exam, Level I, 1993) Compared with the CAPM, in the APT,
   a. Beta is eliminated as a pricing factor.
   b. Inflation is eliminated as a pricing factor.
   c. The risk-free rate loses its significance.
   d. Multiple factors affect the return generation process.
3. (CFA Exam, Level I, 1993) The feature of APT that offers the greatest potential advantage over the CAPM is the
   a. Use of several factors instead of a single market index to explain the risk/return relationship.
   b. Identification of anticipated changes in production, inflation, and term structure as key factors explaining the risk/return relationship.
   c. Superior measurement of the risk-free rate of return over historical time periods.
   d. Variability of coefficients of sensitivity to the APT factors for a given asset over time.
4. (CFA Exam, Level III, 1981) Richard Roll, in an article on using the CAPM to evaluate portfolio performance, indicated that it may not be possible to evaluate portfolio management ability if there is an error in the benchmark chosen for comparison.

a. Describe the general procedure for evaluating portfolio performance, with emphasis on the benchmark used.

b. Explain what Roll meant by benchmark error and identify the specific problem with this benchmark.

c. Draw a graph that shows how a portfolio that has been judged as superior relative to a measured (SML) can be inferior relative to the true SML.

d. Assume that you are informed that a given portfolio manager has been evaluated as superior when compared with the Dow Jones Industrial Average, the S&P 500, and the New York Stock Exchange Composite Index. Explain whether this consensus would make you feel more comfortable regarding the portfolio manager's true ability.

e. Although conceding the possible problem with benchmark errors as set forth by Roll, some contend this does not mean that the CAPM is incorrect, but only that there is a measurement problem when implementing the theory. Others contend that, because of benchmark errors, the whole technique should be scrapped. Take and defend one of these positions.

CRITICAL THINKING EXERCISES

This exercise requires computer work. Open the CAPM worksheet in the Data workbook. The betas are estimated using the S&P 500 Index as the market proxy. Suppose these mutual funds represent portfolios identified in the first pass regression. Run the second pass regression described by Equation 19.5 and answer the question below. Recall Equation 19.5 is

$$M(R_{i,t} - RF_t) = \gamma_0 + \gamma_1 \beta_i \quad \text{for } i = 1, 2, \ldots, N$$

a. What should γ_0 and γ_1 equal if the mutual fund returns follow the CAPM relationship?

b. What are the estimates for γ_0 and γ_1? Does it support the CAPM relationship? Explain.

c. Graph the actual regression line and the theoretical relationship. What conclusions can you draw from the difference?

d. According to Roll's critique of the CAPM, what do the results imply about the market proxy, the S&P 500?

THE INTERNET INVESTOR

Go to an Internet site with stock quotes for five years. Obtain monthly stock price quotes and dividends paid for a stock and for index quotes for the Dow Jones Industrial Average (DJIA) and the S&P 500 Index.

Calculate returns using the formula: $R_{I,t} = \ln(P_{I,t} + DIV_{i,t}) - \ln(P_{i,t-1})$ for the five-year period.

a. Run a market model regression for the stock return using the DJIA as the market portfolio.

b. Run the market model regression for the stock return using the S&P500 Index as the market portfolio.

c. Compare the beta estimates and determine the SD of the regression residual.

d. What can you conclude given the critique of the CAPM?

Part 7

Investment

Management

PART VII DISCUSS HOW INVESTMENT PORT-

FOLIOS SHOULD BE MANAGED AND SERVES

AS A LOGICAL CAPSTONE FOR THE BOOK.

CHAPTER 20 SETS OUT A SYSTEMATIC PROC-

ESS BY WHICH INVESTMENT PORTFOLIOS ARE BUILT AND MANAGED. CHAPTER 21

DESCRIBES IN DETAIL HOW PORTFOLIO PERFORMANCE CAN BE EVALUATED.

BUILDING AND MANAGING AN INVESTMENT PORTFOLIO

PREVIOUSLY . . .

Together the prior three chapters have developed modern portfolio theory (MPT). We discussed concepts such as diversification, efficient frontiers, beta, and arbitrage pricing.

IN THIS CHAPTER . . .

We describe how investment portfolios should be constructed and managed, whether the investor is an individual or an institution and whether the investor takes an active or a more passive approach to investing. This chapter, along with the next chapter, attempts to tie together all of the many themes and issues we've covered.

TO COME . . .

We conclude our journey through the world of investments with a discussion of how to evaluate the performance of investment portfolios.

Chapter Objectives

After reading Chapter 20, you should be able to answer the following questions:

1. What is the process of building and management an investment portfolio?
2. How do investors develop an investment policy?
3. How do capital market assumptions affect the investment process?
4. What is asset allocation?
5. What does monitoring a portfolio involve?

In a sense everything we have done in the prior 19 chapters has set the stage for these final two chapters. We have described risk and return, the wide array of investment alternatives, how securities are bought and sold, how to analyze bonds and common stocks, the purpose of derivative securities, and modern portfolio theory. All of these topics are combined when we build and manage an investment portfolio.

Building and managing an investment portfolio requires that every investor make a series of decisions and complete a set of tasks. The investor must establish investment objectives in light of constraints, preferences, and circumstances. The investor forms expectations concerning the future performance of various investment instruments. Investment funds are allocated and performance evaluated. The overall goal of this process is to create an investment portfolio that comes as close as possible to meeting the investor's objectives. Ultimately, the success of any investment program should be judged by the portfolio's performance, not the performance of the individual investments it contains.

In this chapter, we outline the step-by-step process of building and managing an investment portfolio. Although the specifics will of course vary widely from investor to investor, the basic process is always the same, regardless of whether the investor is an individual or an institution; whether the investor wants to take an active approach or a passive approach; whether the investment horizon is five years or fifty years; and whether an investor invests $10,000 or $10 million.

Constructing and Managing a Portfolio

Exhibit 20.1 outlines the process of building and managing a portfolio. The outline is fairly general; despite varying details, all investors follow the same steps, and follow them in the order shown. The first step is to develop an investment policy. An investment policy blends three elements: the investor's objectives, constraints the investor faces, and the investor's preferences.

Investment objectives are defined in terms of the investor's required return and risk tolerance. Both are heavily influenced by the investor's characteristics. For example, is the investor an individual or an institution? If the investor is an institution, what kind of institution (profit or not for profit)? If the investor is an individual, what are his or her personal characteristics (such things as age and income)? What time horizon does the investor have (short term or long term)? Constraints include the degree of risk aversion, legal or regulatory constraints, the investor's tax situation, and so forth. Preferences include any unique needs or circumstances.

Because investing never occurs in a vacuum, the investor must formulate some expectations concerning the financial markets. For example, how will stocks perform over the investment horizon, relative to bonds and money market instruments? Often investors base their expectations on historical performance data—data we've reviewed frequently throughout the book—because, of course, ex-post returns are the only actual returns we ever have. But remember, historical return data can be problematic. The past must be considered carefully and appropriately; it is never a guarantee of the future.

Portfolio construction is the next step in the process. Investors combine investment policy with market expectations to make strategic and tactical asset allocations decisions. The investor determines the general mix of investments (strategic asset allocation) along with specific investments within each general category (tactical asset allocation). Issues such as diversification and risk/return optimization are also factors in the asset allocation decisions.

The final step in the process is portfolio monitoring. Whether the investor takes an active approach or more of a passive one, the performance of the portfolio should be measured and evaluated. Part of this includes a determination of whether or not the investment objectives are being met. If the portfolio fails to meet investment objectives, changes must be made. The investor should return to the portfolio construction step.

Exhibit 20.1 ✦ An Outline of the Portfolio Construction and Management Process

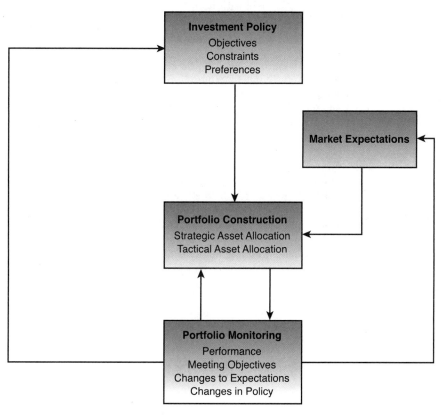

The process shown in Exhibit 20.1 is not a one-way street—it is more of a circle. Changes in investor characteristics lead to changes in investment policy which, in turn, affect asset allocation. For example, as individual investors age, their needs and objectives also change. The investment objectives of a 30-year-old investing for retirement differ significantly from the investment objectives of a 65-year-old who is about to retire.

Financial market expectations also change. A sharp rise in interest rates, for example, usually affects asset allocation, even if investment policy remains essentially unchanged.

Developing an Investment Policy

The first step in the process of building a portfolio is to develop an investment policy. An **investment policy** is a set of guidelines that specifies actions designed to achieve the investor's objectives within the constraints imposed by or on the investor. Both individual and institutional investors should develop investment policies. Important differences between individual investors and institutional investors affect this process. Let's review some of these differences.

investment policy
A set of guidelines that specifies actions to be taken to achieve the investor's objectives within the constraints imposed by or on the investor.

DIFFERENCES BETWEEN INDIVIDUALS AND INSTITUTIONS

Investment professionals often deal with both individual investors as well as institutional investors (such as a pension fund or a not-for-profit organization). Although the overall investment process is essentially the same for both types of investors, many important differences exist. These include:

✦ *Time Horizon.* Individuals don't live forever. An individual investor's time horizon is a function of where that person is in his or her life cycle (for example, beginning a career or about to retire). Individuals can be short-term investors or long-term investors, depending on where they are in the life cycle. On the other hand, most institutions are long-term investors. An institution may have some short-term needs yet still have a long-term horizon.

✦ *Changes in Investor Characteristics.* As individuals progress through the life cycle, investor characteristics such as available resources and life expectancy change dramatically. Institutions, by their very nature, rarely have a life cycle. Consequently, their characteristics change little, if at all, over time.

✦ *Risk and Behavior.* As a *general* rule, individuals investors are more risk-averse than institutional investors. Many individuals view risk as only the possibility than they may lose money. Institutions often take a broader view and deal with risk in a more rational manner than do individual investors, who tend to be more emotional. Conventional wisdom seems to suggest that individual investors, often less experienced than institutional investors, are more prone to falling into the bubble trap and to panicking when prices plunge. However, experience indicates otherwise—institutional investors are just as likely as individual investors to fall into the bubble trap.

✦ *Reasons for Investing.* Individuals often have specific reasons for investing: buying a home, sending a child to college, or retiring early. The reasons institutions invest, on the other hand, may be much more general. As a result, when you develop a profile for an institutional investor, consider not just the characteristics of the institution, but also the characteristics of those who may benefit from the institution's investments.

✦ *Regulatory and Legal Constraints.* Institutions are subject to numerous legal and regulatory constraints on investment decisions. Individuals, on the other hand, have much more investment freedom. Common sense, rather than laws or regulations, is the guiding force for individuals.

✦ *Taxes.* Taxes are an important consideration for individuals because virtually all personal investing has tax implications. Taxes are often much less important for institutional investors. Many, in fact, are tax exempt.

FORMULATING INVESTMENT OBJECTIVES

In general, the three investment objectives are growth in capital, preservation of capital, and current income. As we've noted, inflation erodes investment returns. Consequently, consider all three objectives in real, not nominal terms. If growth in capital is an objective, capital should grow at a rate exceeding the rate of inflation. If capital must be preserved, it should be preserved in real terms. If current income an objective, current income should keep pace with the rate of inflation over time.

All investors must prioritize these three objectives. No single investment instrument is perfect. Money market instruments, for example, preserve capital and produce modest amounts of current income, but they provide no opportunity for capital growth. Common stocks have the potential for substantial capital growth, but many provide little if any current income. And, of course, stock prices don't always go up.

How the investor prioritizes capital growth, capital preservation, and current income depends on the characteristics of the investor and reasons for investing. For individual investors, important characteristics include age, income, martial status, number of dependents, existing assets and liabilities, insurance protection, and current pension benefits. Reasons individuals invest include major purchases, education, and retirement.

There's no escaping the fact that prioritizing investment objectives involves a trade-off between risk and return. One of our recurring themes throughout this book is that risk and return are positively related. Higher returns come at a price: higher risk. Blending individual characteristics with reasons for investing suggests the proper trade-off between risk and return. We can illustrate this point with two hypothetical case studies.

Mark's Retirement

Mark is 25 and just started his career. Like most employers today, Mark's offers a defined contribution retirement plan. In a defined contribution plan, both Mark and his employer make contributions to Mark's retirement account. Mark has a fair degree of control over where the retirement assets are invested. Contributions are tax deductible and investment profits are tax deferred. Mark would like to retire at age 60 and figures he must accumulate at least $1.5 million in his retirement account by then.[1]

Setting priorities among Mark's investment objectives is straightforward. Mark is clearly a long-term investor (his time horizon is 35 years). Current income is not an issue and nor, at this point, is preservation of capital. His clear objective is growth in capital. If Mark and his employer are together contributing $6,000 a year to his retirement account, Mark must earn a minimum of about 9.6 percent per year in order to meet his goal. And because Mark is a long-term investor he can afford to take a fair amount of risk. He's in a position to mostly ignore day-to-day, even year-to-year volatility in the financial markets.

Kim's Daughter's College Education

Here's another simple case study. Kim is in her early 40s and wants to save enough money in five years to send her daughter to college. Kim believes that she'll need about $35,000 in cash at that time and is saving $6,100 per year. What are her investment priorities? Like Mark, current income is not an issue for Kim. On the other hand, Kim has a much shorter-term investment horizon. Although she needs some growth in capital—she must earn about 6.5 percent per year—preservation of capital is also important. Compared to Mark, Kim can take less risk and must be more conservative with her investments.

CONSTRAINTS

Constraints are limitations imposed on the portfolio construction process. Constraints can be self-imposed (imposed by the investor) or imposed by others.

constraints
Limitations imposed on the portfolio construction process.

---

[1]Do you think Mark's goal is ambitious? It's not. If you started working today, the experts say you'll need save a *minimum* of $1 million (in constant dollars) by the time you retire. Company pensions and Social Security will meet only a fraction of your retirement needs.

Investors must operate within constraints and preferences when developing an appropriate investment policy. As we noted earlier, constraints can vary widely from investor to investor, and individual investors face constraints different from those faced by institutional investors. Some major constraints facing both types of investors are discussed below.

Time Horizon

When developing an investment policy, all investors must consider their investment time horizon. Going back to the case studies in the prior section, Mark's time horizon is fairly long (30 to 35 years), whereas Kim's time horizon is fairly short (5 years). As a *general* rule, the longer the time horizon the more risk the investor can afford to take.

Liquidity Needs

The liquidity needs of investors vary widely. An older investor's liquidity needs, for example, might be higher than average. He or she might need liquid assets to meet unexpected medical or long-term care expenses.

Liquidity, as you probably remember from earlier chapters, is defined the ability to turn an asset into cash at a price close to the asset's "true" value. Virtually all financial assets are liquid. However, the price at which shares of common stock can be turned into cash may be unacceptable to the investor. Consequently, investors with greater liquidity needs should keep a greater portion of their portfolios in money market instruments or other near cash assets.

Taxes

As we noted earlier in the chapter, virtually all investment decisions made by individual investors have tax implications. As a *general* rule, the higher the investor's marginal tax bracket, the larger the role played by taxes in investment decisions. Some pertinent tax issues include the following:

✦ Long-term capital gains are taxed at a lower rate than ordinary investment income (dividends and interest).
✦ Only realized capital gains are subject to taxes; unrealized gains are not taxed until the asset is sold.
✦ Most retirement programs offer substantial tax benefits. Contributions may be tax deductible and investment returns are usually tax deferred.
✦ The market value of any investments are part of a person's estate. Federal estate tax rates are much higher than income tax rates.

Although taxes are an important consideration in individual investment decisions, be careful not to allow the tax tail to wag the investment dog. Focusing solely on taxes at the expense of all other factors can lead to poor investment decisions.

Regulatory and Legal Constraints

Other than those relating to taxes, few legal or regulatory restrictions apply to individual investment decisions. Institutional investors, on the other hand, are subject to extensive regulatory and legal constraints, at both the federal and state levels. Most institutions invest money for the benefits of others—a pension fund, for example, invests money on behalf of current and future beneficiaries. Those who invest money for the benefit of others are subject to something known as the **prudent person rule.** This rule states that the institution should act as a prudent person would when making investment decisions. Unfortunately, legal interpretations of the prudent person rule have varied widely from state to state.

An important piece of legislation governing institutional investors in the Employment Retirement Income Security Act (ERISA). In part, ERISA set up rules and standards governing employer sponsored retirement plans, whether these plans are traditional pension plans (so-called defined benefit plans) or retirement savings plans such as 401(k) plans (so-called defined contribution plans).

Special Needs, Circumstances, and Goals

It is not uncommon for investors to have special needs, circumstances, and goals that affect investment decisions. For example, an older investor might want to leave a substantial estate to children or grandchildren. His or her investment choices will obviously be constrained by this goal.

In summary, then, formulating an investment policy is a process by which an investor's circumstances and investment objectives are blended with a set of constraints. The resulting investment policy will go a long way in determining the appropriate asset allocation. But the investment policy isn't the only input into the asset allocation decision. We also must form some expectations concerning the financial markets.

Financial Market Expectations

In the process of forming expectations concerning the financial markets, we can form both *macro-expectations* and *micro-expectations*. **Macro-expectations** involve the future performance for the broad financial asset categories (stocks, bonds, and money market instruments). **Micro-expectations** the future performance of groups and individual securities within the broad asset categories (for example, the future performance of small-company stocks relative to large-company stocks).

MACRO-EXPECTATIONS

A starting point for macro-expectations is the historical record on financial market returns. We summarized much of the historical record in Chapter 2 and have referred to it frequently throughout the book, but it's still worth reiterating the two key results:

✦ Stocks have outperformed bonds and Treasury bills by substantial margins (see Exhibit 20.2). A $1,000 investment in stocks made at the end of 1925 was worth in excess of $2.7 million by the end of 1999. By contrast, a $1,000 investment in bonds made at the end of 1925 was worth less than $40,000 by the end of 1999. Treasury bills did even worse. In fact, Treasury bill returns, on average, have barely kept pace with the rate of inflation since the mid-1920s.

✦ Stock returns have shown much more year-to-year variability than either bonds or Treasury bill returns. This is reflected in higher standard deviations and greater ranges between the highest and lowest annual returns. The standard deviation of stock returns is more than twice the standard deviation of bond returns.

Exhibit 20.2 ✦ HISTORICAL RETURNS FROM STOCKS, BONDS, AND MONEY MARKET INSTRUMENTS: 1926–99 (ANNUAL RETURNS)

	Large Stocks	Small Stocks	Bonds	T-bills
Mean Return	13.3%	17.4%	5.4%	3.8%
Standard Deviation	20.1	33.4	9.1	3.2
Highest Return	54.0	142.2	40.4	14.7
Lowest Return	−43.3	−58.0	−9.2	0.1
Number Positive	54 out of 74	52 out of 74	53 out of 74	74 out of 74

However, the historical record also clearly shows that much of the year-to-year variability in stock returns disappears over longer holding periods. We can clearly see the relationship between volatility and holding period by looking at the data shown in Exhibit 20.3. Notice that both the standard deviation and range drop dramatically as the length of the holding period increases. For example, between 1926 and 1999, twenty years (out of a total of seventy-four years) had negative stock returns. On the other hand, never has one rolling twenty-year period (out of a total of 55 periods) had negative stock returns. Further, the spread annual returns between the best twenty-year period and the worst twenty-year period is only about 14.5 percent. By contrast, the spread in returns between the best year and the worst year for large stocks is almost 100 percent.

If we go back even further in time we notice that stock returns over long periods of time have been remarkably consistent. Exhibit 20.4 shows the nominal and real compound average annual return from common stocks over varying periods between 1802 and 1997. Notice that the real compound average annual return from common stocks has hovered about 7 percent.

Another way of analyzing historical returns is to calculate the probabilities associated with actually earning various rates of returns. If we assume that historical returns are normally distributed, we can calculate probabilities based on the mean and standard deviation of each return series.[2] The probabilities for large-stock investments, for varying holding periods, are shown in Exhibit 20.5. Notice the effect length of holding period has on the probabilities of earning specific rates of return. If you hold stocks for only one year, your odds of earning 5 percent or more are about 66 percent. On the other hand, if you hold stocks for twenty years, your odds of earning at least 5 percent per year are close to 96 percent. Based on historical data, you have virtually no chance of earning negative returns if you invest your money for twenty years. Invest your money in stocks for only one year, and you stand almost a 25 percent chance of losing money.

So, will these patterns hold over the next year, the next five years, the next thirty years, or the next one hundred years? If you're a short-term investor, should you avoid stocks? On the other hand, if you have a long-term time horizon, should you invest most of your money in stocks? No one knows with any certainty what the future will hold, and that's part of the risk associated with all investment decisions.

---

[2]Statistical analysis of historical security returns indicates that the series are fairly close to being normally distributed.

Exhibit 20.3 ✦ The Impact of Holding-Period Length on Large-Stock Risk and Return

	Holding Period			
	1 Year	5 Years	10 Years	20 Years
Mean Return	13.3%	11.0%	11.1%	11.2%
Standard Deviation	20.1	8.5	5.5	3.6
High	54.0	27.5	20.1	17.6
Low	−43.3	−12.5	−0.9	3.1
Number Positive	54 out of 74	63 out of 70	63 out of 65	55 out of 55

Note: All returns are annualized.

Exhibit 20.4 ✦ Summary of Stock Returns since 1802

	Compound Average	Annual Return
Period	Nominal	Real
1802–1870	7.1%	7.0%
1871–1925	7.2	6.6
1926–1997	10.6	7.2
1802–1997	8.4	7.0

Exhibit 20.5 ✦ Probabilities of Earning Minimum Rates of Return

	Holding Period		
Average Annual Return of at Least	1 Year	10 Years	20 Years
5%	65.8%	86.6%	99.5%
10	56.3	58.0	67.8
15	46.4	24.1	5.0

Although our crystal ball is no less clear than anyone else's, we do have some observations and caveats that should help investors form macro-expectations concerning the future returns from financial assets.

1. One clear lesson from the historical record is that stocks are better long-term investments than other financial assets. We don't believe that will change anytime in the foreseeable future. Real stock returns will continue to average between 6 and 8 percent per year. Real bond returns will likely average between 3 and 5 percent per year. Of course, we're not suggesting that stocks will outperform other financial assets next year, or over the next five years. Over longer periods of time—10 to 30 years—we believe stocks will earn substantially higher returns than either bonds or money market instruments.

2. Long-term returns are far more predictable, or if you will less uncertain, than short-term returns. Be careful not to place too much emphasis on short-term trends or patterns. For example, just because stocks did exceptionally well during the last half of the 1990s is no guarantee they'll do well over the next few years. At the same time, don't assume that a period of above-average returns will be followed by a period of below-average returns, or vice-versa.

3. The historical record is just that; it's a record of what happened, not what will happen. Because the financial markets are forward-looking by nature, the past is never a guarantee of the future. If you believe, as we do, that stock prices follow earnings in the long run, future stock returns will be driven by future corporate profits. Interestingly, over long periods of time increases in corporate profits, like stock returns, have been fairly consistent.

MICRO-EXPECTATIONS

If macro-expectations deal with expected returns from general categories of financial assets, micro-expectations deal with expected returns from groups within the general categories. For stocks, for example, examples of micro-expectations include the expected return from large company stocks relative to small company stocks, the expected return from domestic stocks relative to international stocks, or the expected return growth stocks relative to value stocks. An example of micro-expectations for bonds include the expected return on junk bonds relative to investment-grade bonds. Micro-expectations also help select individual securities and to time markets.

As we discussed in the prior section, most investors base their macro-expectations on the historical record. We could base micro-expectations on the historical record as well, but the historical record is far more muddled at the micro level than it is at the macro level. Take, for example, the performance of large-company stocks versus the performance of small-company stocks. On average, between 1926 and 1999, small stocks have returned about 4 percent a year more than large stocks (17.4 percent versus 13.2 percent). Further, small stocks outperformed large stocks in 40 out of the 74 years. Over longer holding periods, small stocks still beat large stocks. For rolling twenty-year holding periods, small-stock returns have averaged almost 15 percent per year. By contrast, large-stock returns have averaged only slightly more than 11 percent per year. Out of the 55 rolling twenty-year periods between 1926 and 1999, small stocks beat large stocks in all but five of the periods.

In recent years, however, the pattern has reversed and large stocks have generally outperformed small stocks. The chart in Exhibit 20.6 shows the compound average annual returns from large and small stocks over varying periods ending on December 31, 1999. Over the five years ending on December 31, 1999, large stocks had an average return of 27.5 percent per year. By contrast, returns from small stocks averaged only about 16 percent per year.

What does the future hold? Will small stocks make a comeback to their dominant position relative to large stocks, or have large stocks become the superior investment? Frankly, your guess is as good as anyone's. We tend to think that small stocks are poised for a comeback, but our conviction isn't terribly strong. We have a lot more confidence in our macro-expectation that stocks will continue to outperform bonds than our micro-expectation that small stocks will again outperform large stocks. Micro-expectations, in addition to being more problematic, require much more careful analysis and research.

One way to avoid problems associated with forming micro-expectations is by investing in index funds. A thirty-year-old investor saving for retirement might invest

Exhibit 20.6 ✦ RECENT RETURNS FROM LARGE AND SMALL STOCKS

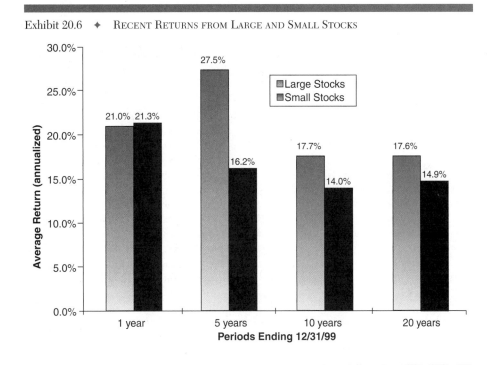

80 percent of her money in a stock index fund and the other 20 percent in a bond index fund. Index funds, as we know, mimic the broad market and have become extremely popular with investors today. The Investment History box on page 590 describes the origins of index funds.

Asset Allocation

Asset allocation involves decisions regarding the percentage of funds to be invested in various financial assets (stocks, bonds, and money market instruments). Asset allocation is the most important part of the portfolio construction process because how funds are allocated among various financial assets determines the investor's return and risk exposure.

As we noted in Chapter 1, investors make two types of asset allocation decisions: strategic asset allocation and tactical asset allocation. In strategic asset allocation decisions regard the general mix of investments that will make up the investor's portfolio. For example, strategic asset allocation might create a portfolio consisting of 70 percent stocks, 20 percent bonds, and 10 percent money market instruments. Tactical asset allocation involves selecting specific investments within each of the general categories of stocks, bonds, and money market instruments. For instance, within the 70 percent of the portfolio invested in stocks, a tactical asset allocation decision might place half of the funds in large stocks and half in small stocks.

Strategic asset allocation considers the investor's objectives, return requirements, time horizon, and risk preferences. In general, investors whose main objective is

asset allocation
Decisions regarding the percentage of funds to be invested in various financial assets.

A Brief History of Index Funds

Index funds—mutual funds designed merely to track a specified index—are extremely popular investment choices today. The largest and oldest index mutual fund, the Vanguard 500 Index Fund, has more than $100 billion in assets, ranking it among the five largest stock mutual funds. Investors are attracted to index funds by low fees, high tax efficiency, and the fact that index funds seem to routinely outperform most managed mutual funds.

In the early 1970s, several banks and investment firms began experimenting with indexing. One of the first was a $6-million index account constructed by Wells Fargo Bank for Samsonite's Corporation's pension fund. Most investment professionals, however, initially dismissed as silly the idea of indexing. The magazine *Pensions & Investments* awarded its "Dubious Achievement Award" in 1972 to Batterymarch Financial Management of Boston for its index-based investing program. Not until 1975 did Batterymarch attract its first index client.

Index fund pioneer and mutual fund maverick John Bogle argues that three seminal articles published in the early to mid-1970s by distinguished authors helped to legitimize the idea of index investing. All three articles pointed out that active investment managers—those managing pension funds and mutual funds—fail to outperform the overall market on a consistent basis. One of authors, the highly respected

Charles Ellis, managing partner of Greenwich Associates, wrote, "The investment management business is built upon a simple and basic belief: professionals can beat the market. That premise appears to be false." In fact, Ellis argued, once you subtract the fees collected by professional money managers, most will consistently underperform the market.

These articles, along with his familiarity of the research on the consistently of mutual fund performance, led John Bogle to create the first index mutual fund, what is now the Vanguard 500 Stock Index Fund. In 1974, Bogle had formed his own mutual fund company, the Vanguard Group. His philosophy was to offer investors low-cost funds. Bogle believed then, and still believes today, that in the long run, low-cost funds would outperform high-cost funds. In his mind, an index fund was the closest real-world investors could come to zero-cost investing.

Bogle's new invention took a while to catch on. Of course, the 1970s weren't the best of decades for stock investors. But even during the 1980s, index funds grew slowly. Not until the mid-1990s did the average investor, helped along by the popular press, "discover" index funds. A headline in a 1995 issue of *Money* magazine read "Bogle wins: Index funds should be the core of most portfolios today." Today, index funds account for more than 7 percent of all mutual fund assets (up from less than 3 percent in 1995). By some accounts, more than 25 percent of all new cash flowing into equity mutual funds went into index funds.

growth in capital will allocate a large share of their investments funds to common stocks. Investors whose main objective is capital preservation, will allocate less money to common stocks, and more to bonds and money market instruments.

Macro-expectations also play a role in strategic asset allocation decisions. An investor who believes, for example, currently finds bonds attractive might choose to allocate a larger share of her portfolio to bonds and a smaller share to stocks than she would normally.

When it comes to tactical asset allocation decisions, micro-expectations play a prominent role. If, for example, an investor believes that small stocks will begin again to outperform large stocks, he might allocate a larger share of the portfolio to smaller stocks, and a smaller share to large stocks. Tactical asset allocation also deals with individual security selection and market timing.

Which is more important, strategic or tactical asset allocation? According to several studies, strategic asset allocation dominates tactical asset allocation. One study

Exhibit 20.7 ✦ A SIMPLE MODEL OF ASSET ALLOCATION

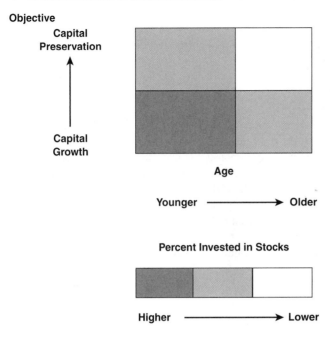

found that virtually all variation in pension plan returns could be explained by strategic asset allocation decisions.[3]

THE LIFE-CYCLE APPROACH TO ASSET ALLOCATION

According to many investment professionals and financial planners, individuals' asset allocation should relate closely to the person's age or stage in life. The life-cycle approach to asset allocation is appealing because of the fairly predictable differences in financial position, investment objectives, and constraints between a sixty-year-old investor and a twenty-five-year-old investor.

Jack Bogle, founder and senior chairman of the Vanguard Group (the nation's second-largest mutual fund company), advocates a simple asset-allocation model based on two factors: the age of the investor, and the whether the investor is in an "accumulation" stage or a "distribution" stage of his or her life cycle. Investors who are in the accumulation stage have as their main objective, growth in capital. Investors who are in the distribution stage have preservation of capital and current income as their primary investment objectives.

Bogle's model is illustrated in Exhibit 20.7. Younger investors in the capital accumulation stage have long-term investment horizons. They have no immediate need for their money and, therefore, can afford greater risks in exchange for higher returns. Consequently, these investors should allocate a large portion of their portfolios to

---

[3]These studies are cited and discussed in John Bogle, *Common Sense on Mutual Funds* (New York: Wiley, 1999), pp. 67–69.

common stocks—perhaps as high as 80 or 90 percent. They should invest the balance of their funds in bonds or money market instruments. Age plays a role for investors in the accumulation stage. The older the investor, the lower the percentage that should be invested in common stocks. However, even older investors in the capital accumulation stage should still invest a majority of their funds in common stocks.

Investors more in the distribution stage have more immediate needs for their money. Short-term volatility and losses are far more significant for an investor in the distribution stage than for one in the accumulation stage. A retired person, for example, may depend on a relatively fixed amount of capital to generate sufficient income to meet daily needs. As a result, investors in the distribution stage should allocate less to stocks and more to bonds and money market instruments. The appropriate mix might be something like 50 percent stocks, 30 percent bonds, and 20 percent money market instruments. Again, the older the investor, the lower the percentage that should be invested in common stocks.

Older investors must avoid becoming too conservative and allocating all of their funds to money market instruments or bonds. Capital growth is important even for a sixty-five-year-old recently retired investor. Here's why. First, although bonds have historically produced the highest current income of any financial asset, bond interest income doesn't increase over time. Considering inflation, real interest income actually declines. Stock income, on the other hand, has historically risen at about the rate of inflation. Consequently, over about a ten year period, dividend income from stocks will generally exceed interest income from bonds. Second, a sixty-five-year-old investor still has a fairly long investment horizon. According to actuarial statistics a healthy person sixty-five years old has a life expectancy of almost twenty years. Financial planners will tell you that you should plan on living into your 90s. Even the sixty-five-year-old, according to the experts, should allocate 40 to 50 percent of her portfolio to common stocks. The Investment Insights box on page 593 lists some suggested portfolios for investors at varying stages of their life.

DIVERSIFICATION AND PORTFOLIO OPTIMIZATION

As you no doubt remember, an important investment truism is that diversification is beneficial. Diversification is a way of reducing a portfolio's risk, without significantly reducing its expected return. All portfolios should, therefore, be diversified. When making asset allocation decisions the investor must ensure an adequate level of diversification. Investing 80 percent of your retirement money in your company's common stock and 20 percent in Treasury bills is probably not adequate diversification.

Fortunately, it is easy to achieve a reasonable level of diversification. As we've seen, even a portfolio of 5 or 6 stocks will be fairly well diversified. And one of the main advantages of investing in mutual funds is diversification. The typical mutual fund holds several hundred different securities. Index funds, another popular choice today, are also by their very nature well diversified. Investing 80 percent of your retirement funds in a stock index fund and the other 20 percent in Treasury bills will likely give you a pretty high level of diversification.

As we discussed in Chapter 17, the two types of diversification are naïve diversification and efficient diversification. Any combination of financial assets will likely result in naïve diversification. On the other hand, efficient diversification is a more systematic process that seeks combinations of investments that minimize risk for a given level of return, or maximize return for a given level of risk. Investors can allocate their funds to construct efficiently diversified portfolios.

INVESTMENT INSIGHTS

SOME SUGGESTED RETIREMENT PORTFOLIOS

Most people cite a financially secure retirement as a major goal for investing. Achieving that requires careful planning and proper asset allocation. Below are some suggested retirement portfolios.

Katie, age 25

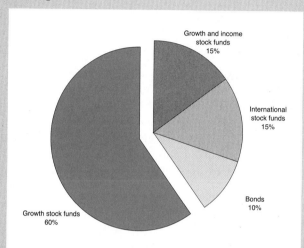

Steven, age 38

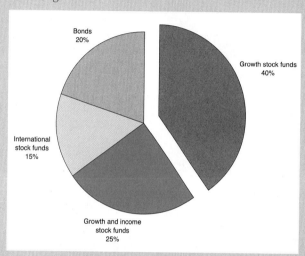

Michele, age 50

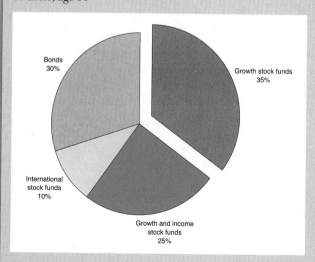

Walter, age 62

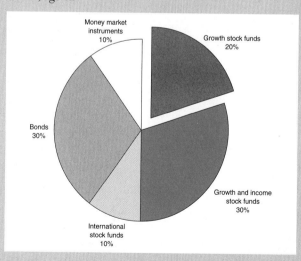

Using historical return data for large stocks, small stocks, bonds, and Treasury bills for 1926 to 1999, Exhibit 20.8 shows the resulting *efficient frontier.*[4] (As we discussed in Chapter 17, the efficient frontier consists of portfolios that maximize return, for a given level of risk, or minimize risk, for a given level of return.) Each of the portfolios, along with efficient frontier, meets the two optimization conditions. The portfolio labeled A on the efficient frontier has the same mean return as a portfolio consisting of 100 percent large stocks (13.2 percent), but has a lower standard deviation (17.2 percent versus 20.1 percent). Portfolio A consists of approximately 56 percent large stocks, 27 percent small stocks, and 17 percent bonds.

Monitoring Portfolios

The last step in the portfolio construction and management process consists of monitoring the investment portfolio. Monitoring a portfolio involves measuring its performance and assessing how well it is meeting investment objectives. In the process of monitoring a portfolio, the investor may decide to make changes to the portfolio based on poor performance or a conclusion that the portfolio has failed to adequately meet the investor's objectives. Investors should also keep tabs on changing market conditions—and resulting changes to macro- or micro-expectations—and investor circumstances. Changes in an investor's circumstances or market conditions may necessitate changes to the investment portfolio.

ACTIVE VERSUS PASSIVE MANAGEMENT

Back in Chapter 1 we discussed the difference between active investors and passive investors. Investors who actively manage their portfolios buy and sell more frequently than more passive investors. Active investors may shift funds between various types of instruments due to shifts in macro- or micro-expectations. To plan these moves, they tend to monitor the performance of their investments more closely, and they may be more concerned about short-term performance than passive investors.

A passive investor, however, tends to buy a portfolio of securities and keep it pretty much intact for a long period of time. This investor may be less inclined to make changes to the portfolio in response to changes in macro- or micro-expectations. Only a significant change to the investor's circumstances will lead to a significant adjustment to the investor's portfolio.

Because active investors make more changes to their investments than passive investors, active investors incur higher transactions costs and may pay more in taxes. Consequently, active investors should earn higher returns than passive investors. Does it pay to be an active investor? Throughout this book we've pondered this question frequently, and our feet are planted firmly in the middle. Some evidence supports arguments in favor of active investing, but equally compelling evidence supports passive investing. Index funds, perhaps the pinnacle of passive investing, often outperform the average actively managed mutual fund.

---

[4]The efficient frontier was constructed using the Optimal Portfolio worksheet in the I-Wizard workbook found on the data disk that accompanies your book.

Exhibit 20.8 ✦ Efficient Frontier: Combinations of Large Stocks, Small Stocks, Bonds, and Bills

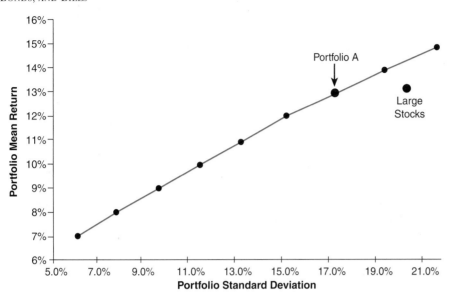

Changes in Investor Circumstances

Both active and passive investors do agree upon that changes in an investor's circumstances may alter an investor's objectives or constraints and lead to changes in asset allocation. Individual circumstances that can change include

- ✦ *Aging.* As investors age, their time horizons shorten. A shorter time horizon means the investor must be somewhat more conservative. As a general rule, as investors age accumulation of capital becomes less important relative to preservation of capital.
- ✦ *Increases or decreases in wealth.* Investor wealth can change dramatically over time, which leads to changes in investment objectives and constraints. For example, an increase in wealth may make an investor less risk averse. Increases in wealth usually push investors into higher tax brackets, and tax issues become a more important consideration in the investment process.
- ✦ *Changes in family status.* The investment objectives of a single person can differ greatly from the investment objectives of someone who has a family.

Rebalancing

Whether you are a passive or an active investor, you may need to occasionally rebalance your portfolio. **Rebalancing** means adjusting your investments to return to your target asset allocation. Although it sounds complicated, rebalancing is actually a fairly simple process. Let's look at an example.

Maria's target asset allocation is 75 percent stocks and 25 percent bonds. Two years ago, she had $75,000 invested in a stock index fund and 25 percent invested in a bond index fund. Over the next two years, the stock index fund had a total return of

rebalancing
Adjusting the contents of a portfolio to return to the investor's target asset allocation.

45 percent, whereas the bond index fund returned 4.5 percent. Now, Maria has more than 75 percent of her money invested in stocks and less than 25 percent invested in bonds. Here's the math:

Stock index fund	Beginning value = $75,000	Ending value = $75,000 × 1.45 = $108,750
Bond index fund	Beginning value = $25,000	Ending value = $25,000 × 1.045 = $26,125
Total portfolio	Beginning value = $100,000 (75 percent stocks, 25 percent bonds)	Ending value = $134,875 (81 percent stocks, 19 percent bonds)

To return to her target asset allocation (75 percent stocks, 25 percent bonds), Maria must rebalance her portfolio. She could either sell some shares of her stock fund and buy bond fund shares or allocate slightly more of any new investment dollars to bond funds until she reaches her target allocation.

PERFORMANCE MEASURE AND EVALUATION

Measuring and evaluating the performance of an investment portfolio is a critical part of the investment process. *All* investors must sit down periodically and carefully measure and evaluate their investments' performance. As we noted, passive investors may do this less frequently than active ones, but even the most passive investor can't avoid this task. Measuring and evaluating performance concerns issues such as overall performance, relative performance, cost, and risk. You must ask yourself whether or not your investment plan meets your investment objectives. If not, you may need to consider some changes.

Measuring and evaluating performance is a logical conclusion to the study of investments. In the concluding chapter we consider how measure and evaluate investment portfolio performance of.

Chapter Summary

1. What is the process of building and managing an investment portfolio?
   The process of building and managing an investment portfolio consists of a series of steps, the details of which can vary from investor to investor. The first step is to develop an investment policy that blends the investor's objectives, constraints the investor faces, and the investor's preferences. Investors consider both the investment policy and expectations concerning future financial market performance when making strategic and tactical asset allocation decisions. The final step of the process is portfolio monitoring. Poor performance, changes in the investor's circumstances, and changing market expectations can lead to changes in the investor's asset allocation.

2. How does an investor develop an investment policy?
   An investment policy blends the investor's objectives with the investors constraints and preferences. Both individual and institutional investors should develop investment policies, but many important differences exist between institutional and individual investors. Three general investment objectives are growth in capital, preservation of capital, and current income. How an investor sets priorities among these three objectives depends on the reasons for investing and the characteristics of

the investor. Balancing investment objectives involves trade-offs between risk and return. Constraints are limitations imposed on the portfolio construction process. Examples of constraints include the time horizon, liquidity needs, taxes, regulatory constraints, and unique needs or preferences.

3. How do capital market assumptions affect the investment process?

You cannot make investment decisions without forming some expectations concerning the future performance of the financial markets. Investors can form both macro- and micro-expectations. Macro-expectations involve future performance of broad financial asset categories (stocks, bonds, and money market instruments). Micro-expectations involve future performance of groups and individuals within the broad asset categories. Investors tend to form expectations based on the historical performance record. Although aspects of the record have been relatively consistent over time, the past is never a guarantee of the future.

4. What is asset allocation?

Asset allocation involves decisions regarding the percentage of an investor's funds to be invested in various financial assets. The two types of asset allocation are: strategic asset allocation—decisions concern the general mix of investments that will make up the portfolio; tactical asset allocation decisions involve selecting specific investments within each of the general categories. Asset allocation decisions are heavily influenced by the investment policy and financial market expectations. One popular approach to asset allocation for individual investors is the so-called life-cycle approach. Younger investors, whose primary objective is capital accumulation, should invest a high proportion of their funds in common stocks. Older investors, whose primary objective is capital distribution and preservation, should invest a smaller proportion of their funds in common stocks. Another factor guiding asset allocation decisions is diversification; all investor's should strive to hold diversified portfolios.

5. What does monitoring a portfolio involve?

Monitoring a portfolio involves measuring its performance and assessing how well it is meeting investment objectives. In the process of monitoring a portfolio, an investor may decide to make changes because of poor performance or a conclusion that the portfolio is not adequately meeting investment objectives. Changes in the investor's circumstances and market expectations may also lead to portfolio changes. The two general approaches to portfolio management are active and passive. Active investors are more adapt to make more frequent changes to their portfolios than passive "buy and hold" investors. All investors must periodically rebalance their portfolios if the actual asset allocation differs significantly from the target asset allocation.

Review Questions and Problems

1. Explain the steps involved in constructing and monitoring an investment portfolio. Is the process a one-way street?

2. Define an *investment policy*. List some differences between individual investors and institutional investors.

3. What are the three main investment objectives? Which objective is most important for a young person investing for retirement?

4. Jill is 25 and wants to begin a retirement investment program (she plans to retire in forty years at age 65). If Jill believes she'll need at least $2.5 million to retire, how much must she invest each year if she can earn 10 percent annually? Convince Jill that she should invest most of her retirement savings—at least initially—in common stocks.

5. John is 65 and plans to retire within the next six months. Currently John has $2.2 million in his 401(k). What is John's primary investment objective? Would investing 100 percent of his money in bonds or money market instruments be a mistake? Why or why not?

6. List some constraints faced by individual and institutional investors. Which type of investor is subject to more regulation?

7. Explain the difference between macro- and micro-expectations. How do most investors form their expectations?

8. What is the different between strategic asset allocation and tactical asset allocation? Give an example of each. Explain how an investor's life cycle affects asset allocation.

9. What steps are involved in the portfolio monitoring stage? Give some reasons why even a passive investor might make some changes to her portfolio.

10. Define *rebalancing*. John wants to maintain an asset allocation of 70 percent stocks and 30 percent bonds. Five years ago, he invested $70,000 in a stock index fund and $30,000 in a bond index fund. Since then stocks have had a compound average annual return of 11.1 percent, whereas bonds have had a compound average annual return of 5.1 percent. What is John's current asset allocation? What changes should he make?

CFA Questions

1. (Level I, 1994) To create an appropriate asset allocation and investment management program, each investor must specify how the objectives and constraints that apply to all investors affect their own particular situations. A useful framework for organizing these objectives and constraints is shown below:

Objectives:	Constraints:
Return	Time Horizon
Risk	Liquidity Needs
	Tax Considerations
	Legal and Regulatory Requirements
	Unique Needs, Preferences, or Circumstances

Assume that you are advising two U.S. clients who are beginning their first investment programs, Iva Jones and the Green Foundation.

a. Iva Jones is a 70-year old widow who has just received the $300,000 insurance proceeds resulting from her husband's recent death. She lives alone in a small mortgage-free house worth $100,000, is in good health, and has no children. The steady income she receives from Social Security and a life annuity meets her minimum living expenses but is not sufficient to allow her to travel or to pursue the hobbies she would like. She has no other income or assets available for investment. A favorite nephew will eventually inherit her estate. Mrs. Jones' income is subject to both federal and state income taxes.

Briefy discuss Mrs. Jones' objectives and constraints, using the framework and the information provided above.

b. Green Foundation has just concluded a successful fund drive and has $1,000,000 to invest. This money represents the foundation's permanent endowment capital, the income from which is used currently to sponsor research projects aimed at developing an improved battery for electric automobiles. The foundation's investment committee wants to maximize long-run total return from the endowment portfolio, but recognizes that the level of the income component will also be important. The foundation is qualified under U.S. law as a tax-exempt entity. It expects to receive no further endowment gifts over the foreseeable future.

Briefly discuss Green Foundation's objectives and constraints, using the framework and the information provided above.

2. (Level III, 1995) Ambrose Green, 63, is a retired engineer and a client of Clayton Asset Management Associates ("Associates"). His accumulated savings are invested in Diversified Global Fund ("the Fund"), an in-house investment vehicle with multiple

portfolio managers through which Associates manage nearly all client assets on a pooled basis. Dividend and capital gain distributions have produced an annual average return to Green of about 8% on his $900,000 original investment in the Fund, made six years ago. The $1,000,000 current value of his Fund interest represents virtually all of Green's net worth.

Green is a widower whose daughter is a single parent living with her young son. While not an extravagant person, Green's spending had exceeded his after-tax income by a considerable margin since his retirement. As a result, his non-Fund financial resources have steadily diminished and now amount to $10,000. Green does not have retirement income from a private pension plan, but does receive taxable government benefits of about $1,000 per month. His marginal tax rate is 40%. He lives comfortably in a rented apartment, travels extensively, and makes frequent cash gifts to his daughter and grandson, to whom he wants to leave an estate of at least $1,000,000.

Green realizes that he needs more income to maintain his lifestyle. He also believes his assets should provide an after-tax cash flow sufficient to meet his present $80,000 annual spending needs, which he is unwilling to reduce. He is uncertain as to how to proceed and has engaged you, a CFA Charterholder with an independent advisory practice, to counsel him.

Your first task is to review Green's investment policy statement.

AMBROSE GREEN'S INVESTMENT POLICY STATEMENT

Objectives:
✦ "I need a maximum return that includes an income element large enough to meet my spending needs, so about a 10% total return is required."
✦ "I want low risk, to minimize the possibility of large losses and preserve the value of my assets for eventual use by my daughter and grandson."

Constraints:
✦ "With my spending needs averaging about $80,000 per year and only $10,000 of cash remaining, I will probably have to sell something soon."
✦ "I am in good health and my non-cancelable health insurance will cover my future medical expenses."

    a. **Identify** and **briefly discuss** *four* key constraints present in Green's situation not adequately treated in his investment policy statement.

    b. Based on your assessment of his situation and the information presented in the Introduction, **create** and **justify** appropriate *return* and *risk* objectives for Green.

CRITICAL THINKING EXERCISE

This exercise requires computer work. Find in the Data Workbook a worksheet entitled Security Returns. The worksheet provides annual returns from large stocks, small stocks, Treasury bonds, and Treasury bills between 1950 and 1999. Use these returns to answer the questions associated with the following case study.

Scott and Shelly are both 45. Their combined annual income is $100,000. Current combined balance in their retirement accounts is $450,000. They are each saving about $7,500 a year (including employer contributions). Bonds make up 40 percent of their investments, stocks 30 percent, and money market instruments 10 percent. Scott and Shelly describe themselves as "conservative" investors. Their main investment goal is to retire financially secure in about twenty years. (They have sufficient resources to meet other major financial goals).

    a. Based on the information provided, how much do you believe Scott and Shelly will need in their retirement accounts by the time they retire? (Most financial planners argue that people need an annual retirement income close to their pre-retirement income. Financial planners also suggest basing retirement plans on the assumption that people will live to be age 90.)

b.   Based on the case information—along with the historical data on stock and bond returns—do you believe Scott and Shelly are saving enough each year?

c.   What is your recommended asset allocation? What kind of risk and return characteristics will it have? What kinds of changes to the portfolio should be made as Scott and Shelly age?

THE INTERNET INVESTOR

1.   Numerous "retirement planners" are available today. Some are software-based programs and others are Internet based. Visit the following web site and, using your plans or those of a friend, go through the retirement planner. Write a brief report on your experience.

     cnnfn.com/markets/personalfinance/tipstools/gateway/retirement.html

2.   When developing an investment policy and allocating assets, investors must consider their tolerance for risk along with other individual characteristics. Visit the following web site and its "Investor Profile Questionnaire." How much would this exercise, in your opinion, help an investor with asset allocation decisions?

     www.schwab.com/schwabnow

3.   Asset allocation can be confusing for many investors, especially novices. A variety of web sites have interactive guides to help investors with asset allocation decisions. Go to the site listed below and complete the asset allocation planner. Write a brief report discussing your reaction to the exercise.

     www.fidelity.com/planning/investment

EVALUATING INVESTMENT PERFORMANCE

Chapter Objectives

After reading Chapter 21, you should be able to answer the following questions:

1. What are some important issues regarding evaluating investment performance?
2. How do analysts measure risk and return?
3. What are three measures of risk-adjusted performance?
4. How good a predictor is past performance of future performance?

Has the "Sage of Omaha" lost his magic touch? That's a question some late-1999 observers were beginning to ask about Warren Buffet, arguably the world's most famous investor, and certainly one of the wealthiest. Why were they questioning Buffet's stock-picking prowess? Perhaps because shares of his company, Berkshire Hathaway were sitting near their 52-week low.[1] Between the end of 1998 and the end

---

[1]Berkshire Hathaway is essentially an investment holding company. It owns 100 percent of several companies and large minority positions in several others. At a price of about $52,000 per share Berkshire Hathaway has the distinction of being the world's most expensive publicly traded stock.

of 1999, shares of Berkshire Hathaway produced a total return of −13 percent. By contrast, the S&P 500 had a total return in 1999 in excess of 23 percent. Two corner-stones of Buffet's investment portfolio—consumer stocks and insurance companies—had miserable years in 1999.

Buffet's investment philosophy has always been to concentrate his investments in a handful of companies whose businesses he considered fairly easy to under-stand and predict. He likes stocks of companies with recognizable brand names and always buys stocks with the intention of holding them for long periods of time. At the end of 1998, Berkshire's largest stock holdings included American Express, Coca-Cola, Gillette, and Wells Fargo. Berkshire is Coke's largest single shareholder. Berkshire also owns controlling interests in two large insurance companies: GEICO and General Re.

By his own admission, Buffet doesn't understand technology very well. He claims that he can't forecast what the technology business will look like in ten years, nor which companies will still be around. As a result, Buffet has avoided technology stocks. But technology stocks have among the best market performers in recent years. The tech-heavy Nasdaq stock market, for example, rose by more than 85 per cent during 1999. Critics suggest that Buffet's investment approach is simply out of date.

Although some suggest that Buffet's time has passed, many others believe in Buffet's approach to investing. Some mutual fund managers, in fact, have used the recent dip in Berkshire's stock as an opportunity to buy additional shares. According to Buffet's defenders, a portfolio that concentrates on a few stocks will have an occa-sional bad year, and what happened during 1999 was merely an aberration not the beginning of a long-term trend. Once the market's fascination with tech stocks ends, Buffet's star will shine brightly again. They advocate ignoring short-term performance and focusing on long-term results. Indeed, even with 1999's poor results factored in, during the 1990s, shares of Berkshire Hathaway outperformed the S&P 500 by a large margin.[2]

The debate over whether the Sage of Omaha still has the golden touch illustrates many of the issues that confront investors when they evaluate the performance of in-vestment portfolios. Properly evaluating investment portfolio performance—the sub-ject of this final chapter—is critical if investors are to make intelligent choices. Although we will focus on evaluating mutual fund performance in this chapter, the material applies to any investment portfolio.

Performance Evaluation Issues

There are no universally agreed upon set of standards for the evaluation of investment portfolios. Government regulators and industry organizations have recently adopted policies designed to make it easier for investors to evaluate and compare perfor-mance. For example, the Association for Investment Management and Research (AIMR) adopted a minimum set of portfolio presentation performance standards in

---

[2]An initial investment of $10,000 in Berkshire Hathaway shares made at the beginning of 1990 was worth in excess of $70,000 by the end of 1999. By contrast, $10,000 invested in the S&P 500 at the beginning of 1990 was worth about $45,000 by the end of 1999.

INVESTMENT INSIGHTS

STANDARDS FOR REPORTING PORTFOLIO PERFORMANCE

In 1993 the Association for Investment Management and Research (AIMR) prepared a list of standards for reporting portfolio performance. These standards, which apply to any investment portfolio, include the following:

✦ Returns reported are total returns (holding period returns).
✦ Ten years of annual returns should be reported.
✦ All fees and expenses should be subtracted from gross portfolio returns.
✦ Cash and cash equivalents are to be included when calculating returns.
✦ Time weighted returns are to be included, at least quarterly and linked geometrically.

The Securities & Exchange Commission has a set of requirements on how mutual fund returns reported in the fund's prospectus. Among these are the following:

✦ Total returns over varying periods of time (one year, three years, five years, and so on).
✦ All fees and expenses are subtracted from gross returns.
✦ Returns calculated on both a before and after tax basis.
✦ For comparison purposes, returns from a benchmark (such as the appropriate market index) are to be included.
✦ A graph comparing the quarter to quarter volatility in the fund's returns relative to the market benchmark is required.

Sources: Association for Investment Management & Research, U.S. Securities & Exchange Commission.

1993.[3] The AIMR standards, as well as standards described by the Securities & Exchange Commission, are listed in the Investment Insights box above.

You must consider several factors when you evaluate mutual fund performance or any other investment portfolio. To illustrate these factors, let's consider the following example. In 1999 the Janus Fund—a large-stock mutual fund—had a total return of slightly more than 47 percent. Another stock mutual fund, the Legg Mason Value Fund, had a total return of 28 percent for 1999. Let's say you're considering investing some of your IRA money in the one of these two stock funds, what should you think about?

TIME PERIODS

Whenever you evaluate performance, and especially when you compare the performance of one mutual fund to another, the time periods must be consistent. You'll often see two different mutual funds both advertising in the same publication that they were the top-performing fund. How can they both make that claim? Simply because each fund used a different time period when promoting its performance.

In addition, we argue that performance over short periods of time, such as a year, is less significant than performance over longer periods such as three, five, or ten

---

[3]AIMR controls and operates the Certified Financial Analyst (or CFA) program. All CFAs are members of AIMR and are, therefore, subject to its standards. Many security analysts, mutual fund managers, and other investment professionals are CFAs. We briefly describe the CFA program in Appendix B.

An Old Star Shines Brightly Again

In the world of mutual funds, the Janus Fund is an old-timer. Janus first sold shares to the investment public in late 1970. Back then, fewer than 200 equity mutual funds traded, with total assets of less than $50 billion. Today almost 4,000 equity funds hold total assets in excess of $2.5 trillion.

The Janus Fund was a trailblazer: one of the first no-load stock funds to sell shares directly to investors, bypassing stockbrokers.

From the beginning, the Janus Fund pursued a growth strategy. It invested in stocks the fund's managers and analysts thought had the potential for rapid earnings growth. The fund's philosophy was simple: In the long run, stock prices will follow earnings. At the same time, the fund believed in capital preservation. If fund managers believed the environment was unfavorable for stocks, the fund would invest a large portion of its assets in money market and other low-risk instruments. During the fund's history, the percentage of the portfolio invested in stocks has ranged from less than 50 percent to virtually 100 percent.

Although the 1970s was generally a forgettable decade for stocks, the Janus Fund more than held its own. Between 1972 and 1981, the fund beat the S&P 500 in seven out of ten years. Its total return was more than twice that of the S&P 500. Between 1982 and 1993, the Janus Fund had a cumulative total return of close to 600 percent. By contrast, the S&P 500 had a cumulative total return of less than 500 percent during the same period. Investors responded by pouring billions of dollars into the Janus Fund. Its net assets more than doubled between 1992 and 1993 alone. By the end of 1993 Janus had close to $10 billion in assets and was one of the largest stock funds.

Then, over the next four years, Janus's performance lagged behind the S&P 500. In 1997, for example, the fund's return was 11 percent less than the S&P 500's. Even more disturbing, the fund trailed its group average. The fund ranked in the bottom third of group stock funds during both 1995 and 1997. Critics wondered if the Janus Fund had simply gotten too large, or if its basic investment approach was no longer working. The Janus Fund even lost its coveted five-star Morningstar rating. Redemptions increased sharply, and the inflow of new money slowed to a trickle. But the fund stayed the course.

Shareholders who stuck with the Janus Fund were rewarded. In both 1998 and 1999 the fund outperformed the S&P 500 by substantial margins (16 percent in 1998 and 26 percent in 1999). The fund also easily beat its group average. In both 1998 and 1999, the Janus Fund ranked in the top quarter among growth stock funds. Money has begun to flow back into the fund. The fund's net assets now exceed $40 billion.

years, or even longer. Both Janus Fund and Legg Mason Value Fund did well during 1999. But how well did they perform over longer periods of time? Actually, over longer periods of time both funds have done well, too. The Legg Mason Value Fund, for example, had an average annual return of almost 36 percent over the five-year period ending in 1999. As we'll see later in the chapter, the Janus Fund's long-term performance record is equally impressive, but during the mid-1990s some investors began to have doubts. The Investment History box above describes how an old star has begun to shine brightly again.

Appropriate Benchmark

In and of themselves, returns tell you little unless you compare them to appropriate benchmarks. For mutual funds the obvious benchmarks are group average and the appropriate market index. Although the Janus Fund's 1999 return was much higher than that of the Legg Mason Value Fund, relative to their respective group averages

Exhibit 21.1 ✦ APPROPRIATE MUTUAL FUND PERFORMANCE BENCHMARKS

Type of Fund	Market Benchmark
Large-stock fund	S&P 500 index
Mid-cap stock fund	S&P Midcap 400 index
Small-stock fund	Russell 2000 index
International stock fund	Morgan Stanley EAFE index
Taxable-bond fund	Lehman Brothers aggregate bond index
Tax-exempt bond fund	Lehman Brothers municipal bond index

Legg Mason actually did better. Morningstar—the well-known mutual fund rating firm—classifies the Janus Fund as a "large-growth" fund, meaning it invests in large-company growth stocks. The average large-growth fund had a total return in 1999 of about 39 percent, so Janus's fund beat the group average by about 8 percent. On the other hand, Morningstar classifies the Legg Mason Value Fund as a "large-value" fund, meaning it invests in large stocks that the fund manager believes are "undervalued" for some reason. The average large-value fund had a total return in 1999 of only 7.4 percent, so the Legg Mason fund beat its group average by more than 20 percent.

The appropriate market index is also another performance benchmark to which you can compare investment portfolio performance. For stock funds, the most commonly used market benchmark is the Standard & Poor's 500 index. (Both the Janus and Legg Mason funds beat the S&P 500 handily in 1999.) Yet the S&P 500 is not the appropriate benchmark for *some* types of stock funds. For example, in the three years ending December 31, 1999, the T. Rowe Price Foreign Equity fund had an average annual return of about 16 percent, well below that of the S&P 500 (its three-year return averaged 27.6 percent per year). But because the T. Rowe Price fund is an international stock fund—meaning the fund invests in companies located outside the United States—its appropriate market benchmark is one of the international stock indexes, such as the Morgan Stanley EAFE Index. That index's average three-year return between 1997 and 1999 was 15.7 percent per year. By comparison to the *appropriate* market benchmark, therefore, the T. Rowe Price Foreign Equity fund did well.[4] Exhibit 21.1 lists the appropriate market indexes for various types of mutual funds.

RISK

A theme we've stressed throughout this book is that investors can't ignore risk when making investment choices. Investors must realize the positive relationship between risk and return and that higher risk must be compensated for in the form of higher returns. Perhaps the Janus Fund and the Legg Mason Value Fund performed well during 1999 only because they are riskier than the market or the average fund in their respective peer groups. You must carefully review the risk of each fund and evaluate whether the fund's *risk adjusted returns* were adequate.

---

[4]The T. Rowe Price Foreign Equity fund also beat its peer-group 1997–99 average, 16 percent per year versus 15.3 per year.

We'll describe methods for evaluating risk adjusted returns a little later in the chapter. As for one measure of risk, both the Janus Fund and the Legg Mason Value Fund have betas of less than one, indicating that they have less systematic (market) risk than average.

OBJECTIVES AND CONSTRAINTS

In the prior chapter we discussed how investment objectives and constraints are blended to form an investment policy which, in turn, has a major impact on asset allocation decisions. Investment performance should always be evaluated within the context of the portfolios objectives and any constraints facing the portfolio manager. For example, many international stock funds are prohibited from investing in U.S. stocks, even if the U.S. market looks more attractive than international markets.

Here's another example. For the three years ending in 1993, Fidelity Asset Manager—an asset allocation fund—beat the S&P 500 by about 4 percent per year, even though the fund had less than half of its portfolio invested in stocks.[5] Investors responded by pouring billions of dollars into the fund. Events soured for Asset Manager, however. In both 1994 and 1995, the fund averaged an annual return of less than 5 percent, compared to 18 percent for the S&P 500. Those who were disappointed with the performance of Asset Manager and redeemed hundreds of thousands of shares failed to understand the fund's primary objective. Asset Manager, like all asset allocation funds, attempts to produce consistent returns over long periods of time, not beat the stock market.

Measuring Risk and Return

Here we will review how to properly measure risk and return when evaluating the performance of investment portfolios. If you need further review, reread Chapters 2, 17, and 18.

RETURN

The best measure of investment return is its total, or holding period return. In Chapter 2 we defined the holding period return, or HPR_t, as follows:

$$HPR_t = \frac{P_t - P_{t-1} + CF_t}{P_{t-1}},$$

where P_t is the price at the end of the period (month, quarter, year, and so on), P_{t-1} is the price at the beginning of the period, and CF_t is the amount of cash received from the investment during the period.[6]

---

[5]Asset allocation funds hold a combination of stocks, bonds, and money market instruments. The percentage invested in each asset category is adjusted to reflect the manager's assessment of changing market conditions.

[6]In Chapter 2 we described how to adjust a holding period return for inflation.

From the holding period return we can construct a total return index, which measures the change in an investors wealth over a period of time. The total return index equals

$$I_t = I_{t-1} \times (1 + HPR_t),$$

where I_{t-1} is the index value at the end of the prior period. The initial index value is set at some arbitrary number (1, 10, 100, 1,000, and so on).

Because returns should be measured over several consecutive time periods, we should also calculate average returns. As we noted in Chapter 2, the two measures of "average" returns are the arithmetic mean (AM) and the geometric mean (GM). The arithmetic mean equals

$$AM = \frac{1}{T} \sum_{t=1}^{T} HPR_t,$$

where T is the number of observations.[7] The geometric mean equals

$$GM = \left[\prod_{t=1}^{T} (1 + HPR_t) \right] - 1.$$

Both averages have their uses. The arithmetic mean is the "typical" return during a period of time. The geometric mean, on the other hand, is the average compound return and measures the actual change in wealth.

RISK

We defined *risk* as meaning that some uncertainty exists regarding what an investment's actual return will be over some period in the future. The greater the uncertainty, the greater the risk. In general, risk is associated with the variability of returns. The more variable the returns, the more risky the investment.

One way of measuring investment risk is to calculate the standard deviation of returns. *Standard deviation* measures the dispersion of a distribution around its mean. The higher the standard deviation, the more variable the returns, and thus the more risky the investment. Standard deviation is found as follows:[8]

$$SD = \left[\frac{1}{T-1} \sum_{t=1}^{T} (HPR_t - AM)^2 \right]^{1/2}.$$

One cornerstone of modern portfolio theory (MPT), which we discussed starting in Chapter 17, is that the total risk of an investment can be broken into two parts. The first part, *unsystematic risk,* can be eliminated through diversification, which comes about when a security is added to a portfolio. The second part, *systematic risk,* cannot

---

[7]We described in Chapter 2 how to annualize the arithmetic mean if it was calculated using data other than annual return data—monthly or quarterly returns, for example.

[8]In Chapter 2 we showed how to annualize the standard deviation if it was calculated using something other than annual return data.

be eliminated through diversification. Standard deviation measures total risk. A measure of systematic, or market risk, we call *beta*. Beta is calculated as follows:

$$Beta_j = Corr(m, j) \frac{SD_j}{SD_m}.$$

where $Corr(m, j)$ is the correlation between returns for investment j; the appropriate market portfolio, SD_j, is the standard deviation of returns for investment j; and SD_m is the standard deviation of returns for the market. The market has, by definition, a beta of one. An investment with a beta of less than one has less systematic risk than the market whereas an investment with a beta greater than one has more systematic risk than the market.

You can measure the degree to which a portfolio is diversified, meaning the degree to which unsystematic risk has been eliminated, by computing the correlation between returns for the portfolio and returns for the market portfolio, $Corr(m, p)$. The square of the correlation coefficient, known as *r-square*, tells you the percentage of the portfolio's total risk that is systematic risk. The closer r-square is to one, the more diversified the portfolio.

RISK AND RETURN MEASURES FOR THE JANUS FUND

As an illustration, let's calculate some risk and return measures for the Janus Fund. Exhibit 21.2 lists annual holding-period returns for the Janus Fund between 1972 and 1999.[9] Annual returns for the S&P 500—the appropriate market benchmark—are also listed in the exhibit. Total return indexes for both the Janus Fund and the S&P 500 are shown graphically in Exhibit 21.3.

First, we'll calculate the arithmetic mean, the geometric mean, and the standard deviation for both return series. The results are shown in the accompanying table.

	Janus Fund	S&P 500
Arithmetic mean	19.1%	15.1%
Geometric mean	17.9	13.9
Standard deviation	17.6	16.3
Value of a $1,000 (year end 1999)	$100,063	$38,178

The Janus Fund averaged higher annual returns than the S&P 500 between 1972 and 1999. For example, Janus had a average annual compound return of almost 18 percent compared to 13.9 percent for the S&P 500. Put another way, $1,000 invested in the Janus Fund at the beginning of 1972 was worth in excess of $100,000 at the end of 1999. A similar $1,000 investment in the S&P 500 grew to "only" about $38,000 in the same 28-year period. At the same time, the Janus Fund had somewhat more risk than the S&P 500. The Janus Fund's standard deviation is 17.6 percent compared to 16.3 percent for the S&P 500. Whether the Janus Fund's additional return is adequate compensation for the additional risk will be discussed in the next section.

---

[9]The Janus Fund is an advantageous example in that it's been around awhile. Most mutual funds today have been in existence for less than ten years; many have been around for less than five years.

Exhibit 21.2 ✦ ANNUAL RETURNS FROM THE JANUS FUND AND THE S&P 500

	Janus Fund		S&P 500	
Year	Annual HPR	Index	Annual HPR	Index
1971		1,000		1,000
1972	35.6%	1,356	19.0%	1,190
1973	−16.0	1,139	−14.7	1,015
1974	−6.7	1,063	−26.5	747
1975	13.4	1,205	37.2	1,024
1976	20.2	1,449	23.8	1,269
1977	3.5	1,499	−7.2	1,177
1978	15.8	1,736	6.6	1,255
1979	34.6	2,337	18.4	1,486
1980	51.6	3,543	32.4	1,968
1981	7.1	3,794	−4.9	1,871
1982	30.6	4,955	21.4	2,272
1983	26.1	6,249	22.5	2,783
1984	−0.1	6,242	6.3	2,958
1985	24.6	7,778	32.2	3,909
1986	12.2	8,727	18.5	4,631
1987	4.2	9,093	5.2	4,873
1988	16.6	10,603	16.8	5,692
1989	46.3	15,512	31.5	7,485
1990	−0.7	15,403	−3.2	7,247
1991	42.8	21,996	30.5	9,461
1992	6.9	23,514	7.7	10,187
1993	10.9	26,077	10.0	11,204
1994	−1.1	25,790	1.3	11,351
1995	29.4	33,372	37.5	15,608
1996	19.6	39,913	23.1	19,208
1997	22.7	48,973	33.4	25,614
1998	38.9	68,024	23.2	31,552
1999	47.1	100,063	21.0	38,178

The correlation of returns between the Janus Fund and the S&P 500 between 1972 and 1999 is .782. Thus, the Janus Fund has a beta of

$$Beta_{Janus} = .782(.176/.163) = .821.$$

The fund's r-square is $(.782)^2 = .611$. So, the Janus Fund has less systematic risk than the overall market (its beta is less than one). And about 61 percent of the fund's total risk is systematic; the rest, about 39 percent, is unsystematic. In the next section we'll examine whether or not the Janus Fund is adequately diversified.

Assessing Risk-Adjusted Performance

Modern portfolio theory has provided three ways of assessing risk-adjusted performance, each named after their respective authors: the Treynor measure, the Sharpe

Exhibit 21.3 ✦ TOTAL RETURN INDEXES FOR THE JANUS FUND AND S&P 500

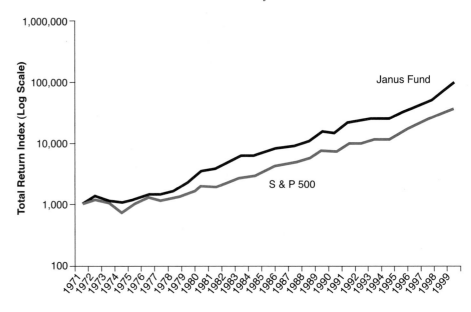

measure, and Jensen's alpha. Although all three measures have their basis in modern portfolio theory, each is slightly different. Let's examine each performance measure individually.

TREYNOR PERFORMANCE MEASURE

Treynor performance measure
A reward-to-risk ratio where the average risk adjusted return from a portfolio is divided by the portfolio's beta.

The **Treynor measure** is essentially a reward-to-risk ratio.[10] It equals:

$$T_p = \frac{AM_p - RF}{\hat{a}_p}. \tag{21.1}$$

where, AM_p is the mean return from a portfolio over a period of time, RF is the risk-free rate, and β_p is the portfolio's beta.

The Treynor measure is based on the capital asset pricing model (CAPM) and security market line (SML) discussed in Chapter 18. Recall that the SML for a portfolio is defined by

$$ER_p = RF + \beta_p[ER_m - RF]$$

where ER_p is the expected (or required) return from the portfolio and ER_m is the expected return from the market. We can rewrite the security market line as

$$[ER_p - RF] = \beta_p[ER_m - RF]. \tag{21.2}$$

---

[10]Jack Treynor, "How to Rate Management of Investment Funds," *Harvard Business Review* (January-February 1965), pp. 119–38.

Essentially Equation 21.2 states that a portfolio's risk premium equals the portfolio's beta multiplied by the market risk premium. Dividing both sides of Equation 21.2 by beta gives us

$$[ER_p - RF]/\beta_p = [ER_m - RF]. \tag{21.3}$$

The left side of Equation 21.3 is the Treynor measure for portfolio p (ER_p replacing AM_p). The right side of Equation 21.3, as you probably remember from Chapter 18, is the slope of the security market line. It's also the Treynor measure for the market because, by definition, the market has a beta of one.

When calculating the Treynor measure we use the *actual (ex-post)* mean return from a portfolio. In a sense we're comparing actual performance to expected performance. Therefore, if a portfolio's Treynor measure equals that of the market, the portfolio lies along the SML. We'd conclude that the portfolio's risk-adjusted performance equaled what it should, given its beta risk. Therefore, the portfolio neither outperformed nor underperformed the market on a risk-adjusted basis. This is shown graphically in Exhibit 21.4.

On the other hand, if the portfolio's Treynor measure is higher than the market's, the portfolio lies above the SML. In that case, we'd conclude that the portfolio's risk-adjusted performance was higher than expected, given its beta risk, and the portfolio, risk adjusted, outperformed the market. (See Exhibit 21.4.) Finally, if the portfolio's Treynor measure is less than the market's, the portfolio lies below the SML. The portfolio's risk-adjusted performance fell below the market's—meaning that its actual return was less than expected given its beta risk. This relationship is graphed in Exhibit 21.4.

Let's evaluate the Janus Fund's risk-adjusted performance using annual returns between 1972 and 1999. We must calculate its Treynor measure and the Treynor measure for the S&P 500. We'll use the return on short-term T-bills as the proxy for the risk-free rate. Between 1972 and 1999, T-bill returns averaged 6.8 percent per year. The Treynor calculations are as follows:

$$\text{Janus Fund: } T_{\text{Janus}} = [19.1\% - 6.8\%]/.821 = .150,$$
$$\text{S\&P 500: } T_{\text{S\&P 500}} = [15.1\% - 6.8\%]/1.00 = .083.$$

The Janus Fund lies above the SML, and its risk-adjusted performance outpaced the market. By how much did it outperform the market? To lie along the SML, the Janus Fund's Treynor measure would have had to equal the market's at .083. A little bit of arithmetic tells us that, given a beta of .821, the Janus Fund's average return would have to have been about 13.6 percent. Subtracting its actual average return, 19.1 percent, from its expected annual return, 13.6 percent, tells us that the Janus Fund's risk-adjusted performance topped the market by about 5.5 percent per year.

SHARPE PERFORMANCE MEASURE

The **Sharpe measure** resembles the Treynor in that it is a reward-to-risk ratio.[11] Instead of using beta as the risk measure, Sharpe substituted total risk, standard deviation. The Sharpe measure equals

$$S_p = [AM_p - RF]/SD_p \tag{21.4}$$

where SD_p is the portfolio's standard deviation.

Sharpe performance measure
A reward-to-risk ratio where the average risk adjusted return from a portfolio is divided by the portfolio's standard deviation.

---

[11]William Sharpe, "Mutual Fund Performance," *Journal of Business* (January 1966), pp. 119–38.

Exhibit 21.4 ✦ INTERPRETING THE TREYNOR MEASURE

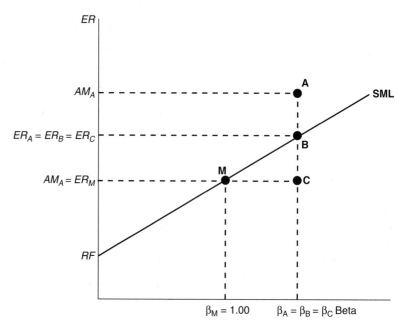

$AM_A > ER_A$, $T_A > T_M$ Outperforms market on a risk-adjusted basis.

$AM_B = ER_B$, $T_B = T_M$ Performs as expected.

$AM_C < ER_C$, $T_C < T_M$ Underperforms market on a risk-adjusted basis.

Sharpe's logic for using total risk instead of only systematic risk lies with the assumption behind beta risk. Beta risk assumes that a portfolio is totally diversified, with no remaining unsystematic risk. Sharpe argues that a portfolio manager whose portfolio is not well-diversified shouldn't be rewarded for exposing investors to unsystematic risk. In other words, a portfolio could have a relatively low beta, but a high standard deviation simply because the portfolio isn't well diversified.

Although the Treynor measure is based on the security market line, the Sharpe measure is based on the capital market line (or CML). In Chapter 18 we defined the capital market line as

$$ER_p = RF + \{[ER_m - RF]/SD_m\}SD_p,$$

where SD_m is the market standard deviation. We can rewrite the CML as

$$[ER_p - RF] = \{[ER_m - RF]/SD_m\}SD_p. \tag{21.5}$$

Dividing both sides of Equation 21.5 gives us

$$[ER_p - RF]/SD_p = [ER_m - RF]/SD_m. \tag{21.6}$$

The left side of Equation 21.6 is the Sharpe measure for the portfolio (with ER_p replacing AM_p). The right side of the equation is the Sharpe measure for the market (again, ER_m replaces AM_m).

As with the Treynor measure, the Sharpe measure is calculated with actual returns. Again, we are in essence using the Sharpe measure to compare actual returns to expected returns. If a portfolio's Sharpe measure equals that of the market, the portfolio lies along the capital market line (see Exhibit 21.5). This means that the portfolio's return equals what would be expected given the portfolio's standard deviation (total risk).

If the portfolio has a higher Sharpe measure than the market, the portfolio lies above the CML. The portfolio's actual return exceeds its expected return, given the total risk of the portfolio. On the other hand, if the portfolio's Sharpe measure is less than the market's, the portfolio lies below the CML. The portfolio's actual return is less than the expected return, given the total risk of the portfolio. Both cases are illustrated in Exhibit 21.5.

Let's compute Sharpe measures for the Janus Fund and the S&P 500 using annual returns between 1972 and 1999. We'll again use the return from T-bills as proxy for the risk-free rate. The mean annual return from T-bills during this period was 6.8 percent. The Sharpe measure calculations are as follows:

$$\text{Janus Fund: } S_{\text{Janus}} = [19.1\% - 6.8\%]/17.6\% = .700$$
$$\text{S\&P 500: } S_{\text{S\&P 500}} = [15.1\% - 6.8\%]/16.3\% = .509$$

Because the Sharpe measure for the Janus Fund exceeded the Sharpe measure for the S&P 500, the Janus Fund's actual return is higher than expected, given its level of total risk, and falls above the capital market line. For the Janus Fund to have a Sharpe measure equal to the market's, its annual return had to average only about 15.8 percent. Given its actual average annual return of 19.1 percent, the Janus Fund, risk adjusted, beat the market by about 3.3 percent per year.

You may recall that according to the Treynor measure, the Janus Fund outperformed the market by an average of more than 5 percent per year. However, according to the Sharpe measure, the Janus Fund beat the market only by about 3.3 percent per year. Why the difference? The answer goes back to the risk measure used and the issue of diversification. The Treynor measure uses beta risk, whereas the Sharpe measure uses total risk. According to the r-square statistic, which measures diversification, the Janus Fund is not totally diversified; if it were, the r-square would be close to one. The Janus Fund has a r-square of .611 meaning almost 40 percent of its total risk is unsystematic.

JENSEN'S ALPHA

The third measure of risk-adjusted performance is Jensen's alpha.[12] As with the Treynor measure, **Jensen's alpha** is derived from the capital asset pricing model (CAPM) and the security market line. We start again with CAPM

$$ER_p = RF + \beta_p[ER_m - RF]$$

and subtract RF from both sides of the equation

$$ER_p - RF = \beta_p[ER_m - RF]$$

Jensen's alpha
A performance measure based on the capital asset pricing model; the expected value of alpha is zero and an alpha greater than zero indicates superior risk adjusted performance.

---

[12]Michael Jensen, "The Performance of Mutual Funds in the Period 1945–1964," *Journal of Finance* (May 1968), pp. 389–415.

Exhibit 21.5 ✦ Interpreting the Sharpe Measure

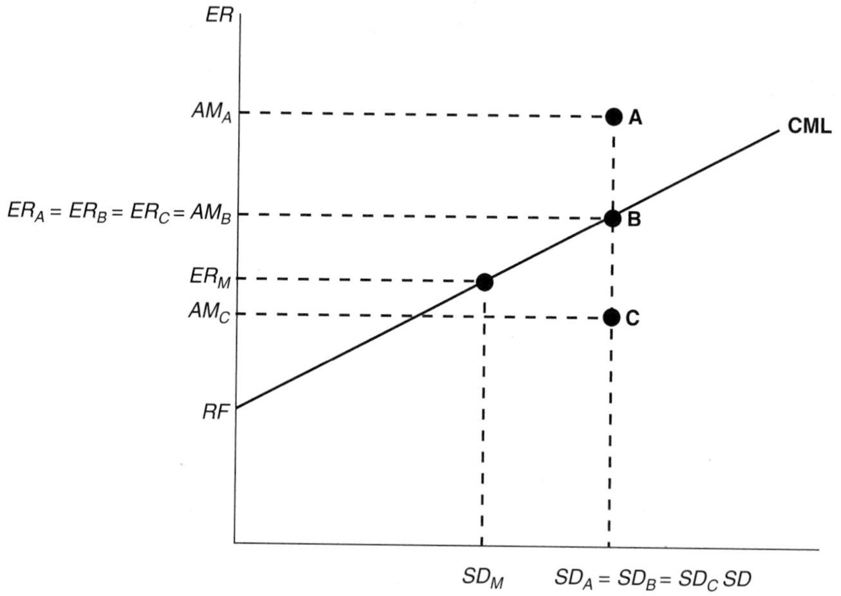

$AM_A > ER_A$, $S_A > S_M$ Outperforms market on a risk-adjusted basis.

$AM_B = ER_B$, $S_B = S_M$ Performs as expected.

$AM_C < ER_C$, $S_C < S_M$ Underperforms market on a risk-adjusted basis.

and we have Equation 21.2 again. Now, let's add another variable, alpha, to Equation 21.2:

$$ER_p - RF = \alpha_p + \beta_p[ER_m - RF] \tag{21.7}$$

In order for Equations 21.2 and 21.7 to equal one another, alpha must equal zero. When the y-axis is defined as the portfolio risk premium ($ER_p - RF$), rather than the portfolio's expected return, the SML's intercept is equal to zero (see Exhibit 21.6). But what happens if alpha isn't equal to zero? If alpha is positive, the portfolio is returning more than it should, given its level of beta risk. In that case, the portfolio lies above the security market line. On the other hand, if alpha is negative the portfolio's return is less than it should be, given its level of beta risk, and the portfolio lies below the SML. So, how is alpha estimated?

In Chapter 18 we described the characteristic line. The *characteristic line* is a regression equation where the return from a security or portfolio is the dependent or Y variable, whereas the return from the market is the independent or X variable. We used the characteristic line as another way of estimating beta, because beta is the slope of the characteristic line.

By making one small modification we can use the characteristic line to estimate alpha. The modified characteristic line is

$$(HPR_p - RF)_t = \alpha + \beta(HPR_m - RF)_t \tag{21.8}$$

Exhibit 21.6 ✦ INTERPRETING JENSEN'S ALPHA

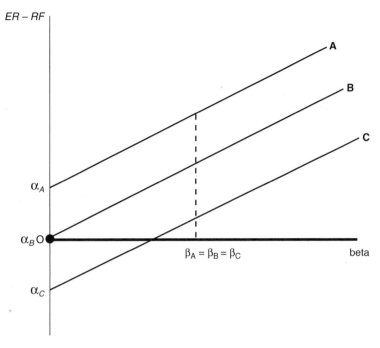

$\alpha_A > O$, Portfolio outperforms market on a risk-adjusted basis.

$\alpha_B = O$, Portfolio performs as expected.

$\alpha_C < O$, Portfolio underperforms market on a risk-adjusted basis.

where α and β are estimated using least squares regression, HPR_p is the holding period return from the portfolio, HPR_m is the holding period return from the market, and t refers to time periods (months, quarters, or years).

Let's estimate alpha for the Janus Fund. Exhibit 21.7 lists the annual returns for the Janus Fund, the S&P 500, and Treasury bills between 1972 and 1999. Also shown is the characteristic line which includes the estimates for alpha and beta. The beta estimate we've seen before. Note that the estimated alpha is .055, indicating that actual returns from the Janus Fund were higher than expected returns given the fund's level of beta risk. In other words, the positive alpha suggests that the Janus Fund, risk adjusted, outperformed the market.

COMPARING TREYNOR, SHARPE, AND JENSEN

To assist in our comparison of the three portfolio performance measures, Exhibit 21.8 lists the performance of ten stock mutual funds, along with the performance of the S&P 500 and T-bills. The three performance measures are calculated for each mutual fund and the measures are ranked from 1 (best) to 10 (worse).

Exhibit 21.7 ✦ Computing Jensen's Alpha for the Janus Fund

	Return − Risk Free Rate	
Year	Janus	S&P 500
1972	31.8%	15.2%
1973	−22.9	−21.6
1974	−14.7	−34.5
1975	7.6	31.4
1976	15.1	18.8
1977	−1.6	−12.3
1978	8.6	−0.6
1979	24.2	8.1
1980	40.4	21.2
1981	−7.6	−19.6
1982	20.1	10.9
1983	17.3	13.7
1984	−10.0	−3.6
1985	16.9	24.4
1986	6.0	12.3
1987	−1.3	−0.2
1988	10.2	10.5
1989	37.9	23.1
1990	−8.5	−11.0
1991	37.2	25.0
1992	3.4	4.2
1993	8.0	7.1
1994	−5.0	−2.6
1995	23.8	31.9
1996	14.4	17.9
1997	17.4	28.0
1998	34.2	18.4
1999	42.2	16.1
Beta	.821	
Alpha	.055	
r-square	.611	

First, recognize that the Treynor measure and Jensen's alpha are closely related to one another. This is because both derive directly from the capital asset pricing model and the security market line. In fact, you may have already noticed that Jensen's alpha is equal to the portfolio's "excess" return (the actual return minus the expected return, given the portfolio's beta risk). We can see this by simply rearranging Equation 21.7 and substituting actual returns for expected returns,

$$\alpha_p = AM_p - RF - \beta_p[AM_m - RF] \tag{21.9}$$

where AM_m is the arithmetic mean return from the market proxy (for example, the S&P 500).

Exhibit 21.8   ✦   PERFORMANCE MEASURES FOR 10 STOCK MUTUAL FUNDS

Fund	Mean Return	Standard Deviation	Beta	r-square	Performance Measures			Ranks		
					Treynor	Sharpe	Jensen	Treynor	Sharpe	Jensen
AIM Value	28.8%	23.4%	1.03	0.89	0.23	1.02	0.04	6	5	6
Berger 100	26.2	30.7	1.22	0.71	0.17	0.69	−0.02	8	8	8
Dreyfus Appreciation	22.5	20.1	0.99	0.93	0.18	0.87	−0.02	7	6	7
Fidelity Fund	29.1	21.9	0.99	0.93	0.24	1.10	0.05	4	2	4
PBHG Select Equity	50.0	72.1	1.54	0.33	0.29	0.62	0.15	1	9	1
Safeco Equity	19.3	18.4	0.88	0.89	0.16	0.78	−0.03	9	7	9
Scudder Large Company Growth	33.7	26.6	1.12	0.88	0.26	1.08	0.07	3	3	3
Strong Growth & Income	31.9	22.7	1.01	0.93	0.27	1.19	0.07	2	1	2
T. Rowe Price Dividend Growth	13.5	14.0	0.66	0.77	0.13	0.61	−0.04	10	10	10
Vanguard US Growth	29.2	22.9	1.03	0.92	0.23	1.06	0.04	5	4	5
S&P 500	24.3	20.6	1.00	1.00	0.19	0.94	0.00			
Treasury bills	5.0									

Because the Treynor measure and Jensen's alpha are so closely related, they will always give you the same ranking when you compare the performance of several portfolios. As an example, take a look at Exhibit 21.8. Notice that the top-ranked fund based on the Treynor measure (PBHG Select Equity) also has the highest Jensen's alpha. The fund with the lowest Treynor measure (T. Rowe Price Dividend Growth) also has the lowest Jensen's alpha.

Where differences in rankings can occur is between Treynor/Jensen and the Sharpe measure. The Sharpe measure relies on the notion that all portfolios *should* be diversified and, consequently, standard deviation rather than beta is the appropriate risk measure. In Exhibit 21.8, the fund rankings based on Treynor/Jensen and Sharpe are fairly consistent, with one notable exception. The PBHG Select Equity fund is the highest-ranked fund based on the Treynor/Jensen measures; it is one of the lowest-ranked funds based on the Sharpe measure. According to the Treynor/Jensen measures, PBHG Select Equity outperformed the market on a risk-adjusted basis. However, according to the Sharpe measure, risk adjusted, the fund under-performed the market. Why? Because the fund is not well diversified—its r-square is only .33—and it has a great deal of unsystematic risk.

PBHG Select Equity has, by far, the highest mean return and the highest standard deviation of any of the ten funds listed in Exhibit 21.8. With a standard deviation of about 72 percent, PBHG Select Equity has more than twice as much total risk as any of the other nine mutual funds—next highest is the Berger 100 with a standard deviation of about 31 percent—and more than three times as much total risk as the

S&P 500. Although PBHG Select Equity has the highest beta of the ten mutual funds, its beta indicates that it has about 1.5 as much systematic risk as the overall market.

If you use the SML to determine the PBHG Select Equity fund's required return, you'd come up with

$$5.0\% + 1.54[24.3\% - 5.0\%] = 34.7\%,$$

which is much less than the fund's actual return, 50 percent. If you use the capital market line, the fund's required return is

$$5.0\% + \{[24.3\% - 5\%]/20.6\%\}72.1\% = 72.6\%.$$

Based on the capital market line, the PBHG Select Equity fund's actual return was more than 22 percent below its required return, given its level of total risk.

Before you conclude that the PBHG Select Equity manager hasn't managed the fund properly, understand that the fund isn't designed to be diversified. As is made quite clear in the prospectus, the fund places large bets on a handful of stocks. Investors are warned that the fund's strategy will likely result in a nondiversified portfolio, one that is riskier than the "average" mutual fund.

The choice of whether to rely on the Treynor/Jensen measures or the Sharpe measure may depend on portfolio objectives. If the portfolio is designed to be diversified, the Sharpe measure is probably the better performance measure. If not, the Treynor measure (or Jensen's alpha) is best.

Past and Future Performance

The performance measures we've just discussed use historical returns and so evaluate *historical* performance. Of course, history may not repeat itself, at least during a particular investment horizon. Thus, the results from using ex-post data even in a theoretically sound technique are dubious at best. Does the past predict the future? As we have seen before, and will seen again, the answer is, alas, both yes and no.

Exhibit 21.9 offers anecdotal evidence on the consistency of mutual fund returns. The exhibit lists the top 10 performing stock mutual funds based on three years ending December 31, 1993 and their subsequent performance during the next six years in three-year periods (1994–96 and 1997–99). How did '93's star funds perform? According to the record, not well. Only one beat the S&P 500 in 1994–96 and only three beat the S&P 500 in 1997–99. On the other hand, six of the ten funds under performed the S&P 500 in *both* 1994–96 and 1997–99.

After an extensive examination of mutual fund returns, John Bogle identifies a tendency for individual mutual fund performance to revert toward the mean. In his words, "there is a profound tendency for the returns of high-performing funds to come down to earth, and, almost as inevitably, for the returns of low-performing funds to come up to earth."[13]

Bogle ranked equity mutual funds by performance during the 1970s and divided the rankings into quartiles. The top quartile beat the S&P 500 by an average of about

---

[13]John Bogle, *Common Sense on Mutual Funds* (New York: Wiley, 1999), p. 226.

Exhibit 21.9 ✦ Subsequent Performance of 1993's Top Performing Funds

Fund	Annualized 3-Year Return (1991–93)	Annualized 3-Year Return (1994–96)	Annualized 3-Year Return (1997–99)
American Heritage	48.5%	−24.8%	3.5%
CGM Capital Development	44.4	11.7	13.3
Oppenheimer Growth & Income	43.0	14.2	22.9
PBHG Growth	42.2	20.0	23.2
Putnam New Opportunities	40.8	18.8	37.3
Montgomery Small Cap	39.0	13.1	20.8
AIM Aggressive Growth	38.0	23.8	19.5
Delaware Investments Trend	37.7	12.4	32.5
MFS Emerging Growth	37.5	18.4	31.1
Skyline Special Equities	37.1	13.6	2.9
S&P 500	15.6	20.4	24.3

5 percent per year. The bottom quartile, by contrast, underperformed the S&P 500 by about 4 percent per year. Bogle then calculated the performance of these funds during the 1980s. Funds in the top quartile, based on 1970s performance, slightly underperformed the S&P 500 during the 1980s. On the other hand, funds in the bottom quartile, based on 1970s performance, actually did better in 1980s, relative to the S&P 500, than in the 1970s.

However, evidence, such as that we reviewed in Chapter 7, also suggests that investors should pay attention to past performance. A study of pension fund managers concluded that money managers with outstanding records are better bets for future gains than those with dismal past performance records.[14] The study measured the results of investing with managers whose performance records over the previous three years placed them in the top 25 percent of all pension funds. This strategy produced a 2.1 percent greater annual return than investing with managers whose performance records for the previous three years placed them in the bottom 25 percent.

We've emphasized throughout this chapter that investors, when analyzing investment performance, should consider *both* return and risk. Several scientific studies of mutual funds returns have used measures of risk-adjusted performance when assessing past performance. One extensive study of stock mutual fund returns found strong evidence of persistence in risk-adjusted performance over time.[15] Using the Sharpe measure performance, the study found that the best predictor of future risk-adjusted performance turned out to be past risk-adjusted performance. However, another scientific study found evidence to the contrary—that past risk-adjusted performance did poorly at predicting future risk-adjusted performance.[16]

---

[14]Josef Lakonishok, et al., "The Structure and Performance of the Money Management Industry," *Brookings Papers on Economic Activity* (1992), pp. 339–91.

[15]James Philpot, *Performance-Related Characteristics of Mutual Funds*, Ph.D. dissertation, University of Arkansas, Fayetteville, AR, 1994.

[16]Mark Carhart, "On the Persistence in Mutual Fund Performance," *Journal of Finance* (March 1997), pp. 57–82.

We believe the primary lesson in this conflicting evidence is this: although past performance isn't a perfect predictor of future performance, it shouldn't be ignored either. Consistently good risk-adjusted performance over a long period of time at the very least tilts the odds of success in the investor's favor.

Chapter Summary

1. What are some issues related to evaluating investment performance?
   Whenever performance is evaluated, the time periods must be consistent with one another. In addition, performance over longer periods of time often provides more useful information than short-term performance. Performance must be compared to the appropriate market benchmark and should be adjusted for risk. Finally, investment objectives and any constraints imposed on the portfolio must be considered.

2. How are risk and return measured?
   Historical performance is evaluated, therefore the appropriate measure of investment return is the holding-period return. A total return index, along with the arithmetic and geometric means also provide useful information. The standard deviation of returns should be calculated along with the portfolio's beta and r-square measure. Beta measures systematic risk and r-square measures the degree to which the portfolio is diversified.

3. What are three measures of risk-adjusted performance?
   The three measures of risk-adjusted performance all derive from modern portfolio theory. The Treynor measure is a reward-to-risk ratio. If the portfolio's Treynor measure is greater than that of the market benchmark, the portfolio's return exceeded its expected return, given the portfolio's beta risk. The Sharpe measure is another reward-to-risk ratio. Instead of using beta, the Sharpe measure uses standard deviation. If a portfolio's Sharpe measure exceeds that of the market, the portfolio's actual return exceeded its expected return, given the portfolio's total risk. Jensen's alpha is based on the capital market asset pricing model. The expected value of alpha is zero. A positive alpha indicates that portfolio's actual return exceeded its expected return, given the portfolio's beta risk.

4. How good a predictor is past performance of future performance?
   All measures of portfolio performance are based on historical returns. Are historical returns good predictors of future returns? The answer is perhaps because evidence supports both positions. A portfolio manager who exhibits consistent, long-term good performance at the very least improves the odds of success for the investor.

Review Questions and Problems

1. List the issues you must consider when evaluating portfolio performance. How could two different mutual funds both claim to be the top performing fund?
2. What is a market benchmark? What is the appropriate benchmark for a small-stock fund? For a large-stock fund?
3. Explain how returns should be measured. What does standard deviation measure? What does beta measure?
4. Assume that a portfolio has a standard deviation of 15 percent. The market portfolio has a standard deviation of 15 percent. If the portfolio has a beta of .80, what is the portfolio's r-square? How well diversified is the portfolio?
5. Compare and contrast the Treynor, Sharpe, and Jensen performance measures. What is Sharpe's rationale for using standard deviation instead of beta?
6. Assume a portfolio has a beta of .80 and a mean return of 20 percent. The market has a mean return of 20 percent. If the risk-free rate is 5 percent, what is the portfolio's Treynor measure? Where does the portfolio lie relative to the security market line?

7. Using the information provided in the prior problem, find and interpret Jensen's alpha.

8. A portfolio has a mean return of 25 percent and a standard deviation of 25 percent. The market portfolio has a mean return of 20 percent and a standard deviation of 18 percent. The risk-free rate is 5 percent. Find the portfolio's Sharpe measure. Did the portfolio out- or underperform the market on a risk-adjusted basis?

9. Assume a portfolio has a Treynor measure of .35 and a Sharpe measure of .25. The market has a Treynor measure of .20 and a Sharpe measure of .30. Explain why the portfolio out-performed the market based on one measure, but under-performed the market based on the other. Is the portfolio's r-square close to one? Why or why not?

10. Is past performance a good guide to future performance? Why is the long-term track record more important than the short-term track record?

CRITICAL THINKING EXERCISES

1. This exercise requires library/Internet research. Using a well-known source of mutual fund information—such as Morningstar or the February issue of *Money* magazine—review data for the three-year period 1997–99. Measured in terms of total return, find the five best-performing stock mutual funds each year (ignore international and sector funds). Record each fund's name and its total one-year return. Also, record the average total return for each fund's group (for example, large growth funds or small value funds), as well as the total return for the appropriate market benchmark.

   a. How did each fund on your list do the following year? For example, how did the top-performing fund in 1997 do in 1998?
   b. Do these one-year returns show any consistent patterns? In other words, do one year's top-performing funds perform well the next year? Discuss your findings.
   c. Assume you buy the best-performing fund from the prior year on January 1 and hold it for the next 12 months. In other words, you would own 1998's top performing fund during 1999. How well do you think this strategy would work?

2. This exercise requires computer work. Open the Mutual Fund worksheet in the Data workbook. The worksheet contains quarterly returns for several mutual funds over a recent ten year period, along with quarterly returns for the S&P 500 and T-bills.

   a. Compute the arithmetic and geometric returns for the funds, the S&P 500, and T-bills. Make sure to annualize the mean returns.
   b. Calculate the annualized standard deviation and beta for each fund.
   c. Calculate the Treynor, Sharpe, and Jensen performance measures. Rank the funds by each measure. Why do the rankings differ from measure to measure?

THE INTERNET INVESTOR

1. Investment writer Robert Markham recently wrote an article that questioned the value of diversification (www.worth.com/articles/z002f01.html). Read the article, along with Jason Zweig's critique (www.pathfinder.com/money). Write a brief report summarizing the pros and cons of diversification. With which point of view do you most agree? Why?

2. The Morningstar web site (www.morningstar.com) has an extensive database of mutual fund performance. Choose ten different stock mutual funds. Visit the Morningstar site and collect the following information: mean return, standard deviation, beta, and r-square. Collect the same information for the S&P 500 (you can use an index fund as a proxy for the S&P 500). Also, find the average return on T-bills. Use these data to calculate the Treynor, Sharpe, and Jensen performance measures for each fund.

3. By now your web-surfing skills should be pretty good. Search the Web, especially the investment-oriented web sites for an answer to this question: Has the Sage of Omaha (Warren Buffet) regained his investment touch? (Hint: The best gauge of Buffet's investment performance is the performance of his company Berkshire Hathaway.)

Appendix A   Sources of Investment Information

This appendix will help you sort through the massive amount of information available to investors today, from economic data to financial news to information on specific companies. We describe both objective sources of investment information and subjective sources of information. We define an objective source as one that provides information and data but no opinions or analysis. A subjective source generally provides both data and opinions.

This appendix is not meant to be comprehensive. The information needs of investors vary substantially. Sources of great importance to certain professional or institutional investors may have little or no value for small individual investors. Many small investors can satisfy all their information needs with general interest periodicals, newspapers, and popular web sites.

SOURCES OF STATISTICAL DATA

A variety of government and private organizations compiles and publishes all kinds of economic and industry data. The amount of data is staggering. You can find the number of housing starts in the United States between 1947 and today, the profits of electric and gas utilities over the past 20 years, or the current yield on Canadian government bonds. Most sources of such information provide objective data (for example, historical economic statistics) rather than subjective opinions and analysis. We start by examining government sources of statistical data about economy-wide and industry-specific conditions and trends.

Government Publications

Several U.S. federal agencies, international organizations, and foreign governments compile and publish statistical data. Some series are reported monthly, some quarterly, and some annually. Some series may have historical data going back many years. Below are several examples.

Survey of Current Business.   The U.S. Department of Commerce publishes the *Survey of Current Business* each month to review recent developments in the U.S. economy (and to a lesser extent, the world economy) and to present data for gross domestic product (GDP), industrial production, employment, wages, interest rates, and so on. The *Survey* also contains detailed data on conditions in specific industries. The *Survey* reports current data and limited historical data, typically going back a couple of years.

Besides the *Survey*, every two years the U.S. Commerce Department publishes *Business Statistics*, which provides longer-term historical economic data. You could find data, for example, on steel production or the unemployment rate from about 1947 to the present.

Federal Reserve Bulletin.   The *Federal Reserve Bulletin* is published monthly by the Board of Governors of the U.S. Federal Reserve System. It is the investor's primary source for current monetary and banking data. The *Bulletin* also presents several other financial data series, both domestic and international.

In addition to banking and financial data, the Bulletin contains articles, written by the staff of the Board of Governors, on contemporary monetary and banking issues.

Announcements, congressional testimony by board members, and so forth are also printed in the Bulletin.

International Publications.   Several international organizations provide detailed data on world economies, including the International Monetary Fund (IMF), United Nations, and World Bank. In addition, the governments of most developed countries, such as Canada, publish statistical data regularly. An example of this type of publication is the IMF's *International Financial Statistics,* which provides country-by-country data regarding inflation, industrial production, unemployment, main components of the country's GDP, and so on.

The average investor may have little interest in these types of international data, but some professionals might be interested. For example, say an analyst for a big Wall Street investment firm follows a company that generates a high percentage of its sales in Europe. Obviously, the prospects for that company, and therefore the investment potential of its stock, will be closely tied to the economic outlook in Europe.

Nongovernment Sources

Economic data are also available from nongovernment sources such as financial institutions, investment firms, securities exchanges, and trade associations. In fact, many of these private organizations provide some of the data that appear in government publications such as the *Survey of Current Business.* Furthermore, many investment advisory services—such as Standard & Poor's and brokerage firms—publish extensive economic data. Unlike government sources of economic data, however, these sources often provide subjective commentary along with statistical information. For example, they may provide data that suggest that European economic growth is accelerating and answer the question of what it means for European stocks.

NEWSPAPERS AND PERIODICALS

Most investors probably get the bulk of their information from newspapers and periodicals. You may well know *Barron's,* the *Wall Street Journal, Business Week,* and such, but hundreds of more specialized publications are published that interest certain investors.

Newspapers

Most daily newspapers report some business and economic news, although the quality and quantity of coverage can vary widely. Many daily papers, even in larger cities, tend to concentrate on local business news, but there are exceptions. The *New York Times,* for example, provides extensive, well-respected coverage of national business and economic news. Many investors prefer daily business newspapers for more in-depth financial information.

The *Wall Street Journal* is arguably the best known, most widely quoted business publication in the world. It is also one of the oldest. Founded in 1885, the *Journal* provides detailed coverage of business and economic news, both national and global. The *Journal* publishes Asian and European editions and carries extensive price quotations for stocks, bonds, options, futures, and mutual funds. It also reports earnings announcements, dividend declarations, new product information, management changes, and other current business news.

Barron's, like the Wall Street Journal, is published by Dow Jones & Company. *Barron's* is a weekly newspaper that covers a wide range of investment topics. A typical issue contains a review of the week's major business and economic developments, interviews with professional investors, recent analyst opinions on stocks, and columns on commodities, mutual funds, options, and so forth. *Barron's* also publishes thorough price quotations on all major types of investments, as well as detailed technical information.

Periodicals

Dozens of periodicals seek to inform investors. These include general interest periodicals such as *Newsweek* and *Time,* business periodicals such as *Business Week, Forbes,* and *Fortune,* and international periodicals such as the *Economist.* All contain news and analysis of contemporary business and economic issues. The business periodicals tend to focus more narrowly on investing, providing articles on specific companies, consumer trends, economic forecasts, and so forth.

Trade periodicals may also interest certain investors. These publications of various trade associations provide in-depth coverage of specific industries and segments of the economy. Two examples of trade periodicals are *Air Transport World* and *Public Utilities Fortnightly.*

In addition to the general business press, some well-known periodicals deal more heavily with personal investing and others aspects of personal finance. These publications include *Money* magazine, *Smart Money,* and *Worth.*

INVESTMENT ADVISORY SERVICES

To supplement published information, investors can consult private companies that specialize in providing investment information and advice. These include the large, well-known financial information services such as Standard & Poor's, brokerage firms such as Merrill Lynch, and investment newsletters such as the *Professional Tapereader.* The cost of these services varies. Many large public and college libraries offer at least some of these publications to patrons. Clients of brokerage firms may have access to some of this information free of charge. Purchasing many of these services as an individual can be quite expensive. A yearly subscription to a typical newsletter costs between $200 and $300. An annual subscription to *The Outlook,* a Standard & Poor's publication, costs almost $300. Any investor should carefully evaluate the cost and benefit of buying any of these publications.

Moody's and Standard & Poor's

Moody's Investors Service and Standard & Poor's (S&P) provide similar publications and information services covering a wide range of investment topics. Moody's and S&P provide both objective information and subjective analysis. As one service, Moody's and S&P each publish basic reference volumes covering most public corporations. Moody's *Manuals* group company information by industry for banking, industrial, international, transportation, and public utility firms. These publications and S&P's *Corporation Reports* both provide detailed historical and current information on revenue, earnings, capitalization, major news developments, and so forth. Moody's and S&P update these reference volumes continuously throughout the year. Both also publish regular reports on the economy and specific industries. S&P's two-volume *Industry Surveys,* for example, provide valuable industry information.

Moody's *Bond Survey* is another example of the many reports and publications of these advisory services. This weekly publication provides extensive information on and analysis of the bond market. A typical issue of the *Bond Survey* includes a list of new bond issues, data on interest rates, and bond ratings under review. In addition to its *Corporation Reports,* S&P publishes *Stock Reports,* two-page summary reports on most public companies. Updated quarterly, these reports provide basic financial information (for example, revenue, assets, dividends), as well as brief assessments of companies' future prospects.

Two other S&P publications are *The Outlook* and *Investor's Monthly.* Unlike *Stock Reports,* these publications tend to offer more subjective analysis of the financial markets and specific stocks and contain less statistical data. A typical issue might analyze conditions in the overall market, make changes in stock recommendations, and highlight special situations.

Value Line

One of the best-known and most widely followed investment advisory services, Value Line, follows more than 1,700 individual stocks in 98 industries. Each weekly report spotlights one or two industries and the companies in those industries. A new report is prepared on each company and industry approximately every three months. Although Value Line reports a great deal of objective information, most investors view it primarily as a source of subjective analysis.

Many users of Value Line rely on several summary measures. Two especially important numbers appear in the upper left corners of its company reports: timeliness (probable price performance in the next 12 months) and safety (probable safety in the future). To develop its timeliness ranking, Value Line uses a computer model to rank each of the stocks it follows, with higher ranks indicating better investment potential. The service assigns ranks of 1 and 5 to the top 100 and bottom 100 stocks, respectively. Ranks of 2 and 4 identify the next 300 stocks from the top and bottom, respectively. The remaining, middle group of about 900 stocks get timeliness ranks of 3. A similar procedure is used to assign safety rankings. We discussed the performance of investment strategies based on the Value Line rankings in Chapter 7.

Brokerage Firms

In Chapter 6, we discussed the difference between full-service brokerage firms, such as Merrill Lynch, and discount firms, such as Charles Schwab. Other than their commission rates, the major difference between the two is the full-service firm's offer of investment advice and information. All full-service firms, for example, maintain lists of stocks that they recommend. Brokers at full-service firms often use some of the sources we have already discussed (for example, S&P and Value Line). Often, however, they rely more on reports prepared by their firm's analysts.

Every major full-service brokerage firm employs a group of security analysts, each of whom concentrates on specific industries and stocks. Each major firm, for example, has at least one analyst who follows Chrysler and the auto industry. Brokerage firms also employ economists, market strategists, technical analysts, bond market analysts, and even weather forecasters to fully serve their clients. The data disk that accompanies the text includes an actual security analysis report on Home Depot (Home Depot.doc)

Mutual Fund Rating Services

Several investment advisory services follow mutual funds almost exclusively. Three of the most firmly established mutual fund rating services are CDA/Wisenberger, Lipper Analytical Services, and Morningstar. In 1993, Value Line began offering a mutual fund rating service similar to the company's well-respected stock rating service. Mutual fund rating services all present objective information and historical results for mutual funds; some also make subjective recommendations.

Newsletters

Investors can subscribe to dozens of investment newsletters. Some of the better-known newsletters include *The Zweig Forecast, The Prudent Speculator, The Chartist,* and *Elliott Wave Theorist.* Newsletters provide subjective analysis and opinion rather than objective information. Newsletters tell investors, for example, what they should buy, what they should avoid (or sell), and whether to hold stocks or cash. Many newsletters, although not all, rely on technical analysis to make their investment recommendations. Subscriptions to investment newsletters are generally fairly expensive, as mentioned above, and many newsletters have less than stellar track records for their advice.

COMPUTER-BASED INFORMATION SOURCES

One of the most significant developments in recent years has been the growth of computer-based sources of investment information. These allow computer users to access large information databases without going to the library or turning a page. Computer-based sources can be divided into two groups: historical databases, and on-line services, including the Internet. Historical databases provide users with financial information on disks or computer tapes, updated periodically.

Traditional Computer Databases

Several computer databases have been around for years. Many universities and large institutions subscribe to these databases, which require mainframe computers. COMPUSTAT, a service of Standard & Poor's, maintains a body of historical financial information on thousands of companies, as well as industry and economic data. It can provide either annual data, going back as far as 20 years, or quarterly data, going back as far as 20 quarters.

Another established computer database is CRSP, developed by the Center for Research in Security Prices at the University of Chicago. CRSP produces computer tapes, updated annually, that report monthly and daily historical security price returns on approximately 5,000 NYSE, AMEX, and over-the-counter stocks. Dividends and closing prices are also included. Some of the series go back as far as 1926.

PC Products

Today, the personal computer is an excellent alternative. During the past few years, personal computers have made sophisticated use of technologies such as CD-ROM and high-speed modems. These services include both on-line services and databases. For example, Standard & Poor's has created a compact disk version of Compustat for use on a personal computer. Called Research Insight, it contains most of the information found on the mainframe version of Compustat. Research Insight has several report and chart builders that can be used in conjunction with Microsoft Excel.

The Internet

For investors, the Internet is one of the greatest information sources currently available. What is more, much of the information you can obtain from the Internet is free to users. All you need is Internet access and one of the popular web browsers. Your college or university probably has both. An alternative is to subscribe to one of the many so-called Internet service providers (ISP). Examples include America Online, Earthlink, and Prodigy.

The amount of information available on the Internet is staggering, and it is growing daily. Getting started is often the hardest part. A good place to begin is Yahoo (www.yahoo.com). Yahoo organizes web sites by category and is updated constantly. Yahoo has a powerful search feature that allows you to comb the web-based on search terms and names you specify.

An excellent source of company information is Edgar (www.sec.gov/edgar). Attached to the SEC's home page, Edgar is an electronic library of SEC filings. If you want to study the most recent annual report for a company, you can find it on Edgar. Furthermore, many companies have home pages. You can read about new products or study the annual report. Microsoft's web site (www.microsoft.com), for example, lets you download its latest annual report as an Excel file.

On the data disk, we have included a file—called Web Sites—you can use with either Netscape or Microsoft's Internet Explorer. It is a set of bookmarks for major investment-oriented web sites. You just open the file and point your mouse to your desired destination.

CRITICAL THINKING EXERCISE

This exercise requires library and/or Internet research. Below is a list of 12 data items. For each item, identify an information source—there may be multiple sources—collect the most recent data you can find, and answer any questions asked.

1. Breakdown of Canadian GDP into the four major components (private consumption, net exports, government spending, and private investment).
2. Japanese and U.S. savings rates. Collect the most recent year's data and data for 1985. Be sure to define *savings rate*.
3. Distribution of U.S. population by age group and projected change in each age group to the year 2005.
4. Performance of the Weitz Value mutual fund from 1990 through the most recent year you can find.
5. U.S. retail sales (seasonally adjusted and not seasonally adjusted). Obtain overall data and sales for specific types of retailers (e.g., discount stores).

6. Revenue, operating expenses, and net income of U.S. electric and gas utilities (overall industry data). Collect the most recent year's data and data for 1990.

7. Stock price index for the computer industry from 1990 through the most recent year. Be sure to specify how the computer industry is defined.

8. Exchange rates between the U.S. dollar and the Japanese yen and between the U.S. dollar and the German mark from 1990 through the most recent year.

9. Earnings and dividends for The Gap from 1990 through the most recent year. Could you construct a total return index using these data?

10. Projection of earnings for The Gap for next year. Why are The Gap's earnings expected to rise or fall?

11. Most recent balance sheet and income statement for Wal-Mart Stores.

12. Industry ratios and averages for the airline industry.

Appendix B Careers in Investments

Many readers may be interested in working in the investments field; it can be a rewarding career. Although it is difficult to estimate exactly the number of full-time investment professionals, a good guess would be several hundred thousand, at least. For example, Merrill Lynch, the nation's largest brokerage and investment company, has about 40,000 employees. Fidelity Investments, the world's largest mutual fund company, which also operates a large discount brokerage firm, employs close to 10,000 people. Of course, not all of these workers are engaged in investment management, but a majority probably are.

In this appendix, we take a brief look at some of the career opportunities in the investments field. Before we begin, however, consider the following: First, competition for most jobs in the investments field is intense. Institutions have many high-quality applicants from whom to choose. Second, the number of investment professionals is not growing especially rapidly; in some job categories, the number of workers may actually be declining. Several well-known investment firms have cut staff in recent years. As a result, you must be flexible in your job search. You must be willing to relocate, be willing to start at the bottom, and be prepared to work hard. Finally, you should be aware that many positions in the investments field require federal or state licenses, or both.

WHO EMPLOYS INVESTMENT PROFESSIONALS?

The obvious employers of investment professionals are brokerage firms, investment banking firms, life insurance companies, pension funds, and mutual funds. Ask your librarian for sources that list the addresses and phone numbers of these organizations. Also, don't forget about banks. Many investment professionals begin work in bank trust departments. Also, many large banks have active bond-trading operations, especially for municipal bonds. Even large, nonfinancial corporations employ investment professionals to manage such areas as investor relations and pension plans.

BROKERAGE AND SALES POSITIONS

The first job that probably comes to mind in the investment field is that of a stockbroker (now called an *account executive* in most brokerage firms). Account executives work mainly with individual investors, though some may handle accounts for small institutional investors as well. Account executives provide advice, execute orders, and help maintain records. Account executives who work for full-service firms such as Merrill Lynch earn most of their compensation through commissions on trades. Successful account executives can do quite well financially, earning six-figure annual incomes. Brokers at discount brokerage firms, on the other hand, are salaried employees. They are responsible for maintaining records, providing price quotations, and executing orders; these are, of course, important services. The distinction between full-service and discount brokerage firms was described in Chapter 6.

Large investment firms also employ salespeople who deal mainly with institutional investors and other workers who execute orders (traders). In any case, a successful account executive or investment salesperson possesses effective selling skills, along with some interest in finance. New account executives often have prior sales or business experience.

A growth area today is the sale of 401(k), and other similar defined-contribution retirement plans, to employers. Most employers have replaced traditional pension plans with defined contribution plans. Large investment firms and mutual fund companies are actively marketing these plans.

ANALYSTS AND PORTFOLIO MANAGERS

Security analysts work for a variety of organizations studying stocks, bonds, options, futures, and so forth. Analysts write research reports for distribution to their organizations' clients. Most analysts specialize in particular securities. Stock analysts, for example, specialize in specific industries and companies, following the pattern described in Chapters 11 through 14. Analysts work for large banks, brokerage firms, life insurance companies, mutual funds, and pension funds. The analyst whose name appears on a research report usually has a staff to assist him or her. Many analysts begin their careers by doing tedious grunt work for the senior analyst. Top analysts can easily command six- or seven-figure salaries.

Portfolio, or money managers, in the view of many, represent the pinnacle of the investments field. Portfolio managers are responsible for managing large pools of funds and work for mutual funds and other large, institutional investors. Most managers have staffs of assistant managers and analysts. The compensation of a top portfolio manager can easily exceed $1 million annually.

INVESTMENT BANKERS

As we discussed in Chapter 3, investment bankers act as intermediaries between issuers of securities and investors. They also advise corporate and government clients on financial strategies. Investment bankers often lead large staffs and are well compensated. Senior investment bankers can make well into the seven figures annually.

FINANCIAL PLANNERS

Many individuals turn to financial planners for help with personal finance issues such as estate planning, taxes, insurance, and investments. Financial planners come from a variety of backgrounds, including accounting and insurance sales. Some work for insurance companies, investment firms, banks, and even public accounting firms. Other financial planners work independently. The demand for financial planners has increased dramatically in recent years and has coincided with the growth in defined contribution retirement plans (such as 401k and 403b plans). Earnings of top financial planners easily reach into six figures.

Financial planner is still a loosely defined term, however. Almost anyone, regardless of qualifications, can call himself or herself a financial planner. Attempts are being made to develop some sort of professional designation for financial planners. The Certified Financial Planner designation means that an individual has met education and experience requirements and has demonstrated a minimum level of knowledge and competence about subjects such as taxes, life insurance, and estate planning. More than 25,000 individuals today hold CFP certificates, and we suggest that anyone with an interest in becoming a financial planner obtain a CFP certificate. For more information, contact the CFP Board, 1700 Broadway, Suite 2100, Denver, CO, 80290-2101; (303) 830-7500; www.cfp-board.org.

CHARTERED FINANCIAL ANALYSTS

There are approximately 20,000 Chartered Financial Analysts (CFAs) in the United States. Obtaining a CFA designation enhances the prestige of an investment professional such as a security analyst or portfolio manager, much as a CPA designation enhances the prestige of an accounting professional. To obtain a CFA designation, you must pass a series of three comprehensive examinations (Levels I, II, and III) over a consecutive three-year period. You must also meet certain educational and experience requirements to reach each level.

Throughout the text we've included sample questions from past CFA exams. These sample questions demonstrate the types of subjects and information a CFA candidate at each level is expected to know.

Although a CFA designation is not necessarily a requirement to enter the investments field, the designation is valued by most investment organizations. It is rare today to find a top analyst or portfolio manager who isn't a CFA. For more information, contact the Association for Investment Management and Research, PO Box 3668, Charlottesville, VA 22903-0668; (804) 980-3668; www.aimr.com.

We wish you the best of luck on whatever career path you decide to take.

Appendix C   Answers to Recap Questions

CHAPTER 2

1. 33 percent.
2. Historical returns are ex-ante returns.
3. Inflation adjusted real return is 29.1 percent.
4. Measured in yen, 16.7 percent; measured in dollars, 12.2 percent.
5. Total return index is as follows:

Year	Total Return Index (Year 0 = 10,000)
1	11,550.00
2	13,860.00
3	12,404.70
4	16,746.35
5	21,351.59

$10,000 invested at the beginning of the period would have been worth in excess of $21,300 by the end of year 5. Total return during the period equals approximately 113.5 percent.

6. Arithmetic mean equals 17.5 percent; geometric mean equals 16.4 percent.
7. The CAAR during the three year period (1996-98) equals 27.4 percent.
8. Credit risk is the risk that the financial health of the issuer will deteriorate lowering the value of the security; interest rate risk is the risk interest rates will risk; market risk is the risk reflected in the daily fluctuations in security prices.
9. The standard deviation equals: 15.9 percent.
10. Annualized standard deviations are: 15.8 percent and 16.9 percent.

CHAPTER 9

1. $854
2. $851.55
3. $872.55
4. 12.17 percent
5. 4.387 years; 4.1 years
6. $20.50 increase for $1,000 face-value bond.

CHAPTER 10

1. The forward rate on a one-year bond one year from today is 6.64 percent; the forward rate on a two-year bond one year from today is 6.5 percent.
2. The investor would sell one two-year bond (receiving $89.05) and buy 1.063 three-year bonds (paying $89.05). In two years, the investor would owe $100; in three years he or she would receive $106.30. The one-year return is 6.3 percent.

CHAPTER 13

1. The compound average annual growth rate equals 15.8 percent; the forecast of 1999 earnings equals $2.55.
2. The estimated regression equals: $-203.224 + .1025(\text{Year})$; the forecast of 1999 earnings equals $1.71.

3. Of the two the forecast derived from the compound average annual growth rate is probably going to be more accurate. The forecast derived from the regression is less than 1998 earnings by over 50 cents per share.
4. Earnings forecast equals $0.966 per share.
5. Earnings forecast equals $1.178 per share.
6. Earnings forecast equals $1.035 per share.

CHAPTER 14

1. Vs0 = $127.68
2. Market price is $102 and intrinsic value is $127, so the stock is undervalued.
3. ROE (22%) > ERs (15%), so it is a growth company.
4. It is a growth stock because it is undervalued.
5. g = 14.46%
6. g = 6.6%
7. g = 13.86%
8. ERs = 14.5%
9. V_{s0} = $127.68
10. Undervalued
11. Vs0 = $44.42
12. JNJ P/E = 32.6
13. JNJ MV/BV = 4.48

CHAPTER 17

1. M_{AOL} = 195.42%
2. SD_{AOL} = 203.65%
3. Yes, Y dominates X because it has a lower risk for the same level of return.
4. CV_Y = 1.2; CV_Z = 1.11. CV_Z is less risky per one percent of return, but it does not dominate stock Y. The choice depends on individual risk preference.
5. Mp = 0.1084
6. SDp = 0.185

CHAPTER 18

1. ERp = 0.09
2. SDp = 0.024
3. Beta = 0.94
4. ERs = 0.171
5. ER_B = 0.22
6. PR_B = 0.18
7. No, it is not a good investment becauser $PR_B < ER_B$.
8. Graph with RF = 0.05 with beta = 0.0 and ER_M = 0.18 at beta = 1.0. Draw a line between the two points and display ER_B = .22 on the line at beta = 0.94.

CREDIT LIST

PP. 97–99	Standard & Poor's NYSE Stock Report © The McGraw-Hill Companies, Inc. Reprinted by permission.
P. 112	Reprinted by permission of Yahoo!
PP. 146–147	Reprinted by permission of Yahoo!
P. 165	© 1981 *Journal of Finance.* Reprinted by permission.
P. 167	Reprinted by permission of American Association of Individual Investors.
P. 170	© The McGraw-Hill Companies, Inc. Reprinted by permission.
P. 171	© The McGraw-Hill Companies, Inc. Reprinted by permission.
P. 194	© The McGraw-Hill Companies, Inc. Reprinted by permission.
P. 231 (top)	Standard & Poor's Debt Rating Criteria © The McGraw-Hill Companies, Inc. Reprinted by permission.
P. 231 (bottom)	© 1991 *Journal of Fixed Income.* Reprinted by permission.
P. 232	© 1992 *Financial Management.* Reprinted by permission.
P. 233	© 1998 The McGraw-Hill Companies, Inc. Reprinted by permission.
P. 257	© 1993 Prentice-Hall, Inc. Adapted by permission.
P. 260	© 1993 Prentice-Hall, Inc. Adapted by permission.
P. 297	© 1997 Richard Irwin. Reprinted by permission.
P. 313	© 1997 Harcourt College Publishers. Reproduced by permission of the publisher.
P. 371	Value Line report for American Home Products reprinted by permission of Value Line, Inc.
P. 406	Reprinted by permission of *The Wall Street Journal.* © 1999 Dow Jones & Company, Inc. All rights reserved worldwide.
P. 408	Reprinted by permission of *The Wall Street Journal.* © 1999 Dow Jones & Company, Inc. All rights reserved worldwide.
P. 436	Chicago Board of Trade 1997 specifications courtesy of Chicago Board of Trade.
P. 538	© 1971 *Journal of Finance.* Reprinted by permission.
P. 539	© 1992 Forbes, Inc. Reprinted by permission of *Forbes* Magazine.
P. 540	© 1992 Forbes, Inc. Reprinted by permission of *Forbes* Magazine.
P. 557	© 1972 Praeger Publishing. Reprinted by permission.
P. 558	© 1972 Praeger Publishing. Reprinted by permission.

NAME AND ORGANIZATION INDEX

Boldface text and page numbers refer to key terms. *Italic* page numbers refer to exhibits.

SUBJECT INDEX

Boldface text and page numbers refer to key terms. *Italic* page numbers refer to exhibits.